Judging the
Supreme Court

Rhetoric and Public Affairs Series

Judging the Supreme Court

Constructions of Motives in *Bush v. Gore*

CLARKE ROUNTREE

Michigan State University Press
East Lansing

Copyright © 2007 by Clarke Rountree

∞ The paper used in this publication meets the minimum requirements of
ANSI/NISO Z39.48-1992 (R 1997) (Permanence of Paper).

 Michigan State University Press
East Lansing, Michigan 48823-5245

Printed and bound in the United States of America.

13 12 11 10 09 08 07   1 2 3 4 5 6 7 8 9 10

LIBRARY OF CONGRESS CATALOGING-IN-PUBLICATION DATA

Rountree, Clarke, 1958–
  Judging the Supreme Court : constructions of motives in Bush v. Gore / Clarke
Rountree.
      p. cm—(Rhetoric and public affairs series)
  Includes bibliographical references and index.
  ISBN 978-0-87013-809-6 (cloth : alk. paper)
  1. Bush, George W. (George Walker), 1946—Trials, litigation, etc. 2. Gore, Albert,
1948—Trials, litigation, etc. 3. Contested elections—United States—History.
4. United States. Supreme Court—History. 5. Political questions and judicial
power—United States—History. I. Title.
KF5074.2.R68 2007
347.73'26—dc22   2007035870

Cover and book design by Sans Serif, Inc.
Cover art courtesy of AP Images

green
press
INITIATIVE Michigan State University Press is a member of the Green Press Initiative and is committed to developing and encouraging ecologically responsible publishing practices. For more information about the Green Press Initiative and the
use of recycled paper in book publishing, please visit
www.greenpressinitiative.org.

Visit Michigan State University Press on the World Wide Web at:
www.msupress.msu.edu

To Jennie,
whose candor and quiet strength
have been a source of inspiration to me
for more than twenty-five years.

Contents

Acknowledgments

Many have provided support during the development of this book. The College of Liberal Arts at the University of Alabama in Huntsville provided me a sabbatical in Fall 2002, allowing me time to get the initial chapters of this book written. I have had the benefit of helpful responses on initial drafts from a number of knowledgeable scholars. Chief among these is Ed Appel, who provided the most extensive feedback on the early chapters. Bob Wess, John Lyne, and Lelon Oliver offered wise advice. The reviewers for Michigan State University Press had concrete suggestions that have greatly improved this book. Marty Medhurst has been a thoughtful and supportive editor. My department colleagues and friends have been very patient listening to me talk about this research over the last five years. Ashley Perry and Christina Ho provided copyediting help in preparing the manuscript for submission. And the talented copyeditors at Michigan State University Press have provided extensive and helpful suggestions for making my prose more readable.

Introduction

A long with the suffering, death, and widespread fear engendered by the tragic events of September 11, 2001, the terrorist attacks and the subsequent war on terrorism gave an indisputable political advantage to the seven-month-old administration of President George W. Bush. It took the wind out of a storm of criticism claiming that the man who occupied 1600 Pennsylvania Avenue was not the man the American people had elected to their highest office. Americans naturally rally around their commander-in-chief when their country is under attack. That rallying reinforced Bush's position as leader and brushed from the front pages things unrelated to the war on terrorism, such as the controversial outcome of the 2000 election.[1]

But for months following Election Day, charges of irregularities were made about the razor-close presidential election in Florida, which was decided by less than one ten-thousandth of the total vote.[2] Those irregularities overwhelmingly favored George W. Bush. There was the infamous "butterfly ballot" in Palm Beach County—designed by a Democrat—that led thousands of elderly Jewish citizens to vote mistakenly for Reform Party candidate Patrick Buchanan instead of Democrat Al Gore or to spoil their ballots.[3] Punchcard-based voting machines used by less affluent, more Democratic-leaning counties were discovered to have produced five times more spoiled ballots than the optical-scan voting systems employed in the more affluent, Republican-leaning counties.[4]

African-American voters, who supported Gore by a nine-to-one margin,[5] complained not only that their ballots were more frequently rejected than those of whites[6] but that they were more likely to be turned away at the polls because they were mistakenly purged from voter lists as "felons."[7] Charges of racism were fueled by the actions of state troopers in Leon County, who set up a vehicle checkpoint on the morning of the election near a predominantly black polling area—one of the few in this overwhelmingly white county—delaying many who were going to vote.[8]

Then there were charges that Republican vote totals were illegally bolstered. In Seminole and Martin Counties, several thousand absentee ballots failed to include voter identification information. Republican election officials in each case allowed Republican Party officials to "correct" these ballots—in plain violation of state law[9]—while not affording the same opportunity to Democratic Party officials.[10] Nassau County officials ignored automatic recount totals when they certified the original vote totals that gave 51 more votes to Bush (justifying that rejection because fewer votes were tallied the second time).[11] Secretary of State Katherine Harris, who was Florida's chief election official and also cochair of Bush's Florida campaign, pushed to have overseas ballots accepted even if they had postmarks after election day, bending the law and changing existing practices; those overseas ballots favored Bush by two to one.[12]

If not for these irregularities, which overwhelmingly favored George W. Bush., conservative judge Richard Posner admits, Gore would have won. He offers that "if the question is what percentage of the people who voted in the Florida election thought they were voting for Gore, the probable answer is more than 50 percent."[13]

Overshadowing all of these concerns about the election, however, were two pivotal legal battles that ensured a Bush victory. The first came one day after the Florida Supreme Court mandated a state-wide manual recount of all undervotes (ballots for which the vote-counting machines did not detect a vote for president). At the request of the Bush legal team, five of the most conservative justices of the U.S. Supreme Court issued a stay order to halt the recounts. Those same justices supported the Texas governor three days later, when the Court handed down its 5-4 verdict in *Bush v. Gore*, the second and decisive battle, which effectively ended all recounts and awarded the highest office in the land to Republican George W. Bush. That decision, issued in an unsigned per curiam ("by the court") opinion, overturned the Florida Supreme Court's ruling ordering recounts on the grounds that the standards for recounting ballots were so vague as to raise equal protection concerns, since different ballots might be recounted using different standards. The Court technically remanded the case back to the Florida Supreme Court, though in doing so, it indicated that the recounts could not be restarted, because it found that Florida law required that certified results be submitted by December 12, which would end two hours after the U.S. Supreme Court's decision was handed down.

Criticism of the decision in *Bush v. Gore* has been swift, harsh, and voluminous.[14] Hundreds of political commentators, lawyers, judges, and legal scholars have publicly denounced the decision.[15] Legal scholars have penned scores of essays criticizing the decision.[16] In the first two years following the decision, lawyers, legal scholars, and political commentators published ten books, most of which criticized the decision.[17] The threat of mass protests at Bush's inauguration led authorities, for the first time in

American history, to declare the ceremony a "National Special Security Event," which required anyone attending to have permission from the government.[18]

The criticisms of the *Bush* decision are based not simply on the result (a victory for Bush) or the ideological split (with the most conservative justices supporting Bush) but on the extraordinary novelty and weakness of the legal reasoning of the majority, the intrusion of the federal court into an issue of state law, and the unwillingness of the Court to allow the recounts to continue. In the absence of good legal reasons for the decision, the critics argued, the decision looks extremely partisan. Thus, Yale Law School professor Bruce Ackerman called the decision "[a] blatantly partisan act, without any legal basis whatsoever"; Harvard Law School's Alan Dershowitz dubbed it "[t]he single most corrupt decision in Supreme Court history"; and American University professor Jamin Raskin called the justices "[b]andits in black robes."[19] Jeffrey Rosen claimed that the majority "have . . . made it impossible for citizens of the United States to sustain any kind of faith in the rule of law as something larger than the self-interested political preferences of William Rehnquist, Antonin Scalia, Clarence Thomas, Anthony Kennedy, and Sandra Day O'Connor."[20] Famed federal prosecutor Vincent Bugliosi accused the Court of committing "the unpardonable sin of being a knowing surrogate for the Republican Party instead of being an impartial arbiter of the law" and insisted that "legal scholars and historians should place this ruling above the Dred Scott case (*Scott v. Sandford*) and *Plessy v. Ferguson* in egregious sins of the Court."[21]

The handful of defenders of the decision, with rare exceptions, have endorsed not the reasoning of the *Bush v. Gore* majority but only the result.[22] Former U.S. District Court judge Frank McGarr admitted "that the U.S. Supreme Court reached out with perhaps challengeable jurisdiction" but insisted that it was required to do so to rein in an out-of-control Florida Supreme Court and to avoid a looming crisis.[23] University of California, Berkeley, law professor John Yoo used that pragmatic defense as well, insisting that "the Court believed that only it could intervene so as to bring the national election controversy to an end in a manner that would be accepted by the nation." Admitting that, Yoo added, "is not to say that the precise reasoning of the per curiam was utterly correct."[24] *National Review* writer Mark Miller acknowledged that "[s]ome conservatives are coming to believe that, at least with respect to *Bush v. Gore*, the Rehnquist Court might have abandoned judicial restraint in an effort to implement a conservative outcome."[25]

The overarching concern with *Bush v. Gore*—and critics and defenders of the decision agree on this point—is less with specific legal arguments and holdings than with judicial motives. That is obvious when we consider a hypothetical scenario whereby the roles of Democrat Al Gore and Republican George W. Bush are reversed. If Gore were ahead and Bush were behind in the vote count, and Gore appealed to the U.S. Supreme Court to halt that recount and received the same judgment as Bush received, then reaction to the decision would be quite different. It is not simply that "liberal" critics would muffle their complaints, as no doubt many would; it is that the conservative five who decided the case would be viewed as ruling against their political interests. Their motives would not be suspect in the way they are now suspect. As it is, defending their motives is much more difficult, whether it is the Court doing the defending or others.

Judicial motives of this sort are not simply something inside the heads of judges; they are rhetorical constructions, crafted by judicial decision-makers, their critics, and their defenders. And there are tangible rhetorical limits on such constructions, which may be thought of as a web of rhetorical possibilities and constraints that give when pulled in one direction, while tightening up from another direction. These webs are complex, drawing in a host of seemingly remote acts that hem in a judge, while allowing him or her to do rhetorical work at the fringes. These constructions of motives are not incidental to American judicial decisions; they are the very lifeblood of them. They draw upon and answer to an American political ideology that values a liberty that comes from answering to no king but only to the law.[26]

Well-constructed judicial motives reinforce the mythology that we live under the rule of law; poorly constructed judicial motives raise questions about the legitimacy not just of individual judicial decisions but of our political system and its romantic[27] reliance on an impartial judiciary. Though it be merely a mythology, the most prejudiced of judges recognizes the limitations it places upon the motives he or she is permitted; thus, the rhetorical demands of that political mythology are real.

As is well illustrated in *Bush v. Gore*, judicial motives may become contested grounds, where judges' constructions are challenged or defended, reformulated, and reinterpreted. This is true as well in ordinary judicial cases, where lawyers, lower courts, and later courts attempt to construe various actions, more or less accurately, but always within a limiting web of motive possibilities.

The contested ground of judicial motives in *Bush v. Gore* is examined here through an extensive analysis of what has been said by various parties about those motives. The great attention given to judicial motives in this case ensured that nearly every possible means of persuasively constructing those motives was deployed by critics and defenders of the decision, yielding the most persuasive accounts we have for the actual motives of the court. Those motives derived less from proper judicial concerns about the law, justice, and laying down rules for the future than from the political and personal concerns of the majority justices. The upshot of this conclusion is that a cadre of conservative justices on the highest court ensured that their favored candidate would ascend to the most powerful office in the United States—indeed, in the world. It means that our democracy, reliant as it is on the rule of law, has been undermined. It serves as a warning for Americans to better guard their form of government, which they may ensure only with news media that do a better job in helping the public understand the mysteries of judicial decision making, so that they may rise up as a people when they are poorly served.

An understanding of judicial motives is inextricably tied with constructions of what law is being followed, of what justice requires for parties (and the larger society) in a given case, of how larger contexts shape (or ought to shape) legal decision making, and other considerations that take us beyond narrow questions of what a judge was thinking in rendering a particular decision. An analysis of this expands beyond a narrow focus on individual motives to include jurisprudential considerations explored by many legal scholars, yet it goes beyond legal analysis in situating the issue of judicial motives within a larger framework of institutional legitimacy. It highlights, as standard legal analyses do not, that judicial opinions are rhetorical performances, that key to those performances are constructions of "proper" judicial motives, and that through rhetorical analysis, judicial motives can be teased out, their propriety assessed, and the quality of judicial opinions as rhetorical performances determined.

Ultimately, the rhetorical performances embodied in judicial opinions are constitutive of the political community. If they are good performances, they help to constitute the U.S. democracy as a good one, supporting the system of government, and assuring citizens that in the United States, they live under the rule of law. Obviously, if they are poor performances, as is the case with *Bush v. Gore*, they undermine the third leg of the tripartite system, threatening the whole notion that Americans live under the rule of law, and rendering the black-robed keepers of that central myth into mere political actors, trading in their own narrow interests, and unworthy of the esteem and lifetime appointments they are given.

This study adds to the extensive literature on *Bush v. Gore* a meta-analysis of the rhetoric of motives in the case: a careful assessment of the most compelling constructions of judicial motives in this case to discern what can most reasonably be concluded about what the majority was doing and why it was doing it. In other words, after legions of critics and defenders, pundits and scholars, and even the Court itself have offered their constructions of what the Court was doing and why it was doing it, this study identifies the most coherent and persuasive accounts of Court motives. It shows that constructions of judicial motives are critical to the assessment of this case and to an understanding of the role of the judiciary in the U.S. democratic system. Finally, such constructions of motives are rhetorical—that is, they aim to persuade an audience of their legitimacy in the face of limits on the rhetorical possibilities for such constructions.

1

Judicial Motives in American Jurisprudence

In his opening statement before a Senate Judiciary Committee that ultimately rejected his nomination to the U.S. Supreme Court, Judge Robert H. Bork nonetheless demonstrated his sensitivity to the constraints on judicial motives in our American political system when he stated: "The judge's authority derives entirely from the fact that he is applying the law and not his personal values. That is why the American public accepts the decisions of its courts, accepts even decisions that nullify the laws a majority of the electors voted for."[1] Indeed, the values reflected in Bork's statement underlie the complaints against the *Bush v. Gore* Court. They were criticized for applying or appearing to apply their personal values and not the law in deciding for Bush, thereby undermining public confidence. Thus, Anthony Amsterdam of the *Los Angeles Times* charged the Court with "masking result-driven, political, unprincipled decisions in the guise of obedience to rules of law."[2] University of Chicago law professor David A. Strauss claimed: "This was not a triumph of the rule of law."[3] And even conservative University of Utah law professor Michael W. McConnell worried that *Bush v. Gore* could "undermine public faith in the rule of law itself."[4]

What should give us pause about Bork's statement and those of these commentators on the majority decision is that they seem to rely on assumptions about law that have long since been invalidated by legal scholars. As Thomas Reed Powell of Columbia University acknowledged as early as 1918 in an article entitled "The Logic and Rhetoric of Constitutional Law": "In determining a great number of the most important questions, there are two or more courses equally open to the Supreme Court, as the constantly recurring division of judicial opinion amply illustrates."[5] This early recognition of the susceptibility of the law to differing interpretations has been amply substantiated by legal skeptics from the legal realists to members of the critical legal studies movement to legal pragmatists.[6] So was Bork, widely heralded as a towering legal intellect, unaware of developments in legal philosophy over the better part of the twentieth century? Certainly not, though we must take pains to explain *why* he—or any other judicial candidate—is virtually required to talk as if the law could simply be "applied" and why charges of failing to heed the rule of law are hurled so readily by journalists and even legal scholars.

Judicial Mythology and the American Political System

The Founding Fathers certainly spoke as if the law could be applied rather straightforwardly. In justifying the substantial constitutional powers proposed for the new Supreme Court, for instance, Alexander Hamilton brushed away concerns about what he called "the least dangerous" branch of government by insisting that the courts would "be bound down by strict rules and precedents which serve to define and point out their duty in every particular case that comes before them."[7] Whether this claim was the product of an Enlightenment mind-set certain that rationality could and would prevail in legal decision making or merely a persuasive strategy this notable lawyer used to sway those considering whether to support the proposed Constitution, it implied that there would be significant constraints upon judicial action.

Courts certainly have worked to bolster their image as impartial decision makers bound down by the law, feeding a powerful judicial mythology with the pomp of courtroom procedure (such as requiring others to stand when judges enter and to address them as "Your Honor"), the furnishing of courtrooms (which place judges behind stately benches often high above those who plead in their courts), and judicial costume (which has given up powdered wigs but maintains the stately black robes).[8] Chief Justice William Rehnquist was particularly sensitive to this symbolism, adding four gold stripes to his own judicial robe prior to the Clinton impeachment hearings in imitation of the Lord Chancellor in a Gilbert and Sullivan operetta, and forbidding cameras in the Supreme Court's courtroom (thereby maintaining the Court's air of mystery), despite the proliferation of such cameras in many other courtrooms and pressure from the networks to open up the *Bush v. Gore* case to public viewing.[9]

The Supreme Court, in particular, has good reason to maintain the image of objectivity and infallibility that this judicial mythology promotes. The Supreme Court of the United States is not directly accountable to "the people." Supreme Court justices are nominated by the president and approved by the Senate, to be sure, but their lifetime appointments ensure that they may serve for decades before the popularly elected branches of government can recall their influence. Although impeachment is an option, it has been tried only once—unsuccessfully, two centuries ago—and it has never been an effective check on Supreme Court power.[10]

Furthermore—and perhaps unforeseen by Hamilton and many of his contemporaries—this "least dangerous" branch of government has grown to become the most powerful adjudicative body in the Western world, reaching questions left to the political branches of government in the British system.[11] Its power of judicial review, in particular, has given it a strong check on democratic processes. Wielding such power without the aid of an army or governmental purse strings to enforce its decisions requires the Court to rely on its authority alone to carry the day, which it has done successfully, with extremely rare exceptions.[12]

Small wonder that the Supreme Court speaks in a "priestly voice"[13] that positions the justices as middlemen between us and the law, that they characterize themselves as interpreters rather than creators of law, that they imply that they are chained to judicial logic rather than free to craft arguments from a rich well of rhetorical resources, that they pretend to be above normal human biases, and that they insist that what they assert about the law *is* the law.[14] In short, the Supreme Court employs a "chaste rhetoric that pretends not to be rhetorical"[15] and characterizes its own motives in deciding cases as severely circumscribed by the law.

One may call this a disingenuous game—pretending that the law requires a given outcome and that the hands of judges are tied by the rule of law—when legal scholars have told us for decades that the law has more flexibility than such pretensions admit.[16] And yet three considerations should give one pause before proclaiming that the judicial emperors have no clothes. First, if it is admitted that the power of the Supreme Court—indeed, of the judiciary more generally—comes from the maintenance of a "rule of law" mythology, one must wonder what will be sacrificed in announcing that the jig is up. Courts may have thwarted the will of the people, but this often has been a good thing, particularly in the area of protecting civil rights from the encroachments of an intolerant majority.[17] Shaking the nation's confidence in the high Court—or at least in the idea that a good Court can follow the law—might give majority-driven branches of government openings to snub unpopular Supreme Court decisions.

Second, if the "rule of law" standard for judging Court decisions is discarded, what standard will be used to judge bad decisions? Writers on jurisprudence from legal realists to "crits" to legal pragmatists have suggested that judges should seek the social good through their decisions (since flexible law does not require particular outcomes), but inevitably, all such theorists must turn to someone's or some group's ultimate value judgments about what that good is. Forgoing the limitations placed on judicial decision making by even an idealized rule of law in favor of this or that group's or judge's conception of the good (consider the gulf between Justice Antonin Scalia's "good" and Justice John Paul Stevens's "good") gains only the advantage of sincerity.[18] Such candor would not ensure that the values to be embraced are any better than those now embraced; indeed, it seems an exchange of one piety (speaking for the law) for another (speaking for good values).

The third reason to pause before abandoning the rule of law as a standard in law concerns the practical implications of embracing the judicial mythology. If judges are not really constrained by the law, they certainly are constrained to meet the rhetorical demands of a political system and a political body that judge them against the idealized standards of their judicial mythology. To maintain their credibility—which is the ultimate basis of their power—judges must look and act as if they are constrained by the law. If they embrace a mythology that suggests that they are forced by law to reach a particular verdict, then they had better make a good case that they are following the law in reaching that verdict. For the U.S. Supreme Court to make such a case involves, ideally, convincing the vast audience of lawyers, lower courts, future Supreme Courts, legal scholars, politicians, litigants, and interested members of the public that its decision follows the law. Indeed, a well-written opinion first convinces fellow judges that such a case has been made, one that will meet the rhetorical demands of facing the larger community of court watchers.

Embodying the Judicial Myth

But what is required for a court to embody the judicial myth in its decisions? Or, stated otherwise, what persuades court watchers that a court has followed the law? The short answer is that a court must persuade others that its actions in deciding a case embody proper judicial motives. This short answer may not seem to take us much further, but it does focus attention on two crucial elements of judicial rhetoric. First, deciding cases involves action—full-blooded action by full-blooded judges. It is not mechanical, clear-cut, or determined; rather, it involves judgment from those who judge. Second, despite the full-bloodedness of the act and its agents, judicial decisions must be proper. Such requirements of propriety stress the need for decisions to be bounded and to respect the sovereign authority of the rule of law. Impartial, fair-minded, knowledgeable jurists are those trusted to follow the law, and when those qualities are seen in a decision, the rule of law appears to be safe.

In a practical sense, embodying proper judicial motives involves much more than simply strategic characterizations of what the court is doing, as in statements such as "We reached the conclusion we did because this controlling precedent requires it." Although such self-descriptive language is common, such assurances alone will not suffice. Courts must take care that their construction of the case, its facts, its precedents, and the like appear appropriate and supportive of their verdicts. So, for example, opinion writers construct precedent decisions to make them fit more neatly with cases to which those judges would apply them. Similarly, they construct legislative acts, constitutional provisions, administrative regulations, and other legally relevant materials so that they apply more readily to the cases before them. These constructions, in turn, shape interpretations of judicial motives. Consider, for example, the advantages of constructing (or reconstructing[19]) a precedent that is an awkward fit with the case at bar. If a court reconfigures that precedent to make it fit more seamlessly with the facts before it—without straining the precedent too much—then following that well-fitting precedent makes it appear that the court is "following the law" more so than if it simply claimed that it "must" follow some ill-fitting precedent.

A good example of this judicial construction is found in an early Supreme Court case involving the admiralty jurisdiction. In *The Genesee Chief v. Fitzhugh*,[20] the High Court considered whether a law extending the admiralty jurisdiction of federal courts to lakes and rivers connecting to the sea was constitutional. Just sixteen years earlier, in *The Thomas Jefferson*,[21] the Supreme Court had ruled, following long-settled English common law, that the admiralty jurisdiction was limited to waters affected by the tide, insisting that "the Admiralty never pretended to claim, nor could it rightfully exercise any jurisdiction, except in cases where the service was substantially performed, or to be performed, upon the sea, or upon waters within the ebb and flow of the tide."[22] Thwarting both a clear precedent and long-standing common law would not make Chief Justice Roger Taney's court appear to be following the rule of law. So Taney set out to reconstruct the common law to make it fit.

The rule limiting the admiralty jurisdiction to the ebb and flow of the tide suited England, Taney insisted, because

> there was no navigable stream in the country beyond the ebb and flow of the tide; nor any place where a port could be established to carry on trade with a foreign nation, and where vessels could enter or depart with cargoes. In England, therefore tide-water and navigable water are synonymous terms, and tide-water, with a few small and unimportant exceptions, meant nothing more than public rivers, as contradistinguished from private ones; and they took the ebb and flow of the tide as the test, because it was a convenient one, and more easily determined the character of the river.[23]

Taney added that when the Constitution was adopted, the seaboard-dominated country could use this same definition, since all navigable rivers on the Atlantic were influenced by the tides. Courts followed this rule, unthinkingly, and "[i]t was under the influence of these precedents and this usage, that the case of the Thomas Jefferson . . . was decided in this court; and the jurisdiction of the courts of admiralty of the United States declared to be limited to the ebb and flow of the tide."[24] The *Thomas Jefferson* decision, Taney insisted, was erroneous, though the Court that decided it could be forgiven, because "the great importance of the question as it now presents itself could not be foreseen; and the subject did not therefore receive that deliberate consideration which at this time would have been given to it by the eminent men who presided here."[25]

Taney's act of overruling *The Thomas Jefferson*, therefore, was recast as an act of refusing to "follow an erroneous decision into which the court fell."[26] Instead of thwarting the law, the Court could suggest that it was upholding the *true* law, newly clarified by shaking off an unthinking adherence to custom without reason.

Understanding what is involved in strategies such as Taney's reconstruction of a common-law rule and a precedent, as well as his own judicial decision (which these earlier reconstructions make possible), provides a perspective for a fruitful approach to the *Bush v. Gore* decision.

Conveniently, the strategies for constructing judicial motives and those for constructing the elements of judicial opinions, such as precedents, draw upon the same rhetorical resources, because both concern action. Looking at judicial opinions in light of the acts they construct is appropriate for two reasons. First, judicial opinions are shot through with constructions of acts and their motives; this is literally the stuff that judicial argument is made of, the evidence upon which it relies.[27] Characterization of these acts, rather than some form of syllogistic or analogical reasoning, is the primary mode of judicial persuasion.[28] Second, focusing on this ubiquitous (though strangely camouflaged) concern of courts with action allows one to see past the technical language of rules, precedents, holdings, dicta, and the like, to where the rhetorical work of judicial argument takes place—where those rules, precedents, holdings, dicta, and other legal distinctions are shaped and reshaped in support of judicial purposes.

Re/Constructing Action in the Judicial Process

Judicial opinions construct, reconstruct, or embody at least ten different acts.[29] An initial set of acts a court considers in deciding a case includes those acts that gave rise to the case. In a criminal case, this may be the killing of one person by another, the embezzlement of corporate funds, or an act of vandalism against public property. For civil cases, this includes the failure to heed a stop sign which leads to the injury of another, the refusal of one party to meet his or her obligations under a contract, or the execution of a contested will. All such acts—the facts of the case—are subject to various constructions by judges that make one party or another appear more or less deserving, more or less liable, more or less guilty, and so forth. Obviously, such constructions play into concerns about whether justice has been done in a given case.

A second set of acts is performed by legal representatives and govern-ment officials. These include the filing of criminal charges through a com-plaint, information, or indictment and the bringing of civil suits, as well as the legal responses to such charges and suits. Such acts may be construed as proper or improper, frivolous or well grounded, ripe or unripe, and so on. Courts may construct these acts as a way to avoid getting to the merits of a case or to ensure that a case is heard.

Trial courts and judges enter in a third set of acts, hearing motions, di-recting verdicts, sending cases to trial, trying cases, rendering decisions, and so on. Such actions are scrutinized for their adherence to the law, and on rare occasions even factual judgments may be second-guessed.

A fourth set of acts arises when appeals are made or certiorari is granted. Again, judicial motives are scrutinized to see if they embody proper judicial motives or not, follow the law or not, in their acts of agreeing to hear cases, of remanding cases back to trial courts, of handing down decisions, and so forth. Depending upon the deference owed to a lower court, these characterizations can be crucial (as they proved to be in *Bush v. Gore*).[30]

Lumped together in a fifth set are a whole host of acts that make up the primary law. Constitutions, laws, and regulations are enactments that can-not be understood apart from the human action that gave them life (though legal discourse often reduces such actions to something more technical and less human). In some cases, this may require searching for the intent of the framers or of a legislative body in records of proceedings, preambles, the words of particular provisions themselves, and so on. Courts may ask questions about motives: What varieties of speech did the framers intend to be protected by the First Amendment? Why did Congress select this particular regulatory agency to oversee this problem? What so-cial concern gave rise to this particular criminal provision? Even judges who eschew original intent approaches nonetheless are frequently forced to deal with law as an enactment.

Precedent decisions are a sixth form of primary law frequently con-strued by judicial opinions. Courts take the constructions of earlier courts, who explain what they were doing and why they were doing it, and re-construct those original constructions in light of new cases and new cir-cumstances (whereby, for example, mere dicta may take on new importance and holdings may be reconstituted in new ways).[31] In a remarkably underestimated (if ordinary) rhetorical strategy, justices make prior courts speak to situations they may never have envisioned, lending authority and the benefits of settled law to the resolution of new problems.

On the other hand, courts may need to undermine the acts of prior courts, as in *The Genesee Chief* in reconstructing the decision in *The Thomas Jefferson* as unwittingly erroneous.

A seventh set of acts includes those of contributors to secondary law: the writers of legal review essays, restatements of the law, model codes, legal encyclopedias, textbooks, and the like. The scrutiny given these acts is typically more in selection than in construction, except where an opposing justice's use of such a source needs to be challenged.

An eighth set of acts that opinion writers construct includes the competing opinions of their brethren. For majority opinion writers, their greatest concern is with dissenting opinions. Dissenting opinions typically reconstruct majority opinions to show that they are not following the law—a serious threat to a majority's ability to present its motives as proper. Majority opinions usually explain dissenters' opinions, typically while maintaining a decorum that finds them "sadly mistaken" rather than "stupid," "malicious," or "motivated by personal interests."[32] Concurrences are not as threatening and typically receive less reconstruction by the majorities from which they diverge, though dissenters may challenge them.

A ninth set of acts is the least tethered by factual or discursive grounding. These are acts discussed in judicial opinions that are merely predicted, proposed, possible, hypothetical, imagined, or generalized. Sometimes these acts involve a past that the Court wishes to characterize, as when the *Bush v. Gore* majority discussed how punchcard voting errors were *likely to have been made* or, propositionally, how punchcard voting was *supposed to go* or *ought to have gone*. Such speculations often deal with an unknown future as well, as when an opinion writer is considering what will happen if the Court reaches one decision or another. For example, an opinion writer might describe the circumstances that will follow if certain types of erotic art are not protected by the First Amendment, if abortion law is returned wholly to state governments, or if federal law-enforcement officials are limited in their ability to use wiretaps against terrorist suspects.

The more fanciful opinion writer may analogize a situation to one from mythology, from history, from fiction, or from other literature. Typically, though, such hypothetical or fictional acts are used to drive home a point, often more effectively than a historical act could, since hypotheticals may adopt particular elements to a given case. Consider Justice Robert Jackson's use of a hypothetical act in *Korematsu v. United States*, the Japanese internment case. Jackson's dissent sought to make clear that the military's decision to arrest Fred Korematsu for failing to leave his

West Coast home and report to a relocation center was based solely upon his race. Jackson noted:

> Had Korematsu been one of four [persons]—the others being, say, a German alien enemy, an Italian alien enemy, and a citizen of American-born ancestors, convicted of treason but out on parole—only Korematsu's presence would have violated the order. The difference between their innocence and his crime would result not from anything he did, said, or thought, different than they, but only in that he was born of different racial stock.[33]

Speculations about a hypothetical future also feed into a tenth and final sort of act. Although these are less commonly included in judicial opinions, judges have to think about how their own motives may be construed by future courts and lawyers. Speculations about future interpretations may lead opinion writers to emphasize the particular facts of the case before the court (suggesting that they were determinative), to display a concern that other courts might try to take the principle underlying its ruling too far (suggesting that those courts should not do so), to offer multiple grounds for a decision (suggesting that many reasons support the court's decision), and so forth.

But beyond simply making clear what was decided and how it was decided (an important administrative function, to be sure), courts construct (and embody) this tenth act—their own act of decision—to demonstrate that their motives are proper; that they are fair, knowledgeable, and just; that they meet the high demands of the rule of law. In their concern for this ultimate act, courts cannot casually ignore rhetorical constraints by appearing to run against the rulings of other cases for no good reason, ignoring the intent of the legislature, or bending the rules for a pitiable or powerful litigant while disregarding the effect of such a ruling on later cases. They understand that what they do influences how they are perceived.

Since judicial opinions indisputably construct these ten types of acts, and do so strategically to support their decisions and their credibility, the chief rhetorical work of the judicial opinion is to embody and characterize actions. And the "evidence" considered in judicial opinions can be fairly described as a plethora of acts and their motives.

Judicial Opinions and the Grammar of Motives

The most widely used approach to analyzing the rhetorical construction of motives comes from Kenneth Burke's theory of "dramatism" and employs

Burke's "pentad"—a heuristic for exploring motives through discourse.[34] Central to pentadic criticism is the conception of action. Burke notes that there are five elements required for something to be considered an "act" at all: it must involve (1) an *act* (2) undertaken by a human *agent* (or humanized agent such as a corporation), (3) within some *scene* or context, (4) through some *agency*, (5) for some *purpose*.[35] Any analysis of human motives, he argues, must use a terminology drawn from one or more of these constituents of action, considering specifically "what was done (act), when or where it was done (scene), who did it (agent), how he did it (agency), and why (purpose)."[36] Burke later extended this pentad to include *attitude*, answering the "how" question in the sense of "in what manner."[37]

Burke does not claim any originality for these pentadic terms or the questions that underlie them; rather, he claims that these questions about human motives are ubiquitous and appear in sources from Aristotle's *Nichomachean Ethics* to Talcott Parsons's *Structure of Social Action*, being fixed in the interim "in the medieval questions: *quis* (agent), *quid* (act), *ubi* (scene defined as place), *quibus auxiliis* (agency), *cur* (purpose), *quo modo* (manner, attitude), *quando* (scene defined temporarily)."[38] Each of these questions must be answered in any fully rounded statement of motives, because, as a whole, they encompass the logical constituents of action; hence, statements that disregard one or more of them are partial accounts and not as fully rounded as they could be.

Because each of these elements is connected in the structure of action (Burke's "grammar of motives"), an understanding of one term influences the understanding of all of the other terms.[39] Thus, whenever we perceive a scene, agent, act, agency, purpose, or attitude as having a given nature or quality, or we characterize one of those elements (or accept another's characterization), we "grammatically" limit potential interpretations of all the other terms. The grammatical limitations produced by perceptions and characterizations of the elements of action, taken as a whole, constitute the motive for the action in question. Motive, then, can best be understood as a configuration of the elements of action in a given case.[40]

Such configurations of motives may arise spontaneously or may be carefully crafted, a product of efforts to understand and explain or of efforts to persuade. We employ them when we account for our own actions, as well as the actions of others, even when those actions or those others are only predicted, proposed, possible, hypothetical, imagined, or generalized.[41] And, although rhetorical critics have looked almost exclusively for such configurations in verbal texts, they are not limited to the verbal—filmmakers, painters, mimes, advertisers, and many others rely upon the nonverbal to represent motives strategically.[42]

Following Burke's method, rhetorical critics seeking to understand the construction of motives in a given case must begin with a text,[43] identify the relevant acts to be analyzed, distinguish the pentadic elements, and then break down the elements of action into pairs or "ratios" for analysis, and interpret the results.[44] Identifying the text is easy for simple analyses of judicial opinions: one gets a copy of the decision and sees what the court said about what it was doing and why it was doing it. More complex analyses look to other texts that defend or question the characterizations of motives made by a court, enlarging the texts relevant to understanding the motives of a court. Such complex analyses are meta-analyses of motives, looking not merely at what a court says about what it is doing and why but at what others say about what the court said (and did not say) about what it was doing and why.

Once a text is located, one must identify the act or acts to be analyzed. In this case, the primary act is the act of the majority in deciding *Bush v. Gore*. However, this act is interpreted in light of other acts constructed by the Court, such as the act of the Florida Supreme Court in the appealed case, the acts of the canvassing boards, the acts of voters, and so forth. Each separate act constitutes a distinct pentadic set, each with its own unique terministic relationships.

The third step in pentadic analysis is to identify the terms embodied in a given pentadic set in the text under analysis. This involves looking in the text for key pentadic terms, which are answers to the questions: what act was done (act), who did it (agent), when and where it was done (scene), how (agency), why (purpose), and in what manner (attitude). There are many ways a text may characterize a pentadic term in answering its related question(s). For example, Burke notes the variety of answers to the questions of when and where, which concern the scene within which an act is done:

> Besides general synonyms for scene that are obviously of a background character, such as "society," or "environment," we often encounter quite specific localizations, words for particular places, situations, or eras. "It is 12:20 P.M." is a "scenic" statement. Milton's *L'Allegro* and *Il Penseroso* are formed about a scenic contrast between morning and night, with a corresponding contrast of actions. Terms for historical epochs, cultural movements, social institutions (such as "Elizabethan period," "romanticism," "capitalism") are scenic, though often with an admixture of properties

overlapping upon the areas covered by the term, agent. If we recall that "ideas" are a property of agents, we can detect this strategic overlap in Locke's expression, "The scene of ideas," the form of which Carl Becker exactly reproduces when referring to "climates of opinion," in *The Heavenly City of the Eighteenth-Century Philosophers.*[45]

The rhetorical critic must take care to look not simply for terms that are scenic or purposive or agency-related, and so on, on their face but for those that *function* within a particular grammar of motives as scene or purpose or agency, and so on. As Burke emphasizes, there is a great deal of overlap among his pentadic terms, and pentadic analyses should reveal *"the strategic spots at which ambiguities necessarily arise."*[46] For example, in the *Korematsu* case, the military's report on its decision to relocate 110,000 people of Japanese origin from the West Coast strategically converted rights-holding individual agents into a group that constituted a dangerous scene.[47] We engage in the same sort of dehumanizing transformation when we complain about a "crowded room," reducing individual people to their function as scenic elements.

After identifying the key pentadic terms of a given act, the fourth step in pentadic analysis involves identifying crucial ratios, or relationships between pentadic terms, taken in pairs for easier analysis. The goal is to see how the characterization of one term shapes our understanding of another term. Here is where the power of characterization is revealed. For example, Burke observes that one's characterization of a given situation "prescribes the range of acts that will seem reasonable, implicit, or necessary in that situation."[48] That is, when rhetors characterize scenes, they make audiences believe that certain actions ought to be taken—even before those actions are recommended.[49] Burke illustrates the workings of the scene-act relationship using an example from judicial rhetoric, taken from the *Korematsu* case:

> In a judgment written by Justice Hugo L. Black, the Supreme Court ruled that it was not "beyond the war powers of Congress and the Executive to exclude those of Japanese ancestry from the West Coast area at the time they did." And by implication, the scene-act ratio was invoked to substantiate the judgment: "When under conditions of modern warfare our shores are threatened by hostile forces, the power to protect must be commensurate with the threatened danger."[50]

Here the Supreme Court suggests that the scene (shores threatened by modern warfare) controls the act (allowing the exclusion of Japanese

Americans from the West Coast). Rhetorically, their characterization of this particular scene provides a justification for what otherwise might be deemed an unconstitutional act. Had the scene been characterized as "well protected" or the enemies inhabiting the scene as "inept" or as "armed with vastly inferior weapons," then the act would find less justification.

The particular way in which one grammatical element shapes another depends on their terministic relationship. Those relationships have general and specific dimensions. General dimensions are described and amply illustrated by Burke in *A Grammar of Motives*. For example, the scene contains the act; means (agencies) are adapted to ends (purposes); agents are the authors of their actions; and attitudes may be a first step to action or serve as a substitute for action. And, of course, terministic relationships flow both ways, so that while scenes may be said to contain acts, an act may create a scene.

Specific dimensions of terministic relations are normative, established by a discourse community's shared beliefs about what goes with what at a given point in time, underlying expectations that one will or should find certain types of agents engaging in certain types of actions, using certain agencies, within certain scenes, for certain purposes, evincing certain attitudes. Think of a burglar, for example—a type of agent—and consider how quickly you can list your own expectations about where you might find him, what he might be doing, when he might be doing it, how he might be doing it, why he might be doing it, and the attitude he might have. If you are successful in generating the list, you will understand how one term (agent) can shape an understanding of all the other terms.[51]

There are specific dimensions in judicial discourse as well, which include, for example, the purpose-agent ratio, which holds that an agent who brings a case to court is expected to have a stake in the outcome of the case under the doctrine of "standing" (the purpose creates an agent with standing). Rhetors rely on such expected terministic relations in persuading audiences to interpret motives in a particular way; on the other hand, if they would sever ties between related terms and question presumptive motives, they face a rhetorical challenge.

Roe v. Wade provides a good illustration of the Court's successful severing of terministic ties on the issue of standing: Dallas County district attorney Henry Wade argued that "Jane Roe" had no standing to bring her lawsuit, because in light of the lengthy appeals process, she was no longer pregnant (hence, this agent had no personal purpose for pursuing this litigation).[52] A dissenting Associate Justice William Rehnquist invoked the purpose-agent ratio as well, agreeing that this was a "hypothetical lawsuit" which rendered the case moot.[53] To sever this presumptive tie between purpose and agent, Associate Justice Harry Blackmun wrote for the majority:

> The usual rule in federal cases is that an actual controversy must exist at stages of appellate or certiorari review, and not simply at the date the action is initiated.
>
> But when, as here, pregnancy is a significant fact in the litigation, the normal 266-day human gestation period is so short that the pregnancy will come to term before the usual appellate process is complete. If that termination makes a case moot, pregnancy litigation seldom will survive much beyond the trial stage, and appellate review will be effectively denied. Our law should not be that rigid. Pregnancy often comes more than once to the same woman, and in the general population, if man is to survive, it will always be with us.
>
> Pregnancy provides a classic justification for a conclusion of nonmootness.[54]

In most instances where motives are at issue, prior discourses, perceptions, and assumptions prefigure particular terministic relations (and their corresponding motives), for to name an agent, to describe a scene, to invoke a purpose, to perceive an agency, or to suggest an act is to ratchet up a grammatical logic that undergirds the human ability to size up a situation. The actions characterized by judges—legislative enactments, the actions of a criminal defendant, the judgments of trial and appellate courts, and so forth—are almost always prefigured by textual accounts and embodiments of those actions. Long lines of judicial decisions account for the motives behind constitutional enactments. Statutory preambles posit the raison d'être of legislation. Trial courts determine the factual questions about what defendants were doing and why they were doing it. Legal scholars prophesy about future actions of persons and corporations if particular judicial decisions are reached. And, of course, competing litigants line up their own divergent constructions of relevant actions for judicial endorsement.

All of this prefiguring may appear a boon to judges, who may sit back and choose among competing characterizations as they like. However, judges must mold together characterizations of divergent actions into a coherent whole that embodies decision making that is understandable and acceptable to the legal community and those who watch it. In this molding process, grammatical choices judges make in characterizing actions carry implications beyond individual pentadic sets (i.e., beyond particular acts and their corresponding scenes, agents, agencies, purposes, and attitudes). For example, a judge intent on finding a criminal guilty of violating a particular statute may construe the criminal's act so that it fits easily into the category of crimes covered by that statute; on the other hand, if the facts surrounding the criminal act require too much straining for that, the judge may construe the legislative act of passing the statute in a way that broadens its coverage to include the criminal act.

Judges cannot strain grammatical logic with impunity, however; rhetorical choices in one or more pentadic sets can become rhetorical constraints in others, particularly in the pentadic set that includes the judge as agent—the judicial decision itself. Ideally, a decision maker's discourse will avoid serious grammatical strains and show unequivocally (1) that prior cases, long-accepted legal principles, legislative statutes, administrative regulations, state and federal constitutions, and their authors (whose intentions are invoked) require the decision; (2) that the decision yields the greatest justice in the instant case (given characterizations of litigants as deserving of legal reward or punishment); and (3) that the decision creates the fairest and most efficacious results in the long run, providing clear direction and a just outcome for all foreseeable cases like it.

If prefiguration, grammatical constraint (within and between pentadic sets), or a lack of inventional ingenuity prevents a judge from reaching this ideal, he or she nonetheless strives toward it, for falling too far short is to shirk judicial responsibility (by failing to follow the law, do justice in the individual case, and lay down rules to guide future conduct and decision making). Generally, the further a judge falls from this ideal—by ignoring or straining the grammatical logic within which he or she must work rhetorically—the less persuasive his or her argument.

2

The Road to *Bush v. Gore*

The 2000 presidential election pitted Democrat Vice President Al Gore against Republican Governor George W. Bush, with third-party runs by Ralph Nader on the left and Patrick Buchanan on the right. In one of the closest presidential elections in history, Bush won the Electoral College and the presidency with 271 electoral votes to Gore's 266, while Gore won the popular vote by more than half a million votes. The election came down to a battle over Florida's 25 electoral votes, which turned on a final 537-vote lead for Bush out of almost 6 million votes cast.[1]

Election 2000's roller coaster ride began at 6:48 P.M. (CST), when NBC called the Florida contest for Gore.[2] Within twelve minutes, all major networks joined in the prediction, relying on the same erroneous Voter News Service numbers as NBC.[3] Two hours later, with egg on their faces, the networks began retracting their call for Gore and said the race was too close to call. At 1:16 A.M., the networks began calling the election for Bush. Fifteen minutes later, Gore called Bush to concede the election. But between the time Gore called Bush and his arrival at Nashville's War Memorial to give his concession speech, Bush's lead had dwindled from 50,000 to less than 2,000, ensuring an automatic recount in Florida. Gore called Bush back at

2:30 A.M. to retract his concession. Gore campaign chairman Bill Daley addressed the waiting crowd at the War Memorial to announce that until the recounts were completed, the campaign would continue.[4]

During the next thirty-six days, Bush never lost his lead, though it fluctuated wildly between its early high of 1,784 votes and its low of 154 votes just before the U.S. Supreme Court intervened.[5] Those fluctuations resulted from changes wrought by automatic recounts, manual recounts, corrections of errors, and the addition of overseas ballots.

The Gore team recruited former secretary of state Warren Christopher to head up the postelection effort; the Bush team countered with its own former secretary of state, James Baker. Daley and Christopher got to work quickly, calling for manual recounts in Broward, Miami-Dade, Palm Beach, and Volusia Counties—Democratic strongholds where Gore had won by large margins. As those counties considered Gore's request and conducted recounts in sample precincts, the automatic recounts were completed. The Associated Press announced on November 10 that Bush's lead had been whittled to 327 votes in the automatic recount.[6]

The Bush team countered these efforts by filing a request in U.S. District Court on November 11 to stop the hand recounts, which was denied. On November 16, they filed an appeal in federal Circuit Court in Atlanta to stop the recounts because of unequal treatment of ballots, which was also denied.[7]

Although they were stymied by the courts at this point, the Bush team had more success with Florida's executive branch, which was led by George W. Bush's brother Jeb. Although the Governor recused himself from the state's Election Commission,[8] the Bush team found an ally in Secretary of State Katherine Harris, a Republican, Florida's chief election officer, and cochair of Bush's Florida campaign. Prodded by a Republican lobbyist sent to Tallahassee by the Bush team to "bring this election in for a landing,"[9] Harris announced that she would not extend the deadline for the slow-moving recounts past November 14, even though under federal law, she could not certify the election until November 17. She also issued an opinion letter, at the request of the state chairman of the Republican Party, that interpreted state law as limiting recounts to correcting tabulation errors that could be traced to the vote-counting machines, not to voter errors in marking ballots.[10] This letter convinced Broward and Palm Beach Counties that they should cancel hand recounts.[11] When required by a county circuit judge to exercise her discretion in considering late returns (instead of summarily dismissing them), Harris asked the recounting counties to state their reasons, reviewed them, and then quickly rejected them, urging that only fraud, statutory violations, or a natural disaster could justify an extension.[12] Contrary to law and long-standing practice, Harris directed counties to accept overseas absentee ballots even if they were not postmarked on or before the election, and these overseas ballots heavily favored Bush.[13] She accepted without question absentee ballots from Seminole County, where Republican Party officials had filled in missing voter identification numbers on thousands of Republican absentee ballot applications in plain violation of state law.[14] She also accepted revised vote totals from Republican-controlled Nassau County, which threw out the mandatory automatic recount totals and reverted to original counts that gave Bush 51 more votes.[15]

Gore got help from allies as well. Florida's Democratic attorney general, Robert A. Butterworth, sent an advisory letter to the canvassing boards countering Harris's claim that recounts were limited to errors traceable to election machinery. By urging that voter error was a valid reason for justifying a recount, he persuaded Palm Beach County to restart its recount.[16] A Democratic lawyer filed a suit to have the Seminole County absentee ballots that were filled out by Republican operatives thrown out.[17] And a Gore lawyer circulated a much-criticized memo that outlined a strategy for mounting legal challenges against absentee ballots, including those from military voters.[18]

In response to Bush's legal efforts, the Gore team initiated a volley of legal suits to ensure that deadlines were extended and that more ballots were reviewed. They unsuccessfully sought an extension of the deadline for recounts at the county circuit court level but won a ruling that the secretary of state could not arbitrarily rule out late returns.[19] They persuaded the Florida Supreme Court to endorse the continuation of manual recounts,[20] to delay certification of the vote,[21] and eventually to order a statewide recount of all undervotes.[22] They were rebuffed by the same court when they asked for a new election in Palm Beach County to remedy the "butterfly ballot" problem,[23] when they asked that Miami-Dade County be forced to resume a recount (which it canceled after a mob of Republicans threatened the canvassing board),[24] and when they requested an immediate recount of 14,000 disputed ballots from South Florida.[25]

When facing the U.S. Supreme Court, Gore batted 0 for 3. First, the High Court vacated the decision of the Florida Supreme Court extending the deadline for recounts and for certification.[26] The High Court intervened a second time after the Florida Supreme Court ordered a statewide recount of all undervotes, staying the recount pending its ruling.[27] Finally, the High Court ruled in *Bush v. Gore* that the recount violated the equal protection clause of the Fourteenth Amendment, because differing standards were used in the recounts.[28] This last decision effectively gave the election to Bush, since the Court asserted that Florida law required that votes be certified by December 12 to take advantage of a federal safe harbor provision (ensuring that the state's electors could not be challenged), and that was the date the decision was handed down.

The day after the *Bush v. Gore* decision, Gore conceded the election.[29] On December 18, the Electoral College cast its votes. On January 6, 2001, Congress counted those votes, thwarting an attempt to block the vote by members of the Congressional Black Caucus who were upset about the disenfranchisement of many African-Americans in Florida.[30] On January 20, 2001, George W. Bush was sworn in as the forty-third president of the United States.

The Florida Supreme Court's Decisions

Because the U.S. Supreme Court's intervention in Election 2000 came as a response to decisions of the Florida Supreme Court, two of the state court's most relevant decisions deserve review in greater detail.

Palm Beach County Canvassing Board v. Harris

Palm Beach County Canvassing Board v. Harris[31] prompted the first intervention by the U.S. Supreme Court.[32] Following the automatic recounts of all Florida votes (required by state law since Bush's lead was less than one-half of one percent), Broward, Miami-Dade, Palm Beach, and Volusia Counties conducted sample recounts of at least one percent of the votes in their districts. On the basis of these sample recounts, Palm Beach and Volusia Counties decided to conduct full manual recounts of votes in their districts. These recounts had scarcely begun on November 13 when Harris announced that all county returns had to be in her office by 5:00 P.M. the next day. Concerned that it could not complete recounts, the Volusia County Canvassing Board asked the Second Circuit Court in Leon County for an injunction to bar the secretary of state from ignoring recounts that came in after that date. The trial court ruled on November 14 that the deadline was mandatory but that the secretary could exercise her discretion in considering whether to accept the late returns. The Canvassing Board appealed this ruling and was joined by the Palm Beach County Canvassing Board.

In the meantime, Harris asked the canvassing boards to state their reasons for filing late returns, reviewed them, and rejected them, announcing that she would certify the election on November 18 after the overseas ballots were counted and added to the totals.[33] On November 16, Gore filed an appeal in the Florida Circuit Court to require Harris to accept amended returns but was denied. Gore appealed, and his case, along with the canvassing boards' case, was heard by the Florida Supreme Court.[34]

The Florida high court considered two primary issues. First was the question of what the Florida statutes meant by an "error in vote tabulation." The justification for a manual recount in Florida is an "error in vote tabulation which could affect the outcome of the election,"[35] so knowing what constituted such an error was critical. The secretary of state's interpretation of "error in vote tabulation" would "exclude the situation where a discrepancy between the original machine return and sample manual recount is due to the manner in which a ballot has been marked or punched."[36] The Florida court rejected this interpretation, insisting: "The plain language of section 102.166(5) refers to an error in the vote tabulation rather than the vote tabulation system. On its face, the statute does not include any words of limitation; rather, it provides a remedy for any type of mistake made in tabulating ballots" (1229). The court added that language in a provision dealing with damaged or defective ballots ensured that "no vote shall be declared invalid or void if there is a clear indication of the intent of the voter as determined by the canvassing board" (quoting Florida Statutes § 101.5614 [5] at 1229). The Florida Supreme Court used this and other provisions of Florida election law, as well as goals reflected in the Florida Constitution and in the idea of democracy more generally to ensure that state power resides in the people (1227–28), to urge that the failure of machines to count improperly marked ballots did encompass an "error in vote tabulation." This ruling meant that county canvassing boards could justify their decisions to recount, despite the secretary's opinion to the contrary.

The second issue to be addressed was the question of the seven-day deadline. Here a poorly wrought statute gave the court an excuse to reconsider the deadlines. The statutes had two problems. First was a conflict between the "shall" and "may" provisions of the election statutes. Section 102.111(1) states that "[i]f the county returns are not received by the Department of State by 5 P.M. of the seventh day following an election, all missing counties *shall* be ignored, and the results shown by the returns on file shall be certified" (emphasis added). That implies that the November 14 deadline was firm. But section 102.112(1) states that "If the returns are not received by the department [of State] by the time specified [i.e., seven days after the election], such returns *may* be ignored and the results on file at that time may be certified by the department" (emphasis added). This latter provision implies that there is flexibility in the November 14 date.

A further discrepancy arose from the deadlines for requesting and completing manual recounts. Florida law requires that a request for a manual recount "must be filed with the canvassing board prior to the time the canvassing board certifies the results for the office being protested or within 72 hours after midnight of the date the election was held, whichever occurs later."[37] That means that Gore could have requested a recount on November 10 or even as late as November 14 if the canvassing boards from which he sought recounts had not certified their vote totals. Yet if the November 14 date was mandatory and no manual recounts could be accepted after that date, this provision appears meaningless. Furthermore, even if a request were filed by the November 10 deadline, it is not clear that large counties (such as Miami-Dade) would have time to conduct a recount.

The Florida Supreme Court resolved these discrepancies by setting a new deadline that would give the canvassing boards a reasonable amount of time to complete the manual recounts. First, addressing the "may" and "shall" conflict, the court noted that the "shall" provision came from a more specific and more recently enacted provision entitled "Deadline for submission of county returns to the Department of State; penalties." Invoking statutory rules that give preference to more specific and more recent provisions, the court supported the more permissive interpretation (1234). It also noted that section 102.112 included provisions for fining tardy canvassing board members $200 per day for each day the returns were late—a provision that would be meaningless if late returns had to be ignored (1234–35).

Noting the discrepancy in the deadline for filing a protest and the deadline for canvassing boards to turn in their totals, the Court found that in the case where a candidate files a protest on the sixth day after the election, "if the mandatory provision in section 102.111 were given effect, the votes of the county would be ignored for the simple reason that the Board was following the dictates of a different section of the Code [i.e., one that permits such last-minute protest filings]. The Legislature could not have intended to penalize County Canvassing Boards for following the dictates of the Code" (1235).

The Florida court raised a red flag to the U.S. Supreme Court when it considered under what circumstances the secretary of state may legally ignore vote totals submitted after the seven-day deadline. The state court relied upon the Florida Constitution's Declaration of Rights, insisting: "The right of suffrage is the preeminent right contained in the Declaration of Rights, for without this basic freedom all others would be diminished" (1236). Given the centrality of the right of suffrage in the Florida Constitution, the court found that the secretary of state was limited in her power to reject late returns by the need to provide adequate time for recounts on the one hand and, on the other hand, the need to ensure time for any contests to the election results to be filed. The court settled on a new deadline of November 26, 2000, for manual recount totals to be submitted.[38]

Bush appealed the Florida decision to the U.S. Supreme Court, citing three grounds. First, he argued that the Florida Supreme Court violated Article II of the U.S. Constitution by changing state election law, when the Constitution requires that the appointment of presidential electors shall be made "in such Manner as the Legislature [and presumably not the judiciary] may direct."[39] Second, Bush argued that the state court did not merely *interpret* but *changed* state law after the election in violation of 3 USC § 5.[40] Finally, raising an issue that would prove critical to the outcome of the election controversy, Bush argued that the lack of clear standards for the recounts was a violation of the due process and equal protection clauses of the U.S. Constitution.[41]

On November 24, the U.S. Supreme Court agreed to hear the case on the first two questions raised by Bush (leaving out the equal protection issue).[42] On the same day, it turned down Bush's appeal from a U.S. Circuit Court decision that refused to stop the manual recounts.[43] By the time the High Court heard oral arguments on December 1, the case was essentially moot, since the Florida Supreme Court's November 26 deadline for recount returns to be filed had passed, and some wondered why Bush did not withdraw the suit.[44] The Court's December 4 decision was unanimous and very modest. It vacated the decision and asked the Florida Supreme Court to clarify the basis for its conclusions; it especially wanted the state court to explain how much it thought the Florida Constitution circumscribed the state legislature's authority to direct the manner of selecting presidential electors and the weight the state court gave to the safe harbor provision (which ensured that state electors certified by December 12 could not be challenged by Congress) in its ruling.[45]

Gore v. Harris

Gore v. Harris involved an appeal from a judgment by a Leon County trial
court that had denied all relief to Gore under the "contest" provisions of
Florida election law. The Florida Supreme Court took up this case on December 7 and handed down a judgment the next day.[46]

The Florida Supreme Court reported that Gore had filed a contest challenge to the election results "on the grounds that the results certified by
the Canvassing Commission included 'a number of illegal votes' and failed
to include 'a number of legal votes sufficient to change or place in doubt
the result of the election'" (1247, citing § 102.168(3)(c), Fla. Stat. [2000]).
Gore argued for five instances in which legal votes had been excluded or illegal votes included in totals. Among the excluded legal votes, Gore contended, were 215 net votes for Gore counted in Palm Beach but rejected by
the secretary of state for missing the submission deadline, 168 others in
Miami-Dade that were rejected for the same reason, 3,300 ballots that allegedly were for Gore but were set aside in Palm Beach because the canvassing board could not discern the voters' intent, and 9,000 ballots from
Miami-Dade County that were never manually counted. Among allegedly
illegal votes included in the totals were the larger Nassau County Election
Night tabulations, which that county's canvassing board submitted instead
of the later, smaller automatic recount totals, thereby giving Bush 51 more
votes.[47]

The Florida Supreme Court held, in a 4-3 per curiam decision, that the
trial court erred as a matter of law in not including the partial recounts
from Palm Beach and Miami-Dade Counties and in not calling for a review
of the 9,000 ballots from Miami-Dade, which presumably included ballots
where voter intent could be discerned. They rejected Gore's appeal for the
3,300 ballots from Miami-Dade County and the Nassau ballots, deferring to
the trial court, because these involved "mixed questions of law and fact"
(1248).

The court began by noting that § 102.168 of the Florida Statutes provided that election contests are to be resolved in a judicial forum (1249).
Indeed, the court noted, the grant of authority is very broad in that statute,
authorizing the circuit court judge to "fashion such orders as he or she
deems necessary to *ensure that each allegation in the complaint is investigated,
examined, or checked, to prevent or correct any alleged wrong, and to provide any
relief appropriate under the circumstances*" (quoting § 102.168[8] with emphasis at 1250). The court cited legislative committee reports noting the importance of accurate recounts (1251).

The court criticized the trial court's standard of review, which had judged the canvassing boards' action by an "abuse of discretion" standard. The court insisted that this was the wrong standard because "[t]he trial court in the contest action does not sit as an appellate court over the decisions of the Canvassing Board. Accordingly, while the Board's actions concerning the elections process may constitute evidence in a contest proceedings, the Board's decisions are not to be accorded the highly deferential 'abuse of discretion' standard of review during a contest proceeding" (1252).

The court also took the trial judge to task for misapplying a second standard. Judge N. Sanders Sauls had ruled at trial that Gore was required to show that there was a "*reasonable probability* that the results of the election would have been changed" (1255; emphasis added). The higher court noted that the judge was relying on a standard used before the 1999 revision of the election statutes. That revision set a specific, new standard: "the '[r]eceipt of a number of illegal votes or rejection of a number of legal votes sufficient to change *or place in doubt* the result of the election'" (quoting with emphasis from § 102.168 [c] at 1255). Given the closeness of the election and the large number of undervotes yet to be counted, the court found that Gore met this threshold requirement (1256). That burden was even easier to meet when the court determined that a recount of undervotes should include not simply the 9,000 ballots in Miami-Dade County but undervotes throughout the state, since "[r]elief would not be 'appropriate under [the] circumstances' if it failed to address the 'otherwise valid exercise of the right of a citizen to vote' of all those citizens of this State who, being similarly situated, have had their legal votes rejected" (1254).

Ultimately, the entire case turned on how the court defined "legal vote." Obviously, the concern for relief for voters who had their legal votes rejected would go away if improperly marked ballots (which typically constituted undervotes) were not legal votes. Florida law does not define a legal vote, so the court searched the statutes for some direction, landing on section 101.5614(5), which deals with the examination of damaged or defective ballots and insists "[n]o vote shall be declared invalid or void if there is a clear indication of the intent of the voter as determined by the canvassing board" (quoted at 1256). The court cited several precedents from Florida and other states to show that "so long as the voter's intent may be discerned from the ballot, the vote constitutes a 'legal vote' that should be counted" (1256). The court concluded that "a legal vote is one in which there is a 'clear indication of the intent of the voter'" (1257).

The case was remanded back to Judge Sauls, who recused himself; the case was reassigned to Judge Terry Lewis, who had previously ruled in favor of Bush in denying that Secretary Harris had abused her discretion in ignoring late recounts. Judge Lewis set in motion a statewide recount of undervotes which began the next morning, December 9. That afternoon, at the request of Bush, the U.S. Supreme Court intervened and granted a stay of the recounts on a 5-4 vote. It heard arguments on December 11 and handed down its election-ending decision on December 12.

The Stay Order

Deploying the pentad provides an initial analysis of the construction of the Court's motives by Justice Scalia in the stay order, as well as the dissent's alternative construction.

A stay is a form of "quick justice" built around an embarrassment and a paradox. The embarrassment is that while judicial processes are central to ensuring justice, they are too slow to do so in some cases. That is, while the formal, deliberate means (agency) of judicial decision making is necessary to the ends of justice (i.e., the purpose requires this agency), those means may actually thwart that purpose in some cases. For example, if a convicted murderer on Death Row appeals his conviction but is executed before a slow-moving appellate court overturns his conviction, that victory will provide little comfort to him given the "irreparable harm" of his execution. Thus, we have the stay to stop such executions so that slow-moving courts have enough time to reach their decisions. Paradoxically, to ensure that justice is met (the ultimate purpose), the stay order shortcuts the process (the agency) by rendering a quick decision without the benefit of substantial briefing, oral argument, thoughtful deliberation, or careful opinion writing. Though such quick decisions do not reflect the sort of deliberation required to meet the demands of justice, paradoxically, without that quickness, a court might miss the chance to offer *any* justice.

Now the paradox and embarrassment of the stay are tempered somewhat by truncation of all of its elements. Thus, working within a restricted scene (little time), we expect a restricted agency (little deliberation), a restricted purpose (to prevent irreparable harm and provide temporary justice), and sometimes even a restricted agent (whereby a single Supreme Court justice might grant a stay, rather than the entire Court). This restricted act of granting a temporary suspension might even bring with it a restricted attitude, which undertakes such action less deliberately and less cautiously.

The rhetorical strategy of the stay takes its character as a restricted form of action for granted; the real rhetorical work goes on in characterizing two related acts. First, the court must construct a believable act of "suffering irreparable harm." This is a proposed or hypothetical act whose harm is not yet realized (if it were, there would be no need for a stay). To construct this harm effectively, the court must show that the hypothetical or proposed act of suffering is likely—that the scene is ripe for it, that the means are in place, that the agent is susceptible to it, and perhaps that it has purpose. Alternatively, and perhaps more typically, the petitioner's potential act of suffering is transformed into the agency of another's actions. In this sense, the passivity of the petitioner is enhanced (making an even more suitably Christlike victim to protect), as his or her suffering serves the purposes of someone else's act. In justifying the grant of stays, courts may wish to show that the actions of others that are likely to cause irreparable harm are driven by questionable motives—illegal agencies, selfish purposes, ruthless attitudes, and so forth. Even if some of these motive characterizations are extralegal in their significance, they still help paint a picture of justice in granting a stay.

The second act the court must construct is its own future act of decision, one in which the outcome would favor the petitioner. This is the requirement that the petitioner show that he or she likely will win the appeal that follows the stay, making permanent the temporary justice provided by the stay. From one perspective, this construction is unproblematic; after all, the court approving the stay is simply predicting what it itself will do in the future.[48] On the other hand, such predictions assume that the conclusions of a deliberate judicial process (ends wrought through appropriately thoughtful means) can be foretold even in the truncated scene, and with the truncated agency, of a stay order.

The one-paragraph stay order of December 9, 2000, suspended the Florida Supreme Court's order to its circuit court and stopped the recount of the votes in Florida.[49] It set dates for the Bush and Gore lawyers to submit briefs and to present oral arguments. It was supported by the five most conservative members of the U.S. Supreme Court: Chief Justice William Rehnquist and Associate Justices Anthony Kennedy, Sandra Day O'Connor, Antonin Scalia, and Clarence Thomas. It was opposed by the most liberal members of the Court, Associate Justices Stephen Breyer, Ruth Bader Ginsburg, David Souter, and John Paul Stevens. Justice Stevens

wrote a scathing dissent from the stay order, which the other three dissenters joined, prompting Justice Scalia to write a brief response, concurring with the stay order's judgment.

Justice Stevens complained that by "stop[ping] the counting of legal
votes, the majority today departs from three venerable rules of judicial restraint that have guided the Court throughout its history" (512). Those traditions are respecting state supreme court rulings interpreting their own
law, deferring to other branches of federal government with jurisdiction to
settle disputes, and declining to rule on constitutional questions "not fairly
presented" (512–13). Stevens's invocation of rules draws upon the power
of agency as a curb on Court action, for to follow a rule is to use it as a
means for directing action (through the agency-act relationship). But
Stevens also calls these rules "venerable," suggesting that they are "tried
and true." These agencies, he implies, have become part of the judicial
scene insofar as they "have guided the Court throughout its history." Technically, we may note, the actions of the Court in following these rules frequently in the past has created a scene within which the current Court
does its work. Stevens does not cite any of those earlier actions of following these rules but implies that they are legion. Thus, there are two "grammatical" imperatives invoked here: one deriving from agency (the Court
ought to employ these rules to guide its conduct) and one deriving from
scene (this history should contain the Court's actions in the present case).
In failing to follow these venerable principles or to adapt its actions to a judicial scene within which they are operative, the majority ordering the stay
flouts "restraint" and engages in inappropriate activism.

Stevens turns next to the claim that Bush would be irreparably harmed
without the stay. Such irreparable harm must take into account not only
the harms avoided by granting the stay but the harms it causes, through a
"balance of equities."[50] Both harms to Bush and to Gore in this stay are hypothetical, requiring both Stevens and Scalia to elaborate the harms attendant to the stay in support of their own positions.

Stevens began not by considering the circumstances under which Bush
might be harmed by the failure to grant a stay but by considering Bush's
act of requesting a stay, finding that he must make "a substantial showing
of a likelihood of irreparable harm" and insisting that he had "failed to
carry that heavy burden" (513). By emphasizing the size of the task Bush
was required to complete (i.e., substantial and heavy), Stevens suggested
that he had failed. Furthermore, the justice noted, "[c]ounting every
legally cast vote cannot constitute irreparable harm," presumably because

what counts as harm itself is circumscribed by the agency that causes it. Using legal means (agency), he implied, cannot yield the sort of harm that is actionable. So even if Bush were harmed, it would not be the sort of harm he could use to justify a stay.

Stevens's construction turns on the assumption that the votes that were being counted were legally cast, since counting illegal votes arguably might cause irreparable harm of the sort recognized for the purposes of a stay. To bolster this characterization, Stevens had to defend the Florida Supreme Court's assertion that the votes being recounted were legally cast. For the purposes of attacking the stay order, Stevens limited his claim to a negative one: "It is certainly not clear that the Florida decision violated federal law" (513). That clarity was necessary for the U.S. Supreme Court to overcome the deference it owed to the state court. Citing numerous statutes and precedents, Stevens argued that the Florida court's ruling followed the policies reflected in Florida's statutes, Florida's court decisions, other states' court decisions, the U.S. Constitution, and the ideals of democracy that "every legal vote should be counted" (513). Thus, according to Stevens, the Florida court was bound by the law—the ultimate agency guiding judicial action.

Giving deference to Florida's highest court and its ruling that the votes being recounted were legally cast supported Stevens's claim that there was no cognizable harm to Bush, and Florida's "justified" ruling redounded upon Stevens's construction of the Court's own stay ruling, suggesting that it was unsupported. Because the U.S. Supreme Court failed to adhere to three venerable principles of judicial restraint and supported a stay where the appellant failed to show irreparable harm, Stevens could claim that the majority was activist and errant in issuing the stay.

Stevens went further to suggest that Gore and the public would be seriously harmed by the stay, implying that the majority had failed to "balance equities" in considering harm in the case. Quoting his own opinion in an earlier Supreme Court case, he insisted that "the entry of the stay would be tantamount to a decision on the merits in favor of the applicants."[51] In other words, approving the stay (the Supreme Court's first act) is equivalent to making the final decision in favor of the petitioner (the Supreme Court's final act), a concern that a precedent Court decision declared problematic. Underlying this claim is an implied concern about scene, for the equivalency of the first and final acts turned on the shortness of time left for Gore to complete the recounts.

As a final consideration on the issue of harm, Stevens predicted that the stay actually might hurt Bush in the long run, noting: "Preventing the recount from being completed will inevitably cast a cloud on the legitimacy of the election." Here the Supreme Court's act (preventing the recount) would create a scene, metaphorically represented as a cloud that would hurt Bush by making his election appear questionable.

Justice Scalia characterized his opinion concurring with the Court's stay as an unusual act, one "not customary" but made "necessary" as a response to Justice Stevens's dissent. Justice Stevens's characterization of the majority's stay decision apparently had undermined the Court's credibility, requiring some repair by Scalia. Scalia's response sought to demonstrate that the Court had met the two criteria for granting a stay: showing (1) that, absent the stay, Bush would suffer irreparable harm and (2) that Bush likely would win his appeal.[52]

Justice Scalia refused to address the merits of the case (as Stevens had, briefly), "since they will shortly be before us in the petition for certiorari we have granted" (512). This is a scenic appeal, suggesting not that the justice had considered the substance of the case but that in a sense he was close to it. It also invokes a sense of order—an agency concern—or a manner of proceeding that makes consideration of the merits premature (where agency and scene overlap, so that one thing must follow another in time).

Tersely, he announced that "[i]t suffices to say that the issuance of the stay suggests that a majority of the Court, while not deciding the issues presented, believe that the petitioner has a substantial probability of success" (512). This act in which the majority is engaging is one of believing, as contrasted with the act of deciding, that Bush will win his appeal. Believing is less deliberate, less formal, and less authoritative than deciding. It does not commit the majority to finding for Bush, though it evinces an attitude that leans in his direction. The agencies of believing are less rigorous than those of deciding, involving a feeling, a sense, an overall ballpark assessment. They do not require an explanation of how one reached a particular belief (as one must normally justify an important decision).

This terse line also connects two acts rather smugly. The issuance of the stay becomes a sign that the majority will rule for Bush. In a sense, this is the symbolic import of the stay: to send a signal that the Court is siding with Bush or his position. In grammatical terms, the Court is evincing an attitude (for they have no agencies of decision, having not considered the substantive issues) which Scalia believes will carry over into the final decision (with attitude controlling act when they get to the ultimate case). Since Scalia is speaking for himself here, it also represents the justice's own construction of what the court was doing in this stay.

If Stevens's discussion of the Florida Supreme Court's law-following act of deciding that legally cast ballots must be recounted supported the denial of Bush's harm and, thereby, the basis for his stay, Scalia's insistence that Bush was likely to win his appeal served the opposite purpose, showing that Bush *would* be harmed because the ballots being counted were "of questionable legality." The similarity to Stevens's argument is striking where Scalia states, "[t]he counting of votes that are of questionable legality does in my view threaten irreparable harm to petitioner, and to the country, by casting a cloud upon what he claims to be the legitimacy of his election" (512). Here Scalia's substitution of a potentially illegal agency (counting questionable votes) for Stevens's legal agency (counting legal votes) yields a cognizable harm, a scenic cloud to match Stevens's own. Scalia bolsters his claim that the agency of recounting might be illegal by accusing the Florida Supreme Court "of letting the standard for determination of voters' intent—dimpled chads, hanging chads, etc—vary from county to county," raising constitutional questions (512).

But Scalia's characterization of an illegal agency yielding a cognizable harm makes an assumption that he refused to note. The irreparable harm in recounting could be realized only if Bush lost his lead in the election. For certainly Bush would not be harmed if the recount showed that he won the election after the additional "questionable" votes were added to the totals. In fact, that would *dispel* the cloud of suspicion (and harm) that so worries Scalia. Although Gore had made gains in the earlier recounts in selected Democratic strongholds, it was not clear that he would continue to make gains in the statewide recount ordered by the state court, which included just as many Republican strongholds. Thus, the new scene of recounts did not support the assumption that the acts of recounting would be qualitatively similar. But perhaps the mere possibility that Gore might take the lead was enough for Scalia and the majority.

That possibility created concerns beyond those of Bush alone, Scalia insisted, warning: "Count first, and rule upon legality afterwards, is not a recipe for producing election results that have the public acceptance democratic stability requires" (512). Again, this assertion rests on the assumption that Gore would take the lead, that the Court would then announce that the Gore lead was achieved by counting illegal votes, and finally that the Court would reverse these election results. This future scenario rests the problem with the public, who may not accept such results and, therefore, may become unstable. Thus, the Court sets itself up as a protector against democratic instability wrought by an American public likely to be unconvinced by the Court's subsequent actions.

A final curiosity is reflected in Scalia's use of the word *recipe*. Scalia imagines the justice system as agent (a chef of sorts), which is both making and following a recipe (an act of creative cooking) to yield the cupcakes of democratic satisfaction. And just as in following a recipe, the order of the steps is crucial, with counting followed by ruling the wrong order.

Both Stevens's and Scalia's opinions involve bootstrapping arguments, whereby assumptions about the legality or illegality of the recounts lead to conclusions about the lack of harm or the harm to Bush. Such assumptions are undoubtedly common for stays, with their truncated deliberation. Those bootstraps are lightly fortified with brief considerations of the probable constitutionality or unconstitutionality of Florida's recount order and by considerations of what might follow from approving or disapproving the stay. Scalia's consideration of harm for Bush is the more speculative, since it is unclear whether the race's leader would change; Stevens could be certain that not counting the votes would hurt Gore by leaving him without a chance to gain the lead and with little time to restart the recounts should the High Court permit it.

3

The U.S. Supreme Court
Decides the Election

Following the stay order of December 9, 2000, the U.S. Supreme Court heard oral arguments on December 11 and handed down its final decision at 10:00 P.M. on December 12, two hours before the end of the safe harbor period for states to submit their vote totals and ensure that no challenges would be made when Congress convened to tally the electoral votes officially on January 6, 2001. Television reporters standing in front of the darkened Supreme Court building struggled to make sense of the text of the decision distributed by the clerk.[1] CNN's Jeff Greenfield remembered an old law school trick and flipped to the dissenting opinions for a stark, anguished statement of what the majority had wrought.[2]

The Bush v. Gore *Majority Opinion*

The *Bush v. Gore* majority opinion begins on an unusual note: it fails to identify its author.[3] Instead, the agent of this monumental decision is an undifferentiated court, the curia in this per curiam decision. Per curiam decisions are normally handed down as unanimous decisions and accompany summary dispositions rather than fully developed opinions.[4] Using the per curiam label for the agent typically lends a sense of broad support for a decision (as a sign of a unanimous decision); but as a representation of the five in a 5-4 split (where three in the majority filed a separate concurrence), it appears almost as if no author wanted to claim it. It functions to hide the roles of Justices Kennedy and O'Connor, whose names appear nowhere in any of the opinions.[5] On the other hand, it mimics the per curiam in the 4-3 Florida decision it overturns, answering camouflaged agent with camouflaged agent.

Reconstructing the History of the Case and the Issues

The majority began with a consideration of the actions and events that led to the controversy before it, including even the previous decision by the state court that had been vacated and remanded back to it for explanation. This review of the history of the case strategically characterized a number of acts to make the election appear less uncertain than it was and the Florida Supreme Court to appear inconsiderate of the requirements of law. On the election results, the majority noted that Bush's 1,784-vote lead from election night was reduced by the automatic recounts, though Bush still led with a "diminished margin" (528). The generality of that term, *diminished margin,* simply may reflect the Court's unwillingness to endorse any of the various postelection numbers, but it also draws attention away from the precipitous drop in Bush's lead (more than 70 percent by the time of certification) and the minuscule size of the lead he unofficially held when the Court stopped the recount (154 votes).

In judging Secretary of State Katherine Harris's role in the election controversy, the Court depicted her actions as passive and law-abiding, noting that "[t]he Secretary declined to waive the November 14 deadline [for final vote tallies] imposed by statute" (528). The majority emphasized the statute's specific deadline, ignoring the concern (which the Florida Supreme Court raised) that this deadline might conflict with other statutory provisions making the legal requirement of that deadline less clear. The majority emphasized the legislature's command here, saying not that the deadline was "set" or "stated" but that it was "imposed." Facing legislative imposition of this deadline, the secretary's passive refusal to waive the deadline was portrayed as appropriate.

This depiction of a law-abiding secretary of state is contrasted with the picture of the Florida Supreme Court, whose motives were questioned even in reviewing the facts of the case. The majority followed its account of the secretary's actions with: "The Florida Supreme Court, however, set the deadline at November 26" (528). In this characterization, the Florida legislature had set a clear deadline, which the secretary followed and the Florida Supreme Court ignored. The majority makes no mention of the Florida court's explanation for why it set the new deadline (because of the "may" and "shall" conflicts; because the recount provisions were poorly written and allowed almost no time for recounts that met the November 14 deadline). Instead, it reminded readers that it previously had vacated and remanded that decision back to the Florida court, "finding considerable uncertainty as to the grounds on which it was based" (528). Although the remand decision voiced concerns that the Florida court might have relied on the Florida Constitution for its judgment (a reliance that, it turns out, was not clearly impermissible),[6] the majority here reconstructed the Court's "uncertainty" to imply that there were no clear grounds, rather than many grounds (some of them perhaps impermissible). Although the majority mentioned that the Florida court had issued a decision on remand a day earlier, it did not review the state court's clarified grounds but only noted that it "reinstat[ed] that date" (528).

Next, the majority turned to a review of the history of the *Gore v. Harris* decision. It noted Vice President Gore's filing of a contest and the denial of relief by the state circuit court. However, it reconstructed the actions of Circuit Court Judge N. Sanders Sauls to make it appear that he applied the same standard as the Florida Supreme Court, directly rejecting the claim that the state supreme court endorsed. It did this by using Gore's act of appeal to frame the judge's subsequent decision. Noting the means for Gore's appeal, the majority stated: "He sought relief pursuant to § 102.168(3)(c), which provides that '[r]eceipt of a number of illegal votes or rejection of a number of legal votes sufficient to change or place in doubt the result of the election' shall be grounds for a contest" (528). It continued, "[t]he Circuit Court denied relief, stating that Vice President Gore failed to meet his burden of proof" (528). The implication is that the grounds for appeal relied upon by Gore were the grounds for judgment applied by the circuit court, which concluded that "Gore failed to meet his burden of proof"; Gore's agency becomes the circuit court's agency.

This construction makes it appear that the Florida Supreme Court's reversal, holding "that Vice President Gore had satisfied his burden of proof

under § 102.168(3)(c)" (noted in *Bush v. Gore,* 528), was simply a difference of opinion about whether that particular burden had been met. As
noted earlier, the standard that Judge Sauls used came from a 1982 Florida
precedent, which the Florida Supreme Court noted had been superseded
by the 1999 revision of the election laws. Sauls had ruled that Gore was required to show that there was a *"reasonable probability* that the results of the
election would have been changed" by a recount."[7] In implying that the
two state courts had applied the same means for judging Gore's appeal, but
reached different conclusions, the majority raised questions about the
Florida Supreme Court's motives. With the agency-act relationship severed
(i.e., the means did not constrain the judgment), other terministic relationships were brought to the fore, notably agent (i.e., who is doing the judging) and attitude (i.e., the court's feelings about the appellant and his
party).

The majority reviewed the various orders of the Florida Supreme Court,
taking particular note of its definition of a legal vote: "A 'legal vote,' as determined by the [Florida] Supreme Court, is 'one in which there is a clear
indication of the intent of the voter'" (528). The state court did not merely
"state," "note," or "interpret" what a legal vote was; it "determined" that,
taking an active role. The majority deflected attention from the direct reliance of the Florida Supreme Court on the language of a Florida statute,
emphasizing the state court's act.

Finally, in setting out the matters for review, the majority agreed to review two issues:

> Whether the Florida Supreme Court established new standards for resolving
> Presidential election contests, thereby violating Art. II, § 1, cl. 2, of the
> United States Constitution and failing to comply with 3 U.S.C. § 5, and
> whether the use of standardless manual recounts violates the Equal Protec-
> tion and Due Process Clauses. With respect to the equal protection question,
> we find a violation of the Equal Protection Clause. (529)

Two constructions are notable here. First, by hearing two issues but rejecting one, the majority embodied "the reasonable court," one that will
not simply rule against the Florida court at every turn but will consider the
merits of each claim and reject those it finds wanting. Second, in phrasing
the second issue as concerned with "the use of standardless manual recounts," the majority already evinced a judgment on the issue. The Florida
Supreme Court and Gore could argue that "intent of the voter" *is* a standard for manual recounts—that, in fact, it is the legislatively mandated

standard—though it may be a looser standard that some would like. But the majority's adjective glosses over those possibilities in framing this purportedly neutral issue on the recounts.

Constructing the Law

The majority began its consideration of the legal issues by noting "a common, if heretofore unnoticed, phenomenon": that 2 percent of ballots nationally do not register a vote for president (529). The majority reconstructed the acts that lead to not registering a presidential vote to include "deliberately choosing no candidate at all or some voter error, such as voting for two candidates or insufficiently marking a ballot" (529). The reasons for the failure to register votes, then, are traceable to acts by the voters, either erring or choosing not to choose. Although there is no suggestion that the machines themselves might fail to count properly marked ballots, the majority does connect the act of voting incorrectly to "punch card balloting machines [that] can produce an unfortunate number of ballots which are not punched in a clean, complete way by the voter" (529). Here the majority struggled with a motivational tension that connects erroneous acts with an error-producing agency, not indicating exactly where to place blame. The punchcard balloting machines produce errors; but the failure to punch in a clean, complete way is attributed to the voter. This issue is important since machine-caused errors create less culpability on the part of voters and suggest that in counting their votes, we might give them the benefit of the doubt.

The majority warned that "[i]n certifying election results, the votes eligible for inclusion in the certification are the votes meeting the properly established legal requirements" (529). This statement serves two functions. First, it prepares us for limits on what will count as a legal vote, by noting the need to meet properly established legal requirements. This otherwise uncontroversial statement prepares us to distinguish a category of votes that are *ineligible* for inclusion because they fail to meet such requirements. Second, it implies that the actions of voters may have rendered their votes ineligible, even if the punchcard machines contributed somewhat to voter errors.

The next section of the majority's opinion explained the source of the right to vote and the limitations placed on states to ensure that right. The majority starts with some constitutional history, noting that the state legislature is given plenary power to choose the manner of selecting presidential electors through Article II of the U.S. Constitution.[8] While state legislatures could choose presidential electors themselves, over time all have decided to use popular election as the means for choosing those electors (529). After states choose this method, the majority insisted, "the right to vote as the legislature has prescribed is fundamental; and one source of its fundamental nature lies in the equal weight accorded to each vote and the equal dignity owed to each voter" (529).

The majority shifts from the legislature's act of granting the vote in presidential elections to its means of implementing that right in noting that "[t]he right to vote is protected in more than the initial allocation of the franchise. Equal protection applies as well to the *manner* of its exercise" (530; emphasis added). Here the majority drew upon the ubiquitous concern for agency in legal argument, a concern with the *how* of action. If equal protection of all citizens under state law is a central purpose of the Fourteenth Amendment, courts often have looked at how states craft and implement their laws to ensure that this equal protection purpose is met, through an agency-purpose or means-ends interpretation of state action.

Drawing on two voting rights cases from the 1960s, the majority tried to specify the limits the equal protection clause places on state means. First, quoting the *Harper v. Virginia Board of Elections*[9] statement that "[o]nce the franchise is granted to the electorate, lines may not be drawn which are inconsistent with the Equal Protection Clause of the Fourteenth Amendment," the majority concluded that "the State may not, by later arbitrary and disparate treatment, value one person's vote over that of another" (quoting 665 at 530). Next, the majority reiterated the *Reynolds v. Sims's*[10] statement that "the right of suffrage can be denied by a debasement or dilution of the weight of a citizen's vote just as effectively as wholly prohibiting the free exercise of the franchise" (quoting 555 at 530).

Citing a precedent is perhaps the most frequently used strategy in judicial argument, though its rhetorical power is rarely appreciated. As a mode of constructing motives—which is central to the aspect of judicial argument examined here—citing a precedent is complex. Citing a precedent supports a decision in two ways:

> [F]irst, by urging that two different actions—that giving rise to the precedent case and that giving rise to the case at bar—are substantially the same; second, by urging that two judicial acts—the decision in the precedent case and the decision in the case at bar—*ought* to be the same. In making "consubstantial" [i.e., "of one substance"] the acts giving rise to the two cases, opinion writers point up similarities in the acts, scenes, agents, agencies, purposes, and attitudes involved and downplay differences. In following

previous decisions, judges divide their rhetorical labor (by building upon and deferring to what was done before), identify their legal reasoning with that already endorsed, and support the consistency of the law over time and across different courts.[11]

In citing *Harper* and *Reynolds,* the majority elided its motives and standards of judgment with those of more liberal courts in the heyday of the civil rights movement (an ideological inconsistency many commentators would note). It endorsed seemingly unobjectionable standards of fairness, standards about which, it asserted, "[t]here is no difference [of opinion] between the two sides of the present controversy" (530). And it would be attacked both for selectively and incompletely drawing the means for assessing unequal treatment and for ignoring the spirit as well as the letter of the law of these precedent cases. But on its face, the majority's construction of its own motives demonstrates a concern for fair means and a just end.

Applying the Law

The lessons of these precedent cases are applied to the Florida recount order when the majority asks "whether the recount procedures the Florida Supreme Court has adopted are consistent with its obligations to avoid arbitrary and disparate treatment of the members of its electorate" (530). The majority states that "[t]he Florida Supreme Court has ordered that the intent of the voter be discerned from [ballots with chads] hanging, say, by two corners [and those with] just an indentation" (530). This strategic construction of what the Florida Supreme Court was doing in its remand to the county circuit court positions the high state court as an agent demanding the application of a standard that the majority finds constitutionally problematic. Consider, alternatively, the Florida Supreme Court's actual words in the remand: "In tabulating the ballots and in making a determination of what is a 'legal' vote, the standard to be employed is that established by the Legislature in our Election Code which is that the vote shall be counted as a 'legal' vote if there is 'clear indication of the intent of the voter'" (Section 101.5614[5], Florida Statutes [2000]).[12]

In constructing the state court's actions, the majority downplays the state court's manifest reliance on a Florida statute for the "intent of the voter" standard. The only reference the majority makes to this standard's sources are to *Gore v. Harris,* with no qualifications such as "quoting § 101.5614(5)" (530). The unstated implication is that this standard is judge-made; and if so, the majority could wonder more easily why that standard was not better adapted to the difficulties of the recount—notably, determining specific rules for what is to count as a vote.

The majority's statement that the state court "ordered that the intent of the voter be discerned from [ballots]" implies that every ballot requires a judgment of intent—a tall order, indeed. Not only does it leave off the important qualifier *"clear indication of* the intent of the voter" (a more specific standard than merely "intent of the voter"), but it implies that the state court might not accept the judgment that "no intent" could be discerned from a recounted ballot—clearly an erroneous conclusion in light of the state court's rejection of 3,300 Palm Beach County ballots from which the canvassing board failed to discern voter intent.[13]

At this point, the Supreme Court majority addressed a strain in the argument it was developing against the "intent of the voter" standard: the fact that intent is a widely used standard in legal judgments. In a sense, intent is a proven agency, a constitutionally valid means for reaching even decisions that would send a convicted criminal to his or her death. To discount the application of this venerable standard to the recount case, the majority drew a distinction based on the object of the inference of intent and the acts of those discerning intent.

> The law does not refrain from searching for the intent of the actor in a multitude of circumstances: and in some cases the general command to ascertain intent is not susceptible to much further refinement. In this instance, however, the question is not whether to believe a witness but how to interpret the marks or holes or scratches on an inanimate object, a piece of cardboard or paper which, it is said, might not have registered as a vote during the machine count. The factfinder confronts a thing, not a person. The search for intent can be confined by specific rules designed to ensure uniform treatment. (530)

The majority's contrast between the generalized acts of a fact finder confronting a person and confronting an inanimate object, between believing a witness and interpreting marks or holes or scratches, and between following adequately refined rules and inadequately refined rules, is stark and effective. It distinguishes the two types of acts through this antithesis and makes a case for carving out this difference. But of course, just because more refined rules for interpreting ballots *could* be developed, it did not follow that they *must* be. Nor does it follow that loose standards in recounts violate the equal protection clause. That argument had to be developed further.

The majority bolstered its case by asserting that "[t]he want of those rules here has led to unequal evaluations of ballots in various respects" (530). In support of this claim, the majority cited Florida Supreme Court Chief Justice Charles Wells's dissenting opinion in *Gore v. Harris,* the oral argument, and the trial record (530–31). Particularly damning was its example from Palm Beach County, which, the majority reported, "began the process with a 1990 guideline which precluded counting completely attached chads, switched to a rule that considered a vote to be legal if any light could be seen through a chad, changed back to the 1990 rule, and then abandoned any pretense of a *per se* rule, only to have a court order that the county consider dimpled chads legal" (531).

Of course, this example of changing standards concerned the recounts *prior to* the *Gore v. Harris* order, not *under* that state court order, so this evidence was not a clear strike against the Florida court's recount order (though the majority implies that it is). It *was* a strike against the inclusion of prior recounts made under these differing standards, though the majority does not make this distinction. Nevertheless, in noting multiple acts of changing standards, the majority implied that the county canvassing boards were afforded latitude for switching standards and, indeed, might exercise that latitude. Thus, the majority concluded, "[t]his is not a process with sufficient guarantees of equal treatment" (531).

At this point, the majority returned again to its precedents to suggest that such unequal treatment of voters violated equal protection. Citing *Gray v. Sanders*[14] the majority urged that "[t]he Court found a constitutional violation" because "a State accorded arbitrary and disparate treatment to voters in its different counties" (531). In *Moore v. Ogilvie,*[15] which involved a presidential election, the majority noted, "we invalidated a county-based procedure that diluted the influence of citizens in larger counties in the nominating process, [observing] '[t]he idea that one group can be granted greater voting strength than another is hostile to the one man, one vote basis of our representative government'" (quoting 819 at 531). As reconstructed by the majority, these cases both supported the idea that states cannot treat groups disparately—they cannot favor the voters of one county over those of another (*Gray*) or voters in small counties over those in large counties (*Moore*). Additionally, *Gray* is used to stand for the proposition that arbitrary treatment of voters in different counties is problematic.

In applying these precedents to the Florida case, the majority faced a challenge, as many later commentators would note. It needed to establish that discernible groups had been arbitrarily and disparately treated by vote counters.[16] It began by noting that earlier recount totals from Miami-Dade, Palm Beach, and Broward Counties were to be included in the new certified vote count, even though "each of the counties used varying standards to determine what was a legal vote" (531). To illustrate the impact of these different standards, the majority noted that Broward County's "more forgiving standard" led it to recover "almost three times as many new votes [as Palm Beach County], a result markedly disproportionate to the difference in population between the counties" (531).

In addition to the disparities in treatment among these three counties, the majority noted, there were differences of treatment between these three counties and the rest of the state's counties conducting a recount under the Florida Supreme Court's recount order. While those three counties recounted all their ballots, the rest of the state was recounting only undervotes. This left out overvotes (where more than one candidate had been marked), leading to disparate treatment between overvoters in those three counties and those in the rest of the state. Also, the majority suggested, there was differential treatment of overvoters and undervoters, since

> the citizen whose ballot was not read by a machine because he failed to vote for a candidate in a way readable by a machine [i.e., an undervoter] may still have his vote counted in a manual recount; on the other hand, the citizen who marks two candidates in a way discernible by the machine [i.e., an overvoter] will not have the same opportunity to have his vote count, even if a manual examination of the ballot would reveal the requisite indicia of intent. (531)

Finally, the majority noted a disparity in the treatment of hand-recounted ballots and machine-counted ballots, describing a hypothetical act: "the citizen who marks two candidates, only one of which is discernible by the machine, will have his vote counted even though it should have been read as an invalid ballot" (531). Oddly, this assertion challenges the presumption of correctness implicitly given to the certified vote tallies, which were made up almost exclusively of machine-counted votes. To meet all of the majority's concerns, presumably, all ballots in all counties would have to be recounted using a single standard in order to avoid the arbitrary and disparate treatment forbidden by the equal protection clause. Such a requirement appears quite impractical for any statewide Florida election, given the shortness of time allowed for recounts under Florida law, as the majority reads it.

Unlike the precedent cases of *Gray* and *Moore,* the majority did not indicate a single group that had been discriminated against through this unequal treatment but offered a shotgun approach to identifying differences of treatment, between Miami-Dade, Palm Beach, and Broward Counties on the one hand and the rest of the state's counties on the other; between undervoters and overvoters; between voters whose ballots were machine-tallied and those whose ballots were hand-tallied. This arbitrary and disparate treatment was endorsed by the Florida court: "The State Supreme Court's inclusion of vote counts based on these variant standards exemplifies concerns with the remedial processes that were under way" (531).

As a final equal protection concern, the majority highlighted a potential difference of treatment between those whose votes were recounted and those whose votes were not. Noting the Florida Supreme Court's inclusion of a partial recount from Miami-Dade County, the majority pointed to a hypothetical future act it found troubling: that the Florida Supreme Court might accept incomplete final recount totals.[17] That is, a past act of accepting partial recounts in Miami-Dade was taken as evidence of an attitude toward accepting such incomplete recounts in the future, giving the majority "no assurance" (532) that this questionable act would not be used for a final certification. So the concern was not that the state court *had* violated equal protection in this way but that it *might.* Indeed, the majority "interpret[ed] the Florida Supreme Court's decision [in *Gore v. Harris*] to permit this" (532).

Constructing State Court Motives

The majority elaborated further on what the state court was doing in order to dismiss its reasoning, insisting: "This accommodation [accepting partial returns] no doubt results from the truncated contest period established by the Florida Supreme Court in [*Palm Beach County Canvassing Board v. Harris*], at [Gore's] own urging" (532). That is, the state court extended the protest period in the first case and thereby truncated the contest period, creating a severely restricted scene (limited by time) which it then claimed as a constraint requiring it to "accommodate" partial returns. The majority debunked this scene-act rationale (which it attributed to the state court) by insisting that it was a scene of the state court's and Gore's own making. The majority added that purpose must control agency in these matters, since "[a] desire for speed [i.e., how you get there] is not a general excuse for ignoring equal protection guarantees [i.e., the ultimate purpose of the act]" (532).

If endorsing past acts of differential treatment and threatening to do impermissible acts in the future were not troublesome enough, the majority insisted, ongoing recounts had problems as well, primarily with the means by which the state court's orders were carried out: "That [recount] order did not specify who would recount the ballots. The county canvassing boards were forced to pull together ad hoc teams comprised of judges from various Circuits who had no previous training in handling and interpreting ballots. Furthermore, while others were permitted to observe, they were prohibited from objecting during the recount" (532). While a different construction of this order might have interpreted it as deferring to the county canvassing boards or to Judge Terry Lewis, whom the state court put in charge of the process, the majority painted the act as inadequate in its control, leading to troublesome implementation. Although circuit judges might be a commendable choice as presumably neutral agents of the law operating as fair agencies for counting votes, the majority emphasized their lack of experience and the lack of rules in grouping them. The majority did not consider the qualifications of any alternative counters (say, the county canvassing boards, which were dominated by members of one party or another). Nor did it consider the qualifications or motives of those who might object during the recounting.

With past, present, and future actions put in doubt, the majority concluded: "The recount process, in its features here described, is inconsistent with the minimum procedures necessary to protect the fundamental right of each voter in the special instance of a statewide recount under the authority of a single judicial officer" (532). Two features of this conclusion about the equal protection problems of the Florida Supreme Court's decision are noteworthy. First is the emphasis on the right of "each voter," which downplays *Gray's* and *Moore's* emphasis on groups of voters (say, those in large counties versus small counties) in favor of the individual voter. This emphasis would become a point of key concern for critics of the decision.

Second, the majority's specification that the equal protection problem it found involved "a statewide recount under the authority of a single judicial officer" seems odd, since no mention of the "single judicial officer" was made in its discussion of these problems. Emphasizing the oversight of a single judicial officer might have threatened the majority's claim that the recount was arbitrary, since a single judicial officer could provide his own judgment as the basis for an ultimate, shared standard, if a single agent may be so "reduced" to an agency of judgment or standard here. And in leaving out a consideration of his role, the majority's construction of equal protection problems does not appear to hinge on this feature of the recount order, making the late inclusion of that element suspicious.

Such suspicions are confirmed when we read this narrow language as a setup for the limitation the majority adds next: "Our consideration is limited to the present circumstances [which include a single judicial officer], for the problem of equal protection in election processes generally presents many complexities" (532). By insisting that its actions in determining an equal protection violation involved specific features of this case, the majority sought to keep its decision from being used as a precedent in the future. This attempt to negate the precedential value of the *Bush v. Gore* decision would be cited by critics as strong evidence that this decision was politically motivated, operating for the benefit of Bush alone, rather than for the benefit of justice more generally (that is, for similarly situated voters in the future).

At this point, the majority took on a challenge raised by dissenters (and to be raised by scores of legal commentators) that the use of different types of voting machines created more inequality in the treatment of ballots than was wrought through the recounts. Even the majority admitted that the punchcard system produced a much larger number of rejected ballots than the optical-scan system. Here the majority glosses over that concern and redirects the issue to actions by the state court, insisting:

> The question before the Court is not whether local entities, in the exercise of their expertise, may develop different systems for implementing elections. Instead, we are presented with a situation where a state court with the power to assure uniformity has ordered a statewide recount with minimal procedural safeguards. When a court orders a statewide remedy, there must be at least some assurance that the rudimentary requirements of equal treatment and fundamental fairness are satisfied. (532)

The issue of different voting machines is dismissed by invoking the "expertise" of "local entities," whereby qualified agents choose the most appropriate agencies for their own elections, presumably based on their expertise (rather than, say, on economic considerations). This approved exercise of an agent using a well-chosen agency is contrasted with another that is disapproved, whereby the Florida Supreme Court (the agent) did not use its power (the agency) to provide uniformity in the recount, to meet the purpose of providing equal protection to the state's citizen voters. Two assumptions are hidden in this construction: first, that "clear indication of the intent of the voter" (or "intent of the voter," as the majority characterized it) is not a standard sufficient to ensure uniformity and, second, that the state court had the power to set standards. The majority, no doubt, used its review of the disparate treatment of ballots to substantiate the first assumption. For the second, it invoked a purpose-agency relationship that suggested that meeting the constitutional goal of ensuring equal treatment and fundamental fairness necessitated a means for achieving that and, hence, implied a judicial power for doing so.

In addition to failing to ensure equal treatment, the majority added, "[t]he contest provision, as it was mandated by the State Supreme Court, is not well calculated to sustain the confidence that all citizens must have in the outcome of the elections" (532). This reference back to the stay order's political concerns suggests that the majority's equal protection problems are not merely constitutional but entail a larger purpose; thus, the state court's means must be adapted to meet both the constitutional purposes of equal protection and the related political goal of ensuring public confidence in the election. The state court should have known better, the majority insisted, given dissenting Chief Justice Wells's reminder, for example, that the unrecounted overvotes needed to be addressed (532).

The overall picture of the Florida Supreme Court is of a body with the power to act to ensure that constitutional and political purposes were met, that was even warned by its leader to take care in such matters, but that chose instead to provide only vague direction to recounters and to endorse questionable partial recount totals and vote counting based on disparate standards. The majority did not explicitly state that the Florida court acted in bad faith or for political purposes but only that it acted erroneously; thus, it was not evil but only foolish.[18]

Providing a Remedy

The majority insisted that making the recount constitutional would require "substantial additional work" (532):

> It would require not only the adoption (after opportunity for argument) of adequate statewide standards for determining what is a legal vote, and practicable procedures to implement them, but also orderly judicial review of any disputed matters that might arise. In addition, the Secretary of State has advised that the recount of only a portion of the ballots requires that the vote tabulation equipment be used to screen out undervotes, a function for

which the machines were not designed. If a recount of overvotes were also required, perhaps even a second screening would be necessary. Use of the equipment for this purpose, and for any new software developed for it, would have to be evaluated for accuracy by the Secretary of State, as required by Fla. Stat. § 101.015 (2000). (532–33)

By refusing to announce what kind of recount its decision requires—all ballots, all undervotes, both undervotes and overvotes—the majority lengthens its list of what might have to be done, amassing a catalogue of tasks likely to prolong seriously any recount process. Alternatively, had it required that all ballots be recounted by hand to meet the equal protection concerns it previously raised, then the last three steps (setting up software to screen for undervotes and overvotes and to have the secretary evaluate that) would drop out. The use of vote-counting equipment to screen undervotes and overvotes—"a function for which the machines were not designed" (a bad agency-purpose connection)—would drop away. The majority would be left with standard setting, legal challenges, and a big pile of ballots to be recounted as its only time-consuming tasks at this late point in the election. Yet, with fewer steps, it would appear less daunting in the short time remaining. The majority strategically characterized the job as daunting.

The majority did not indicate which ballots had to be counted, because it did not intend for the recounts to go forward. In the most controversial holding of the case, the majority found that Florida law required that certified vote totals be submitted by the federal safe harbor date of December 12, which was the date the majority handed down its opinion. Ironically, the majority used the Florida court to justify its reading of Florida law, noting: "The Supreme Court of Florida has said that the legislature intended the State's electors to 'participat[e] fully in the federal election process,' as provided in 3 U.S.C. § 5" (citing *Gore v. Harris* at 533). In citing the state court's statement from *Gore v. Harris,* the majority did not consider whether that goal of meeting the safe harbor provision trumped all other goals (such as getting an accurate tally of votes). In fact, it flatly ignored the repeated theme in all of the Florida Supreme Court's opinions that the right to have one's vote counted was supreme.

Taking the goal of meeting the safe harbor deadline as an absolute command of the Florida legislature, the majority rejected Justice Breyer's proposal to allow the recounts to restart under new guidelines, because that would violate Florida law in not meeting this safe harbor deadline. By insisting upon this interpretation of Florida law—ostensibly supported by the

Florida Supreme Court itself—the majority could stand by the law, shut down the recounts, and end the election controversy.

Constructing Its Own Motives

The majority ended its opinion by directly and explicitly constructing its own motives. First, in the face of the 5-4 split that pitted conservatives against their liberal counterparts, the majority sought to bolster its numbers, noting: "[s]even Justices of the Court agree that there are constitutional problems with the recount ordered by the Florida Supreme Court that demand a remedy" (533). Indeed, dissenting Justices Breyer and Souter did think that equal protection problems existed, though they thought that a remand to continue the recount under new guidelines was required. The difference between these dissenters and the majority was sufficient so that Breyer and Souter did not choose to concur in part (on equal protection) and dissent in part (on the remedy and other matters)—a mechanism that would have bolstered the majority greatly. But by enlisting the two as agents in this controversial, election-ending decision, the majority was able to claim a near consensus. Of course, critics would question whether it was proper to enlist these two when their opinions on the remedy and other matters differed so greatly from the majority's.

With coagents enlisted and their ranks swelled somewhat, the majority turned to characterize its attitude in the decision, offering a final assurance that it was acting with proper judicial motives:

> None are more conscious of the vital limits on judicial authority than are members of this Court, and none stand more in admiration of the Constitution's design to leave the selection of the President to the people, through their legislatures, and to the political sphere. When contending parties invoke the process of the courts, however, it becomes our unsought responsibility to resolve the federal and constitutional issues the judicial system has been forced to confront. (533)

This attitude of reluctance and obligation suggested that the case was foisted upon the Court, that the majority was constrained by law to act. It downplays the rarity with which the Supreme Court accepts *any* case and the number of outs the Court had in justifiably avoiding the controversy altogether—as almost all legal commentators knew, assuring the public that the Supreme Court would never become embroiled in this highly politicized case.[19]

In meeting the ideals of judicial action—speaking to the past, present, and future by following the law; providing justice in the instant case; and providing sound principles for future judges—the majority fell considerably short, even based on this cursory examination of its opinion. It was strongest in invoking the past, construing equal protection to require uniform treatment of voters' ballots, even though these conservatives ironically drew on liberal court decisions and did not follow those decisions in emphatically identifying the groups harmed. The idea of treating each ballot equally has a strong appeal to fairness, though the remedy of effectively throwing out all uncounted ballots (for lack of time) gutted any sense of justice. The majority's list of equal protection requirements for a recount, which appeared to necessitate recounting all ballots in all counties manually, using a single standard established after hearing arguments from all parties, employing trained ballot handlers, allowing objections by observers, and allowing time for legal contests following the recounts, requires a means unsuited to the limited scene of a protest or contest period in a presidential election. In this sense, electoral justice through recounts is merely an ideal, unrealizable in any actual election. Finally, the majority's direct, inexplicable attempt to limit the reach of an otherwise fair-minded (if in any sense practicable) rule to the present case ensured that no future justice would make up for the lack of justice in the present case.

Rehnquist's Concurring Opinion

The concurring opinion of Chief Justice Rehnquist was joined by Justices Scalia and Thomas. Although this opinion does little to construct the majority's actions further, it is important in noting additional grounds for the decision. Many defenders of the outcome of the case prefer the legal reasoning of the concurring opinion, suggesting that the majority opinion's shortcomings should be overlooked, since the "correct" outcome was reached in any case. Such defenses reconstitute the majority's actions, in a way, by denying that any harm followed from its use of the wrong legal agency, making them important to an overall evaluation of majority motives.

Rehnquist's concurring opinion sought to enumerate "additional grounds that require us to reverse the Florida Supreme Court's decision" (533). A concurrence might serve as a challenge to a majority opinion, in suggesting that different grounds are more appropriate for the decision. However, in this case, the three concurring justices also joined the majority opinion and simply suggested that there were "additional" reasons to reach the majority's conclusion.

Justifying the Supreme Court's Intervention

Rehnquist began with a more developed justification for intervening in the election than the majority offered, invoking the scene-act ratio in insisting: "We deal here not with an ordinary election, but with an election for the President of the United States" (533). This insistence that the scene of a presidential election required the extraordinary act of federal intervention in a state election dispute found particularly appropriate support in the cited Supreme Court case of *Anderson v. Celebrezze*, which stated: "[I]n the *context* of a Presidential election, state-imposed restrictions implicate a uniquely important national interest."[20]

Rehnquist played upon this distinction between the ordinary and the extraordinary, insisting that "[i]n *most* cases, comity and respect for federalism compel us to defer to the decisions of state courts on issues of state law," and "in *ordinary* cases the distribution of powers among the branches of a State's government raises no questions of federal constitutional law," yet holding that "*exceptional* cases in which the Constitution imposes a duty or confers a power on a particular branch of government" require the extraordinary federal judicial action the Court is taking (534; emphasis added).

With that justification for intervention offered, Rehnquist turned to reconstructing a constitutional enactment to show that the Florida Supreme Court had usurped the power of the Florida legislature, contrary to federal law. Rehnquist quoted Article II, § 1, cl. 2, with emphasis, declaring: "'[e]ach State shall appoint, in such Manner as the *Legislature* thereof may direct' electors for President and Vice President" (534). This, he insisted, means that "the text of the election law itself, and not just its interpretation by the courts of the States, takes on independent significance" (534).

In attempting to draw a bright red line between the legislature's commands and the judiciary's interpretation of them, Rehnquist embodies the strict constructionist. No doubt, he believes that the interpretation he gave to Article II just before was literal, tied to the text, and not merely a matter of "interpretation by the courts." He assumes that the statutory text, a record of Florida's legislative act, is identical to that act and "speaks for itself" (as the majority's paper ballots could not). He relies on a distinction in judicial action as well, between simply reading what the legislature requires and interpreting the same. Rehnquist would take this abstract distinction and apply it to the Florida case to show that the Florida court overstepped its constitutional authority in ordering the recounts. Foreshadowing this argument and providing one final justification for federal intervention, Rehnquist cited the 1892 case of *McPherson v. Blacker*[21] in support of the claim that "[a] significant departure from the legislative scheme for appointing Presidential electors presents a federal constitutional question" (534).

Finding the Discrepancy between the Legislature and the Judiciary

Once Rehnquist established that this extraordinary election case justified an extraordinary act of intervention under Article II and that a distinction could be made between the Florida legislature's wishes and the Florida Supreme Court's interpretation of those wishes, all he needed to do was construct the legislature's enactment and show a discrepancy between what it intended and what Florida's high court *said* it intended. He was aware that this intervention and second-guessing suggested a lack of faith in the state court but insisted that "[t]his inquiry does not imply a disrespect for state *courts* but rather a respect for the constitutionally prescribed role of state *legislatures*" (535). He cited two civil rights cases in which the Supreme Court protected African-American litigants from hostile Southern courts to show that such interventions were sometimes necessary and not unprecedented.[22]

After a lengthy review of the Florida election statutes (535–36), Rehnquist began detailing several points at which the Florida Supreme Court departed from the legislative scheme. First, he argued that the state court departed from the legislative scheme in failing to give presumption to the certification of Governor George W. Bush in the contest period, "empt[ying] certification of all legal consequence during the contest, and in doing so depart[ing] from the provisions enacted by the Florida Legislature" (537). Oddly, Rehnquist did not cite a smoking-gun statutory provision to support this conclusion but inferred it from the state court's ruling in *Palm Beach County Canvassing Board v. Harris*, which effectively lengthened the protest (and therefore the certification) period and shortened the contest period. Rehnquist concluded: "Underlying the extension of the certification deadline and the shortchanging of the contest period was, presumably, the clear implication that certification was a matter of significance. The certified winner would enjoy presumptive validity, making a contest proceeding by the losing candidate an uphill battle" (536–37).

The juxtaposition of "presumably" and "clear" is almost as strange as the bold inference he draws from the state court's actions (wherein "extension" means significance, which equals presumptive validity). Despite the tenuousness of this claim, it did allow him to complain about an earlier state decision (not now before the Court) as a "modification of the code" in "extend[ing] the 7-day statutory certification deadline established by the legislature" (536), marking the first step in a pattern by the state court of ignoring legislative intent. Rhetorically, it was weak in being the first such claim to follow the section assuring readers that a clear line could be drawn between what the legislature intended and what the state court said it intended.

Rehnquist had an easier time with his second claim of discrepancy, which held that the state court usurped legislative authority in the recount order. While the state court ordered statewide recounts, Rehnquist insisted that "the election code clearly vests discretion whether to recount in the [canvassing] boards" (537). Additionally, the Florida court's inclusion of late recount totals usurped "the Secretary's discretion to disregard recounts that violate [the certification deadline]" (537).

Rehnquist next rejected the Florida court's interpretation of "legal vote" for "plainly depart[ing] from the legislative scheme" (537). In support of this charge, Rehnquist blurred the distinction between legal requirements and actual Election Day processes when he stated:

> Each Florida precinct before election day provides instructions on how properly to cast a vote, § 101.46; each polling place on election day contains a working model of the voting machine it uses, § 101.5611; and each voting booth contains a sample ballot, § 101.46. In precincts using punch-card ballots, voters are instructed to punch out the ballot cleanly:
>
> > AFTER VOTING, CHECK YOUR BALLOT CARD TO BE SURE YOUR VOTING SELECTIONS ARE CLEARLY AND CLEANLY PUNCHED AND THERE ARE NO CHIPS LEFT HANGING ON THE BACK OF YOUR CARD.
>
> Instructions to Voters, quoted in *Touchston v. McDermott.*(537)

Note that Rehnquist asserts in each case that such instructions *are* provided, not that they are *supposed* to be provided; the legislature's admonitions to action are taken as descriptions of action. Given widespread reports of Election Day problems in Florida,[23] that is a generous assumption. But it is an assumption Rehnquist needs to make if he is to place full responsibility for uncounted ballots with the voters for whom he would deny relief and to construct the law of Florida as excluding them from the counting.

For Rehnquist, the only votes that are legal votes are those that a machine can count, and he offered the "reasonable person" to judge that construction: "No reasonable person would call it 'an error in the vote tabulation,' FLA. STAT. § 102.166(5), or a 'rejection of legal votes,' FLA. STAT. § 102.168(3)(c), when electronic or electromechanical equipment performs precisely in the manner designed, and fails to count those ballots that are not marked in the manner that these voting instructions explicitly and prominently specify" (537). The reasonable person here is made to recognize two agency-act relationships, whereby properly working machines count legal votes and no others, and properly punched ballots constitute legal votes but no others. Thus, the person who tries to vote but fails to follow guidelines has not legally voted, and his or her vote can be rejected under Florida laws. Rehnquist's construction carries an idea of just deserts, whereby agents too inept to follow directions (which are "explicit" and "prominent") lose the chance for their votes to be counted. Here is where Rehnquist's earlier veiled insistence that what the law requires is what actually happens on Election Day pays off, as he can smugly dismiss the errant voter who could not be educated, despite the state's many attempts to do so.

Rehnquist's prescription as actual practice was deployed a second time in his complaint that:

[t]he scheme that the Florida Supreme Court's opinion attributes to the legislature is one in which machines are *required* to be "capable of correctly counting votes," § 101.5606(4), but which nonetheless regularly produces elections in which legal votes are predictably *not* tabulated, so that in close elections manual recounts are regularly required. This is of course absurd. (537)

Because vote-counting machines must be capable of correctly counting votes, Rehnquist reasons, those it cannot count are not legal votes. The absurdity of holding otherwise is reflected in Rehnquist's generalized act of having to recount in close elections. He construes this recounting task as "regularly required"—presumably an act that would occur often, defeating the efficiency of a voting system, and rendering it "absurd." However, this characterization is strategically placed: only in close elections are manual recounts regularly required. Close elections might be rare indeed (certainly, this presidential election was); but when they happen, recounts would be regularly required. If recounts were required only in rarely seen close elections, then the Florida Supreme Court's construction would not seem so absurd.

Rehnquist built on this claimed absurdity to show the state court's lack of deference to the secretary of state, "who is authorized by law to issue binding interpretations of the election code" (537). Deference would not be necessary, presumably, if the court had relied on a plain reading of the statute (for Rehnquist, the legislature's obvious intent); but it relied on this "peculiar reading," undermining any judicial excuse for failing to defer to her "reasonable interpretation" (537).

Note that this construction of the secretary's interpretation of state law as reasonable means that her understanding and that of the legislature are identical. This is critical, since, as a member of the executive branch, Harris was no more authorized to depart from the legislative scheme (empowered by Article II) than was the state judiciary. The reasonableness of her interpretation (a good attitude) and the grant of authority to her to interpret the election code (making her an authorized agent) ensured that questions of her motives as cochair of Bush's Florida election campaign were irrelevant. As an agent, Rehnquist implied, she was authorized, reasonable, fair, and correct.

Rehnquist refused to grapple directly with the Florida court's reliance on § 101.5614(5) in its "peculiar reading," the provision dealing with damaged or defective ballots which held that "no vote shall be declared invalid or void if there is a clear indication of the intent of the voter as determined by the canvassing board." In finding legal votes outside what the machine could count, that provision threatened Rehnquist's construction of legal votes as machine-countable votes. He dismissed that argument by noting that Florida Supreme Court Chief Justice Wells's dissent found that provision "entirely irrelevant" (538). He also refused to "parse [the] analysis" the Florida court made of the rest of the election code.

In reducing legal votes to machine-countable votes, Rehnquist appears to gut manual recounts of any purpose, except perhaps in cases where the machinery breaks down. Rehnquist never addresses this discrepancy—which would seem to make most of the legislature's provisions about manual recounting irrelevant.

Finally, Rehnquist followed the per curiam decision's lead in insisting that the Florida legislature had mandated December 12 as the final deadline for the election results to be finalized. Like the majority, Rehnquist turned to the earlier Florida Supreme Court opinion in substantiating this "legislative wish" (538). Unlike the majority, which used this argument to justify stopping the recounts, Rehnquist deployed it to show again that the Florida Supreme Court had thwarted the legislature's intent in violation of Article II. He attacked its legal justification in ordering the recount by selectively quoting from the authorizing statute, noting: "The Supreme Court of Florida ordered this additional recount under the provision of the election code giving the circuit judge the authority to provide relief that is 'appropriate under such circumstances.' Fla. Stat. § 102.168(8) (2000)" (538). What he left out was the more expansive grant of authority implied in a fuller rendering of the provision: "the circuit judge to whom the contest is presented *may fashion such orders as he or she deems necessary* to ensure that each allegation in the complaint is investigated, examined, or checked, to prevent or correct any alleged wrong, and *to provide any relief appropriate under such circumstances*" (emphasis added). In the fuller statutory language, Rehnquist's scenic limitation (to "such circumstances") gives way to agent expansions (whereby a judgment is made to "fashion such orders as he or she deems necessary") and a broader act (affording "any relief").

Mimicking the per curiam opinion's rejection of a continued recount, Rehnquist enlarged the actions that needed to be completed as he limited the scene of the recount period available after the state court's December 8 decision, noting: "In light of the inevitable legal challenges and the ensuing appeals to the Supreme Court of Florida and petitions for certiorari to this Court, the entire recounting process could not possibly be completed by that [December 12] date" (538). Noting that a local election dispute in Florida once took sixteen months to resolve, Rehnquist added that the federal deadlines in this election shortened the period even further (538). Thus, with a small scene and many substantial acts, the state court's recount order was not an "appropriate" one under the authorizing statute (539). Rehnquist quoted dissenters from the Florida decision in support of that scene-act construction (539). He ended by agreeing with the majority's reversal of the state court decision, reminding his readers that his arguments were to be added to those of the majority, with whom he, Justice Scalia, and Justice Thomas joined.

Constructing Florida's Supreme Court and His Own Concurrence

In Rehnquist's construction, a good Florida court would have deferred to the secretary of state and the canvassing boards. It would have drawn the plain meaning of "legal vote" from the election code as "machine-countable vote" and would not have read the "Florida statutes as requiring the counting of improperly marked ballots" (538). It would have realized the impossibility of continuing the recount and rejected it as an inappropriate remedy. This good Florida court would not have thwarted the clear intent of the legislature, running afoul of Article II's grant of exclusive authority in presidential elections to the state legislature and forcing an intervention by the federal courts.

In maintaining this construction, it was critical for Rehnquist to make the case unequivocally, for he was second-guessing a state court interpreting its own state law. Terms such as "clear," "plain," "absurd" polarized his opinion, portraying his judgment as emphatic and absolute. To maintain this level of certainty, Rehnquist refused even to address Florida's arguments to the contrary. He left the rejection of § 101.5614(5) to Chief Justice Wells. Although he quoted extensively from the election code in his review of the statutes, he refused to consider the implications drawn from the most important of them by the Florida court. Notably, his emphasis on the legislative grant of authority to the secretary of state ignored the legislative grant of authority to the judiciary to hear contest disputes in § 102.168(1). And he did not give full voice to the expansive authority given to the courts in § 102.168(8) of the contest provisions.

It is not that arguments could not be made against the Florida court's invocation of these statutes; they certainly could be (as Posner and others would demonstrate). But to engage those arguments would be to muddy the waters, and Rehnquist needed unquestioned clarity if his own motives in failing to defer to a state court interpreting its own state law were to appear legitimate. This initial examination of his arguments suggest that he overplayed his hand. The arguments he offered to justify this unusual overturning of a state court's interpretation of its own law were weaker than needed and much weaker than he implied.

Assessing the Court's Constructions

Despite the weaknesses of his arguments, Rehnquist fared better than the majority in meeting the ideals of judicial action. In constructing constitutional law, he was in virgin territory, as Article II, § 1, cl. 2, has scarcely been interpreted. Unlike the majority, which wrenched earlier liberal Court decisions to meet its needs, Rehnquist could provide an original interpretation of Article II's provisions, milking the constitutional term *legislature* for all it was worth. He was on weaker ground in telling a state court what its law really meant and in attempting to draw a bright line between following legislative mandates and interpreting the law. Like the majority opinion's cataloguing of instances of differential treatment of various congeries of voters, Rehnquist's opinion piled up a series of discrepancies he saw between what the legislature mandated and what the state court *said* it mandated. While the line was blurrier than he averred, it carried the image of a substantial case against the Florida Supreme Court, as shotgun arguments are wont to do.

Justice in resolving the case was easier to defend for Rehnquist than for the majority, since the voters (with their uncounted ballots) were moved out of the picture in a way that their centrality to the majority decision would not allow. Rehnquist's justice was stopping an out-of-control Florida Supreme Court bent on thwarting the will of the constitutionally empowered Florida legislature. His remedy of stopping the recounts followed simply as a matter of law, not to thwart voters but to ensure that the state court would toe the constitutional line.

Nor did Rehnquist attempt to limit the reach of his decision, offering Article II justice for anyone who cared to call upon his argument in the future. Rehnquist's justice was not for this case and this case alone but for posterity, meeting the goals of laying down clear law.

Overall, in embodying judicial motives, Rehnquist emerged stronger than the majority, and many defenders of the Court would rely on his reasoning. But, of course, his was not the opinion that attracted five justices, so his remained a supporting role.

4

The Dissent Reconstructs Majority Action

Four separate dissents were written by the most liberal justices on the Court, one each by Justices Stevens, Souter, Breyer, and Ginsburg. Each dissent was joined by all dissenters in whole or in part, with the exception of Justice Stevens's scathing dissent, which Justice Souter refused to join. As a whole, these dissents focused much more attention on the concurring opinion of Chief Justice Rehnquist than on the majority opinion, suggesting that the quick turnaround for this decision may have left the question of which opinion would win a majority in the air until the last moment.

The focus here is on the dissent's reconstruction of majority action but not as systematically upon the dissent's embodiment of its own actions, for two reasons. First, the dissenting opinions did not reflect the decision of the Court and, therefore, do not represent the law of *Bush v. Gore*. Second, tracking down embodiments and constructions of motives by all those who have constructed the majority's motives would be far beyond the scope of this analysis.

Stevens's Dissenting Opinion

Justice Stevens's dissent takes on both the majority and Rehnquist, disputing their legal judgments, denying their characterizations of the Florida Supreme Court's actions, and challenging the propriety of their judicial actions. Justices Ginsburg and Breyer joined this dissent, though Justice Souter did not.

Reconstructing Rehnquist

Stevens rejected Rehnquist's second-guessing of the Florida Supreme Court's interpretation of its own law, noting "it is our settled practice to accept the opinions of the highest courts of the States as providing the final answers [about the meaning of state laws]."[1] And whereas Rehnquist had depicted the situation as "exceptional," given the "context" of a presidential election and the Article II requirements that had been violated, and had insisted that this situation demanded the extraordinary act of federal intervention, Stevens severed that scene-act logic on the scene side, insisting tersely, "[t]his is not such an occasion" (539). His opinion sought to substantiate that scenic claim.

In response to Rehnquist's strategic emphasis in quoting Article II, § 1, cl. 2, to say that "[e]ach State shall appoint [presidential electors], in such Manner as the *Legislature* thereof may direct" (emphasizing the agent with the power to direct), Stevens countered with his own: "Each State shall appoint [presidential and vice-presidential electors], in such Manner as the Legislature *thereof* may direct," emphasizing the scenic constraints on that agent's role. It is the *state's* legislature that has the power, making the legislature an agent limited by its governmental scene. Thus, Article II "does not create state legislatures out of whole cloth, but rather takes them as they come—as creatures born of, and constrained by, their state constitutions" (539).

If the leap from "legislatures of states" to "legislatures of state constitutions" was too quick, Stevens immediately cited support from *McPherson v. Blacker*[2]—the same case relied on by Rehnquist in insisting that significant departures from the state legislature's presidential election laws were forbidden. Quoting *McPherson*, Stevens insisted "that '[w]hat is forbidden or required to be done by a State' in the Article II context 'is forbidden or required of the legislative power under state constitutions as they exist'" (quoting 25 at 539). Citing *McPherson* served two purposes. First, it shored up his claim that the Florida legislature was not an independent agent, freed from its state constitutional moorings to mandate whatever it wished. Second, it implied that Rehnquist had strategically selected parts of this precedent to use, while ignoring other parts. Stevens's own construction did not require a denial of the claim Rehnquist drew from the precedent, a move that might have undermined its value as a precedent; however, the claim he drew from *McPherson* did challenge Rehnquist's suggestion that the legislature was independent of normal state constitutional processes. Thus, Rehnquist was implicitly portrayed as a manipulator of this precedent decision, one willing to use the parts he found supportive and ignore others he did not.

Stevens spelled out the implications for the present case of this distinction between a free Article II legislature and one born of the state constitution:

> The legislative power in Florida is subject to judicial review pursuant to Article V of the Florida Constitution, and nothing in Article II of the Federal Constitution frees the state legislature from the constraints in the state constitution that created it. . . . The Florida Supreme Court's exercise of appellate jurisdiction therefore was wholly consistent with, and indeed contemplated by the grant of authority under Article II. (540)

Not only did the Founding Fathers and the *McPherson* court support this view, but, Stevens added, "the Florida Legislature's own decision to employ a unitary code for all elections indicated that it intended the Florida Supreme Court to play the same role in Presidential elections that it has historically played in resolving electoral disputes" (540). This argument appeals to means and ends, for if the Florida Legislature intended for the courts to play a different role in presidential elections than in other elections, it would have provided a separate code of regulations to govern them.

Stevens added to this collection of agents endorsing judicial involvement in presidential election disputes the U.S. Congress, which, in the safe harbor statute relied on by both Rehnquist and the majority, requires that states wishing to protect their electors from congressional challenges must meet the safe harbor deadline and "select electors in contested elections 'by judicial or other methods' established by laws prior to the election day" (quoting 3 U.S.C. § 5 at 540).

In light of this congressional recognition of the judiciary's role in presidential elections, Rehnquist presumably would have had to hold as unconstitutional 3 U.S.C. § 5's provision for judicial involvement to silence the threat to his reading of Article II—something he would be loath to attempt, even in a nonbinding concurring opinion. Yet Rehnquist still had a slender limb to stand on, despite this chorus of voices singing of the judicial role: he could reluctantly admit that role but insist that it was limited to a strict construction of what the legislature had mandated.

Challenging Rehnquist's assertion that the state court had changed Florida election law in its rulings, Stevens insisted that "neither in this case, nor in its earlier opinion in *Palm Beach County Canvassing Board v. Harris* . . . did the Florida Supreme Court make any substantive change in Florida electoral law" (542). Citing a U.S. Supreme Court–endorsed legal assumption from a previous case, Stevens suggested that, for example, in resolving the "may" and "shall" conflict in the protest provisions, the state court merely announced what the law had always been, because "[l]ike any other judicial interpretation of a statute, its opinion was an authoritative interpretation of what the statute's relevant provisions have meant since they were enacted."[3]

This last rebuff to Rehnquist was an elegant, if strategic, construction of motives. It started with the question of whether law had been changed. It located the law in what the statutes originally meant (or, by extension, what the legislature originally intended). In order to learn what a statute means, it suggested one ask an authoritative interpreter of the law, in this case the state supreme court. Once it had ruled on what the law meant, that was not merely a new understanding of the law but an unearthing of what that law had been all along. By definition, then, the Florida court's interpretation could not change the law, because it simply discovered the law laid down by the legislature since the beginning. Thus, the court's new action yielded an old legislative purpose, connecting across pentadic sets.

If this argument proved too much—for it might mean that no state court could ever get it wrong, since it bootstraps historical legislative intent— Stevens does say more about the Florida court's rulings in particular.[4] He insisted "[i]ts decisions were rooted in long-established precedent and were consistent with the relevant statutory provisions taken as a whole" (540). Like Rehnquist, he did not delve into particulars to support this claim, though his final qualification attempted to broaden the scene within which the court's decisions on particular provisions were judged, including especially provisions supporting the "legislature's intent to leave no legally cast vote uncounted" (542). Finally, he compared the state court's actions with a generalized view of judicial action drawn from *Marbury v. Madison*,[5] insisting the Florida court "did what courts do" (542), namely, "say what the law is" (quoting *Marbury* 177 at 542, n. 7). This emphasis on an agent doing what it does (the act following from the nature of the agent) ties back to the grant of authority given by many voices to this judicial oversight. Thus, when the Founding Fathers, the U.S. Congress, the authors of Florida's constitution, the Florida legislature, and the Florida judiciary all say that the state courts have a voice in interpreting election law, then it follows that those courts will say what the law is and that that law will be what the legislature meant from the start, with no change of law.

Although these constructions cut to the heart of Rehnquist's characterization of the law and of the Florida court's decision, Stevens never referred to the chief justice or his opinion directly. He maintained an attitude of reasoned and civil judicial propriety, though he would be somewhat more direct with the majority.

Reconstructing the Majority

Stevens's attack on the majority position began by aiming not at the majority but at the "petitioners" (i.e., Bush and his colleagues), who erred "in asserting that the failure of the Florida Supreme Court to specify in detail the precise manner in which the 'intent of the voter,' Fla. Stat. § 101.5614(5) (Supp. 2001), is to be determined rises to the level of a constitutional violation" (540). In a page-long list of references, he noted that a majority of states "apply either an 'intent of the voter' standard or an 'impossible to determine the elector's choice' standard in ballot recounts" (540, n. 2). The unstated implication of citing dozens of state acts is powerful: (1) that overturning that "intent of the voter" standard would be to throw into question statutes in a majority of states (significantly changing the quality of the Court's act); (2) that in light of the widespread use of this standard, it is strange that no other court ever questioned this standard (the scene should have led to a judicial act if there were a problem); (3) that in endorsing the legislative standard, the Florida court acted reasonably, as did dozens of legislatures that passed the same standards and other courts that let them stand. All these agents could not be wrong, he implied.

Stevens sought to sever the tie to the *Reynolds v. Sims* precedent, which the majority invoked to suggest that a denial of suffrage could be wrought through "a debasement or dilution of the weight of a citizen's vote" as well as outright disenfranchisement. Although he admitted that that case prohibited the unequal weighting of votes, he insisted, "we have never before called into question the substantive standard by which a State determines that a vote has been legally cast" (540). Thus, Stevens depicted the majority not as simply following a landmark civil rights case but as making a completely new equal protection claim.

Whereas the majority took pains to distinguish the use of intent as a standard in this setting (where paper ballots were the signifier of that intent) from its use in other settings (such as criminal trials), Stevens analogized the two:

> [T]here is no reason to think that the guidance provided to the factfinders, specifically the various canvassing boards, by the "intent of the voter" standard is any less sufficient—or will lead to results any less uniform—than, for example, the "beyond a reasonable doubt" standard employed every day by ordinary citizens in courtrooms across this country. (541)

The majority had focused on a hypothetical act, what could have been done by the state court in further specifying standards. Stevens took what *was* done and compared it to what *is* done every day in other settings. Hypothetical acts trade on ideals, which can set high standards; actual acts bring those standards down to earth. In a footnote, Stevens cited a Supreme Court precedent recognizing that the "beyond a reasonable doubt" standard might be further clarified but that the Court held that it need not be, offering a lesson for the Florida case.[6]

Taking on the majority's primary objection to the use of the "intent of the voter" standard, Stevens admitted that "the use of differing substandards for determining voter intent in different counties employing similar voting systems may raise serious concerns" (541). But, he insisted, raising a point that the majority ignored in all but the final statement of the holding, "[t]hose concerns are alleviated—if not eliminated—by the fact that a single impartial magistrate will ultimately adjudicate all objections arising from the recount process" (541). This magistrate was offered as the ultimate standard, or agency, for determining the intent of the voter. And even if clear substandards (say, "only cleanly punched cards") were objective, then so was this "impartial magistrate."[7]

Finally, Stevens noted, if constitutional principles were interpreted too literally on this recount standard, "Florida's decision to leave to each county the determination of what balloting system to employ—despite enormous differences in accuracy—might run afoul of equal protection," as would other states' delegations of the same authority (541). Quoting a Supreme Court precedent, he urged that "the machinery of government would not work if it were not allowed a little play in its joints."[8] The analogy to the decisions on which voting systems to use—which would be used by many critics who found greater equal protection concerns there—invoked the need for fairness and consistency in the application of equal protection rules. The generalized statement about the workings of government urged metaphorically (and with the benefit of precedent) that standards that were too tight were unworkable or unwarranted.

Stevens also called for consistency of action in the remedy, reminding his readers of what the majority found:

> As the majority explicitly holds, once a state legislature determines to select electors through a popular vote, the right to have one's vote counted is of constitutional stature. As the majority further acknowledges, Florida law holds that all ballots that reveal the intent of the voter constitute valid votes. Recognizing these principles, the majority nonetheless orders the termination of the contest proceeding before all such votes have been tabulated. (541)

The majority's actions in recognizing the importance of voting rights and the existence of uncounted legal votes were inconsistent with its act of halting the recount, in this construction. The purpose of counting constitutionally protected votes was at odds with the act of stopping the recounts. If "stopping" suggested a simple denial of troublesome action by the majority, Stevens offered a more active characterization, accusing the majority of "effectively order[ing] the disenfranchisement of an unknown number of voters whose ballots reveal their intent" (541).

Of course, the majority had offered its justification: that Florida law required vote totals to be completed by December 12, 2000, the day the decision was handed down. Instead of addressing the Florida Supreme Court's alleged act of interpreting Florida law to require that the deadline be met (which the majority used), Stevens implied that the majority was reading 3 U.S.C. § 5 as some kind of mandate to states (or reading Florida law as reading this as a mandate). He insisted that the safe harbor statute was not addressed to states at all but to Congress, since "those provisions merely provide rules of decision for Congress to follow when selecting among conflicting slates of electors [and they] do not prohibit a State from counting what the majority concedes to be legal votes until a bona fide winner is determined" (541). He gave the example of Hawaii in the 1960 presidential election, which did not certify its electors until January 4, 1961, "well after the Title 3 deadlines" (541). That analogy was weak to the extent that Hawaii's delay did not affect the determination that John F.

Kennedy had won the election, though it did show that very late returns had previously been accepted.

Stevens's reconstruction of the safe harbor provision as an act addressed to Congress and not binding on the states did not directly challenge the majority's argument that the Florida legislature wanted to adhere to that federal guideline, even if it was not binding. It did provide a basis for reinterpreting what the state court was doing when it discussed the significance of the safe harbor deadline (which was not endorsed by any Florida law). Another dissenter (and some critics) would take on the majority's reading of Florida law more directly.

In the closing paragraph of his dissent, Stevens criticized the implicit motives of both the petitioners and the majority in a two-step condemnation. First, on the petitioners, he insisted: "What must underlie petitioners' entire federal assault on the Florida election procedures is an unstated lack of confidence in the impartiality and capacity of the state judges who would make the critical decisions if the vote count were to proceed. Otherwise, their position is wholly without merit" (542). The petitioners' attitude of doubt respecting the state judges, Stevens insisted, underlies all concerns about unclear standards. The state judges who would conduct and oversee the recounts would yield an unproblematic result, Stevens suggested, unless one assumed they were corrupt or inept. Thus, the act of challenging on equal protection grounds was actually an act of implicitly condemning the judges—a troubling prospect for this elderly judge.

The second step allowed Stevens to transfer blame for this unsavory attitude to the majority as well, whose "endorsement of that position . . . can only lend credence to the most cynical appraisal of the work of judges throughout the land" (542). This attitude of not trusting judges, embodied by the petitioners and endorsed by the majority, would spread to a larger scene, bolstering those who mistrust judges. The effect of this High Court endorsement was a diminished confidence in "the men and women who administer the judicial system [whose work is] the true backbone of the rule of law" (542). In a widely quoted ending flourish, Stevens predicted the dire consequences of the majority's decision:

> Time will one day heal the wound to that confidence that will be inflicted by today's decision. One thing, however, is certain. Although we may never know with complete certainty the identity of the winner of this year's Presidential election, the identity of the loser is perfectly clear. It is the Nation's confidence in the judge as an impartial guardian of the rule of law. (542)

Although Stevens had begun with the petitioner's lack of confidence and dubbed the majority's decision an endorsement of that lack of confidence, here he implicitly went beyond both. It is not just that a Supreme Court decision that turns on skepticism about state judges inspires others to such skepticism, it is the judge in a general sense who is implicated. And the majority justices, as judges, were among those implicated. Thus, Stevens's respectful dissent comes as close as his judicial propriety will allow to saying that these majority justices are raising questions about their own impartiality. But, strategically, he allows their own skepticism about state court judges to condemn them by extension.

Souter's Dissenting Opinion

Justice Souter's dissent was joined by Justices Breyer, Stevens, and Ginsburg, though the latter two did not agree with Souter's finding of equal protection concerns. Despite those concerns, Souter insisted that the Court should not have heard either the previous Florida case or this case, characterizing the latter as "another erroneous decision" (543).

Souter divided his opinion into three issues: safe harbor, Article II, and equal protection. The first he dismissed in one paragraph, sounding like Stevens in insisting that "no State is required to conform to § 5 if it cannot do that (for whatever reason)" (543). Like Stevens, he did not address the majority's contention that Florida law requires that this deadline be met. The next two issues were dealt with more extensively, by reconstructing the Florida Supreme Court's action in interpreting the election code and by reconstructing a hypothetical recount under new provisions that avoid the equal protection problems he also found.

Reconstructing Florida's High Court

Souter began his reconstruction of the Florida court's motives by tossing out many of the statutory interpretations implicitly questioned in the majority's review of the case's history (which included the prior Florida case which the federal court vacated), noting "there is no question here about the state court's interpretation of related provisions dealing with the antecedent process of 'protesting' particular vote counts, § 102.166, which was involved in the previous case, *Bush v. Palm Beach County Canvassing Board*" (543). The majority had catalogued all of its complaints against the Florida court (such as its resolution of the certification deadline) in its history of the case in an effort to show a pattern of thwarting clear legislative intent (such as the seven-day deadline for certification). Such judicial sins (if they were sins), Souter suggested, were irrelevant here because they have nothing to do with the appeal accepted by the *Bush v. Gore* court.

With the defensible ground so limited, Souter turned to a close analysis of the Florida Court's interpretation of § 102.168, which governs election contests. He framed this analysis with a rereading of the petitioner's contention through a scenic—specifically a spatial—metaphor. In asserting an Article II violation that substituted the state court's interpretation for the state legislature's intentions, he postulated, "[w]hat Bush does argue, as I understand it, is that the interpretation of § 102.168 was so unreasonable as to transcend the accepted bounds of statutory interpretation, to the point of being a nonjudicial act and producing law untethered to the legislative act in question" (543). Here, judicial action is imagined within the bounded field of the reasonable, with statutory interpretation tied to a legislative enactment (presumably, somewhere in the center of that field). To be reasonable is to stay within that field, tethered to the legislative act, acting as a judge; to be unreasonable, by implication, is to wander outside that field, to break ties to the legislative act, and to engage in nonjudicial action. We should note that, unlike the strict constructionist Rehnquist, Souter does not suggest that a reasonable judge must be tethered to the text; his characterization makes the act something greater than the words or statutory text alone, though (as he demonstrated) those are important signifiers of the act.

In interpreting § 102.168's conditions for justifying a recount, namely, the "rejection of a number of legal votes sufficient to change or place in doubt the result of the election," he asserted that "[n]one of the state court's interpretations is unreasonable *to the point of displacing* the legislative enactment quoted" (543–44). He added that "the majority view is in each instance *within the bounds* of reasonable interpretation" (544; emphasis added). The Florida court's interpretation of "rejection" as "a failure to count" was "*within the bounds* of common sense . . ." (544; emphasis added). On the state court's reading of "votes sufficient to change or place in doubt [the results of the election]" as meaning that the number of uncounted ballots must make it "reasonably possible" that the outcome would change, Souter said that "there is no warrant for saying [this reading] *transcends the limits* of reasonable statutory interpretation to the point of supplanting the statute enacted by the 'legislature' within the meaning of Article II" (544; emphasis added). Although these constructions appear to work within a scene-act logic, whereby the bounded scene of reason determines the act of reasonable interpretation, it actually works the other way around: the act of reasonable interpretation invokes the scene of reason, demarcating boundaries as the justices enact reasoned interpretations.

Souter admitted that saying the Court was within this scene of reason and common sense did not imply that alternative, or even better, interpretations were not possible. In fact, the field of reason was broad enough to encompass several possible readings; "the two dissents from the majority opinion of that [state] court and various briefs submitted to us set out alternatives" (544). Thus, he notes, "other interpretations were of course possible"; "[i]t is perfectly true that the majority might have chosen a different reading"; "[t]he majority might have concluded that 'rejection' should refer to machine malfunction"; and "the majority might have thought (as the trial judge did) that a probability, not a possibility, should be necessary to justify a contest" (544). Nevertheless, Souter held, "the majority view is in each instance within the bounds of reasonable interpretation, and the law as declared is consistent with Article II" (544). Furthermore, Souter asserted, citing Justice Ginsburg's dissent, the Court's "customary respect for state interpretations of state law counsels against rejection of the Florida court's determinations in this case" (545).

Souter embodies the antithesis of the certain, swaggering, strict constructionist who finds definitive, singular meaning in statutory language. Because his rhetorical task is simply to defend a state supreme court who deserves deference from its federal counterpart, he does not have to evince an attitude of certainty about his findings concerning Florida law or the state court's interpretation of it; he simply has to show that what it determined was reasonable or, even less, not unreasonable. He embodies the respectful judge in two ways. First, in admitting that many interpretations are reasonable, he does not have to show error on anyone's part and may respect others' constructions, if not their conclusions. Second, he shows respect for the state court, even as he oversees its work.

Reconstructing the Recount

Souter even shows respect to his colleagues in the majority in agreeing with their equal protection finding. In doing so, he departs from two of his dissenting colleagues, remarking of the various substandards for recounting ballots (i.e., indentations, hanging chads, fully punched chads, etc.): "I can conceive of no legitimate state interest served by these differing treatments of the expressions of voters' fundamental rights. The differences appear wholly arbitrary" (545). Even in condemning these differences, Souter did not fault the state court. Instead of saying that they failed to impose a standard, he said that a disparity "obtains" based on the vague "intent of the voter" standard. The closest he came to blaming the state court for failing to provide a standard was in a parenthetical summary of a hearing, which involved "soliciting from county canvassing boards proposed protocols for determining voters' intent but declining to provide a precise, uniform standard" (545). This statement emphasized not a positive act of implementing a vague standard but a negative act of declining, much as the majority had strategically characterized the secretary of state as declining to waive a deadline.

Souter insisted that these disparities in recount standards were distinguishable from those created by the use of different voting systems, challenging Stevens's opinion, since "local variety can be justified by concerns about cost, the potential value of innovation, and so on" (545). The distinction here concerns purpose, which arbitrary choices (such as different substandards) lack. If a county chose punchcard systems because they cost less, while another, more affluent county chose optical-scan machines for reliability, then those different but reasonable purposes could justify the distinction. But if one county chose to count dimpled chads, while other county chose to count only fully punched chads, then that difference in treatment appeared arbitrary.

It is not inconceivable that a purpose could have been imagined for the different substandards. Counties might rely on their own prior years' standards for the recounts (which may have diverged on such criteria), county canvassing boards might have different levels of confidence in their ability to discern intent based on various signs of intent, and counties might have noticed differences in the sort of errors manifested on the ballots in their particular precincts—errors, say, that might have been connected to particular instructions given by poll workers, practices in servicing punchcard machines (such as emptying chad trays regularly or not), and so forth. On this last point, consider journalist Jeffrey Toobin's account of the Broward County recount experience:

> At first, the Broward board operated by a very narrow standard, one that recognized votes only if two corners of a chad were dislodged. In one precinct, many ballots were just punctured through—they had no dislodged chads at all—and the mottled backs looked like pages of Braille. Obviously, a voting machine had been miscalibrated, and legitimate votes were not being counted, even though the voters' intent was easy to discern.[9]

Souter did not imagine these differences but only the similarity of the recount situations, as he described a common scene with "identical types of ballots used in identical brands of machines and exhibiting identical physical characteristics" (545). And scene controlled purpose for Souter, not agents (with their different experiences) or agencies (variations in standards used in the past) or attitudes (with their different levels of confidence).

Souter departed from his majority colleagues when it came to a remedy. In doing so, he painted a more optimistic future scene for recounts. First, he took the Electoral College's counting day, December 18, 2000, as the final deadline, not the safe harbor day, with no explanation (though perhaps he relied on other dissenters to reject the earlier deadline). Second, unlike the majority, which recited a litany of tasks to be completed in any recount, Souter pared down the work. He referred to trial transcripts, noting that the undervotes numbered only 60,000 statewide, dismissing an earlier figure of 170,000 by insisting that it included overvotes (545). Overvotes, he insisted, did not have to be recounted, because, as Justice Breyer would argue, "no showing has been made of legal overvotes uncounted" (545).

He did not review concerns about reprogramming the machines to screen for undervotes, hearing arguments over standards, leaving time for lawsuits, and so forth, as the majority had done. Yet he admitted that "[t]o recount these manually would be a tall order, but before this Court stayed the effort to do that the courts of Florida were ready to do their best to get that job done" (545). Souter sidestepped the point that the halted recounts were unconstitutional, on his own reading. Instead, he used the remark to characterize the attitude of the state courts, suggesting that their eagerness to do the work made the swift completion of that work more likely (with attitude controlling how the recount was done).

Overall, Souter insisted that this state supreme court, due deference from the High Court, acted within a scene of reason in interpreting its own law. And although the state court's standards in directing the recounts needed to be grounded in a purpose that treated voters equally, it should have been given time to complete what the majority made it difficult for it to complete.

Ginsburg's Dissenting Opinion

Justice Ginsburg's dissent was joined by Justice Stevens in whole and Justices Breyer and Souter in part (the latter two diverging on her rejection of an equal protection problem). She was direct and adamant in her attack on Chief Justice Rehnquist's concurring opinion, avoiding the more indirect approach of Stevens and Souter (who focused more on the Florida Court than on the majority, characterizing the latter mostly indirectly). The remainder of her opinion explained why she saw no equal protection problem. She ended her spirited dissent differently from her three colleagues. Whereas they each announced, "I respectfully dissent," she showed her disdain by pronouncing simply, "I dissent."

Reconstructing Rehnquist

Justice Ginsburg's opinion opens with a direct characterization of Chief Justice Rehnquist's dissent, demonstrating his inconsistency in noting:

> The Chief Justice acknowledges that provisions of Florida's Election Code "may well admit of more than one interpretation." *Ante*, at 3. But instead of respecting the state high court's province to say what the State's Election Code means, the Chief Justice maintains that Florida's Supreme Court has veered so far from the ordinary practice of judicial review that what it did cannot properly be called judging. (546)

Rather than turn to an analysis of Florida's interpretation to dispute Rehnquist's characterization of the state court's reading of its own law, Ginsburg simply insisted that "[t]here is no cause here to believe that the members of Florida's high court have done less than 'their mortal best to discharge their oath of office.'"[10] She kept the focus on Rehnquist's act, rather than turning to the state court's act.

Ginsburg's approach was to show that Rehnquist's failure to defer to the state supreme court's interpretation of Florida's law was itself improper and inconsistent both with long-standing Supreme Court practice and with the conservative majority's opinions respecting state authority. She began with a consideration of the justices' duty in this case, insisting, "I might join the Chief Justice were it my commission to interpret Florida law" (546). The act of interpreting state law was inconsistent with the Supreme Court justices as agents, since they had no commission to do so. In establishing that this commission does not include such second-guessing, and, therefore, that Rehnquist's act was inappropriate, Ginsburg contrasted this failure to defer with prior examples of deference and reminded her readers of the reasons this deference is given.

Reviewing precedents inconsistent with some criticized judicial action supports that criticism in three ways. First, it draws on the powerful charge of inconsistency, showing that many other judges view the law one way, while the criticized judge views it another way, marginalizing his or her reading and suggesting that it (and he or she) is errant, peculiar, or deviant. Second, since past precedents establish what the law is, such deviations may be shown to violate the law. Finally, in treating some party in a present case differently from how a similarly situated party was treated in the past, the inconsistent judge can be charged with unfairness.

The inconsistency Ginsburg wished to highlight was between the Court's past practice of deferring to state courts' interpretations of law and Rehnquist's own failure to defer to the Florida Supreme Court's reading of its election law. She also sought to show a discrepancy in prior courts' attitudes toward state courts and Rehnquist's attitude toward the Florida Supreme Court.

Ginsburg insisted that "[t]his Court more than occasionally affirms statutory, and even constitutional, interpretations with which it disagrees" (546). To substantiate this claim, she noted the Court's deference to federal administrative agencies, "unless their interpretation violates 'the unambiguously expressed intent of Congress.'"[11] Since this deference has been given despite Article I's vesting of all legislative power in the Congress, Ginsburg could argue analogously for the lesser case, that "[s]urely the Constitution does not call upon us to pay more respect to a federal administrative agency's construction of federal law than to a state high court's interpretation of its own state's laws" (546). More directly, she cited cases where "we let stand state-court interpretations of *federal* law with which we might disagree" (546), especially habeas corpus laws (546–47).

For the latter proposition, she recruited one of Rehnquist's conservative majority colleagues, former state court judge Sandra Day O'Connor, whose 1981 law review article entitled "Trends in the Relationship between the Federal and State Courts from the Perspective of a State Court Judge" is cited for the proposition that "[t]here is no reason to assume that state court judges cannot and will not provide a hospitable forum in litigating federal constitutional questions."[12] Although O'Connor did not join Rehnquist's concurring opinion, the suggestion that even his conservative colleagues on the bench disagreed with his lack of deference to the state court further marginalized him, in this characterization.

If Rehnquist's actions were inconsistent with these precedents, so was his attitude. Even when the Supreme Court "examine[s] state law to protect federal rights," Ginsburg argued, "we have dealt with such cases ever mindful of the full measure of respect we owe to interpretations of state law by a State's highest court" (547). Thus, in a contract clause case, she noted, "the Court 'accord[ed] respectful consideration and great weight to the views of the State's highest court,'"[13] and in a case that led to the forfeiture of federal constitutional rights, she noted the Court's insistence that "the state court's declaration 'should bind us unless so unfair or unreasonable in its application to those asserting a federal right as to obstruct it.'"[14]

Ginsburg added to the inconsistent acts and attitude of Rehnquist a failure to recognize the ultimate purposes for that deference. First, she insisted, the Supreme Court defers to state courts in interpreting state law because as state agents, they are better positioned as interpreters of state law, since "we appropriately recognize that this [U.S. Supreme] Court acts as an 'outside[r]' lacking the common exposure to local law which comes from sitting in the jurisdiction."[15] Using a scenic, spatial metaphor that Souter no doubt would approve, the scene (in the jurisdiction) creates an appropriate agent (state court) for interpreting state law. The U.S. Supreme Court is outside this scene and does not gain the benefits of working there.

A second purpose that Rehnquist failed to recognize was that of keeping good relations between the federal and state governments. Quoting two cases, Ginsburg noted that "the federal tribunal risks friction-generating error when it endeavors to construe a novel state Act not yet reviewed by the State's highest court,"[16] while deferring "helps build a cooperative judicial federalism."[17]

In summary, Ginsburg suggested that Rehnquist was the wrong agent (lacking a commission), working in the wrong scene (not in the jurisdiction), engaging in the wrong act (as contrary court actions showed), with the wrong attitude (not deferential), for the wrong purpose (not supporting a cooperative judicial federalism or leaving the decision to the better agent). In fully developing this portrait of Rehnquist's errant actions, Ginsburg made her characterization more believable, stabilizing her image with many grammatical strands.

Rehnquist, of course, could challenge this characterization by appealing to the exceptional, claiming that the peculiarities of this case led him to depart from traditional practices. To justify this departure, Rehnquist had cited three precedents where the Court had intervened. Ginsburg turned next to those cases to discount this "exceptional" argument.

Rehnquist had relied on one very early case and two from the modern civil rights period. Ginsburg scrutinized the manner by which the chief justice cited the cases, noting, "The Chief Justice's *casual citation* of these cases might lead one to think they are part of a larger collection of cases in which we said that the Constitution impelled us to train a skeptical eye on a state court's portrayal of state law. But one would be hard pressed, I think, to find additional cases that fit the mold" (548; emphasis added). This bit of grammatical analysis subtly exposed an attitude-act relationship, whereby the manner in which Rehnquist cited the case implied a larger act of pointing to many cases, though, as Ginsburg argued, "[r]arely has this Court rejected outright an interpretation of state law by a state high court" (548).

In addition to severing this grammatical connection and its implications, Ginsburg showed that the three cases relied upon were inapplicable to the current case. She did so primarily through a scene-act argument that opened up those precedent cases to more thorough analysis. Using scenic language, she insisted that "those cases are embedded in historical contexts hardly comparable to the situation here" (548). She explained those contexts, beginning with the 1813 case of *Fairfax's Devisee v. Hunter's Lessee*,[18] in which a Virginia court "misconstrued its own forfeiture laws to deprive a British subject of lands secured to him by federal treaties" (548). Virginia's motives must be understood in light of the scene, Ginsburg insisted; the decision came "amidst vociferous States' rights attacks on the Marshall Court" (548). That scenic description was bolstered with support from a well-known constitutional law book[19] and from the outcome of the case, which "led to the Court's pathmarking decision in *Martin v. Hunter's Lessee*."[20]

The civil rights cases were decided "in the face of Southern resistance to the civil rights movement," another scene of resistance by Southern states' rights advocates that required a strong response from the Court. In the 1958 case of *NAACP v. Alabama ex rel. Patterson*,[21] Ginsburg noted, the U.S. Supreme Court "held that the Alabama Supreme Court irregularly applied its own procedural rules to deny review of a contempt order against the NAACP arising from its refusal to disclose membership lists" (548). The second case, *Bouie v. City of Columbia*,[22] was decided "at the height of the civil rights movement" in 1964. There, the South Carolina Supreme Court allowed criminal trespass laws to be applied to lunch counter sit-ins, "criminalizing conduct not covered by the text of an otherwise clear statute" (548). In this well-documented scene of unfairness by recalcitrant and racist Southern courts, Ginsburg argued, these exceptional decisions not to defer were made. In the much different scene of the 2000 presidential election, Ginsburg could insist, "[t]he [Florida] court surely should not be bracketed with state high courts of the Jim Crow South" (548).

Still in the historical mode, Ginsburg turned from scene to purpose, challenging Rehnquist's interpretation of Article II as requiring the Court not to give deference to the state court (lest the Court "abdicate our responsibility to enforce the explicit requirements of Article II").[23] She cited

Articles III and IV and *The Federalist Papers* to urge that "[t]he Framers of our Constitution . . . understood that in a republican form of government, the judiciary would construe the legislature's enactments" (549). She also suggested that invoking Article II to protect the state legislature from the state judiciary "contradicts the basic principle that a State may organize itself as it sees fit" (549). Drawing on a second conservative colleague of Rehnquist's, Ginsburg quoted Justice Kennedy on the division of sovereignty between the state and federal governments which the Founding Fathers, in their "genius," endorsed.[24]

If Rehnquist missed the mark in interpreting the Constitution, Ginsburg had a scenic explanation: "[t]he extraordinary setting of this case has obscured the ordinary principle that dictates its proper resolution: Federal courts defer to state high courts' interpretations of their state's own law" (549). Broadening her condemnation, Ginsburg noted: "Were the other members of this Court as mindful as they generally are of our system of dual sovereignty, they would affirm the judgment of the Florida Supreme Court" (549). Here she hinted at what many commentators would note: a discrepancy between the states' rights ideology espoused by this conservative majority and this decision which treads on states' rights, an agent-act inconsistency (since states' rights advocates are supposed to support states' rights). Ginsburg challenged Rehnquist's attempt to have it both ways, in insisting he was supporting the rights of the state legislature, charging: "The Chief Justice's solicitude for the Florida Legislature comes at the expense of the more fundamental solicitude we owe to the legislature's sovereign" (549). That "sovereign" (as Justice Stevens had argued) was the state as a whole, since under Article II, "[e]ach *State* shall appoint, in such Manner as the Legislature *thereof* may direct [the electors for president and vice president]" (quoted with emphasis at 549).

Reconstructing the Recount

Justice Ginsburg's consideration of the equal protection claim relied on Justice Stevens's argument that the problem was not substantial, admitting that in an "imperfect world . . . in which thousands of votes have not been counted, perfection could not be expected in the vote tallies" (550). However, she denied that the Florida court-ordered recount, "flawed as it may be, would yield a result any less fair or precise than the certification that preceded that recount" (550). Ginsburg's refusal to paint a more appealing outcome for a completed recount does not help her case, since it fails to provide a sense of the justice lost in the majority's failure to allow the recount to go forward. For her, allowing the recount to continue was not a means to justice in the sense of better assessing voter intent (as the Florida Court argued); instead, deferring to the state court by allowing the recount to continue would support justice, as well as vindicating the law and ensuring continuing good relations between the federal government and the states.

On the December 12 deadline she referred to her dissenting colleagues, suggesting that the deadline was not mandatory and that the Supreme Court's stay prevented "an able circuit judge in Leon County" from completing the recount (550). Her particular complaint about halting the recounts continued her "failure of deference" theme, insisting that the decision by the majority "ultimately turns on its own judgment about the practical realities of implementing a recount, not the judgment of those much closer to the process" (550). This construction uses scenic proximity (as used before in saying who is in a better position to judge Florida law) to give greater credibility to the Florida agents handling the recount, discounting the federal court's credibility in this matter.

Ginsburg also offered a reading of the December 12 deadline that suggested other "significant dates" from various sections of chapter 3 of the U.S. Code that might just as well be used:

> § 7 (specifying December 18 as the date electors "shall meet and give their votes"); § 12 (specifying "the fourth Wednesday in December"—this year, December 27—as the date on which Congress, if it has not received a State's electoral votes, shall request the state secretary of state to send a certified return immediately). But none of these dates has ultimate significance in light of Congress' detailed provisions for determining, on "the sixth day of January," the validity of electoral votes. § 15. (550)

Because Congress was required to count electoral votes turned in after December 12 unless the votes "ha[d] not been . . . regularly given" (quoting 3 U.S.C. § 15 at 550), any of these dates could be used, even up to January 6, 2001, insisted Ginsburg. This expansion of the scene within which the recounts legitimately could take place meant that the majority's contention that there was no time to continue the recount was wrong; indeed, plenty of time remained to meet even the long list of tasks the majority required for a constitutionally defensible recount.

Finally, Ginsburg characterized the agents involved in the lawsuits and the recounts as hardworking, suggesting that they could have finished a recount in an orderly, timely fashion—an easy thing to do with her newly enlarged scene. Although she might have complained about the secretary of state or the Bush team's efforts to delay the process and keep the recounts from being completed (as many commentators did), she did not. On the contrary, she asserted that "no one has doubted the good faith and diligence with which Florida election officials, attorneys for all sides of this controversy, and the courts of law have performed their duties. Notably, the Florida Supreme Court has produced two substantial opinions within 29 hours of oral argument" (550). This positive assessment kept her on the high road but also supported her rejection of the majority argument that a recount was impractical as an "untested prophecy" (550), by portraying these agents as more angelic and more cooperative than the record supported.

Breyer's Dissenting Opinion

Justice Breyer joined Justice Souter (as Souter joined him) in recognizing the equal protection problem raised by the majority. Justices Stevens and Ginsburg joined him on all but this point. Breyer used less than a quarter of this, the longest dissent, to deal with the equal protection issue (and that primarily to reject the majority's remedy). The remainder joined Justice Ginsburg's dissent in an attack on Rehnquist's Article II argument. Breyer used historical arguments, even more than Ginsburg, to put Article II and 3 U.S.C. § 5 into context.

Reconstructing the Majority

Whereas Stevens and Souter focused on what the Florida court was doing to defend the state court's decision, indirectly criticizing the actions of the majority that second-guessed its decision, Breyer focused on what the majority was doing in this case, beginning bluntly: "The Court was wrong to take this case. It was wrong to grant a stay. It should now vacate that stay and permit the Florida Supreme Court to decide whether the recount should continue" (550–51). Although the majority had included Breyer among the "seven" recognizing equal protection problems in the Florida recount, they distorted Breyer somewhat in suggesting that his "only disagreement is as to the remedy" (533). Obviously, in saying here that "the Court was wrong to take this case," he went beyond a mere "remedy" disagreement.

Instead of focusing on what the petitioners were claiming, as Stevens had done, Breyer placed the action squarely in the majority's hands, noting:

> The majority raises three Equal Protection problems with the Florida Supreme Court's recount order: first, the failure to include overvotes in the manual recount; second, the fact that *all* ballots, rather than simply the undervotes, were recounted in some, but not all counties; and third, the absence of a uniform, specific standard to guide the recounts. (551)

This division of the majority's actions went further than other dissents, which focused primarily on the equal protection issue involving the lack of a uniform substandard for recounting votes.[25] In separating out different acts of allegedly undermining equal protection, Breyer was able to take the punch out of the majority's shotgun approach to establishing equal protection problems.

To reject the overvote problem, Breyer noted a lack of any factual basis for supporting that claim, since "petitioners presented no evidence, to this Court or to any Florida court, that a manual recount of overvotes would identify additional legal votes" (551). Thus, while the recount process had uncovered new votes, and this was shown in the trial, there was no legally established basis for assuming that one might recover votes from overvotes. This was a tidy and powerful argument against that aspect of the majority's equal protection concerns.

Breyer's rejection of the second equal protection problem built on his argument against the overvote problem. This second majority concern was that all ballots had been recounted in some counties; therefore, those living in the state-ordered undervote recount counties were being treated differently. He rejected that claim by reference to the first, saying "[t]he same is true of the second [claim]" (551). His point appears to be that absent a finding that overvote recounting produces more votes, counting all ballots does not yield a difference. This glosses over the majority's claim that recounting even ballots that were not rejected as undervotes or overvotes might yield different results, since, for example, "the citizen who marks two candidates, only one of which is discernible by the machine, will have his vote counted even though it should have been read as an invalid ballot" (per curiam, 531). However, because this was speculative and not established at trial, Breyer could reject it for the same reason he rejected the overvote problem.

Finally, Breyer turned to the issue of using differing standards in the recount, which he admitted "does implicate principles of fundamental fairness" (551). Oddly, even in agreeing with the majority's concern, he gives
the most accurate and most generous reading of all the opinion writers
(dissenters included) of the standard employed by the Florida Supreme
Court, which he characterized as "the uniform general standard of the
'clear intent of the voter'" (551). In his reading, this is not only a "standard" but a "uniform" standard that looks for not merely the "intent of the
voter" but the "clear intent of the voter."[26]

Breyer goes further to explain why the Florida Supreme Court followed
that standard instead of providing "uniform substandards" (551), shifting
some blame to the U.S. Supreme Court itself: "In light of our previous remand, the Florida Supreme Court may have been reluctant to adopt a
more specific standard than that provided for by the legislature for fear of
exceeding its authority under Article II" (551). The U.S. Supreme Court
had questioned the state court's reliance on the Florida Constitution in justifying its lengthening of the protest period from November 14 to November 26. Breyer's characterization provides a broader context of action
within which to understand Florida's choice to stick to the one basic standard for finding legal votes it could find in the election code. The high federal court made the state court gun-shy, Breyer suggested, by criticizing
them for changing standards drawn from specific legislative language. Indeed, as some critics would argue, it may have placed the state court in a
Catch-22, whereby if they had developed a substandard, Rehnquist could
have attacked them for violating Article II; whereas when they did not,
they could be criticized for violating equal protection.

Despite Breyer's explanation for the state court's actions and his implication of the Supreme Court in fostering those actions, he nonetheless asserted that "basic principles of fairness may well have counseled the
adoption of a uniform standard to address the problem" (551). Those fairness issues were relevant because of Breyer's belief that "the use of different standards could favor one or the other of the candidates" (551). Breyer
gave no explanation for this assumption. Although the actions of Gore and
of Democrat-controlled counties where the initial recounts took place suggested that they believed a looser standard would benefit them, it is hardly
clear that this would be the case in a statewide recount. Indeed, the most
respected recount by the media after the election controversy ended
suggested that Bush, not Gore, would have benefited from a looser standard statewide.[27]

Ironically, Breyer in dissent did a better job of tying vote recount standards to particular groups of voters than did the majority, making the equal protection more compatible with the voting rights precedents invoked by the per curiam. But the majority did not follow him on this, perhaps because identifying Republicans or Democrats as beneficiaries of these standards would have reminded court watchers that this was a decision with partisan consequences.

With that unnecessary pitch for a majority who, he asserted, should not even have taken this case (a rhetorical blunder), Breyer quickly returned to castigating the majority, this time over the remedy. He insisted that "there is no justification for the majority's remedy, which is simply to reverse the lower court and halt the recount entirely" (551). Breyer's remedy would be to remand the case to the state court so it could set a uniform substandard for a recount of all undervotes in the state—including even those in the previously recounted counties (presumably to dispel any remaining concern over the equal treatment of all counties and their voters) (551).

Like Ginsburg, he relied on a scene-agent argument to bolster the state court's opinion on a recount and discount the majority's, since the majority lacks "*any* record of evidence that the recount could not have been completed" (552), and "state courts are in a far better position to address" such factual issues (552). And while Breyer's dissenting colleagues missed the majority's particular claim that the Florida Supreme Court had found that Florida law required it to meet the safe harbor deadline, Breyer did not, insisting that "whether, under Florida law, Florida could or could not take further action [in light of the December 12 deadline] is obviously a matter for Florida courts, not this Court, to decide" (552).[28]

Breyer accused the majority of unfairness and imprudence in "craft[ing] a remedy out of proportion to the asserted harm [especially since] that remedy harms the very fairness interests the Court is attempting to protect" (552). As many critics would note, throwing out the votes of those whose interests one purports to be protecting is not a good means to the ends of justice. And in the interest of fairness, as Justice Stevens had argued, the majority was fiddling around with a minor equal protection concern while Rome burned in the larger equal protection problem of different voting machines with their differing levels of accuracy and reliability. But while Stevens would use the comparison to reject both equal protection concerns, Breyer would cleverly connect the two. He did so by agreeing that the use of different voting systems meant that "voters already

arrive at the polls with an unequal chance that their votes will be counted"
(552). Instead of playing one concern against the other, as Stevens did, he
proposed to kill two birds with one stone (a single agency to meet two purposes) by having the state court set a new substandard for recounting and
restarting the recount to "redress" the "inequity" caused by different voting
systems (552).

Breyer was the only justice specifically to note that recounting would
overcome the problem of different voting systems by recovering those ballots that were rejected in greater numbers in the punchcard counties. And
he tied this fact to a reshaped characterization of the Florida Supreme
Court's recount order, which had as its purpose not only the identification
of every uncounted vote, but the redress of this voting system-related
inequity.

Reconstructing Rehnquist

The large remainder of Breyer's dissent was directed to a refutation of
Rehnquist's concurring opinion. Breyer first considered Rehnquist's justification for reviewing the Florida Court's decision under Article II, turned to
the merits of the claim that the Florida court usurped legislative power,
and ended with a consideration of why federal courts should stay out of
such controversies.

Breyer characterized Rehnquist's review of state law as "unusual" and
scrutinized his justification for failing to give the usual deference to the
state court. The means by which Rehnquist justified this review was "some
combination of Art. II, § 1, and 3 U.S.C. § 5" (552). Specifically, Rehnquist
relied on a "strained" reading of the plain text of Article II (Breyer directed
us to Stevens on this point) and on *McPherson v. Blacker* for "the conclusion
that Article II grants unlimited power to the legislature, devoid of any state
constitutional limitations, to select the manner of appointing electors"
(552). As Stevens had done, Breyer pointed out *McPherson's* recognition of
state constitutional limitations on legislative power in selecting the manner
of appointing electors. Relying on a different section of *McPherson* from
Stevens, Breyer noted that the precedent "specifically refer[s] to [a] state
constitutional provision in upholding [a] state law regarding [the] selection
of electors."[29] Just as in Stevens's dissent, this correction of Rehnquist's
reading of *McPherson* implied bad faith on the chief justice's part.

Breyer turned next to untangle a complex web of actions constructed
and connected by Rehnquist to justify (1) enforcing the safe harbor provision and (2) castigating the Florida court for "changing the law" (in

violation of Article II) in failing to enforce the safe harbor deadline. The distinct acts discussed in this reconstruction are labeled below to highlight the grammatical complexity of this argument:

> The concurrence's treatment [act 1] of § 5 [act 2] as "informing" its inter-pretation of Article II, § 1, cl. 2 [act 3], ante, at 3 (Rehnquist, C. J., concur-ring), is no more convincing [than his "plain" reading of Article II or his use of *McPherson*]. The Chief Justice contends [act 1a] that our opinion in *Bush v. Palm Beach County Canvassing Bd.* [act 4], ante, p., (per curiam) (*Bush I*), in which we stated that "a legislative wish [act 5] to take advantage of [§ 5] would counsel against" a construction of Florida law [act 6] that Congress might deem to be a change in law [act 7], id., (slip op. at 6), now means that *this Court* "must ensure that post-election state court actions do not frustrate the legislative desire to attain the 'safe harbor' provided by § 5." [act 8] Ante, at 3. (552–53)

Breyer explicitly attributed two related acts to Rehnquist here—1 and 1a, in which the chief justice "treat[s]" of and "contends" for two interpreta-tions of law. Rehnquist's construction of the remaining acts are shown to support these primary acts. Rehnquist, we are told, reads Article II *through* § 5 (act 3 through act 2), understanding an act of the Founding Fathers through an act of Congress. He uses *Bush I* (act 4) to interpret the Florida legislature's act of wishing to meet the safe harbor (act 5), so he can direct the Court's interpretation of Florida law (act 6) to avoid a conflict with a hypothetical congressional act (act 7) and implement a Court directive to correct the state court (act 8).

Not only does Breyer's characterization of Rehnquist's reconstruction show the complexity of the interpretive claim made by the chief justice, but it also allows him to sever the connections Rehnquist is deemed to have made. That is done by reconstructing the acts themselves. He first re-constructs act 2 in noting that "§ 5 is part of the rules that govern Con-gress' recognition of slates of electors" (553). That is, § 5 is scenically connected ("part") of rules (agencies or means) that support a particular purpose (governing Congress); its place, means, and ends connect it to Congress, not to the states (as Rehnquist would have it).

Next, he turns to act 4, insisting: "Nowhere in *Bush I* did we establish that *this Court* had the authority to enforce § 5" (553). This goes to the act of the court itself (discovered after surveying the textual scene of *Bush I*), considering what was done and not done by the court. Breyer's emphasis on "this Court" (for the second time in this section) pointed to a separate act—what the Court might do if it did not lack the authority. This is the rejected act, the nonact for Breyer.

He continued in further characterizing the Court's act in *Bush I:* "Nor did we suggest that the permissive 'counsel against' could be transformed into the mandatory 'must ensure'" (553). This construction follows from the unique opportunity in judicial argument for post hoc disconfirming analyses to show what a court was not doing. Here, it takes Rehnquist's putative reliance on *Bush I* (a reliance emphasized by Breyer's reconstruction) in concluding that the Supreme Court "must ensure that postelection state court actions do not frustrate the legislative desire to attain the 'safe harbor' provided by § 5" (quoting Rehnquist at 553). Emulating the "plain reading" approach of a strict constructionist, Breyer laid Rehnquist's statement next to the *Bush I* statement "that 'a legislative wish to take advantage of [§ 5] would counsel against' a construction of Florida law that Congress might deem to be a change in law" (quoting Rehnquist at 553), complaining that under Rehnquist's construction, "counsel against" now means "must ensure" (553). The contrast between the "permissive" and the "mandatory" suggests an unwarranted leap by Rehnquist that "turns the presumption that legislatures would wish to take advantage of § 5's 'safe harbor' provision into a mandate that trumps other statutory provisions and overrides the intent that the legislature *did* express" (553). Breyer's antithesis between "counsel against" and "must ensure," the "permissive" and the "mandatory," and Rehnquist's "presumption" and the legislature's "express[ed]" intent suggested a gap between the law and Rehnquist's construction of the law.

Having thrown into doubt Rehnquist's claim that the federal court could legally intervene to enforce an Article II violation, Breyer next turned to consider an "even if" argument.[30] "Even if" arguments follow challenges to legal or factual claims, considering the implications for a case even if those legal or factual claims were true. This approach, popular in legal argument, provides a more thoroughgoing attack on an opponent's argument because it undermines more than one leg upon which that argument stands. Thus, if the judge's argument against a legal or factual claim were found wanting, he or she could rely on the "even if" argument to challenge an opponent's position.

Breyer's "even if" argument assumed as true Rehnquist's claim to have the authority to review the Florida court's interpretation of state law to ensure that it did not impermissibly distort what the state legislature intended. Even under that assumption, Breyer urged, Rehnquist's application of that hypothetical law reached the wrong conclusion (553). Rehnquist had asserted that "the Florida Supreme Court's interpretation of the Florida election laws impermissibly distorted them beyond what a fair reading required, in violation of Article II" (quoting 535 at 553). Breyer stated that "apparently" there were three elements of this alleged distortion. First, the change of the election certification date from November 14 to November 26 was said to be a distortion. What Rehnquist overlooked in this allegation, Breyer stated, was a "plain conflict in the language of different statutes" (namely, the "may" and "shall" provisions and the recount option with the too-short window to exercise it). Even if the concurrence ignored that basis for interpreting the statute, it was irrelevant, since "that issue no longer has any practical importance and cannot justify the reversal of the different Florida court decision before us now" (553). In other words, the concurrence was seeking to reverse Florida based on past "sins" irrelevant to the current controversy.

The second distortion, Rehnquist had alleged, was the state court's order to recount the ballots despite the fact that it could not have been fully completed by the safe harbor deadline. Here Breyer followed Souter in blaming his colleagues for preventing a complete recount, insisting that "the inability of the Florida courts to conduct the recount on time is, in significant part, a problem of the Court's own making" given its "improvidently entered . . . stay" (553). Rehnquist's characterization implied bad faith on the part of the Florida court in ordering to be done what could not be done in the limited time available. Breyer rebutted this implied characterization, insisting that "[t]he Florida Supreme Court thought that the recount could be completed on time, and, within hours, the Florida Circuit Court was moving in an orderly fashion to meet the deadline" (553). In this construction, the attitude and the agency of the recount challenged the bad faith suggestion of Rehnquist. Breyer missed an opportunity here to add that the Florida court's own reading of Florida law did not necessarily hold December 12 as the final deadline (i.e., the scene was larger than suggested by either Rehnquist or Breyer).

The third distortion identified by Rehnquist presented a greater challenge, requiring a lengthier response: that "the Florida court, in the opinion now under review, failed to give adequate deference to the determinations of the canvassing boards and the Secretary" (553). Dividing the question, Breyer insisted, "there are two sides to the opinion's argument that the Florida Supreme Court 'virtually eliminated the Secretary's discretion'" (553). He went on to consider the conflict over the definition of "legal vote." However, Breyer was a bit imprecise here. Breyer's quotation of Rehnquist was slightly different from the original statement, which charged the state court with "virtually eliminating both the [certification] deadline and the Secretary's discretion to disregard recounts that violate it" (537). The discretion in question, for Rehnquist, was a choice of whether to accept late recounts. Breyer took "discretion" in a broader sense than specifically used in the incompletely quoted statement to suggest more generally the secretary's power to which the state court was accused of "fail[ing] to give adequate deference" (553).

Perhaps he used this pointed statement by Rehnquist to reflect the chief justice's general attitude toward the state court's treatment of the secretary. Or perhaps he took liberties because the chief justice took liberties in condemning the state court for past sins (since the certification deadline was not raised in the *Bush v. Gore* appeal, which dealt with the contest period but had been raised in *Bush I*, which dealt with the protest period). Or perhaps this was the language of the last draft of Rehnquist's opinion that Breyer got to see prior to its publication. In any case, Breyer is conflating two acts, using Rehnquist's protest complaint to stand in for his contest complaint. Breyer had stressed that his concern over these three "distortions" involved "the opinion now under review" (553).

The framing of the issue as one of discretion was not ideal for Breyer as he turned to a consideration of the secretary's and the Florida Supreme Court's competing interpretations of "legal vote." For "discretion" suggests that the secretary's exercise of authority is "uncontrolled by the judgment or conscience of others."[31] Breyer never refuted the questionable implication—which his construction suggested—that the secretary had discretion in establishing what a legal vote is (rather than, as Rehnquist stated, in deciding whether to accept vote tallies after the certification deadline).

With that clumsy beginning, Breyer noted that the secretary "claimed that a 'legal vote' is a vote 'properly executed in accordance with the instructions provided to all registered voters'" (554). In characterizing the secretary's act as claiming rather than holding, finding, or establishing, Breyer downplayed suggestions that her interpretations of law were binding (as Rehnquist had suggested)[32] and played up the idea that she was a mere advocate for this position. "The Florida Supreme Court did not accept her definition," he noted, though "it had a reason" (554). Here Breyer ambiguously presented the state court's role in interpreting the state's election code, implying that it was in a position to accept or reject the secretary's definition but indicating that "a reason" supported that (suggesting, perhaps, that the court could not simply reject out of hand but needed to justify its decision).

Breyer clarified the deference due to the secretary later, when he insisted that "nothing in Florida law requires the Florida Supreme Court to accept as determinative the Secretary's view on such a matter" (554). Breyer's assertion, which cited no law on the issue, was a weak counter to Rehnquist's insistence that the secretary's interpretations were "binding," pointing to § 97.012 and § 106.23 of the election code and insisting that a 1993 state court precedent required them to "defer to the Secretary's interpretations."[33] And although good arguments could have been offered against Rehnquist's reading of these authorities, Breyer provided none.[34]

Breyer did offer reasons for the Florida court's alternative interpretation of "legal vote." Relying on the state court's arguments, he noted

> that a different provision of Florida election law (a provision that addresses damaged or defective ballots) says that no vote shall be disregarded "if there is a clear indication of the intent of the voter as determined by the canvassing board" (adding that ballots should not be counted "if it is impossible to determine the elector's choice"). Fla. Stat. § 101.5614(5) (2000). (554)

The characterization of this subsection as "a different provision" distinguished it from the provision detailing the grounds for a contest, though it did not indicate why this particular provision, with its specific concern for "damaged or defective ballots," ought to control the definition of "legal vote" for the entire election code. An act-agency argument could have urged that this means of determining a legal vote was limited to the act of examining damaged and defective ballots.

Justice Souter, by contrast, had more fully developed an explanation for what the state court was doing when it landed on the defective ballot provision, noting: "The statute does not define a 'legal vote,' the rejection of which may affect the election. The State Supreme Court was therefore required to define it" (544). Instead of merely landing on "a different provision," the Florida court landed on perhaps the *only* provision that provided an indication of what a legal vote was. Admittedly, a division of labor would allow Breyer to rely on Souter's previous argument, but there was no explicit reliance of this sort, and Breyer's characterization looked weak by comparison.

Breyer did a bit better in citing court cases supporting this definition of "legal vote," including a "roughly analogous [Florida] judicial precedent

. . . and somewhat similar determinations by courts throughout the Nation" (554). These cases and the statutory language, Breyer insisted, led
"the Florida Supreme Court [to conclude] that the term 'legal vote' means
a vote recorded on a ballot that clearly reflects what the voter intended"
(554). Thus, the state court was constructed as following the law and not
"impermissibly distort[ing]" the law, contrary to Article II (554).

Breyer next took on the charge that the Florida court had failed to give
proper deference to the canvassing boards. He had an easier time here by
scenically distinguishing two periods: the protest period and the contest period. He insisted that "[t]he boards retain their traditional discretionary authority during the protest period," but the contest period was different. If a
candidate could show that there were enough uncounted legal votes to
place in doubt the results of the election, then the canvassing boards' earlier decisions not to recount could be set aside (554). Breyer insisted: "To
limit the local canvassing board's discretion in this way is not to eliminate
that discretion. At the least, one could reasonably so believe" (554). With
this distinction between the acts of limitation and of elimination, Breyer
could challenge Rehnquist's insistence that this was a distortion of state
law.

Breyer took advantage of the generous language of the contest provision, emphasizing the state court's authority in this matter to "fashion such
orders as he or she deems necessary to ensure that each allegation . . . is *investigated, examined, or checked* . . . and to provide any relief appropriate"
(quoting § 102.168[8] with emphasis in original, at 554). Breyer's emphasis elided the act of recounting with those of investigating, examining, and
checking authorized by the statute, insisting that "[t]he Florida Supreme
Court did just that" (554).

Like Souter, Breyer admitted that "[o]ne might reasonably disagree with
the Florida Supreme Court's interpretation of these, or other, words in the
statute," but insisted, "I do not see how one could call its plain language interpretation of a 1999 statutory change so misguided as no longer to qual-
ify as judicial interpretation or as a usurpation of the authority of the State
Legislature" (554). To bolster this claim, he noted that other states "have
interpreted roughly similar state statutes in similar ways," citing two by
way of illustration. By noting other state courts' declarations that "the purpose of the voting process is to ascertain the intent of the voters" and that
"whether a ballot shall be counted . . . depends on the intent of the voter,"
Breyer places the Florida court among reasonable peers.[35]

Reconstructing the Petitioners, Himself, and the "Road Map"

In continuing his challenge to Rehnquist's concurring opinion, Breyer turned in the second section of his opinion to a consideration of how such election disputes should properly be resolved. This agency concern would be transformed into an agent concern, where who did the resolving determined whether the means were proper. Breyer would reject the involvement of federal courts while endorsing the involvement of state courts and the U.S. Congress. He did so through yet another rereading of Article II and an in-depth historical analysis of the Electoral Count Act.

Breyer began by rejecting Rehnquist's claim that this case demanded intervention because it involved "an election for the President of the United States" (555). As a national act, Rehnquist could claim, it invoked federal interests, it had broad implications for the nation as a whole, and it was unique (whereas, say, congressional races were much more common and much more local in character). Breyer did not dispute that but insisted that its "importance is political, not legal" (555). The High Court has a long-standing policy of avoiding "political" issues, so this distinction implied that this was a case outside the Court's jurisdiction.

Breyer admitted that there was one legal issue worthy of concern—the equal protection claim—though he held that this was balanced by "a competing fundamental consideration—the need to determine the voter's true intent" (555). Most of the petitioners' concerns did not involve such basic rights but rather "the constitutional allocation of power" (555). Rather than separate out the equal protection wheat from the power allocation chaff, Breyer suggested that the latter diluted the former, so that the two sides were engaged in "a tangential legal [dispute]" (555). The converse rhetorical strategy used by judges is to toss aside the chaff to focus better on the real issue, freeing oneself from such irrelevant scenic distractions. Or, to use a different metaphor, Breyer's approach was one that rejected another's shotgun argument—many minor arguments trying to collect into something significant—by tossing aside many irrelevant pellets (in this case, the "power allocation" subarguments) and finding only one pellet left. One pellet could not fell the legal beast the petitioners' sought to win.

Given the small threat of this singular constitutional pellet, Breyer reasoned, the equal protection issue "might have been left to the state court to resolve if and when it was discovered to have mattered" (555). The smaller size of the threat ensured that a state court, unassisted by the U.S. Supreme Court, might handle the issue.

The majority had identified Breyer as one of "[s]even Justices of the Court [who] agree that there are constitutional problems with the recount ordered by the Florida Supreme Court that demand a remedy," with the caveat that two of the justices (Breyer being one of them) "disagree[d] as to the remedy" (per curiam, 533). Breyer's construction of his own motives set him up for such use by the majority from whom he dissented, particularly in his statement that the equal protection issue "does implicate principles of fundamental fairness" (551). However, the majority's assertion that Breyer's concern over equal protection "demand[s] a remedy" might be overstated in light of his argument that (1) the federal court should not have taken the case, (2) the case involved "a tangential legal [dispute]," and (3) the state court could have addressed the problem itself "when it was discovered to have mattered." Breyer's suggestion that the state court could address the issue was an alternative remedy that the majority could contend was covered in its caveat on disagreement about the remedy, though his "when it was discovered to have mattered" seems to imply that it might never have mattered, so that no remedy would be necessary. A stronger claim would have been "*if* it was discovered to have mattered"; but Breyer left the majority with enough wiggle room to construct his motives to their advantage.

If Breyer believed that the constitutional issues were not enough to warrant the Supreme Court's intervention, he also believed that federal law counseled judicial restraint by indicating that other institutions were responsible for resolving such election disputes. Invoking a metaphor, Breyer insisted that "[t]he Constitution and federal statutes . . . set forth a road map of how to resolve disputes about electors, even after an election as close as this one" (555). The image of a road map served a scenic function here, suggesting proper direction and the relative placement of legal players on this field. A road map also serves as an agency, telling one how to get from one place to the other. Unlike statutes and constitutions, which must be interpreted, road maps need only be read. The implication is that the law on this road map was clear and not in dispute; the Supreme Court had only to follow proper directions.

In looking for direction, Breyer began by noting that the "road map foresees resolution of electoral disputes by *state* courts" (555). In support of this reading, following Stevens, he cited 3 U.S.C. § 5's reference to "the appointment of . . . electors . . . by *judicial* or other methods" (555). A second congressional act reinforced this state court role and brought Congress's role to the fore. Breyer noted that "the Electoral Count Act, enacted after the close 1876 Hayes-Tilden Presidential election, specifies that, after States have tried to resolve disputes (through 'judicial' or other means), Congress is the body primarily authorized to resolve remaining disputes."[36] Finally, bringing the Constitution to bear as well, Breyer noted that "the Twelfth Amendment commits to Congress the authority and responsibility to count electoral votes" (555). Thus, three acts (two statutory, one constitutional) shored up Breyer's road map, which, he added, "nowhere provides for involvement by the United States Supreme Court" (555).

In addition to an absence of any statement in the statutes or the Constitution regarding the U.S. Supreme Court's role in such election disputes, Breyer offered a reading of legislative history to suggest that a court role had been positively rejected. He quoted an 1886 House Select Committee on the Election of President and Vice-President rejecting other bodies: "The two Houses are, by the Constitution, authorized to make the count of electoral votes. They can only count legal votes, and in doing so must determine from the best evidence to be had, what are legal votes. . . . The power to determine rests with the two Houses, and there is no other constitutional tribunal."[37] This statement, while not conclusive evidence of what Congress intended, suggested that the means for settling these dispute rested solely with Congress. Those means were bolstered when connected to a purpose for this particular choice, which Breyer found in a quotation from the member of Congress who introduced the Act:

> The interests of all the States in their relations to each other in the Federal Union demand that the ultimate tribunal to decide upon the election of President should be a constituent body, in which the States in their federal relationships and the people in their sovereign capacity should be represented.
>
> Under the Constitution who else could decide? Who is nearer to the State in determining a question of vital importance to the whole union of States than the constituent body upon whom the Constitution has devolved the duty to count the vote?[38]

Putting the two quotations side-by-side, Breyer bolstered the quoted characterizations of means and ends through the grammatical logic that connected them: Congress is the agency for recounts because of the need for a national constituent body to determine this question "of vital importance to the whole union of States."

Of course, this statute would stand up only if the Constitution permitted it. Congress has not infrequently passed statutes that failed to meet constitutional muster, and ones that increase their own power might require the most scrutiny from constitutional watchdogs. To meet this concern, which is only implicit in this dissenting opinion, Breyer had included with the lengthy quotation above an explanation of the constitutional basis for the power offered by the congressman who introduced the legislation, insisting that "[t]he power to judge of the legality of the votes is a *necessary consequent* of the [constitutionally authorized] power to count" (quoted at 556). This argument draws on the act-agency relationship, whereby authorizing Congress to count entails authorizing congressional means to do so. A final fleshing out of the constitutional act by the legislator added a purpose to this act and agency: "The existence of this power is of absolute necessity to the preservation of the Government" (quoted at 556). Thus, implied Breyer through this legislator's words, Article II gives Congress the power to count, that counting requires means for determining what a legal vote is, and those means ensure that the purpose of preserving the government is met (no doubt a real concern only twenty-one years after the Civil War ended).

After empowering the congressional role in resolving electoral disputes, Breyer turned again to reject the federal judicial role. This time, he reversed the grammatical strategy, drawing the character of the act out of the means. After reviewing in detail the Electoral Count Act's elaborate rules for settling electoral disputes, he concluded: "Given the detailed, comprehensive scheme for counting electoral votes, there is no reason to believe that federal law either foresees or requires resolution of such a political issue by this Court" (556). As this logic goes, if Congress had intended Court intervention, why did this elaborate scheme not mention the Court? Or, from another reading, why would Congress provide such detailed direction if it did not intend that to be followed?

On this point, Breyer explicitly turned to constitutional questions, insisting: "Nor, for that matter, is there any reason to think that the Constitution's Framers would have reached a different conclusion" (556). Breyer offered one powerful example to support this claim: "Madison, at least, believed that allowing the judiciary to choose the presidential electors 'was out of the question.'"[39] Restating the purpose connection, he insisted that this approach "is as wise as it is clear," since Congress would "[express] the people's will far more accurately than does an unelected court. And the people's will is what elections are about" (556). The judiciary was, by this reckoning, an inappropriate agency for resolving such disputes, because it was unelected and removed from "the people's will"; Breyer's endorsement of Congress thus provides a basis for the rejection of the judiciary.

Not only was the judicial role inappropriate, Breyer argued, but the 1887 Congress (which passed the Electoral Count Act) believed it was "danger[ous] [to] ask judges, unarmed with appropriate legal standards, to resolve a hotly contested Presidential election contest" (556). Breyer here suggested the image of a judge without law to guide him or her. The agent-agency connection is closer than a first glance might suggest, for our American judicial mythology holds that a judge acts as a judge only insofar as he or she follows the law. Without appropriate legal standards to guide judges, they stand naked, as mere mortals, stripped of the arms that make them judges (much as a sharpshooter without a weapon ceases to be the agent we would recognize as a sharpshooter). Thus, the agency makes the agent, just as much as the agent implies the agency.

To establish that the legislature that passed the Electoral Count Act worried about this danger, Breyer reviewed the circumstances surrounding the 1876 presidential election dispute to characterize the scene within which the legislators passed that act. He noted that three states sent two slates of electors to Washington in the election contest between Rutherford B. Hayes and Samuel Tilden, throwing the close election into Congress's hands. Congress appointed a commission of five senators, five representatives, and five Supreme Court justices to resolve the dispute. The commission was evenly split between Democrats and Republicans, with Justice David Davis, an independent, as the deciding vote. Davis was elected to the Senate by the Illinois legislature and was replaced by Justice Joseph P. Bradley, a Republican, who threw the election to the Republican, Hayes. Although, as Breyer noted (citing Alexander Bickel), Bradley relied on a legal principle and was probably honest and impartial, he brought disdain on himself and the judiciary:

> Justice Bradley immediately became the subject of vociferous attacks. Bradley was accused of accepting bribes, of being captured by railroad interests, and of an eleventh-hour change in position after a night in which his house "was surrounded by the carriages" of Republican partisans and railroad officials. (557)

The moral of the story for the *Bush v. Gore* court was clear:

> [P]articipation in the work of the electoral commission by five Justices, including Justice Bradley, did not lend that process legitimacy. Nor did it

assure the public that the process had worked fairly, guided by the law.
Rather, it simply embroiled Members of the Court in partisan conflict,
thereby undermining respect for the judicial process. And the congress that
later enacted the Electoral Count Act knew it. (557)

Rhetorically, the implications of that story, and Breyer's use of it, are manifold. First, the story served as an elaborate account of the historical scene
within which the 1887 Congress passed the Electoral Count Act. This scene
of concern over the judiciary (as well as the lack of clear standards for deciding close elections) controlled the act that followed eleven years later.
The point of the legislation, as Breyer constructed it, was not simply to
avoid another debacle like that in 1876 but to avoid "embroil[ing] Members of the Court in partisan conflict." Whether that was a central concern
of most legislators is unclear, but Breyer's construction of the events, with
its key focus on Justice Bradley, made that element loom large in this legislative scene.

The reconstructed events in the 1876 election dispute not only carried
implications for Breyer's reading of the Electoral Count Act, but it also told
a story with a clear moral for the Court's actions in 2000. As Breyer told it,
an otherwise honest and impartial judge was thrown into this controversy
without the appropriate legal standards to justify his election-deciding
vote. He and the Court suffered as a result. This story was directly applicable to the *Bush v. Gore* majority, who jumped into the election conflict
and—from Breyer's and the other dissenters' readings—were weakly
armed with appropriate legal standards. Indeed, Breyer explicitly added
that "the Court is not acting to vindicate a fundamental constitutional
principle" (557). The majority justices may have considered themselves
honest and impartial, like Bradley; nevertheless, they and the Court could
suffer as Bradley and his Court had. Moreover, Breyer added, this "self-
inflicted wound . . . may harm not just the Court, but the Nation" (557).

Breyer was concerned not only about a majority decision he found
wanting but also about the 5-4 split, insisting, "in this highly politicized
matter, the appearance of a split decision runs the risk of undermining the
public's confidence in the Court itself. That confidence is a public treasure
[that] has been built up slowly over many years" (557). Breyer treads carefully here, never directly pointing to his conservative colleagues' political
leanings (though the disaster that found Republican Bradley supporting
Republican Hayes might have given a hint in that direction). Instead, he
notes that the "matter" itself is "politicized" and is worried about "appearance[s]." The threat to the "public treasure" Breyer would defend is made

more significant by the time involved in building it up, suggesting a long recovery for a Court damaged by this controversy.

In illustrating what a diminished Court might face, Breyer drew on an oft-repeated quotation of President Andrew Jackson, who, upset with the Court's ruling in favor of the protection of the Cherokee Indians, was reported to have said, "John Marshall has made his decision; now let him enforce it!"[40] Although Breyer admitted "[w]e run no risk of returning to [those] days," the quotation suggested how far the Court could fall.

Breyer's closing paragraph suggested that the Court had acted "in order to bring this agonizingly long election process to a definitive conclusion," but had "not adequately attended to that necessary 'check upon our own exercise of power[:] our own sense of self-restraint.'"[41] In short, he suggested, the majority's purpose controlled its act, rather than a proper judicial attitude of self-restraint. He ended by stating that he would permit the recount to continue under new standards (558).

The Dissenters' Reconstructions of Majority and Concurring Opinions

Overall, the dissenters gave much more attention to Rehnquist's concurring opinion than to the majority opinion, perhaps because they thought that the chief justice's view would prevail and stand as the majority decision. Justice Ginsburg was the most direct in attacking Rehnquist's opinion for failing to defer to the state courts (as history indicated the Court traditionally had done), for misapplying civil rights era precedents (and equating Florida with a recalcitrant Jim Crow South), and for his inconsistency in ignoring his own states' rights ideology.

Justice Souter was the strongest defender of the Florida Court's interpretations of its state election laws, finding that it operated with the bounds of reasonable interpretation. With Ginsburg and Stevens, he emphasized that what the state court was doing in interpreting its own law constituted appropriate judicial action. He challenged Rehnquist's shotgun approach to finding fault with the Florida court by throwing out the protest concerns he had smuggled into this contest decision.

Breyer made the strongest argument challenging Rehnquist's reading of Article II and of 3 U.S.C. § 5, delving into the motives of the Founding Fathers and legislators to establish that they intended Congress, not the Supreme Court, to settle such election disputes. Ginsburg and Stevens supported such views by changing Rehnquist's emphasis in reading Article II's grant to legislatures as a grant to the state, from which the legislature is born, constrained by the state constitution that gave it birth. Breyer and Stevens both provided a devastating challenge to the chief justice's reading of the *McPherson* precedent, showing that he had ignored specific sections of the opinion where the precedent court recognized the state constitutional limitations on the legislature's power in selecting electors.

The attack on the majority's position was weaker, particularly in light of Souter and Breyer's finding of equal protection problems in the recount. Whereas Stevens and Ginsburg found variations in the recount standards constitutionally inconsequential and overshadowed by differences in the reliability of voting systems (which also lacked an equal protection violation), Souter and Breyer thought a recount based on a new, uniform standard was needed. Breyer provided both support and challenges to the majority's equal protection concerns. First, he undermined their shotgun of equal protection concerns by throwing out overvote concerns as not factually established and the counting of different types of votes in some counties as irrelevant (given the overvote finding). He also blamed the Supreme Court itself for making the state court gun-shy about setting more specific recount standards by rebuking the state court for setting a new certification deadline in *Bush I*. On the other hand, he helped the majority by going further than they had in suggesting that different recount standards might favor one candidate or the other, providing more easily identified groups of voters discriminated against than the majority's overvoters and residents of different counties.

Curiously, none of the dissenting justices pointed to the inconsistency of the majority's equal protection holding with earlier Court decisions requiring a finding of intent to establish an equal protection violation. Perhaps this liberal minority left out those concerns because they themselves did not support the intent rule. Or perhaps in the rush to get out their opinions, they overlooked this argument. In any case, they missed an opportunity to support further their charge of inconsistency against the majority.

All of the dissenting justices rejected the safe harbor deadline that prevented a recount from proceeding, though only Justice Breyer challenged the specific argument of the majority that the Florida Supreme Court itself had held that Florida law required that the safe harbor deadline be met. By throwing out this deadline, the dissenters showed that there was time for a recount. Justice Souter in particular painted an optimistic picture of the speed of the recount, and most dissenters noted the diligent attitude of those engaged in the recounts.

The dissent painted a picture of the majority as perhaps overstating the equal protection problems, as manufacturing a phony deadline to prevent a recount, and as disrespecting the state court. On this last point, the chief justice was the worst, failing to defer to the state court (as was the High Court's tradition), as well as misconstruing Article II and 3 U.S.C. § 5. All of the conservative five were criticized for their inconsistency in failing to respect states' rights.

5

Reporters Reconstruct the Supreme Court's Action

If the U.S. Supreme Court's power ultimately rests upon the American public's perception of its authority, then that public is a critical audience of the Supreme Court's decisions. However, legal discourse is rarely adapted for a lay audience. Although the average American may have a gut sense of what is fair and unfair in a given case, he or she can hardly be expected to fathom the legal nuances of the *Bush* Court's equal protection holding or Rehnquist's Article II argument. The American people rely on an intermediary—the news media—to explain what the Court was doing and why it was doing it in a given case.

In constructing motives, the news media face a different rhetorical challenge from that of the High Court. While they share the Court's need to appear objective and fair, they also are concerned to grab and keep their readers' interest; after all, they are—with minor exceptions—money-making corporations selling stories to the public. Therefore, they tend to dramatize stories, focusing on key agents and emphasizing conflict, rather than engaging in dry technical analyses.[1]

The postelection roller coaster, with its final showdown in the Supreme Court, was a bonanza for the news media. It offered a drama of twists and turns, with the most powerful office in the world hanging in the balance. It featured colorful key players, including the candidates, their former secretaries of state, celebrated legal counsel (including David Boies, Laurence Tribe, and Ted Olson), slow-talking southern judges, diligent ballot counters, hordes of chanting supporters (for both sides), and an army of talking heads. And although cameras did not catch them in action, the powerful and mysterious "wizards" of the U.S. Supreme Court were given voice through audio recordings of the oral arguments and lengthy quotations from their opinions.

Reporters and the Stay

News reporting on the *Bush v. Gore* case sought to present itself as objective and fair. In the interest of objectivity, most stories quoted key segments of the majority and dissenting opinions, as well as the stay. They focused upon key legal issues that explained the outcome of the decision, particularly the equal protection concerns and the safe harbor deadline. In the interest of fairness, they quoted both critics and defenders of the majority's opinion. To avoid the perception of judging what they witnessed, they used the words of others to do so.

Despite journalistic goals to be objective and fair, there is no ultimately neutral vocabulary for describing motives. Reporters have to use words to describe what the Court was doing and why it was doing it, and in choosing those words, they necessarily convey a particular view of the Court's motives.[2] They are much more subtle than editorialists, but they are rhetorical nonetheless.

On the day after the Supreme Court issued its stay order halting the Florida recounts, reporters began predicting the High Court's future action in *Bush v. Gore,* reading into the stay their attitudes, purposes, and agencies; considering their political affiliations; and comparing possible actions to those of earlier courts. John Farrell of the *Boston Globe* focused less on what the stay did than on what it portended, relying on scholars and Scalia's concurrence in concluding that the 5-4 majority "have probably already reached a verdict . . . on the claims in the case of *Bush v. Gore* that they will hear tomorrow."[3] Farrell enhanced this prediction of future action by emphasizing the solidarity of the majority, whom he called a "bloc of conservative justices" and a "firm majority." Reflecting Kenneth Burke's conception of attitude as "incipient action,"[4] the justices were "poised" to reverse the Florida court. In Justice Scalia's concurring opinion defending the majority's stay, Farrell noted, Scalia had been "blunt" about the probability of a Bush victory. The conservative justice was driven by a purpose (as his colleagues, in their unity, presumably were as well) to end a dispute that was "threatening the legitimacy of a Bush presidency and harming American democracy." Thus, Farrell painted a majority on the brink of action, with an attitude of unity and certainty, driven by patriotic, and perhaps political, purposes.

Although Charles Lane of the *Washington Post* agreed that "Scalia . . . all but predicted the outcome," he emphasized the division of the Court rather than the unity of the majority, highlighting the political wrangling over the stay, opening with: "Abandoning all pretense of unanimity, the U.S. Supreme Court's liberal and conservative members openly attacked each other yesterday over whether to stop the manual recounting of ballots in Florida."[5] Dramatizing the conflict, Lane characterized the agents in dispute and their actions: "The center-left . . . 80-year-old Justice John Paul Stevens[, who] publicly dissented from the five-member center-right majority's decision" and "Justice Antonin Scalia, the court's most dynamic conservative, [who] fired back with an opinion defending the majority's decision." Stevens did not merely dissent, he publicly dissented; Scalia did not merely explain the majority position, he fired back. Emphasizing Stevens's advanced age and Scalia's dynamism, as well as their ideological leanings, constructed a conflict between old and young, liberal and conservative.

Adding an ironic twist to this drama, Lane insisted that the two justices shared a common purpose: "to save the country from the disaster that would befall it if a questionable electoral process were to go forward, producing a president whose legitimacy would be widely doubted." Lane connected this last statement of purpose to the legal issue of irreparable harm, noting that each side's lawyers claimed such harm would befall their client. Numerous citations of arguments by Bush and Gore lawyers further defined the grounds of the conflict in the stay and in the case to come. Near the end of his lengthy article, Lane reiterated the dramatic conflict, noting: "Constitutional scholars expressed astonishment at the forcefulness with which the court's majority intervened in the case, and at the unmistakably angry way in which the minority objected." This passionate division might prove troublesome, Lane predicted, since "[h]istory suggests that, if the court is to play an effective role as national arbiter of politically charged legal disputes, it is better to do so through unanimous decision-making."

Thus, Lane implied, the Court was headed for a dramatic but ineffective resolution of the election dispute.

Writing for the Associated Press, Laura Meckler began by putting the stay into a larger historical context: "The U.S. Supreme Court's long-standing reputation for operating above the political fray is being tested mightily in the case that could decide the presidency."[6] This framing of the dispute immediately cast the majority's action as unusual and questionable, with the implications of this divergence from the past clearly noted. Meckler followed this opening by noting that "conservative justices lined up with George W. Bush and liberal justices backed Al Gore as the court suspended the hand count of thousands of Florida ballots that may contain undetected votes for president." Here, the unusual agent-act relationship that found the Supreme Court involving itself in a political matter was made politically explicable by narrowing the agents and their acts, whereby conservatives support Republicans and liberals support Democrats. Meckler was much more explicit than Farrell or Lane in highlighting this political connection, which is made even tighter by the larger scene (of prior court actions) within which she situates it.

Meckler's characterization of the scene in Florida as perhaps containing "undetected votes for president" made the conservatives' actions more problematic than the liberals', even if both might reflect political purposes. Rather than explicitly drawing out the implications of the partisan story she was developing, she did what good reporters do and let others voice those concerns. Specifically, she looked to the American public, not directly but through the eyes of legal scholars:

> "I do think its image is tarnished in the eyes of many people," Erwin Chemerinsky, law professor at the University of Southern California, said of the court. "It's seen as another political player." "The court doesn't have many resources, but what it does have is the good will and the good faith of the people," said Mary Cheh, a law professor at George Washington University. "It's a very fragile thing, so you don't want to lose it."

Later in the story Meckler gave voice to defenders of the Court, who insisted that the Court's image was diminished only "for those who disagree with the court's action." She allowed them to offer an alternative characterization of the action, namely, "a flawed Florida Supreme Court decision to order hand counts across the state," which, according to George Mason University law professor Daniel Polsby, "thrust the judicial system very far into the political thicket."

However, Meckler quickly offered Democratic support for the partisan view of the majority's actions, noting that "Gore supporters smell hypocrisy. They suggest that conservatives on the Supreme Court who usually favor returning power to the states are usurping state authority in this case." This agent-act inconsistency, whereby defenders of states' rights usurp state authority, adds another support to the construction by implying that a political purpose underlies these agents' decision to do something antithetical to their own ideological beliefs. This is made understandable in another statement from Chemerinsky, that "[t]his seems to be much more naked political power being exercised by five Republican justices and that's what I think is so damaging,"

Meckler's construction, we might say, was only drawing out the implications of the grammatical relationships formed by the actions of the Supreme Court. Conservatives *did* side with the most conservative candidate, and liberals *did* side with the most liberal candidate. The Supreme Court historically *has* stayed out of political disputes. The conservative majority *has* espoused a support for states' rights. And "many people" (especially Democrats) certainly *were* complaining that the Court was playing politics in halting the recounts. While this is an obvious and easy construction to make, it is not the only possible construction. She might have emphasized the uniqueness of the presidential dispute as calling forth this unusual action (as Rehnquist would later argue). As Farrell did, she might have focused on predicting future action by the Court. As Lane did, she might have focused on the immediate conflict between a majority and a dissent ironically sharing the same purpose, rather than upon the political alliances that gave the two factions diverging purposes.

All three reporters characterized the stay as a split decision with serious consequences for the presidential election and for the Court's standing in public opinion. They all indicated the ideological split, though Meckler tied that explicitly to a political split. They all spoke to the historical uniqueness of the case. And they all suggested that the stay was an indication of probable alignments in a final *Bush* decision. Later characterizations reversed this reading, by using the decision in *Bush v. Gore* to reread what the Court was doing in the stay.

Reporters and Bush v. Gore

Bush v. Gore was a gold mine for reporters hoping to dramatize this final chapter in the thirty-six-day postelection controversy. It involved the most

powerful judicial body in the world in an unprecedented, controversial ruling that awarded the highest office in the land to a man with whom the
Court majority appeared ideologically and politically allied. It gave a victory to the Republicans while dashing the hopes of Gore supporters in an
election where the country was evenly split about who it wanted for president. And it released a flood of criticism, creating a postdecision drama
that questioned the legitimacy of the *Bush* majority. While news stories
generally refused to take sides explicitly on the correctness of the decision,
they quoted enough from the majority, the dissenters, and legal commentators to expose (and intensify) the controversy surrounding it. And their
language revealed subtle constructions of their own making

The Significance of *Bush v. Gore*

The question of significance addressed how the act of decision ought to be
regarded within a larger historical scene. While the act called for historical
comparisons, the historical scene that reporters constructed shaped how
the act could be interpreted. So here the reporters would be suggesting
qualities of the act and looking to a history (which they constructed) to
judge it. Using this grammatical logic, reporters characterized *Bush v. Gore*
as historic, unusual, unexpected, and controversial. Finlay Lewis of the *San
Diego Union-Tribune* noted that this was "the first time that the U.S.
Supreme Court has taken action to affect the outcome of a presidential
election."[7] Robert G. Kaiser of the *Washington Post* said that it was "without
precedent in law or politics."[8] Linda Greenhouse of the *New York Times*
noted the situation, the Court's action, and the manner in which the decision was reached and announced in orienting the case to its larger historical scene, insisting: "Nothing about this case, Bush v. Gore, No. 00-949,
was ordinary: not its context, not its acceptance over the weekend, not the
enormously accelerated schedule with argument on Monday, and not the
way the decision was released to the public tonight."[9]

If the decision was significant and unusual, it also was unexpected, reported Anne Gearan of the Associated Press. Just by taking the case, she
noted, "[t]he justices stunned nearly everyone, including many in the
campaigns themselves."[10] *Newsweek* reporters Evan Thomas and Michael
Isikoff concurred, adding that "[e]ven Bush's own lawyer, Ted Olson, was
surprised when the High Court issued an unusual emergency order to stop
the manual ballot recount in Florida on Dec. 9."[11] Thus did reporters use
reactions to characterize the actions of the High Court.

The characterization of the case as controversial involved a consideration of the arguments of the majority and the dissenters, the reaction of
the legal community, and speculations about the motives of the five conservatives who effectively handed the election to Republican George W.
Bush. Most reporters began with the most pertinent fact indicating controversy: the 5-4 split. Reporters said this split exposed "a profoundly divided
court,"[12] "deeply fractured"[13] by an "internal divide"[14] that "decided the
next president of the United States . . . by the narrowest of margins."[15] The
scenic quality of their terminology was joined with agent terms reflecting
philosophical leanings in reports calling this "deep divide"[16] an "ideological
gulf,"[17] defined by "searing ideological lines"[18] and a "well-established lib-
eral-conservative fault line."[19] If division was a reflection of ideology, the
act of dividing was a cause or a sign of negative attitudes, some reporters
suggested. Thus, Joan Biskupic of *USA Today* spoke of the Court's "bitter division."[20] *Boston Globe* reporters Mary Leonard and John Farrell said this
"bitter split" was reflected in the Court's "hydra-headed ruling . . . with
[its] multiple dissents and concurrences."[21] Reconstructions of the dissents
enhanced the sense of controversy and division. The dissents were characterized as "sharp,"[22] "scathing,"[23] "bitter,"[24] and "stern,"[25] in "attacking
what they saw as contradictions or outright hypocrisy in the majority's
reasoning."[26]

This division appeared more profound when contrasted with the unanimity of the Supreme Court's decision in *Bush v. Palm Beach County Canvassing Board* (or *Bush I*). As Charles Lane of the *Washington Post* noted:

> When it first considered the election dispute eight days ago [in *Bush I*], the
> court managed to preserve the appearance of unanimity by issuing an un-
> signed opinion. In that case, the court simply returned the issue to the
> state's supreme court with instructions to bring its ruling into conformity
> with the U.S. Supreme Court's reading of the Constitution and federal law.
>   Over the weekend, the court split 5-4, with a conservative majority fa-
> voring a halt to new manual recounts requested by Vice President Gore and
> ordered by the Florida court, and a liberal minority openly dissenting.[27]

Lane's suggestion that the Court had tried "to preserve the appearance
of unanimity" in *Bush I* was an inference about what the Court was doing
in that previous case. But it was an inference based on historical analogies
that others noted. For example, *Time* magazine noted that "Chief Justice
Earl Warren worked mightily behind the scenes to extract a unanimous decision [in *Brown v. Board of Education*]," because, the magazine insisted,
"[t]here's always considerable pressure on the Supreme Court, in very

important cases, to rise above—or at least appear to rise above—political divisions."[28]

Given this purpose for rising above political divisions (or appearing to do so), Linda Greenhouse speculated that the *Bush v. Gore* decision was a failed compromise, urging that "the court's day and a half of deliberations yielded . . . a messy product that bore the earmarks of a failed attempt at a compromise solution that would have permitted the vote counting to continue."[29] Finlay Lewis agreed, pointing to the oral arguments for evidence:

> During Monday's oral arguments, Souter and Breyer floated a possible compromise under which the case would be sent back to the Florida court with instructions to lay out a single statewide standard for discerning voter intent on the contested ballots.
>
> The majority ignored that suggestion.[30]

Again, this was speculation, but it was reasoned speculation, taking statements by Souter and Breyer not as expressions of opinion to counsel or for the public record but as appeals to their conservative colleagues for reaching some consensus on this case. The failure to reach a compromise led to the split decision and to this "hydra-headed ruling," which reporters called "a complex and scattered series of opinions,"[31] a "tangled and elaborate ruling,"[32] and "a tangle of six different majority, concurring and dissenting opinions."[33]

Frank J. Murray of the conservative *Washington Times* downplayed the divisions by relying on the argument offered by the majority itself, complaining: "Many of those who joined yesterday's uproar focused on the one-vote margin to reverse the lower court, overlooking the 7-2 vote that ruled the Florida vote setup violated the Equal Protection Clause of the 14th Amendment."[34] He quoted Republican senator Olympia Snow's statement that "seven of the Supreme Court justices recognized that there were some serious constitutional issues with respect to the counting standards and Equal Protection Clause" and former White House Counsel C. Boyden Gray's insistence, "I would take a 7-2 decision anytime. I don't think it is divisive at all."

Anne Gearan qualified that 7-2 distinction, noting that there were "limited areas of agreement among seven justices."[35] Charles Lane of the more liberal *Washington Post* went further in tying the 7-2 characterization to the majority, suggesting that the "unsigned opinion for the court seemed to exaggerate the degree of agreement between [Souter and Breyer] and the majority."[36] Linda Greenhouse of the *New York Times* went even further to note that

> [the majority's] opinion later caused some confusion by its reference to "seven justices of the court" who "agree that there are constitutional problems with the recount." That was true, but it was also beside the point, because by then the only question was whether there was a remedy for those problems, in the form of a restructured but continuing recount. On that question, the vote remained 5 to 4.[37]

Murray and other reporters provided larger scenes within which to interpret this split decision, implying that such splits were not so rare (and, perhaps, should not be judged as unusual). Murray followed his article with a list of landmark Supreme Court cases, many of which were split 5-4 or 7-2, including *Dred Scott* and *Roe v. Wade* (7-2) and the *Miranda* and *Bakke* decisions (5-4). His placement of *Bush v. Gore* on this list implied that it also is a landmark. However, he also included several important unanimous decisions, such as *Marbury v. Madison, McCulloch v. Maryland, Brown v. Board of Education, Gideon v. Wainwright,* and *U.S. v. Nixon.* At best, this suggests that some landmark decisions have been split, though it also shows that many have not.

Marianne Lavelle and Chitra Ragavan of *U.S. News & World Report* offered a similar list, though they limited their examples to 5-4 splits alone. Of the six they listed, three were decided by the current Court (two from the same year as *Bush v. Gore*).[38] Gearan identified a trend implicit in this listing, remarking that "[i]n the most recent court term, 20 of 73 signed decisions were reached by 5-4 votes, the highest percentage of one-vote outcomes in more than a decade, with O'Connor and Kennedy joining the Rehnquist bloc in 13 of those votes."[39] As we move from Murray's construction to Gearan's, we shift from scene as a container of the action (whereby this is but one split decision among many) to agent as container of this action (whereby this Court has a penchant for split decisions). The agent characterization does indeed moderate the judgment of the *Bush* decision as unusual in its divisiveness, though only by indicting the Court itself for being divisive. Thus, the act is saved from a harsher judgment (based on the split alone) at the expense of the agents (polarized and divisive as they are).

The Outcome of *Bush v. Gore*

If simply hearing the case and reaching a split decision marked *Bush v. Gore* as historic, unusual, unexpected, and controversial, the outcome of the case itself would provide fodder for those who would question the Court's motives. An outcome may be construed as a purpose—something an agent sought. It also may be constructed as an effect—an unintended, unforeseen, accidental, or incidental outcome. Or it might be offered as something in between, as when one reacts to the actions of others, leading to consequences that one would not seek otherwise.

All reporters announced that the election had effectively been awarded to Bush through the decision. For example, Finlay Lewis noted, "[t]he language of the majority all but awards the victory to Bush."[40] In a move that Lewis would repeat, this characterization shifted responsibility for giving the election to Bush from the Supreme Court to (in this case) the agency (the "language") rather than the agents. Alternatively, Lyle Denniston of the *Baltimore Sun* portrayed the Court's intervention as active and obstructive: "The majority set up a series of barriers that will have the effect of barring any more counting."[41] In a bit of grammatical analysis of his own, Denniston suggested that the majority attempted to appear passive in this work: "The majority *said* it was accepting a responsibility it did not seek in deciding the case. But it *found a way* to assign primary responsibility to the Florida Supreme Court and the Florida Legislature."[42]

Lewis found other agents to blame for the decision as well, specifically the voters and the calendar.[43] He insisted that "[t]he problems [that led to this case] arose because voters had not properly pushed out a piece of the ballot punch card—or chad—corresponding to a presidential candidate." He did not mention difficulties with the punchcard system itself, any failures by election officials to instruct voters properly, or any failure of the recount process to assess the inadequately punched ballots. Instead, it was voters who were blameworthy.

Another candidate Lewis offered for blame was time, for "despite the arcane legalistic wrangling reflected in the 65 pages of ruling and dissents, the calendar emerged as the biggest obstacle to a recount." Contrast that with Denniston's remarks quoted above that the High Court had set up "barriers" to a recount. Thus, whereas Denniston would name the Supreme Court as the agent of the controversial act, Lewis would blame another agent (voters) and the scene (time).

The *Economist* magazine's characterization of the majority also shifted blame, pointing to the Florida court and relieving the federal Court of some of its responsibility for this controversial act. Using a scenic metaphor, the magazine contended that "the Florida recount put [the U.S. Supreme Court] in an impossible position." It bolstered the already favorable 7-2 split on the equal protection issue by noting that "even the dissenting Justice Ginsburg called [the recount] flawed." And it listed equal protection problems along with Article II concerns as a group, amassing a number of reasons for the reversal and declaring: "[n]o wonder the US Supreme Court struck [the Florida decision] down."[44] Of course, this construction grouped agents who did not agree with the Court's actions (especially Ginsburg and Breyer but also Souter). And it implied that equal protection and Article II concerns could be lumped together to explain the purposes for the Court's decision (though only three justices supported the Article II reasons). Together this enlarged group of agents with their enlarged purposes suggested near unanimity in support of appropriate legal conclusions.

Other reporters whose constructions provided a defense for the Court almost erased the active agent in focusing on a welcome outcome, namely, an end to the controversy. Thus, Richard L. Berke of the *New York Times* noted Senator Kay Bailey Hutchison of Texas's statement that "[t]he country has needed closure on the presidential election of 2000 and the Supreme Court of the United States has delivered that closure tonight."[45] Joan Biskupic quoted conservative Berkeley law professor John Yoo's terse statement that "[i]t's over."[46] Emphasizing *what* was over, David G. Savage and Henry Weinstein of the *Los Angeles Times* noted that "[d]efenders of the ruling say the court did the nation a service by resolving a seemingly *intractable dispute*."[47] And the *St. Louis Post-Dispatch* proclaimed that "[d]espite [some] shortcomings, the decision did bring an orderly end to an unsettling dispute that threatened to throw the election into Congress."[48]

Of course, closure also entailed the shattering of Gore's hopes for the White House. Thus, Leonard and Farrell of the *Boston Globe* called the decision a "near-mortal blow" for Gore's presidential hopes.[49] Gearan noted that if the decision ended the election controversy, it also ended "Democrat Al Gore's hopes for the White House."[50] Editorialists would emphasize that Gore's loss was also democracy's loss.

If closure was a defensible end in itself, so was avoidance of the crisis toward which this last statement pointed. Avoidance could be validated as a purpose, however, only if the crisis to be avoided was significant. Here the news media offered their versions of a future scene without court intervention. The *Economist* described that scene as "the nightmare possibility of having a divided Congress choose between competing slates of electors in January."[51] That scenario had been elaborated by the media for weeks, *Time* reminded us, noting that Court defenders assured the public that "[t]he court's decisive ruling forestalled the nightmare scenarios that TV talking heads had been gleefully spinning. Rival sets of Florida electors. A tie vote in Congress. Constitutional deadlock."[52]

Reconstructing Legal Arguments in *Bush v. Gore*

Although the significance of the decision and the outcome were the leading points made by reporters narrating this high drama, most news organizations offered at least a cursory account of the legal arguments upon which the case turned. Typically, this involved selective quotations summarizing the equal protection finding, the safe harbor deadline, the remedy imposed by the majority, and the limitation of the precedential value of the case. Shorter stories offered little more than a passing reference to Rehnquist's concurring opinion, though many cited the dissenting opinions' disagreements with the majority's arguments. The construction of those legal arguments and the disagreements with them set the stage for a final assessment of Court motives.

Speaking generally, several reporters characterized the Court's legal arguments as weak. The *Economist*, which had shifted much of the blame to the state court, nonetheless urged (focusing on the act more than the agent) that "the case has raised serious doubts about its reasoning, its remedy, and even some of the judicial philosophy that informed its decision."[53] In summarizing its reading of *Bush v. Gore*, the British magazine was more direct in placing the majority in the driver's seat:

> In short, the US Supreme Court has rejected the ballots of some voters, stretched arguments in such a way as almost to make new law and has arguably shown disrespect to the legislative branch by imposing its own interpretation of what the Florida legislature wanted. It has done exactly what it overruled the Florida state court for doing.[54]

Despite these concerns over *how* the Court acted in *Bush v. Gore*, the *Economist* accepted this questionable action as "the cost of bringing an end to the election."[55] Thus, the ends (purpose) justified the means (agency), following the old grammatical saw.

Robert G. Kaiser of the *Washington Post* relied on legal scholars for his assessment. For example, he cited the parallel drawn by University of Chicago law professor Cass Sunstein between *Bush v. Gore* and *Roe v. Wade*: "The court in both cases intervened aggressively without having a constitutional provision that authorizes [the intervention]."[56] While this characterization implicitly condemned unwarranted aggression by the Court, it also appeared to trade conservative tit for liberal tat, whereby the conservative aggression of *Bush* answered the liberal aggression of *Roe*. Kaiser found Sunstein admitting, in any case, that the majority ruling may not hold up very well, though, the professor added (following the *Economist*'s logic), "as a matter of statesmanship [which cleaned up a messy political situation] it may well be vindicated."

Almost a year after the decision, Stuart J. Taylor of *Newsweek* summarized the position of the defenders of the decision:

> Conservatives generally defend the result. There are dissenters, but the most forceful ones don't want their names in the newspaper. In the judgment of one such conservative legal thinker, the court's equal-protection argument was "laughable," and, he adds: "I think history will judge the decision harshly." He and many others have suggested that the court's conservatives would have handed down a far different ruling if Bush had been the one demanding a manual recount, and Gore had been demanding that it be stopped.[57]

Although this retrospective assessment could not influence public constructions of motives in the immediate aftermath of the decision, it did provide a fair summary of the ends-means construction of the conservatives he referred to, though it expanded the ends a bit. The *Economist* and Sunstein had endorsed an ends-means interpretation that found ending an intractable election contest as a purpose justifying the questionable means employed by the majority. Here, Taylor added to that purpose not merely closure but handing the election to Bush. This is a terministic distinction deserving scrutiny. For conservatives seeking to defend the Court, the emphasis had to be on the purpose of closure, with the election of Bush merely incidental to that finalizing of the contest. But critics could reverse the emphasis, insisting that the election of Bush was the Court's purpose, while ending the contest was merely an agency for accomplishing that.

Reporters' characterizations of specific legal arguments gave greatest attention to the equal protection claim upon which the majority decision turned. Many noted the unequal treatment of ballots that bothered the Court. Reporters noted that the recount standards were "different,"[58] "varying,"[59] and "unequal."[60] Reporting the majority's position, Charles Lane noted "an unconstitutional lack of uniform criteria for determining voter intent."[61] The *Economist* implicitly explained the problematic standards (the agency of recounts) with reference to the limited scene, noting that the recounts "had been arranged *at the last minute* under varying standards for counting ballots."[62] Leonard and Farrell of the *Boston Globe* were less generous in calling the recount standards "haphazard,"[63] though they did not implicate any particular agent for this but focused on the process.

Lavelle and Ragavan of *U.S. News & World Report* offered a construction of the recount problems that actually made the Bush team a contributor to the inequality:

> In its argument to the court, the Bush legal team tapped into the rich tradition of civil rights law. Pepperdine Law School's Douglas Kmiec, one of the advisers to the Bush team, says this was a key reason Bush's lawyers refused to ask for a statewide recount, even after members of the Florida Supreme Court suggested it. Accepting a statewide recount would have made it more difficult to argue that the process was unfair, robbing Bush's team of its most potent legal weapon.[64]

Although the Florida Supreme Court *had* ordered a statewide recount of undervotes, this characterization of Bush as ensuring more inequality to bolster his legal case threw suspicion over their equal protection claims more generally.

Lavelle and Ragavan also provided the most sophisticated of the news media's analyses of equal protection law in this case. Many news organizations barely mentioned the basis for the holding. Those that did typically reported simply that the majority had found that using different standards in the recounts violated equal protection by not treating ballots the same.[65] The *U.S. News & World Report* team scrutinized the law of equal protection, with the help of a legal expert:

> Bruce Fein, a former Justice Department official in the Reagan administration and a Supreme Court expert, points out that in 1976, the Supreme Court made clear that litigants had an equal-protection claim only if they could prove that there was an intent to discriminate against them. Discrepancies due to voting-machine differences "aren't pro-Democratic or pro-Republican," Fein says. "They are random errors."[66]

The use of a Reagan-era official made this characterization more credible. And the reporters further balanced this construction by raising the concern for equal treatment of ballots in a new way, again relying on Fein to note a "potential for intentional discrimination in the hand-counting process as the Florida Supreme Court established it because there was no specific standard on what counted as a vote."[67]

This construction might have been connected to Justice Stevens's concern over "an unstated lack of confidence in the impartiality and capacity of the state judges who would make the critical decisions if the vote count were to proceed."[68] While Stevens attributed this lack of confidence to the petitioners, obviously it would serve the majority's ostensible need to establish discriminatory intent. But the majority had chosen not to implicate the recount officials, probably for fear of weakening its case since there was no incontrovertible evidence of partisanship on the part of the counters and of needing to show that one candidate (presumably Bush) would be discriminated against.[69] And almost all reporters went along with this.

The ever-vigilant *Economist* raised its own concerns about the equal protection argument: "Originally, the equal protection clause provided for equality under the law. That notion has been used to require 'one man, one vote.' But to go from there—as the Supreme Court did—to forbid varying standards of vote counting in a statewide election is a stretch."[70] The magazine added the concern that *not counting* uncounted ballots amounted to unequal treatment of voters as well. Furthermore, there was the likelihood of opening the floodgates to lawsuits in every close election. Finally, the magazine raised a concern over consistency: "the court stretched the meaning of the equal protection part of the constitution far, far beyond anything that a strict constructionalist would tolerate. Yet it was the constructionalists on the court—people who stick closely to the original wording of the constitution—who developed this argument."[71]

This agent-act concern—in this instance involving a strict constructionist who fails to follow the constitution by stretching its meaning—would be used again and again to suggest hypocrisy or a failure of fair dealing on the part of the majority. *Time* magazine invoked this ratio in its report on the equal protection holding as well:

> The conservatives performed a[n] . . . about-face on the Constitution's Equal-Protection Clause. The conservative camp, headed by Chief Justice William Rehnquist and Antonin Scalia, is generally skeptical of even well-established equal-protection claims, but in this case they found an entirely new equal-protection right: the right to uniform standards in a manual vote recount. The conservatives have previously not been receptive to pleas of unequal treatment in other areas, even when the most important rights are at stake. In McCleskey v. Kemp, for example, a black man on death row showed that capital punishment is administered without uniform standards from one jurisdiction to the next and is more often applied to blacks than whites for the same crime. But a conservative majority held that this did not violate the Constitution.[72]

This construction used a general statement and an example to illustrate the conservative majority's hostile attitude toward equal protection claims, even when those claims involve issues of life and death. That attitude was shown to be inconsistent with the act of ruling in *Bush* on the basis of an equal protection claim. Such constructions would contribute the groundwork for editorials decrying the decision as partisan.

To explain this change of attitude and action, *Time's* news analysts turned to the claims of civil rights' advocates "that the conservative Justices, long reluctant to apply the law's protections to minorities, were eager to cite its protections when the victim was a wealthy white Ivy League political candidate."[73] Thus, the reporters began building a case for purpose, whereby inconsistent judicial actions are explained by reference to particular ends they seek.

William Glaberson of the *New York Times* found a different kind of grammatical inconsistency in this equal protection ruling, which also laid the groundwork for a new interpretation of purpose, this one spanning two different acts by the Court. Reviewing the majority's actions in *Bush I*, Glaberson noted that "the Supreme Court did not then suggest, as it did last night, that the recounts Florida was conducting were constitutionally flawed because different standards were being used in different counties."[74] The Supreme Court agreed to hear *Bush I* on only two of the three issues raised by the Bush team (the Article II and 3 USC § 5 issues), rejecting the equal protection issue. The Court's two actions in dealing with the same election dispute appeared inconsistent. Defenders might appeal to differences in scenes, purposes, agencies, and so forth; but on its face, the Court's actions appeared as inconsistent as the recount standards they condemned.[75]

Glaberson also raised another issue that would attract the attention of several reporters: the safe harbor deadline that the High Court used to justify ending all recounts. Glaberson noted that "some legal experts have said [December 12] was not really a deadline at all." He quoted New York University law professor Barry Friedman's damning comment that "[i]t is remarkable . . . that the Supreme Court decided for the State of Florida that the Dec. 12 deadline was more important than finding the will of the voters." Friedman's construction challenged the majority in two ways: First, it suggested that the wrong agent was determining Florida law (because the federal court "*decided for* the State of Florida"). The *Economist* noted the same problem, remarking that "the high court's ruling seems to set itself up as a better judge of what the Florida legislature intended than the Florida Supreme Court."[76] Obviously, the magazine implied, interpreting Florida's legislative intent was best done by the Florida high court (the act determining the best agent). Such deference to the state court was particularly appropriate, Glaberson added, for those (like the conservative majority) who call themselves supporters of states' rights (raising another agent-act inconsistency).

The second issue raised by Glaberson's statement involved purpose, with the reporter urging that one purpose ("finding the will of the voters") actually should have taken precedence over the other purpose (meeting the deadline). In other words, the ends should have controlled the means, and one needed to start with the right ends. Here, the *Economist* again concurred, delving back into the Florida Court's decision to support a different interpretation of its motives: "The Florida court *mentioned* the legislature when justifying its decision according to law. But it did not *imply or say* that it thought the legislature's adoption of a 'safe harbour' trumped everything else."[77]

Here the British periodical noted something that most of the Court's dissenters seemed to miss when they argued against the majority by insisting that the safe harbor deadline was not a constitutional requirement, namely, the per curiam's specific claim that the Florida Supreme Court itself had found that the Florida legislature intended to meet the December 12 deadline. Glaberson drew this distinction as well, adding an irony pointed out by University of Iowa law professor Randall Bezanson: the majority's purported finding of legislative intent relied on the Florida court's opinion in *Palm Beach County Canvassing Board v. Harris,* and "the justices in Washington had overturned [that case]." Thus, even if they were not substituting their judgment for the Florida court's, they were nonetheless relying on a decision they themselves had vacated.

If the equal protection and safe harbor issues drew scrutiny from a few astute news sources, the remedy itself did not. This is surprising, since the Court's "remedy" for treating ballots unequally was a ruling that ensured that those unequally treated ballots were never counted—a troublesome species of justice, to be sure. Irony provides effective drama, and reporters seek drama; but no mainstream reporter noted this irony. Even otherwise incisive reports missed this mark. For example, the *Economist* noted that "the justices' remedy seemed no better than the one offered in Florida."[78] However, instead of pointing to the irony of protecting voters by ignoring their ballots, the magazine looked to political consequences, worrying that "[b]oth Mr. Bush and the court itself could be harmed by [the remedy]." *Time* magazine ignored these voters as well, noting the Court's insistence that the deadline had arrived in a section entitled "Not Every Wrong Has a Legal Remedy."[79]

Most news organizations simply quoted or paraphrased the dissenters' *legal* arguments that the deadline was incorrect and that the voting should continue, not questioning the *fairness* of the remedy. For example, Charles Lane of the *Washington Post* quoted Justice Breyer's statement: "What it does today . . . the Court should have left undone. I would repair the damage done as best we now can, by permitting the Florida recount to continue under uniform standards."[80] Lyle Denniston of the *Baltimore Sun* summarized the legal arguments as well, noting that

> two of those seven [justices] wanted to remedy that [equal protection] violation by letting recounts resume under a new, uniform standard to be laid down by Florida state courts. The five others who found a constitutional violation opposed that remedy.
>
> The court's two other justices said the recounts should be allowed to resume just as the Florida Supreme Court had outlined. Those two found no constitutional problems with the recounts completed so far, or with the standard used for judging ballots.[81]

Again, no mention of the voters.

Another legal issue largely ignored by reporters concerned the "political question" doctrine, whereby the Supreme Court traditionally has refused to intervene in issues better suited to resolution by other branches of government. Savage and Weinstein's article in the *Los Angeles Times* was a rare exception here, citing critics who "say the court departed from its usual conservative principles by resolving the type of 'political question' that the justices have shunned in other cases."[82] Again, an agent-act inconsistency was invoked to suggest that the justices were acting out of character.

A final legal issue discussed by reporters was the unusual attempt to limit the precedential reach of the opinion. *Time* magazine put the majority limitation into a broader framework of generalized judicial action:

> Generally speaking, Supreme Court decisions establish principles and precedents that can then be used to apply broadly to other cases. But the majority in Bush v. Gore, in a few throwaway lines, cautioned that "our consideration is limited to the present circumstances." In other words, unless you are a presidential candidate whose opponent has persuaded a court to order a statewide recount without uniform standards, this case might not apply to you at all.[83]

This last line was an interpretation of what the majority meant by its limitation—for it was not spelled out by the Court. Insofar as the case involved equal protection in election recounting, it might be broader than the presidential elections noted by the story. Nonetheless, the story captured the attitude of the limitation (if not the actual act), implying that the application would effectively be limited to the *Bush* case alone.

Lavelle and Ragavan of *U.S. News & World Report* relied on Supreme Court scholar Edward Lazarus to suggest that "the court purposely created 'an out' for itself."[84] With that characterization of action, they added an explanation of purpose from Lazarus: "I think they recognize they have dipped their toe into extremely deep waters . . . and they don't know where the bottom is." Thus, the purpose of avoiding an unknown extension of equal protection claims based upon this ruling led the majority to add its limitation as an out. The picture of a Supreme Court willing to pronounce law to reach a controversial decision in a present case, while giving itself an out should future litigants invoke the same law offered an easy target for critics. Even Linda Greenhouse of the *New York Times* could report a year later, as a matter of "fact," that "[t]he outcome was clearly one of convenience rather than the opening shot in a Rehnquist court equal-protection revolution."[85]

Reconstructing the Majority in *Bush v. Gore*

Reporters' characterizations of the case, its outcome, and the legal arguments all set the stage for an overall judgment of the Court itself in this decision. Here the reporters connected the dots of their earlier characterizations, turning from a consideration of what the majority did and how they did it to a consideration of who they are and why they did it. The *who* and *why* questions involved issues of reputation, credibility, and legitimacy.

Leonard and Farrell of the *Boston Globe* noted that the Court was aware of the potential links between what they did in the *Bush* case and how they would be perceived: "The justices were cognizant that the court's reputation could be damaged by a ruling the public perceived as partisan."[86] Indeed, noted Anne Gearan of the Associated Press, "[t]he unsigned majority opinion [itself] acknowledges the court is in an awkward position as it delves into an election."[87] Thus, although "the high court help[ed] to choose the next president," reported David Shribman of the *Boston Globe*, "[they made] efforts to seem not to do so. . . ."[88]

Of course, the majority could not escape the grammatical implications of the act-agent ratio, or what Kenneth Burke sometimes calls the *actus-status* relationship: inevitably, what one does carries implications for how one is perceived, and vice versa.[89] While as a group they could not escape that connection, individually they could temper it. They did so, some reporters implied, by using the per curiam format, failing to indicate who, exactly, was responsible for this controversial majority opinion.

Most reports noted that the opinion was unsigned.[90] Many acknowledged that Justice Kennedy or Justice O'Connor or both were the authors. For example, Charles Lane noted: "It was only by process of elimination that the public could learn that O'Connor and Kennedy had provided the fourth and fifth votes to decide the case for Bush. Their names appeared nowhere in the opinions explaining the court's reasoning."[91] Thomas and Isikoff of *Newsweek* identified the likely authors and explained the unusual use of the per curiam form:

> The name of the likely author of the majority opinion—Justice Anthony Kennedy—was entirely missing from court documents. Kennedy might have had some help from O'Connor, but court watchers can only guess, since her name is also absent. The opinion was labeled "per curiam," meaning "by the court." Normally, per curiam opinions are unanimous and uncontroversial. Kennedy's (and/or O'Connor's) [role in this case] will be the source of controversy and debate for years.[92]

The *Newsweek* characterization noted the atypical use of the per curiam in this split and the controversial decision to imply that some distancing might have been going on. Gearan was more direct, quoting Yale law professor Jack Balkin's assertion: "Kennedy and O'Connor decided it, but they are hiding. It's a stealth 5-4 opinion."[93] That act, she added, was judged by other scholars as lacking courage.[94] Hiding here is readily accounted for as a means for the fearful to avoid direct criticism for writing this controversial opinion.

Reporters relied heavily on legal scholars and other commentators to suggest that in the *Bush* decision, the Court had been activist, ideological, inconsistent, political, partisan, and self-serving. Stuart Taylor Jr. of *Newsweek* relied on Republicans to characterize the majority as activist, noting: "Many conservative Republicans, who have long fought against liberal judicial activism, are equally uncomfortable with the activist aura of the court's decision—no matter how pleased they may be with the outcome."[95]

The Court's activism was driven, many reporters suggested, by its ideological commitments. Biskupic of *USA Today* noted that "[t]he five justices

[are] all ideological, if not political, conservatives."[96] Many called them "conservatives,"[97] led by "the court's three-member conservative wing," those "staunch conservatives, Chief Justice William Rehnquist and justices Antonin Scalia and Clarence Thomas."[98] Gearan connected their ideology and their act, quoting Jerome Barron, law professor and former dean at Georgetown University, in noting that "[t]his is basically five ideological conservatives picking a conservative president."[99]

There is an ambiguity here which these reporters did not clarify in applying the term *ideological* to the majority judges. The term might refer to judges' political beliefs or to their judicial beliefs (or both), with obvious overlaps between the two. The distinction is important because it supports grammatical consistency in these reporters' description of the *Bush v. Gore* decision under one reading of ideology, while violating grammatical consistency from another. Insofar as ideology is associated with an agent (as in "an ideological conservative"), then that agent's acts are grammatically explicable to the extent that they follow those ideological commitments. We find such consistency in Gearan's quotation of Barron, who found "five ideological conservatives picking a conservative president." Here their ideology represents political commitments and an outlook shared with George W. Bush.

This agent-act relationship breaks down, however, when we consider the judicial ideology the reporters associated with the majority justices. That is, characterizations of these conservative judges' fundamental beliefs about the law were shown to clash with the actions they undertook, creating an agent-act inconsistency. The most noted inconsistencies were those involving the majority's position on states' rights and on equal protection law.

Time magazine, for example, stressed this inconsistency with respect to the majority's states' rights beliefs:

> the Justices seemed to contradict their long-held positions on important legal principles to reach the result they wanted. The conservatives on the court, for example, have been on a crusade to shift power from the Federal Government to the states. Their states-rights agenda has led them to strike down as infringements on state sovereignty such federal laws as the Violence Against Women Act and to defer repeatedly to state courts' interpretations of state statutes. But in Bush v. Gore, the conservatives didn't hesitate to strike down the Florida Supreme Court's interpretation of Florida election law.[100]

Here, *Time* educates its readers and illustrates the Court's ideological inconsistency by using acts (past decisions) to characterize agents (and their ideologies); then noting the inconsistency between those ideological agents
and their act in *Bush*. From another perspective, we may say that there is
an act-act inconsistency, whereby what was done before was not done in
the *Bush* case, though the inconsistency runs grammatically through the
agents who are the presumptive authors of consistent actions.

Many other reporters highlighted the same problem, describing the
agents and their act as inconsistent. William Carlsen of the *San Francisco
Chronicle* called this inconsistency an "unusual twist," because the majority
was "a faction that in the past has championed states' rights to determine
their own laws, [yet they] ultimately voted to reverse the Florida Supreme
Court and stop the court-ordered manual recount."[101] Warren Richey of
the *Christian Science Monitor* quoted a law professor on the "inconsistency
between the Rehnquist court's general solicitousness for states and the outcome in this case."[102] Lyle Denniston of the *Baltimore Sun* noted that "[t]he
same five justices, in opinion after opinion over the past eight years, have
sought to shore up state sovereignty against federal intrusion."[103] Jonathan
Ringel of the *Fulton County Daily Report* cited a liberal law professor's reference to "the majority's typical states-rights stance."[104] Gearan distinguished specific justices in noting that "[i]n recent years, O'Connor and
Kennedy have sided with the court's three most conservative jurists in a
series of 5-4 rulings championing state power over that of the federal
government."[105]

Reports of inconsistency on equal protection were less frequent, appearing only in longer news stories by mainstream news magazines. For example, after discussing the majority's inconsistency on states' rights, *Time*
noted a "similar about-face on the Constitution's Equal-Protection Clause"
from a Court typically "skeptical of even well-established equal-protection
claims."[106] Lavelle and Ragavan of *U.S. News & World Report* reported the
"delicious irony" that "[a] court [that] hasn't exactly been an aggressive
champion of civil rights . . . may have opened the door now to a host of
new [equal protection] lawsuits by minorities."[107]

The agent-act inconsistency on the judicial ideology side set the stage for
establishing an agent-act consistency on the political ideology side,
whereby charges of partisanship could account for the outcome and
explain the majority's divergence from its earlier positions. And, although
many would recite charges of partisanship in their news reports, very few
actually established a clear political affiliation to support that reading.

Newsweek and the Associated Press offered rare references to the fact that the majority justices had been appointed by Republican presidents.[108] Charles Lane of the *Washington Post* only mentioned those political affiliations months later in his review of the 2000–2001 U.S. Supreme Court term.[109] Instead, the link seemed to ride on the political ideology connecting the majority justices and the Republican governor of Texas.

In maintaining their reportorial objectivity, news organizations turned to others to voice partisanship concerns, connecting the majority justices to the future president. *Time* magazine stated that "a sizable number of critics, from law professors to some of the court's own members, have attacked the ruling as antidemocratic and politically motivated."[110] Similarly, Savage and Weinstein of the *Los Angeles Times* cited simply "[c]ritics [who] say the five justices in the majority decided what result they wanted to reach—an end to ballot recounts—and then cobbled together a weak rationale to get there."[111] Gearan cited a general source and tied the Court's judgment to the stay as well: "[t]he court had already compromised its nonpartisan reputation by agreeing to hear disputes over the election twice—both times at Bush's request, scholars said."[112] Joan Biskupic of *USA Today* cited a specific source, New York University law professor E. Joshua Rosenkranz, who was concerned that the 5-4 decision along ideological lines "can only convey to the public that judges are simply politicians in black robes."[113] Robert Kaiser cited a partisan source but allowed that source ostensibly to speak for "Americans":

> Liberal legal scholars decried the ruling as a politically motivated power grab unmoored in precedent or the law. Sen. Patrick J. Leahy (Vt.), the ranking Democrat on the Senate Judiciary Committee, said, "The majority has dealt the court a serious blow by taking actions many Americans will consider to be political rather than judicial."[114]

Kaiser balanced that liberal source with a conservative source equally concerned, noting that President Ronald Reagan's former White House counsel A. B. Culvahouse expected the Court to remain above the political fray, but admitted that "[h]ere they're very much in the fray [in a way that can] call into question the impartiality of the court."[115] David Shribman of the *Boston Globe* defended his sources and generalized their sentiments in insisting that "ordinarily sober voices in the American conversation are complaining that the Supreme Court has taken a fateful, partisan step."[116]

A conservative newspaper and a liberal one used surprisingly similar tactics in making partisan charges (i.e., acts) an element of the scene.

Frank Murray of the *Washington Times* focused on the majority preparation for a hostile scene, noting that "the majority in the Bush v. Gore ruling already is girding against cries of hypocrisy and partisanship."[117] Richard Berke of the *New York Times* noted that the decision "exposed veteran judges to accusations of partisan taint."[118] The difference in these two characterizations is that in the latter, liberal interpretation, the decision itself created the scene of exposure for the Court. In the former, the focus is on judges protecting themselves from an already threatening scene.

A few reports cited defenders of the decision who denied that politics played a role. Kaiser of the *Washington Post* noted that Republican senator Orrin Hatch, who chaired the Judiciary Committee, "rejected any suggestion that the court's decision was political."[119] Gearan quoted Pepperdine University constitutional scholar Douglas Kmiec, who insisted, "[n]ot only do I believe they decided this issue on law, not politics . . . but I think the composition of this court at the moment reflects a very nice and workable balance of opinion."[120] This second source appeared more objective than he might otherwise have appeared, since Gearan did not mention that Kmiec was an advisor to the Bush legal team, something two other reports did note.[121] The *Boston Globe*'s Shribman tempered the accusations of partisanship somewhat by pointing to a larger historical scene of Supreme Court action, urging that "[i]n truth, the court has never been a politically sterile redoubt."[122]

Beyond the general charge of partisanship leveled at the majority, a few reporters suggested that the justices had personal interests in the outcome of the election. Specifically, the reports suggested, their interest revolved around who would shape the Supreme Court in the future. Julian Borger of the *Guardian* noted that "[m]ore than that of any other case before the supreme court, the outcome of Bush v Gore has had a direct impact on the future of the judiciary."[123] Warren Richey of the *Christian Science Monitor* tied that impact to judicial motives in the *Bush* decision, noting that because "[t]he Supreme Court itself was a key campaign issue, with warnings about the broad implications of certain justices retiring . . . any justice contemplating retirement during the next four years has a vested interest in who becomes president."[124] Stuart Taylor Jr. of *Newsweek* named two potential retirees, citing "speculation that both 76-year-old conservative Chief Justice William H. Rehnquist and 70-year-old centrist Justice Sandra Day O'Connor may retire in the next year or two."[125] *Time* magazine focused on Justice O'Connor in particular, giving her a purpose for finding for Bush in noting: "[A]ccording to the *Wall Street Journal*, O'Connor's husband said

at an election-night party that his wife, a 70-year-old breast-cancer survivor, would like to retire but that she would be reluctant to leave if a Democrat won the presidency and got to select her successor."[126]

Borger added Scalia to this list of potential retirees and raised a second
motive for finding for Bush: "Mr. Bush's election could have a direct bearing on Mr. Scalia's career. Earlier this year he told the *Washingtonian* magazine that if Al Gore won the election he would retire as he would have no
chance of winning the coveted position of chief justice."[127] Kaiser of the
Washington Post also mentioned Scalia's interest in the chief justice position,
though he thought Scalia's role in the *Bush* decision had made such an appointment untenable. He did not speculate about whether Scalia had taken
this problem of "appearances" into account, though it potentially could
challenge charges that supporting a promotion was a motive of Scalia's
given this "Catch-22."[128] Taylor added Kennedy to the list of chief justice
hopefuls, noting that even conservatives thought of him "as more ambi-
tious for promotion than devoted to principle."[129]

Beyond retirement and promotion purposes in ruling for *Bush,* several
reporters cited family ties that raised potential conflicts of interest for the
majority justices. *Time* magazine noted a conflict involving Justice
Thomas's wife:

> Thomas' wife draws a paycheck from the conservative Heritage Foundation,
> where she has been vetting resumes for positions in a Bush Administration—
> an Administration her husband's vote helped usher in. Mrs. Thomas denies
> her work is for Bush and says she and her husband don't discuss his cases. But
> Lisa Lerman, a legal-ethics expert at Catholic University, calls the situation
> "unseemly."[130]

Both *Time* and Borger mentioned a conflict involving Justice Scalia's
sons. *Time* said that Scalia had two sons working for law firms that supported the Bush postelection litigation, while Borger mentioned only one
son, Eugene, who was "a partner in the Washington office of Ted Olson,
who acted for Mr. Bush in the two cases he brought to the court in the past
two weeks."[131] *Time* did temper its list of conflicts by admitting that "by the
very fact of the nomination process, all the Justices have links to one political side or the other."[132]

The Justices Speak Out

In view of these media reconstructions of High Court motives, almost all
justices departed from their usual reticence in discussing specific decisions

and made public statements on it, providing their own spin on what they were doing and why they were doing it. Reporters eagerly conveyed these statements to offer new insight into the high drama that unfolded in the High Court.

Linda Greenhouse of the *New York Times* suggested that the justices sought two reconstructions of their actions through their various remarks, urging "first, that the court was engaged in an appropriately judicial act rather than an illegitimately political one (significantly, this message was delivered by the Bush v. Gore dissenters); and second, that despite their sharp disagreement, the justices can still get along and their institutional bond remains strong."[133] Some justices succeeded better than others on both scores.

Justice Thomas was the first to speak out—unusual for a justice who never asks questions during oral arguments. He had scheduled a C-SPAN presentation to high school students before *Bush* arose. In it, he drew a distinction between the Supreme Court and Congress, saying that they were "entirely different worlds," because politicians "have no influence on us. The last political act we engage in is confirmation. That is the last act. And I have yet to hear any discussion, in nine years, of partisan politics in this—among members of this court."[134]

Reporters added their own interpretations to his remarks. Kaiser of the *Washington Post* called this an "unusual step [in] denying that politics was a factor in their decision."[135] Frank Murray of the *Washington Times* described Thomas's purpose as seeking "to minimize any role of politics in the outcome or the appearance that the Bush v. Gore case engendered bitterness."[136] Thomas and Isikoff of *Newsweek* thought his remarks might be considered "defensive."[137]

Kaiser also reported Rehnquist's first postdecision statement, as the chief justice watched Justice Thomas on C-SPAN with reporters in the Supreme Court's public affairs office. The journalists asked Rehnquist if he agreed with Thomas on the issue of politics, and he responded: "Absolutely . . . absolutely."[138]

Justice Kennedy offered comments in a congressional hearing in which he and Justice Thomas were testifying to a House appropriations subcommittee regarding a request for more than $100 million dollars to renovate the aging U.S. Supreme Court building. Charles Lane reported that Kennedy "told a congressional hearing . . . that the court intervened because the case posed 'constitutional issues of the gravest importance' that the court had a 'responsibility' to resolve."[139] Kennedy continued the theme of reluctant intervention (featured in the majority opinion), insisting: "Sometimes it is easy to enhance your prestige by not exercising your responsibility, but that has not been the tradition of our court."[140] Paul Leavitt and Kathy Kiely of *USA Today* added his statement that "it was our responsibility to take the case" and his qualification that *Bush v. Gore* "was not the most difficult decision that the court has made."[141] This last remark sought to make the case less extraordinary and the closeness of the call appear less controversial.

Thomas concurred with Kennedy on the responsibility thrust upon the Court by *Bush v. Gore*, insisting that "[i]t is on difficult issues that the court is required to be the court."[142] However, he admitted that he personally would have avoided getting involved in the decision if that were possible.[143]

Justice Scalia was speaking to the Economic Club of Grand Rapids when he admitted: "I don't have any fears that the long-term reputation of the court will suffer because of Bush v. Gore," adding, "I think the opinion was the right one."[144] In fact, he offered a metaphor to suggest that the Court's reputation ought to be "used" because it was not "some shiny piece of trophy armor mounted above the fireplace [but] working armor . . . meant to be used and sometimes dented in the service of the public."[145]

O'Connor, the fifth majority justice, spoke on two occasions reported by the press. First, she told the *Arizona Republic*, the leading newspaper in her home state, that she had no plans to retire.[146] This may have been an attempt to respond to the story in *Newsweek* about her reaction to Gore's apparent victory on Election Night.[147] Her husband told others she wished to retire but did not want a Democrat naming her replacement, explaining her exasperated response. Charles Lane, who related her comments in a *Washington Post* story, noted the absence of any reference to the *Newsweek* story, connecting the two by implication.[148] An Associated Press story used a scholar's commentary to interpret the justice's remarks further:

> "It may be that she wanted to put some distance between herself and that highly controversial ruling," said George Washington University law professor Mary Cheh. "Because of the appearance of a quid pro quo, it might put her in an awkward position if she retired now, and she is doing what she can to separate the two events."[149]

O'Connor commented on the case directly in a rare interview with television's *Dateline*, which Reuters reported, admitting "she wished the justices had never had to make the decision that all but delivered the White

House to George W. Bush," adding: "There was a great deal of criticism. It
was a difficult case. It's too bad that it came up." Maintaining the theme of
reluctantly doing one's duty, O'Connor added, "We don't always have a
choice in what comes here."[150]

In her remarks at the University of Melbourne Law School in Australia,
Justice Ginsburg did not challenge the majority's portrayal of itself as re-
luctant judges, but she did not support it, either. She passed up an oppor-
tunity to comment on the harm *Bush v. Gore* might have done to the
Court's legitimacy, noting that it "awaits history's judgment."[151] Charles
Lane summarized her presentation:

> Reviewing politically contentious Supreme Court cases of the recent past,
> she noted approvingly that justices appointed by President Richard M.
> Nixon had ruled against him in the 1974 Watergate tapes case, precipitating
> Nixon's resignation, and that two appointees of President Harry S. Truman
> had tipped the balance against him in the 1952 "steel seizure case."[152]

Refusing the opportunity to connect these remarks to the majority justices,
Lane noted: "She made no analogous comment about the Bush v. Gore
majority, remarking instead that two of the dissenters, Stevens and David
H. Souter, were appointed by Republicans and could be considered to have
crossed what she called 'party lines.'"[153] Linda Greenhouse noted an edge
in Ginsburg's measured remarks, insisting that the justice had "in no way
receded from her view that the decision was seriously misguided."[154]

Justice Breyer's remarks at a law school in Lawrence, Kansas, were less
nuanced and more supportive of the aims of preserving the Court's credibility. He reassured his listeners that the explanation for the *Bush* decision
"isn't ideology and it isn't politics."[155]

Justice Souter's remarks on the case came to the mainstream press
through a convoluted route. *Newsweek* reporter David Kaplan wrote a book
about the election, *The Accidental President*, which included a controversial
quotation from Souter. *Newsweek* excerpted part of the book that included
this quotation, which other news organizations picked up. Kaplan's account came from a story about Souter's visit to the Choate preparatory
school, in which he is said to have explained his frustration at being unable
to get Justice Kennedy to join his opinion to allow the recounts to continue. Kaplan reported: "If he'd had 'one more day—one more day,' Souter
now told the Choate students, he believed he would have prevailed." In
the most damning post-decision remark, Kaplan quoted Souter as telling
students: "It should be a political branch that issues political decisions."[156]

Kaplan's story became controversial when a teacher from Choate wrote the *Washington Post,* denying that Souter had made the statement about possibly turning Kennedy with one more day. Kaplan stood by his story. Souter never clarified his statements.

With the exception of Souter's somewhat unintentional construction of events and Ginsburg's measured reservations, the justices did try bolster the Court's image, denying that politics played a part, that tensions continued, and that they wanted to get involved. Of course, their remarks could be seen as self-serving, especially for the majority, which sought to rehabilitate its tarnished image.

Reporters Extract Drama from Bush v. Gore

Overall, reporters provided a fairly full account of judicial action in *Bush v. Gore,* noting what kind of act was involved, the means used to complete the act, the sort of agents who did it, and some of the purposes. These constructions, with a few exceptions, were fairly consistent. The act was unprecedented, historic, unexpected, controversial, and divided, perhaps the product of a failed compromise. While the conservative press stressed the 7-2 agreement on equal protection problems (with the *Economist* actually implying an 8-1 agreement by noting Ginsburg's remark that the recount was "flawed"), others noted that the areas of agreement were limited. While some reporters stressed the Court's active role in halting the recounts and preventing Gore from possibly becoming president, others shifted the blame to the Florida court, to the calendar, or to the voters themselves. While many reporters pointed to the closure provided by the opinion and the "nightmare" of a political resolution that the decision avoided, others stressed the awarding of the presidency to Bush.

Remarkably little analysis was made of the legal arguments themselves—how the Court reached its decision. Most stories simply relied upon statements by the majority and the dissenters to frame the discussion (with very little coverage of Rehnquist's concurring opinion).[157] For example, few went beyond the majority's claim that varying standards for recounts constituted an equal protection violation. Only exceptional analyses compared this holding to earlier Supreme Court decisions. Most reporters characterized the standards as variable, even haphazard, and used that finding to account for the Court's concerns. The safe harbor deadline received greater criticism, typically from scholars quoted by the reporters, and a few stories pointed out that the federal court was substituting its judgment of what Florida law was for the state court's judgment. No general reports considered the irony of the remedy in halting recounts to protect voters. A few reporters noted that the limitation of precedent seemed very ends-oriented.

These considerations of the legal bases for the decision, brief though they were, nonetheless provided enough information for reporters to indicate inconsistencies. These ideologically conservative justices—some of them "staunch conservatives"—acted uncharacteristically like liberals, finding equal protection problems, second-guessing a state court, and taking an active role in resolving a presidential election. Those inconsistent actions were explicable if this judicial action were given a political purpose of putting Bush in the White House, some stories implied or stated through the critics they quoted. Here, conservative sources stressed closure as the primary purpose, whereas liberal sources stressed giving the presidency to a Republican as the primary purpose. Stories of these conservatives wanting to retire or to gain promotion to the chief justiceship bolstered the political purpose.

In this focus on judicial action, scene emerged as the least important pentadic term. Aside from passing references to the High Court as an ultimate judicial scene, the larger historical context for this unprecedented decision, and the short window for this speedy decision, little was said about it. However, if the scene did not contain the act of decision, the act did create a scene. The scene emerged from the act (rather than the reverse), with ideological gulfs, hordes of Court critics (so many that the agents constituted a scene), and a Court exposed to charges of partisanship as the scenic consequences of the decision.

The most important grammatical ratios in these constructions of majority motives were either suggested implicitly or taken from the mouths of sources, invoking agent-act, agent-purpose, and purpose-agency relationships. Agent-act, the relationship between who the agents of the decision were and what they decided, worked through two related constructions. First, the inconsistency between who the agents were and what they did in the decision created a problem, for these conservatives were acting like liberals, actively intervening, thwarting a state court's interpretation of its own law, and finding equal protection problems (as they rarely had before). That inconsistency threw into relief another aspect of these agents: their conservative politics, which connected them to Bush. These conservative agents, some stories suggested, were acting on behalf of their political allegiances. This more consistent construction supported an agent-purpose relationship, whereby conservatives wanted to elect Bush, though reporters did not draw out this grammatical connection themselves. In stories portraying the conservative justices as seeking to retire or get promoted—something they appeared ready to do only if a Republican president were in office—their purpose of putting Bush in the White House was bolstered. Finally, the purpose-agency ratio explained the unusual ruling. If the majority wanted a Republican president, then that purpose led them to adopt any agency required to realize that end, from "liberal" judgments (on equal protection and states' rights) to weakly supported claims, such as the safe harbor deadline and the precedential limitation of their decision.

Such damning conclusions, insinuated by the news media's drama, suggested a government institution illicitly wielding its considerable power to determine who would hold the most powerful office in the world. These news reports held out the possibility that ending the election controversy might have been a blessing, though they did not resolve the question of whether these ends justified the means. Editorialists commenting on the decision would be much more direct in offering such assessments.

6

Editorialists Reconstruct *Bush v. Gore*

If reporters had to rely largely on the grammatical implications of their constructions and quotations from others to portray *Bush v. Gore* as a dramatic and controversial decision, editorialists were not so limited. They were much more explicit in their constructions of what was done, who did it, how they did it, and why. They did not merely leave grammatical implications to their readers but drew the connections explicitly to condemn or defend the majority justices.

While editorials argue and take sides, they typically do not rely heavily on elaborate considerations of the evidence. Newspapers and magazines rarely provide sufficient space for editorialists to support their contentions thoroughly. Footnotes or even explanatory references are extremely rare. Instead of relying on *logos* to carry the day, editorialists rely on their own *ethos* and simple characterizations of motives. Frequently, editorialists are experts in the area they are discussing or, alternatively, columnists whose reputations precede them (for better or worse).

The *Bush v. Gore* decision generated a barrage of editorials in large daily newspapers, mainstream newsmagazines, and magazines catering to those on the left and on the right of the political spectrum. Unsurprisingly,

left-leaning publications tended to criticize the decision, while right-lean-
ing publications tended to defend it. Overall, the criticisms overwhelmed
the defenses both in number and in zeal.

In reconstructing the motives of the *Bush* Court, critics and defenders
used notably different strategies. Defenders tended to focus on what the
Florida Supreme Court did, while critics focused more on what the U.S.
Supreme Court did. Defenders tended to focus on the purposes for the
Bush Court's actions, while critics focused on the means. Defenders tended
to cast doubt on the work of those conducting recounts, while critics defended them as proceeding apace to discover what the Florida voters really
intended.

Court Defenders and the Bush Majority

Defenders of the Court spent less time focused on what the Court did than
on what others had done, seeking to shift both the focus and the blame
from the majority's actions. What they did say about the Court's actions
suggested that those actions were forced; that is, the true motives were located in the actions of others, rather than in the High Court, which simply
responded to the actions of others. Thus, *USA Today* urged that "[t]he justices were forced into the case, and while they handled it poorly, their
choices were few."[1] Jim Wooten, columnist for the *Atlanta Journal and Constitution*, named the forcers, charging that the Florida Supreme Court
"forced the U.S. Supreme Court to waste its capital and credibility on a dispute that never should have been back there."[2] Debra J. Saunders of the
San Francisco Chronicle imagined this forcing in scenic terms, insisting that
the Florida Supreme Court "placed the U.S. Supremes in an impossible position."[3] Obviously, rhetorical work in constructing the Florida Supreme
Court's motives would contribute to this scene-act construction, whereby a
scene created by the state court led to an act by the U.S. Supreme Court.

Also useful in constructing the *Bush* majority's motives as having been
forced was an emphasis on their attitude as reluctant. Wooten claimed the
Court was "drawn . . . reluctantly and regrettably . . . into presidential election politics."[4] Harvard law professor Charles Fried, who served as counsel
for the Florida legislature in resisting Al Gore's efforts to challenge the election results, echoed Wooten's assessment of the majority's attitude, insisting, "I see the Court as having reluctantly done the job its commission
required of it."[5] Fried's construction notably adds that the court was required by its commission to reach this decision; that is, as agents with

particular responsibilities (Supreme Court justices), they had no choice but to reach this decision. Between the act of being forced and the attitude of reluctance, there emerges an image of a Court trying to do its duty under difficult circumstances.

Like the majority decision itself, the Court's defenders challenged reports that the decision was split 5-4, stressing instead the 7-2 division on the issue of equal protection. Nat Hentoff, writing for the conservative *Washington Times,* complained that "much of the media has downplayed or ignored the fact that the Supreme Court vote was 7-2 on the crucial constitutional issue."[6] Ronald Rotunda, a visiting fellow at the Cato Institute writing for the *Christian Science Monitor,* used the 7-2 construction to deny partisanship in the decision and to attack earlier commentators:

> When the US Supreme Court decided Bush v. Gore on Dec. 12, it did not divide along partisan lines, no matter what the pundits claimed the next morning. On the constitutional question, the court ruled 7 to 2 that Florida's recount violated the "equal protection" clause—that is, ballots were treated differently in different counties.[7]

The problematic act in this construction comes from a news media that misrepresented the decision's support, rather than from the Court's actions. Rotunda's scenic reference ("the next morning") provides an image of a quick, ill-considered characterization of the Court as split. He also equates the act of treating ballots differently in different counties with violating the equal protection clause (though there is a legal leap involved in that).

Randolph May of the Progress and Freedom Foundation in Washington, writing for the *Legal Times,* was a bit more careful in his characterization of the split for the legal audience he addressed, admitting that Justices Breyer and Souter were not in total agreement with the majority: "While both of these justices would have favored a remedy for violation of the constitutional norms other than halting further manual recounts, the fact that seven justices determined that the manual vote recounting was arbitrary and fundamentally unfair gives the Court's action legitimacy."[8] May plays here upon an agent-act relationship, whereby the number of judges in agreement (that is, who is reaching this conclusion) challenges the idea that the decision was partisan and makes the act more acceptable. This construction responds to the conservative-versus-liberal account of the decision suggested by news reports and editorials focused on the five justices who joined the majority and the four who dissented.

Additional work on characterizing the majority as agents of the decision expanded the scene within which their actions would be judged. Instead of focusing on their controversial act in *Bush v. Gore,* these editorialists framed the decision and its agents in terms of other decisions made by the conservative majority, suggesting that the conservative-liberal division supporting a charge of partisanship was baseless. Clinton prosecutor Kenneth Starr was most elaborate in this reframing strategy, urging in a *Wall Street Journal* editorial:

> for all the fireworks and breathless reporting surrounding Bush vs. Gore, the Supreme Court's work has been remarkably conventional and restrained. A sober look at the court's work as a whole yields up the conclusion—contrary to conventional wisdom—that the court's guiding principle, in all areas of the law, has been "don't rock the boat." With regard to issues such as abortion and school prayer, the Rehnquist Court has flatly declined to overturn controversial decisions from the Warren and Burger eras. Perhaps the best example of the don't-rock-the-boat principle came last year, in the Court's remarkable decision in Dickerson vs. United States, which reaffirmed the Warren Court's landmark ruling in Miranda vs. Arizona. Chief Justice William Rehnquist, a long-time Miranda critic, wrote a majority opinion that shows the court is fiercely determined, even at the expense of intellectual rigor and doctrinal consistency, to stay the course. Along the same lines, the justices have acquiesced in the Warren Court's extension of the "exclusionary rule" to state courts, thereby barring the inclusion of illegally obtained evidence despite the absence of any express constitutional provision to that effect—and notwithstanding Justice Benjamin Cardozo's withering criticism that this rule permits the guilty to go free just because "the constable blundered."[9]

Starr's construction of the conservative justices draws attention away from the controversy over *Bush v. Gore* and suggests that a broader view of their rulings shows that they are less conservative or partisan than some have claimed. This larger context of action shows purportedly conservative justices maintaining precedents set by more liberal courts, even when they disagree with them. The implications for our view of these agents and for this particularly troublesome election-ending act are clear: the agents are not so conservative, and their decision in *Bush* was not driven by partisanship or ideology. Grammatically, prior acts are used to redefine these agents (an acts-agents ratio); in turn, those redefined agents should determine our view of their election-ending act (an agents-act ratio).

Fried, whose editorial was a response to legal scholar Ronald Dworkin's own editorial, uses the same scene-enlarging strategy to deny charges of partisanship. In challenging Dworkin's emphasis on the conservative-versus-liberal divide in *Bush v. Gore,* he insists:

> in fact the divide is not at all neat. For instance, on the most bitterly contested issue dividing the Court for several decades now, the right to choose established in Roe v. Wade, two members of the majority are committed to a version of the same position Professor Dworkin espouses and the dissenters favor. Indeed, there are ideas and whole phrases in the O'Connor, Kennedy, Souter joint opinion in the Casey case that might have come straight out of Professor Dworkin's writings. The same might be said about Justice O'Connor's opinion in the "right to die" cases. Surely neither she nor Justice Kennedy can fairly be readily relegated to some caricatural conservative pigeonhole. And for that matter Justices Scalia and Thomas are a good bit more "liberal" (if one must use these degraded and inaccurate labels) than Justices O'Connor and Breyer on a number of issues, such as free speech.[10]

Starr and Fried's enlarged scenes import other acts to assure readers that the *Bush* majority is not simply a conservative junta seeking to keep liberals out of the White House. Indeed, they suggest, the picture is more complicated. And it is the news media and Dworkin who have misled the country on who these agents are and what their motives in *Bush* might have been.

With all the focus on other judicial acts and the acts of others, very little attention was given by the defenders of the Court to the means by which the majority reached its decision. That is unsurprising given the controversy surrounding the equal protection claim, the safe harbor deadline, the insistence on stopping all recounts following the remand, and the denial of the decision's precedential value. Fried grappled more directly than anyone else with one issue of agency, noting:

> Dworkin disagrees with the Court's judgment that the kind of recount ordered by the Florida Supreme Court was a denial of equal protection because it "puts no class of voters, in advance, at either an advantage or disadvantage." But the Supreme Court has made clear—as recently as last year in a unanimous opinion in a jejune case involving one family's sewer connection—that disparate treatment may violate the Constitution's guarantee of equal protection even if no identifiable class of persons is the target of the intentional disparity.[11]

This characterization suggests that the agency of finding an equal protection claim where no identifiable class is harmed is appropriate because an earlier act of the Supreme Court—a unanimous one, no less—had said so.

The claim had the scholarly support of a footnote to the sewer case. For casual readers of this editorial, such an invocation of a prior decision shifted the burden to those who would disprove it, given that no answer would be forthcoming in the present issue. Fried's construction of this appropriate agency of finding equal protection was weak insofar as it failed to cite other cases to demonstrate the trend he implies is illustrated by this recent example, the many cases that suggested a contrary holding (as critics would note), and his own stretching of the cited case's findings.[12]

Rotunda examined the charge that the Court had no jurisdiction to hear this case because no federal issue was involved. Instead of addressing the Supreme Court's own rationale for hearing the case, he also drew attention to a different act, insisting: "Anyone who saw the televised hearing with Florida Judge N. Sanders Sauls knew that he and the attorneys regularly talked about equal protection, just like the Supreme Court."[13] This is a commonsense appeal that refers to television viewers' judgments about trial court proceedings and assumes that "equal protection" *talk* at the trial level justifies federal appellate jurisdiction at the U.S. Supreme Court level. The agency of Supreme Court jurisdiction is drawn out of a scene within which such issues are found.

May, writing for the *Legal Times,* took on what was perhaps the most contentious charge of all in addressing the controversial safe harbor deadline invoked by the Court. Like Fried and Rotunda before him, he shifted the action to the Florida Supreme Court, insisting:

> Even the Florida Supreme Court did not discount the importance of this deadline. Lost in the shuffle of the U.S. Supreme Court's Dec. 12 decision was the Florida Supreme Court's Dec. 11 decision responding to the remand from the first U.S. Supreme Court decision. The Florida court adhered to the importance of Dec. 12 "as the date for final determination of any state's dispute concerning its electors in order for that determination to be given conclusive effect in Congress."[14]

May is indirect and cautious here. He does not focus on a Florida Supreme Court holding concerning the deadline (an act of the state court); rather, he discusses what the state court did not do. To bolster this reading, he quotes the Florida Court's recognition of December 12 as a dispute-avoiding deadline. The state court's failure to discount that deadline (conceived here not as a lack of action but as an act of omission) and its recognition that meeting this deadline was necessary to avoid disputes (whereby a recognition of a statute's purpose is taken as an embracing of that purpose over all other purposes) were used to imply that the Florida court embraced this deadline as mandatory and, consequently, the U.S. Supreme Court read that as a requirement of Florida law (relying, ironically, on the state supreme court it would second-guess).

If the Court's defenders said little about the means by which the Court reached its decision, and what they said was stated indirectly, they were more assured of the ends that were either sought or simply came as a consequence of the decision; and in their constructions, the ends apparently justified the unexamined means. For these commentators, the consequences of inaction on the Supreme Court's part was a constitutional crisis. Thus, Michael Uhlmann, a California professor of government writing for the *Pittsburgh Post-Gazette,* applauded the Supreme Court for "hav[ing] ended the scorched-earth legal maneuvering that threatened to convert this turmoil into a full-blown constitutional crisis."[15] Charles Krauthammer of *Time* magazine insisted that the chief justice in particular sought to avoid "a constitutional train-wreck."[16] A *Newsday* editorial painted a more vivid picture, noting that "the nation would have gone through another month of electoral agony only to have the same result. In that sense the court's action saved the nation considerable turmoil."[17] *USA Today* insisted that "[w]hatever one thinks of the court's decision, it brings an end to the most flawed and contentious election in more than a century."[18] These constructions do not pretend to get at the true purposes of the *Bush* majority. Instead, by extending a hypothetical scene into the future, the editorialists seek to provide a context from which that practical purpose could be drawn (a scene-purpose ratio).

The picture that emerges from these defenders' constructions of the majority's act in *Bush v. Gore* is rather threadbare. We learn that a large majority of the Court acted (or reacted) because it was forced to do so by the Florida court and the lack of equal treatment of ballots. This majority entered the election controversy reluctantly. The means it used in hearing and deciding the case followed the Florida Supreme Court, the state trial court, and its own earlier decision. And the decision avoided a constitutional crisis.

The picture is further fleshed out not by additional consideration of what the *Bush* majority was doing but by a consideration of what others were doing. The actions of others created a scene within which the Court was required to act. In this sense, the indirection involved in addressing others' actions in order to understand the majority's actions is part of an overall rhetorical strategy of showing that the scene controlled the majority's actions. This is a typical strategy for shifting the blame from an otherwise answerable agent. For example, David Ling shows that Senator Edward Kennedy used that scene-act strategy to shift blame away from himself and toward the physical context in the Chappaquiddick incident.[19] The acts of the Florida Supreme Court, the vote counters, the voters, the dissenters, and even Gore's attorneys are scrutinized to show how they contributed to a scene in which the majority was compelled to take action.

Court Defenders and the
Florida Supreme Court Majority

The greatest attention was given to the Florida Supreme Court's ruling. While defenders of the High Court insisted on the near unanimity of its 7-2 decision on the equal protection issue, they emphasized the 4-3 split in the Florida decision. May called the decision "fractured."[20] Uhlmann stressed the split in noting that "*four* Florida justices decided that [the election] rules somehow frustrated the electorate's will . . . and simply rewrote the rules governing election contests."[21]

While the Court defenders largely ignored how the *Bush* majority reached its decision, they focused extensively on the Florida Supreme Court's agency. A *Denver Rocky Mountain News* editorial noted "the seat-of-the-pants quality of the Florida high court's latest ruling." The same editorial stated that the Florida ruling "did not treat all votes equally" and that it ignored overvotes.[22] Saunders compared what the state court did with what it could have done, noting: "If the state court had wanted a statewide recount that didn't look like a fix, it would have outlined objective statewide standards."[23] Uhlmann charged the state court with "changing important rules after the fact."[24]

An elaboration of these troublesome means was necessary to support the defenders' characterization of even more troubling state court purposes. Here they did not focus simply on consequences, as they had in their brief consideration of the *Bush* majority's purpose. Rather, they considered specific goals. Saunders charged that "the Florida Supreme Court's activist ruling [was] clearly designed solely to move Al Gore into the Oval Office."[25] Here the agency (an activist ruling) was adapted to the purpose of winning a Democratic victory. Wooten stressed the state court split in urging that "four judges on the Florida Supreme Court reopened all the partisans' wounds and dangled the absurd proposition before them that, hey, maybe it would be possible to win this election in the courts."[26]

Saunders built upon her construction of a troubling agency in adding an attitude to these political purposes, insisting that the state court had a "hunger to hand Gore the election by any means necessary."[27]

The contrast between these editorialists' treatment of the *Bush* majority's agency and purpose (and the relationship between its means and ends) and those of the state court majority is noteworthy. They either did not discuss the High Court's agency, or, if they did, they did not connect it directly to the purpose of avoiding a crisis. On the other hand, in discussing state court actions, they elaborated both the troubling means used by the Florida four and the political ends they sought, connecting the two explicitly, as in Saunders's phrase connecting a purpose ("hand[ing] Gore the election") to an agency ("by any means necessary"). This draws attention away from what the *Bush* majority was doing, and toward what the state court majority was doing, setting the latter up as the scene-generating impetus to federal court action.

On the other hand, the defenders of the Court readily elaborated High Court motives in discussing the first U.S. Supreme Court decision in *Bush v. Palm Beach County Canvassing Board,* because this provided grounds for explaining the state court's transgressions and for characterizing its attitude in ordering a statewide recount as troubling. In that prior decision, the defenders stated, the High Court showed "traditional deference"[28] and used "a mere query . . . to keep from humiliating its Florida subordinate."[29] Nevertheless, said Krauthammer, this per curiam decision "sent a pointed message to the willful Florida justices."[30] But, urged Fried, the state court "refused to take the hint."[31] Instead, Uhlmann argued, they ignored this "spanking," and the "four Florida justices walked into the valley of death: They revised Florida's election code a second time in a manner even more egregious than the first."[32]

This construction of U.S. Supreme Court motives in *Bush I* shows the High Court as tolerant, as reluctant to intervene, and as considerate of the state court's authority. It also shows the Florida Supreme Court's attitude in "walk[ing] into the valley of death" as troubling. Fried the academic was the mildest, insisting that the "lower court appear[ed] to the Justices to be taking its direction in less than a wholehearted spirit."[33] Krauthammer called them "willful."[34] Uhlmann specifically rejected the need to conclude that the state court had "sinister partisan motives" and chose instead to describe it as "free-wheeling," "irresponsible," and "sloppy."[35] These latter characterizations fit with Wooten's adjective of "naïve" to describe the state court majority, though when connected with the partisan purposes he had given them, theirs was a naiveté respecting means, not ends.[36]

By characterizing the Florida majority's decision as an obstinate response to an earlier Supreme Court warning, the defenders of the *Bush* majority could suggest that the High Court was forced to intervene to stop an out-of-control four-person state court majority willing to use any means necessary to put Gore in the White House. That condemnation of the state court was supported by the defenders' extensive consideration of the troubling vote recounting acts that the state court's decision put into motion.

Court Defenders and the Vote Recount

Editorialists' reconstruction of the vote recount attempted to show that the Florida Supreme Court majority's order that the recount officials discern "the clear intent of the voter" on recounted ballots led to troublesome results in the recounting. These commentators focused almost exclusively on the agency of the recount—how it was being carried out—though that view of agency had implications for how one viewed the purposes of the recounters. Krauthammer said the ballot counting was done "by microscope and horoscope."[37] Saunders charged that Palm Beach County changed its standard three times.[38] Both Saunders and Rotunda rapped Broward County for using partisan means for partisan ends. Saunders charged that in "recognizing rogue indentations, Broward County found three times as many new votes and netted Gore 567 extra votes."[39] Rotunda insisted that in Broward, "[i]f some of the vote counters saw several clean punches for Democrats and no punch for Gore, not even an indentation, but they saw a 'scratch' near his name, they called it for Gore."[40]

Fried avoided charges against particular counties but pointed to the general problem of variability in ensuring a consistent judgment about what to count as votes, noting that the intent standard was "[a]pplied by many scores of variously trained, instructed, and supervised ballot counters to punched pieces of cardboard [making the intent standard] manifestly out of place, to say the least."[41] Hentoff, like Rotunda, used an appeal to television viewers' common sense to made a legal inference:

> During the repeated hand recounts that had already taken place, television viewers could plainly see there were different standards for deciding which votes were legal from county to county—and in some counting rooms, from table to table. Clearly, those recounts were not treating voters equally under the U.S. Constitution's guarantee of "equal protection under the laws."[42]

A couple of commentators used a description of the recounts to suggest that there was no time to finish them, as the U.S. Supreme Court had declared. The basic grammatical argument was that the scene could not contain the act, at least temporally. Hentoff insisted that "even if the deadline had been extended to Dec. 18, there would not have been time to promulgate those standards, implement them and provide appellate review by all the courts of the inevitable challenges to the results of that recount."[43]

Unlike most Court defenders, Fried admitted that the *Bush* majority's argument that a recount had to meet the safe harbor deadline was "the least convincing portion of the Court's opinion." But, he insisted, if all the legal arguments and recounting "miraculously" could have been accomplished by the next deadline, December 18, then "that fact itself would have occasioned a complaint to the Supreme Court that the Florida court had once again failed to comply with the preexisting standards of Florida law." Therefore, the scene could not contain the recount act even with some extension. Indeed, Fried goes so far as to claim that the closeness of the election ensured that more recounts would yield no more accuracy. Thus, recounting as a means would not support an end of finding out who really received the most votes.[44] Like the majority opinion, Fried's assessment constructs such vote recounts as theoretical only, and practically unattainable.

Court Defenders and Other Acts

In addition to shifting blame to the Florida Supreme Court and those conducting the recounts, some editorialists mentioned other possible scapegoats. Wooten and Uhlmann blamed the voters. Wooten characterized their acts as leading to the problem, because they "departed from clearly stated instructions" and caused the undervote problem.[45] Uhlmann agreed that voters may have failed to follow instructions but also noted that they may have chosen not to vote for a presidential candidate or that a machine may have been the cause of the error. In any case, Uhlmann insisted, the undervote "carries no moral significance."[46] To diminish the significance of the undervotes—either because the voters brought this problem down upon themselves or because such errors do not constitute a problem that must be acknowledged—serves to support indirectly the actions of the Supreme Court majority in rejecting the current recounts and keeping new recounts from beginning. The issue becomes not what the Supreme Court did in *Bush v. Gore* but what the voters did to invalidate their own votes. This is a problematic construction inasmuch as Uhlmann admits that machines may have caused errors. He does not explain this incongruity, except perhaps to imply that voter error combined with machine error made those votes less valid.

USA Today shifted blame to both the public and the government for their "inattention to the most vital process of democracy: voting."[47] Starr blamed Gore's lawyer, David Boies, who "made a critical concession at oral argument: namely, that the standards being followed by the Florida vote-counters varied wildly."[48] The first shift of blame implicated the whole election scene as a creation of agents who had failed to watch over some of the most important governmental functions. The second was much narrower, implicating the lawyer of the loser in creating a scene that would hurt his client and providing a "just deserts" narrative wherein the legal maneuverings of contestant lawyers left the Supreme Court with findings it could not ignore.

A couple of commentators focused on the four dissenters in the case, not simply to discredit their complaints but to turn the tables on Court critics. Fried offered a classic table-turning response to Dworkin:

> [Dworkin] relentlessly casts the disagreement as one between the five "conservative" and the four "liberal" Justices, with only the former moved by partisan motives. Even if the divide were as neat as he says, one wonders why exactly the same charge of partisanship could not be leveled against the four dissenters.[49]

Hentoff took on Justice Stevens particularly, showing an inconsistency between his present concerns and an earlier opinion, insisting that

> those charging that the United States Supreme Court should not have interfered in the state court's decisions were answered in a 1983 decision by Justice John Paul Stevens, who is now a bitter dissenter in Bush vs. Gore. Back then, in Anderson vs. Celebrezze, Mr. Stevens emphasized that since "the president and vice president are the only elected officials who represent all the voters in the nation, the state has a less important interest in regulating presidential elections than state or local elections because the outcomes of the former are largely determined by voters beyond the state's boundaries."[50]

At its worst, such a strategy functions as a *tu quoque*, saying, in effect, "You're guilty of that, too!" On a grammatical level, it identifies the acts of critics and defenders in terms of agency, suggesting that both are applying the same criteria (an agency) in assessing motives. Thus, to hate what I do is to hate what you do. Or, alternatively, to fail to apply the same basis for judgment to both camps is to be unfair, where the fairness of the act is determined by the means by which it is carried out.

Overall, the editorialists defending the Court characterized *Bush v. Gore* as a decision supported by a large majority of the Court but forced upon the reluctant justices by a partisan state supreme court, by partisan vote counters, by a limited time period (scene) that would not contain the recounts, by a state government and public inattentive to the mechanisms of democracy, by errant voters, and by Gore's ineffective legal counsel. Although little was said directly about the Supreme Court majority's action, the consequences of its actions were lauded for avoiding an inevitable constitutional crisis.

Court Critics and the Stay Decision

To say that editorialists criticizing the *Bush v. Gore* decision were bitter is an understatement. They charged that the decision was partisan, with no basis in law. They urged that the High Court was willing to use any means necessary to ensure that Bush became the next president of the United States, not simply for the sake of their own Republican Party but for personal reasons as well. Famed federal prosecutor Vincent Bugliosi, writing for *The Nation*, was the most vehement, calling the majority's actions "a judicial coup d'état" and accusing the conservative justices of committing "one of the biggest and most serious crimes this nation has ever seen—pure and simple, the theft of the presidency."[51]

Like some of the defenders of the Court, critics would expand the scene within which to judge the *Bush* majority's actions, though they generally would draw the lines around acts directly related to the postelection dispute. For example, many critics focused on the December 9 stay of the recount, through which they would read the final decision in *Bush* in assessing majority motives. Justice Scalia's concurrence in the stay claimed that stopping the recount was necessary because counting votes of questionable legality "threaten[s] irreparable harm to petitioner [Bush] by casting a cloud upon what he claims to be the legitimacy of his election."[52]

Bugliosi was the most thoroughgoing in his critique of this position:

> With the haste of a criminal, Justice Scalia, in trying to justify the Court's shutting down of the vote counting, wrote, unbelievably, that counting these votes would "threaten irreparable harm to petitioner (Bush) by casting a cloud upon what *he* claims to be the legitimacy of *his* election." [Emphasis added by Bugliosi.] In other words, although the election had not yet

been decided, the absolutely incredible Scalia was presupposing that Bush had won the election—indeed, had a right to win it—and any recount that showed Gore got more votes in Florida than Bush could "cloud" Bush's presidency.[53]

Several grammatical threads attempt to tie down the idea that Scalia's action was inappropriate: The act involved an attitude of presumption (i.e., that Bush had won), unwarranted in this scene where the election had not yet been decided. The quickness of Scalia's act (reflecting both a particular agency and a hurried attitude) is likened to the haste of a criminal. The agent himself is called absolutely incredible, a judgment grammatically supported by Bugliosi's characterizations of the act, scene, agency, and attitude.

If conclusions about Scalia's motives were not clear enough, Bugliosi provided additional mutually supporting links among agent, agency, act, and attitude, insisting: "Only a criminal on the run, rushed for time and acting in desperation, could possibly write the embarrassing words Scalia did, language showing that he knew he had no legal basis for what he was doing, but that getting something down in writing, even as intellectually flabby and fatuous as it was, was better than nothing at all."[54] Here is a story of an agent (a criminal) using means such agents use (rushing and acting in desperation) to reach an act for fear that not acting (failing to state any reasons) would be worse (his purpose).

Bugliosi's pentadic characterizations rely on one another in urging a negative assessment of Scalia's statement justifying the stay. Because these characterizations are incendiary, Bugliosi ran the risk of being dismissed as merely a liberal critic of the conservative majority. To bolster his assessment of the inadequacy of Scalia's justification, Bugliosi did what most good advocates do: he cited outside support. Grammatically, this strategy works by drawing on another's characterization of the same act. It also draws attention to the act of characterizing itself, recognizing that the agent undertaking the characterization may be thought to harbor motives, just as those he or she characterizes are said to harbor particular motives. At its most effective, this strategy draws on someone whose motives would seem to be at odds with the interpretation they give. In this case, Bugliosi relies on a conservative to analyze the conservative Scalia's motives, noting:

Terrance Sandalow, former dean of the University of Michigan Law School and a judicial conservative who opposed *Roe v. Wade* and supported the nomination to the Court of right-wing icon Robert Bork, said that "the balance of harms so unmistakably were on the side of Gore" that the granting of the stay was "incomprehensible," going on to call the stay "an unmistakably partisan decision without any foundation in law."

Here Sandalow is characterized as a conservative (an agent with particular attitudes). This agent characterization is bolstered by two conservative acts by him (opposing *Roe* and supporting Bork), whereby acts define who this agent is. And Sandalow, who presumably would support conservatives like Scalia, is quoted to support the idea that the stay was wrongheaded and partisan.[55]

Bugliosi also relied on a characterization of the stay by *New York Times* news analyst Linda Greenhouse. Greenhouse was more cautious than the irate Bugliosi, however, drawing attention to troublesome appearances instead of straightforwardly attributing improper motives to Justice Scalia. She noted:

> That [stay's] justification put the court in the position of seeming to protect Mr. Bush—who has endorsed Justices Scalia and Clarence Thomas, named to the court by his father, as his ideal justices—from whatever uncomfortable truth the uncounted ballots might reveal. The fact that the justices entered the stay at midafternoon Saturday, with the counting under way and most of it expected to conclude at 2 P.M. on Sunday, gave the court the appearance of racing to beat the clock before an unwelcome truth could come out.[56]

If Greenhouse was more guarded than Bugliosi, she made up for it through grammatical constructions that lent support to negative interpretations of Scalia's motives. She went beyond Bugliosi in connecting Scalia with Bush, noting that the latter extolled the former and that the justices had been appointed by his father. This act of endorsement and the agent connection to them through Bush's father suggest a common substance (and perhaps a common purpose). Greenhouse's careful, scenic description (midafternoon Saturday when counting was to conclude at 2:00 P.M. Sunday) supported her subsequent characterization of the means (racing) and the purpose (avoiding an unwelcome truth).

Andrew Stephen, writing for the *New Statesman,* focused on the hypothetical future act Scalia sought to avoid as a means to critique the justice, noting: "Put simply, the learned Scalia believed that the American masses simply could not be trusted to know election recounts—lest, presumably, instability results if and when they discover that the wrong man is to be in the White House."[57] Scalia's presumed distrust of the American masses is presented as an attitude we should disdain.

Attitude was the focus of many Court critics of the stay. For example, Eric Foner, writing for *The Nation*, claimed that "never has there been a public statement as partisan as Antonin Scalia's when first suspending the recounts that the Court needed to insure 'public acceptance' of a Bush presidency."[58] Paul Starr, Princeton sociologist and co-founder of the *American Prospect*, used attitude to challenge the purported purpose in stating that the ruling was "[h]ypocritically justified as avoiding 'irreparable harm' to Bush, [yet] the stay did irreparable harm to Gore—as became apparent when the Court issued its final decision and said there was no time for a remedy."[59]

Mike Godwin, a policy fellow at the Center for Democracy and Technology, used a *Reason* magazine article to attack Scalia's agency-purpose logic in using a stay to prevent counting that might cast a cloud over the legitimacy of Bush's election, noting: "If improperly conducted recounts risk generating such a cloud, a court-mandated halt of the recounts is not exactly clear-skied if legitimacy is your concern."[60]

Overall, critics of the stay characterized the act as unjustified, hasty, incomprehensible, and not founded on law; undertaken with a presumptuous and partisan attitude, by a conservative, criminal-like agent admired by (and perhaps allied with) Bush; through a hypocritical and hurried agency that was adapted to protecting Bush from harm (while ignoring the harm to Gore) by avoiding finding the truth about who really won the election (lest it unsettle American voters), in a scene where the presidential election had yet to be decided. Scalia's ideological leanings, his membership in the Republican Party, and the praise given him by Bush (as well as the appointment connection to the elder Bush) combined with the effect of the stay ruling to make him open to the charge of partisanship. But his failure to address explicitly the balance of harms issue—considering potential harms to Gore as well as to Bush—made this act and its means vulnerable to critics' negative constructions.

Court Critics and the Bush *Majority*

Most critics of the *Bush* decision focused on the majority decision itself, rather than the Florida court decision, the dissents, the vote counting, or other acts, drawing attention away from a potentially troubling scene drawn out by the state court's actions. Complaints voiced a range of concerns from disappointment to outrage. CBS News anchor Dan Rather, writing an editorial for the *Houston Chronicle*, was among the most moderate, claiming: "This was a decision with more than enough in it to disappoint everyone." Focusing on the decision itself and not its agents, and on reactions to the decision rather than what was actively done by the justices, moderated Rather's complaint. Part of Rather's concern over the decision was the lack of unanimity, as he noted:

> Historically, there have been times when, at least in hindsight, the high court has acted with a discernible political character. Seldom, though, has the court weighed in on matters so squarely in the political arena, and when it has—the Watergate tapes decision comes to mind—it has generally done so with unanimity.[61]

Rather's construction blends the scene and the act, whereby the metaphorical location of the issues in the political arena determined the character of the act. In such scenes, Rather suggested, unanimity has been the rule. In invoking history, Rather drew attention to the *Bush* Court's departure from the norm he invoked. Again, this is indirect criticism, but the grammatical point is made.

The *New Republic*'s unsigned editorial was more direct, urging that "morally and historically speaking, we have witnessed an outrage." It called the decision "Orwellian" and supported its concerns through a series of contrasts between what the majority said and what it did:

> The justices cite precedents affirming "the one man, one vote basis of our representative government," and then they proceed to nullify the votes of thousands of men and women. They castigate the contest provision of the Florida Supreme Court for failing to "sustain the confidence that all citizens must have in the outcome of elections," and then they proceed to shatter the confidence that all citizens must have in the outcome of elections. They protest that "none are more conscious of the vital limits on judicial authority than are the members of this Court," and then they proceed to extend judicial authority into the very heart of American politics—an extension so vast and so unprecedented that it can only be described as un-American.[62]

Grammatically, this contrast constructs an agency-act disjunction, whereby what they say (i.e., the means by which they reach their conclusion) and what they do (i.e., the actual act and its outcomes) are shown to be at odds. Such grammatical inconsistencies radiate out into other terms, implying that the agents are insincere or hypocritical, that means are poorly adapted to stated purposes, and that judicial attitudes may be improper.

Harvard law professor Randall Kennedy, writing for the *American Prospect*, focused especially on the decision's "unusual" mandate that the recounts not be restarted, insisting "[t]hat act of judicial fiat crystallizes, more than anything else, the outrageousness of Bush v. Gore."[63] Implied by "fiat" is the idea that the means for reaching this decision was arbitrary, yet Kennedy focuses on the act itself as outrageous, not simply how it was done but that it was done.

Stephen of the *New Statesman* also focused on the act itself, calling it

> a supreme fait accompli [because] it would be impossible to resume and complete the recount the Supreme Court itself had halted more than three days before, even though, at that stage, only a few hours had been required to complete the recount that might well have given the 43rd presidency to Al Gore.[64]

Stephen's juxtaposition of the Court's stay (where the Court itself halted the recounts) and its later decision that it would be impossible to resume recounts (which had previously been a few hours from completion) suggested that the Court's earlier act created a scene within which recounts would be impossible. His suggestion that the election might well have gone to Gore points up what was at stake in the Court's self-sustaining actions. Characterizing the act as a supreme fait accompli suggested the bootstrapping and far-reaching nature of the act.

If Stephen's "fait accompli" suggested an act tightly controlled by the Court, so did two separate editorials that noted a Catch-22 character in the decision. *USA Today* connected the stay decision to the final decision in saying that the latter "ruling of the court's five-justice majority—the same five who suspended the recount last week—read as if it came straight from the pages of Catch-22." The editorial explained this characterization: "The justices said a recount could be conducted if done under uniform standards, which the Florida courts had failed to provide. But they went on to say there's no time left under the Constitution to conduct that count, to the exasperation of four dissenting justices."[65] Like Stephen, *USA Today* connected the stay to the *Bush* decision as one continuous act, though here the emphasis is on a conflict between a recount agency and the scene. The Court required an agency (uniform standards) that could not be used in the scene (where there's no time left).

Also as in Stephen, the implication of the act's label (as a Catch-22) is used to play up the Court's role in creating the untenable scene (as the same five who suspended the recount the previous week). To further implicate the Court in the creation of this time-crunched scene, the newspaper also accused them of working at a "leisurely pace in handling its part of the case." This characterization is difficult to sustain in historical terms, under which the speed of the Court must be judged as incredibly swift. The *Boston Globe* endorsed this strained construction, bolstering it by accusing other agents of delaying when it insisted: "Much of the reason that time ran out, as Justice Ruth Bader Ginsburg said, can be laid to the court's own tortured shilly-shallying, and also to the delaying tactics of the Bush forces."[66]

The *Denver Post* also invoked the Catch-22 charge:

> [f]or Vice President Al Gore, the decision was little more than a bitter taunt. While apparently conceding [a] recount might have been held, the court issued its ruling two hours before the Dec. 12 "safe harbor" period expired. The unsigned opinion then went on to say that it was the immediacy of that very deadline that made the task of conducting a legal count impossible. The court, essentially, authored its own new edition of "Catch-22."[67]

The *Post* described the scene in more detail than *USA Today* (two hours before the December 12 safe harbor period expired), contextualizing the act so that the means for resolving the recount problem was shown to be an exercise in futility. Again, a scene-agency disjunction proved to be the problem, though as author of the Catch-22, the Court's role in creating this troublesome scene was highlighted.

Bugliosi drew on religious language to convey his condemnation of the decision, calling it an "egregious [sin] of the Court" worse than *Dred Scott* and *Plessy v. Ferguson*.[68] The *Atlanta Journal and Constitution* focused on the outcome of the case in calling it "a shotgun wedding," whereby Bush was married to the American polity.[69] Both constructions drew on acts offered as analogues. For Bugliosi, the decision was like a sin, but it also was similar to (though worse than) two other highly controversial decisions. The *Atlanta Journal*'s comparison to a shotgun wedding functions as a metaphor that highlights the forcing involved and the consequences of the Court's actions.

Overall, the act itself was held to be disappointing and outrageous, a two-step judicial fiat (starting with the stay) that was an egregious sin which created a Catch-22. The decision also functioned as a shotgun wedding, joining Bush to a reluctant polity. The primary basis for these complaints about the judicial act can be traced to how the decision was reached. Agency concerns, in turn, carried implications for reading judicial

purposes, agents, and attitudes. The scene functioned primarily as a backdrop for understanding what was at stake and how the decision could have
happened.

The means by which a decision are reached is critical to the maintenance of judicial ethos. In the popular imagination, the courts follow the
law, apply the law, and are constrained by the law. The law leads, and they
follow. The law determines the outcomes of cases. So it is unsurprising that
the negative assessments of the *Bush* Court's opinion drew largely on
damning constructions of how that decision was reached. Jeffrey Rosen of
the *New Republic* cut to the heart of the rhetorical problem for judges perceived as failing to follow the law:

> [B]y not even bothering to cloak their willfulness in legal arguments intelli-
> gible to people of good faith who do not share their views, these four vain
> men and one vain woman have not only cast a cloud over the presidency of
> George W. Bush. They have, far more importantly, made it impossible for
> citizens of the United States to sustain any kind of faith in the rule of law as
> something larger than the self-interested political preferences of William
> Rehnquist, Antonin Scalia, Clarence Thomas, Anthony Kennedy, and San-
> dra Day O'Connor.[70]

In the absence of a guiding agency (or at least intelligible legal arguments),
agent and purpose loom large in the assessment of judicial motives, as the
evasion of the constraints of following the law give way to willfulness and
self-interested political preferences.

Paul Starr also made agency primary in noting that "[n]othing about the
2000 election matters nearly as much as the ugly means by which it was
brought to an end." Those means were tainted by partisanship and were
inconsistent with the majority justices' judicial philosophy, Starr explained:

> No one would feel that sense of betrayal if the majority of the Court had
> acted consistently with its judicial philosophy. Suppose the facts had been
> reversed and Al Gore had been leading by a small margin in Florida when
> he appealed to the Supreme Court to stop a recount requested by Bush.
> Suppose he had also argued that differences among counties in standards
> for judging ballots represented a violation of constitutional guarantees of
> equal protection. Consistent with their past decisions, Justices Scalia,
> Thomas, Rehnquist, Kennedy, and O'Connor could have ruled that states'
> rights precluded federal jurisdiction. Likewise, they could have dismissed
> the equal-protection claim as lacking merit as well as precedent. Who seri-
> ously doubts that this is precisely what they would have done? Such a deci-
> sion would have helped Bush and hurt Gore, but because of its intellectual

consistency with the justices' previous opinions, no one would have had any basis for questioning the integrity of the Court.[71]

Here Starr works at the intersection of agent and agency, whereby an agent attribute, judicial philosophy, becomes the means by which to reach consistent decisions. Yet the majority justices, ruling inconsistently regarding their positions on states' rights and equal protection, laid aside this means for ensuring consistency and decided for Bush. An inconsistency between past means and present means, between the agents' judicial philosophy and their actions, and between how they would have treated Gore (in this hypothetical act) and how they treated Bush raises concerns about judicial integrity.

The *Atlanta Journal and Constitution* also cited agency problems, insisting that the decision was "deeply unsatisfying, less because of the conclusion than the tangled means by which it was reached." Unlike Starr, the *Journal* did not point to judicial philosophy but to a slavish adherence to calendars, complaining that the Court's decision "was based not on the issue of justice, or on the U.S. Constitution, or even on Florida law, but on the basis of the calendar."[72]

Rather's commentary also focused on agency, insisting that "with its confusing and sometimes contradictory decision in Bush v. Gore, the Rehnquist court damaged its own reputation and that of the court as an institution. Not by what it decided—but how."[73]

Most commentaries focusing on the means by which the decision was reached looked at particular legal bases for the decision invoked by the Court. The greatest attention was given to the majority's claim that Florida's recount violated the equal protection clause of the Fourteenth Amendment—the central constitutional problem addressed by the majority. Insofar as the *Bush* majority could claim that an equal protection violation was occurring—that is, that the Constitution prohibited the sort of recounts that the Florida Supreme Court ordered—then they could claim to be following the law. The editorialists attacking the decision sought to show that this was not a violation of equal protection, that the precedents did not support such a finding, and that the remedy was worse than the problem itself.

Before addressing the merits of the Court's findings, Bugliosi alone questioned the Court's recognition of Bush's standing to raise an equal protection argument, drawing on his own experience in claiming:

Now, in the equal protection cases I've seen, the aggrieved party, the one who is being harmed and discriminated against, almost invariably brings the action. But no Florida voter I'm aware of brought any action under the equal protection clause claiming he was disfranchised because of the different standards being employed. What happened here is that Bush leaped in and tried to profit from a hypothetical wrong inflicted on someone else.[74]

Bugliosi set up a norm, based on the cases he had seen, whereby those who are not treated equally are the parties with standing to bring a suit. Bush was not such an agent, raising questions about whether he could rightly bring a suit to oppose the wrong done to voters by variable recount standards. A purpose-agent relationship is necessary for standing. Insofar as the case turned on harm to voters arising from the use of unconstitutional differences in vote-counting standards, Bugliosi's construction challenges the purpose-agent relationship supportive of Bush's standing. However, he avoided claiming outright that there is no basis for standing (e.g., such as a third-party standing claim). That argument would be left to more scholarly assessments of the decision.

Underlying the muddled standing issue was an unstated assumption that Bush himself would be harmed by the recounts. This assumption was embodied in the arguments of editorialists supporting the *Bush* decision that the recounting teams were unfairly attempting to eke out more votes for Gore. Godwin took on this charge, questioning the implied relationship between the disparate counting standards and the harm to candidates. He insisted: "Whatever rule might be used (counting dimpled chads, say, or refusing to count them), the rule itself won't inherently favor one candidate over another and thus won't favor one candidate's voters over the others."[75] This misses the mark in terms of addressing the Court's explicit concern that a variable agency for recounts will harm voters (e.g., by giving voters in one county a better chance than those in another county that their undervote will be recounted). However, it goes to the heart of the agency-purpose relationship implied in the stay decision, that recounting was likely to cause irreparable harm to Bush's claim to the election (where purpose is drawn out of an agency favoring one over another).

In attacking the Court's equal protection claim, other commentators also turned to the recounting processes themselves. Neal Kumar Katyal, one of Gore's lawyers writing in the *Washington Post*, urged that "different counties use different procedures all the time. They use different ballots, have different registrars, different members of their canvassing boards and they open and close their polls at different times. But that does not make any of these actions unconstitutional."[76] Bugliosi expanded this voting scene tem- porally in asserting: "Varying methods to cast and count votes have been going on in every state of the union for the past two centuries, and the Supreme Court has been as silent as a church mouse on the matter, never even hinting that there might be a right under the equal protection clause that was being violated."[77] Katyal and Bugliosi used a scene-agency rela- tionship to suggest that the use of different standards for voting and count- ing votes is widespread, making the variability in Florida's recount standards ordinary. Bugliosi implicated the Supreme Court in implicitly en- dorsing (or at least not dismissing) such variances, making the Court's complaint in *Bush* surprising.

A couple of commentators in more narrowly targeted publications took on the specific majority claim that not counting overvotes amounted to treating voters differently. Godwin, writing for *Reason*, noted that "the dis- senters rightly pointed out that no one had presented evidence of an over- vote problem. In other words, the majority was so eager to find an equal protection violation that they assumed facts not in evidence."[78] Carlos Ball, writing for the *Gay & Lesbian Review*, insisted:

> there is a rational reason for treating overvotes differently from undervotes: in the former, the person has voted for more than one candidate, clearly vi- olating the rule to vote for one candidate only, rendering the vote void. In the latter, the voter may well have abided by the rules; the problem is that the machine may have failed to read the voter's intent.[79]

Both commentators used constructions of others' actions: Godwin of the dissenters, Ball of overvoters and undervoters. Godwin constructed major- ity attitudes as eager and partisan. Ball simply presented two different agency-act relationships—one for overvoters and one for undervoters—to show the greater culpability of the overvoters and to reject the majority's claim that their votes needed to be recounted in the interest of equal protection.

The Supreme Court had cited four precedents to try to show that it was following the law in finding an equal protection violation. Several com- mentators challenged this move. Most simply dismissed the notion that any precedent supported the decision. For example, Rosen insisted: "The reason the conservatives can find not a single precedent to support their equal protection theory is because the theory is made up for this case only."[80] The *Boston Globe* argued: "The notion that there needs to be a sin- gle standard for casting and counting votes runs counter to law and practice since Article II of the US Constitution first gave authority over elections to individual states in 1787."[81] Katyal also invoked long-standing traditions, urging: "The Supreme Court has never, in its 200-year history, decided that if ballots cannot be counted with absolute perfection, they cannot be counted at all."[82] These three editorials described a scene of action within which no precedents supporting the majority decision can be found; on the contrary, they urged, tradition and practice make up a scene within which such a precedent could not arise.

Bugliosi's lengthy editorial was one of the only popular sources that addressed the particular precedents invoked by the Court:

> In a feeble, desperate effort to support their decision, the Court cited four of its previous cases as legal precedent, but not one of them bears even the slightest resemblance to Bush v. Gore. In one (Gray v. Sanders), the state of Georgia had a system where the vote of each citizen counted for less and less as the population of his or her county increased. In another (Moore v. Ogilvie), the residents of smaller counties in Illinois were able to form a new party to elect candidates, something residents of larger counties could not do. Another (Reynolds v. Sims) was an apportionment case, and the fourth (Harper v. Virginia) involved the payment of a poll tax as a qualification for voting. If a first-year law student ever cited completely inapplicable authority like this, any thoughtful professor would encourage him not to waste two more years trying to become a lawyer. As Yale law professor Akhil Reed Amar noted, the five conservative Justices "failed to cite a single case that, on its facts, comes close to supporting its analysis and result."[83]

Although Bugliosi went so far as to list and describe each of the precedents cited by the per curiam opinion, his dismissal of them was accomplished through an editorial flourish rather than a reasoned analysis. He relied on a simple contrast between these four precedents (which are individual judicial acts) and the *Bush* case, which did not clearly line up factually (as precedents often do not). He did bolster this dismissal with a reference to learned authority, implying that Amar, too, would dismiss the Court's citations just as a first-year law student citing them would be dismissed.

Bugliosi also suggested that the *Bush* court was not even following its own lead in *Bush v. Palm Beach County Canvassing Board*, decided a week earlier:

> The proof that the Court itself knew its equal protection argument had no merit whatsoever is that when Bush first asked the Court, on November 22, to consider three objections of his to the earlier, more limited Florida recount then taking place, the Court only denied review on his third

objection—yeah, you guessed it, that the lack of a uniform standard to determine the voter's intent violated the equal protection clause of the Fourteenth Amendment. Since the Court, on November 22, felt that this objection was so devoid of merit that it was unworthy of even being considered by it, what did these learned Justices subsequently learn about the equal protection clause they apparently did not know in November that caused them just three weeks later, on December 12, to embrace and endorse it so enthusiastically? The election was finally on the line on December 12 and they knew they had to come up with something, anything, to save the day for their man.[84]

Bugliosi took the Court's earlier rejection of the equal protection argument to reflect its opinion of the quality of that means for deciding the case. He elaborated a changed scene and partisan purposes to account for the change of heart that made this holding central to the final decision. He ignored the rationale, mentioned in the previous chapter, that the equal protection issue was not ripe because it was under review by a lower court.

Even if the Court's critics could show that the equal protection argument was novel, they still did not have a smoking gun for labeling this a partisan decision. To further their case, the editorialists needed to show that this agency not only lacked a connection to the past (an agency drawn from past precedents) but also lacked a connection to the present and to the future. While connecting to the past by following the law involves an agency-act relationship (whereby applying a precedent determines the judicial act), connecting to the present and the future involves a purpose-agency relationship (whereby judicial means are adapted to judicial ends, such as justice in the individual case or in future cases).

The overarching end sought in *Bush v. Gore*, according to the majority opinion, was fairness in the treatment of voters' ballots, which was required to avoid the constitutional problems. In a narrow sense, the means the Court used to meet this end were to order that a uniform standard for recounting ballots be applied. In a larger sense, as critics would complain, the Court's means involved stopping the recounts altogether and ensuring that those differentially treated ballots would never be counted at all. Effectively, they argued, the means were not adapted to the Court's stated ends. Thus, Katyal complained that "[i]n the ironic name of equality, the Rehnquist court deprived thousands of Florida voters of their right to be heard."[85] Godwin paraphrased the Court's troublesome ends-means reasoning: "We had to refuse to count your (possibly incorrectly rejected) votes in order to vindicate your right to have your votes counted fairly."[86]

Because even the per curiam recognized the significantly higher rejection rate for punchcard voting systems when compared with optical-scan voting systems, critics charged that the Court's means for resolving the case actually led to greater inequality of treatment than the inequality it sought to rectify. For example, Rosen claimed that "[b]y preventing states from correcting the counting errors that result from different voting technologies, the conservatives have precipitated a violation of equal treatment far larger than the one they claim to avoid."[87] On the same grounds, Godwin insisted that "[t]he Supreme Court's order blocking manual recounts ensured that votes in one county are more likely to count than votes in another county."[88]

The *Boston Globe* applied that ends-means logic to the future and found it wanting: "That finding [of an equal protection problem] throws into question the electoral systems in virtually every state, all of which have their own customized methods of voting, whether by machine, punch card, hand-written mark, or absentee ballot."[89] Many more critics would complain about the Court's limitation of this precedent, which ameliorated the *Globe*'s concern while raising more serious concerns.

The second most criticized means used in the Court decision was the invocation of the safe harbor provision to prevent the recounts from restarting. Starr insisted that December 12 "was only a deadline for states to secure guaranteed acceptance of their certified electors by Congress; the electors were not actually going to vote for another week, and Congress has in the past accepted later changes in electoral votes."[90] Noting the majority's reliance on the Florida Supreme Court's reference to the safe harbor deadline, Rosen insisted:

> O'Connor and Kennedy [presumed authors of the per curiam] had converted the Florida court's passing reference to the federal law telling Congress which electoral slate to count in the event that a controversy was resolved before December 12 into a barrier, now mysteriously embedded in state law, that prevented the Florida Supreme Court from completing manual recounts after December 12.[91]

Gail Schoettler of *The Denver Post* complained that "[d]espite the unequivocal language of Florida law, the U.S. Supreme Court decided a 'safe harbor' date was more important than the right to have your vote counted."[92] Bugliosi drew on legal authorities to make this case:

> Writing in the Wall Street Journal, University of Utah law professor Michael McConnell, a legal conservative, pointed out that the December 12

"deadline" is only a deadline "for receiving 'safe harbor' protection for the state's electors" (i.e., if a state certifies its electors by that date, Congress can't question them), not a federal deadline that must be met. New York University law professor Larry Kramer observed that if a state does not make that deadline, "nothing happens. The counting could continue."[93]

Many commentators added that the Supreme Court itself contributed to the failure to meet deadlines. For example, Rosen suggested that "for the Court to announce this rule at ten o'clock at night on December 12, after having stopped the count two precious days earlier, only added to the gallows humor."[94] Schoettler agreed that "[t]his lack of time . . . was a result of the Supreme Court's stopping the recount in the first place."[95]

Finally, a number of commentators criticized the majority's limitation of the *Bush* precedent "to present circumstances." Bugliosi, noting the Court's justification that "the problem of equal protection in election processes generally presents many complexities," insisted: "That's pure, unadulterated moonshine. The ruling sets forth a very simple, noncomplex proposition—that if there are varying standards to count votes, this violates the equal protection clause of the Fourteenth Amendment." After rejecting that purpose for this means of ending the election, Bugliosi offered another:

> the Court knew that its ruling (that differing standards for counting votes violate the equal protection clause) could not possibly be a constitutional principle cited in the future by themselves, other courts or litigants. Since different methods of counting votes exist throughout the fifty states (e.g., Texas counts dimpled chads, California does not), forty-four out of the fifty states do not have uniform voting methods, and voting equipment and mechanisms in all states necessarily vary in design, upkeep and performance, to apply the equal protection ruling of Bush v. Gore would necessarily invalidate virtually all elections throughout the country.[96]

The equal protection ruling was found troublesome by the *Boston Globe* because of such far-reaching implications; here, Bugliosi used those implications to explain why the Court really limited the decision to the *Bush* case alone. Reading the equal protection holding together with the "limited to present circumstances" restriction suggested insincerity on the Court's part. This means of resolving the *Bush* case could not become a means for resolving other cases, because that was far-reaching and impractical. Thus, Bugliosi suggested, a means for limiting its reach had to be used. Yet Bugliosi had shown that such a limitation did not follow from the complexity of the case, as the majority had said, but only from the breadth of its potential application to a scene rife with such equal protection problems.

Godwin used a paraphrase to attack the limitation: "In other words, the majority seems to be saying, we believe Florida's election code issues add up to an equal protection problem only insofar as they raise the possibility that George Bush might not win Florida. But don't expect us to be bound by this decision in future cases."[97]

In summary, how the conservative majority reached its controversial decision was construed as more significant than what it did, though those agencies of majority action would be used to reach conclusions about the Court's purposes, the character of the judges, and the attitudes of the judges, ultimately redounding upon the interpretation of this judicial act as outrageous. A larger scene was investigated to shed light on the majority's agencies of decision, notably its members' prior positions on equal protection and states' rights, their use of four voting rights precedents, their rejection of equal protection in *Bush I*, and their application of this new equal protection standard in a scene within which states regularly use various methods for voting and vote counting. The means adapted by the Court to ensure fairness were justifiably criticized—allowing *no* recounts to ensure *fair* recounts. The safe harbor means for ending the recounts was rejected as a misunderstanding of the purpose of that federal statute and of the Florida Court's interpretation of it in light of Florida state law. The lack of precedential value accorded this new decision by the majority also was scrutinized for overstating the difficulty of its future application and for reining in what was certain to be a far-reaching new equal protection standard.

In turning from the means to the ends of the decision, critics took two general approaches. Some focused on the real purposes behind the majority decision, suggesting they were partisan. Others looked at consequences, which might be intended or unintended outcomes. Typically, editorialists relied on constructions of the means to reach conclusions about purposes.

Bugliosi, ever reliant on outside sources to bolster his constructions, quoted a December 25, 2000, article from *Time* magazine that found "[a] sizable number of critics, from law professors to some of the Court's own members, have attacked the ruling as . . . politically motivated."[98] Citing a disjunction between the Court's means and purported ends, Bugliosi insisted:

[I]f the Court's five-member majority was concerned not about Bush but the voters themselves, as they fervently claimed to be, then under what conceivable theory would they, in effect, tell these voters, "We're so concerned that some of you undervoters may lose your vote under the different Florida county standards that we're going to solve the problem by making sure that none of you undervoters have your votes counted"? Isn't this exactly what the Court did?[99]

The *Boston Globe* also noted this disjunction: "the court's goal should have been a fair election, counting as many legal votes as possible. To apply so much distorted thinking and convoluted law only to deny this simple desire is perverse."[100] Randall Kennedy, a Harvard law professor writing in the *American Prospect,* connected these means to the Court's true ends to explain the connection. The means, he averred, were a "hypocritical mishmash of ideas that even some of [the majority's] ideological allies—for instance, Einer Elhauge, a Harvard Law School professor who represented the Republican-dominated Florida legislature—have criticized as being poorly written and thinly reasoned." The ends wrought by these hypocritical means reflected a commitment to "clearing away any last-minute impediments to the ascendancy of George W. Bush." [101]

Novelist, historian, and playwright Gore Vidal also found partisan purposes at work, charging that "[the] Bush campaign [was] loyally aided and abetted by a 5-to-4 majority of the Supreme Court" in keeping the ballots . of minority voters from being counted.[102] Harold Meyerson, in the *American Spectator,* relied on the dissenting opinions in leveling his charges of partisanship, insisting that "[t]aken together, the four dissenting opinions from these politically moderate jurists make unmistakably clear their belief that the five justices in the majority twisted, flouted, and mocked the law to make George W. Bush president."[103] The *New Republic* flatly asserted: "This ruling was designed to bring about a political outcome, and it is an insult to the intelligence of the American people to suggest otherwise."[104] In the face of Justice Thomas's denial that politics was involved in the decision, Kennedy charged "that assertion rings ridiculously hollow."[105] Bugliosi was more acerbic, claiming of the conservative majority that "at least we know they can lie as well as they can steal."[106]

Many commentators looked to consequences, rather than to political purposes, for grounds to criticize the Court. Consequences stand uneasily between purpose and scene. They function as purpose insofar as we interpret these outcomes as something that was sought by the agents. However, there are unintended consequences, which we normally do not label purposes for action. When not assigned under the heading of purpose, these outcomes become part of a scene created by the actions in question. As part of the scene, they do not function as a container of action, shaping what the agents do, because they come later in time. That makes them an effect rather than a cause of action. An act may create a scene, in a reversal of the normal terministic relationship. Thus, whether the Supreme Court majority intended it or not, commentators charged it with injuring voters (especially African-American voters), the U.S. Supreme Court, and even Bush.

Katyal charged that the majority "deprived thousands of Florida voters of their right to be heard."[107] Even if they did not intend it, Bugliosi alleged that the conservative five "*knowingly transform[ed]* the votes of 50 million Americans into nothing and [threw] out all of the Florida undervotes."[108] *Boston Globe* columnist Adrian Walker noted that African-Americans, who voted 9 to 1 for Gore in Florida, were most disserved by the decision: "For those voters, many of them only a generation or two removed from systematic violation of their voting rights, this decision, and the election it decides, comes as sorry news. Faith is fragile, and too many people have been given too much reason to lose faith."[109] The *Denver Post* noted that voters were divided and asserted that the *Bush* decision "will exacerbate, rather than ease, our national division."[110]

Many commentators worried, as Justice Stevens had, about the damage to the judiciary, particularly the Supreme Court. Rather stated: "the Rehnquist court damaged its own reputation and that of the court as an institution."[111] Schoettler claimed that the "treasure" of positive public opinion toward the Court was "badly tarnished."[112] Katyal worried about specific implications of this loss of credibility:

> The price of George W. Bush's victory has been the immolation of America's last great standing institution: the Supreme Court. By elevating politics over principle, the court revealed itself to be no better than any other institution or actor that touched this election. Its decision will prompt an attack on the court from Congress, lower court judges and scholars. And the court has only itself to blame.

He added to these concerns claims that lower courts might begin ignoring Supreme Court decisions and that lawsuits over election disputes could flood the High Court.[113]

The *Denver Post* thought that "the court itself may be the biggest loser."[114] The *Boston Globe* agreed:

The greatest casualty of the court's midnight decision may be the public's belief in the judiciary's ability to be an impartial judge of the law. Before this year most Americans believed, naively perhaps, that the US Supreme Court was the best in the world, transcending partisanship to dwell pristine in the law.

Today, it has left the presidency compromised and its own reputation sullied.[115]

This final concern, about compromising the presidency, was echoed by others. The *Denver Post* claimed: "The court . . . did Texas Gov. George W. Bush no favors. He has been handed a hollow victory, based more on the ill-concealed partisanship of the justices than on the merits of the law and facts. For Bush to pull a successful presidency out of the court's cynical ruling will take a miracle."[116] The *Boston Globe* indicated similar concerns in its lead sentence, calling the *Bush* ruling a "murky decision that will not give George W. Bush the firm endorsement he needs to govern."[117]

Overall, Court critics found the *Bush* Court's actions to be partisan, motivated by a desire to install Bush in the White House, and detrimental to voters, the Court itself, and even Bush. The agencies these critics found so troubling in ensuring fairness to voters were found explicable when the purpose of electing a Republican was joined with these means. Such purposes were easily attributed to agents these critics found partisan and self-interested.

Characterizations of the conservative majority and the justices themselves sought to find a motive within them, collectively and individually, as agents. Grouping them as a conservative "Gang of Five," commentators sought to explain the outcome by looking at how they worked as collective agents. Thus, the *New Republic* noted the 5-4 split, emphasizing that "this was a 5-4 decision, not a 7-2 decision, as some Republican spinners would have us believe, on the utterly false assumption that every justice who acknowledged the chaos in the standards of counting concurred in shutting the counting down."[118] The *San Francisco Chronicle* also noted this split, particularly on the recount issue, which it found to be "falling so cleanly on ideological lines."[119] Others characterized the majority as "intensely partisan," "five right-wing justices," "Republican larcenists," and "criminals."[120]

Kennedy invoked a sports metaphor, calling the five conservatives "downfield blockers" who cleared the way for a Bush presidency.[121] Columnist Ellen Goodman also drew a sports metaphor from the mouth of one of her sources, Harvard law professor Martha Minow, whom she quoted as saying: "Somebody has to be umpire. If the umpire is a parent on one team, you can't play anymore. The game's over."[122] The *New Republic* also emphasized the Court's partisanship, asking: "Are the justices, then, hypocrites? Alas, they are not. They are—sub silentio, as they might say—Republicans."[123]

One of the biggest charges against the conservatives was that they were inconsistent. Schoettler noted the majority's about-face on states' rights in intervening in a state court's interpretation of state law, complaining: "This same majority has staunchly defended states' rights."[124] Foner also noted this inconsistency, citing "the majority's disdain for the principle of federalism these very Justices have trumpeted for the past several years."[125] University of Texas law professor Sanford Levinson endorsed this concern:

> How can one take seriously the majority's claims that their award of the presidency to Bush is based on their deep concern for safeguarding the fundamental values of equality? This majority has been infamous in recent years for relentlessly defending states' rights against the invocation of national legal or constitutional norms.[126]

Meyerson also complained about "arguments that contradict everything the justices normally stand for but that had to be made in order to stop the count. The Rehnquist-Scalia gang, for instance, has penned a succession of controversial five-to-four decisions over the past half-decade asserting the rights of states over the federal government."[127]

Kennedy extended the charge of inconsistency to the equal protection issue: "Chief Justice William Rehnquist and Company are typically unmoved by alleged Equal Protection Clause violations (except when the plaintiffs are whites charging so-called reverse discrimination)."[128] Foner seconded this accusation: "The current Court's concept of equal protection has essentially boiled down to supporting white plaintiffs who claim to be disadvantaged by affirmative action."[129]

The charge of inconsistency is centered in the agents because they are the vessels of tendency who, in this case, are running against their tendencies. Judicial agents with a history are found to stand for something. They have beliefs and values about the law, and perhaps even a judicial philosophy. Here, these agents with particular tendencies run against those tendencies and raise charges that they are acting inconsistently in this special case for particular, partisan purposes. Of course, agents can change, and their views can evolve, but when they do so at propitious times, their motives may rightly be scrutinized, as they were by these critics.

Beyond these partisan interest charges, Starr also accused the majority of acting in its own self-interest:

> Everyone knew during the past year that the election was in substantial measure about the future of the Supreme Court. Delicately balanced between conservative and moderate factions, the Court would likely be tipped one way by Gore's nominees, the other way by Bush's. The most straightforward explanation for the decision in Bush v. Gore is that the five justices in the majority acted in their own long-term self-interest, ensuring that their side will continue to dominate the Court.[130]

Levinson endorsed this view by noting specifically that "at least two of [the conservative five] are eager to retire and be replaced by Republicans nominated by a Republican President."[131] That charge was easiest to sustain against Justice O'Connor, whose husband was reported by the *Wall Street Journal* and *Newsweek* magazine to have said that the breast-cancer survivor wished to retire only if a Republican could replace her.[132]

Even more troubling than general charges of self-interested actions were charges of personal conflicts of interest. Vidal was the most vivid in describing the conflicted agents:

> Justice Antonin Scalia—both name and visage reminiscent of a Puccini villain—affirmed family values by not recusing himself from the Bush-Gore case even though his son works for the same law firm that represented Bush before the Court. Meanwhile, Justice Clarence Thomas's wife works for a far-right think tank, the Heritage Foundation, and even as her husband attended gravely to arguments, she was vetting candidates for office in the Bush Administration.[133]

Vidal did not get into the requirements for recusal but used family relationships to indicate that these agents had more at stake than the political shape of the Court.

Overall, these descriptions of partisan and self-interested agents suggested different purposes at work from simply deciding this case fairly. Indeed, agent descriptions (e.g., right-wing) carry implications for attitudes (e.g., partisan) and purposes (e.g., to help one's family; to shape the court). A final characterization of who was doing the act involved a criticism of the per curiam form of the decision. Rosen charged that that anonymous form was used because the opinion writers "were afraid to sign their names."[134] This fear of being held responsible for a partisan act completed a picture the Court critics sought to paint. It suggested that the justices knew what they were doing was wrong but did it anyway, hiding behind the unusual per curiam screen to avoid personal responsibility for twisting the law in order to hand Bush the presidency.

Scene was not a significant focus for critics. The *Atlanta Journal and Constitution* used scene to remind readers of the cache of uncounted votes:

> somewhere in Florida, in courthouses and warehouses and election offices scattered across the state, 45,000 ballots that were legally cast by U.S. citizens who expected their voices to be heard still sit uncounted this morning. Those ballots could have—and should have—brought this election to a far more conclusive ending.[135]

This morning-after scene speaks for silenced voices and lost opportunities. It is a scene created by the conservative majority's act.

Walker used a scenic description to support a negative characterization of the conservative majority's motives, noting in a headline: "The US Supreme Court Decision That Ended the 2000 Presidential Election Was Issued under Cover of Darkness, After the Justices Had Slipped Out the Back Door."[136] Because darkness and slipping out the back door are associated with secretive processes and evildoing, this scenic description supports the characterization of Court actions as questionable. Walker did not simply invoke the darkness; the decision was issued under cover of darkness, as if there were something to hide.

Vidal's cynical view of American history painted a scene within which the conservative majority's actions were consistent with ongoing attempts to keep democracy at bay:

> American politics is essentially a family affair, as are most oligarchies. When the father of the Constitution, James Madison, was asked how on earth any business could get done in Congress when the country contained a hundred million people whose representatives would number half a thousand, Madison took the line that oligarchy's iron law always obtains. A few people invariably run the show; and keep it, if they can, in the family.
>
> Finally, those founders, to whom we like to advert, had such a fear and loathing of democracy that they invented the Electoral College so that the popular voice of the people could be throttled, much as the Supreme Court throttled the Floridians on December 12. We were to be neither a democracy, subject to majoritarian tyranny, nor a dictatorship, subject to Caesarean folly. John Adams said we were to be a nation of laws, not men, which has since boiled down to a nation of lawyers, not people—or, at least, of people who count or get counted in elections.[137]

Vidal's characterization of this so-called American democracy makes *Bush* consistent with its historical container, while critiquing such antidemocratic tendencies.

Constructions of the *Bush* majority decision by editorialists criticizing the Court showed the act as disappointing and outrageous primarily because of the means used to reach the decision. These means were troublesome, critics said, for several reasons: the justices failed to follow their earlier decisions and their judicial philosophies (especially concerning states' rights and equal protection), the precedents they relied on were unsupportive, the justices previously had rejected the equal protection argument (in *Bush I*), the safe harbor provision was not applicable, and they had no legal basis for limiting the precedential value of the decision. The critics found that ending all recounts was a poor means of ensuring fairness, though it was a good means for supporting the political purpose of putting Bush in the White House, which was the conservative majority's goal. The majority justices were the type of agents likely to have this as a goal, the critics claimed: they were right-wing partisans who wanted the Court to remain in Republican hands. Additionally, some of them had personal interests in the outcome of the case. Yet, fearing for their reputations in signing off on this controversial decision, Justices O'Connor and Kennedy hid behind the cloak of a per curiam ruling and did their work under the cloak of darkness. They left thousands of valid votes uncounted and did a disservice to the voters, the Supreme Court as an institution, and Bush as future president.

Court Critics and the
Florida Supreme Court Decision

If defenders of the Court largely ignored its actions in *Bush v. Gore* and focused their attention on the actions of the Florida Supreme Court, critics of the Court did the opposite. The lengthy diatribes against the conservative majority's transgressions were not matched by a well-developed defense of the Florida court's actions. Like their counterparts, they drew attention to actions they would question, rather than actions they would defend. Walker, for example, admitted that the reasoning of the Florida Supreme Court was "tortured" but argued that "they surely were correct in holding that the right to cast a vote and have that vote count overrode every other electoral consideration."[138] That is, the ends were correct even if the means were problematic.

Stephen indirectly defended the Florida Supreme Court by criticizing Republican critics of Florida judges more generally:

> James Baker, Boy George's 70-year-old frontman, never hesitated to impugn the integrity of the Florida courts when decisions went against Boy George: one judge hearing a case brought by a Democrat privately (seeking to throw out votes because of Republican ballot fiddling) was publicly lambasted before she heard the case, on the grounds that she was a black woman who had been passed over for promotion by Bush's kid brother, Governor Jeb. She could not possibly rule fairly, Republicans wailed—before she threw out the case and was then promptly upheld by those equally suspect Florida Supreme Court judges.[139]

Stephen's defense never even gets to the Florida court's decision in the overruled *Gore v. Harris*. Rather, he seeks to show that Republican critics of the state court are prejudiced against Democratic judges, and unreasonably so.

Godwin was one of the only editorialists criticizing *Bush v. Gore* to focus on what the Florida court did. He began, much as defenders of the U.S. Supreme Court had, by urging that the Florida court was forced by others to deal with some sticky issues. First, he noted, "the Florida legislature had presented the courts with a crazy quilt of ambiguous and/or self-contradictory election laws." These laws required judicial interpretation. Second, the trial court, whose ruling was overturned by the Florida Supreme Court, put the state court in an awkward position:

> [T]he Florida Supreme Court was faced with a decision in which a trial court judge (in the word of the majority opinion) "did not make any findings as to the factual allegations made in the complaint and did not reference any of the testimony adduced in the two-day evidentiary hearing, other than to summarily state that the plaintiffs failed to meet their burden of proof." Apart from seeming to dispense with his role as fact-finder, Judge N. Sanders Sauls also seemed to conflate the "protest" and "contest" phases of disputing an election in Florida (and the differing burdens of proof required in each phase). When a trial court judge reaches factual and legal conclusions in a summary, arbitrary, or legally questionable way, he creates the kind of issues that state appellate courts were created to sort out.

Thus, like the *Bush* majority (as constructed by Court defenders), the state court was obligated to render a "corrective" judgment.[140]

To challenge the charge of partisanship, Godwin noted that "[o]f the five arguments made by Gore's team, the Florida Supreme Court's four-justice majority accepted only three." Considering a hypothetical act, he noted that "[i]f the Florida Supremes were really the judicial-activist, partisan-Democrat meddlers its GOP critics say they were, they would have come up with some chad-centric standard as to how to interpret ballots that vote-counting machines rejected."[141] Thus, through their actions and their nonactions, the state court showed itself to be nonpartisan (through an act-agent relationship).

Godwin also challenged the claim that "[t]he Florida Supreme Court usurped the prerogative of the Florida legislature to decide how its state's electors are chosen, in violation of both state and federal law." Interpreting the act they were to follow (where following makes this the agency of action), Godwin claimed the state court "was doing just what it was supposed to do, consistent with Article II of the U.S. Constitution, with the federal elector-selection statute, and with state election law." To support that interpretation, he noted:

> Title 3, Sec. 5, of the U.S. Code, for example, contemplates that disputes arising from state elector-election contests may be decided by a state's judiciary, provided that the law under which that contest is decided was in place before Election Day. As it happens, Section 102.168 of the Florida Statutes— in place before Nov. 7—allows for Florida elections, other than those for the state's house and senate, to be contested in Florida courts. The same Florida election statute authorizes a judge to "fashion such orders as he . . . deems necessary to ensure that each allegation in the complaint is investigated, examined, or checked, to prevent or correct any alleged wrong, and to provide any relief appropriate under the circumstances."[142]

Godwin also looked at how the state court did its job, and its attitude:

> When you read the Florida Supreme Court's majority opinion, you see an immense effort to adhere to what the court believes the Florida legislature has defined its role in election-law questions to be. "This essential principle, that the outcome of elections be determined by the will of the voters, forms the foundation of the election code enacted by the Florida Legislature and has been consistently applied by this Court in resolving elections disputes," the Florida majority writes. Both the majority decision and the dissenters' opinions in Gore v. Harris, even though they reach differing conclusions, are reasoning in ways consistent with standard jurisprudential principles. As important, they are laboring to adhere both to their own judiciary's general body of precedent and to the specific legal and factual constraints of the case before them.[143]

The Florida majority's immense effort, its attempt to follow standard jurisprudential principles, and its laboring with the law and facts are evidence of its fairness in this case.

The critics' brief treatment of the Florida majority's actions suggested that
it was forced by the poor work of the legislature and the trial court judge to
take action. It suggested that the means for resolving this case were reasonable and their purpose appropriately judicial. Republican critics of the state
court, they suggested, simply had a prejudiced view of Democratic judges.

No other acts received significant attention from the Court's critics—not by
the voters, the vote counters, or the lawyers. Strategically, they focused on
the *Bush* court almost exclusively, drawing attention to their sins and away
from the alleged sins of others. With rare exceptions, they had little to say
about the Florida court, even though the Court's defenders had relied extensively on attacking the state court to support the claim that the U.S. Supreme
Court was obliged to intervene to rein in an out-of-control state court.

Editorialists Talk Past Each Other

To a great extent, supporters and defenders of the Court talked past each
other, constructing different sets of acts. There were a few areas where
characterizations collided. For example, defenders of the Court characterized the act and attitude of the *Bush* majority as reluctant, while critics
called them willful. Despite this difference, the two groups sustained their
characterizations along different grammatical pathways. The defenders had
focused on the Florida court's actions as creating a scene that forced the
majority to take reluctant action. Critics had drawn on the controversial
means used by the majority and tied that in with their political affiliations
(an agent concern) and with accusations of partisan purposes to render the
act and attitude willful. Neither position challenged the other's grounds but
only its conclusions about the act and attitude of the Court.

Supporters and defenders clearly clashed on the 5-4 versus 7-2 split of
the Court. Rotunda, for example, sought to challenge the 5-4 characterization by arguing that the critics decrying the split had made a hasty decision
("the next morning").[144] May was the most even-handed of the defenders,
telling the readers of the *Legal Times* that "seven justices determined that
the manual vote recounting was arbitrary and fundamentally unfair," even
if Breyer and Souter did not like the remedy.[145] The *New Republic* used the
same information to reach the opposite conclusion: "this was a 5-4 decision, not a 7-2 decision, as some Republican spinners would have us

believe, on the utterly false assumption that every justice who acknowledged the chaos in the standards of counting concurred in shutting the
counting down."[146] Note that, like Rotunda, they also used an attack on
opponents ("Republican spinners") to challenge the characterization.

The difference between the two sides turns on how one defines the act
of decision. For Court defenders, acknowledgment of an equal protection
problem by Souter and Breyer made them part of the decision on equal
protection. For Court critics, the equal protection decision could not be
separated from the determination to stop the counting. Defenders used a
smaller "circumference" for the decisional act than the critics.[147] Neither
side went deeply enough into the language of Souter and Breyer to justify
their inclusion or exclusion from this seven-justice grouping.

A third area of some overlap concerns the conservatism of the majority
justices. Fried and Kenneth Starr drew on other decisions by the majority
to show that they were not so conservative, or at least not partisan. Court
critics talked more about judicial philosophy and political affiliations to
suggest that they were conservative and partisan. Because they did not
compare specific cases or statements on judicial philosophy, the tensions in
these variant constructions cannot be explored. It is ironic, however, to
note that the decision in *Bush v. Gore* itself flew in the face of both sides'
constructions. Kenneth Starr used other cases to show that these justices
don't rock the boat; but this was perhaps the biggest boat-rocking case in
Court history. Court critics urged that these justices were states' rights advocates who were weak on enforcing equal protection; but this was a case
where they overrode states' rights and supported a novel new equal protection ruling.

The rhetorical lesson of these editorials is clear: If you are defending
someone faced with evidence that he, she, or they have engaged in an inappropriate act, move attention away from that particular act and toward
(1) other acts that might have created a situation in which those you are
defending were reluctantly forced to act or (2) other acts of the accused
suggesting that they do not have the motives attributed to them in the particular case. On the other hand, if you are attacking them, focus attention
on the act itself and away from the acts of others that may have contributed to a situation requiring a response from the accused.

7

Scholars Reconstruct the Stay Decision

S cholars constructing motives have two key advantages over journalists and editorialists: space and time. Books and scholarly journals provide space for arguments to be elaborated, evidence to be adduced, and sources to be enumerated. And, unlike journalists and editorialists, who normally face deadlines, scholars typically have considerable leisure to ponder, research, write, and revise their rhetorical constructions. They also benefit from a better-educated audience, especially those knowledgeable in the law.

This enviable space and time provide an opportunity for scholars to scrutinize the work of judges, which they frequently do, deploying the same basic tools for reconstructing motives that we found in judicial opinions, news reports, and editorials. However, if the same grammatical means are used in such reconstructions, there is a difference in the meticulousness of scholarly reconstructions. What Kenneth Burke has said of theological discourse applies equally to scholarly discourse about the law: both are "example[s] of words used with thoroughness."[1]

Scholars exerted a great deal of effort examining *Bush v. Gore* and the acts surrounding it. A number of scholarly books and scores of law review essays analyze the case.[2] Many scholarly analyses reflect frustration or

anger over the Supreme Court's ruling in this monumental case and provide withering criticisms of its arguments and of the Court itself. Ronald
Dworkin noted: "I know of no other instance in which so many distinguished academic and professional critics have criticized the Court in such
angry and intemperate language, or even suggested, as they did in this
case, that some justices had decided for personal and self-serving reasons."[3]
Others have called the overwhelming scholarly denunciation of the per curiam decision "scathing,"[4] "vehement,"[5] "inflamed,"[6] "angry,"[7] and "without precedent."[8] Judge Richard Posner called it "the most execrated
modern decision of the Supreme Court."[9]

If the liberal bent of most constitutional scholars explains some of this
anger,[10] it does not explain why almost no conservatives who spoke in defense of *Bush v. Gore* supported the reasoning of the per curiam. Nelson
Lund, who defended "every last jot and tittle"[11] of the majority opinion,
complained that "[c]onservatives have frequently defended the result and
certain aspects of the decision, but have generally been unwilling to endorse the legal reasoning offered by the Court as the basis for its decision."[12] Pamela Karlan agreed with that assessment, noting that "even
those scholars who defend the Court's judgment—such as Richard Epstein
and Richard Posner—do so without embracing fully its reasoning."[13] Peter
Berkowitz and Benjamin Wittes added that "[l]eading conservative professors of constitutional law were not much heard from," and when they did
speak, "they were comparatively measured in their statements [finding] in
Bush v. Gore a reasonable though flawed ruling."[14]

Whether liberal or conservative, legal scholars, as scholars, are expected
to provide reasons for their positions. And in that reason giving, not all
scholars took sides in this struggle (though many did so). As a group, they
were much more willing to concede weaknesses in the side they defended
or strengths in the side they attacked than their editorialist counterparts.
However, in the end, they usually weighed in on the question of whether
the Supreme Court did the right thing or not. Grammatically, that reason
giving is understandable as a form of motive reconstruction, as scholarly
commentators on the decision sought to explain what the majority was
doing and why it was doing it.

The stay order that preceded the *Bush v. Gore* decision was "the first genuinely extraordinary action taken by the United States Supreme Court."[15]
The stay order, which stopped the statewide recounting that was just beginning in Florida, was shocking to many commentators. Their constructions harshly scrutinized the questionable means by which it was justified

by Justice Scalia's concurring opinion. A stay is issued where a petitioner can show that, absent the stay, he or she will suffer irreparable harm and also that he or she is likely to win the case to which the stay gives rise. Most critics focused on Scalia's claim that irreparable harm would come to Bush absent the stay. Cass Sunstein of the University of Chicago made this his focus, arguing that the stay "is difficult to defend on conventional legal grounds—not because Bush lacked a substantial probability of success, but because he had shown no irreparable harm."[16] Scholars identified several problems with this claim of harm. First, as Elizabeth Garrett argued, it was far from clear that Bush would lose his lead in the recount, and absent such a loss, no harm would follow; thus, she contended, the harm was "more speculative than real under the circumstances."[17] Dworkin also highlighted this questionable assumption.[18] Neither Garrett nor Dworkin reconstructed the recount scene to show why this was questionable, though Garrett appeared to be making a post hoc judgment.[19] On the other hand, Scalia had not constructed the scene to support the harmful outcome the stay sought to avoid, so presumption did not clearly rest with his side, either.

Scalia rests his claim of harm on the assumption that counting the ballots in an unconstitutional manner (i.e., one violating equal protection) would cast the harmful cloud over Bush's election that Scalia sought to avoid, for if the counting were legal, no cognizable harm could be claimed. On this point, Garrett tried to undermine the harm claim by insisting that an unconstitutional recount might not have occurred after all, since "Judge Lewis [who oversaw the recounts] might have imposed standards that would have satisfied, or at least ameliorated, the equal protection concerns articulated by the seven justices."[20] Because the stay stopped the recount before its character was revealed, she averred, Scalia was basing the harm to Bush on hypothetical acts and hypothetical agencies. A trustworthy agent, such as Judge Lewis, might ensure that the recount met constitutional standards (for example, by resolving disputed ballot claims in a consistent manner, statewide). Scalia's stay opinion had focused not on what had occurred or might occur in the recount but on what "the Florida Supreme Court opinion, as interpreted by the Circuit Court, permits" (namely, recounting using varying standards).[21] No doubt, Scalia could have effectively invoked the recent recount to show that what is permitted might come to pass. And, in any case, stays often must anticipate harms based on assumptions about what will come to pass.[22]

Using another approach, several scholars sought to trump Bush's harm claim with a constitutional claim. For example, Dworkin contended:

> Public knowledge that Gore would have won, if the recounts had continued and been accepted, would produce doubt about a Bush election only if the public disagreed with the Court's judgment that the recount was illegal; and it is constitutionally improper for the Court to keep truthful information from the public just because the information might lead it to conclude that the election was a mistake or that the Court was wrong.[23]

Here, Dworkin elaborated Scalia's act that leads to harm, drawing attention to those feared by the conservative majority: the public. This construction pits an elite Supreme Court against a public they appear not to trust, but it does so by smuggling in the characterization of truthful information, which would prove a bone of contention for Scalia (who would say it was "misleading information" based on a faulty recount).

David Strauss used the same term, construing *truthful* in a more limited way, and connected the agency to a questionable purpose: "The premise of this argument is that there is a legitimate interest in suppressing truthful information—information about what the recount ordered by the Florida Supreme Court would have disclosed—in order to protect the President of the United States from political harm."[24] Here, *truthful* refers simply to an accurate reporting of what the recount disclosed, whether or not that recount was constitutionally acceptable.

Laurence Tribe, the Harvard law professor who was on Gore's legal team, avoided the issue of truthfulness altogether, opting for information. He also specified the constitutional problem at stake, arguing that Scalia's position

> seems irreconcilable with the First Amendment, for the Court could set the record straight later by announcing that the recounted "votes" had not been tallied in a lawful manner should that be its ultimate conclusion, and the freedoms of speech and press plainly prevent government from suppressing information lying at the political core of free expression on the theory that the minds of adult citizens would be so polluted by learning of it that no subsequent refutation could undo the "harm."[25]

As we move from Dworkin to Strauss to Tribe in this argument, we get a less and less objectionable characterization of the information they would allow the public to see. Furthermore, Tribe reconstructed the stay as an act not simply of avoiding harm to Bush but of "suppressing information lying at the political core of free expression." He teased out the implications of Scalia's simple concern for the "public acceptance" that ensures "democratic stability,"[26] finding unwarranted and unconstitutional paternalism. Scalia's skepticism of democratic processes foreshadows a theme many commentators would find in the majority and concurring opinions of *Bush v. Gore*. However, if Scalia's construction of the public did not reflect our democratic ideals, it did have a practical appeal: mass audiences certainly may not appreciate legal distinctions well enough to accept a reversal of an apparent victory in such a monumental election. Bush's fortune in hanging on to his slender lead in Florida is testament to the power of momentum in ensuring a grudging public acquiescence in his claim of victory.

To win this argument, Scalia was forced to reduce the mass American public to an element of scene, whereby potential opinions became the basis for future instability, which might constrain lawful Court action in the future. Dworkin, Strauss, and Tribe sought to keep the public as democratic agents, neither victims of scenic circumstances nor components of a scene. From their perspective, Scalia was not treating the public like some dehumanized scene so much as treating them like volatile children. Both constructions had their appeal, though Scalia's construction challenged the idea that democracy not only trusts the public but is constituted through public knowledge and participation in the political process.

Critics launched another assault on harm over the "balance of equities" issue, whereby the majority was obliged to consider the potential harm to Gore of granting the stay. Strauss argued it succinctly: "the potential harm to Vice President Gore was vastly greater [than that to Bush]. Had Vice President Gore prevailed on the merits in the Supreme Court, the stay might easily have deprived him of his victory, by preventing the counting of the ballots before the electors were to cast their votes on December 18."[27]

Scalia's construction could win this rhetorical battle as well, but not without losing the war on the stay issue. The battle could be won through Scalia's construction of Bush's probability of success in his assertion: "It suffices to say that the issuance of the stay suggests that a majority of the Court, while not deciding the issues presented, believe that the petitioner has a substantial probability of success."[28] If it was clear that Gore would not win because the Supreme Court would decide that the recount was unconstitutional, then no cognizable harm could come to Gore from stopping the recount. As Jack Balkin explained, "[t]his view [of the harm issue] makes perfect sense if the Court had already made up its mind that

Bush would win the case and become president."[29] Lund elaborated this position, though in a decidedly post hoc analysis:

> Contrary to a lot of heated commentary, this order had no adverse effects on Gore's legal rights. Seven members of the Supreme Court subsequently agreed that the suspended recount was inconsistent with constitutional standards, and nobody can have a right to something that is itself illegal. The counting that would have been done after the stay order and before the Court's decision on the merits would have been legally void, and Gore could have had no legal right to the results of an illegal recount.[30]

Lund here reset the stay decision within a later scene, trying to explain the halt of the recount in light of what the Court subsequently did. Technically, we can represent this strategy as follows: If the stay is act 1 undertaken in scene 1, and the *Bush v. Gore* decision is act 2 undertaken in scene 2, then his argument works through a scene 2–act 1 logic, which is impossible.[31] Of course, this logic might be defended if we consider that the majority supporting the stay was the majority supporting the Bush decision, so that, effectively, they could create the scene necessary to make Lund's logic work. However, that is not his construction of motives here—he did not say "they knew what they were going to do." And, making such self-fulfilling prophecies was problematic in any case.

The stay majority trades strength on the harm argument for weakness on the majority's construction of its own motives in staying the decision. Dworkin hinted at this problem: "Their first major ruling, on Saturday, December 9 (soon after the recounting began), was to halt the recount even before they heard argument in Bush's appeal of the Florida Supreme Court decision ordering those recounts."[32] This reconstruction characterized the Court's actions in temporal sequence: the majority found that Bush had a substantial probability of success in his appeal even before they heard argument in that appeal. Recall that to reject the "harm to Gore" argument required a strong certainty that the recount would be found unconstitutional; but as Dworkin implied, how could that certainty be so strong if they had yet to hear arguments in the case?

Strauss admitted that "[i]t is probably pretty common for justices to know, from reading the certiorari petition, how they will vote in a case." However, he drew a distinction between common cases and this case:

> But this was not a run-of-the-mill case presenting a slight variant on a subject that the justices have thought about dozens of times. The Florida Supreme Court's decision in *Bush v. Gore* concerned a state election law

statute with which the justices surely had no prior familiarity—even from *Bush v. Palm Beach County Canvassing Board,* which concerned an entirely different state statute. Governor Bush's arguments also drew on broader aspects of Florida election law and Florida administrative law; he argued, for example, that the Florida Supreme Court should have required deference to the decisions of the county canvassing boards even though the contest statute did not say so explicitly. The equal protection argument that was the basis of the majority's opinion depended on a detailed familiarity with the facts about the various recounts that had been underway, as well as an assessment of what was "practicable."

The Florida Supreme Court issued the opinion at 4:00 P.M. on December 8. The United States Supreme Court granted the stay at 2:45 P.M. on December 9. In less than twenty-three hours, five justices evidently had decided that Governor Bush was sure to prevail, because in view of the harm to the Vice President, the stay could not possibly be justified if there had been any doubt. The justices reached this decision even though they had little or no prior familiarity with the state law involved, and even though they were acting on the basis of a very hastily prepared stay application and opposition. It is hard to resist the conclusion that they knew all along what they were going to do.[33]

Here, Strauss drew attention to the scene-act problem: the justices could not possibly have reached a decision on Bush's appeal given the shortness of the time and their lack of familiarity with the law and the facts in the case. His detail in describing the scene (less than twenty-three hours) and the act (involving the consideration of a variety of substantive, esoteric legal issues and not one but five justices all deciding that Governor Bush was sure to prevail) made this construction of motives compelling. He even rejected their reliance on the agency of the Bush team's brief, which was hastily prepared. If the act did not fit the scene, Strauss suggested, it did fit the purpose of finding for Bush. Yet Strauss constructed his own motives not as jumping to that grammatically obvious conclusion (i.e., purpose controlling act) but as being drawn to it because it is hard to resist.

As Strauss's construction highlighted, Scalia was in a rhetorical bind. To the extent that he strengthened his case for rejecting Gore's claim to harm, he would weaken his characterization of the majority's deliberations as fair. Perhaps he recognized the bind, since he only admitted that Bush had a substantial probability of victory, rather than something stronger. But if we take him at his word, even that probability should have allowed room for Gore to argue possible harm, should greater study of the issues lead the case to be decided the other way. However, if we take Scalia's rejection of any harm to Gore as further endorsement of his certainty about Bush's victory (for he cannot withstand the arguments without that certainty), then scene becomes a critical factor, and the unfairness of a too-quick judgment supports negative conclusions about the majority's purposes.

If the stay opinion revealed questionable purposes on the majority's part, the per curiam opinion in *Bush v. Gore* was constructed by scholars as confirming those questionable purposes, especially the analysis of the means-ends or agency-purpose ratio. This agency focus is typical for legal scholars concerned with whether the decision followed the law and how the High Court's interpretations might reshape the law, providing agencies to be followed in the future. These agency constructions radiated out into constructions of judicial purposes, judicial agents, judicial attitudes, the act of decision itself, and, to a lesser extent, the scene. The handful of scholarly defenders had trouble constructing their case by focusing on the means by which the decision was reached and tried to make either respectable judicial agents or an enlarged scene the controlling term.

8

Scholars Reconstruct How the Court Reached Its Decision

The per curiam decision in *Bush v. Gore* was criticized by scholars primarily for its misuse of agency, or how the Court reached its decision. Five issues received the most attention as scholars considered how the majority reached its decision: justiciability, equal protection, the safe harbor deadline, the remedy, and the limitation of the precedential value of the case. These issues involve agency in the sense that they are concerned with following the law (or failing to do so), which grounds judicial action in the ultimate ratio, agency-act, which suggests that acts ought to follow the law, adhere to it, be constrained by it. The law lays down the rules for determining what judicial agents should do and how agents ought to be judged when they fail to follow those rules.

Justiciability

A handful of scholars seriously questioned whether the Court should have heard this case in the first place. One reason for rejecting the case, according to Pamela Karlan, is that Bush did not clearly have standing to sue. Standing rests on an established purpose-agent ratio, whereby an agent who brings a case to court is expected to have a stake in the outcome of the case in order to make it a "case or controversy" justiciable by the court; that purpose creates an agent with standing. Obviously, if Bush could prevent any more counting and become president, he had a stake in the election case. But the agent's purpose also must be related to the agency involved, which in this case is defending the constitutional rights of voters to have their ballots counted in a consistent manner. As Karlan noted of Bush: "He is not an excluded voter himself."[1] That is, he was not an agent with a purpose to protect his own voting rights, but rather he seeks to stand in for others. Gene Nichol also wondered, more narrowly,

> why candidate Bush had standing to assert the equality claims of voters in particular Florida counties. Broward County, according to the Court, "uncovered almost three times as many new votes" as did Palm Beach. One would suppose, therefore, that some unknown Palm Beach county voters were denied equal treatment by the state. Those voters, however, were not before the United States Supreme Court; George W. Bush was.[2]

Vincent Bugliosi, the federal prosecutor of Charles Manson whose scathing article in *The Nation* was reprinted and added to his equally scathing book, *The Betrayal of America*, was one of the first to raise the standing issue, insisting that "no Florida voter I'm aware of brought any action under the equal protection clause claiming he was disfranchised because of the different standards being employed. What happened here is that Bush leaped in and tried to profit from a hypothetical wrong inflicted on someone else."[3]

While it is clear that Bush did not have the standing of voters in the controversy, who were the agents purportedly harmed by the equal protection violations of the state court, he could argue for third-party standing, as even Laurence Tribe, who served on Gore's legal team, admitted:

> Although, as Professor Karlan points out, Bush was not a registered voter in any of the challenged counties in Florida . . . , he surely had third-party standing. His injury was obvious: the Florida Supreme Court was in essence forcing the Governor of Texas to exchange twenty-five electoral votes the Florida Secretary of State had certified as his on November 26—a number sufficient to make him the next president—for a recount to be conducted by a process he regarded as an unconstitutional roulette game rigged in favor of his opponent. Bush potentially had standing on this theory to represent at least those who had voted for him and whose votes stood to be devalued

during a recount. More generally, he shared with all the voters a sufficiently common interest in protecting the integrity of the vote count to ensure his standing as third-party plaintiff.[4]

Tribe drew on a precedent to support this contention, urging that Bush's "standing was analogous to that of the defendant in *Powers v. Ohio*, in which the Court allowed a white criminal defendant to represent black voters excluded from the jury pool on the basis of their shared interest in eliminating racial discrimination from the courtroom."[5]

Tribe's generous construction ascribed a pragmatic purpose to Bush (to save the electoral votes he had been awarded), born of a troublesome re-counting scene (an unconstitutional roulette game). Tribe was not troubled by eliding this particularly personal purpose with the larger public purpose of protecting the integrity of the vote count, suggesting both can live comfortably together. And he was content to rely on *Powers v. Ohio* despite the fact that Chief Justice Rehnquist and Justice Scalia—two key votes in this 5-4 majority—dissented in that case, finding that Powers did not meet the third-party standing requirement because he lacked an "injury in fact."[6] Either Tribe was generous to a (rhetorical) fault, or it was more important for him to endorse a position on third-party standing with which he agreed than to win this initial battle over *Bush v. Gore*.

Despite Tribe's position, other scholars were not ready to concede the point, and they bolstered their arguments by reconstructing the actions of Bush as a third party, considering Bush's purpose of protecting his own voters or the voting process more generally. As Karlan urged:

> [U]nless and until the Supreme Court is prepared to say that [Bush's] supporters are disproportionately likely not to have their votes recovered under the prescribed process—and the Court made no such finding—he is an especially unlikely candidate for third-party standing. It is hard to see George W. Bush as the champion of a claim by undervoters in overwhelmingly Democratic Palm Beach County that they are being denied equal protection because their votes would have been included under the more liberal Broward County standard. Indeed, Bush's third-party complaint in *Gore v. Harris*—the source of his intervention in the case which the Supreme Court decided in *Bush v. Gore*—alleged, among other things, that the standard used in Broward County was partisan, inconsistent, and unfair. The relief he sought was a declaration that "the illegal votes counted in Broward County under the new rules established after the election should be excluded under the Due Process Clause and 3 U.S.C. § 5." Nothing in that proposed remedy vindicates the rights of excluded voters in Palm Beach County or elsewhere except in the brute realist sense that they might be content to have their

votes excluded if that means that a disproportionate number of votes by the other guy's supporters get excluded as well. [7]

Karlan's reconstruction looked more specifically at the Bush legal team's means—its arguments and its recommendations (of means) for the Court to resolve the issue. The remedy of throwing out votes does not fit with standing up (or in) for voters except, as Karlan noted, where throwing out votes on both sides serves voters. This is a purpose-agent disjunction as Karlan constructed it, whereby the purpose of excluding votes does not yield an agent who is standing for the voters. On the other hand, if excluding votes is construed as ensuring the integrity of the vote count, as Tribe would have it, then that larger purpose might give Bush standing, though this begs the question of what injury to particular persons might come from not excluding these votes.

Frank Michelman attacked the notion that any injury to voters was threatened, making Bush's standing in for voters problematic. He contended that the only maltreatment a voter might face was

> the chance that her ballot would undergo appraisal by an intent-of-the-voter standard, honestly applied by whoever would be applying it. True, her ballot stands possibly to be rejected by the official who happens to be the one to pick it up, whereas it might have been accepted if another official had been the one to pick it up first, because of differing rules of thumb in use by the two, each of them reasonably and impartially adopted and applied. These are eventualities about which our voter will never know, and it is not clear why she has any reason to care about them, either, given that the anticipated vagaries of ballot appraisal are utterly random with respect to partisan voter interest.[8]

While this might appear an overly optimistic construction of the recounting taking place, Michelman drew on the *Bush* majority itself to support that construction:

> All [the majority] found legally wrong was that the intent-of-the-voter standard—they thought unnecessarily—allows different honest counters, or groups of them, to make different dispositions of identical ballots, on a basis that is utterly random with respect to voter interest. No one's equal dignity is impugned by this practice, and only Humpty Dumpty would describe it as valuing one person's vote over another's.[9]

Michelman thus used the majority's legal finding that the recount standard alone was problematic to conclude that no injury was threatened and, by extension, that Bush had no basis for standing in, even as a third party, for these voters, or for himself. This is a complex route, to be sure: Michelman used the majority to construct the recounting act as harming neither Bush nor voters; this, in turn, constructed Bush's purpose as neither avoiding harm to himself nor avoiding harm to the voters; without the avoidance of either harm as a purpose, Bush lacks standing (through the purpose-agent relationship).

Even if Karlan's focus on Bush's means and Michelman's focus on Bush's purposes did not undermine the standing endorsed by Tribe, the failure of the majority even to raise the standing issue was troubling to some. For example, Nichol admitted:

> Bush did have a powerful stake in the outcome of the case [and he may] have satisfied standing law's immensely illusive and inconsistently applied third-party rule. But the Justices never even bothered to ask. Matters were too vital, too crucial, too hurried, and too important. Both federalism and separation of powers concerns melted away.[10]

Nichol criticized the Court even as he used the time-starved scene and the significance of the act to explain (if not forgive) the lack of treatment. He also contrasted this lack of concern by the majority over standing with their greater concern in other cases, involving less affluent plaintiffs.[11]

Francis Beytagh focused on the agents alone in finding the Court's silence on standing troublesome:

> [Bush and Cheney] were not Florida residents or voters. Could they assert their supporters' federal constitutional rights, under some third-party standing theory? If so, it was never mentioned, by anyone. Could they claim a denial of equal protection as candidates, since the rights of potential voters for them were implicated? Again, no reference to this possibility either, anywhere.[12]

Mark Tushnet also found "the silence in *Bush v. Gore* about justiciability is quite remarkable."[13] Here, the majority's silence (and the silence of the dissenters as well) was taken not merely as no action but as an act of omission. The entire Court was charged with acting questionably because it failed to discuss an obvious legal issue. The fact that the dissenters did not raise a concern over this issue and that Gore's own attorney, Tribe, rejected it as a concern, undermines the forcefulness of this construction of omission and gives support to Nichol's emphasis on the temporally limited scene as explaining (if not justifying) this oversight.

A second issue of justiciability was no less contentious: the political question doctrine. As Karlan noted, "much of the criticism of *Bush v. Gore* both explicitly and implicitly invokes the political question doctrine, arguing that the Supreme Court ought to have left to Congress the question of how to handle the Florida controversy."[14] This doctrine, detailed in the 1962 case of *Baker v. Carr*, describes conditions when it is justifiable for a court to involve itself in political issues. Notably, the doctrine runs against intervention in instances where clear textual commitments place responsibility with other branches of government, such as the Electoral Act of 1887, which gave Congress responsibility for settling presidential election disputes.[15] Tribe believed that in light of this act and its constitutional underpinnings, "[t]he requisite textual commitment to a political branch could hardly have been clearer."[16] Given that clarity, Samuel Issacharoff contended, "other institutional actors were amply well positioned to address the claimed harm."[17]

Just because other agents could have addressed the problem did not mean that they must. Defenders of the Court relied on *Baker* and its progeny to show just how involved the High Court had become in issues that formerly had been political hot potatoes. Richard Pildes, for example, painted a post-*Baker* scene of court action that seemed to provide precedent for the *Bush* court's intervention:

> *Baker v Carr* dramatically lowered the "political question" barrier to judicial oversight of politics. More recently, that constitutionalization has increased in pace, as issues like the status of political parties, the regulation of campaign finance, the role of race and partisanship in drawing election districts—and now, the counting of individual ballots—have been transformed into grist for the constitutional mill.[18]

Pildes's scene includes lowered barriers, constitutional doctrine in motion (increasing in pace), and a gristmill to emphasize changes that make the *Bush* Court's actions appear acceptable (through a scene-act perspective).

Karlan, who is often critical of the Rehnquist Court, emphasized the current Court's contribution to the creation of this scene of political intervention:

> the Supreme Court is now embroiled in the very heart of the political thicket. A substantial share of the Court's docket consists of cases involving the regulation of politics—restrictions on campaign spending, redistricting, ballot access, candidates' speech, and so on. If anything, recent history reveals a Court that seems willing to head even deeper into the woods.[19]

Like Pildes, Karlan was scenic, describing place (in the very heart of the political thicket), docket size (as a share of the whole), and direction (even deeper into the woods). Karlan's distinct emphasis was that this was a scene of the Court's own making, which added the idea that the agents involved are being consistent in their treatment of *Bush v. Gore*, though, for her, it was an unfortunate consistency.

Even Issacharoff, who made the most extensive study of this question for *Bush v. Gore*, acknowledged a post-*Baker* "demise of the political question doctrine," admitting that "[i]t is not that the Court *cannot* enter the domain of politics, but that there are often compelling reasons why it *should not*."[20] At most, he accused the majority of "seriously lacking in the appropriate spirit of reluctance [to intervene in a political question]."[21] With too little rhetorical room to restructure the scene to support his complaint, Issacharoff retreated to issues of moral or prudential action (what the Court should not do) and proper attitude (reluctance).

If the political question issue were not sufficiently undermined by scenic considerations, Nelson Lund added that *Baker*, like *Bush v. Gore*, involved a vote-dilution issue, so that the Court's unwillingness to avoid intervention there carries a precedent (or at least a moral) for the *Bush* Court as well.[22] Attempting to draw such analogies is problematic—more problematic than the approaches that pull back and take a broad look at the constitutional law scene—because drawing attention to that similarity reminds us that there is a key difference in the two cases. In *Baker*, the Court intervened because urban voters in Tennessee had no other recourse when the state legislature refused to reapportion political districts for more than half a century, leaving political power in rural areas despite tremendous growth in cities like Nashville. The Tennessee courts would not do anything, so voters turned to the federal courts as a last resort. The voters purportedly represented by Bush's lawsuit did have recourse—the Electoral Act of 1887 specifically provided for a congressional remedy for such problems. Lund also was ham-handed in describing the political question doctrine used to challenge *Bush*. While even *Bush* critics admitted that the doctrine had become very broad—providing a ready agency for the majority to follow in hearing the case—Lund sought to undermine the credibility of the doctrine as a whole, asserting with the voice of an insider:

> The real theory, well known to sophisticated students of law and political science, is that the Supreme Court should refuse to decide certain politically sensitive cases, especially those involving the constitutional allocation of power between the federal and state governments, in order to conserve the Court's political resources for more important tasks, especially those involving the protection of certain "individual liberties." In practice, what this means is that the Court should sometimes allow the Constitution to be

violated when Congress infringes on the rights of the states, while protecting judicially selected "individual liberties" that often have no basis in the Constitution.[23]

Lund's position undermined a line of legal cases which the *Bush* majority or its defenders could invoke in this case involving individual liberties. He viewed the political question doctrine as an agency of limitation, where others construed it as an agency of permission. He even impugned the majority which he would support with the implication that its individual liberties claim might have no constitutional basis. Louise Weinberg's terse statement, by contrast, was much more supportive of *Bush:* "It is clear enough after *Baker* that courts can and do adjudicate election controversies."[24]

Arguably, Bush had standing, and the Court was justified in hearing the *Bush* appeal, though the majority should have made a case for that in light of standing and political question concerns. If the case was justiciable, how did the Court fare in explaining the means by which it concluded that the Florida Supreme Court recount order violated the equal protection clause?

Equal Protection

The equal protection argument that was central to the per curiam decision for Bush had embarrassingly little support among conservatives seeking to justify the decision. Richard Epstein, who mounted what he called a "qualified rear-guard defense of the outcome in *Bush v. Gore,*" admitted: "Quite simply, I regard that argument as a confused nonstarter at best, which deserves much of the scorn that has been heaped upon it."[25] John Yoo, a Berkeley law professor who clerked for Justice Clarence Thomas, emphasized the advantages of a quick resolution to the election controversy but conceded that "[t]his is not to say that the precise reasoning of the per curiam was utterly correct."[26] Martin Carcieri recognized the weakness of the case and appealed to the shortened time frame, explaining in a scene-act apologia: "The Court could not fully develop its case, of course, since it was under a tight deadline."[27] Michael McConnell also stressed the scene's role in his defense, urging that "the Fourteenth Amendment holding, while not very clearly explained in the hastily prepared opinion, was both sensible and persuasive."[28] Only Lund unabashedly endorsed the majority's equal protection analysis as "quite straightforward, and firmly grounded in precedent."[29]

The clash over constructions of the majority's motives in its equal protection holding occurred on a number of pentadic fronts, constructing four major acts: (1) the recount, (2) the Florida Supreme Court's recount order, (3) the equal protection precedents, and (4) the original vote count. This focus on major acts related to the equal protection ruling represents one of the clearest examples of what Kenneth Burke called "the paradox of substance"[30]—where a great deal of attention was expended characterizing collateral acts in order to strategically construct the primary act involved in the equal protection holding of the per curiam. The paradox is that we define action in terms of what it is not. But, drawing on this paradox is particularly useful where a defense has been mounted for an act, such as the per curiam, that has proven difficult to defend. Drawing attention away from what the Court was doing was useful to the defense, and critics followed them away. Such indirection also should be expected in discussing judicial motives generally, since legal justification typically takes the form of showing how one is constrained to follow a particular course. Eventually, critics turn away from constraints (which they would challenge), and focus on the direct actions of the majority as well, with few defenders following them.

The Recount

Court defenders mounted their strongest stand in characterizing the recount itself as troublesome. Because the equal protection ruling turned on the idea that Florida's recount mechanisms were arbitrary and unfair in allowing different substandards to be employed in assessing voter intent, Court defenders sought to establish problems with the recount to lay a foundation for the Court's equal protection concerns. Court critics challenged those assertions.

Judge Richard Posner painted a picture of the recounting that drew on images from television coverage of the initial recounts in three Democratic counties, allowing the hypothetical act he constructed to stand synecdochically for the whole process:

> inferring a voter's intention from a merely dimpled chad or, even worse, from indentations next to a candidates's chad (rather than indentations on the chads themselves), is highly questionable. A faint dimple or other slight indentation might be created by the handling of the ballot or by its being repeatedly passed through the vote-counting machines. Or the voter may have started to vote for the candidate but then changed his mind, perhaps realizing he had made a mistake and started to punch the wrong candidate's chad. And of the many undecided voters in the 2000 Presidential election,

some may have gone into the voting booth still undecided and, in the end, "decided" they could not make up their minds. And no doubt some voters—probably many more than the undecideds—misunderstood or simply neglected to comply with the ballot instructions, even though they were clear and if followed would ensure that a vote would be registered.[31]

Posner's construction was loaded with strategic characterizations to throw into question the accuracy of the recounting process. Because this construction was wholly hypothetical rather than descriptive of an actual act, he could shape it to the rhetorical demands of the case he wished to make against the recount and even go inside the heads of his hypothetical voters. His story included ballots inadvertently marked by the counting and recounting process (accidents rather than acts), ballot counters discerning intent from the most minuscule signs (perhaps zealous officials using improper means to assess intent), and voters changing their minds, choosing not to vote, or voting improperly (voters who did not want or deserve to have their ballots counted). The picture is of a scene fraught with problems.

The rhetorical choices Posner made in this characterization of the recount scene can usefully be thrown into relief by contrasting his description with that of journalist Jeffrey Toobin, who described actual ballots in the Broward County recount as follows: "In one precinct, many ballots were just punctured through—they had no dislodged chads at all—and the mottled backs looked like pages of Braille. Obviously, a voting machine had been miscalibrated, and legitimate votes were not being counted, even though the voters' intent was easy to discern."[32] Posner made the most questionable ballots—those with scratches or indentations—central. His focus on a single faint dimple or other slight indentation drew attention away from patterns of indentations, on either a single ballot or collections of ballots. He implied that ballots had been handled a great deal and passed through counting machine many times. They certainly were handled by recounters, although, as the television images showed, the recounters treated them gingerly. And most ballots had been through the counting machines twice—for the original count and in the automatic recount, though Posner's term *repeatedly* appears to imply more and to suggest that, somehow, such processing was ill advised (given the delicacy he attributed to the ballots).[33]

While Toobin stated that many uncounted ballots had voter intentions that were readily discernible, Posner implied, with his careful characterization, that discerning voter intention was difficult. He also tried to establish a means by which dimples, scratches, or indentations might have appeared on the ballots not as failed votes but as accidents. First, he suggested that the handling and recounting might have created these erroneous signs of voter intent. This description is weak to the extent that it fails to account for two problems with this account of agency. One is the problem of the fortuitous location of these errant marks. If such handling or processing marks are created, what is the chance that they will show up directly next to a presidential candidate's name on the ballot? Another problem is the sheer randomness of those marks that do appear by a candidate's name. Why would they favor one candidate rather than another? Would they not simply be random and, to that extent, unimportant to influencing the final vote count?[34]

Posner's second strategy was to explain possible voter actions that might lead to erroneous marks. His description of the voter who starts to punch out a chad and then realizes he or she is punching the wrong one was poorly constructed, because if the voter stopped because of a mistake, would he or she not then punch out the correct chad (having caught the error) and either avoid an undervote or at least make a greater indentation in an alternative candidate's chad?

Posner's construction of the undecided voter who fails to vote for any presidential candidate is certainly credible, since most of the undervotes yielded no new votes at all but were rejected as showing no clear intent. [35] However, he seemed to imply that ballots with discernible markings nonetheless may represent these undecided voters, and he offered no account of how such marks might appear (other than the random marks discussed before).

Finally, Posner constructed the errant voter who fails to follow "clear" instructions and receives his or her just deserts (i.e., losing his or her vote) as a consequence. This construction, like that of Rehnquist's concurring opinion, assumes government compliance with Florida regulations that others would challenge, moving the debate to yet another collateral act. Tribe, Schwartz, and the U.S. Commission on Civil Rights painted a different picture of the voting scene, undermining Posner's simple claim of clarity in instruction while moving responsibility away from voters (through a scene-act argument). Tribe noted that "the [voting] instructions were not uniform from county to county and may have been provided only in English in areas with large Hispanic populations, despite the legal requirement that they also be printed in Spanish."[36] Paul M. Schwartz quoted the *Los Angeles Times*'s finding that "[n]early every county was swamped by complaints of inexperienced poll workers who couldn't answer questions, didn't know the law and unfairly turned away registered voters."[37] Schwartz also specifically blamed canvassing officials in Duval County, who "managed to publish a sample ballot in newspapers that contained incorrect instructions; when these instructions were followed, an invalid vote resulted."[38] The Commission on Civil Rights noted a number of obstacles to voting, many flowing from inadequate financial resources made available to county canvassing boards for training poll workers and educating voters.[39] A statement in the commission's majority report challenged Posner's characterization of voter error with respect to minorities particularly (whose votes were rejected in disproportionate numbers), noting that "Governor Jeb Bush's Select Task Force on Election Procedures, Standards and Technology revealed that less than 1 percent of the problems minority voters faced during the election resulted from 'voter error.'"[40] Effectively, these challenges move responsibility from Posner's errant voter to the scene and the agencies of the electoral process.

Pildes described the motives of a different set of agents in expressing his concern over the recount process. Instead of focusing on the voters, he turned to the counters, calling them "partisan officials, free to adopt and apply different and highly subjective standards in a context in which everyone knew (or thought they knew) which way those standards would cut on an issue in which all were intensely interested."[41] This concise construction links partisan agents to partisan means (differential counting) adapted to partisan purposes (giving an advantage to their candidate) within a scene (context) where they knew (or thought they knew) which recount standards would favor their candidate. Characterizations of agents, agency, purpose, and scene are mutually reinforcing, creating a motivational web that yields a troubling act.

Critics of the High Court offer two constructions that challenge Pildes's story of a tainted recount. Michelman called the *Bush* majority itself as a witness for the recounters:

> In *Bush v Gore*, to go by the doctrinal proposition there declared, the majority intervened not on behalf of the would-be Gore voters whose votes were being weeded out by biased Republican counters, or would-be Bush voters whose votes were being weeded out by biased Democratic counters. All they found legally wrong was that the intent-of-the-voter standard—they thought unnecessarily—allows different honest counters, or groups of them, to make different dispositions of identical ballots, on a basis that is utterly random with respect to voter interest.[42]

Michelman built on the failure of the High Court to criticize the motives of recounters, but he offered no support for the actual honesty of the officials or the randomness in the recount standards' outcomes. For the former, he simply relied on the narrowness of the per curiam ruling, which cited only the failure to specify recount standards as the equal protection problem rather than impugning the recount officials' motives. Jack Balkin recognized the care with which the Court discussed the recount officials, noting "[t]he Court did not make these accusations directly in its opinion"; but, he admitted, "[i]t is quite possible that the U.S. Supreme Court actually did not trust the Democratic canvassing boards and trusted recounts by Democratic judges even less, even if the latter recounts were held using a single standard."[43] Michelman seemed to rely on the letter of the opinion, ignoring its spirit, which Justice Stevens criticized for appearing to endorse the Bush team's "unstated lack of confidence in the impartiality and capacity of the state judges who would make the critical decisions if the vote count were to proceed."[44] In short, Michelman took the Court at its literal word.

Michelman's claim that various standards would yield random results also had no direct support, though it built on the "honest officials" claim to the extent that those agents would not choose a standard strategically to effect a particular outcome (i.e., there was no partisan agent to use partisan means for partisan ends). Additionally, from a post hoc perspective, it is easy to make the case for Michelman's randomness—or at least for a lack of clear strategic choices in setting standards—since the postelection media recounts suggested that a looser standard actually favored Bush rather than Gore, contrary to what many assumed.[45]

Tribe made a similar move in defense of the counters' motives when he cited a Florida precedent that interpreted the state election code as requiring "a presumption of proper performance."[46] Like Michelman, Tribe was attempting to trump factual judgments with legal judgments. Grammatically, this connects two acts: the act of a legal authority and the act of recounting, interpreting the latter through the eyes of the former. In Tribe's case, he attempted to render judgment on a whole class of acts (recounting in Florida), of which this particular recount is a member. In Michelman's case, the legal act was tied to the specific recounting act in question. In neither case can we dismiss the possibility of recounter partisanship as an underlying concern in the Court's decision, though both supply grounds for casting concerns over partisanship as legally irrelevant.

Tribe offered a second, more developed construction of the recount process to counter Pildes's concerns. He noted that the recount teams themselves were required by the state election code to consist of members of both parties.[47] That supported his explanation about the legislature's lack of concern about partisanship by suggesting that

> the election code of Florida attempts to harness rather than to exile partisan motives and political self-interest, while providing safeguards against partisan fervor. The principal safeguard rests in reliance on the integrity of the members of county canvassing boards, with public scrutiny helping keep those board members honest. . . . The state's election statutes simultaneously reveal the legislature's confidence that, even in the midst of partisan wrangling, closely watched election officials will perform their duties in an ethical manner. [48]

Tribe's curious construction was stretched between individual agents and the scenes within which they work in fixing the source of honesty in the process, whereby the state relies on the integrity of members, but uses public scrutiny to "keep those board members honest"; the officials will be "ethical," but they must be "closely watched." Grammatically, the public scene creates the ethical agent. Because integrity does not flow from the agent, scenic constraints are necessary to keep the process honest, and Tribe suggested that these are built into the system.

Dworkin's approach to the problem of partisan motives in the recount was much more elegant. He focused on the fact that this was a statewide recount, which included both Democrat-leaning and Republican-leaning counties, and suggested that "different political biases [might] cancel themselves out across the state."[49] For him, the scene did not create ethical agents but acted as a medium of equilibrium so that, on the whole, partisan biases had little impact. Given the razor-thin closeness of the election in Florida, such a balancing of political biases in the state appears credible.

It is easy for critics of the recount process to suggest that partisanship is involved, since the entire state electoral process is predicated on party members running canvassing boards and holding responsibility for elections and recounts. In the face of this challenge, those defending the recounts (and criticizing the High Court for stopping them), often drew a distinction between the ordinary recounting process and the one that was put in place by Judge Terry Lewis, which provided special judicial oversight. Peter Shane described the process set in place by Lewis as follows:

> Both the Gore and Bush campaigns would be entitled to have observers watching every counting team. Objections to the treatment of any ballot could be registered in writing by either observer and filed with the Clerk of

the Leon County Circuit Court for Judge Lewis's review. If questions arose with regard to any ballot, they would be reviewed in each county by two circuit judges who, if they could not agree, would refer the matter for determination to Judge Lewis, who would preside over the statewide recount.[50]

In this construction, judges (rather than mere partisans) participate in a process that allows input from both parties and offers a final arbiter to settle disputes. Shane did not take the politics out the process, but his construction implied that politics takes a back seat to judicial judgment. He did not indicate that the judges, who are elected in Florida, might themselves be partisans; however, in emphasizing their judicial role (a particular kind of agent or partisan), he suggested fairness and objectivity. Dworkin supported this characterization in calling the final judicial arbiter, Judge Lewis, "a highly reputable state court judge (who, incidentally, had already decided in Bush's favor in an earlier, important, ruling)."[51] Indeed, if Lewis was a partisan, then he might be said to lean in favor of Bush, undermining complaints from conservatives who sought to stop the recount.

Pildes was not impressed with such assurances. In a classic scene-act construction, he suggested that the rushed recount would make such theoretical oversight yield to practical concerns:

> In theory, judges would be available to oversee the recount process at the last stage. But if county boards were engaging in partisan manipulation in either the standards they adopted or the way they applied those standards to specific ballots, any possibility that judges would have been able to revisit that count to bring uniformity and consistency to it, under the exceptional time pressures involved, seems speculative at best.[52]

This was a major theme of the majority, the concurring opinion, and defenders of the Court: time was too limited to do what the Florida court proposed.

This was a fortuitous theme for Bush supporters, because it provided a Catch-22 for recounters. If they did not allow sufficient opportunities for objections from party officials observing the recounts—a check on the partisan manipulation that concerned Pildes—then critics could claim that the recount was partisan and unchecked. On the other hand, if officials allowed more time for addressing such objections, Pildes and others could claim that they could not possibly finish the recount. Judge Lewis's order recognized this dilemma and compromised, ordering that party officials "may not make a verbal objection or challenge to any particular ballot determination nor in any way disrupt or interfere with the counting process," though he allowed them to make objections and challenges in writing.[53]

The major problem of Pildes's construction here, and those of other Court defenders, is that his judgment itself about what the recounters could do is speculative. Whether the Florida Supreme Court could accomplish the task it set for itself in a constitutional manner within the limited time frame would be borne out in the counting itself; but Pildes's speculation could never be tested. It stands on the persuasiveness of the construction alone. It builds on Pildes's previous construction of recount officials as partisan, suggesting that they would use both the choice of recount standards and the application of those standards to help their candidates. It assumes that any intervention by judges would be after the fact (rather than, as Shane would have it, ongoing as differences of opinion arose). And it assumes that the limited scene could not contain such acts. Although the entire construction turns on scene (for if time were not short, judges could check partisan problems), the only description he gave is of exceptional time pressures, begging the question of exactly how much time he believed the recounters had. He did not answer that question, and his construction was weaker because of that.

An agent concern involving the recount that the Court did mention was the use of judges as recounters, not because they might be biased but because they were not specifically trained to conduct recounts. Dworkin claimed that this complaint involved "stretching for any objection to the recount procedures [the conservative majority] could find" and dismissed it by considering the alternative, noting that "(as the vivid television pictures we all saw confirmed) the local election officials were hardly experienced either, and it was not unreasonable to expect that judges could learn as quickly as anyone else could."[54] This agent-act argument does not speak directly to the qualities of the judicial agents to justify their use in the recounting act but only to their relative abilities when compared with those local election officials whose televised acts of recounting did not support their qualities as trained recounters (through an act-agent relationship).

The crux of the recount concerns constructed here comes back to an alleged failure on the part of the Florida Supreme Court to provide trained recounters and a more specific standard for judging whether or not a given undervote ballot should be deemed to represent a legal vote. Grammatically, the state court's agency in directing the untrained agents did not control the act of recounting sufficiently to avoid mistakes and unfairness. Defenders of the recount enlarged the notion of agency to include not just a criteria for judging what counts as a vote but an entire process involving partisan participants who nonetheless were kept in line by oversight processes that included a final, respected judicial magistrate. They also supported the idea that the judges conducting recounts were at least as qualified as previous recounters.

The battles over the propriety of the "intent of the voter" standard laid down by the state court would occur in constructions of what that court did in its recount order. Keep in mind, though, the obvious overlap in the acts of the court and the acts of the counters whom they would direct, as constructions of the recount and the recount order carry implications for understanding both.

The Florida Supreme Court's Recount Order

Posner reiterated the concerns of the Supreme Court over the recount order issued by the state supreme court: "The Florida court refused to establish criteria for recovering votes from spoiled ballots more specific than the intent of the voter."[55] Lund went further in attaching a purpose to this refusal to specify a substandard:

> If the Florida Supreme Court had actually been seeking to ascertain the "will of the voters" of Florida, it would have designed a statewide recount that could believably be called more accurate or more reliable than the initial machine counts. At an absolute minimum, that would have required reexamining all the "overvotes" (where the machines detected a vote for more than one candidate, and therefore recorded no vote) as well as the "undervotes" (where the machines detected no vote for any candidate). Once one assumes that the "intent of the voter" should be honored even when the voter failed to comply with the instructions on how to vote, these two categories of ballots become logically indistinguishable.[56]

Between Posner and Lund, we have a construction of state court action in terms of not what it positively did but what it failed to do.

Lund implicated a different purpose: seeking something other than to ascertain the will of the voters. Posner's description was weak insofar as it simply reported what the state court did not do, without providing an explanation for why it chose the standard it did. Lund at least alluded to a purpose—a political one, presumably—though it is a nondescript purpose.

Defenders of the state court provided detailed descriptions of what the state court actually did. Dworkin reflected the views of many who pointed to the Florida statute in explaining why the state court did not adopt a more specific standard than intent of the voter:

It might well have thought that it was not its role to do that. The Florida statute, after all, laid down nothing more specific than the voter-intention test, and the court might have thought it more in keeping with the spirit of that instruction to allow individual counters to decide, with the evidence of ballot before them, how best to achieve that task. The Florida court had already been attacked as being political, moreover, and it might well have thought that it would encourage rather than defuse that criticism if it made any one choice for the whole state that might be thought to favor one candidate or the other. It may well have decided that the wisest course, as well as the course most in keeping with the statute, was simply to pass on the statute's instructions to those who would study the ballots at first hand.[57]

Dworkin's characterization portrayed the state court as possibly going through a number of serious considerations before concluding that it would not set down a more specific standard—quite a contrast to (and more compelling than) Posner's simple refusal or Lund's refusal for vague political reasons. Here the Florida court not only acts as a general judicial agent but reflects on its role as a particular judicial agent—using that reflection to clarify what such agents do to ensure that their actions follow from that role.

Unlike Posner and Lund, Dworkin did not set out the state court as a lone player but noted others' actions in explaining its act of decision. He emphasized what the Florida legislature (through its statute) had done, in laying down "nothing more specific than the voter-intention test." Not only does he have the state court taking notice of the letter of the law, but he has it assessing the spirit of the law, thereby extending and supporting legislative purposes to leave the judgment to the "individual counters" who, he noted "would study the ballots at first hand." This latter characterization portrays the counters as more appropriate for determining what is a vote, since they have "the evidence of the ballots before them" (a scene-agent relationship). Dworkin cast the state court not as defying the legislature (as Rehnquist in particular charged) but as cautiously deferring to it.

Dworkin played up this cautious attitude on the court's part by surrounding it with a scene within which the state court had been attacked as political (a scene-attitude relationship), suggesting that this attitude, rather than some questionable purpose, led it to stick to the statutory standard. That cautious attitude informs Dworkin's consideration of a hypothetical act of setting a more specific standard, where he noted that whatever choice was made, it "might be thought to favor one candidate or the other," and he had the court thoughtfully avoiding that choice and its motivational entail-ments. Thus, the scene provides the impetus for judicial caution and the basis for counters to do a more effective job than the court in choosing stan-dards. It contains a thoughtful judicial agent reflecting on its role and decid-ing to adopt an agency for the recount given to it by the legislature.

Epstein gave left-handed support to Dworkin's concern over possible perceptions of partisanship if the state court had laid down specific recount guidelines: "It takes little imagination to predict that, if it had been forced to adopt a uniform standard for all punchcard ballots, the Florida Supreme Court could leap to that standard that maximized the number of under-votes that were included in the final tally."[58] His view of the Florida Supreme Court as partisan led him not to support a more specific recount standard, because that would have given the state court leave to choose a standard that helped Gore. So, while Dworkin would have the state court avoid appearances of partisanship, Epstein would follow his lead to avoid giving them an opportunity for partisanship.

Several High Court critics took on the per curiam's particular assertion that "[t]he [recounting] factfinder confronts a thing [i.e., a ballot], not a person," making intent more difficult to discern, since he or she cannot question the ballot as he or she would question a witness. Herman Schwartz drew on an exchange between Dworkin and Fried in noting the frequency with which the law relies on paper rather than witnesses, citing Dworkin's "classic example of a contested last will and testament; the de-ceased testator is no more present than the anonymous Florida voter who left behind a punch card, optical scanner ballot, or paper ballot."[59] Tribe took on complaints about the unresponsive paper ballot and the generality of the "intent of the voter" standard in noting that

> our society jails people for years, sometimes even executes them, on the basis of how a given jury interprets and applies a general standard like "proof beyond a reasonable doubt," or on the basis of how a particular jury infers the intent of the accused from pieces of circumstantial evidence at least as susceptible to different readings as are the marks on a ballot.[60]

Dworkin, Schwartz, and Tribe all appealed to consistency between how the Court treats other acts and how it treats this similar one. Tribe's example drew on Aristotle's argument from the greater and the lesser,[61] suggesting that if we use a general standard to put someone to death, surely we can use a similarly general standard to record a vote.

Other state court defenders emphasize the source of the "intent of the voter" standard, throwing into relief the fact that the Court ignored the statutory bases of the standard. As University of Virginia law professor Richard Schragger emphasized: "Of course, the Florida Supreme Court's 'intent of the voter' standard did not come out of thin air: it had ample precedent in state case law and statutory provisions, and it embodied a state constitutional value that encouraged the counting of all possible votes."[62] Schragger and many others would point to the legal bases for this standard. Many relied on the statute cited by the state court itself, § 101.5614(5), which dealt with damaged ballots that could not be counted by the tabulating machines and required that they not be disregarded if there were a "clear indication of the intent of the voter."[63]

Lund challenged this legal basis for the "intent of the voter" rules, charging: "that provision applies only to cases where the ballot itself is damaged or defective, which simply reinforces the conclusion that the Florida laws did not contemplate manual recounts designed to correct errors by voters."[64] Posner made the same point, urging that "the provision about recording a vote when there is a clear indication of the voter's intent is for cases in which the ballot is damaged or defective, which is different from its being spoiled by the voter, and is indeed a kind of tabulating error."[65] The argument, which suggests that this particular agency (finding the intent of the voter) is adapted to the narrow purposes indicated by the provision's focus on damaged and defective ballots, urges (in good purpose-agency form) that this criteria for recounting is used only when an intrinsic problem with the ballot (not one caused by a voter) leads to its exclusion in counting.

Tribe responded to Posner particularly, citing a precedent that expanded the reach of "damaged or defective ballot":

> In *Beckstrom v. Volusia County Canvassing Board,* the Florida Supreme Court "construed 'defective ballot' to include a ballot which is marked in a manner such that it cannot be read by a scanner." This definition clearly encompasses incompletely punched-through ballots. . . . Judge Posner . . . dismisses *Beckstrom* by opining, in essence, that Florida's highest court could not really have meant what it said in 1998. His contention is a wholly unsupported assertion whose only virtue is that it permits him to advance his far more rigid interpretation with a straight face.[66]

Tribe's reliance on this recent, authoritative interpretation of the statute in question indeed is difficult to dismiss. Posner attempted to overcome this precedent by suggesting that such an interpretation meant "that the canvassing board has a duty to inspect all such ballots"; since he believed this requirement was unreasonable, he urged that such a reading "cannot be and apparently never has been taken seriously," citing a *Miami Herald* article to support this judgment.[67] On the narrower reading of Tribe, that indeed the highest state court ruled on the meaning of "defective ballot," Tribe has the better construction, given the clear statement that even Posner could not reconstruct and must try to dismiss. Furthermore, there is no Florida ruling that supports the particular interpretation that Posner made. And one may work around the troubling implication that recounts would be frequently required if this rule were followed (a purpose he found unacceptable), for example, by finding that an attendant duty to count such ballots is limited to very close elections or elections where a contest or protest has been made (a scenic construction that would contain that purpose within more reasonable bounds).

Schragger added to Tribe's statutory source § 101.011(2), a provision that "indicat[es] that paper ballots not properly marked with an 'X' may nevertheless be valid 'so long as there is a clear indication . . . that the person marking such ballot has made a definite choice,'" as well as a 1940 Florida case which ruled "that a nonconforming marking on the ballot should have been counted because it was clear whom the voter intended to vote for."[68] Even McConnell, who defended the per curiam's equal protection argument, admitted that "[t]he Florida Election Code [in § 102.166(7)(b)] provides that in conducting a manual recount, the counting team's duty is 'to determine a voter's intent in casting a ballot.'"[69] McConnell was surprised that the Florida Supreme Court did not cite this provision, since it deals with manual recounts more generally than the damaged and defective ballot provision.[70]

If Florida relied on the "intent of the voter" standard, so had a great many other states, as Justice Stevens's decision noted.[71] Many Court critics noted Stevens's reference to thirty-three states with a similar requirement,[72] and their emphasis on this legal scene carries implications for three acts: (1) Florida law, which is not unusual in this respect, (2) the Florida Supreme Court's reliance on this standard, which was well grounded and typical, and (3) the U.S. Supreme Court's criticism of this standard, which defied the scene. Michael Klarman was typical in noting the terministic disjunction suggested by the High Court's construction of the "intent of the voter" standard within this scene: "The plethora of states employing the 'intent of the voter' standard in a wide variety of contexts, including manual recounts and the counting of write-in and absentee ballots, no doubt were surprised to learn that they have been acting un-constitutionally all along." Based on this surprise, Klarman found the majority's position unpersuasive.[73]

The majority opinion implied that the voter intent standard was judge-made and therefore suspect. But with three statutory provisions, two precedent cases, and a plethora of similar state laws supporting the legal basis of the "intent of the voter" standard, it is hard to deny that these constructions of the law supported the state court's reading. The Florida court could insist that the legal scene and a legislatively mandated agency determined its decision to adopt this standard.

Working the construction of the Florida Court from another angle, Shane noted that specifying a stricter standard would have changed Florida law, as his hypothetical example shows:

> [S]ubsidiary standards consistent with the law might have provided, for example, that dimpled chads, in and of themselves, should not automatically be deemed conclusive as to voter intent. It might well have violated Florida law, however, to deny either party the possibility, even under subsidiary standards, of arguing that a dimpled chad on a particular ballot did meet the Florida statutory standard of "clear intent of the voter." To deny that possibility would have been to amend Florida's statutory standard.[74]

This characterization moves the state court's action from the passive adoption of a legal standard to a positive refusal to rewrite the law. Shane's hypothetical example points to the problem of conclusiveness in such substandards in ruling out what the broader language of the law permits, and allows him to shift any blame for the broad standard to the Florida legislature that passed it. Changing the standard, at this point, he insisted, would have raised concerns about changing the rules after the election.[75]

Even if it meant refusing to follow state law, an argument still might be made that the Florida court should have ignored this well-grounded standard in light of concerns that counters would choose and apply standards haphazardly (or worse, with an eye to partisan interest), leading to disparate and unfair treatment of voters whose ballots they were examining. Thus, Justice Souter, in dissent, had complained that the vagueness of the "intent of the voter" standard opened the door to differential judgments in counting votes: "I can conceive of no legitimate state interest served by these differing treatments of the expressions of voters' fundamental rights. The differences appear wholly arbitrary."[76] So, even if this voter intent agency grew out of a well-grounded legal scene and adopted the agency mandated by the legislature, it yet might have a troublesome purpose—or lack of purpose—which led to acts of unconstitutionally divergent treatments of similarly situated voters. In short, it was differential, and perhaps unfair, for no good reason. Thus, even if the "intent of the voter" standard is grounded in law, perhaps the law itself is bad and needs to be checked by the supreme law of the Constitution.

Grammatically, the Constitution is often the most important constituent of the legal scene, shaping our understanding of all laws, no matter how well grounded they are. It often has been invoked to determine the proper shape of state agencies. Unfortunately, the Constitution itself is often so vague that it creates a huge and threatening scenic trump to state laws. Critics of the High Court's use of this trump sought to show that there were good reasons to use this more general standard and that it did not lead to unfairness.

The commentators who urged that there were good reasons to leave the recount standard vague relied on two terministic points: scene and purpose. Tribe, for example, divided up the statewide scene of the recounts into different precinct-based scenes that require correspondingly different acts, noting:

> [U]niform statewide rules [more specific than "intent of the voter"] would necessarily introduce their own distinct inequalities. In any given county, unusually many of the punch-card voting machines might be outdated or in poor repair; or the chads might have been cleared out less recently than the statewide norm; or more of the voters might be elderly or frail; or voting instructions, which the law required to have been printed in Spanish *and* English, may have been written in English only—as was the case in Osceola County, with a 29 percent Hispanic population. For an election canvasser in such a precinct to use a more inclusive standard than the one applied by a canvasser in another precinct, where an identical-looking ballot could have an entirely different history, might be the best way to respect, not violate, the principle of "one person, one vote."[77]

Because such scenes may differ in a variety of ways, Tribe insisted, having the recounting act constrained by a narrow agency (say, requiring only cleanly punched-out ballots) would not do justice to differences in those scenes. Fairness for Tribe is taking into consideration the circumstances within which judgments are made on ballots and adapting to those circumstances. Agencies must be adapted to scenes, and those scenes differ, he suggested.

If such scenes demanded a flexible agency, then so did the ultimate purpose of getting an accurate vote count. As Dworkin argued:

> [A] state might rationally decide that accuracy would be improved overall by using a general standard rather than trying to anticipate in detail all the evidence that a ballot might present: a set of concrete tests might not have allowed, for example, for the Florida voter who wrote "I vote for Al Gore" across his otherwise unmarked and unpunched ballot.[78]

Dworkin's hypothetical gets at a critical point stressed by many commentators: any rule narrower than "intent of the voter" necessarily would exclude attempts to vote that nonetheless would clearly indicate intent. Thus, a narrow agency such as "count only chads connected by two corners or less," would miss the written note "I vote for Al Gore," even though that would clearly indicate intent and even though such a clear indication of intent would meet the statutory requirement. Terministically, the narrow agency is not adapted to the broader purpose. Tribe explained how to adapt the counting agency to the counting purpose: "The only way to accommodate cases that merit exceptional treatment [e.g., someone circling 'Bush' or 'Gore' on their ballot but not punching cleanly] is to demote the uniform rules to the status of mere guidelines, all to be applied with a dollop of subjective judgment and a pile of common sense."[79]

Both Tribe's and Dworkin's examples highlight the most obvious of irregular signs of intent, downplaying the scratches or indentations that worried Posner. And to that extent, they fail to consider the more ambiguous signs of intent that Posner would keep out of the hands of partisan counters. On the other hand, Tribe's construction, while admitting subjectivity in the standard, nonetheless appeals for common sense to be brought into the act of counting. And, with his earlier emphasis on harnessing partisanship through recount mechanisms that allow Democrats and Republicans to keep a close eye on each other, he swaps standards adaptive to varying needs for the certainty, and inevitable inaccuracy, of more rigid approaches. Such adaptive standards also provide a basis for fairness in the count, to the extent that voters who make good faith efforts to let their intent be known (even if they fall short of meeting requirements necessary to the machine count) would not be left out but would have an opportunity for their votes to be counted.

Fairness finds its home in a number of grammatical terms. It may be a purpose—to have fair laws or a fair recount system. It may be a property of agents, who may be deemed fair or unfair. Various scenes may support or undermine fairness, for example, when courts seek to keep newspapers and magazines away from jurors. And acts often are judged as fair or unfair. It is a quality of agency to the extent that how people are treated is the basis for judgments of fairness. In the law, this is where fairness is often located—in procedures, rules, practices, and other agencies. This is where Posner located fairness, as Rehnquist did before him, in suggesting that adherence to rules by voters and vote counters ensures fairness and that those voters who fail to follow the rules of voting do not suffer unfairness when their votes are thrown out. But if we accept earlier descriptions of a troubling scene within which voters were not properly instructed, poll workers were ill trained, precincts failed to provide Spanish instructions, and old machines worked poorly, then fairness would seem to support going the extra mile to make up for earlier unfairness. Unsurprisingly, we find advocates on both sides of the *Bush* case arguing about what voters deserve and how far the state should go on their behalf. Posner and Rehnquist can maintain their position just so long as they can gloss over voting problems by emphasizing what was supposed to happen or what intelligent voters should have done. If Tribe's scenic description is compelling, then fairness requires more effort.

Surprisingly, Dworkin took a position that reveals an underlying and unexamined assumption by both sides: that looser recount standards benefit rejected voters. Cass Sunstein embodied this assumption in the following hypothetical:

> Suppose, for example, that in one country [sic], a vote will not count unless the stylus goes all the way through, whereas in another country [sic], a vote counts merely because it contains a highly visible "dimple." If this is the situation, some voters can legitimately object that they are being treated unequally for no good reason. On what basis are their ballots not being counted, when other, identical ballots are being registered as votes?[80]

Likewise, Lund complained that "voters who cast 'dimpled chad' ballots in Broward were treated more favorably than those who cast similar ballots in Palm Beach."[81] Even the per curiam used this language, noting that "Broward County used a more forgiving standard than Palm Beach County."[82] This assumption by Sunstein, Lund, and the per curiam leads to the terministic tug-of-war over the scene, the proper agencies of recount, the culpability of voters, and so forth. But Dworkin was the only scholar to challenge this assumption in discussing fairness to the voters. He made this argument using two hypothetical counties: County X, which has a looser recount standard, and County Y, which has a stricter recount standard. He noted that "[e]ach County's rule of thumb runs a risk—in County X that an unintended vote will be counted, and in County Y that an intended vote will not be counted. In each case the character of the risk is the same: a voter's intention may be contradicted."[83] Dworkin's reframing of the issue in terms of finding or contradicting the voter's intention (whether counting an unintended vote or not counting an intended vote) demonstrates that standards adopted by counties can cut both ways, so that looser standards cannot be said to be more favorable to voters (as they might find unintended votes) than tighter standards (as they might exclude intended votes). Because differing standards cut both ways in terms of disadvantaging voters, Dworkin's construction challenges the argument that using differential standards was itself unfair and, indeed, violative of the equal protection clause.

Dworkin reminded his readers that differential treatment alone does not constitute a harm:

> Fairness does not require that government treat all citizens in exactly the same way in all circumstances. On the contrary, different cities and towns within any particular state inevitably adopt very different laws—criminal laws and other regulations, for example, as well as voting and recount procedures—and the state does not violate any duty to treat all its citizens with equal concern and respect when it permits that. Fairness requires not that all a state's citizens be treated the same, but that none of them be disadvantaged vis-à-vis other citizens—by laws that are either irrational, or that discriminate against them on some suspect ground, like their race, or in the exercise or value of some fundamental right, like the right to vote. That moral requirement cannot be violated unless a law or legal structure damages some person or puts him at some disadvantage in some way. Being treated differently is not automatically being treated unequally or unfairly. No Florida citizen could sensibly make the objection that Sunstein puts in his mouth—that he has been treated "unequally"—unless he could show, not just that different rules of thumb for identifying voters' intentions were used in his county from those used in other counties, but that the difference in some way constituted a harm or disadvantage to him.[84]

Dworkin described a larger scene within which differential treatment of citizens by states is common and insisted that the use of different recount standards does not harm or disadvantage anyone.

In addition to complaining about differential standards for recounting under the Florida Supreme Court's order, the High Court had found equal protection violations in the exclusion of overvotes from the recount order and the inclusion of partial recounts in the vote totals. Although the per curiam focused on the unequal treatment of ballots, Lund drew attention to the consequences of this unequal treatment in the form of vote dilution, which he analogized to stuffing the ballot box:

> For at least forty years, the Supreme Court has treated the stuffing of ballot boxes as a paradigmatic violation of the Equal Protection Clause. Much more subtle and indirect forms of vote dilution have also been outlawed. Like some of those practices, the selective and partial recount ordered by the Florida Supreme Court may have been an inadvertent form of vote dilution. But that recount had effects that were virtually indistinguishable from those in the paradigmatic case. There is no meaningful difference between adding illegal votes to the count and selectively adding legal votes, which is what the Florida court was doing. The Supreme Court rightly concluded that the vote dilution in this case violated well-established equal protection principles.[85]

Analogies such as this attempt to make two acts consubstantial. They succeed insofar as the acts, agents, agencies, purposes, scenes, and/or attitudes of both acts are shown to have similarities more important than their differences. Lund's analogy found overlap in the effects of both acts, which he found virtually indistinguishable. Grammatically, however, the distinctions are pretty stark: stuffing the ballot box always carries a purpose, whereas even Lund called the Florida case a possibly "inadvertent form of vote dilution." Mark Tushnet also pointed to this distinction, insisting that "the analogy to classic vote fraud, is misleading [because] [t]he Court's equal protection analysis . . . does not make anything turn on an intent to deny any identifiable group its vote."[86]

There also is a qualitative difference between having legal votes counted and such bogus votes counted: legal votes come from legal voters and should always be included if possible, whereas bogus votes come from cheaters and should always be excluded; legal votes are expressions of the will of the voters, whereas bogus votes are the machinations of those who would corrupt the voting process. What is being diluted is not legal votes but, possibly, the ratio of votes for particular candidates in a preexisting vote count. Lund's phrase about "selectively adding legal votes" smuggles in a sense of purposive action that is at odds with the earlier use of the term, though this characterization is important to his indictment of the state court's actions.

Lund bolstered his claim of selective vote dilution in reiterating the High Court's complaints about the inclusion of partial recounts and the exclusion of overvotes:

> the Florida court devised an extremely complex system of weighting, in which certain kinds of ballots were more likely to be counted as legal votes in some places than in others, thus discriminating for and against different groups of voters based on where they happened to reside. Most obviously, voters who cast "overvote" ballots in Broward, Palm Beach, and Miami-Dade Counties were treated more favorably than those who cast similar ballots elsewhere. Similarly, voters who cast "dimpled chad" ballots in Broward were treated more favorably than those who cast similar ballots in Palm Beach. Voters living in the unrecounted (and more Republican) precincts of Miami-Dade were disadvantaged in comparison with those living in the recounted (and more Democratic) precincts. The complexity of the vote dilution involved did not convert it into something other than vote dilution.[87]

Lund's characterization is quite similar to that of the per curiam, offering a shotgun approach to explaining which voters would be discriminated against. Unlike the majority, he emphasized the implications of such counting for the overall vote count and the vote dilution that would follow,[88] drawing attention to the consequences for the election—something the majority took pains to avoid. In characterizing the state court's action as complex, he implies that the court's means were in some way sophisticated, or carefully constructed for a political (or at least unconstitutional) purpose which is weakly suggested (through an agency-purpose relationship).

Many commentators responded to the concerns of the majority and Lund on the issues of partial recounts and overvotes. For the former, the majority had found troubling the inclusion of totals from three counties where Gore had requested recounts, because they were full recounts that included overvotes (ballots for which the counting machine detected two votes for president), because Broward County's count was finished after the certification deadline, and because the Miami-Dade County count was partial. This final point also made the High Court worry that the recount it had stayed might be concluded by adding in partial recounts.[89]

Shane gave the most thorough defense of the state court's inclusion of partial recounts. He began by characterizing the recounting act as continuing, rather than complete:

> [T]he [U.S. Supreme] Court objected that "the Florida Supreme Court's decision thus gives no assurance that the recounts included in a final

certification must be complete." It might equally be said, however, that nothing in the Florida Supreme Court's decision suggested that anything else would be the case. The Court's mandatory inclusion in the statewide certified totals of the precertification partial recount in Miami-Dade was simply consistent with its decision to include the results from all the precertification recounts. It was emphatically not the case, however, that the Miami-Dade partial recount was the end of the matter for Miami-Dade County. With regard to the remaining undervotes in Miami-Dade, Miami-Dade was to complete its recount in the same manner as every other county: by reviewing all the undervotes. There would, in other words, be a complete and not a partial total in Miami-Dade.[90]

Because a complete recount would satisfy the majority's (and Lund's) concerns about partial recounts, Shane's characterization of the act as incomplete, ongoing, and yet to be completed directly addressed those concerns. He suggested that the Supreme Court was misreading the state court's motives in presuming they might include final, partial recount totals. Shane reread state court motives through past acts, calling them consistent with the practice of including all precertification totals (removing the primary source for the High Court's "misreading").

Shane next took on the inclusion of recounts that involved overvotes as well as undervotes, not by extending an act (as he had done previously) but by dividing one:

> A second objection was that the Broward, Palm Beach, and partial Miami-Dade totals were included based on a comprehensive review of the ballots in question, while the recounts under Judge Lewis's supervision would be limited to undervotes in all other counties not recounted prior to certification. There was, however, an obvious rationale for this difference. The counties that completed comprehensive recounts prior to certification were directed to do so by the statutory provisions governing precertification election protests.[91]

Here, instead of extending the act of recounting, he divided the recount into protest and contest phases. Under provisions of the protest phase of recounting, candidates were allowed to request recounts in selected counties. Lund and the Supreme Court ignored the statutory option available to both candidates and the choice of Bush not to request any recounts. The selectivity of these recounts was thereby condemned as unfair to Bush and unequal in its treatment of voters, despite the fact that it followed statutory processes and reflected strategic choices by the Republican candidate condemning the process. Although these divergent rhetorical strategies (enlarging or dividing an act) may raise suspicions, the statutory basis for his distinction is strong. The enlarged act simply becomes the recounting of the contest period, which Shane showed stretching into the future until completed.

Tribe brought an entirely different argument to bear on the overvote problem, changing its very nature:

> [W]hile it may be true that three counties' recounts included overvotes, it is also true that thirty-four counties examined overvotes for mistakes during the original machine count and subsequently included, in their initial vote tallies, overvotes that revealed the voter's intent. Despite this fact, the Court tried to have it both ways: If the three counties erred by including their overvotes, then surely the thirty-four counties erred as well. And if the Constitution requires the recount to be invalidated because of selective inclusion, then the initial count must be invalidated on exactly the same ground.[92]

Tribe's basis for this factual claim was a June 1, 2001, *Washington Post* article reviewing the Florida election,[93] so it is unclear whether this information was available to the U.S. Supreme Court. Nonetheless, Tribe's post hoc analysis indicted the High Court's uninformed view and struck a theme that will reappear frequently: that the initial count the recount would replace was flawed.

Tribe turned to the per curiam argument not that overvotes were included in partial recounts but that overvotes were excluded from the statewide recount, even though they might contain evidence of the intent of voters as well. Tribe insisted that by "taking the Court on its own terms, a recount standard that uniformly excludes overvotes should be perfectly constitutional—each overvote is treated the same as every other."[94] Tribe supported this argument by making "overvote" a classification scheme equivalent to "dimpled chads":

> The Court's insistence that there be a uniform standard more specific than the "clear intent of the voter"—and its holding that, so far as equal protection is concerned, any standard sufficiently objective and uniform would do—assumes that whole classes of certain "ballot markings" may properly be excluded. One must wonder how the Court could require a uniform standard that would undoubtedly exclude a "class" of ballots (say, dimpled chads) and yet find a constitutional violation in the state legislature's decision to exclude a different class of ballots (that is, overvotes).[95]

This argument relies on a construction of a nonchalant Supreme Court, willing to accept "any standard sufficiently objective and uniform." While objectivity was a key goal of the majority, it does not follow that just any standard would be acceptable. There are reasons to distinguish overvotes as a class of ballots with particular voter errors from dimpled chads as a class. For example, some overvotes might more clearly reveal a voter's choice than ballots with dimpled chads.

Dworkin offered an approach that better justified a distinction between undervotes and overvotes, suggesting that the recount might reasonably be limited to the former "if there is reason to think either that mistakes are particularly likely in that category, or that evidence of such mistakes are particularly likely to appear on ballots in that category, or both." To make this argument applicable to the focus on undervotes and the exclusion of overvotes, he wrote:

> It is distinctly more likely that a voter would mistakenly fail to punch a chad through or not mark his candidate's box on the ballot strongly enough for a machine to register the vote than that he would mistakenly punch through two chads or make two independent marks, each of which is strong enough to be registered. It is also much more likely that a mistake of the first kind would leave evidence of intention on the ballot, in the shape of a partially detached or even dimpled chad, for example, or a weak mark on a candidate's box, or a strong mark very close to it, than it is that a mistake of the second kind would leave such evidence behind.[96]

Dworkin's generalized description of voters' hypothetical acts of voting is compelling in its narrative of how marks come to appear (or fail to do so). In describing likely actions by voters, Dworkin demonstrated how the scene might be set for recounters, who are required to interpret marks. His construction suggests that the distinction between overvotes and undervotes is reasonable, in part, because the marks left by undervoters will be easier to interpret and more frequent.

When Dworkin's hypothetical voters are compared with postelection recounts by the *Miami Herald,* his construction is partly challenged and partly vindicated. Although, as his description suggested, it takes much more effort to overvote than to undervote, statewide undervotes totaled less than 65,000 while overvotes totaled 110,000.[97] Dworkin's particular description of overvoting left out the case where voters punched out two candidates' chads because they thought they were supposed to do so (for example, to vote for the vice-presidential candidate as well) or because they were punching out a chad for a candidate in a different race—both of which were likely mistakes.[98] On the other hand, recovering those overvotes was, as Dworkin suggested, more difficult than for undervotes. A recount of overvotes by the *Miami Herald* and several other news organizations found about 3,000 ballots were clear regarding voter intent, compared with the recovery of as much as a majority of the undervotes.[99]

Balkin offered a third argument for excluding overvotes that brings the legislature's intent into play. He suggested that the legislature specifically forbade the recounting of overvotes:

> section 101.5614(6) provides that "if an elector marks more names than there are persons to be elected to an office or if it is impossible to determine the elector's choice, the elector's ballot shall not be counted for that office." This implies that "overvotes"—where more than one name was punched on the ballot—and votes where the voter's intent could not be determined were not "legal votes." That part of the statutory text is important because the Florida Supreme Court's December 8 decision ordered the recount of undervotes, but not overvotes. Section 101.5614(6) seems to offer textual support for that approach.[100]

Based on this construction, the Florida court was simply following the law in not requiring the counting of overvotes, a straightforward agency-act construction.

Schwartz was one of the few scholars to recite what is perhaps the most compelling argument for excluding overvotes from the recount process: the dissent's position that no evidence had been presented at trial to show that any overvotes had been overlooked. Schwartz made this procedural issue a constraint on state court action: "The lack of any legal showing about the possibility of valid votes among the overvotes limited the kind of relief that the Florida court could order."[101]

Overall, High Court critics provided a strong argument for the Florida court's decision to exclude overvotes from the recount. The state court was simply following the law in not including overvotes, because the state legislature had called for rejecting overvotes in § 101.5614(6), and no legal showing was made to suggest that recoverable votes could be found in overvotes. The Florida Supreme Court was using an agency approved by the U.S. Supreme Court in offering an objective standard for rejecting some ballots—in this case, all overvotes—and there was good reason for excluding this class, since it would be hard to recover votes from overvote ballots.

Undoubtedly, as Court defenders could note, there were recoverable votes on overvote ballots, and the Florida Supreme Court's emphasis on finding the will of the voters would be consistent with counting overvotes. Court critics could respond that time was short, and this limited scene might properly contain the state court's action in attempting to streamline the process and make the recount as efficient as possible. However, the U.S. Supreme Court's position seemed to allow for no such efficiencies when it insisted: "A desire for speed is not a general excuse for ignoring equal protection guarantees."[102] Indeed, the Court's idealized vision of what the recount must be would almost preclude any actual recount from ever taking place, even in a more extended period of time than most presidential elections allow, so this construction must be scrutinized closely.

On the whole, critics of the High Court defending the state court's act in ordering a recount of the undervotes using the "clear intent of the voter" standard had a well-wrought account of the Florida Supreme Court's actions: The state court was primarily constrained by *agency*—the most powerful motive term in law—in following the law laid down in three statutory provisions, two precedent cases, and the provisions of thirty-three other states. It also followed the law in following statutory provisions that allowed more thorough recounts in three counties selected by Gore (under which Bush also might have requested recounts) and in not recounting overvotes (which nonetheless had been recounted by dozens of other counties). In following the law, the court showed deference to the legislature—evincing the right attitude. It also avoided acting in a way that might favor, or appear to favor, one candidate or the other. In other words, it was sensitive to a scene within which its actions would be judged and conformed to a legal scene within which the voter intent standard was long accepted and at least as rigorous as standards used to judge criminal defendants in death penalty cases. Although the standard the state court followed from the legislative mandate allowed variability in counting, that would not favor any one group of citizens over others, because looser standards are not any more favorable than stricter standards if the purpose is to assess voter intent (since both approaches can lead to mistakes but not favoritism). In not choosing a standard that might favor one or the other, the state court's purpose was appropriately judicial, and these judicial agents acted as judges.

Defenders of the per curiam critical of the state court's ruling tried to make the state court's role in laying down the standard more proactive, suggesting that it refused to act to avoid the problems of a general standard. This construction fails in refusing to address directly the statutory basis of the voter intent standard and in providing weak reasons for rejecting Florida precedents that support the use of that standard. None of the state Court critics considered the implications of adopting a specific substandard for counting votes in terms of due process (changing the law after the fact—something they complained about mightily elsewhere) or in terms of the potential for partisanship in the selection of such a standard. Lund's attempt to characterize the state court's action as a form of stuffing the ballot box was weak to the extent that it required a partisan purpose, which relied on a partisan method, which even he admitted might have been inadvertent in favoring one candidate or the other. He followed the per curiam in attempting to shotgun the problem of differential treatment, bringing many weak arguments about various potential victims, instead of a single strong one about any one of them, hoping that the breadth or complexity of the act would suggest its impropriety.

The Equal Protection Precedents

Whether or not the Florida Supreme Court violated the equal protection clause of the Fourteenth Amendment in failing to provide subsidiary standards for the vote recount, in excluding the overvotes, and by including partial recounts depends not just on what the state court did but also on what the equal protection clause requires. In theory, the equal protection clause should have circumscribed the Florida Supreme Court's action in *Gore v. Harris,* which, in turn, should have circumscribed the recounters' actions. If the state court flouted the constitution in its recount order, then that order gave leave to recounters to act unconstitutionally. Grammatically, these three related acts—as if their convoluted terministic relations were not complicated enough—became linked to a fourth set of acts: those explaining what the equal protection clause requires. These are U.S. Supreme Court precedents that give life and meaning to the 1868 amendment passed on the heels of the Thirteenth Amendment's abolition of slavery in the United States. Unsurprisingly, the High Court and its defenders read these precedents differently from their critics. For at this fount of the law, rhetors on both sides of the issue can construct what is to be followed and do so in a way that finds the state court well grounded or out of bounds, and the Supreme Court that overturned them in one or the other category. Terministically, the Fourteenth Amendment is an act (or enactment) that yields an agency of action for future courts and the state agents who follow their orders.

Precedents provide a rich ground for reconstructing the law, because they involve full-fledged judicial acts whose scenes, agents, agencies, attitudes, and purposes can be construed this way or that to reconstruct strategically what the precedent courts were doing and why they were doing it. Additionally, those reconstructing the law can highlight precedents that support their readings and, to some extent, ignore those that do not.

The conservative majority opinion relies, ironically, on four Warren Court decisions to support its equal protection ruling: *Gray v. Sanders* (1963), *Reynolds v. Sims* (1964), *Harper v. Virginia Board of Elections* (1966), and *Moore v. Ogilvie* (1969). The Court discusses these precedents and their implications for equal protection in two places. First, in referencing *Harper* and *Reynolds:*

> The right to vote is protected in more than the initial allocation of the franchise. Equal protection applies as well to the manner of its exercise. Having once granted the right to vote on equal terms, the State may not, by later arbitrary and disparate treatment, value one person's vote over that of another. See, e.g., *Harper v. Virginia Bd. of Elections*, 383 U.S. 663, 665, 16 L. Ed. 2d 169, 86 S. Ct. 1079 (1966) ("Once the franchise is granted to the electorate, lines may not be drawn which are inconsistent with the Equal Protection Clause of the Fourteenth Amendment"). It must be remembered that "the right of suffrage can be denied by a debasement or dilution of the weight of a citizen's vote just as effectively as by wholly prohibiting the free exercise of the franchise." *Reynolds v. Sims*, 377 U.S. 533, 555, 12 L. Ed. 2d 506, 84 S. Ct. 1362 (1964).[103]

Later, referring to *Gray* and *Moore:*

> An early case in our one person, one vote jurisprudence arose when a State accorded arbitrary and disparate treatment to voters in its different counties. *Gray v. Sanders*, 372 U.S. 368, 9 L. Ed. 2d 821, 83 S. Ct. 801 (1963). The Court found a constitutional violation. We relied on these principles in the context of the Presidential selection process in *Moore v. Ogilvie*, 394 U.S. 814, 23 L. Ed. 2d 1, 89 S. Ct. 1493 (1969), where we invalidated a county-based procedure that diluted the influence of citizens in larger counties in the nominating process. There we observed that "the idea that one group can be granted greater voting strength than another is hostile to the one man, one vote basis of our representative government." 394 U.S. at 819.[104]

Critics of the High Court were skeptical, even dismissive, of the per curiam reliance on these precedents. Elizabeth Garrett noted that "so many courts had dismissed the equal protection argument, in part because precedent seemed to strongly disfavor this analysis."[105] Dworkin claimed flatly: "There was no precedent [for the equal protection claim] in any past judicial decision."[106] Bugliosi insisted that of the four civil rights cases cited by the Court, "not one of them bears even the slightest resemblance to *Bush v. Gore.*"[107] Tribe suggested that "[t]he cases the Court chose to enlist . . .

simply do not support its cause."[108] Even Epstein noted that "there is an obvious gulf between the cases cited by the Supreme Court majority and the unfortunate electoral situation as it developed in Florida."[109]

Many commentators simply noted the significant factual disparities between *Bush* and the precedent cases. Bugliosi, the most caustic critic, was among these:

> In a feeble, desperate effort to support their decision, the Court cited four of its previous cases as legal precedent, but not one of them bears even the slightest resemblance to *Bush v. Gore*. In one (*Gray v. Sanders*), the state of Georgia had a system where the vote of each citizen counted for less and less as the population of his or her county increased. In another (*Moore v. Ogilvie*), the residents of smaller counties in Illinois were able to form a new party to elect candidates, something residents of larger counties could not do. Another (*Reynolds v. Sims*) was an apportionment case, and the fourth (*Harper v. Virginia*) involved the payment of a poll tax as a qualification for voting. If a first-year law student ever cited completely inapplicable authority like this, any thoughtful professor would encourage him not to waste two more years trying to become a lawyer. As Yale law professor Akhil Reed Amar noted, the five conservative Justices "failed to cite a single case that, on its facts, comes close to supporting its analysis and result."[110]

Bugliosi's characterization of these cases as some sort of fig leaf to cover a partisan decision fit with his overall attack on the motives of the High Court. Of course, there are always factual differences between precedents and the cases that cite them, so the issue becomes one of determining which facts, and the principles and holdings derived from them, are critical and which are unimportant.

Part of the difficulty is that the majority did too little to explain the connection between the precedents it cited and the application it made of them to the *Bush* case. As Michael Abramowicz and Maxwell Stearns noted:

> Although the Court alludes to its "one person, one vote" jurisprudence, it offers no analysis of any of the cases developing that rule. Instead, the majority simply states: "The question before us . . . is whether the recount procedures the Florida Supreme Court has adopted are consistent with its obligation to avoid arbitrary and disparate treatment of the members of its electorate." Most notably, the majority did not explain the origin of its "arbitrary and disparate treatment" approach.[111]

The failure of the per curiam to better explain the connection between the precedents it cites and its reasoning provides grounds for complaint. This is particularly true where the Court seems to be going beyond the precedents, as Abramowicz and Stearns noted, in its novel "arbitrary and disparate treatment" standard, which appears in no Supreme Court cases involving equal protection.[112]

Tribe suggested that the majority mischaracterized the precedents in order to draw out the standard it applied in this case. He noted that "[t]he Court cited *Gray v. Sanders* for the proposition that the Equal Protection Clause forbids 'arbitrary and disparate treatment of voters in [a state's] different counties,'" and admitted that "*Gray* did involve disparate treatment of urban and rural residents." However, he added, "it did not involve arbitrary treatment. Indeed, the state legislature had in place a careful plan which had the effect of diluting the votes of urban residents."[113] Tribe's description of a careful plan suggested that the errant authority in that case was being the opposite of arbitrary in its distinctions between urban and rural residents; it was being strategic in favoring the latter over the former.

Turning to the second case, Tribe noted that "[t]he Court also quoted *Moore v. Ogilvie* for the proposition that granting 'one group . . . greater voting strength than another is hostile to the one man, one vote basis of our representative government.'" Tribe admitted that "[i]n *Moore,* while the Court did describe the law at issue as 'arbitrary,'" it also found that it "discriminates against the residents of the populous counties of the State in favor of rural sections."[114] Tribe's description of the effects of the law implies a purpose (to favor rural voters), which, in turn, challenges the term *arbitrary* through a purpose-agency relationship (whereby a given purpose implies an agency devised to meet that purpose).

Tribe's characterization of both cases drew attention to purpose, urging that "in each case the law at issue targeted a specific group—urban voters—for disparate treatment," while *Bush v. Gore* "did not single out any class for disparate treatment."[115] He turned to the recount acts in question to verify this, noting that "[n]othing in the record indicated that the Florida Legislature, the state judiciary, or the county recount teams intended to discriminate against any class, suspect or otherwise."[116] Tribe offered a classic refutation of a precedent's value: highlight the most important element of the precedent (in this case, the discriminatory purpose), show that the case in question lacked that element, and conclude that it is inapplicable. Thus, while the per curiam emphasized the arbitrariness (or purposelessness) of the act (an element of agency and perhaps attitude), Tribe made purpose primary and even read back into agency a sense of means adapted to ends (with the careful plan from *Gray* and the implied control in *Moore*).

Dworkin argued in a similar vein, though he did not directly address purpose but rather its cousin, effect. An effect may be something sought, the ultimate end of someone's purpose, or it may simply be a byproduct of a scene within which causal relations yield outcomes. It is more tangible than purpose, in that it is theoretically measurable, whereas purpose must be derived from statements or actions that are signs of intent. In the precedent cases, Dworkin notes, the effect is a harm: "The five conservative justices cited a variety of earlier decisions in an attempt to justify their equal protection claim in *Bush v. Gore*, but in every one of these the plaintiffs had been harmed."[117] Dworkin illustrated this harm with the *Reynolds* case, noting that it involved a denial of equal protection because the state "create[d] voting districts with more people in some districts than in others [causing] those who live in more populous districts [to] suffer a greater dilution of their votes."[118]

Epstein examined the individual precedents relied on by the per curiam and found each distinguishable from *Bush*. In the *Harper* precedent, for example, he found a "suspect" classification by the state triggered scrutiny of state law there, adding:

> *Harper* has scant relevance to the probity of Florida's recount procedures. It is one thing to find a serious affront to equal protection from a wealth test that is uniform in its application [i.e., because everyone had to pay the same $1.50] but disparate in its impact [i.e., because poor people are denied the franchise]. It is quite another to find an equal protection violation in a process that does not take into account wealth (or for that matter, race) in deciding what counts as a valid vote. In a word, the Florida scheme is devoid of any suspect classification needed to trigger the equal protection analysis.[119]

Recall that the per curiam had tried to identify various groups of differentially treated voters: overvoters (whose votes were not to be recounted) versus undervoters; voters in counties using one recount substandard versus those in counties using a different one; and voters in Gore's early recount counties (where full recounts were made) versus those in the rest of the state. None of these groups, Epstein noted, is "suspect."

Epstein next turned to *Reynolds*, which he found "far afield":

> That case dealt with the refusal of state legislatures to reapportion themselves, in ways that perpetuated massive differences in the size of legislative

districts. The obvious imbalance is that all individuals who reside in populous counties systematically have much less political influence than their peers who reside in less populous counties. It is possible therefore to identify unambiguously the winners and losers from the state practice, and to demand in principle at least some justification for imbalances consciously perpetuated by the refusal of the dominant legislative coalition to initiate electoral reforms that would necessarily cut into its own power.[120]

Here Epstein moved from means (suspect classifications) to purpose, emphasizing that an entrenched power base (particular agents—the dominant legislative coalition) was seeking to hold onto its power through a means that favored its voting base, namely, less populous counties. Lest the lesson be missed, Epstein explained that the Florida recount involved "no conscious form of ex ante discrimination. From the ex ante perspective no one can identify the determinate class of individuals who benefit from or are burdened by the choice of this or that standard for counting ballots. It is not as though one standard was used for Gore voters and another for Bush voters."[121]

Epstein's final point drove home the connection he sought between the precedents and the current case, which most scholars danced around: Was there an identifiable, invidious purpose for conducting the recount in the way it was conducted? Here we find a cautious discourse of civil rights precedents reflected in scholars' careful descriptions of what these precedents involved—at least, until the issue is brought down to fundamental grammatical principles at work. *Suspect classification* is a term describing a means often connected to a racist purpose.[122] It suggests, though does not explicitly state, "We believe that a white majority is using this classification for the purpose of limiting the power of minorities."[123] Epstein's example from *Reynolds* was more explicit, revealing a political purpose in favoring less populous counties. Although constitutional scholars might violate the letter of constitutional law if they find purpose central to these cases (when the Supreme Court precedents do not explicitly endorse a finding of purpose), at the very least, purpose lurks in the background, shedding light on our understanding of what constitutes a troubling classification.[124]

Michelman went beyond Epstein's consideration of the cases cited by the High Court to provide an overall summary of the Court's jurisprudence on such equal protection issues:

So far as I am aware, in no case prior to *Bush v. Gore* has the Court recognized a claim to unequal protection of voting rights in which there was on the state's part no explicit or implicit act of what the jargon calls "classification"—that is, ex ante division of a population of actual or would-be voters into groups (defined by race, party, place of residence, wealth, or financial capability) to whose members the state accords differentially advantageous treatment within the general voting scheme.[125]

Michelman's construction of voting rights precedents encompassed the four cases cited by the per curiam (which involved the identified groups he mentioned) and highlighted the novelty of the Supreme Court decision, which is to say it was unprecedented and does not rest upon *Reynolds* or the other cases cited. The precedents, he averred, require a well-developed act: the state must be the agent that acts, explicitly or implicitly, to classify identifiable groups of voters (the means) to provide advantageous treatment of one group over another (the purpose). This construction adequately describes the four civil rights precedents, where voters in more populous counties were disadvantaged when compared with those in less populous counties (*Gray, Moore,* and *Reynolds*) or poor voters who had trouble paying the poll tax were disadvantaged when compared to wealthier voters (*Harper*).

Shane did not try to summarize all equal protection cases but instead contrasted *Bush v. Gore* with "typical equal protection cases," insisting that it

> does not exhibit any obvious link between a challenged classification or criterion for treatment and any group's systematic advantage or disadvantage. The majority opinion identifies three sources of differentiation in the treatment of voters by different counties: differential standards for evaluating contested ballots, differences between recounts limited to undervotes and recounts that reexamined all of the ballots cast, and differences between tabulations based on partial recounts versus tabulations based on completed recounts. Legally speaking, these may be phenomena worth noting, but it is hard to predict who will be hurt by them. There was no allegation that any amounted to an intentionally invidious discriminatory practice—the kind of practice that the Court normally requires before it elevates the intensity of its constitutional scrutiny of state practices under the Equal Protection Clause.[126]

Here a lack of intent on the state court's part is derived from a lack of knowledge within a scene where differential treatment of voters does not allow predictions regarding alleged harms. Shane worked from the typical or normal case in insisting that a discriminatory purpose must be found. He added that any differences in the vote counting process were not intentional but "were the by-product of a feature of state governance long treated as reasonable, namely, state deference to county administrative discretion in the implementation of statewide administrative mandates."[127] That is, the act of deference itself yielded the outcome, not a discriminatory purpose.

Sunstein illustrated the state of the law with a hypothetical case of a state attorney general candidate who complains to a federal court about differential vote-counting standards, insisting that the court would likely say:

> "No previous decision of any court supports the view that the Constitution requires uniformity in methods for ascertaining the will of the voter. There is no violation here of the principle of one-person, one-vote. Nor is there any sign of discrimination against poor people or members of any identifiable group. There is no demonstration of fraud or favoritism or self-dealing. In the absence of such evidence, varying local standards, chosen reasonably and in good faith by local officials, do not give rise to a violation of the federal Constitution. In addition, a finding of an equal protection violation would entangle federal courts in what has, for many decades, been seen as a matter for state and local government."[128]

In giving voice to the federal court in this hypothetical case, Sunstein portrayed an act that illustrates the state of the law and the usual reluctance of federal courts to involve themselves in such processes. This enactment features a cautious judicial agent, drawing upon well-established rules, and rejecting the hypothetical candidate's plea—a model offered for the Supreme Court, no doubt.

Issacharoff did not try to infer the rule of law from the Warren Court precedents cited by the per curiam, but he undermined their value as precedents and, thereby, reframed the Court's action in citing them: "the Court revived the fundamental rights line of cases from the 1960s, most notably *Reynolds* and *Harper v Virginia Board of Elections.*"[129] They needed revival, he argued, because their line of cases "had essentially collapsed of its own weight decades ago."[130] That collapse came, he argued, from an "unsuccessful attempt to extend fundamental rights claims to everything from privacy to wealth distinctions." Eventually, he argued, "the fundamental rights line of cases succumbed to the emergence of intent-based equal protection review after *Washington v Davis.*"[131] A collapsed line of cases that succumbed to another standard suggests an old agency that has outlived its usefulness. Although he did not claim that these cases had been overruled, he did suggest that newer cases had taken the law they represented in new directions. Indeed, Issacharoff's characterization of the *Bush* court's citation of these cases as a revival draws attention to their age and the fact that more recent precedents were not relied upon by the Court—even precedents that might have drawn on *Reynolds* and the other civil rights cases, applying them to more recent problems.

Issacharoff's construction of the *Washington* precedent is strong. The case involved African-American candidates for police positions in Washington, D.C., who, it was alleged, had been discriminated against by a written test of verbal skills which they failed more often than their white counterparts. The Circuit Court found a constitutional violation, and the Supreme Court reversed, clarifying equal protection in both the Fifth and Fourteenth Amendments:

> The central purpose of the Equal Protection Clause of the Fourteenth Amendment is the prevention of official conduct discriminating on the basis of race. It is also true that the Due Process Clause of the Fifth Amendment contains an equal protection component prohibiting the United States from invidiously discriminating between individuals or groups. *Bolling* v. *Sharpe,* 347 U.S. 497 (1954). But our cases have not embraced the proposition that a law or other official act, without regard to whether it reflects a racially discriminatory purpose, is unconstitutional *solely* because it has a racially disproportionate impact.[132]

By extension, equal protection claims that indicate "disproportionate impacts" on overvoters versus undervoters, voters in early recount counties versus other counties, and voters in different counties (employing different subsidiary standards) presumably should demonstrate that the state was invidiously discriminating between these groups.

The most damning characterizations of the Court's use of equal protection precedents did not simply suggest that earlier cases were distinguishable in requiring an intent to discriminate but that recent rulings made by the conservative justices themselves demanded a showing of individualized harm. For example, Dworkin quoted the 1995 Supreme Court case of *U.S. v. Hays,* which rejected an equal protection claim in insisting: "Appellees point us to no authority for the proposition that an equal protection challenge may go forward in federal court absent the showing of individualized harm, and we decline appellees' invitation to approve that proposition in this litigation."[133] That opinion, he noted, was supported by "Scalia and the other majority justices."[134] Indeed, all five per curiam justices, as well as Souter and Breyer, supported the opinion, written by Justice O'Connor. Dworkin's construction highlights an apparent inconsistency and an embarrassment: that the agents of this earlier act employed an agency (the harm standard) which they now appear to ignore; rendering the acts inconsistent, the agents inconsistent, and the control of this ruling (the agency to be followed) ineffectual. This construction builds upon Dworkin's earlier characterization of the Florida recount standard as harming no one in particular. It diminishes the stature of these "inconsistent" justices to whom Court defenders would have us defer in the judgment of what the law demands. Such inconsistency would raise the specter of judicial purpose, leading critics to wonder at the exception to the equal protection rule made by these conservative justices. That is, if the means did not control the act, perhaps a political purpose did.

Communication scholars Theodore Prosise and Craig Smith added more precedents to the list, noting that Rehnquist joined the decision requiring a finding of invidious discrimination in *Washington v. Davis*. After *Bush v. Gore*, Prosise and Smith argued, the majority returned to *Washington*'s understanding of the equal protection standard. For example, they noted that in the 2001 case of *Board of Trustees of the University of Alabama et al. v. Patricia Garrett et al.*, "Justice Kennedy, in his concurring opinion, wrote: 'the failure of a state to revise policies now seen as incorrect' fails to 'constitute the purposeful and intentional action required to make out a violation of the equal protection clause.'"[135] Indeed, Kennedy cited *Washington* as his precedent for this position, reaffirming what the Court seemed to have forgotten in *Bush*.

Defenders of the High Court used two strategies, either bolstering the precedents or recasting the *Bush* case in a way that allowed the use of a more amenable standard. Lund, for example, used the bolstering strategy, refusing to moderate his judgments in insisting that the Court was relying on "well-known and long-established case law."[136] As acts, Lund suggested, they are old and respectable, but that does not mean they have not been overturned. Indeed, Lund addressed one contrary precedent cited by other scholars, stating in an endnote: "Commentators who assume that the 'discriminatory purpose' requirement of *Washington v. Davis*, 426 U.S. 229 (1976) is applicable in this area are mistaken. See, e.g., Shane, supra note 2."[137]

Lund's reference to Shane's essay in the *Florida State University Law Review* deferred the argument to another who presumably had made it before, providing a scholarly division of labor.[138] His offering of Shane as an example of such an argument against the applicability of the discriminatory purpose requirement of the *Washington* case, implied that others had

made the argument as well (Shane being merely one example of this argument). Thus, Lund constructed Shane's essay as a particular kind of act. He
used this construction of one scholar's action to shed light on the law of
equal protection which, in turn, shed light on the U.S. Supreme Court's actions in the *Bush* case. The specific implication is that *Washington*'s "invidious discrimination" requirement is the wrong standard for judging this
equal protection case, and the *Bush* Court ruled correctly in applying equal
protection where no discrimination was found.

Lund's construction of Shane was seriously misleading, however. Lund
implied that Shane found the *Washington* standard inapplicable to *Bush* because some other equal protection standard was more appropriate. But
Shane's essay argued that *Bush* was not really an equal protection case at
all (in part because the *Washington* standard was not applicable in light of
the facts of the case); instead, he suggested that it involved a due process
issue.

Shane mentioned the *Washington* case only twice, and both times in end
notes. The first reference was a description of the majority's finding in
Bush: "The majority purported to address an equal protection problem in
Bush v. Gore, although none of the practices being challenged amounted,
under anyone's account, to a form of explicit or otherwise intentional discrimination against Bush voters—the sort of harm typically addressed
through an equal protection rubric."[139] In another statement that referred
to the *Washington* case, Shane insisted: "There was no allegation that any
[of the actions under scrutiny in the case] amounted to an intentionally invidious discriminatory practice—the kind of practice that the Court normally requires before it elevates the intensity of its constitutional scrutiny
of state practices under the Equal Protection Clause."[140] Thus, while Lund
implied that the *Washington* standard was the *wrong equal protection standard*
to apply to *Bush v. Gore,* Shane argued that *equal protection itself* was the
wrong approach to judging the Florida case and that the requirement of intentionally invidious discrimination had not been met in the *Bush* case.
Shane's emphasis on the per curiam "purport[ing] to address an equal protection problem" and on its deviation from "the kind of practice that the
Court normally requires" in such cases clearly indicated that he believed
the equal protection standard applied by the Court was wrong, contrary to
Lund's suggestion that Shane found the discrimination-based standard itself wrong.

Lund did admit that *"Bush v. Gore* did not involve the application of a
preexisting rule that systematically discriminated against an identifiable

class of voters, such as those residing in more sparsely populated jurisdictions [as in the *Gray, Moore,* and *Reynolds* cases cited by the per curiam]. But," he insisted, "nothing in the rationale underlying the vote dilution cases limits it to such cases."[141] To support this extension, he cited a 1983 case for the proposition that "[u]nconstitutional vote dilution has been found, for example, where there is no systematic discrimination against a class of voters with shared political interests."[142] Technically, this description is accurate. The *act* did involve unconstitutional vote dilution with no systematic discrimination. However, the cited case, *Karcher v. Daggett,* was not decided on equal protection grounds but rather on an interpretation of Article I, section 2, of the U.S. Constitution—a different agency. As the majority opinion stated: "The question presented by this appeal is whether an apportionment plan for congressional districts satisfies Art. I, § 2, of the Constitution without need for further justification if the population of the largest district is less than one percent greater than the population of the smallest district."[143] Only Justice Stevens's lone concurring opinion invoked equal protection.[144] Because the *Bush* case concerned standards developed under an equal protection analysis, Lund's glossing over of this agency difference is problematic. Standards for providing equal protection to citizens and for meeting the requirements of Article I may justifiably be different, and they certainly have developed through different lines of precedents. Thus, the *Karcher* precedent has limited value for informing about whether the *Bush* Court followed the law.

Lund drew on another precedent to support an even more curious argument. Referring to the per curiam reminder that the Constitution forbids "sophisticated as well as simpleminded modes of discrimination," Lund asserted that "'sophisticated' modes of discrimination include those that are unintentionally discriminatory."[145] The per curiam construction seems to stress a purpose-agency relationship, whereby the character of the agency (be it simple-minded or sophisticated) is secondary to the purpose that drives that agency (discrimination); both means are problematic if the purpose is discriminatory. Lund made purposelessness (unintended discrimination) an agency of sophistication. Purpose, which previously had driven the agency (as clever discriminators discovered sneaky ways to meet their purposes), dropped out of the equation for Lund. To support this odd claim, Lund cited a 1974 U.S. Supreme Court case from New York in which

> state law permitted absentee voting only by those who were absent from their county of residence on election day. When applied to persons in jail, it had the odd and unforeseen effect of discriminating between those who

were jailed in their county of residence and those who were jailed elsewhere. Without even suggesting that the legislature's intent was relevant,
the Court held that this application of the statute violated equal
protection.[146]

Two things are notable about this case's relevance to Lund's "sophisticated,
unintentional discrimination": First, there is a notable lack of sophistication
in a law that merely leaves out a group in its absentee voting provisions.
Obviously, because inmates housed outside their county of residence could
vote, this was not a sneaky way to discriminate against prisoners in general; rather, it appears to be an oversight. Second, Lund failed to mention
that an identifiable class was involved in this case: prisoners housed in
their own counties. Perhaps because this cut against his previous arguments about identifiable groups being unnecessary to the application of
equal protection, he ignored that element.

Lund did raise an issue that others would address more directly concerning the possibility of an equal protection problem where no invidious
discriminatory intent is evident. This approach seeks a more amenable
standard for equal protection's application. Understanding this issue requires a bit of legal context. Equal protection law developed largely to protect minorities from majority discrimination (as one would assume, with
the Fourteenth Amendment passed to protect recently freed slaves from
state discrimination). At least since the 1938 case of *U.S. v. Carolene Products
Co.*, the Supreme Court has suggested that there are suspect classifications
that should raise flags for those determining whether a state has treated
certain groups of its citizens equally.[147] Suspect classifications made by a
state (such as race) and classifications impinging on fundamental constitutional rights, are given "strict scrutiny" from courts seeking to determine
their constitutionality, requiring that governmental actions be closely related to a compelling government interest. *Washington v. Davis* added a requirement to strict scrutiny that the government's purpose be assessed to
see if discrimination is intentional or merely incidental.[148]

Before the development of strict scrutiny, and since then in cases not involving suspect classifications or fundamental rights, courts generally used
a "rational" test that applied ordinary scrutiny, considering whether legislative means are reasonably related to some appropriate legislative ends. As
Gerald Gunther described the test: "A minimal 'fit' or 'congruence' must
exist between the classifying means and the legislative ends."[149] Under the
rational test, where the government enjoys presumption, most legislation
was deemed constitutional; under strict scrutiny, where the government

carries the burden of proof, many legislative acts have been struck down (though less often than before the *Washington* intentional discrimination requirement). These two standards both have been applied in equal protection cases, where, Mark Tushnet noted, "one assesses purported justifications by invoking either rational-basis review or strict scrutiny."[150] Scholars have turned to one standard or the other to explain the *Bush* decision, Tushnet suggested, because

> [t]he U.S. Supreme Court waffled on the standard it applied. In one paragraph, it characterized the right to vote as "fundamental," which would imply that only the strongest justifications could be provided for disparate treatment. Yet, in the next paragraph, the Court suggested that Florida's procedures were "arbitrary," a term associated with rational-basis review.[151]

This lengthy prelude explains a second avenue that defenders of the *Bush* majority have taken: the rational test route. As Weinberg reported:

> My colleague, Ernie Young, tells me that he believes the *Bush v. Gore* Court found the recount so irrational that it was not necessary to find it intentionally discriminatory as well. But he does not argue that *Bush v. Gore* should be read as a due process case. Rather, he relies on *Shaw v. Reno*, 509 U.S. 630, 658 (1993), to furnish a precedent for rational basis review of an equal protection voting rights claim.[152]

Shaw had rejected a race-conscious redistricting effort that sought to increase minority representation. The conservative Court, according to this report of Young's position, did not need to find intentional discrimination (as expected after *Washington*) but relied on the rational test alone. Ironically, the rational test gives more leeway to state agencies (such as the Florida Supreme Court) by shifting the burden of proving an unconstitutional purpose to others; but, for a Supreme Court that cannot or will not attribute an intent to discriminate against voters whose ballots are being recounted, this test actually may prove easier to apply in striking down the Florida court's action.

Weinberg, who reported this position of her colleague, quickly rejected it by reconstructing *Shaw:*

> To be sure, in *Shaw v. Reno* the Court held that a gerrymandered district was so irrational as to be inexplicable except as an intentional racial separation. No further scrutiny was necessary. But *Shaw* was not about the unintended consequences of traditional American voting practices and standards. Rather, *Shaw*, in effect, held that that gerrymander was so extreme as to support an inference of intentional discrimination. Nothing in *Shaw* changes

the position that it is invidious discrimination that is actionable under the Equal Protection Clause. Human blundering is not. That is a main reason why commentators have found the Court's equal protection rationale in *Bush v. Gore* to be unprecedented.[153]

Once again, the terministic battle has shifted away from *Bush*—in this case, as a means to criticize *Bush*—reconstructing a colleague's argument about a rational test by reconstructing a precedent case relied on to support that test's applicability. The reconstruction turns on agency (how the Court came to reject the redistricting plan—by inferring intentional discrimination) to shape the act in a different way (through an agency-act relationship), making *Shaw* a case that continues to support *Washington*'s intent requirement rather than supporting the "rational" test that might justify the *Bush* decision. Weinberg bolstered her own position by referring to commentators who also believed *Bush* was unprecedented, naming Epstein and Michelman particularly,[154] two scholars whose rejection of precedents cited by the per curiam already has been noted.

McConnell relied on yet another precedent to argue that a rational test may be sufficient and, further, that discrimination against a particular group is unnecessary:

> It may be true that the Equal Protection Clause typically protects against discrimination against identifiable groups, but as recently as last year, the Court summarily affirmed the principle that it also protects against "irrational and wholly arbitrary" state action, even where the plaintiff does not allege that the unequal treatment was on account of "membership in a class or group."[155]

As in other constructions of the equal protection standard, McConnell relied on a reference to the case alone, rather than a detailed reconstruction of the Court's action, suggesting clarity where there was actually ambiguity.

McConnell used two strategic constructions here. One emphasized that in the cited case, the plaintiff did not allege that the unequal treatment was on account of membership in a class or group. Although the plaintiff did not make this allegation, the Court in *Village of Willowbrook v. Olech* recognized Olech as "a class of one" and took pains to "note that the complaint in this case could be read to allege a class of five."[156] A second construction emphasized the irrational and wholly arbitrary nature of the state action in this case, which, indeed, was recognized by the Court. What McConnell did not mention was the Court's recognition "that the Village *intentionally* demanded a 33-foot easement as a condition of connecting her [Olech's] property to the municipal water supply where the Village required only a 15-foot easement from other similarly situated property owners."[157] Thus, under McConnell's brief rendition, the *Willowbrook* precedent appears to allow cases involving irrational and arbitrary acts against individuals not recognized as classes. As in Lund's construction, the agency of discrimination (irrational and arbitrary) is paramount, and purpose is eliminated (by ignoring intention and ignoring a class against whom intention might be aimed). A more accurate construction of that precedent recognizes the Court as allowing an equal protection claim against small classes of people (but classes, nonetheless) that are intentionally treated in an irrational and arbitrary manner, bringing purpose back into the standard.

Ironically, a third strategy for urging that the Court was following the law came from a Court critic, Karlan, who both bolstered precedents and located a more amenable standard. She admitted: "Unfortunately for equal protection law, *Bush v. Gore* is not an aberration. Rather, it is yet another manifestation of the newest model of equal protection, a model laid out in the Court's decisions regarding race-conscious redistricting and Congress's power to enforce the Fourteenth Amendment."[158]

Karlan supported this contention primarily with *Shaw v. Reno*, which Weinberg had rejected as allowing an inference of intentional discrimination because of its radical gerrymandering (the purpose deriving from the agency). Karlan quoted the *Shaw* Court's position:

[A] plaintiff challenging a reapportionment statute under the Equal Protection Clause may state a claim by alleging that the legislation, though race-neutral on its face, rationally cannot be understood as anything other than an effort to separate voters into different districts on the basis of race, and that the separation lacks sufficient justification.[159]

Given this position, Karlan insisted that "[p]laintiffs in *Shaw* cases need not prove either that they were denied the right to vote or that their votes were diluted. In fact, despite the Court's reliance on prior vote dilution and disenfranchisement decisions, the real character of a *Shaw* case is not a claim about voting rights at all."[160]

Karlan was straining against two terministic constructions that threaten her novel reading. First, the quoted section appears to derive illegitimate action from the means, with the effort to separate voters into different districts on the basis of race as the act the justices found troubling, derived from a legislative agency that was only race-neutral on its face (the character of the action determined by a race-based agency which only appeared race-neutral). The second terministic challenge Karlan faced was the *Shaw* Court's reliance on prior vote dilution and disenfranchisement decisions, suggesting that the agency of those precedent cases was the agency in these cases. Karlan ignored the Court's stated reliance on these precedents, which implied, effectively, "This is how we decided the earlier cases, and this is how we are deciding the present case" (following the legal agency, as judges seek to do).

Karlan's reconstruction of Supreme Court motives reflects the painstaking work of legal scholars faced with poorly written legal opinions, seeking to piece together into a coherent doctrine—or at least a predictable direction—the actions of our highest court. In the *Bush* case, where the Court appears to have created a Frankenstein mixing of the strict scrutiny and the rational basis tests, Karlan strained to fit the Court within a new, third line of cases that requires neither the intent of the strict scrutiny test nor the minimal test of fit between Florida law and the recount's purposes. Missing from this construction is the Court's own reference to this new line. *Shaw* is not cited in the *Bush* case. The Court does not mention "structural" tests. So, scholars like Karlan read between the lines to see what the Court was really doing and to predict what it may do in the future.[161]

All of this complex reconstruction was too much for Heather Gerken, who reminded her colleagues that "the Court has not yet explicitly accepted scholars' invitation to think of democracy in structural terms, and the [*Bush*] opinion itself offers no hint that it is taking a structural view."[162] To support this claim, she offered a comparison between *Bush v. Gore*, which "discuss[es] injury in terms of [the] individual right to vote" and an explicitly structural argument by Justice Breyer in *Nixon v. Shrink Missouri Government PAC et al.*, where he "suggest[s] that campaign finance doctrine should be recast as a principle 'to protect the integrity of the electoral process—the means through which a free society democratically translates political speech into concrete governmental action.'"[163] No language similar to Breyer's is found in *Bush v. Gore*, so *Bush v. Gore* really is not about structural issues, she insisted.

A great deal of energy was expended by scholars (though not so much by the High Court) in reconstructing the equal protection precedents in this case. If those precedents supported the Supreme Court's conclusion that Florida's failure to specify subsidiary standards for recounting ballots violated the Constitution, then the per curiam could be said to be following the law and the state supreme court could be criticized for failing to do so. While most *Bush* critics—and even some defenders—dismissed the

Warren-era precedents cited by the majority as inapplicable, Lund attempted a simple characterization of the cases as "well-known and long-established." Such minimal verbal work could not overcome the better-developed constructions of critics who found the civil-rights-era cases involved distinct, identifiable groups who were discriminated against for clear political purposes (specifically, to maintain the status quo in power relations) and suffered harm as a result. Even Epstein, who supported the outcome of *Bush v. Gore,* noted that the voters identified by the Court as suffering harm (e.g., overvoters) did not constitute a suspect class or a group that clearly would suffer harm.

Then there was the problem of the uncited precedents, which explained where the law of equal protection had moved since the Warren years. Especially notable is *Washington v. Davis,* an early case which Rehnquist joined, which established a standard for equal protection judgments that required a showing of intentional invidious discrimination. Because the per curiam did not assert or find that the Florida Court (or the legislature that wrote the voter intent standard) was intending to discriminate against anyone, the *Bush* ruling seems to flout this precedent. Indeed, cases cited by critics suggest that the members of the conservative majority themselves supported the *Washington* standard, both before and after *Bush.* Lund's assurance that another scholar had undermined the *Washington* case's application was misleading. His reliance on *Karcher v. Daggett* also proved a dead end. And his attempt to construct unintended discrimination as "sophisticated" gave up too much in the way of purpose.

The only reconstructive strategy left for Court defenders was to suggest that there were yet newer precedents that allowed a different standard to be applied to *Bush. Shaw v. Reno* was invoked to support this alternative approach, first through a simple rational test. However, Weinberg showed that the Court could simply infer intentional discrimination from the extreme gerrymandering of the state legislature in that case and avoid this new test. More contested is the idea that *Shaw* supports a third, "structural" approach to equal protection, especially coming as it does from a Court critic. If the High Court is following this line, it certainly did not invoke it in *Bush v. Gore,* and, as Gerken showed, it probably has not bought into the idea elsewhere, either.

Ultimately, the precedents cited by the per curiam are not explained well enough to make it clear that existing law was being followed here. Indeed, further examination seems to suggest that they are poor precedents for the kind of action the Court took. And if the Court was following some version of structural equal protection identified by Karlan, it has given little indication of that, failing either to cite *Shaw* or its progeny or to use the language of structural equal protection.

The Original Vote Count

Even if critics of the per curiam decision had been willing to concede that the equal protection precedents might somehow be construed to support the Court's finding, they would not have conceded to the High Court's focus on problems with the recount alone in light of seemingly more significant problems with the original count. The Court had made an agency-act claim that, essentially, "The law says that treating ballots differently is wrong, and we are applying that law." However, critics pointed out that the Court was applying this agency inconsistently, ignoring a more serious case of treating ballots differently, notably in allowing the use of different voting systems (e.g., optical-scan versus punchcard balloting systems) which led to significant differences in the number of rejected ballots and hurt identifiable groups.

Critics had an advantage in constructing this sense of inconsistency, because the majority conceded a problem in the election scene: "that punch card balloting machines can produce an unfortunate number of ballots which are not punched in a clean, complete way by the voter."[164] Critics elaborated on this unfortunate number and contrasted it with the number of rejected ballots in counties using more advanced technologies, piling up statistics to sharpen the picture of this troublesome scene. Klarman cited studies showing "that undervotes were five times more likely in Florida counties using punch-card ballots than in those using more modern, optical-scan ballots."[165] Sunstein clarified that comparison, noting rejection rates of 15 ballots per 1000 for punchcard ballots, versus 3 ballots per 1000 for optical scan ballots.[166]

Mark Levine, an attorney whose construction of the Supreme Court's decision in a question-and-answer dialogue was e-mailed and forwarded to thousands of readers around the world, sharpened the distinction between the two trouble spots in the scene—one embraced by the majority and the other dismissed by it—to highlight the inconsistency:

> The problem was neither the butterfly ballot nor the 3% of Democrats (largely African-American) disenfranchised. The problem is that somewhat less than .005% of the ballots may have been determined under slightly different standards because judges sworn to uphold the law and doing their

best to accomplish the legislative mandate of "clear intent of the voter" may have a slightly different opinion about the voter's intent.[167]

Levine's statistical descriptions defined comparative elements of the problematic scene to which the per curiam was a response, adding a characterization of law-bound judges hard at work to suggest how small a problem the Court addressed and how large a problem it ignored, even though both problems were part of the same scene containing its judicial action.

Issacharoff reminded readers of the standard the Court was applying in highlighting this inconsistency:

> The claimed wrong in Florida, the disparity in the standards for counting contested ballots, pales before other disparities in access to a meaningful vote, most notably the well-documented failure of voting machines used in one part, but not in another, of many states, Florida included. That clearly would fall under the Court's new injunction that states have an obligation "to avoid arbitrary and disparate treatment of the members" of the electorate.[168]

Here, the Court's new legal agency was characterized scenically as encompassing actions that fall under its control. If the state's use of different voting technologies amounted to arbitrary and disparate treatment of voters, this difference of treatment was problematic under the Court's own standard.

Not only did these differences represent disparate treatment of voters in counties employing different voting systems, but certain classes of voters were put at a disadvantage. And these were classes traditionally recognized by the Court in equal protection cases: African-Americans, the poor, and members of a particular political party (in this case, Democrats). Klarman noted, for example, that "county-to-county disparities . . . were correlated with race; heavily Black precincts across Florida were more likely to use antiquated voting equipment, which substantially increased the chances of ballots failing to register a vote in the presidential election."[169] Schwartz focused on the biggest comparative disparity:

> voters in Florida's Gadsden County had a sixty-eight times greater chance of having their votes invalidated than voters in adjoining Leon County. Gadsden County, which is Florida's only majority-black county, depended on unreliable voting technology, while Leon County, a majority-white county, benefited from state-of-the-art voting machines.[170]

Karlan also emphasized the "racially disparate impact" created by different voting technologies and suggested that "the newest equal protection

[established in *Bush*] vindicates the interests of middle-class, politically po-
tent voters, while ignoring the interests of the clause's original beneficiaries."[171] If *Bush* follows *Shaw*'s legal agency, Karlan urged, it does not follow
the equal protection clause's purposes (to benefit African-Americans).

Lani Guinier related the disparities to wealth: "The vast disparity from
county to county between the voting technology available to poor and rich
voters discourages many less-educated voters from even attempting to cast
a ballot. Yet this Court has not shown the same solicitude to assure uniform access to the ballot for the voters themselves."[172] Schwartz cited a
Miami Herald analysis of uncounted ballots which found that "ballots in
precincts with high poverty were discarded at a rate nearly double that of
better-off precincts."[173]

McConnell, a defender of the per curiam ruling, admitted that the differences in voting machines hurt Democrats:

> Every voting system has its flaws, but in ordinary cases the effects are ran-
> domly distributed. The problem in Florida arose because the optical scan-
> ning system is predominantly used in more Republican areas, while the
> punchcard system is predominantly used in more Democratic areas. Thus,
> the errors were not randomly distributed.[174]

McConnell endorsed the idea of having a uniform voting system through
the state, though he rejected the equal protection concerns raised by not
having them.

Because victims of this troubling scene were from classes of voters traditionally recognized in equal protection cases, the failure of the Supreme
Court to consider this larger and more traditional voting rights problem is
constructed as inexplicable. Karlan, who had suggested that *Shaw* could be
seen as a precedent for the Court's structural equal protection holding,
nonetheless condemned the Court's inconsistency: "A Court that believes
that the real problem in Florida was the disparities in the manual recount
standards, rather than the disparities in a voter's overall chance of casting a
ballot that is actually counted for the candidate for whom he intended to
vote, has strained at a gnat only to swallow an elephant."[175] Karlan's construction described the Court's act as denying an obvious problem while
easily finding a less obvious problem. Guinier added to Karlan's description
of perverse actions descriptions of perverse attitudes: "The Court's impa-
tience with nonuniform vote counting standards stands in marked contrast
to its tolerance of chaotic balloting mechanisms in the voting booth."[176]
The first scene involving nonuniform vote-counting standards made the

court impatient, while the chaotic balloting scene left it tolerant, the scene controlling attitude only in the former.

Sunstein turned the Court's passivity in ignoring the larger equal protection problem into positive, troubling action, urging that the *Bush* decision "might well have authorized equality problems as serious as those it prevented." As he explained, "the Court's decision, forbidding manual recounts, ensured that the relevant inequalities would not be corrected."[177]

Overall, critics painted a picture of the Supreme Court fiddling around with a minor equal protection problem while a much larger problem burned. They showed not only that significant, tangible harms were attributable to the state's decision to allow different counties to use different voting systems but that those harms were much more likely to hurt minorities, the poor, and Democrats. Furthermore, they suggested that not only did the Court ignore this larger problem, but in stopping the recounts, it prevented the problem from being ameliorated, actually creating more equal protection problems than it sought to cure.

While the per curiam opinion recognized the "unfortunate" discrepancy in the number of ballots rejected by the different voting systems, it never hinted that this represented a cognizable problem. It assured that "[a]fter the current counting, it is likely legislative bodies nationwide will examine ways to improve the mechanisms and machinery for voting,"[178] but it never suggested that they must address this problem. The closest the Court came to considering the issue involved a procedural dodge: "The question before the Court is not whether local entities, in the exercise of their expertise, may develop different systems for implementing elections."[179] The implication is that expertise, rather than some arbitrary action, guided the development of systems that yielded such different levels of accuracy.

Lund relied on characterization alone to carry his defense of the per curiam here:

> there may be latent forms of inequality associated with particular kinds of voting machines, or in the use of different kinds of machines in different counties. But it does not follow that such relatively minor and speculative inequality can permissibly be "corrected" with the kind of gross and palpable inequality that pervaded the Florida court's recount process.[180]

Lund did not explain why the statistically demonstrable differences in ballot rejection rates between counties using punchcard systems and those using optical-scan systems—differences recognized by the per curiam itself—are minor or speculative, though he assured his readers that what the county canvassing boards were doing was quite substantial.

Posner took a different defensive tack. He admitted that counties that chose to use punchcard technology "not only hurt Gore but hurt him through disenfranchising a disproportionate percentage of blacks who were eligible to vote."[181] This was partly because of technology that is harder to use and partly because of feedback given to voters at the precinct level. Wealthier counties used machines that spit back erroneous ballots to errant voters at the precinct level, providing an opportunity for revoting, while poorer counties typically centralized their ballot counting to save money. In the face of this difference, Posner still rejected equal protection concerns by insisting that "[t]he choice of voting technology and counting site cannot be attributed to deliberate racial discrimination or even to indirect discrimination, as might be inferred if the choice were correlated with literacy."[182] Although the per curiam obviously did not require intentional discrimination for its equal protection finding, Posner did. Posner can do so and maintain his own consistency (if not the Court's) since he rejected the per curiam's equal protection argument over the recounts as well, mounting his defense of the outcome elsewhere.

A novel argument defending the per curiam's failure to consider this larger equal protection concern came from McConnell, who insisted that "the Equal Protection Clause requires equality of treatment within a jurisdiction, but not between jurisdictions."[183] Because Florida law gives counties authority over elections, he asserted, "there is no constitutional problem if different counties adopt different voting systems."[184] He also insisted that there was no remedy for such a problem in any case—except for the radical solution of a revote—and that such concerns should have been raised before the election, when they could be addressed.[185]

McConnell attempted to support his claim that the law requires equality of treatment only within a jurisdiction by citing two 1970s cases involving school funding, and then he admitted that this holding was only "implicit," as he rejected the "ostensible explanation" in one of the cases.[186] In short, McConnell's construction of the law as excusing the Supreme Court's failure to consider this equal protection problem was weak. His remedy argument actually sidestepped the issue of whether or not equal protection is violated by the use of different voting systems. The *Bush* decision itself had a poor remedy (ending all recounts because of time), yet the Court reached a decision on the merits.

This must stand as one of the weakest aspects of the per curiam's equal protection argument. For even if we accepted the construction that this case was following the law of equal protection (as Karlan urged, left-handedly), the fact that greater equal protection concerns existed in the form of voting technologies with significantly different levels of reliability, and that those different technologies involved not only many more voters but voters from distinct groups—including groups traditionally protected under the Fourteenth Amendment—undermined the majority's construction of its own actions. Inconsistency in (1) the application of a legal agency (equal protection), (2) the agents who treated the concerns completely differently, and (3) the act of finding equal protection problems in the one case but not finding them in the other case undermined the sense that the Court was dealing fairly. The weak defenses of Lund's verbal characterization and McConnell's invocation of implicit law justifying the differential treatment were no match for the palpable descriptions of serious problems that the majority swallowed easily while straining at the gnat of recount discrepancies.

Overall, defenders of the equal protection ruling painted the recount as untethered by rules, subjective, and at the mercy of partisan, untrained counters. They found that the state court actively refused to lay down a more specific standard that would have limited subjectivity and partisanship. They relied on Warren-era precedents, rational-basis tests, or structural equal protection to ground the decision in the law. They had a more difficult time dismissing the equal protection concerns involving the voting machines, doing no better than the per curiam insistence that county officials exercise their expertise in deciding which voting technologies to buy. Many notable defenders of the outcome of *Bush v. Gore* nonetheless rejected the equal protection argument, including Posner, Yoo, Epstein, and Pildes.

The critics of the per curiam constructed an equal protection ruling perhaps explicable only by considering political motives. They suggested that the judges doing the recounting could apply common sense in discerning intent from ballots at least as easily as a jury discerns criminal intent from circumstantial evidence. And though partisans might be involved in the recounting, the system was set to check that partisanship through written objections, a balancing of Republican- and Democrat-dominated counties, and the ultimate judicial overseer, Judge Lewis. They noted that the recounters were following standards set down not by the Florida Supreme Court but by the Florida legislature and used in thirty-three other states. In refusing to set substandards for counting, the state court was acting deferentially and cautiously, avoiding the appearance of choosing a standard that might favor one or the other candidate. Court critics argued that the High Court was on weak legal grounds in finding an equal protection violation, because the most relevant precedents (which the conservative majority ignored) required a finding of invidious discrimination against identifiable groups (preferably, minority groups), while no coherent group (certainly not overvoters) was harmed by differential standards. Arguments that a rational test alone would find a violation were challenged by different voting scenes in different counties that might justify different recount standards, not to mention the policy of deferring such decisions to county officials with statutory authority to make them. And, finally, if the *Bush* majority was so concerned about equal protection, how could it ignore the unequal voting systems, whose impact was hundreds of times worse?

The Safe Harbor Deadline

The equal protection argument was less controversial than another determination that led to a refusal to restart the recounts. This was the "safe harbor deadline" argument that the High Court used to put an ultimate stopping date on recounts—December 12, 2000, the date the *Bush* decision was handed down.

Grammatically, constructions of the safe harbor argument were complex in implicating a number of interrelated acts. Logically, the interpretation begins with the safe harbor provision in federal law (3 U.S.C. § 5), which would provide an incentive to states to report votes early to ensure that Congress would not challenge a state's electoral slate when it counted votes in January. Next, in this case, come the acts (or omissions) of the Florida legislature in indicating when the vote tallies were due and what might justifiably be sacrificed to meet the deadline. The Florida Supreme Court, in turn, would interpret the Florida legislature's purposes in this respect, along with state constitutional considerations, to determine what Florida law said about this issue. Finally, the U.S. Supreme Court would interpret what the Florida Supreme Court said about this deadline. The High Court strung together these first three acts in its decision, concluding that "[t]he Supreme Court of Florida has said that the legislature intended the State's electors to 'participat[e] fully in the federal election process,' as provided in 3 U.S.C. § 5."[187] Holding this deadline as sacrosanct, the conservative majority insisted that recounts could not restart, since the safe harbor deadline would end two hours after it handed down their opinion.

Several other acts were implicated in this decision: (1) the Florida constitution, an enactment that reflected the state's values in weighing deadlines against other considerations; (2) the recount itself, where defenders would wonder whether any extension would have allowed a completion of the work; (3) the Supreme Court's actions in *Bush v. Palm Beach County Canvassing Board*, which some construed as influencing the state court's statements on the safe harbor deadline; (4) a possible restart to the recount; and even (5) the current Florida legislature's actions, which might have undermined any extension.

In discussing the 1887 Electoral Count Act passed by Congress, not a single scholar claimed that the December 12 deadline was mandatory. As Dworkin explained, "the safe harbor provision is not mandatory; it does not provide that a state loses its electoral votes if they are not submitted by December 12, but only that its votes, if submitted after that date, might conceivably be challenged in Congress, if reason can be found to challenge them."[188] He implied in another essay that December 18 might have been a more pertinent date, noting that "[r]esults certified to Congress after [December 12] but before December 18, the date on which the electoral college actually votes, might well have been perfectly valid, though they would not have been immune from a challenge in Congress."[189] Weinberg emphatically supported both of Dworkin's points:

> Nothing in Section 5 would require a state to resolve its election by December 12. Nothing in Section 5 would prohibit a state that has yet to resolve its election from proceeding in due course with a constitutional recount after December 12. Absent a controversy to be resolved by Congress, as long as Florida's electors were chosen by December 18—the date set for convening the electoral college in 2000—the votes of Florida's electors would be counted.[190]

Even defenders of *Bush v. Gore* endorsed Dworkin's and Weinberg's readings. McConnell stated that "[a]s a matter of federal law, the December 12 date is not a strict deadline, but merely a 'safe harbor' date insulating electors chosen by that date from congressional challenge."[191] Notably, Lund, the staunchest defender of the per curiam decision, called December 12 a "non-binding deadline," though he added that "federal law required that all presidential electors meet and cast their votes on December 18."[192]

Levine would go beyond statement and characterization to challenge the December 18 deadline, invoking an old (nonlegal) precedent in insisting that the final deadline was January 6 (when Congress convenes to count the votes), noting (as Justice Stevens had, in his *Bush* dissent) that in the 1960 presidential election, Hawaii turned in its electoral votes on January 4, 1961.[193] Here, he used an earlier act to enlarge the outside deadlines for turning in votes, suggesting not simply what the law says, but what has been done in practice.

Tribe took a different tack, reconstructing the 1887 act itself in questioning whether the safe harbor deadline could be enforced. He insisted that "concluding all election contests by that safe harbor date wouldn't in any event guarantee that Congress would honor the promise made by the 1887 Congress in the Safe Harbor Act." He argued that, legally, one Congress could not bind another; thus, the 1887 Congress could not tell the 2001 Congress that it must recognize those slates of electors turned in by states by December 12.[194]

Whether or not the federal statute mandated that votes be submitted by December 12, the Florida legislature might have wanted to adopt that deadline and could have made it part of the state's law to do so. But, as liberal and conservative commentators noted, the Florida legislature did not express its intent on this question through the means of statutes, laws, or rules. Klarman noted, "[t]he text of Florida election law does not say a word about the federal safe harbor provision."[195] Tribe went even further:

> You can read the Florida statutes backwards and forwards without finding the slightest clue that the state legislature ever decreed all recounts in a contested presidential election must stop by December 12. For that matter, nowhere does the legislature indicate that recounts must stop at any time before the electors meet to vote on December 18 or before Congress counts the votes on January 6.[196]

Despite the lack of legislation on the matter, many commentators inferred a legislative purpose to meet the deadline if possible. For example, McConnell noted: "No doubt the Florida legislature hoped to take advantage of that safe harbor, but it passed no statute embodying that intention."[197] Dworkin qualified that position: "Certainly the Florida legislature would wish to meet the December 12 deadline if it fairly could."[198] This qualification about the Florida legislature's purposes would become a bone of contention, since this legislative wish to meet the deadline would be balanced against competing wishes by those criticizing the safe harbor position of the per curiam.

Dworkin took pains to note that legislative intentions, as reflected in Florida law in 2000, were not to be understood as circumscribed by the current, Republican-dominated Florida legislature's intentions. Querying Florida law about the need to meet the safe harbor deadline, he insisted,

> asks not whether the present Florida legislature, dominated by Republicans who seemed anxious to deliver their state to Bush in any way possible, would make that choice [to meet the safe harbor deadline], but whether it would be justified by sound legal interpretation of existing Florida law, which cannot appeal to partisan political motives of that character.[199]

Indeed, Dworkin's lesson about proper interpretation of law was not ignored by any defenders of the *Bush* decision. However, Lund did use the intentions of the current Florida legislature to make a different argument. He warned that "the passing of the December 12 'safe harbor' deadline would virtually have assured intervention by the Florida legislature," and he insisted, "it is safe to assume that a slate of electors pledged to Bush would have been selected."[200] His point was that ignoring the safe harbor deadline would not have provided any advantage to Gore's team, in any case, and it would lead to a series of fractious political disputes that might pull the Supreme Court even deeper into a political quagmire. Thus did Lund resurrect legislative purpose as relevant to the safe harbor deadline, though admittedly not as a question of what the law in Florida was on the issue but rather what kind of workable solution might be wrought to end the controversy.

Now, even if the Florida legislature did not mandate that December 12 was a final deadline, the Florida Supreme Court might have interpreted it to say so. Indeed, this is where Lund hung his hat. He claimed that "the Florida Supreme Court had already concluded, as a matter of state law, that recounts had to be concluded by December 12."[201] To support this conclusion, Lund attempted to construct a Florida Supreme Court stating that this deadline was sacrosanct. For that, he turned to the state court's revised ruling in the *Palm Beach County Canvassing Board v. Harris* case:

> In that opinion, the Florida court had interpreted state law to allow the late filing of amended election returns by county officials in only two circumstances: where a late filing would preclude someone from exercising his rights under the statutory "contest" provisions, and where the late filing would "result in Florida voters not participating fully in the federal electoral process, as provided in 3 U.S.C. 5 [the safe harbor provision of federal law]."[202]

This account was strategically constructed to suggest that Florida law did not allow late filings that violated the safe harbor deadline. Lund left one important element out of this construction of the state court's conditions for rejecting late filings: an agent. Specifically, Lund failed to mention the role of the Department of Elections in the state court's construction. The referenced passages were taken from the Florida court opinion's explanation of what constitutes a "reasoned basis for the exercise of the Department's discretion to ignore amended returns"[203]—the court was, after all, trying to decide whether Secretary of State Katherine Harris could simply toss out late filings by appealing to the "shall" provision of the election code that mandated a particular deadline. Thus, it was not that Florida law said that late filings could never be accepted (as Lund implied); rather, the state court's interpretation of Florida law gave the Department of Elections a justification for rejecting late returns. Here, a strategic choice not to reconstruct the context of the action served Lund's rhetorical purposes of characterizing Florida law (or the state court's reading of that law) as demanding the deadline.

Lund also relied on two quotations from footnotes in the revised *Palm Beach County Canvassing Board v. Harris* decision. First, he quotes the state court's statement:

> What is a reasonable time required for completion will, in part, depend on whether the election is for a statewide office, for a federal office, or for presidential electors. In the case of the presidential election, the determination of reasonableness must be circumscribed by the provisions of 3 U.S.C. 5, which sets December 12, 2000, as the date for final determination of any state's dispute concerning its electors in order for that determination to be given conclusive effect in Congress.[204]

Lund drew on the court's statement that the safe harbor deadline circumscribed what was a reasonable deadline to suggest that the court believed that this was a critical date to meet.

Lund found additional support a few pages later, emphasizing how protest and contest provisions must work together, in the court's warning:

> As always, it is necessary to read all provisions of the [Florida] elections code in pari materia. In this case, that comprehensive reading required that there be time for an elections contest pursuant to section 102.168, which all parties had agreed was a necessary component of the statutory scheme and to accommodate the outside deadline set forth in 3 U.S.C. 5 of December 12, 2000.[205]

Lund did not attempt to analyze this construction, other than to suggest that it showed that "the Florida Supreme Court had already concluded, as a matter of state law, that recounts had to be concluded by December 12."[206]

Critics on both sides of the controversy admitted that the state court had shown some consideration for the safe harbor deadline, though they were more cautious than Lund. Posner offered, for example, that "[t]he Florida Supreme Court's opinions in the election litigation had seemed to treat December 12 as the deadline for determining the state's electors, lest the determination be rejected by Congress."[207] By qualifying his interpretation of state court motives (speaking not of what they *did* but of what they *seemed to do*) and emphasizing a primary purpose for the deadline (tying the deadline to a specific purpose, which might be narrower than other judicial purposes), Posner fell short of Lund's claim that the state court had embraced the deadline as a matter of state law.

Most commentators took Sunstein's position, admitting, "It is true that the Florida Supreme Court had emphasized the importance, for the Florida legislature, of the safe harbor provision," while qualifying that "the Florida courts had never been asked to say whether they would interpret Florida law to require a cessation in the counting of votes, if the consequence of the counting would be to extend the choice of electors past December 12."[208] Rhetorically, he defined the Florida court's act—parts of which were quoted by Lund—as a limited one. He defined those limits by what the court "had never been asked [to do]," namely, to determine whether that deadline was absolute, or whether other factors could be weighed against the interest of meeting the safe harbor deadline. In this way, Sunstein and others could acknowledge that the Florida Supreme Court saw the December 12 deadline as important but construe that attitude as constrained by other important considerations.

Sunstein balanced the court's attitude about the safe harbor provision against its attitude about counting all the votes, trumping the former with the latter in urging that "the Florida Court's pervasive emphasis on the need to ensure the inclusion of lawful votes would seem to indicate that if a choice must be made between the safe harbor and the inclusion of votes, the latter might have priority."[209] The term *pervasive emphasis* suggests a quality of strength in the state court's conviction about counting votes (to be balanced against its concern about the deadline). Dworkin made a similar argument in admitting that "the Florida legislature would wish to meet the December 12 deadline if it fairly could"[210] (as any fair construction of the court's statements must admit) but insisting that "it hardly follows—nor did the Florida Supreme Court suggest—that the legislature would have wanted to gain the immunity at any cost, including compromising the fairness and accuracy of its election."[211] The metaphor of cost connects ends to means, suggesting that these particular ends did not justify the means (or costs) but that other ends were at stake as well. In other words, Lund's construction worked insofar as he depicted the Florida Supreme Court as single-minded in its ends, willing to pay any price to meet the deadline. Dworkin's construction was more nuanced, suggesting competing ends that tugged against the purpose-agency logic Lund attributed to the state court.

David Strauss emphasized just what these costs were: supporting the safe harbor deadline meant stopping the election and possibly "awarding the state's electoral votes to the candidate who lost the election—'lost' according to the state's election laws, as interpreted by the highest court and modified by any federal constitutional requirements." He concluded, "[t]hat is an unlikely intention for any legislature to have."[212] By emphasizing the possibility that this act of stopping the recounts might award the election to the loser of the Florida election, Strauss magnified the possible tradeoff, putting a heavy weight on the recount side as against the side for meeting the safe harbor deadline.

In light of this tug-of-war over the Florida Supreme Court's act of determining whether state law did or did not require that the safe harbor deadline be met, commentators defended or chastised the U.S. Supreme Court for finding that the state court found that a "legislative wish" to take advantage of the safe harbor provision trumped all other considerations. In characterizing the High Court's actions, Tribe focused on the attitude behind the act and the agency of its implementation:

> the per curiam disingenuously translated the Florida court's opinion that the legislature wanted all recounts to be completed by December 12 (so as to take advantage of the promise contained in Congress's safe harbor statute) into a bright-line rule halting the recount at midnight, December 11 [sic]— at the cost of throwing out countless legal votes.[213]

The idea that the U.S. Supreme Court did not genuinely believe its interpretation of Florida law through its reading of the Florida Supreme Court's opinion was echoed by Klarman as well, who called the safe harbor concern "a complete fabrication"[214] and bolstered this interpretation with another instance of inconsistency:

> One can only marvel at the disingenuousness of this conclusion [on the safe harbor deadline]. [T]here is enormous irony in the Bush majority's

eagerness to defer entirely to the Florida court's supposed conclusion regarding the significance of the December 12 safe harbor deadline under state election law. Three members of that majority could identify no other aspect of the state court's interpretation of state election law that warranted similar deference. The majority's posture on this issue is especially remarkable given the concurring Justices' statement that, in light of Article II concerns, "the text of the election law itself, and not just its interpretation by the courts of the States, takes on independent significance." The text of Florida election law does not say a word about the federal safe harbor provision.[215]

Here, Klarman drew on an agent-act inconsistency, whereby earlier insistence upon legislated law trumping state court interpretations gave way in this case to deferring to a questionable interpretation of state law (attributed to the state court) where no textual authority supports that interpretation. That agent-act charge is directed against Rehnquist, Scalia, and Thomas, whose concurring opinion drew a distinction between the legislature's intentions and those of the state court.

The irony is made richer still in Klarman's construction when he blamed the U.S. Supreme Court for the state court's statements highlighting the safe harbor deadline:

> [T]o the extent that the Florida Supreme Court did emphasize in its opinion the significance of the December 12 deadline, it plainly was responding to the Supreme Court's earlier intervention in *Bush v. Palm Beach County Canvassing Board*, which essentially had coerced the Florida court, upon threat of reversal, to acknowledge the importance of the safe harbor provision. Thus, the Supreme Court first forced the Florida jurists to acknowledge the significance of the December 12 deadline, and then insisted that its own hands were tied with regard to permitting the manual recount to continue, given the Florida court's interpretation of the significance of the December 12 deadline. This is a nifty trick.[216]

Klarman did not support this characterization of coercion with evidence, though it is true that the original *Palm Beach County Canvassing Board v. Harris* decision (prior to the "corrected" version submitted on December 11, 2000) made no mention at all of December 12 or of the safe harbor provision. The inclusion of safe harbor language was part of the state court's response to the High Court, and it genuflects to federal law (which is certainly what the High Court expected the state court to do); however, it also may have been a response to the time pressures that were less of a concern when the original *Palm Beach County Canvassing Board v. Harris* decision was handed down.

Tribe made the U.S. Supreme Court culpable in a different way. He insisted that "even if the Florida court *had* explicitly read the December 12 deadline as a binding deadline, deferring to that 'interpretation' contradicted the Court's equal protection holding."[217] He urged:

> Under the *Court's own reasoning* . . . the Fourteenth Amendment would preclude any legislative or judicial determination to put the state's interest in finality above the rights of those voters to have *all* of their ballots counted. As the Supreme Court itself had told the Florida high court: "The press of time does not diminish the constitutional concern."[218]

This appeal for consistency of action provided a purpose for the High Court not to defer to what it said was the state court's interpretation.

Lund tried to shore up his position, in the face of what he appeared to admit was a weak safe harbor position (while insisting that this was what the Florida court said about the deadline), by invoking actions by the state court—a tit to Tribe's tat in invoking the High Court's actions. He used characterization to speak not of what the proper law is in this case but of what a different ruling on safe harbor could portend:

> [T]he Florida court had already proved to be highly aggressive and irresponsible in dealing with federal law and with the U.S. Supreme Court. It is therefore quite possible that [had the December 12 deadline not be enforced] the next stab at a statewide recount would have been infected with new constitutional problems, which the U.S. Supreme Court would then have had to deal with under time pressures even greater than those it faced in *Bush v. Gore* itself.[219]

This "things could be worse" argument was a final, necessarily hypothetical retreat for argument against strong constructions suggesting that (1) the safe harbor deadline was not a mandate, (2) the legislature said nothing about the deadline, (3) the state court thought it was important but not clearly more important than other things, and (4) the High Court was acting inconsistently with respect to (a) its deference to this interpretation and other state court interpretations and (b) its holding on this deadline and its equal protection holding that time did not diminish constitutional concerns.[220] It relied on an agent-act-scene relationship, where irresponsibility led to erroneous actions which led to a more constrained scene within which a future High Court would have to work. The entire construction relied on Lund's characterization of the state court as highly aggressive and irresponsible, which he tried to demonstrate in his essay on the case.

However, Lund's constructions had weaknesses that did not provide strong supports for this characterization of the Florida Court's actions.

The Remedy

The safe harbor ruling provided the High Court with a basis for denying that the recount be restarted under new, constitutionally acceptable standards by building on the safe harbor ruling. The per curiam claimed:

> Because the Florida Supreme Court has said that the Florida Legislature intended to obtain the safe-harbor benefits of 3 U.S.C. § 5, Justice Breyer's proposed remedy—remanding to the Florida Supreme Court for its ordering of a constitutionally proper contest until December 18—contemplates action in violation of the Florida election code, and hence could not be part of an "appropriate" order authorized by Fla. Stat. § 102.168(8) (2000).[221]

Here, the majority read the legislature's intention from the safe harbor provision and through the Florida Supreme Court to find that its own hands were tied in remanding the case back to the state court for a new recount.

Even Posner admitted that "the natural remedy [to the state court's constitutionally flawed recount order] would have been to direct the Florida Supreme Court to redo the order."[222] Pildes agreed with this characterization, suggesting that in an "ordinary case," the High Court "likely would have . . . sent the case back to have that constitutional recount process carried out under the supervision of Florida judicial and executive officials."[223] Weinberg called this "the logical and necessary remedy."[224] These characterizations of what should have been done as natural, likely, logical, and necessary, suggest that this means of remedy flowed from the case whose outcome the majority determined. Contrasted with this obvious remedy was the High Court's decision to stop all recounts, which Ward Farnsworth called "an extraordinary measure."[225]

Beyond characterization, commentators considered the outcomes of the remedy. Tribe was most colorful in suggesting that "the Court devised a remedy that sent the Titanic's deck chairs—on whose salvaging the Court had so myopically focused—down with the ship."[226] Tribe described an agency with an attitude (myopic focusing) to explain the act. Weinberg used another clichéd metaphor, noting that "under the Court's ruling, some unknown large quantity of concededly legal votes in Florida would never be counted, to protect George W. Bush from the counting of some unknown lesser quantity of disputable votes—the baby thrown out on a suspicion of the bath-water."[227]

American University professor Jamin Raskin highlighted the disjunction between the Court's means and its presumed ends (justice):

> If voters are threatened with constitutional injury by potentially not having their votes counted in an election when similarly situated votes in other counties are being counted, that injury becomes absolutely certain when the Court's relief is to order that the votes not be counted. How are the rights of pregnant chad voters vindicated by judicial relief compelling their automatic exclusion from the election?[228]

Thus, for Raskin, the baby would certainly be thrown out with the bathwater, making the agency-purpose relationship troubled.

Bugliosi amplified this discrepancy between means (the remedy) and ends (preserving the right to vote) by calculating the number of voters wronged: "The Court majority, after knowingly transforming the votes of 50 million Americans into nothing and throwing out all of the Florida undervotes (around 60,000), actually wrote that their ruling was intended to preserve 'the fundamental right' to vote."[229] Bugliosi amplified the purposefulness of the Court's act in noting its knowledge of what they did and played up the discrepancy between its stated purpose of preserving the right to vote with its means for accomplishing that: throwing out 60,000 Florida undervotes.

Posner, while admitting that the obvious remedy would be to return the case to the Florida state court, challenged suggestions that any such babies were lost with this bathwater, urging that recounting would not necessarily have yielded any more accurate results. He warned that "[h]uman counters can be fatigued, biased, or simply unable to infer the voter's intent with any approach to certainty from a ballot that the machine refused to count; so they can make many errors too [as presumably the original counting machines had]—some deliberate, which is beyond a machine's capacity."[230] Moreover, he insisted that there was evidence that recounting (either by machine or by hand) could dislodge chads, leading to a deterioration of the ballots and greater inaccuracy.[231] Grammatically, Posner here shifted attention away from the act of remanding the case to the state court for a recount—which he admitted would be the "natural" remedy—to the proposed act of remedying that might have followed that natural order, implying that following the natural course might not have led to results any more accurate. Stated otherwise, if the purpose of reaching an accurate count was primary, then this agency of a human recount would not clearly serve that purpose. Consequently, even if the Court did not follow the natural path, it probably was for the best.

Constructions of the original count suggest that the high rejection rate was problematic and perhaps needed correction through a human count. And there may be reasons for believing that even a count by fallible humans would yield a fairly accurate overall result (for example, because of oversight by competing parties and trustworthy judicial officers, because of balancing between Republican and Democrat counties, etc.). In any event, constructions of the results do not bear directly on interpretations of what the Court ought to have done, even if they may diminish concerns about the negative results of its actions.

By far the most creative argument came from Lund, who urged that "[c]ontrary to a widespread misperception, the Supreme Court did not forbid the Florida court from attempting to conduct a statewide recount under constitutionally permissible standards."[232] Lund based this construction on the assumption that the Florida Supreme Court could have told the U.S. Supreme Court that it had misinterpreted the state court's ruling on December 11, or even for the state court to overrule that December 11 decision.[233] This was an interesting argument, essentially retreating again outside the act in question to reconstruct that act: by making a bold state court the agent under orders from the High Court, Lund could suggest some theoretical leeway in the High Court's decision, even if this was practically unthinkable.

Farnsworth expanded this theoretical line a bit by going to the next act in the progression: after the bold state court took action—since it was the obvious interpreter of Florida law—he speculated that the High Court might have backed down. He suggested that such backpedaling would be a product of "uncertainty" about federal authority to overrule a state court on its own law. But he quickly qualified any hint that this uncertainty reflected hesitant attitudes; instead, he suggested a more insidious act was at work, namely, "a game of chicken [which] the Supreme Court won."[234]

Since both conservative and liberal scholars described a remedy that returned the case to the state court for further recounting under a new standard as the appropriate course, the per curiam decision to remedy Florida's infringements on the fundamental right to vote by ending all recounts was cast as inappropriate. Posner's suggestion that it would not make any difference simply seeks to mitigate the sense of damage wrought by this decision, while not condoning it. And Lund grasped at technical straws in suggesting that the High Court left enough wiggle room for the state court to restart the recount—this surely would not have been viewed as prudent on the part of the lower court (now rebuked a second time by the federal court), given the High Court's ruling that under Florida law (which it read for the state court), "remanding to the Florida Supreme Court for its ordering of a constitutionally proper contest until December 18 . . . contemplates action in violation of the Florida election code, and hence could not be part of an 'appropriate' order authorized by Fla. Stat. § 102.168(8) (2000)."[235]

Limitation to the Present Case

The final major construction of how the High Court decided *Bush v. Gore* involved its attempt to limit the precedential value of the case. It stated that its ruling was "limited to present circumstances, for the problem of equal protection in election processes generally presents many complexities."[236] Both liberals and conservatives insisted that this limitation was unprincipled. Sunstein noted that it lacked "a sense of principle."[237] Strauss said it had "barely a fig leaf of principle."[238] Posner noted that this caveat "made the opinion appear unprincipled."[239] Issacharoff said the limitation lacked "doctrinal mooring."[240] In short, there was no clear agency to support this act of limitation. Perhaps this explains Lund's silence on the issue.[241]

Bugliosi attacked the idea that these so-called complexities meant that a clear precedent could not be laid down. He offered his own reading for the Court: "[I]f there are varying standards to count votes, this violates the equal protection clause of the Fourteenth Amendment."[242] Karlan tried to explain why the Court would not want to lay down this otherwise clear rule: "The most generous explanation for this extraordinary paragraph is that the Court was acting under tremendous time pressure and was hesitant to announce a rule that could swiftly throw into doubt the constitutionality of a huge number of state election systems."[243] This generous reading suggested that the scene (time pressure) created an attitude (hesitancy) that led to an act (limiting the case's precedential value, not throwing into doubt other state elections) that refused to provide a future agency (precedent) for other equal protection arguments. Many other scholars would note the far-reaching implications of the Court's reasoning, suggesting, for example, that "they would invalidate virtually every close election in our past and our future, since there is always considerable disparity among voting machines and standards employed to count and recount votes."[244]

Less generous explanations suggested that the Court "went out of its way to try to limit its ruling to the facts of *Bush v. Gore*,"[245] "trying to free itself from the discipline of stare decisis,"[246] and creating the equal protection argument "as a cynical vessel used to engage in result-oriented judging by decree."[247] Many commentators suggested that this was a paradigm case of what Justice Owen Roberts complained about in his famous dissent in *Smith v. Allwright*:

> The reason for my concern is that the instant decision, overruling that announced about nine years ago [in *Grovey v. Townsend*], tends to bring adjudications of this tribunal into the same class as a restricted railroad ticket, good for this day and train only. I have no assurance, in view of current decisions, that the opinion announced today may not shortly be repudiated and overruled by justices who deem they have new light on the subject.[248]

Karlan quoted Roberts's dissent, noting that these words of warning were "ironically written by a Justice in another voting-rights case nearly sixty years earlier."[249] Issacharoff called the limitation a "classic 'good for this train, and this train only' offer."[250] Farnsworth complained: "The decision paid no tribute to the past, and in offering so little by way of explanation it seemed meant to have as little future force as the Court can give to one of its rulings—a decision 'good for this day and train only.'"[251] Klarman argued that "the Justices in the majority made clear their intention to treat the decision as 'good for this day and train only.'"[252] And Tribe discussed the limitation in a section entitled "Good for This Day and Train Only."[253]

Relying on Roberts provides a number of rhetorical advantages. First, it draws the words of condemnation from the mouth of a Supreme Court justice; thus, it is not merely critics of *Bush* who are concerned about such limitations, it is members of the Court. Second, as a classic admonition against deciding cases without drawing on existing law or laying down new law, it reminds readers of a basic legal principle that the Court ought to heed. And finally, the metaphor of a train ticket good for this day and train only provides a colorful (if somewhat anachronistic) way of highlighting the implications of such practices.

Alan Dershowitz offered a paraphrase of the Court's limitation to highlight what he believed even the justices would admit was its disingenuous character: "In future election cases, don't try to hold the Court to what it said in *this* case, because it decided this case not on general principles applicable to all cases, but on a principle that has never before been recognized by any court and that will never again be recognized by this court."[254] Here, Dershowitz highlighted the ultimate limitation of agency in the *Bush* case: an agency uniquely tailored to settle this election dispute and not to be used again. The act of *Bush v. Gore*, therefore, would be circumscribed, its agencies not deployed for future cases. However, if the Court might try to amputate this agency arm of its act (and it is not clear that it could), it could not amputate the agent arm, for its decision would carry implications for how the justices would be perceived.

Dershowitz extended one strand of the agent arm of *Bush* to the past to suggest inconsistency on the part of Scalia in particular. He noted that Scalia wrote in *United States v. Virginia*: "The Supreme Court of the United States does not sit to announce 'unique' dispositions. Its principal function is to establish *precedent*—that is, to set forth principles of law that every court in America must follow."[255] Posner, acknowledging Dershowitz's point, admitted:

> How does [Scalia's position] square with the statement in the majority opinion in *Bush v. Gore*, which Scalia joined reluctantly, that "Our consideration is limited to the present circumstances, for the problem of equal protection in election processes generally presents many complexities?" It doesn't, inviting charges of hypocrisy, or worse—the charge of rank partisanship leveled against Scalia by Dershowitz on insufficient evidence, but plausible enough to resonate with the millions of Americans who already profoundly distrust the good faith of all government officials.[256]

Posner did manage to suggest that such inconsistency was reluctant on Scalia's part (an attitude that may suggest the agent who acted inconsistently at least did not do so happily). Nonetheless, Posner recognized how this limitation—an act using a particular agency of the decision—carries implications for the public view of the agents of the decision.

Agency and the Per Curiam Decision

Agency is central to judicial argument, because judicial decision making is supposed to be about following the law, applying rules, adhering to precedent—in short, allowing judicial action to be constrained by the law laid down. Agency also operates in a prospective sense, potentially laying down law, rules, and precedents to be followed.

Because *Bush v. Gore* involved a number of issues concerned with what the law to be followed was, a number of agency considerations were

raised. One the Court itself did not raise was whether the Court was justified in hearing the case at all. The per curiam never raised the question of
whether Bush had standing to sue on behalf of those whose ballots were
recounted using differential standards, nor did it consider whether this political question was justiciable under its standards. Nonetheless, a case
could be made that the Court acted justifiably in hearing the case, even if
the Court itself did not bother to make it.

The most exhaustive issue addressed by scholars was the agency that
served as the central legal holding of the case: that the recount order issued
by the Florida Supreme Court violated the equal protection clause. Defenders and critics of the Court wrangled over how partisan or arbitrary
the recount was, whether a subsidiary recount standard (more specific
than voter intent) issued by the state court would have been appropriate,
and whether safeguards in place (especially Judge Lewis's ultimate oversight) could check these problems. Defenders had a hard time denying that
the standard used by the Florida Supreme Court was drawn from Florida
law and had been widely used by other states and for many years. Defenders also had a hard time denying that more recent precedents seemed to
require a showing of intent to discriminate against identifiable groups as a
crucial element in equal protection cases—cases that made the Warren-era
precedents the per curiam cited appear as questionable authority, especially for this conservative court. Oddly, the greatest support for the High
Court's finding came from critics such as Karlan, who inferred that the
Court had developed a structural approach to equal protection, though
that support was strongly questioned as well and was never invoked by the
Court itself. Defenders also had difficulty distinguishing the equal protection problem of different voting machines used in different counties (especially in poor and minority counties)—which affected a huge number of
voters—from the smaller equal protection problem identified in the recount. Indeed, it appeared that allowing a recount actually might address
some of the problems associated with the use of different voting machines,
so that the Court's decision to end the recounts actually exacerbated the
problem. On the whole, defenders had a much weaker construction of the
equal protection claim, explaining why almost no conservative defenders
supported that finding.

The means for ending the recounts were especially troublesome. The per
curiam had insisted that Florida state law, as interpreted by the state
supreme court it was overruling, required that all vote counting be completed by the safe harbor deadline. Almost all defenders of the High Court

simply suggested that the Florida legislature would want to make this deadline if it could, though no one argued that this deadline trumped every other consideration.[257] Yet the High Court used its construction of state law in suggesting that it was forced to conclude that there was no time for recounting. Court critics found this one of the most egregious constructions of agency, suggesting that the Court was acting disingenuously and politically. This means of ending the controversy was disconnected from the purpose of meting out justice in this case, since ending the recount meant throwing out the ballots of the very voters the High Court seemed to be trying to protect from unequal treatment. Finally, limiting the precedential value of the case suggested justice tailor-made for Bush alone, flying against a more principled approach for which Scalia himself had called.

9

Scholars Reconstruct Why
the Court Reached Its Decision

Although agency is central to judicial argument, it is closely connected to, or at least readily implies, purpose. Means are to be related to ends; we adapt particular means to reach particular ends. We may emphasize those ends to suggest that purpose determines means, whereby we seek particular ends and find the means to reach them. Or we may derive purposes from agencies, whereby purposes are inherent in, implied by, or a consequence of the agencies we use.

The heavy reliance of legal opinions on precedents tends to embed purposes within agencies. In a case involving some truly novel legal problem, where a court is forced to consider law's purposes as primary in figuring out how to dispose of a case (as the means for simply following some earlier line are unavailable), purpose in that case leads to the development of particular agencies. However, when a similar issue arises in the future, the Court can almost ignore purpose and follow the law (i.e., apply the agency developed beforehand). In a sense, that agency carries over the earlier purpose to a different situation. When done too slavishly, it may lead to a response that Burke likens to a "frozen parry" in a fencing match, whereby the same agency ("parrying in a particular way") is used even where the "thrust" one would thwart (in responding to the particulars of a case) is different.[1]

Of course, purpose is related to all the other grammatical terms as well, underlying acts, embodying attitudes, revealing the nature of particular agents while springing from them, or even deriving from scenes.

Generally, defenders of the *Bush v. Gore* decision chose to speak of good outcomes, rather than particular purposes, moving purpose closer to scene (specifically, future scenes fraught with problems the decision sought to avoid), rather than toward agent, with its emphasis on choice of outcomes. Specifically, they suggested that the Court helped the nation avoid a crisis and provided what Posner dubbed "rough justice."[2] Critics of the per curiam decision focused on outcomes to some extent, denying the alleged crisis while playing up the damage to the Supreme Court and to democratic institutions and rejecting any claim that justice had been done. However, many went further to claim explicitly that the majority wanted to make the Republican candidate president as a means to further its members' conservative goals on the Court through his future judicial appointments.

Because many Court defenders relied on describing negative outcomes avoided by the decision, they tended to draw the Court's purpose out of a hypothetical future scene. Posner was the most elaborate in depicting a worst-case scenario that might follow without the High Court's intervention. He admitted that "[b]ecause the Supreme Court halted the recount for good on December 12, we do not know what would have ensued had the Court allowed it to resume," adding, "We know only what *could* have ensued—and what could have ensued is fairly described as chaos, providing a practical argument in defense of the Court's remedy."[3] Posner's parade of horribles runs on for the better part of a chapter. He suggested that if the Florida Supreme Court had been allowed to carry on its recounts, it probably would have missed the safe harbor deadline, because of the time involved in developing a new standard, implementing it, and handling objections and legal challenges. This, in turn, would lead the Republican-dominated Florida legislature to appoint its own slate of electors favoring Bush. The state court might have objected to this, raising a new legal conflict, or the issue might have left the U.S. Congress to decide which slate of electors to choose (especially if the safe harbor deadline had been missed and they were not bound to support the first slate), assuming one slate was for Gore and the other for Bush.

If the recounting led to the missing of the December 18 deadline for the Electoral College to meet as well, he insisted that might have led to a conflict with Article II's requirement that "the day on which the electors vote 'shall be the same throughout the United States,'" leading to another legal battle. More legal challenges might have been made as Congress worked on January 6 to resolve the controversy. With the Republican-controlled House likely to support Bush and the Democrat-controlled Senate likely to support Gore (with Vice President Gore's tie-breaking vote, no less), then Florida's chief executive (Governor Jeb Bush) would resolve the deadlock, giving the election to his brother. But, insisted Posner, the Florida Supreme Court might intervene again and declare the governor's certification invalid, which the Florida legislature might try to prevent by withdrawing judicial jurisdiction.[4]

Posner added that the congressional battle could have continued for more than two weeks, requiring that an acting president be named, and he assured his readers that Speaker of the House Dennis Hastert and President Pro Tempore of the Senate Strom Thurmond would have declined the temporary post, leaving the position to pass over Secretary of State Madeleine Albright (who was foreign-born and ineligible) to Secretary of the Treasury Lawrence Summers. When resolution finally came, Posner worried, "[t]he new President would have started behind the eight ball, with an irregular and disputed accession, an abbreviated term of office, and no transition."[5]

Elsewhere, Posner described the situation similarly, admitting that it was "a worst-case scenario" but asserting "that [it] is by no means fantastic, or even highly improbable."[6] The upshot of this wrangling, he insisted, would be that

> the forty-third president would have taken office after long delay, with no transition, with greatly impaired authority, perhaps amidst unprecedented partisan bickering and bitterness, leaving a trail of poisonous suspicion of covert deals and corrupt maneuvers, and after an interregnum unsettling to the global and U.S. domestic economy and possibly threatening to world peace. (How would the crisis over the Chinese seizure of our surveillance plane have been resolved by Acting President Summers? And would other hostile foreign powers or groups [have] tried to test us during the interregnum?)[7]

Posner filled his worst-case scenario (a scene) with contentious acts, the cumulative effect of which would delay the transfer of presidential power and give heart to America's enemies. He assumed that partisanship (a contention-bolstering attitude of agents with partisan purposes) would reign in all political and judicial bodies (save, perhaps, the U.S. Supreme Court) and that such contentiousness would extend the scene of uncertain presidential leadership farther and farther into the future.

By circumscribing agents, attitudes, purposes, and actions within the troublesome scene he portrayed—a scene marked with a trail of poisonous suspicion of covert deals and corrupt maneuvers—Posner drew attention to what may be (scenically), rather than who the agents he describes were, what attitudes they held, what purposes they sought, and what actions they were apt to take. A primary focus on who the agents were (notably, the state court, Congress, the governor of Florida) might highlight questions about whether they were given constitutional authority to make such decisions. A primary focus on attitudes or purposes is liable to raise the question of whether partisanship is the only important attitude here (rather than, say, patriotism or a concern for justice) or whether political victory is the only outcome they might seek. A primary focus on actions might raise the question of whether statesmanship (judicial, legislative, or executive) might not prevail. Posner's rhetorical strategy emphasized how things might look rather than closely examining how or why they developed.

Cass Sunstein offers what would become a controversial (though less elaborate) characterization of the threatening future scene, insisting that "[t]he Court might even have avoided a genuine *constitutional crisis*" in "the chaotic post-election period of 2000." The Court was a good agent for ending the election, he insisted, and "it probably did so in a way that carried more simplicity and authority than anything that might have been expected from the United States Congress."[8]

John Yoo also focused on the abilities of these particular judicial agents to avoid "events [that] threatened to spiral out of control." For him, the troublesome alternative scene is a function of its partisan agents, because

> [a]ll of the institutions that could control the outcome of the election—the legislature, the Florida Secretary of State, the Florida Supreme Court, the local election officials and Congress—were subject to charges of partisan bias. Although these institutions are popularly elected, their partisan nature might have allowed the election process to drag on.[9]

Yoo seemed to imply that the less partisan Supreme Court was less likely to drag out the process and more likely to rule fairly—a contention other commentators would challenge.

Yoo went further than Posner in ascribing a particular purpose to the Court, rather than simply weighing possible outcomes: "No doubt that the

Court believed that only it could intervene so as to bring the national election controversy to an end in a manner that would be accepted by the nation, as indeed it has been."[10] This last point provided a "good outcome" to contrast with the troublesome scene absent Court intervention, emphasizing purpose by contrasting two possible outcomes (essentially a choice confronting the High Court). Yoo also attributed a thought process that set the Court up as a unique and benevolent savior for the presidency and the nation.

Richard Epstein enhanced his characterization of majority purposes by dovetailing them with the purposes of election laws, which he admitted seek "to expand the franchise" but also try to meet "the twin interests of finality and probity." If these competing interests are not always met to everyone's satisfaction (as some would contend they were not here), Epstein insisted, it is because "an election code has to contend with grubby realities as well as lofty aspirations."[11] By pitting finality and probity against expansion of the franchise (through continuing the recount), Epstein suggested a competition over law's purposes, where the Supreme Court was required to choose sides. A vindication of this choice was offered in Epstein's characterization of the public response to *Bush v. Gore* as "widespread relief and not widespread protest."[12]

Michael McConnell also came down on the side of finality and "a prompt resolution," by noting the significance "of selecting the president-elect of the world's greatest power." He insisted that "[a] smooth transition to a new administration takes time" and warned of the consequences of delay: "uncertainty about who is to be the next president is profoundly unsettling to the nation, and to the world."[13] Thus, the significant nature of the act (involving the selection of the leader of the world's greatest power) is what threatens the scene.

Ronald Cass, who also supported the outcome but not the majority's reasoning, similarly endorsed the benefits of closure, insisting that "[t]he majority no doubt did the nation a service in bringing to a close a vote-recount process that had kept the election from a conclusion for more than a month, even after it became clear that, by one route or another, George Bush would in all likelihood emerge as the victor."[14] Cass added something that would become a theme for Court defenders: that even if the recounting had gone ahead, Bush would have won in the end. Such assurances suggested that the consequences of the High Court's intervention were negligible in terms of who took office and very positive in terms of providing closure and time for a smooth transition of power.

Posner used statistical inferences based on Broward County's recount to suggest that Gore had only a 1 in 20 chance of overtaking Bush in a recount.[15] McConnell based a similar claim on the media recounts, to suggest that "George W. Bush almost certainly would have won the election in Florida even if Vice President Gore had gotten everything his lawyers asked for in court."[16] Of course, these outcomes have nothing to do with the justifiability of the Court's legal decision or the propriety of its endorsement of finality as a primary purpose. It does, however, offer a mitigating factor to consider when assessing the consequences of the Court's decision. Indeed, it provides a basis for what Posner offered as the strongest defense of the Court's decision: that it provided "rough justice."

Critics of the High Court challenged the idea that a crisis was at hand in the postelection dispute. Farnsworth argued that there was no crisis justifying the Court's "lawless" intervention:

> Here there was no apparent danger of a junta, of riots, or of a collapse of civil order; however, there was no threat of instability, except in the sense of prolonged uncertainty and controversy. If Florida had sent two slates of electors to the electoral college, some protests in the streets no doubt would have occurred regardless of the final outcome. But protests and instability are not at all the same thing. Protests can represent a healthy public interest in the outcome of the election. They may be annoying, but unless they turn lawless, they cannot be considered a judicially cognizable cost of recounting.[17]

Farnsworth here drew a tight connection between means and ends, implying that if there had been a danger of a junta, of riots, or of a collapse of civil order, then a purpose of avoiding those consequences might have justified the Court's lawless means to end the controversy, for the good of the country. But simple protests could not justify this kind of heavy-handed intervention.

Farnsworth next turned to the issue of an alleged constitutional crisis: "The usual definition of a constitutional crisis is a dispute between coequal branches of government about the Constitution's meaning that calls into question the authority of either one to trump the other. Nothing quite like that appeared to be in the offing here."[18] He admitted that a tie between the Senate and the House that required Jeb Bush to break it "would have been awkward," but he noted that "there were statutory rules providing for all this; at least at the time of the Court's decision, the country did not appear headed into a controversy where the rules gave out and left different branches of government at loggerheads."[19] Thus, against the chaos and constitutional crisis of Court defenders, Farnsworth offered mere protests and awkward actions that nonetheless were grounded in clear agencies.

McConnell, who was concerned about delays in reaching a decision on the matter, nonetheless questioned the claim by defenders of the Court that the intervention in *Bush v. Gore* avoided a constitutional crisis. He did so partly by questioning characterizations of likely partisan actions that Posner and others used to construct a story of crisis: "I do not assume that all members of Congress would necessarily vote the party line [if they were asked to choose between two slates of Florida electors]." By not assuming the worst (in a partisan sense) from Congress, he was able to conclude that "[w]hether following politically contentious—but legal—procedures would constitute a constitutional crisis is not obvious," insisting that "[it] might well depend on how Congress rose to the occasion."[20]

Elizabeth Garrett agreed with Farnsworth and McConnell in suggesting that "this line of argument overstate[s] the seriousness of the election mess by elevating it to the level of 'constitutional crisis,'" and added a second set of outcomes overlooked by defenders of the Court, namely, the "potential negative long-term consequences for the Court and the political branches."[21] Those consequences are manifold and serious, she noted:

> It leads to an environment of low expectations for elected officials, in which we no longer hold them to an acceptable standard of responsiveness and re-flective judgment or require them to enact and oversee wise policies. We leave that to the unelected judges who work in an institution ill-designed to craft comprehensive policies that can be modified and improved over time. Moreover, by requiring the justices to save us from a political "crisis," we ask the Court to make decisions that will be characterized as partisan and may reduce judicial legitimacy, undermining the justices when they act within their proper sphere.[22]

Garrett's environment depicted a scene to be avoided by forgoing Supreme Court involvement to counter the scene Posner and others would avoid by approving Supreme Court involvement. And whereas Posner's scene was concerned with a short-term setting that opened up the election dispute to partisan wrangling (until the dispute was settled, perhaps after January 6), Garrett's scene stretched on into an indeterminate future, shaping both legislative and judicial motives. Garrett's argument was reminiscent of the argument about balancing harms, which critics said the High Court failed to do in issuing the stay (which considered the potential harm to Bush but not the potential harm to Gore).

Frank Michelman also saw legislative and judicial damage resulting from the Court's actions: "they may have caused injury to public confidence either in the Court's supposed special guardianship of the rule of law or in the capacity of Congress to carry the burden of political leadership in conditions of constitutional stress."[23] Pamela Karlan agreed, saying that the High Court had "short-circuit[ed] the normal, albeit potentially contentious and messy, process of self-government. And once again, the Court's decision left in its wake weakened institutions."[24]

Ronald Dworkin and many others would focus on the damage to the High Court particularly, given the unique role it has played in American history. Dworkin wrote:

> The people's general willingness in the past to accept the Court's view of the Constitution—sometimes grudgingly but for the most part unreservedly— are sources of wonder in other parts of the world. Whatever else we may say about *Bush v. Gore*, it has put at risk a vital and perhaps indispensable part of America's domestic political capital.[25]

Francis Beytagh insisted that "the Court did itself considerable institutional harm in the *Bush* case, and that it will take some time for that 'self-inflicted' wound to heal."[26] That wound, Garrett suggested, may "undermin[e] the justices [even] when they act within their proper sphere."[27]

Others voiced additional concerns for alternative negative consequences. Laurence Tribe worried about the effect on the public, not merely the public's perception of other players, arguing that it was "predictable [that] the decision was sure to polarize the polity."[28] Peter Shane agreed, arguing that "[t]he precedent of such judicial usurpation poses grave long-term peril to both democracy and the rule of law that is not susceptible to ready eradication in the short run."[29] Even McConnell concurred with this latter concern, "that rather than stimulating serious reflection on the role of the Court, *Bush v. Gore* may exacerbate the already corrosive cynicism about public institutions and undermine public faith in the rule of law itself."[30]

Overall, Court critics sought to diminish the threat of the scenario Posner and others described and to paint their own picture of negative consequences that would follow Court intervention. Defenders had a weak case insofar as their hypotheticals assumed the worst (perhaps an unreasonable assumption) and relied on a series of troublesome events for their scenario to become problematic, particularly for a constitutional crisis to arise. Critics had a weak case to the extent that the actual realized outcomes they feared—outcomes they believed the Court should have kept in mind as it deliberated what to do—may not have been borne out by subsequent history. Indeed, a regular argument made by Court defenders in the months and years after *Bush* was handed down was that it had no discernible and lasting effect on the Supreme Court's reputation. While this is difficult to assess, defenders were able to point to polls showing that the Court's reputation dipped just after the decision but bounced back to typical levels within a few months. Peter Berkowitz and Benjamin Wittes made the strongest case for such resilience:

> Nor has the Court itself fared badly in the public's eye. The Pew Center for the People and the Press has been measuring the Court's approval rating since 1987. In that time, the rating has fluctuated from a low of 65 percent in 1990 to a high of 80 percent in 1994. In January 2001, the Court's favorability rating stood at 68 percent. Three months later, it stood at 72 percent. More interestingly, the Court was viewed favorably by 67 percent of Democrats.[31]

Critics might rightly object that it is not the opinions of the unwashed masses that matter but rather the opinions of those in legal circles who understand what went wrong in this case. Berkowitz and Wittes had an answer for them as well:

> The academics worrying themselves about the crisis of the Court's legitimacy present as a sociological claim what is really normative criticism: The Court deserves to lose the public's confidence, or, put differently, as a result of *Bush v. Gore* the Court has lost legitimacy in the eyes of the majority of academic pundits (namely, themselves) whom the public ought to follow.[32]

While it is not clear that significant institutional harm must rest solely in public opinion (rather than also in the opinions of legal academics), this defense did challenge the extent of the alleged injury to the Court.

Curiously, some critics of the Court suggested that there may have been positive consequences offsetting these negative consequences of the decision, primarily in the Court's setting a new equal protection precedent (even if it tried to limit that precedent). Samuel Issacharoff, for example, suggested that "[t]o the extent that *Bush v. Gore* revitalizes a non-race-based standard of constitutional protection of rights in the political process, the resulting diminution in the need to dress up all claims of wrongdoing in racial garb could be quite welcome."[33] Sunstein noted the usefulness of this precedent for voting rights particularly, suggesting that "the Court appears to have created the most expansive voting rights in many decades."[34]

He believed that "[i]t would be a nice irony if the Court's weak and un-precedented opinion, properly condemned on democratic grounds, led to significant social improvements from the democratic point of view [such as ensuring equality in voting technology]."[35] Court defender Epstein admit-ted that such a precedent would be appealing to the *Bush* dissenters, urging that the opinion is "ripe to be pressed into the service of causes that are championed by [the majority's] more liberal brethren."[36]

Overall, Court defenders tended to draw purpose out of future negative scenes that the High Court sought to avoid, while Court critics challenged these negative characterizations (particularly of a constitutional crisis) and offered negative scenes of their own which they suggested would or did follow from the Court's decision, though they admitted that establishing a new voting rights or equal protection precedent might be a thin silver lin-ing to an otherwise gray outlook.

One outcome that was rendered secondary in this clash between Court defenders and critics was one that is generally thought to be central to ju-dicial purposes: justice. Courts have not infrequently ignored precedents or forgone the advantages of setting down a clear and easily applied rule for future cases simply to ensure that justice is done in the case before them, that those deserving of mercy or punishment, reward or loss, receive such.[37] Of course, not even critics of the High Court were ready to claim that they sought injustice, even if that was an outcome. Yet defenders of the Court had a difficult time claiming that justice was done for the voters whose ballots were thrown out to prevent their suffering from differential treatment in recounting. The best the defenders could do was follow the earlier pattern of arguing for avoiding worse outcomes, suggesting that in-justice was avoided by the decision. On this basis, Posner, and those who endorsed him, stood ready to claim that something less than justice—"rough justice"—was achieved.

Posner defended the justice of the Court's position by arguing that the majority's actions prevented injustice. Posner claimed that the Florida Supreme Court "was deforming Florida's election law," so that "[t]he result of the Supreme Court's intervention was . . . at the least, rough justice" (which may or may not involve legal justice).[38] Although Posner rejected the reasoning of the per curiam, he still believed that the outcome was positive in preventing the injustice of the state court's twisting of Florida's election law. This was a difficult position to sustain in light of Posner's crit-icism of the per curiam reasoning. For if the state court was "deforming Florida's election law" and thereby causing injustice (in not following the law), then why was the per curiam's alleged failure to follow the law not also a basis for injustice? Posner claimed that the result of the decision was the correct one, even if the majority's rationale for that result was flawed. He half-heartedly threw his support to Chief Justice Rehnquist's concurring opinion as a plausible basis to justify the outcome and his assurance that rough justice was achieved.[39] Additionally, Posner forgave the majority for its incorrect application of the law, noting that "[t]he Court was operating under great time pressure—and it shows," while insisting, "But there was no injustice."[40] Note that the Florida Supreme Court, which also worked under great time pressure, was not granted such forgiveness by Posner for its failure to follow the law.

Issacharoff endorsed Posner's characterization and bolstered it by claiming that the Florida Supreme Court was acting politically, that "[p]articularly in light of the peculiar claims for selected recounts under shifting procedures, the Florida scenario was ripe for claims that the integrity of the process was being compromised for partisan aims"; thus, he agreed with Posner that rough justice was done.[41] Issacharoff created a distinction that might justify the difference in Posner's treatment of the time-starved state and federal courts, since the former is alleged to have been driven by a political purpose. However, like Posner, Issacharoff failed to apply the same standard to the High Court, whose conservative majority of Republicans acted in a fashion to put their own man in the White House—certainly as political, on its face, as the state court's motives.

David Strauss, who criticized the decision, nonetheless endorsed this "negative" strategy as the most coherent reading of the Court's motives: "As an effort to thwart, by any means necessary, a perceived illegitimate act by the Florida Supreme Court, it begins to make sense."[42] Where he differed was on the issue of justice. Justice, or the avoidance of injustice, was not the Court's aim. Rather, Strauss claimed, reversing the state court was primary, as "[t]he majority's actions in the litigation show a relentless search for some reason that could be put forward to justify a decision reversing the Florida Supreme Court." He contended that "[t]he outcome was a foregone conclusion."[43] Purpose drives agency here, and it is a reactionary purpose.

Critics of the Court who complained of the injustice of the decision typically pointed to the remedy of stopping the recount. Alan Dershowitz, for example, insisted: "It would be absurd for a court to tell citizens whose votes might be in danger of some dilution from the counting of other votes that the remedy is not to count any of the votes, including theirs. Such a 'remedy' substitutes disenfranchisement for dilution in the name of equal protection."[44]

Vincent Bugliosi highlighted the hypocrisy of the Court's claim to be rendering justice in protecting voters' rights: "The Court majority, *after knowingly transforming* the votes of 50 million Americans into nothing and throwing out all of the Florida undervotes (around 60,000), actually wrote that their ruling was intended to preserve 'the fundamental right' to vote."[45] Sunstein countered Court defenders' claims that the High Court avoided the injustice of the state court's ruling with a reminder of the justice the High Court undermined: "By preventing states from correcting the counting errors that result from different voting technologies, the conservatives have precipitated a violation of equal treatment far larger than the one they claim to avoid."[46]

Douglas Kellner, a philosopher who wrote a book on the election, elaborated the injustice of the per curiam decision and pointed to a judicial purpose more specific than achieving justice:

> The scandal [of obsolete voting equipment nationwide] was multiplied by the fact that the older equipment was largely in place in poor and minority, largely African American, districts, but such concerns did not bother the Partisan Supremes, who were more interested in putting their conservative ally George W. Bush in the White House than addressing the injustices of the American way of voting and crisis of democracy evident in Florida—a crisis that the conservative majority Supreme Court decision immensely intensified.[47]

Most legal commentators who highlighted the political purposes of the High Court—both in putting Bush in the White House and in ensuring that a Republican would be in charge of making appointments to the aging Supreme Court—treaded more carefully than Kellner and Bugliosi in making the partisan charge. Michelman, for example, subordinated such speculation to a footnote, where he said of the per curiam decision:

> The silence here [on the Article II issue endorsed by Rehnquist, Scalia, and Thomas] of Justices O'Connor and Kennedy is fully consistent with suspicion that they acted in *Bush v. Gore* (a) as judicial conservatives and (b) out of preference for a Bush presidency. They stood ready to assert on other grounds in support of an order terminating the election controversy in Bush's favor.[48]

Instead of saying that O'Connor and Kennedy's purpose in the per curiam was to put Bush in the White House, he suggested simply that their failure to support Rehnquist's concurring opinion was "fully consistent with" such conservative, partisan motives—recognizing an act-purpose relationship.[49]

Dworkin avoided a direct claim of partisan purposes by attributing that judgment to others, insisting that the weak defenses of the *Bush v. Gore* decision

> are not enough, singly or together, to dislodge the conviction of most American lawyers and citizens that the five justices acted cynically—not in defense of established law, as they claimed, or even of conservative principles of jurisprudence or political philosophy to which they were otherwise committed, but with a distinct, partisan, and self-interested political goal in mind. On this view, the conservative justices decided as they did in order to elect the president who was most in sympathy with their own political convictions, and who would be likely, when he appointed future Supreme Court justices, to appoint those who would join them, to strengthen their control of the Court, rather than with their more liberal rivals.[50]

Dworkin's cautious argument was, in a way, more damning than a direct charge of partisanship, for it attributed this interpretation of motives broadly (to most American lawyers and citizens), suggesting, perhaps, that this was the most obvious or most popular or most plausible reading of the motives embodied in the High Court's actions.

Elsewhere, Dworkin provided more support for this claim of partisanship, though he allowed his readers to connect the dots. He noted longer-term goals of the conservative majority that might easily be connected to the installation of Bush in the White House, insisting that their "aim [is] to transform constitutional law, not as the Warren Court did, to strengthen civil liberties and individual rights, but rather to expand the power of states against Congress, shrink the rights of accused criminals, and enlarge their own powers of judicial intervention."[51] Lest the connection be missed, Dworkin explained the agency required to reach these purposes:

> The prospects of future success for the conservatives' radical program crucially depend on the Court appointments that the new president will almost certainly make. Those appointments will determine whether the conservatives' activism will flourish (even adding, perhaps, the two new votes that would be needed to overrule abortion rights so long as O'Connor and Kennedy refuse to take that particular step) or whether it will be checked or reversed. Bush long ago signaled, in naming Scalia his favorite justice, his intention that it flourish.[52]

Dworkin was coy here, demonstrating long-term purposes, explaining the means required for reaching those purposes, yet drawing back from personally endorsing the obvious connection between the two. Indeed, he explicitly rejected the connection, suggesting that "[i]t is . . . inherently im- plausible that any—let alone all—of them [the conservatives] would stain the Court's reputation for such a sordid reason [as furthering their political aims]."[53] Yet he ended his essay with an admonition paired with a trou- bling conclusion: "We must try, as I said, not to compound the injury to the Court with reckless accusations against any of its members. But those of us who have been arguing for many years that the Supreme Court makes America a nation of principle have a special reason for sorrow."[54]

So, in Dworkin's construction, the decision lacked principle, was made by judges with a long-term goal of transforming constitutional law—a pur- pose that could only be wrought by ensuring that a Republican president held the power to replace the aging justices—and, in fact, "ensured . . . a Bush victory."[55] Given Dworkin's construction, calling the accusation of partisanship reckless seems inconsistent, except, perhaps, inasmuch as it serves to discourage "compound[ing] the injury to the Court." Such an ac- cusation, under Dworkin's construction, would be justified, though per- haps reckless in its harmfulness.

Tribe also was cautious in considering partisan purposes. He admitted that it was possible "that the action of those justices was overdetermined, being a product both of self-aggrandizing proclivities and of a preference for candidate Bush. No doubt, the justices in the majority shared, at a min- imum, that baseline preference." Calling a Bush presidency a preference rather than a goal of the majority diminishes its influence over the deci- sion, while still highlighting its potential role in motivating the Court to decide as it did. Tribe backed farther away from this implication, however, by psychologizing the decision-making process, insisting that "the role that this shared preference played in each justice's mind remains ultimately unknowable—probably even to that justice."[56] Thus, even if this purpose guided their decision, he suggested, it may have done so unconsciously. This fairly removes premeditation (and the attendant responsibility that goes with it) from the act.

As Dworkin did, Tribe laid the obvious resources for constructing parti- san motives on the table, even as he discounted them. In another passage, he noted that alternative means for reaching a Bush presidency were available:

> [L]eaving the matter to Congress looked like a fairly secure way to hand the election to Bush [and thereby] underscores the fact that the Court's dramatic intervention need not have reflected a wish to assure a Bush

presidency (and hence to secure the almost incestuous appointment of like-minded successors to the Court), but could well have reflected nothing beyond dismay at the very processes that lay ahead regardless of their result, including a wish to have the presumed Bush succession unmarred by what Justice Scalia described—in an opinion accompanying the December 9 decision of a bare majority of the Court to issue a stay—as "a cloud upon . . . the legitimacy of [Bush's] election."[57]

Tribe's words were measured: the obvious purpose need not have been to put Bush in the White House; it could well have reflected dismay over the processes to follow. On the other hand, he implied, it could have embodied that political purpose, and it might not have involved dismay over processes. Overall, his construction suggested that there was another means to reach the favored political conclusion, and perhaps the Court did not even seek that conclusion (acting regardless of the result). At the same time, the Court wished, perhaps, to reach that conclusion in a way that least threatened *Bush's* legitimacy (where there was no intimation that an alternative result would protect Gore's legitimacy). Tribe's curious construction is analogous to attributing these motives to a car buyer: "I don't necessarily want to buy a sports car, but I'd like it to be a *red* sports car."

Balkin was among the most direct of the legal scholars to critique the Court's potentially partisan motives, elaborating on its political purposes and the means to reach them. He began by noting the potential conflicts of interest in the case, reiterating (and thereby highlighting) them even as he rejected some of them:

> Justice Scalia's son worked at the same law firm as Theodore Olson, who represented the Bush team before the Court. Justice Thomas's wife was employed by the Bush transition team. Neither of these two conflicts is particularly important; at most they demonstrate that Scalia and Thomas are well connected to conservative elements within the Republican Party, which should surprise no one. But the most important conflict of interest applied to all of the Justices. By effectively deciding who would become the next president, they were also effectively deciding who would appoint their replacements and future colleagues. It was widely speculated that Chief Justice Rehnquist and Justice O'Connor had been considering retirement in the next four years. They would much rather retire under a Republican president than a Democratic one.[58]

Conflict of interest here was the basis for a personal purpose, which nonetheless was widely shared by the majority. The media reports about Rehnquist and O'Connor retiring in the future sharpened Balkin's construction of their personal interests, in this account. For O'Connor in particular, Balkin repeated in a footnote the news story about her dismay on learning that Gore had taken the lead in the presidential election and her husband's assertion that she wanted to retire and did not want a Democratic president to appoint her successor.[59]

As damning as Balkin's construction of purpose was, he too pulled back, in a manner, in explaining their actions, calling it

> no isolated fender bender in which a local judge helped out the son of a former law partner. Rather, the case decided the outcome of a presidential election and may well have determined who would sit on the Supreme Court and the lower federal courts for decades to come. Moreover, unlike the judge deciding the case of a fender bender in some obscure venue, the Court could not have failed to recognize that all eyes were upon it. That the conservative Justices acted as they did suggested that their partisanship was so thorough and pervasive that it blinded them to their own biases. It seemed as if they had lost all sense of perspective.[60]

Balkin's pull-back comes in the sense of lost perspective, as if the justices acted not thoughtfully, purposefully, and maliciously but blindly. The analogy to an explicit fix by a local court condemned the judges' motives in the harshest sense, as they acted in partisan fashion before the whole world. So much for a pull-back.

Balkin also took on the frequent claim that, of course, Supreme Court opinions have political consequences, for such decisions typically carry social, economic, political, cultural, and other implications. However, Balkin drew a "distinction . . . between the 'high' politics of political principle and the 'low' politics of partisan advantage."[61] Balkin applied the distinction to the Rehnquist Court:

> The same five conservative Justices who formed the majority in *Bush v. Gore* had been engaged, for over a decade, in a veritable revolution in constitutional doctrines concerning civil rights and federalism. In those decisions, the five conservatives had been promoting a relatively consistent set of ideological positions like colorblindness, respect for state autonomy from federal interference, and protection of state governmental processes from federal supervision. But the decision in *Bush v. Gore* did not seem to further those values, at least not directly. Rather, the five conservatives seemed to adopt whatever legal arguments would further the election of the Republican candidate, George W. Bush.[62]

Here, the purpose controls the agency, as the justices ignored their own ideological positions in adopting whatever legal arguments would put Bush in the White House.

Other scholars adopted the same argument, that the majority ignored its typical ideological positions in reaching a conclusion that would put Bush in the Oval Office. Two communication scholars, Theodore Prosise and Craig Smith, noted that "these justices were not merely settling a question of law; they were participating in a decision to determine who would be president, and thus who would make the next appointments to the Court." They added that "[t]he justices were no doubt aware that their decision would influence the direction of the Court for years to come."[63] Michael Klarman, a legal scholar, called "the *Bush* outcome . . . a product of these Justices' partisan political preference for George W. Bush, which, for at least a couple of them [notably O'Connor and Rehnquist], may have been enhanced by their desire to retire from the Court while a Republican President is in office to choose their replacements."[64]

Garrett endorsed this specific partisan purpose by noting something unique about the *Bush* case that underlies claims of a partisanship: "Rarely does the Court actually know that its decision will result in the immediate election of one or the other individual who is a party in the case. In *Bush v. Gore,* however, the Court must have been aware that each decision it rendered helped George Bush and harmed Al Gore."[65] The immediacy of the result, Garrett suggested, bolstered the idea that this was the Court's aim. Because the next president was likely to select additional Supreme Court justices, she noted, the Court had a personal interest in the outcome of the election. And this purpose, by the majority, of continuing its legacy was dear to them, because "the future membership [of the Court] determines whether a retiring justice's jurisprudential legacy will live on and whether remaining justices will be able to assemble majorities for their opinions."[66] This partisan judicial purpose, then, led to the adoption of these particular means for continuing the conservatives' legacy.

Louise Weinberg took this judicial purpose of shaping future appointments to the High Court for granted and suggested that such a purpose offended the Constitution:

[An] offense to Article III occurs when, in choosing the President, majority Justices try to influence the choice of their own future brethren and successors, and so fasten on the country their own ideology and politics—their own interpretations of the Constitution and laws—for the future, beyond the ordinary reach of stare decisis and their own lifetimes. There is

offense to Article III in this because life tenure is all the temporal power the
Constitution bestows upon a Justice of the Supreme Court.[67]

Weinberg distinguished this from simple strategic resignations:

> It is one thing for a single Justice to plan a strategic resignation. It is quite
> another for the majority of Justices, sitting within the jurisdiction of the
> Supreme Court of the United States, cloaked in all the majesty of Article III,
> to make the Court, as an institution, their instrument in putting their pre-
> ferred candidate into the presidency, in order to facilitate their own strategic
> resignations.[68]

Weinberg warned that such a practice could set up the Court "like a caste
of Janissaries, future and present kingmakers in potential perpetuity."[69] If
such a caste of judges controlled both their successors and the presidential
election, they would become "self-perpetuating lawgiver and kingmaker
both."[70] Weinberg's highly speculative scenario sounded much like the
worst-case scenarios for a continuing recount spun by Court defenders,
and she defended it similarly: "These unconstitutional opportunities are
hardly exaggerated or fanciful, since the Court has now availed itself of
them, or at least shown itself willing to disregard the appearance of having
availed itself of them, in *Bush v. Gore*."[71] The only advantage Weinberg's
claim had over, for example, Posner's "parade of horribles" (which he similarly characterized as "by no means fantastic, or even highly improbable")
is that she can cite a precedent for this action in *Bush v. Gore*, whereas Posner had to consider logically what could happen, with no precedents for
those events.

Purpose was constructed largely in terms of outcomes or future scenes.
Both sides pointed to negative future scenes, with Court defenders warning of an awkward, lengthy, problematic conclusion to the election, possibly involving a constitutional crisis, absent the High Court's intervention,
and Court critics' predictions that the Court, the rule of law, democratic institutions, and the public were actually harmed by the decision. Analogously, Court defenders described injustice avoided by the Court's slapping
down of the out-of-control state court, while Court critics described the injustice of disenfranchising undervoters and ignoring the will of 50 million
Americans who voted for Gore. Finally, Court critics noted that the conservative majority on the court voted its preference for president and may
have done so to ensure future appointments to the court that would continue their conservative legacy.

10

Scholars Reconstruct
Who Decided *Bush v. Gore*

The agents in the *Bush v. Gore* case were the High Court, the majority and dissent, and individual justices. We typically assume that particular kinds of agents have particular kinds of purposes, or that those with particular purposes ought to be seen as particular kind of agents. We characterize the agent who seeks justice differently from the agent who seeks political advantage, for example. We also define agents by the way they group themselves (e.g., into majority ranks or dissenter ranks) or the way they may be grouped by others (e.g., as conservatives or liberals). We draw on actions, agencies, purposes, attitudes, and scenes to define who agents are or to situate them within a framework that reveals something about them.

Closely connected to constructions of who agents are is their manner or attitudes. We may think of attitudes in a general or a particular way: as reflecting persistent character traits, such as disdaining chaotic democratic processes in general, or as closely connected to particular action, such as disdaining chaotic democratic processes in Florida's recount.

Agents in Bush v. Gore

As did the editorialists writing before them, scholars characterized the agents of the *Bush v. Gore* decision in light of how they divided on the decision, where their political and ideological allegiances lay, and what their actions revealed about their character. They went further than their editorialist counterparts in using elaborate claims of consistency and inconsistency on the part of the agents of the *Bush* decision to suggest that these were admirable or contemptible judges.

Court critics claimed that the decision was divided 5-4 along well-recognized ideological and political fault lines, while Court defenders stressed a 7-2 split on the equal protection issue and played down ideological and political differences. Jack Balkin made the case for a stark 5-4 division in *Bush v. Gore*, which he highlighted by comparing that division with other landmark constitutional law cases:

> Thus, unlike *Brown v. Board of Education* and the Nixon tapes case [which were unanimous], the decision in *Bush v. Gore* was far from unanimous. Indeed, it was divided along strictly ideological lines. Justices Kennedy and O'Connor proved decisive in forming a five-person conservative majority; as they have in so many other recent cases upholding states' rights, limiting federal regulatory power, and constricting federal constitutional claims.[1]

Balkin's characterization of the decision made it appear unusual in its split over a momentous constitutional decision (where earlier decisions had been unanimous) and suggested that the alignment was typical (having occurred in so many other recent cases) and ideological. Balkin cited thirteen examples of "revolutionary" constitutional cases in which the conservative majority voted as a bloc,[2] using (past) act-agent ratios to justify the group characterization as "a five-person conservative majority."

Other Court critics made the same point. Douglas Kellner noted that the *Bush* decision was "split across the usual ideological lines"[3] and referred to the conservative bloc as a "Gang of Five."[4] David Strauss said that the court was "splintered along ideological lines."[5] Frank Michelman characterized the per curiam as attracting "a bare majority of justices" and insisted that the decision reflected "a Supreme Court exactly split into the familiar, identifiably ideological wings."[6] Theodore Prosise and Craig Smith added purpose to their characterization, arguing that "[i]n *Bush v. Gore*, the justices not only divided along ideological lines, but they divided in a way suggesting self-serving political motives."[7]

Even Michael McConnell, who supported the decision, acknowledged the 5-4 split, which, he said, "created the appearance—whether or not justified—that the Court voted its politics instead of the law."[8] McConnell noted, as Balkin had implied, that a more unified opinion would have been better for this high-profile case:

> If the five justices in the majority had joined with Justices Souter and Breyer, and remanded to the Florida courts to conduct a recount under strict constitutional standards, the near unanimity of the decision would have been vastly reassuring to the American people. And whichever candidate had won would enter office with far greater public confidence in the legitimacy of his election.[9]

McConnell here was concerned about appearances and the possibility (which Prosise and Smith noted) that the decision could be seen as political. The ideological split identified by many scholars could be used to suggest that agents who share a particular ideological perspective also may share political purposes.

Overall, this strategy of grouping five individual justices implied that they were either working together in a common cause here or that they shared ideological perspectives or motives (called conservative) that would account for their joining—in short, that they are ideological agents, with the purposes and attitudes, and perhaps agencies and actions, associated with such agents. These are the kinds of agents who might be driven by their ideology or who might be seeking to embrace and propagate the values of their shared ideology. Ideology functions both as the identifying characteristic that justifies the grouping and the motivational force that drove them together. It also provides a touchstone for connecting the majority to candidate George W. Bush, who might be said to share their conservative ideology.

Samuel Issacharoff drew out the political alliances implicit in this ideological divide when he asked: "[D]id the Court accomplish anything more than the delivery of a resolution to the dispute that placed in office the candidate most in keeping with the Court's philosophical predilections?"[10] Michelman offered the same extension in noting "that the justices who cast the pro-Bush votes include all and only the five who are commonly identified as composing the conservative wing of an ideologically polarized Court."[11] Both scholars drew on the agent-act ratio, suggesting that ideological or philosophical leanings might have led to the act of casting a pro-Bush vote. The strategy drew from the agent side, where ideological or philosophical biases previously had been established, to account for their voting behavior. They did not do the reverse, namely, taking the vote on behalf of Bush to determine that these were ideologically aligned agents in an act-agent logic. Rather, the prior establishment of the ideological grouping provided the terministic ground from which they worked. Such a terministic strategy undergirded Michelman's later statement: "Out of uncertainty's jaws, then, the conservative majority's action drew a clean win for the candidate whom any judicial conservative could fairly be supposed to prefer, other things being in their mind more-or-less equal."[12]

Ronald Cass, who wrote about the *Bush* case in a book on the rule of law in America, launched one of the strongest attacks on the claim that the court was divided and partisan. To challenge the characterization of this decision as splintered, enhance the idea of judicial consensus, and downplay claims about the ideological character of the majority justices, Cass began with the earlier Supreme Court case on the election controversy before turning to the case at hand:

> all nine of the justices on the Supreme Court agreed in the first case, *Bush v. Palm Beach Canvassing Board* (*Bush I*) that the Florida Supreme Court's decision at least might have rested on an incorrect construction of the law. And seven of the nine justices in the second case, *Bush v. Gore* (*Bush II*), concluded that the Florida decision did violate federal law.[13]

Cass admitted that "[t]he justices disagreed sharply over the standard to use in reviewing the Florida Court's construction of Florida law in *Bush II*," but he noted that "that disagreement did not affect the outcome." Furthermore, he emphasized:

> Despite differences over other issues, seven justices agreed that the use of different standards to count votes violated the equal-protection clause of the Fourteenth Amendment to the Constitution. Although that conclusion was debatable under the precedents of equal-protection law, it had sufficient grounding in those precedents (and the outcome of the Florida decision seemed sufficiently at odds with core concepts of equal treatment) to secure a strong consensus.[14]

By beginning with *Bush I* as a standard and emphasizing the seven-judge agreement on the constitutional problem in *Bush II*, Cass's arrangement implied that only two votes were "lost" in moving from the first to the second case. In this sense, the second case had potential unanimity, which was lost with the two defectors. Admittedly, he noted the sharp disagreement on remedy, though instead of emphasizing that a bare majority

endorsed the outcome, he simply noted that this singular disagreement did
not affect it. While some commentators would note that the "agreement"
was more like a "failed compromise" that could not be repaired at the last
minute[15] (where that compromise contributed to the appearance of greater
genuine unanimity than we might attribute to the seven),[16] Cass offers a
rationale for the strong consensus in the sufficient (if debatable) grounding
in equal protection precedents. That is, the agency of equal protection
precedents explains why these seven judicial agents coalesced around this
constitutional finding. Because neither of the two dissenting judges who
are counted among this seven-member group, Breyer and Souter, ever
mentioned any of the equal protection precedents cited by the majority,
this construction is weak.

Cass attempted to build on this characterization of the Court as enjoying
consensus, reiterating that they were "largely of one mind on that critical
issue," by attacking the partisanship claim. He did this by noting that not
only were the five justices in the majority Republicans, but Justices
Stevens and Souter also were appointed by Republicans. Hence, he concluded, the decision did not yield a party-line vote (which would have
been 7-2), especially since Breyer, a Democrat, joined the majority on the
equal protection finding.[17] Cass's construction seemed to rule out the possibility that the majority five could have voted as they did for partisan reasons, while Stevens and Souter voted as they did for other reasons.

Cass qualified this claim in distinguishing between partisan allegiances
and the political ideologies of the justices:

> one would predict exactly the division that occurred on the remedy in *Bush
> II*. The justices voting against the immediate end to recounts were the four
> who tend to align with more politically liberal interests, interests generally
> congruent with Democratic policies. The justices voting for the immediate
> end to recounts were the five who tend to align with more politically con-
> servative interests, interests generally congruent with Republican policies.[18]

Through ideological alliances, Cass admitted through the back door the
possibility that the "justices' personal preferences [might have contributed]
to the result."[19] But he quickly closed that back door by insisting on the
"broad consensus on the decisive issue of law," by emphasizing the unusual nature of the case and the short time frame for action (which did not
give the Court "the opportunity to find ground that would blunt some of
the rough edges visible in the opinions"), and, finally, by insisting that
"the outcome was seen generally as sufficiently dictated by law to be

conclusive." To support this last claim, he pointed to "the overwhelming majority of the public and both of the principals [who] conceded . . . the authority of the courts (federal and state) to resolve arguments over the election."[20]

The first argument simply reiterated the previous claim of strong consensus, while downplaying the central point of contention, the remedy. The second argument forgave the Court for not better explaining itself and for failing to attract more colleagues to the majority position, using a scene-agency construction to explain why the Court did not do better (because the short time frame led to a decision with rough edges). Others could use the same short time frame to claim that without a more reflective and thoroughgoing analysis of the issues at stake, the majority simply went with its political preferences.[21] And the final claim relied largely on nonlawyers to judge the sufficiency of the legal claims, while ignoring the fact that Gore publicly denounced the Court's legal findings, even as he accepted the verdict.[22]

McConnell also stressed the support on the constitutional issue to deny partisanship: "In light of the 7-2 vote [on the equal protection problems], the Court's judgment cannot plausibly be attributed to base partisan motives."[23] By combining the Court's arguments over a number of issues (equal protection, safe harbor deadline, remedy) under the broad phrase "the Court's judgment" (rather than, say, "the Court's judgment on equal protection matters"), McConnell moved from (seven) agents to (generalized) act (of judgment) to downplay the potential for partisanship. Had he treated the issues individually in this characterization and discussed the 5-4 split on issues such as remedy and safe harbor, this agent-act argument would be much weaker.

After asserting the implausibility of claims that the majority was driven by "base partisan motives," McConnell admitted that when a court has options and knows the outcome of embracing one or the other option, "it would not be surprising to find that their judgment is affected [by the knowledge of those results]." And he despaired that even if it were not so affected, "there will be no way to prove it to the disappointed faction."[24] Thus, a scene that reveals the outcomes of acting one way or another may yield a partisan purpose. And to those who maintained that the High Court had such a purpose—which McConnell admitted he could not dispel— then McConnell offered a *tu quoque*, insisting parenthetically:

I strongly suspect that, if a state supreme court composed entirely of Republican appointees had rendered crucial decisions of dubious legal validity, which had delivered the state to Bush, Justice Stevens and Ginsburg, and many others who complained of Supreme Court meddling, would have seen the necessity of federal court review.[25]

This turning of the tables strategically characterized the state court's actions, by suggesting that they would have delivered the state to their preferred candidate, rather than, for example, ensuring that all undervotes were counted regardless of the outcome. His argument, then, was: "No, the *Bush* majority did not have partisan motives, but even if they did, the dissenters would have had them as well."

Perhaps the strongest source for Court critics arguing that the decision was partisan involved not linking two pentadic terms, such as agent and purpose (whereby a Republican judge might support a Republican presidential candidate), but de-linking two terms, notably agent-act and agent-agency. The argument was simply stated by Strauss, who said that the Court's extension of equal protection to ensure consistent standards in an election recount was "wildly out of character" for the conservative majority.[26] That is, these agents are not the sort one would expect to find an equal protection problem (an act) or to apply the equal protection clause (an agency) to a finding that the state had failed in its duties to voters. He suggested, alternatively, that such an act and a means would more likely be applied by the liberal Warren Court.

Michelman noted the same disjunction: "Taking one by one the issues of law that crucially divided the majority from the dissenters in *Bush v Gore*, it seems that ideological alignment either doesn't predict a vote at all or that it predicts the opposite of the votes cast by conservatives."[27] Michelman illustrated this disjunction by referring to the conservative majority's other decisions:

> it's not particularly to the Court's conservative ideological wing that you would normally look for a somewhat daring doctrinal innovation on behalf of voting rights. Conservative activism on behalf of individual rights claims has been confined to property rights and rights against ("reverse") racial classification. The current conservatives have displayed no special tenderness for voting rights.[28]

Michelman illustrated this last claim with two notable constitutional cases, *Adarand Constructors, Inc. v. Pena* and *City of Richmond v. J. A. Crosson Co.*[29] Thus, Michelman worked through two ratios: (past) acts-agents, which showed the constitutional preferences of these agents; then agents-act, which showed a violation of these preferences in the present case, leaving something other than these agents' constitutional leanings to explain the decision.

Other critics listed other types of agent-act inconsistencies in the majority opinion. Levine noted the conservative majority's tendency to defend states' rights over federal intervention, which they did not do here. He began by establishing past acts that showed this states' rights leaning:

> These five justices have held that the federal government has no business telling a sovereign state university it can't steal trade secrets just because such stealing is prohibited by law. Nor does the federal government have any business telling a state that it should bar guns in schools. Nor can the federal government use the equal protection clause to force states to take measures to stop violence against women.[30]

In intervening in a case involving Florida state law, Levine suggested, the justices were acting out of character. Prosise and Smith endorsed this charge of inconsistency as well, noting that "[t]he conservative majority of Rehnquist, Scalia, Thomas, O'Connor, and Kennedy have generally supported strict construction and the sovereign immunity of states" and citing several cases as well.[31] Weinberg agreed with the latter assessment, citing "the difficulty of squaring the opinion with the principles previously professed by the Rehnquist Court majority—certainly its customary concern for state autonomy as against federal interference."[32]

John Yoo in particular took on the charge of inconsistency with respect to strict construction and states' rights issues. He approached the strict construction issue in a left-handed way, tarnishing the Court's image to keep it from being more severely battered. He started by distinguishing what the Court said from what it did: "If not by deeds, certainly by its rhetoric, the Rehnquist Court has promoted the idea of judicial restraint."[33] He even admitted that the per curiam opinion "genuflects to this ideal."[34] However, he insisted, "[c]ritics of Bush v Gore . . . should not have been surprised by the Court's lack of restraint. The Court has done everything but hide behind the passive virtues." Yoo listed a series of cases where the High Court had been anything but restrained:

> It has reaffirmed the right to abortion and has placed limits on religion in the public sphere. In the federalism area, it has invalidated a series of federal laws in order both to protect state sovereignty and to limit the powers of the national government. One of the laws, the Violence Against Women Act,

passed Congress by large majorities in both houses of Congress. In the race area, the Court has invalidated affirmative action in federal contracting and struck down redistricting that sought to maximize minority representation. On the First Amendment, the Court has invalidated federal laws so as to expand commercial speech and to protect indecent or pornographic material. It has risked confrontation with the political branches by striking down federal laws solely on the ground that they violate separation of powers. Hence, the Court has invalidated the Line Item Veto Act and reversed an effort to expand religious freedoms that the Court had cut back.[35]

Yoo used this long list of aggressive judgments to conclude that "[t]his Court has been anything but shy in flexing its powers of judicial review to intervene in some of the most contentious issues of the day."[36] Ironically, Yoo was able to use the Violence Against Women Act to support an argument that the Court had been consistent in not exercising judicial restraint, whereas Levine had used that and other cases to argue for inconsistency on the states' rights front. The grammatical implication of Yoo's argument is clear: these acts are those of activist justices, not those who practice judicial constraint. Yoo was willing to let the Court suffer from failing to practice what it preached (in claiming to exercise judicial restraint or in philosophically supporting this position) in order to demonstrate consistency between these past involvements in contentious acts and the *Bush* case for which it was so criticized.

Yoo also took on the claim that the conservative majority was acting inconsistently with respect to its generally recognized support of states' rights over the federal government.[37] Rather than denying that the conservative majority supported states' rights (changing the agents), Yoo worked on the act side, distinguishing this act from those supporting states' rights. After admitting that the Rehnquist court had defined itself, in large part, by "protecting states as institutions from federal judicial power," Yoo drew a distinction:

> A principled adherence to federalism, however, does not require the Court to refuse to review the presidential election procedures used by states. Federalism does not create a free-fire zone where states may do anything they please. Rather, federalism is about the appropriate balance of power between federal and state authority, so that neither government abuses its own power at the expense of the rights of the people.[38]

By defining the majority's traditional support of states' rights as "balanc[ing] power between federal and state authority," Yoo suggested that what the Court did was not inconsistent.

Yoo attempted to bolster his argument by insisting that voting is a special case when it comes to federalism, that "our constitutional system today permits substantial federal intervention into state elections." To support this, Yoo cited three cases where the Supreme Court intervened in state election issues.[39] Unfortunately, Yoo attempted to prove too much. Of the three cases he cited, only one was from the Rehnquist Court (the others coming from the Warren Court), and this was *Shaw v. Reno,* where the High Court prevented states from taking race into account when creating political districts, even as they attempted to give minorities more political power.[40] Critics would admit that the Rehnquist Court defied states' rights when it came to beating back programs that affirmatively sought to support minority power, though they would distinguish this decision which did not.

Yoo's strategy attempted to blur the agents here, by making the Supreme Court in general synonymous with the Rehnquist Court, whereby the Supreme Court is consistent in its involvement in state election issues (based on the cases he listed),[41] in previous cases and in the *Bush* case. Obviously, critics could distinguish the Rehnquist Court as the one acting out of character.

Other critics looked at the inconsistency of particular majority justices. Michelman quoted Justice Scalia's concurring opinion in a 1990 case urging that the Supreme Court "need not . . . inject itself into every field of human activity where irrationality and oppression may theoretically occur."[42] Given this stated position on judicial restraint, why, he asks, would Scalia wish to do so "in a case, of all cases, where a presidential election hangs in the balance?"[43]

Cass Sunstein looked at both Scalia's and Thomas's approaches to constitutional interpretation, notably "their commitment to 'originalism' as a method of constitutional interpretation," which, he suggested, was inconsistent with their approach to this case:[44]

> There is no reason to think that by adopting the Equal Protection Clause, the nation thought that it was requiring clear and specific standards in the context of manual recounts in statewide elections. In fact it is controversial to say that the Fourteenth Amendment applies to voting at all. The failure of Justices Scalia and Thomas to suggest the relevance of originalism, their preferred method, raises many puzzles.[45]

Because Scalia and Thomas did not employ their preferred method in this constitutional case, there was an agent-agency inconsistency which Sunstein called "[o]ne of the real oddities of the majority opinion."[46]

In light of the attack on the conservative majority's inconsistency in applying its judicial philosophy to *Bush v. Gore*, Richard Pildes offered a different kind of consistency, rooted in fundamental values about the American system of democracy. He urged that the conservative majority had consistently defended the key value of order in democratic processes, as they did in *Bush*. He cited the 2000 case of *California Democratic Party v. Jones*, which concerned the constitutionality of a ballot initiative approved by California voters to implement a "blanket primary" system, whereby voters voting in primaries could choose which party's primary they wanted to vote in, office by office, rather than voting exclusively in one (e.g., the Democratic primary).[47] Pildes noted that the U.S. Supreme Court reversed the district court's decision and the court of appeals' affirmation to support the initiative, with the seven Supreme Court justices who supported the equal protection claim in *Bush* siding against Stevens and Ginsburg. Pildes contrasted the district court's "celebrat[ion]" of the state's "experiment[s] in democratic government" with the High Court's concerns for ensuring order in democratic processes. He noted that the High Court cast "the State" as an "active agent" that challenged the "'rights' of political parties."[48] Pildes suggested that the Court viewed "democratic politics and political organizations as fragile and potentially unstable entities that require judicial protection [because] a single election in a blanket primary 'could be enough to destroy the party.'"[49]

Pildes next reviewed the High Court's position on fusion candidates—where a single candidate is put on the tickets of more than one party (typically a major party and a third party). A unanimous court of appeals rejected a state's ban on fusion candidates, only to be reversed by the Supreme Court 6-3 (the conservative five plus Breyer). The Court again worried about order, Pildes noted, insisting that "states must surely be able to 'temper the destabilizing effects of party splintering and excessive factionalism.'"[50]

In yet a third case, Pildes showed that the conservative majority, plus Breyer, supported the exclusion of a third-party candidate from a debate on public television. The majority again worried about order, noting that "public broadcasters would be faced with 'the prospect of a cacophony . . .'" if [the third-party candidate's] First Amendment claim were accepted [and

the television station was forced to include him and others in their televised debates]."[51]

These three examples drew a lesson about these conservative agents
(through an acts-agents relationship), that perhaps it was not political
leanings or illicit purposes that guided the *Bush* decision but "different cultural assumptions about how important order and stability, as opposed to
competition and fluidity, are to democracy."[52] Pildes's construction fit well
with constructions of judicial purposes developed by defenders urging that
the Court sought to avoid political chaos, a constitutional crisis, or a
drawn-out contest that might have left the country without an elected
leader—all concerns about order in our democracy. Indeed, he tied these
conservative agents to such purposes:

> When the Court envisioned a political resolution of *Bush v Gore,* the election,
> how much was it moved by a cultural view, not a narrowly partisan prefer-
> ence, that "democracy" required judicially ensured order, stability, and cer-
> tainty, rather than judicial acceptance of the "crisis" that partisan political
> resolution might be feared by some to have entailed? If the Court were so
> moved—by the country's perceived need for what Frank Michelman calls
> "judicial salvation"—*Bush v Gore* would be of a piece with the Court's gen-
> eral vision of democratic politics and the role of constitutional law.[53]

Pildes recreated a sense of consistency among the conservative justices' actions, situating them as agents with a particular vision of democracy and
turning to apply that vision to a *Bush* decision now made consistent with
those justices' views. He raised and rejected the narrowly partisan preference view that would find consistency in conservative Republicans supporting the conservative Republican presidential candidate.

Even some critics of *Bush v. Gore* conceded Pildes's point about the conservative majority's attitudes toward order in democracy. Laurence Tribe
reviewed precedents in election cases supported by the majority and found
that their "signature concerns were the avoidance of political ferment and
fragmentation, the preservation of established hierarchy, and the imposition, whenever possible, of formally realizable, mechanical rules instead
of contextual standards requiring discretion and subjectivity in their
application."[54]

If this agreement provided an attitude-act consistency that explained the
Bush decision, Court critics were not willing to concede that it justified the
decision. For example, Guinier admitted that stability was important to the
conservative majority but urged that the emphasis on stability undermined
democracy:

The elevation of stability and measured change as *the* primary goal of politics disconnects democracy from its participatory ideal. The combination of a thin and mechanistic view of democracy governed by a similarly thin and mechanistic view of equality simply reinforces the ability of the elite within the two major parties to compete among themselves for the reigns of power, while manipulating elections to assure the desired outcome.[55]

Thus, Guinier would trump the attitude-act explanation with a concern for purpose-act, whereby the Court ought to be concerned with ensuring that the participatory ideal of democracy is not overridden by a concern for stability. Other scholars would address the "order over law" argument in considering *Bush v. Gore* as an act.

A final group of characterizations of the conservative majority were decidedly more personal, going beyond their actions as justices to connect other elements to the construction of their individual characters. These came from the least scholarly of the critics: Vincent Bugliosi, whose book on the election grew out of a *Nation* editorial; Levine, a lawyer who disseminated his views via a very popular e-mail; Kellner, a philosopher whose book defined the *Bush* decision as a "theft"; and Alan Dershowitz, whose Oxford University Press book was pitched to a lay audience.[56] Scholars writing for law journals were much less willing to explore the biographies of the justices in accounting for Court motives.

Bugliosi, Kellner, and Dershowitz all noted media reports that Sandra Day O'Connor was upset on hearing (erroneously) that Gore had won the election, leaving her husband to explain that she wanted to retire but did not want a Democrat replacing her. This reference suggested that O'Connor was an agent with particular, personal motives in the *Bush* case. Bugliosi called it a "fact that O'Connor, per the *Wall Street Journal,* said before the election that she wanted to retire but did not want to do so if a Democrat would be selecting her successor."[57]

Kellner quoted *Newsweek*'s report quoting O'Connor in response to the news of a Gore victory as exclaiming, "This is terrible." He included the magazine's report of her husband's explanation "that his 'wife was upset because they wanted to retire to Arizona, and a Gore win meant they'd have to wait another four years' because O'Connor 'did not want a Democrat to name her successor.'"[58] Kellner claimed that in taking her role in the *Bush* decision, O'Connor "forever disgraced herself in the face of the public."[59] For Kellner, O'Connor was an agent with a particular, personal interest in the election.

Dershowitz offered the most extensive consideration of O'Connor, devoting a seven-page section of his book to her (he considers each of the conservative justices separately). He tied together several possible motives in claiming that "[t]he patriotic-partisan motive alone might well have caused Sandra Day O'Connor to decide the case in favor of Bush, even if she had not also had a unique personal motive to help guarantee and Bush victory." Dershowitz quoted a lengthy excerpt from the *Newsweek* article, which added to Kellner's factual account that O'Connor reacted to the Gore victory "with an air of obvious disgust," and noted that she had been "Republican majority leader of the Arizona State Senate and a 1981 Ronald Reagan appointee." The excerpt also noted that two witnesses described this incident.[60]

Maintaining his scholarly stance, Dershowitz did not conclude, based on this attitude-agent or past agent-present agent relationship and his character description, that O'Connor sided with the *Bush* majority for personal reasons, but he did believe the circumstances "raise a serious question about the appearance of justice." He drew on colleagues' comments to help unpack O'Connor's motives, finding that "her *personal* motives may have not been the deciding factor, since she already had a strong *political* inclination toward favoring a Bush victory, and what she meant by 'terrible' was terrible for the country, not terrible for her and her retirement plans."[61] He endorsed this reading by calling her a "lifelong Republican" who was "extremely active in the Arizona Republican Party and in [two Republican presidential campaigns]"; a legislator and a potential (past) "Republican candidate for governor"; a "'very political animal,'" who began as a moderate and "'moved toward the right.'"[62]

Dershowitz went further in painting O'Connor as a partisan who was not "the first politically active elected official to serve on the high court." However, he sought to make O'Connor a special case:

> [T]raditionally politicians have left their partisanship behind when joining the Court. Not so with O'Connor. While serving as a justice, she has been criticized by judicial ethics experts on at least two occasions for using her position as a justice to support partisan Republican causes. Such criticism is rare in the Court's history.[63]

Dershowitz reviewed the two incidents at issue. The first involved her agreement to give a "private briefing" on the Court for Republicans giving at least $10,000 to a political action committee in 1987. She backed out of the engagement after the American Bar Association criticized her for violating its Judicial Code of Conduct, "but not until after her name had been used successfully in the fundraising solicitation," Dershowitz added. The second involved the writing of a letter, requested by an Arizona Republican, supporting "a Republican Party resolution declaring the United States to be 'a Christian Nation . . . based on the absolute law of the Bible, not a democracy.'" Dershowitz noted that she wrote this letter "on Court stationery," and it was used in a state party campaign. She later disavowed the letter, Dershowitz reported, by saying "she had 'had no idea' the letter would be used politically." Dershowitz insisted: "The available evidence points to the opposite conclusion," noting the clarity of the request (which he reproduced).[64]

Dershowitz summarized his indictment by concluding: "Justice O'Connor has thus twice publicly endorsed partisan Republican causes."[65] Thus, past acts inform us about a present agent's character, which, in turn, suggests something about her motives in *Bush v. Gore*. While Dershowitz admitted that she "has not repeated her openly partisan mistakes in recent years," he used her reported comments on the apparent Gore victory to show "that her allegiance to her old party is still strong."[66]

Dershowitz used this examination of O'Connor's partisanship to suggest an either/or conclusion that no Court defender would accept:

> Of course, even if the personal could be separated from the partisan, the suggestion that the deciding factor in her decision was her partisan support for the Republican candidate rather than her personal desire to retire does not put O'Connor in much better light. Her judicial vote was improper if it was influenced by *either* personal or partisan political considerations.[67]

Her only redemption, Dershowitz suggested, would be if she would have voted the same way had Gore been ahead and Bush sought to continue the recount. But he found this position hard to defend, because she did not vote in this case as she had in other cases.[68] Thus, through acts in the distant and recent past, constructions of her attitude toward Gore, and constructions of her persona as a political agent, Dershowitz constructed her motives as tainted in the *Bush* case.

Justice Scalia received considerable scrutiny from these Court critics as well. All four drew attention to a potential conflict of interest involving his sons, both of whom worked for law firms representing Bush.[69] Kellner called them "key" law firms, including "the Florida law firm that included the highly visible Bush lawyer Barry Richards, Bush's point man in the

Florida cases."[70] Kellner cited "(futile) demands for him to recuse himself" from the case.[71]

Dershowitz offered another either/or that qualified his own concern about this paternal conflict of interest, "find[ing] it difficult to believe he was actually motivated by such personal factors." Instead, he suggested, "Scalia's primary motive is to pack the high court, as well as the lower courts, with judges who share his ideology."[72] Once again, Dershowitz embodied the even-handed scholar, who nonetheless found grounds for condemning Scalia. He found support for this concern from Scalia's former University of Chicago colleague, Judge Richard Posner, who told *Harper's Magazine* that "justices are not indifferent to their colleagues and successors, and the president [who] appoints them. That's an inherent serious conflict [and] you can't exclude the possibility of an unconscious influence."[73]

Yet Dershowitz wanted to go beyond this unconscious influence, to suggest that Scalia's conservative ideology, which was "'of the Old World European sort, rooted in the authority of the Church and the military.'"[74] Indeed, Dershowitz wanted to trace Scalia's ideological bent back to his childhood, where he reported that a friend at the "'elite church-run military prep school in Manhattan'" that Scalia attended "remembered him at age seventeen as 'an archconservative Catholic [who] could have been a member of the curia.'"[75] So, this agent with an ideological bent that went back to his teenage years, Dershowitz suggested, was likely to have acted "when necessary to get his candidate elected," even if doing so flew in the face of his judicial philosophy.[76] He concluded:

> Scalia's vote in *Bush v. Gore* has shown that the most accurate guide to predicting his judicial decisions is to follow his political and personal preferences rather than his lofty rhetoric about judicial restraint, originalism, and other abstract aspects of his so-called constraining judicial philosophy, which turns out to be little more than a cover for his politics and his desire to pack the Court with like-minded justices.[77]

Kellner endorsed that view of Scalia's partisanship, characterizing Scalia and Clarence Thomas as "nothing more than transparent shills for the right wing of the Republican Party," while reinjecting the personal as well, claiming "Antonin Scalia was itching to succeed Rehnquist as chief justice."[78] He claimed that "Scalia had reportedly said that he would resign if a Democrat was elected president, which would block his ascent up the Court ladder, hence his entire maneuvering and power play could be read as brute self-interest."[79] Although Kellner cited no source for the resignation threat claim, a *Washingtonian* magazine article from March 2000 provided support for it.[80] Thus, for Kellner, personal and political purposes merged to explain Scalia's actions and to construct him as a particular kind of agent.

Similar charges of a personal conflict of interest were launched against Justice Thomas by all four Court critics. All noted that Thomas's wife had a job at the conservative Heritage Foundation, collecting applications from conservatives seeking jobs in a new Bush Administration.[81] The implication was that Mrs. Thomas's job hinged on the success of Bush's appeal, giving Thomas a personal reason for supporting the Bush position. Dershowitz claimed that Mrs. Thomas had a "substantial interest in a Bush victory."[82]

Dershowitz went much further than the other critics in explaining Thomas's motives. He insisted that "Thomas divides the world into friends and enemies."[83] He demonstrated Thomas's ties to his "friends," serving as a regular speaker to many conservative organizations, including the Claremont Institute, "a group that was actively seeking President Clinton's impeachment." Dershowitz noted that Thomas spoke to that group "just three days before the impeachment vote," ignoring the Judicial Code of Conduct, "which prohibits a judge from 'being a speaker or guest of honor at an organization's fundraising events' or 'making speeches for a political organization.'"[84] Thomas owed his seat on the Court, Dershowitz noted, to the first President Bush and was identified by George W. Bush as one of his "two favorite justices" (Scalia being the second).[85]

Democratic presidential candidate Al Gore and his running mate, Joseph Lieberman, on the other hand, had voted against Thomas's confirmation by the Senate, making an enemy of Thurgood Marshall's conservative replacement. Dershowitz claimed that Thomas had an "abiding hatred for Gore and Lieberman," which contrasted with "his deep sense of loyalty to the Bush family."[86] Dershowitz quoted Jeffrey Toobin to identify the origin of Thomas's hatred, saying that the confirmation hearings "damaged" him, "hurt [him] more deeply than anyone could comprehend," and caused him to "churn within."[87] The result, Dershowitz suggested, was that "[a]fter that transforming event [the Senate hearings that featured Anita Hill], he became consumed with anger, hatred, and revenge."[88] Thus, Dershowitz described an agent with particular attitudes and purposes that account for his act of siding with Bush. He even had Toobin give him an agency for taking action: "The heart of Thomas's strategy for striking back at his liberal critics is, of course, to utilize the Supreme Court itself."[89]

Dershowitz was less certain of Justice Kennedy's personal purposes, though he did note his earlier Republican work as a lobbyist who caught the attention of the Reagan administration. He suggested that Kennedy told his friends that he wanted to become chief justice—something a Democratic president would make problematic. And he found a conservative source to support that ambition in Robert Novak, who observed that "Kennedy's recent swing to the right [in his court decisions] led court-watchers to conclude that he was readying himself for a chief justice vacancy in a Republican administration.'"[90] Dershowitz did not claim that Kennedy was motivated by this purpose but warned that "if he in fact chose personal ambition or party loyalty over principle, then he has, in my view, morally disqualified himself from becoming chief justice or earning a place of honor in the history of the Supreme Court."[91]

Little was said about Rehnquist's personal motives, aside from his interest in retiring and, presumably, in being replaced by a Republican who could continue his judicial legacy.[92] Dershowitz simply insisted that Rehnquist was "a sure thing for the Republican candidate" because of his political leanings. He quoted an exchange between Henry Kissinger and H. R. Haldeman on the Nixon tapes, where the secretary of state asked whether Rehnquist was "pretty far right"; Dershowitz reported that "Haldeman replied, 'Oh, Christ, he's way to the right of Pat Buchanan.'"[93]

Kellner used actions of the newly installed President Bush to support the idea that political motives were in play, scornfully suggesting that

> to properly award his Supreme Court Godfathers, Bush responded to the Scalia-Rehnquist coup by appointing Eugene Scalia, Don Scalia's son, as solicitor of labor, the top legal position at the Department of Labor, while Janet Rehnquist, the Chief Executioner's daughter, was nominated to be inspector general of the Department of Health and Human Services. No subtlety or false decorum for the brazen Bush syndicate, ruled by the law of the properly greased hand.[94]

A decidedly postelection action by Bush was used here to cast doubt on the motives of the justices as they decided the case, perhaps suggesting a quid pro quo arrangement or, at the very least, an unsought reward for sufficiently political behavior. Such innuendo and contemptuous language moved Kellner's constructions away from the scholarly form, though this philosophy professor nevertheless attempted to document the facts on which his damning characterizations were based, unlike the editorialists whose language he mimicked.

One final, decidedly different approach to characterizing the agents in *Bush v. Gore* came from scholars claiming that the Supreme Court was the wrong agent to deal with the presidential election dispute. This relates to an issue of justiciability, though it emphasizes the quality and character of the agents engaging in the action, showing through a contrast that the *Bush* Court (indeed, any Supreme Court) was simply the wrong agent for the action of resolving a presidential election dispute.

Elizabeth Garrett's chapter in *The Vote: Bush, Gore & the Supreme Court* centered on this criticism under the title "Leaving the Decision to Congress." Garrett cited two lines of cases that demonstrated that the Supreme Court was the wrong agent to handle such issues. First, she noted that in the campaign finance reform arena, the High Court had rendered "ineffectual and often counterproductive jurisprudence . . . in part [because of its] institutional limitations."[95] Those limitations included a lack of "comprehensive structures and extensive factfinding" (which *are* available to policymakers).[96] She stated flatly: "Courts are not institutionally suited for this kind of decisionmaking. Instead, they work piecemeal, without sufficient awareness of the effects of their holdings, leading several scholars to point to the campaign finance cases as among the best of examples of the law of unintended consequences."[97] Thus, because of how they work (agencies) and the limited reach of their awareness (a scenic dimension), such cases (resolution actions) are ill suited to these agents.

Garrett expanded this concern to include issues involving "the mechanics of how states conduct their elections." She quoted a federal circuit court decision warning:

> intervention in state electoral processes, other than in extraordinary circumstances, would "thrust [federal judges] into the details of virtually every election, tinkering with the state's election machinery, reviewing petitions, registration cards, vote tallies, and certificates of election for all manner of error and insufficiency under state and federal law."[98]

Grappling with the minutia of election processes threatened to pull the courts down a slippery slope of endless interventions, which could clog the courts with issues best left to legislative bodies and commissions.

Garrett not only made the case that the High Court (and any court, for that matter) was ill suited to do this type of work, but she also made a positive case for Congress as a proper agent to settle presidential election disputes. Garrett challenged the notion that a neutral, independent group (such as a court) was needed to settle this dispute. She looked to the 1887

Electoral Count Act passed in the wake of the Hayes-Tilden presidential dispute of 1876 to argue that the legislators did not intend to avoid politics but to harness it appropriately. She insisted that "[b]y trying to reduce the naked partisanship that characterized the Hayes-Tilden decision, Congress was not trying to depoliticize the decision. Electing a president is a political act, and it should be left to the people and their representatives." She further explained that appropriate agent-act relationship:

> The electoral connection between the people and members of Congress provides another corrective. If some members of Congress had gotten out of hand, then voters could have sent a strong message when the lawmakers stood for election in 2002. Political pressure can be brought to bear through communications to legislators during congressional deliberations as the public watches elected officials on television.[99]

Thus, because the legislature is political, it is a more appropriate agent, since it must be responsive to the people in a way that the Supreme Court could not be. The resolution of this election crisis, then, also should reflect popular will, which the legislature is more likely to reflect. Garrett gave the example of the Clinton impeachment, which led to the "punishing" of some of the members of Congress who pushed impeachment in the 2000 elections.[100]

Michelman made a similar act-agent argument but brought in the conflict of interest (purpose) concern as well:

> senators and representatives caring to retain their offices would have had to face the judgments of voters on their manner of settling the election. In the circumstances of this case, that is a tremendous advantage of institutional competency or fitness. Whatever benefit may be claimed in other settings for the independence of the judiciary, this is one setting—the choosing not only of a political chief executive but of a maker of future members of the judiciary—in which insulation from the voters seems just about disqualifying.[101]

Issacharoff endorsed this agent-act relationship as well, by looking at the Electoral Count Act more closely, insisting that it involved "a coherent attempt made to place responsibility for resolving contested presidential elections in the domain of politics."[102] Sounding much like Garrett in connecting this act to a suitable agent, he argued that "Congress clearly concluded that such decisions would have an inevitable political cast and should therefore be kept clearly confined within the political branches."[103] The difference in his construction was that he brought in the nineteenth-century Congress's purposes to establish this agent-act ratio, rather than simply arguing from suitability.

Issacharoff also argued that the old congressional act specifically excluded the Supreme Court as an appropriate agent in such disputes, quoting the sponsor of the legislation, Senator John Sherman:

> But there is a feeling in this country that we ought not to mingle our great judicial tribunal with political questions, and therefore this proposition [to have the Supreme Court settle such disputes] has not met with much favor. It would be a very grave fault indeed and a very serious objection to refer a political question in which the people of the country were aroused, about which their feelings were excited, to this great tribunal, which after all has to sit upon the life and property of all the people of the United States. It would tend to bring that court into public odium of one or the other of the two great parties. Therefore that plan may probably be rejected as an unwise provision.[104]

Issacharoff used an examination of legislative purposes in choosing Congress as the appropriate agent for resolving presidential election disputes to establish the lack of wisdom of this judicial route.

Even Pildes, who supported the outcome in *Bush v. Gore*, agreed with Issacharoff on the legislative intentions of the Electoral Count Act, agreeing that Congress "chose exactly this political solution for disputed presidential elections in the Electoral Count Act, specifically rejecting the alternative of United States Supreme Court resolution."[105] And, he insisted, this follows the Constitution's explicit approach for disputes over congressional elections as well, which "makes both the United States House and Senate 'the Judge'—not the intriguing choice of words—'of the Elections, Returns, and Qualifications of its own members.'"[106]

Posner and Yoo attempted to bolster the case for the Court as proper agent of this act of resolving the presidential election. Posner qualified the nineteenth-century legislative act by challenging constructions of legislative intention:

> Completely unforeseen [by the 1887 legislature] was the possibility that a deadlock in the Presidential election might arise not from skullduggery (as in the 1876 election), not from a failure of any candidate to obtain a majority of the electoral votes, not from runaway electors, and not from an actual tie in the popular vote in a key state, but from innocent defects in electoral mechanics, whether defects in the design of a ballot, the staffing of the polling places, or the design, maintenance, or operation of voting and vote-tabulating machines, or gaps and ambiguities in the state statutes

regulating the administration of elections and the resolution of election disputes.[107]

Posner did not explain why this difference matters. The innocence of the problems does not make the Court any more politically responsive to the voters, whose will (we might suppose) ought to have an influence on the outcome.

The only serious concern Posner raised for Congress as the ultimate arbiter was that this election was "time-sensitive," and waiting until January 6, 2001, might not have been wise.[108] That is, the scene might require a quicker resolution than Congress could provide to ensure a smooth transition of presidential power; thus, the judicial agent is superior to the legislative agent in this case.

Yoo also took a stab at defending the Court as agent of resolution here, though not in a way that justifies so much as explains the *Bush* intervention. Citing earlier controversial cases where the Court intervened in national disputes, Yoo essentially argued that the Court had sufficient power to "pull off" this decision and still "survive with its legitimacy more or less intact . . . bring[ing] the election dispute to a final conclusion."[109] Thus, the power of this agent made it appropriate for Yoo, rather than whether it was more suitable than Congress. Yoo also stressed the benefits of ending a dispute that the Court "feared was tearing the country apart."[110]

Thus, in the dispute over the propriety of the agent of dispute resolution, advocates of the congressional route looked directly at the suitability of the agent—in terms of its character, its constitutional mandate, and its legislative propriety—while the defenders of court intervention looked at other acts, attempting to chip away at legislative propriety, highlighting the purpose of ending a dispute on a short deadline, or (least convincingly) of exercising power at its disposal.

Overall, Court critics portrayed the conservative five as partisans and ideologues who were politically and personally motivated and willing to act in ways inconsistent with their stated beliefs or past actions in order to ensure a Bush victory, the continuation of their conservative legacy, or their ascendancy to the chief justice position on the Court. They also characterized the Court as the wrong agent to engage in this act of dispute resolution, since Congress had been designated by the Electoral Count Act of 1887, was more representative of the people's will, and was politically answerable for its actions. Court defenders had their strongest argument in suggesting that these were agents who consistently sought to ensure order in politics and government, even at the expense of democracy. Yoo admitted that the five conservatives did not necessarily practice what they preached in terms of judicial restraint—indeed, they were activists who acted very much in character in *Bush v. Gore*. Others tried, less successfully, to play down the 5-4 split by emphasizing the seven votes for an equal protection problem. Finally, defenders questioned the propriety of having Congress settle the dispute, given its urgency. Past acts were drawn on by both sides, to show political activity, indications of political purposes, and prior decisions either consistent or inconsistent with action in the *Bush* case.

Attitudes of the Bush *Court*

Characterizations of agents involved in *Bush v. Gore* supported characterizations of the attitudes of those agents in acting as they did. To say, for example, that a justice is a partisan is to say that he or she has a partisan attitude. Characterizations of the attitudes of the agents in *Bush v. Gore* served to support particular characterizations of those agents or followed from describing those agents in a particular way. Attitudes also are tied to acts; one who engages in reckless acts, for example, could be charged with having a reckless attitude. As Burke noted, attitudes are "*incipient* acts," which means "an attitude can be the *substitute* for an act, [and] it can likewise be the *first step towards* an act."[111]

All other grammatical terms connect to attitude as well. The use of certain agencies may suggest particular attitudes (e.g., car bombs used to support political change may reflect indifference to the value of human life). Certain scenes may contain or give rise to particular attitudes (e.g., a dangerous scene yields a fearful attitude). Certain purposes (e.g., murder) are associated with certain attitudes (e.g., heartlessness).

In constructing attitudes, defenders had very little to say, while critics used a variety of constructions to suggest that the Court had problematic attitudes. Some characterizations readily lead to attitude attribution, suggesting that the Court may have been partisan and self-serving in its attitudes. Additionally, critical accounts of its attitudes revolved around "unjustified confidence" and "aggression" in the Court's intervention into the election. Issacharoff noted the Court's "swaggeringly confident intervention into Election 2000,"[112] tying attitude with the primary act. Tribe more fully described that act in speaking of "the Rehnquist Court's staggering confidence in its own ability to define and prioritize values of constitutional magnitude, and to decide which measures are needed to realize them."[113] Mark Tush-net spoke not of confidence but of a lack of proper attitude, since "[no one] on the Court demonstrate[d] self-doubt or a sense of inner vulnerability."[114]

Jack Balkin and Sanford Levinson also noted that the majority members were "confident of their power" but go further in suggesting that they were "brazen in their authority."[115] Ward Farnsworth urged that they acted despite an apparent conflict of interest, which made their actions "imprudent."[116] Peter Shane spoke of "[t]he arrogance of five Justices in bringing a presidential election to a halt by a one-vote judicial majority." He contrasted this with the majority's attitude in other cases, where they displayed "solicitousness toward protecting political processes against judi-cial intervention, especially at the state and local level."[117] Shane insisted that the Court was "not merely wrong, but reckless."[118]

Michelman called the majority "arrogant" and "rash."[119] However, he qualified his characterization of attitude to avoid the implication that the Court was acting simply on instinct or reacting in a thoughtless manner, since that might take away some of its responsibility to the extent that it knew not what it did. Instead, he painted the majority as strategic, insisting that it "intervened aggressively, decisively, and knowingly to resolve a presidential election in favor of the contestant who had named two of them as judicial models by which he would select future justices."[120] Here, in implying a political purpose, Michelman rendered their actions strategic as well as aggressive.

Garrett also connected attitude to an implicit purpose, describing the majority's "aggressive role in the selection of the forty-third president." She noted that the Court denied that it wanted to get involved in the political process but insisted that "[t]hese words sound strange" in light of what the Court did.[121] Michelman, commenting on the same majority claim that this was an "unsought responsibility," drew out the attitudinal implication more explicitly, saying that the majority "cannot be sincere."[122] Tribe sug-gested that such disclaimers were "insult[ing]."[123] In discussing the safe harbor deadline in particular, Tribe urged that

> the per curiam *disingenuously* translated the Florida court's opinion that the legislature wanted all recounts to be completed by December 12 (so as to take advantage of the promise contained in Congress's safe harbor statute) into a bright-line rule halting the recount at midnight, December 11—at the cost of throwing out countless legal votes.[124]

Both Tribe and Pildes agreed that the Court had an inappropriate attitude toward democracy. Pildes worried that "[t]he current Supreme Court consistently now acts as if the greatest threat is that democracy will become too unstructured, too excessive," and he asked, following *Bush v. Gore,* "whether that is the cultural attitude toward democracy we want our judges—including our Supreme Court—to take."[125] Tribe described the same concern as a "disdain for the meaningful participation of other actors in the constitutional debate [such as Congress]."[126] Boston College law professor Aviam Soifer believed that "[a]t its base, the Court's end-justifies-the-means initiative reveals a lack of respect for the decisions of the elected national political branches—or, for that matter, for state decision-makers."[127] Thus, Soifer made purpose primary, noted the problematic means adapted to that purpose, and suggested that this yielded an attitude of disrespect.

Court defenders had little to say about the Court's attitude, with a few exceptions. To the extent that they supported the reasoning of the majority, Court defenders implied that the majority had a reasonable attitude. Because Lund was the only scholar to endorse the entirety of the majority's decision, he most implied this reasonableness (though he never stated it explicitly).

Posner put a positive spin on claims of aggressiveness, brazenness, and arrogance: "The Court thrust itself boldly into the center of a political struggle."[128] He also implied that the majority acted not analytically but intuitively, because the "[f]ive justices in *Bush v. Gore sensed* that the Florida supreme court was embarked on a path that impaired rather than promoted constitutional values."[129]

The majority of characterizations that accounted for the attitudes of the Court, even if they did not necessarily justify them, turned to the scene as the source of attitudes. Pildes, for example, said that "the Court's actions seem to manifest *anxiety* about the capacity of other institutions, including political ones such as Congress, to avoid unleashing what the Court might well have perceived as 'the furies of civil commotion, chaos, and grave dangers.'"[130]

The most frequently mentioned scenic source of High Court attitudes was the Florida Supreme Court, whose actions were said to have led to the U.S. Supreme Court's attitude in this case. Strauss claimed that the majority "did not trust the Florida Court to play it straight."[131] That distrustful attitude inspired the involvement in the election dispute, as the scene of state court action led to a High Court attitude which led to High Court action.

Ronald Dworkin explained more than defended the majority when he noted that "[t]he five conservative Supreme Court justices who decided for Bush are widely reported to have been *infuriated* by the Florida court, and there is some evidence of that state of mind in the comments some of them made in oral argument in hearings before them."[132] Dworkin went beyond Strauss's distrust to suggest anger on the part of the High Court, drawing on others' reports about its members and their attitudes during oral arguments. Weinberg endorsed this view, calling the Court "clearly . . . *outraged* by the Florida Supreme Court's action, which it apparently perceived as partisan."[133] Weinberg put together the anger with the distrust, whereby perceived partisanship on the state court's part led to anger on the High Court's part. Insofar as the state court's actions became part of the scene of Supreme Court action (or created a scene), Weinberg offered a scene-attitude explanation.

Yoo, a true defender of the majority, made an argument about attitude very similar to the one he made about the consistency of the agents (who, he claimed, always were activist, despite their rhetoric to the contrary). In the face of claims that the majority had an arrogant attitude in the *Bush* case, he suggested that it had an arrogant attitude in many other cases as well, which he traced to its assumptions about judicial supremacy: "Claims to judicial supremacy bespeak an arrogance that the Court has a special role in the American political system, one borne not just out of its unique function in deciding cases or controversies, but out of some vague vision of itself as the final resolver of national issues."[134] Thus, in the face of claims that the conservative five were arrogant in *Bush v. Gore,* Yoo conceded that and added, in effect, yes, but they have always been that way. Thus, the Court's arrogant attitude was not a function of its posture toward Bush or Gore or of its frustration with the state court's rulings but rather of the agents themselves, who were consistently arrogant. Thus, agent, not scene or purpose, controls attitude here.

At best, then, following these characterizations, the majority was bold yet reasonable. Perhaps its actions were a function of anger at the apparent partisanship of the state court or anxiety about the chaos its members thought might ensue without a quick end to the postelection dispute. At worst, they were overly confident and arrogant, aggressive and rash, partisan and self-serving, and distrustful of democracy, the state court, and Congress.

11

Scholars Reconstruct When and Where the Court Reached Its Decision and What It Was Doing

⁂

S cene and act together constitute one of the most frequently used ratios of motives in our science-dominated society. Scene, it is often suggested, contains the act. Thus, socially unacceptable behaviors are often said to be the product of errant chemicals in our brains, such as neurotransmitters. Those chemicals become the material scene that explains actions; changing those chemicals—with antidepressant drugs, Ritalin, or other medicines—changes the neurochemical scene of our actions, "correcting" the "problem."

We invoke scene-act explanations in unscientific accounts of motives as well. Following the attack on the World Trade Center on September 11, 2001, there were horrific examples of a scene containing acts, as people trapped in the towers leaped to their deaths to escape the suffocating smoke and approaching flames. It was not a desire to die that led to these tragic deaths but rather a desire to escape an unbearable scene.

An opportunity exists for reversing this ratio as well. The suicide attackers who flew the planes into the twin towers engaged in an act that created the terrible scene. Similarly, Court defenders would argue that the Florida Supreme Court's actions created a scene that forced the U.S. Supreme Court to act.

Constructions of the Scene of Action

Scene received the least amount of discussion by Court critics, because they did not want to divert attention from the choices and actions of the majority. Court defenders, on the other hand, often mentioned scene, because they wanted to argue that *Bush v. Gore* was "contained" by the scene—that its qualities, some of which they would concede were bad, were a result of factors beyond the Court's control. The most frequent reference to scene is to the short amount of time the High Court had to act. Richard Posner, for example, explained that "[t]he Court was operating under great time pressure—and it shows."[1] He admitted that the majority decision was weak ("it shows") but blamed that not on the agents, their attitudes, or their purposes but on the temporal scene. Richard Pildes spoke of "the press of time," which explained why the decision was brief and less thorough than one might like.[2] Ward Farnsworth admitted that "[t]he shortness of time for decision in *Bush v. Gore* made any errors more pardonable," though he added that it "also brought with it obligations to try and ameliorate its effects."[3]

Nelson Lund went farther than describing the short window of time, describing a scene fraught with complexities:

> A great many novel legal issues were raised in a large number of lawsuits filed by the candidates and their supporters. Furthermore, unlike most other election disputes, those involving the electoral college must be resolved very quickly. *Bush v. Gore* itself was probably decided faster than any comparably important decision in history, and it came at the end of a series of judgments that had themselves been made in unusual haste.[4]

While this challenging scene gave Lund a platform for explaining this less-than-ideal decision (through a scene-act explanation), he did not mount that platform. Instead, he insisted that it was "remarkable . . . how easily defensible [the decision] is."[5] Lund's constant, never-give-an-inch strategy nonetheless set up an argument for those less certain of the strength of the majority's decision.

The most curious scenic argument by a Court defender has to be that of Posner, who used a scenic description of the case to challenge criticisms of the decision by legal scholars: "The narrow perspective of the typical legal professional is inadequate for evaluating the performance of the Supreme Court in so 'big' a case as Bush v Gore—'big' in the sense of involving a dispute whose consequences seem to dwarf the strictly 'legal' considerations bearing on its sound resolution."[6] Posner's reference to size (a scenic dimension) was an attempt to take the evaluation of the decision beyond the strictly legal to additional considerations, which he used to frame his "pragmatic" justification of the outcome of the case (even as he criticizes the legal reasons given by the Court for its decision). This scenic emphasis ties back to the discussion of Posner's characterization of the Court's purpose as centrally concerned with avoiding a future scene of extended disputes, a constitutional crisis, and a government without a leader at a time when its enemies could strike (as China did in capturing a U.S. military aircraft).

Essentially, Posner used an extralegal justification to defend this Supreme Court decision. To justify his reliance on extralegal considerations, Posner substituted his larger political scene for the legal scene. Thus, the scene contains this judicial act, but the scene is not constructed simply (or perhaps even primarily) of laws, constitutions, and judicial precedents but rather of determined enemies, a government in need of a leader, and a concerned citizenry. By changing the quality of the scene, Posner changed the quality of the act, judging it less in terms of its consonance with the law than its adaptation to "a looming political and constitutional crisis."[7]

Defending this approach involved Posner in a complex elaboration of his particular philosophy of judicial pragmatism. Indeed, it appears that Posner shaped this philosophy particularly with an eye to his defense of *Bush v. Gore.*[8] He explained:

> What the good pragmatist judge tries to do . . . is to balance the good effects of steady adherence to the "rule of law" virtues, which tug in favor of standing pat [i.e., "following the law"], against the bad consequences of failing to innovate when faced with disputes to which the canonical texts and precedents are not well adapted.[9]

Posner admitted that giving less weight to the rule of law "will horrify most legal professionals as a belittlement of legal reasoning, and hence an insult to their mystery"; but, he insisted, "law could do with some demystification."[10]

Posner's demystification included weighing, quite candidly, the consequences of the Court issuing what it knew to be a disingenuous decision against the pragmatic concerns for avoiding a crisis and ensuring a "good" outcome. For example, he appeared to believe that Rehnquist, with Scalia and Thomas, who joined in his concurring opinion in *Bush v. Gore*, did not really believe in the majority opinion they endorsed. But in doing so, they developed at least a minimal majority to support the outcome. Posner wondered:

> If all that matters are consequences, then dishonesty, which might seem the correct term for subscribing to a judicial opinion that one thinks all wrong, while no doubt regrettable becomes just another factor in the calculus of decision. But maybe this *is* the right way to think about judicial honesty, or more precisely candor (for *honesty* has financial connotations that are irrelevant to the subject under discussion). A judge will often join an opinion with which he doesn't agree, because he doesn't think a dissent will have any effect, or because he thinks a dissent would merely draw attention to a majority opinion otherwise likely to be ignored, or because he doesn't think the issue important enough to warrant the bother of writing a dissent and doesn't want to encourage other judges to dissent at the drop of a hat. These are pragmatic judgments, and such judgments suffuse the writing of a judicial opinion as well, where tact and candor are frequent opponents. Are these bows to the practical to be regarded as tokens of dishonesty, of a subtle form of corruption brought about by yielding to the pragmatic Sirens? If not, perhaps the decision of the conservative justices to join the majority opinion in *Bush v. Gore*, a momentous decision, is defensible even if they had to hold their breath to do so.[11]

Posner's quite remarkable support of judicial dishonesty that yields an overall good outcome is problematic enough, but almost as problematic is circumscribing what properly may be taken into account in determining what constitutes a good outcome for the pragmatic judge willing to use deception to reach it. Ronald Dworkin, for example, noted that a thoroughly pragmatic judge would want to take into account who was likely to become president given one decision or another in making a judgment of possible outcomes. He argued: "if Posner is right that the justices had a responsibility to reach a 'pragmatic' result in this case, then it would have been irresponsible of them *not* to have allowed [a consideration of who would win and how he would govern] to make a crucial difference [in their decision]."[12] Having reached that conclusion, under Posner's apparent assumptions, he still noted that "[i]t is thought to be a devastating criticism of the five justices, if true, that it made a crucial difference to them which candidate would win if they stopped the recounts."[13]

Dworkin noted that Posner recognized the possibility of a pragmatist judge taking into account who would be elected but then dismissed it as an inappropriate consideration. Dworkin insisted that "his defense is unconvincing,"[14] asking again from the perspective of pragmatist theory:

> Why is it not better in the long run to allow a very occasional minor derangement [of the balance of powers], hidden as well as possible [as Posner suggested], when that will save the nation from a calamitous presidency [as the conservatives might perceive with Gore]? Posner's argument seems driven more by the need, at all costs, to deny that a pragmatist judge would ever base his decisions on partisan political grounds than by any actual pragmatic case for that denial.[15]

Dworkin took on Posner's last line of defense regarding this pragmatist approach, relying on "rule-consequentialism":

> Rule-consequentialism [which Posner invoked to defend against political considerations entering into pragmatic judicial decisions] provides an argument for not judging consequences case by case, but deciding in accordance with fixed rules instead. But Posner is now proposing something very different: a hybrid process in which judges decide by assessing consequences, case by case, but adopt a rule [against political considerations] that requires them to leave the most important consequences out. That is perverse.

Dworkin offered an analogy to illustrate this perversity, saying that Posner's position was "like asking a doctor to choose between alternate medicines for a patient by comparing their prices, availability, and ease of administration, without also asking which will cure and which will kill him."[16]

Ultimately, Dworkin believed the biggest problem with Posner's pragmatic approach to *Bush* (and to cases in general) was that "since judges, like everyone else, disagree about the relative value of different possible consequences of their decisions, telling them to decide by weighing consequences is only—as Posner conceded many people think it is—an invitation to lawlessness."[17] Dworkin did not claim that judges should ignore consequences completely, "but they may only [consider consequences] as directed by principles embedded in the law as a whole, principles that adjudicate which consequences are relevant and how these should be weighed, rather than by their own political or personal preferences."[18]

Posner's pragmatism implicated purpose (to which he would subordinate agency—using even deceptive means to reach a valued end), bringing
us back to that term. But insofar as consequences are part of a scene that is
made larger by considering political, and not merely legal, factors, scene
hovers about Posner's construction of motives, promising to contain the act
of decision. Dworkin would only acknowledge the elements of scene that a
consideration of "principles embedded in the law as a whole" make relevant to a judicial decision.

Posner's approach to scene was much more complex than simply claiming that the Court had too little time to do a good job (which is easy to establish), yet it still relied on a scene-act relationship to account for motives.
But, as Dworkin demonstrated, it potentially brings a great deal of ethically
(and politically) troubling baggage.

Finally, it is time to tie the threads of this lengthy discussion of the elements of judicial action in *Bush v. Gore* back to the hub that ultimately
grounds (even if it does not control) the drama: the act.

Constructions of the Act

Ultimately, if only on theoretical grounds, act must be the hub of any account of motives. We may describe, for example the scene of an accident,
who was involved in it, what their attitudes were at the time, and how it
happened, but accidents, insofar as they are purely accidents, have no purpose and cannot properly be called acts. And if we were strict about it, we
might not even say that agents were involved, since such agents would be
having something done to them more than doing something. Means related to how an accident unfolds are not related to a purpose of having the
accident (unless, of course, it was an intentional accident, in which case it
was not really an accident).

For something so complex and deliberate as a Supreme Court decision,
what the Court did could hardly be described as an accident.[19] Rather, it is
an act, which may be characterized in various ways but will be construed
in light of characterizations of scene, agent, agency, purpose, and attitude,
just as characterizations of those elements must bend to the constructions
of the act to which they are tied through the grammar of motives. In this
sense, act is the alpha and the omega of motives, though various rhetors
can begin with any term they wish to promote above the others. For
example, they may start by emphasizing that the justices are "fair judges"
and follow by constructing the act as a "fair decision" (where agent

determines the nature of the act). Alternatively, they may begin by describing the act as a "judicial coup d'état" and conclude that the judicial agents are "traitors to our democratic system" (an act-agent relationship).

Court critics had several colorful, negative descriptions of the act represented by *Bush v. Gore*, which sought to show that the majority acted improperly or at least imprudently. Court defenders said less about the act itself, but when they did, they attempted to construct it as proper, prudent, or at least small or inconsequential.

Defending the Court's Act

Court defenders took a defensive posture in describing the Court's action in *Bush v. Gore*, constructing appropriate Court motives within a symbolic context already saturated with damning constructions of that same action. Posner claimed that "the U.S. Supreme Court's interventions in the post-election struggle were not the outrages that its liberal critics have claimed them to be."[20] John Yoo insisted that the majority was not "acting hypocritically and lawlessly."[21] Lund acknowledged this negative criticism and attempted to turn it into a scene of heroic action for the Court:

> The *Bush v. Gore* majority had to know that a decision in Bush's favor would trigger an avalanche of scurrilous accusations and politically motivated attacks, and endless insinuations about their personal integrity. They were thus faced with a very unpleasant choice: if they *enforced the law,* they ran the risk of acquiring a reputation for having done the opposite, but if they refused to *enforce the law,* they would preserve their reputation for judiciousness. In deciding to hear the case, and then resolving it *in accordance with the law,* the majority demonstrated genuine integrity and impartiality in exactly those circumstances where it is most difficult to practice.[22]

Lund's characterization of what the Court did as simply enforcing the law brushes aside any issues over the controversy concerning whether the Court "got it right" with respect to the law (though his article tried to argue that the case was clear-cut), reducing the Court's action to something accepted and uncontroversial, something courts are expected to do. By constructing the majority's action as undertaken with an awareness of the threat to its members' reputations, Lund used a future scene (where motives would be misunderstood) to suggest an attitude (resolute, self-sacrificing, and committed to doing what is right) built on a "proper" act (enforcing the law).

Posner also drew on scene to construct the majority's actions as appropriate, calling them "a pragmatically defensible series of responses to a

looming political and constitutional crisis."[23] In painting a future scene of
political and constitutional crisis, Posner emphasized what the Court
sought to avoid, implicating purpose. But his deployment of scene here
was meant to reflect its constraint on action, whereby this problematic future scene determined the Court's responses. In responding, the Court was
not being active and aggressive but rather passive and defensive. No doubt
because of his own concerns about the weakness of the majority's position,
Posner did not call the decision proper, correct, or reasonable but only defensible and only pragmatically defensible at that. The pragmatic defense
that Posner offered for the decision tied tightly to the crisis it sought to
avoid, so that this became an act whose means were adapted to a scene it
sought to avoid (with that avoidance standing as its ultimate purpose).

If Posner offered a straightforward scene-act relationship (whereby the
looming future scene controlled the responsive act), Lund rejected that relationship. For despite the fact that Lund emphasized a future scene of a
majority dogged by criticism, he suggested that that scene did not control
the justices' actions; on the contrary, as agents, they dominated that scene
and did what was right. Such a contrast in grammatical strategies is understandable if we think of Lund's strategy as taking the offensive and Posner's
as taking the defensive. Posner offered the stronger construction, because
he admitted the obvious weaknesses of the majority decision, while Lund's
construction admitted no weaknesses, even in the face of overwhelming
constructions to the contrary.

Pildes looked to the past to explain and defend the *Bush* decision. He
claimed that the present act by the present Court did not diverge from past
acts by the same Court. This strategy tried to make *Bush* and the Court's
earlier decisions consubstantial in insisting that *Bush* "expresses characteristic practices and assumptions of the current Court."[24] He reviewed cases,
such as *California Democratic Party v. Jones*,[25] to show that "it has become
routine for the Court to conclude that constitutional law should determine
the basic institutional arrangements of democracy," making it "no great
leap for the [*Bush*] Court to conclude that presidential election contests too
could appropriately be resolved through Supreme Court decision."[26] This
past act-present act relationship defends the decision by insisting that it reflects consistency on the Court's part, rather than some departure for questionable motives.

Yoo's construction of the majority's actions attempted to minimize those
actions, so that even if they were wrong, it was a little wrong. As did Posner and Lund, he focused on a future scene, which, he assured his readers,

this decision would not change, describing *Bush v. Gore* as rendering "a fairly narrow decision in a one-of-a-kind case . . . that is not likely to reappear in our lifetimes."[27] Yoo's assurances rested on diminished size (fairly narrow) and uniqueness (one-of-a-kind case) to suggest that it carried no implications beyond this decision. He contrasted this lack of future influence with cases where "substantive issues" have been decided—"abortion or privacy rights, for example—that call upon the Court to remain continually at the center of political controversy for years."[28] Yoo sought to diminish the significance of *Bush* through a contrast with more controversial cases that situated the Court in an uncomfortable scene, "at the center of political controversy for years" (in which the where and when of the scene played up the alternatives). *Bush* should not concern us, in short, because it carries no consequences beyond this troublesome current scene. Furthermore, he implied, "if you think this act is controversial, compare it to really controversial acts (like *Roe v. Wade*)." Thus, he distinguished between controversial acts and "this act" to put the latter in a better light.

Posner, in his book on the case, also sought to minimize the consequences of the decision. In chapter 2 on "The Deadlocked Election," Posner analyzed the votes recovered in various recounts, considered possible scenarios for the recovery of additional (uncounted) votes, and found: "The safest conclusion, on the basis of the analysis to this point, is that hand recounts of undervotes using objective criteria would have been unlikely to change the outcome of the election."[29] Posner went on to argue, through a complex statistical analysis, that poverty and illiteracy were correlated with ballots that were unreadable, that using cheaper methods of tallying votes (such as counting at the county level, rather than the precinct level) led to unreadable ballots as well, and that recounting overvotes (which Gore never requested) would have helped him.[30] But the upshot of his analysis is that even if Gore had been granted his recount request, he would not have won anyway.

While all of this is irrelevant to whether the U.S. Supreme Court was justified in intervening in the election and in finding for Bush, it does serve to minimize the consequences of its troublesome actions. Posner could urge that the High Court did not hand the election to Bush, since Bush probably would have won in any case. Instead, it simply shortened an otherwise lengthy and disorderly process that would eventuate in Bush assuming the presidency in any case.

George Priest of Yale Law School made a more complex defense of the consequences of the *Bush* decision, which, he admitted, offered "an

inexpressive and not fully worked out opinion."[31] He did so by relying
heavily on *Bush v. Palm Beach County Canvassing Board*, where the Florida
Supreme Court had extended the deadline for filing late returns and required the inclusion of partial recounts, overruling the actions of the secretary of state on those issues. That case, which was unanimously vacated by
the U.S. Supreme Court (which asked for clarification of the basis for the
state court's ruling), is grouped together with *Bush v. Gore* where Priest
claimed that the latter decision, "in essence, restored the democratic accountability central to the political process theory by reinstating the discretionary decision of the Secretary of State."[32] Priest's phrase "in essence" is
a caveat that admits that the *Bush* decision did not legally or technically do
this, though thwarting the state court led to an outcome that would be the
same as if it had done so. By eliding the two cases, Priest sought stronger
ground from which to defend the Court, relying on a unanimous prior decision (rather than the divisive later decision) and essentially importing its
issues into the present case by focusing on outcomes.

Kenneth Burke spent one section of his *A Grammar of Motives* on strategies such as Priest's that claim that something is the case "in essence." In
"The Rhetoric of Substance," Burke explained the rhetorical function of
using terms such as "substantially," "essentially," "in principle," and "in the
long run." He argued that

> one may say "it is *substantially* true" precisely at a time when on the basis of
> the evidence, it would be much more accurate to say, "it is not true." And
> even a human slave could be defined in Christian doctrine as "substantially"
> free, by reasons of qualities which he had inherited "substantially" from his
> creator. Even in cases where the nature of the case does not justify the
> usage grammatically, it can be used without strain for rhetorical purposes.
> What handier linguistic resource could a rhetorician want than an ambigu-
> ity whereby he can say "The state of affairs is substantially such-and-such,"
> instead of having to say "The state of affairs *is* and/or *is not* such-and-
> such"?[33]

As Burke suggested, there is a grammatical problem with this strategy.
Priest wanted to elide two separate acts to make the second act appear
more defensible. But different acts have their own scenes, agencies, purposes, and so forth. There may be overlap, of course, as when justices in
one legal decision are the same agents in another legal decision. But Priest
was attempting to tie the purpose, or at least the outcome, of *Bush v. Gore*
to a purpose or outcome of the *Bush v. Palm Beach* case.

Priest recognized the stretch implied by this move, admitting that "the United States Supreme Court did not justify its decision in these terms"; that is, there was no ends-means relationship suggested by the Court in its decision between restoring political accountability and deciding the case as it did.[34] Indeed, it claimed to be vindicating the right of voters to have their ballots counted in a similar fashion, saying nothing about returning authority to the secretary of state. Absent such a connection, Priest used language that attempted to make the two decisions consubstantial so that such a purpose might be said to be shared (at least "in essence"). Thus, he spoke of "the set of events leading up to *Bush v. Gore*"; he asserted that "[t]he Florida Supreme Court . . . claimed through its decisions that it, not the elected Secretary of State, should make the determinative political judgment as to how the Florida election process was to be managed"; and he noted that the U.S. Supreme Court "overruled the Florida Supreme Court's various decisions."[35] By pluralizing the object of his remarks, Priest attempted to blur the distinctions between the two cases and to endorse the Court in *Bush v. Gore* for what it did in *Bush v. Palm Beach*.

Priest's references to these joined decisions contrasted with the claims of two other scholars, to whom he was responding, that *Bush v. Gore* itself abrogated the political process. Here Priest complained: "they claim that the Court's decision violated the standards of political process by arrogating to themselves—not to democratically elected officials—decisionmaking power over the election. This criticism, I believe, is wrong."[36] Priest was careful to state that these critics focused on *Bush v. Gore* itself (the decision), while Priest's own construction slipped furtively into language that yoked that case with the earlier case, providing the grounds for a defense that rested on a fallacy of composition.[37] For although the Court's decision to vacate the state court's ruling in *Bush v. Palm Beach* may be said to vindicate the secretary of state (by overruling judgments that directly overruled her own decisions), *Bush v. Gore* had nothing to do with the secretary of state but rather involved recounting processes that, but for the lack of time (said the Court), might constitutionally be allowed to continue with clearer standards.

Priest's construction also traded on one type of political process (where voters could throw out those making bad decisions) for another, and the trade-off was a bad one. On the one hand, he suggested, Florida voters who did not like Secretary of State Harris's decisions could make her politically responsive to them by not returning her to office in the future.[38] The fact that the candidate she supported—a man who might not actually have earned the highest office in the land—would be made president was not a consideration on this model. On the other hand—and this hand Priest did not weigh—Congress, duly empowered by the Electoral Acts of 1887, could decide whether to accept Florida's slate (or choose among competing slates). In this way, a national political process would be in place, holding members of Congress responsible for which votes they endorsed and whom they put into office.[39]

Here, admittedly, judgments about which kinds of political processes are best come into play. Court defenders would stress that the congressional route was fraught with at least two significant problems: first and foremost, the length of time it would have required for a final resolution (and what that would mean for the country) and, second, the possibility that a constitutional crisis might ensue. Court critics could deny the doomsday scenarios that Court defenders were so certain would follow a completion of the recounting.

Cass Sunstein, who had a fairly balanced position on the case, recognized the potential crisis to be avoided but noted a trade-off that was central to the Court's decision: "From the standpoint of constitutional order, the Court might well have done the nation a service. From the standpoint of legal reasoning, the Court's decision was very bad. In short, the Court's decision produced order without law."[40] Pildes would hedge Sunstein's construction of the law side a bit in defending the Court, emphasizing a consistency with earlier Court decisions:

> when we examine the decision in the full tapestry of the Supreme Court's emerging and increasingly active role in the constitutionalization of democratic politics—a role initiated forty years ago in *Baker v. Carr*—we can see images, metaphors, and assumptions about democracy that consistently recur. These images of the relationship between law and order—constitutional law and judicially structured order—to democracy are aspects of a broader jurisprudential culture.[41]

Pildes explained the Court's view of democracy, insisting that "the Court sees democratic politics as fragile and potentially unstable entities that require judicial protection."[42] Here, agent characterizations combined with characterizations of past Supreme Court actions to suggest that, indeed, order was important to the Court and that *Bush v. Gore* followed in that preference for order, and to this extent, it was consistent with the law that the High Court had carved out on this issue.

Pildes even engaged in a bit of rhetorical analysis of his own to defend this particular reading of *Bush v. Gore*. He looked at an earlier decision by the Court on fusion candidates—candidates supported by two different political parties, typically a minor party and a major party.[43] He asked his readers to

> consider how democracy appeared to the decisive Supreme Court [in this prior case]—this time, the *Bush v Gore* majority plus Justice Breyer. The central image in this opinion is not that of invigorated democracy through "political competition," but that of a system whose crucial "political stability" is easily threatened. The word "stable" (and variations of it) appears a remarkable ten times in the brief majority opinion.[44]

Even Laurence Tribe endorsed this "order over law" view to explain what the majority in *Bush* was doing, though not to justify it:

> One can only surmise that, to five justices, images of ballots across the state being counted in front of a nationwide TV audience—images that, for many others, conjured thrilling memories of the voting-rights struggles of decades past—must have brought to mind instead dismaying thoughts of chaos, partisan manipulation, and mob rule. And the spectacle of Congress sorting out the mess at the end probably seemed no more reassuring. Anything so visibly threatening to stability, good order, the established hierarchy, and stately decorum qualified as a "crisis" this Court had jurisdiction to halt.[45]

But Tribe did not leave the matter there, with the motives of the majority accounted for. He went further to note the threats to order that the Court conveniently ignored:

> Never mind about the partisan maneuvering, less open and visible but not less real, that had led to the radical maldistribution of reliable voting machines and methods among Florida's sixty-seven counties, or about such other less apparent sources of inequality and political favoritism as the subjective and variable standard for deciding which absentee ballots to accept. *Those* machinations evidently seemed to the Court part *of* the stable order to be preserved, not a threat *to* it.[46]

Tribe's last points highlighted the flexibility of ideas of order and what it might mean to ensure that the nation had it. Such flexibility returns us to questions of perspective, ideology, and agent when thinking about what the Court was doing.

Dworkin rejected the "order over law" justification/explanation of the Court's motives, denying that the Court actually had favored order over law in the cases cited by Pildes and Tribe, since in those cases the conservative justices did not have to ignore established law, as they did in *Bush v. Gore*, in order to protect the stability of some feature of traditional American democracy, like the two-party system. They rather cited the importance of that feature, as in *Timmons*, to explain why, on perfectly traditional grounds, the Constitution either permitted or prohibited some state action. In *Bush v. Gore*, on the other hand, they could not present their preference as part of any argument. It had to operate, if at all, entirely as a hidden, behind-the-scenes motive.[47]

If Dworkin rejected the consistency argument that would defend or explain the Court's motives by comparing *Bush* with earlier judicial acts, he also rejected the idea of order as a motive because, he insisted, order was not provided, since "the Court's decision in *Bush v. Gore* destabilized rather than stabilized the political process" by setting aside a state court's interpretation of its own law and making manual recounts across the country constitutionally suspect.[48] By distinguishing *Bush* from earlier cases (a present act-past act distinction) and severing the connection of the decision to the purpose of ensuring order, Dworkin opened the door to more questionable motives for Court action, notably "more personal motives."[49] Additionally, as he noted, they did not make such order concerns explicit in their opinion.

Louise Weinberg also rejected Pildes's argument that order led the Court to intervene as it did, for two reasons: "First, the procedures prescribed for political resolution of the election, however chaotic, were the procedures prescribed. Second, if anything threatened the constitutional 'order' it was not the counting of votes, but rather the Court's deciding a presidential election."[50] When combined with Dworkin's concerns about second-guessing state court interpretations of state law and challenging a manual recount standard used in thirty-three states, this provided a strong argument about the narrowness of the Court's vision of what kinds of disorder ought to be avoided.

For defenders of the Court, then, the decision was grounded primarily in considerations of a future scene and represented an act that either maintained order or avoided disorder, that bravely accepted the condemnation that would follow from enforcing the law, that was consistent with earlier decisions in favoring order (though perhaps at the expense of law), and that restored political accountability to the process (by effectively reinstating the secretary of state's decisions). It was inconsequential, in the larger scheme of things, because it would not draw the judiciary into the center of an ongoing political controversy (as *Roe v. Wade* had), nor would it change the result of the election. All it would do was shorten the process for naming the next president and save the country from additional turmoil and perhaps a constitutional crisis.

Court critics would already meet defenders on this slender ground, denying that order was maintained or that a crisis was avoided, rejecting constructions of the majority as brave and righteous, and questioning its adherence to political process theory. While they might admit that the controversy would be short-lived, they did believe it would hurt the Supreme Court, and they would reject as irrelevant the claims that it did not ultimately decide the election. They would add to these characterizations of majority action claims of political and legal impropriety and imprudence.

Attacking the Court's Act

Critics of the per curiam decision described it as surprising, controversial, unpersuasive, inconsistent, shameful, unfair, anarchic, lawless, and illegitimate, suggesting that the act itself was problematic and inappropriate. They accused the Court of plunging in, picking the president through a constitutional coup, and betraying fairness and democracy.

At their mildest, critics noted that the decision was a surprise. Frank Michelman confessed:

> To me, as to many, the majority's action was surprising. Abstention—or dismissal—is the course that, from the beginning, I fully expected the Court to take, at least in the event that the members found themselves without clear and compelling grounds for decisive intervention, commanding agreement from some majority other than that particular majority of five.[51]

Michelman's claim about the surprising nature of the case was grounded in his personal reaction (which he attributed to others as well) and also relied on agency-act and agent-act relationships, whereby compelling grounds (a means for justification) and a group larger than the conservative five would be needed to make the act more acceptable and less surprising.

Sunstein called the decision "the most controversial judicial decision in several decades," assuring his readers that "[i]n the fullness of time, the decision is likely to rank among the most controversial decisions in the entire history of the Supreme Court."[52] As Michelman did, he rested this characterization on his own assessment, placing the decision in an enlarged scene (of decades and the entire history of the Supreme Court).

Dworkin, appealing to his own, learned experience, called *Bush* "one of the least persuasive Supreme Court opinions that I have ever read."[53] Jack

Balkin and Sanford Levinson said the decision was "not only unpersuasive; it is an embarrassment to legal reasoning."[54] Even Posner admitted that *Bush* was unpersuasive:

> Neither the per curiam majority opinion nor the concurring opinion of Rehnquist, Scalia, and Thomas is convincing. The majority opinion adopts a ground (equal protection) neither persuasive in itself nor consistent with the judicial philosophy of the conservative justices, particularly the three just named, who joined the majority opinion without reservation while writing separately. Neither opinion discusses the pragmatic benefit of ending the deadlock, though without that benefit it is hard to see why the Supreme Court agreed to take the case, let alone why it decided it as it did.[55]

Posner's characterization did make way for his own defense of the case on pragmatic grounds, but it went further than Dworkin or Balkin and Levinson in noting the inconsistency of the agents in this case.

Many scholars would note that the decision was inconsistent. This criticism compared the act to previous acts to demonstrate a difference that yielded the inconsistency and raised questions about the majority's motives for the difference in treatment. Theodore Prosise and Craig Smith, for example, focused on the equal protection cases as inconsistent: "The five conservatives—Rehnquist, Thomas, Scalia, O'Connor, and Kennedy—had rejected the equal protection argument in cases ranging from drug convictions, to gay rights in the military, to gay membership in the Boy Scouts, to unequal property taxes."[56] Michael Klarman also saw equal protection inconsistencies: "The majority's equal protection rationale is objectionable not because it represents new law, but rather because it represents bad law—law that the conservative Justices almost certainly would have rejected in any other setting."[57] He was particularly critical of Justice Scalia's inconsistency in this matter, noting that the justice was "on record as rejecting novel constitutional interpretations that forbid longstanding practices [such as using the voter intent standard]."[58] Klarman cited two dissenting opinions as examples where Scalia had rejected such novelty.[59]

Pildes argued against the charge that *Bush* was inconsistent with earlier decisions, urging instead that it "is best understood . . . as the most dramatic crystallization of a deeper, more enduring pattern in the contemporary relationships between democratic politics and constitutional law. This pattern might be called the 'constitutionalization of democracy.'"[60] Pildes reviewed decisions by the Rehnquist Court on blanket primaries, fusion candidates, and the participation of third-party candidates in publicly sponsored debates, showing that, in each case, a majority of the Court ruled against challenges to existing two-party practices, supporting order over attempts to broaden democratic participation and relying on interpretations of constitutional law to support them.[61]

Pildes's argument elided decisions he generalized as involving the constitutionalization of democracy, while downplaying the equal protection basis of *Bush* (which is not found in the cases he cited). His construction worked by rising above the decisions as acts to consider what these acts say about the justices (as agents) and their attitudes toward democracy. As he summarized this construction:

> In case after case, a majority of the current Court—the five justices who voted to end the election litigation, joined at times by Justices Breyer and Souter—has worried about the "stability" of American democracy and the risk of "excessive fragmentation" of American politics. Where other judges have seen competitive practices that ensure a robust and vital democratic system, the current Court has seen threats to orderly democratic processes. The suggestion here is that it is these kind of concerns, assumptions, beliefs, and values [that] played a contributing role in *Bush v. Gore*. When the Court stared at other institutions that might have settled the election, particularly Congress, it did not see a healthy democratic mechanism for political struggle and stable resolution. Instead, the Court saw the specter of disorder, constitutional "crisis," and dangerous instability.[62]

Pildes was able to gloss over inconsistent equal protection precedents by the Court by moving his concern to the higher level of judicial attitudes toward democratic processes, finding that their outlook consistently reflected fear of disorder. Thus, the acts that Pildes would find consistent with *Bush v. Gore* were less about how a decision was reached (i.e., following equal protection precedents, which troubled Klarman and others) than about the manner in which it was reached (with an attitude that worried about disorderly democracy).

Critics also compared the *Bush* decision with hypothetical acts to suggest inconsistency. Many considered a hypothetical reversal of the roles of Bush and Gore. For example, Klarman asked:

> Had all the other facts in the Florida election imbroglio remained the same, but the situation of the two presidential candidates been reversed, does anyone seriously believe that the conservative Justices would have reached the same result? It is telling how even Republican commentators defending Bush generally have refrained from arguing for this conclusion.[63]

Farnsworth agreed with this hypothetical reversal, asking: "Would the thought of effectively ordering a Gore victory have made the decision seem

a little less appealing to even one member of the majority? All one can do
is wonder, but I regret to say that I know of few students of the Court who
think its lineup would have been the same under those circumstances, and
none who think so with any confidence."[64] Vincent Bugliosi made a similar point with respect to the stay as well, challenging in his colorful
fashion:

> [T]ry to imagine Al Gore's and George Bush's roles being reversed and ask
> yourself if you can conceive of Justice Antonin Scalia and his four conserva-
> tive brethren issuing an emergency order on December 9 stopping the
> counting of ballots (at a time when Gore's lead had shrunk to 154 votes) on
> the grounds that if it continued, Gore could suffer "irreparable harm," and
> then subsequently, on December 12, bequeathing the election to Gore on
> equal protection grounds. If you can, then I suppose you can also imagine
> seeing a man jumping away from his own shadow, Frenchmen no longer
> drinking wine.[65]

This act-hypothetical act comparison traded on a dubious agent-act relationship: conservative justices or Scalia ruling in favor of "President Gore"
or stopping the shrinkage of his lead.

Klarman offered a different hypothetical act for comparison, this one involving the Florida Supreme Court: "It is worth pointing out that had the
Florida Supreme Court prescribed a more specific formula for ascertaining
the 'intent of the voter,' the conservative Justices probably would have
ruled that the state court was changing state law and thus violating Article
II."[66] In short, the state court was the victim of a Catch–22, whereby either
setting a standard or refusing to set a standard would land it in constitutional hot water (on either equal protection or Article II grounds). Klarman
noted that the *Bush* majority refused to decide whether the Florida court
had the authority to set new manual recount standards and that in *Gore v.
Harris*, the Florida court was worried about changing the election rules
after the election was over.[67]

Douglas Kellner charged the majority with a different kind of Catch–22:

> Opponents of the ruling bitterly complained that it was precisely the U.S.
> Supreme Court halting the recount that made it impossible to certify the
> count of the uncounted ballots before December 12 and that the court had
> sprung a Catch–22 trap that made it impossible to do what it claimed had to
> be done (i.e., finish the counting by December 12).[68]

Both kinds of Catch–22 suggested a Court that was going to reach a decision for Bush whatever happened. Kellner went further in describing this

as a trap, implying a disingenuous and ethically troubling act on the part of the majority. [69]

Several scholars worded their contempt for the Court's decision tersely, discussing the problems with the case before reaching their damning conclusions. Thus, Peter Shane charged: "It is shameful that the Supreme Court of the United States spurned [the] commitments [of the Florida court to find the will of the voters]" and that the Court was the "primary agent of unfairness in this episode."[70] Aviam Soifer criticized the Court not only for what it did in *Bush v. Gore* but for what it had done in the past as well: "*Bush v. Gore* [seems] like only one of many slashes in the Court's ongoing anarchic arrogation of authority."[71] And David Strauss claimed that "the best that can be said is that the Court trumped the supposed lawlessness of the Florida Supreme Court with lawlessness of its own."[72] Thus, we get simple characterizations of the decision as shameful, unfair, anarchic, and lawless.

Dworkin made an elaborate case that the decision lacked legitimacy. He started with a model of what a legitimate decision should look like (a generalized act), applied that to the *Bush* case, and found it wanting. He linked legitimacy to "the discipline of argument," claiming that courts must satisfy two conditions to make their decisions legitimate:

> The first is sincerity. They must themselves believe, after searching self-examination, that these arguments justify what they do, and they must stand ready to do what the arguments justify in later, perhaps very different, cases as well, when their own personal preferences or politics are differently engaged. The second condition is transparency. The arguments they themselves find convincing must be exactly the arguments that they present to the professional and lay public in their opinions, in as much detail as is necessary to allow that public to judge the adequacy and future promise of those arguments for themselves.[73]

Dworkin's discussion of the legitimate judicial decision described private supporting acts (belief, searching self-examination, self-convinced) that fused with public acts (what the judges say). It excluded "ulterior" motives as illegitimate, perhaps because they are necessarily dishonest and because they are antithetical to the public nature of judicial tribunals, which ultimately must be answerable to the people and the legal community.

When Dworkin applied these conditions to the *Bush* case, he found problems: "Their most fervent supporters describe motives for their decision, like their distrust of the Florida Supreme Court justices, or their anxiety to end the uncertainty and trauma of the postelection period, that are not only not good arguments, but are not even reasons that they would publicly embrace."[74] Here Dworkin confronted, most directly, Posner's claim that the Court acted in a "pragmatically defensible" manner, even though their pragmatic purposes were hidden from the public and they offered weak legal reasons for their conclusions.

Dworkin's eloquent rendering of the problem of legitimacy raises a critical question: How are hidden motives to be assessed in judging what the Court was doing and why it was doing it? Strictly speaking, answering the question "What is the Court doing, and why is it doing it?" may involve any motives constructed by rhetors—patent, hidden, or unconscious. However, hidden motives carry with them an implicit judgment of disingenuousness. For Dworkin (and perhaps a majority of scholars), this lack of sincerity itself is a basis for condemnation. Yet Posner's pragmatic philosophy of jurisprudence is more forgiving, as the hiding of motives simply becomes swallowed up by larger issues of what is pragmatic. He admitted of judicial pragmatism: "If all that matters are consequences, then dishonesty, which might seem the correct term for subscribing to a judicial opinion that one thinks all wrong, while no doubt regrettable becomes just another factor in the calculus of decision."[75]

Yoo, who also was critical of the per curiam's rationale, tried to rescue the legitimacy of the decision by defining that judgment in "sociological or even psychological" terms, specifically, "whether people will think the Court's decision in *Bush v Gore* was legitimate, and as a result will obey it." He distinguished this approach from that of Dworkin and others, which he called "philosophical legitimacy, in which one is concerned with moral obligations to follow the law."[76] On this basis, he turned to the Gallup polls to show that the Court still garnered more confidence than the president or the Congress and that it suffered a mere three-point drop in credibility from August 2000 to January 2001. He admitted that Democrats' respect dropped precipitously while Republicans' jumped, but held, "I think it more likely that the drop in Democratic opinions toward the Court will prove to be a temporary blip."[77]

Thus, while Dworkin was concerned about the manner and means (agency and attitude) for reaching a legitimate decision, Yoo reduced it to considerations of whether the act of decision yielded a problematic scene, in which the opinions of the citizens were not considered individually but as a mass. Quality gave way to quantity, as acts of approval or disapproval were reduced to components of a scene that would or would not support the continued work of the courts.

These negative, general characterizations of the *Bush* decision were qualified by more specific characterizations of what precisely the Court was doing. For example, Strauss and Tribe both used the metaphor of *plunging* to describe the majority's action. Strauss described the action with vivid verbs: "In *Bush v Gore*, a majority of the Court, prompted by a general and unjustified sense that something needed to be done, plunged in, splintered along ideological lines, and played a prominent role in deciding the election. This was not a triumph of the rule of law."[78] The metaphor of *plunging in* suggests an unthinking reaction, a construction bolstered by its connection to the majority's sense (as opposed to opinion or conclusion) that something needed to be done.

Tribe described the Court's plunging differently:

> By plunging ahead in the face of such overwhelming institutional reasons to stay out, and by rationalizing its action in such painfully weak terms, the Court seemed to dishonor a legal tradition to which most of us had devoted our lives, leading many of us to question, at least momentarily, our long-held "constitutional faith."[79]

Tribe emphasized the irrational nature of the Court's action by highlighting the reasons it ignored for staying out and the weak rationalization of its actions. By noting the Court's threat to constitutional faith, Tribe tied in his personal reactions with those of others (he posited) and suggested larger ethical and political consequences of the majority's plunging.

Klarman, Shane, and Weinberg characterized the Court's central action as *picking the president.* Klarman noted the unprecedented nature of this act:

> On December 12, 2000, the United States Supreme Court, for the first time in its history, picked a president. By shutting down the statewide manual recount that had been ordered just days earlier by the Florida Supreme Court, the High Court Justices ensured that George W. Bush would become the forty-third president of the United States.[80]

Klarman offered an agency-act argument to justify his characterization, whereby shutting down the recount ensured Bush's victory, which Klarman equated to picking the president.

Shane described what the majority did as "adjudicat[ing] which person shall be entitled to name their successors."[81] Shane connected act here to purpose, bolstering the former by emphasizing the personal and institutional interests the justices had in the latter. Picking the president is an act that becomes a means to the ends of controlling Supreme Court appointments.

Weinberg was the most elaborate in detailing what this presidential selection entailed. She distinguished this selection from what the Court
claimed to be doing:

> In its final decision of December 12, 2000, the United States Supreme Court
> purported to remand *Bush v. Gore* to the Florida Supreme Court. But, at the
> same time, the Court declared that to permit any further counting of Florida
> votes would be an improper interpretation of Florida law. In this high-
> handed way the Court rendered the remand a hollow formality and took
> the election unto itself. In effectively making permanent its stay of the elec-
> toral process, the Supreme Court handed the election to the certified win-
> ner, George W. Bush. But this was to pronounce a result in a challenged
> election without permitting the prescribed resolution, or any resolution, of
> the challenge.[82]

Weinburg's construction made the election an act in process, which was
never resolved by the Court. Because it was never completed, Weinberg
was able to draw a distinction between what the Court did and what it was
permitted to do: "While a court may validate a completed election, and
make the judgment winner also the election winner, a court may not make
a judgment winner also an election winner in the absence of a completed
election."[83] She warned that "[a] court cannot put itself in the position of
protecting a candidate from the electorate—as the Supreme Court did in
Bush v. Gore."[84]

To sustain her characterization of the Court's illegal selection of Bush for
president, Weinberg took on the claim that there was no valid process to
which the election could be returned, calling that "nonsense":

> The court itself will either have held that the process is valid or it will have
> held that the process is invalid and must be corrected. Once a court has
> stopped an election and ruled it invalid, it can have no option of making the
> judgment winner the election winner without first allowing the election—
> under a corrected process—to reach completion.[85]

Not only did the Court not allow the election to be completed, Weinberg
contended, but

> the Court actively prevented the completion of a halted state recount, never
> having ruled on the merits either of the challenge or the election and never
> having adjudicated the validity of Bush's certification or Gore's request for a
> recount. Instead, the Court selected the next President of the United States
> in the absence of a completed election—the ultimate political act.[86]

Thus, Weinberg contrasted crucial acts not completed by the Court with an ultimate political act that it did engage in, playing "judicial kingmaker," which "is not within the power of the judiciary." [87]

Because the Court effectively made Bush president, Balkin and Levinson asserted in 2001, "Simply put, a constitutional coup occurred last year."[88] The majority was aided by the Florida Republicans, though there was no evidence of a conspiracy, the authors admitted. They insisted that "[t]his does not, however, diminish the importance of the fact that together they undermined a presidential election and installed a person in the White House who had no demonstrable constitutional right to that office."[89] Weinberg urged that the Court's actions undermined Bush's legitimacy, because "even a unanimous court could not have conferred legitimacy on a judicial coup d'état, achieved by stopping and displacing an election."[90] Francis Beytagh added that the framers of the Constitution would never support such a move, and was surprised that "originalists such as Chief Justice Rehnquist and Justices Scalia and Thomas would be in the vanguard of this judicial coup d'état."[91]

Priest challenged the characterization of the *Bush* decision as a coup by involving other agents in the construction of the judicial act:

> No one doubts that Florida's voters possess the rightful authority to determine the winner of the Florida election. And if the only actors in the drama were the United States Supreme Court and Florida's voters, the claim of "coup" might possess some plausibility. Once again, however, the claim ignores the role of other institutional actors in the Florida election, in particular, the Florida Secretary of State and the Florida Supreme Court.[92]

Priest shifts his focus to the Florida Supreme Court (drawing attention away from the *Bush* majority's actions), asserting: "One can accuse the United States Supreme Court of a Constitutional coup only if one can defend without reservation the legitimacy of the decisions of the Florida Supreme Court overruling the Secretary of State."[93] The bar Priest set for this accusation is particularly high if we consider not simply whether the Florida Supreme Court did an adequate job (and, for Priest, there must be no reservations) but the propriety of the High Court's intervention in light of provisions of the Constitution and the Electoral Count Act in making Congress the final authority for determining whether the state court's rulings yield a valid electoral slate. Priest sidestepped these with an argument that an erroneous correction of the state court's error was defensible (two wrongs do make a right here).

Priest bolstered his position by insisting that the majority's decision followed many arguments of Chief Justice Wells's dissenting opinion on the overturned state court decision.[94] It was on this basis that he mounted his primary defense against the claim of a coup:

> [T]he strongest defense to the claim that the five-person, conservative, Republican majority of the United States Supreme Court acted as partisans, seized power, or executed a Constitutional coup is that the Chief Justice of the Florida Supreme Court, a Democrat, seems to be the architect of the coup. There is not an argument in favor of cutting off the Florida recount in the United States Supreme Court's opinion in *Bush v. Gore II* that was not presaged by Chief Justice Wells's dissent in *Gore v. Harris*. This is a very peculiar form of political coup.[95]

In this interesting strategy, Priest made Wells an agent of the U.S. Supreme Court opinion (its architect). He emphasized that Wells was both the chief justice of the Florida Supreme Court and a Democrat, bolstering the state court judge's stature (in opposing his presumptive political interests) as he was named as central actor in a federal court decision where otherwise he had no formal role. The majority justices, then, were merely following Wells's lead. Because a Democrat state judge could not be thought to be leading a judicial coup to install a Republican president, Priest suggested that neither could the Republicans who followed that lead be thought to do so.

This strategy downplayed the actions of the High Court, reducing them to a following role. It ignored differences between the state and federal agents, particularly with respect to their authority in interpreting state law. It stressed quality of agent over quantity, as four of Wells's colleagues ruled differently from him. And it ignored the criticism of the legal basis of the decision which even conservative defenders acknowledged.

Critics who believed the Court overstepped its constitutional bounds in *Bush* described the Court's actions as undermining democracy. Shane claimed "the *Bush v. Gore* majority betrayed democracy."[96] Weinberg asserted that the "basic right [to vote] is violated when any court displaces the electorate by halting any election and deciding the outcome itself," as the Court did in *Bush*.[97] Tribe urged that "in a democracy, politics exists to be attempted, not circumvented," as it was in this case.[98] And Balkin and Levinson suggested that democracy's influence over the Constitution's interpretation was undermined:

By seizing control of the election, the five conservatives severed the connections between their constitutional revolution and popular will. They insulated themselves from the normal checks and balances between the political branches and the judiciary. Their self-entrenching behavior created a real danger that their constitutional revolution would be propelled forward into the future without sustained and continuing popular support.[99]

This last concern highlighted the role of democracy as an ultimate check on the courts, a check that Balkin and Levinson thought had been unjustly stayed.

In constructing the majority decision in *Bush v. Gore,* Court defenders realized they had an uphill battle to justify the Court's actions, noting trenchant criticism the per curiam received. Only Lund tried to turn this to an advantage by saying the justices stuck to what was right, despite the consequences to their reputations. But his misleading characterization of the decision as merely enforcing the law would not garner much support among his fellow defenders, who admitted the decision was weak but insisted that the Court avoided a crisis of either political or constitutional disorder (as it sought to do in previous decisions) and, in any case, did not affect the outcome of the election (since Bush probably would have won) or put the Court into the middle of an ongoing controversy (as *Roe v. Wade* had). Others, like Priest, shifted blame to the state court for its questionable rulings (sometimes drawing on *Bush v. Palm Beach* to tar the *Bush v. Gore* case with the sins of the former). Ultimately, however, as Dworkin pointed out, defenders relied on grounds the Court itself did not mention. Overall, defenders relied heavily on constructions of future scenes to be avoided to explain the Court's actions.

Court critics denied that order was restored (and they charged that law was thrown aside, rather than traded for order), since the Court overthrew a state court's interpretation of its own law, threw into question a recount standard used by thirty-three states, and effectively decided a presidential election (as courts should not do). They focused primarily on the act of the *Bush* Court, saying it violated everyone's expectations and did so on weak grounds that were inconsistent with the Court's prior decisions, unfair and shameful, insincere and illegitimate. Effectively, they argued, this was a judicial coup d'état, an aggressive action that picked the president without allowing the election to be completed, that violated the Constitution, and that was unfair to voters and severed their influence over the judiciary.

Critics' constructions of *Bush* meshed easily with constructions of agency as failing to follow the law; of partisan, ideological, or political purposes; of the aggressive, angry, ideological attitudes of conservative, self-serving judicial agents operating within a scene that did not require their intervention. Defenders' constructions of *Bush* relied on characterizations of the state court as creating a troublesome and time-constrained scene that required the High Court's intervention; on unstated purposes of avoiding disorder, using perhaps problematic agencies but creating "rough justice" nonetheless.

Terministic Constructions as a Rhetorical Strategy

Scholarly reconstructions of the motives of the per curiam did not support a facial acceptance of the per curiam's own construction of its motives. Despite Lund's attempts to defend "every jot and tittle" of the opinion, there were too many holes in his construction to maintain its structure. Not even Lund, for example, was willing to venture a justification for the majority's limitation of the case's precedential value. And when he did try blindly to defend the precedents as strong or the safe harbor claim as solidly grounded in the state court's rulings, he ignored problems his fellow defenders could not. It is not surprising, therefore, that defenders of the per curiam turned invariably to scene to explain what the Court was doing and why it was doing it.

Scene provided a purpose for the Court, even if the agencies adapted to those purposes were hard to defend (except as means subordinated completely to ends). For Court defenders first, the scene was filled with troubling recounts and acts of manipulation by a Florida Supreme Court attempting to keep Gore's presidential election hopes alive. The recounts, they claimed, featured changing standards (notably, in Palm Beach County) that seemed to be adjusted to best support the recovery of Democratic votes. Because Bush was ahead in the count, continued counting could serve only to challenge his claim to victory, giving the entire recount a partisan cast.

In attacking the Florida Supreme Court's recount order, Court defenders sought to draw on what they viewed as the egregious sins of *Bush v. Palm Beach Canvassing Board* (*Bush I*), where the Florida Supreme Court overturned a ruling of the secretary of state that vote returns had to meet a specified deadline, trumping her order with general state constitutional concerns over the power of the people and setting an entirely new deadline to allow more time to recount votes. Some scholars tried simply to elide the two acts, treating them as one continuing act of partisanship, despite the significant differences in the issues, rulings, and situations. Court defenders were on stronger ground in relying on this earlier case to support a "pattern of behavior" claim that painted the state judges as un-trustworthy and politically motivated in the recount that was challenged in *Bush v. Gore.* Court defenders sought to build on this characterization to warn that the state judges might include partial recounts in the final totals—something that would not give equal protection to those undervot-ers the state court claimed to be protecting (since some would have their votes counted, while others would not). This outcome was speculative, of course, but that speculation was bolstered by the state court's earlier inclu-sion of partial recounts and a scene in which time was quickly running out and a complete recount might be impossible. Constructions of ultimate deadlines such as December 12 or December 18 helped to support this argument.

Court defenders had a harder time arguing that the "clear intent of the voter" standard was chosen for partisan reasons, since it came from state statutes and state court precedents and was the standard used by dozens of states. Furthermore, as even Richard Epstein noted, requiring the state court to choose a more specific standard might have given it leave to choose a standard presumed to be supportive of Gore's election.[100] How-ever, Court defenders could claim that the voter-intent standard left lee-way for county-level manipulations that could influence the number of votes recovered. (They had to downplay Judge Lewis's ultimate role in en-suring that the voter-intent rule was consistently applied.)

The second scenic focus of Court defenders was based not on present scenes but on future scenes (which, arguably, could be projected based on current scenes). The future, they warned, would see delays in the transfer of executive power, threatening the government and the world order, and a constitutional crisis that could find Governor Jeb Bush signing over Florida's electors to his brother and the Florida Supreme Court ruling his actions illegal. This last possible action by the state court, they argued, could lead to the standoff by equal branches of the state government (a constitutional crisis) that worried Court defenders, and its likelihood was bolstered to the extent that the defenders were successful in painting the Florida court as partisan.

To stave off these crises, the High Court intervened, on what Court de-fenders conceded were weak grounds, offered weak reasons for ending the recounts, and yet carried enough political weight to push all parties to agree to the election results it endorsed, without losing too much credibility with the public (if not with the more liberal legal academy). Although this appeared to be a partisan act, defenders contended, the majority justices had previously been similarly aggressive and activist in ensuring order in democracy, and, therefore, they were not acting out of character. And they might have done better, had the scene not been so short.

The scene-act grammar of this rhetorical strategy supports a situational ethics explanation of action, moving responsibility away from agents, and even discounting the means they use to respond to the scene. In this strategy, "the scene contains the act," as Burke noted,[101] with its purposes, agencies, attitudes, and even agents falling into line with the demands of that container. It matters less how one responds to the scene, because the scene itself demands some kind of response, so that means become a secondary consideration. Rhetorically, it is a last-ditch retreat for those justifying actions where agents, purposes, agencies, and attitudes are suspect. It implies that whoever faced such a situation would be forced to do the same thing, since the scene contains the act. That implication is weakened to the extent that Court critics could urge that had the positions of the presidential candidates been reversed, the majority would not have reached the same conclusion, and no Court defenders specifically refuted that charge.

Unsurprisingly, this scene-act rationale has been invoked to defend other controversial acts. For example, David Ling argued that Senator Edward Kennedy used this grammatical rationale to explain his actions in the Chappaquiddick incident.[102] As I have summarized elsewhere:

> Faced with the *act* of leaving the scene of an accident that killed Mary Jo Kopechne, Kennedy directed attention to a *scene* of a narrow, unlighted bridge over cold, dark, rushing water that left him nearly drowned and not thinking straight. That terministic focus attempted to draw attention away from alternative terms, such as agent (Kennedy as irresponsible), agency (driving under the influence), attitude (careless), and so forth. It also sought to characterize a term (the scene, as life-threatening and overwhelming) and to characterize a terministic relationship (clearly implying that the scene controlled the act, as Kennedy staggered away in a daze).[103]

The scene-act ratio also has been used to justify Supreme Court decisions, as in the controversial World War II case involving the internment of Japanese-Americans, *Korematsu v. United States.* Burke himself cited this then-recent case when discussing the scene-act ratio in *A Grammar of Motives,* noting:

In a judgment written by Justice Hugo L. Black, the Supreme Court ruled that it was not "beyond the war powers of Congress and the Executive to exclude those of Japanese ancestry from the West Coast area at the time they did." And by implication, the scene-act ratio was invoked to substantiate the judgment: "When under conditions of modern warfare our shores are threatened by hostile forces, the power to protect must be commensurate with the threatened danger."[104]

When it comes to justifying a Supreme Court decision, a scene-act argument is troublesome. For although political and military leaders are expected to be responsive to the changing fortunes represented by current and future crises, judges are expected to be grounded in something more permanent, namely, the law. And although Justice Jackson explained the military's unconstitutional actions in interning Japanese-Americans by acknowledging that "[t]he armed services must protect a society, not merely its Constitution,"[105] he held that it *was* the responsibility of the Supreme Court to protect that Constitution, rather than buckling to the demands of a troubling scene.

A second problem with the construction of motives by scholarly defenders of the *Bush* decision was that it ignored what the per curiam itself said, justifying the Court's actions not on the grounds that it provided but on grounds it never acknowledged nor which, according to Dworkin, "they would publicly embrace."[106] This is particularly troublesome because of the unique role that court-constructed motives play in judicial opinions. When appellate courts hand down decisions, courts below them within their jurisdiction are required to follow those decisions. But what a decision was turns upon what the court was doing and why it was doing it—that is, the court's decision as full-blown action. The primary evidence for what a court was doing is what it says it was doing—this is why precedent courts are quoted so frequently on points of law. So, for example, if the *Bush* court was actually motivated by fear of disorder and a constitutional crisis yet failed to mention those concerns, it would be difficult for lower courts to follow the law of *Bush* in later cases by citing that as a relevant factor in understanding what the law is.[107] Thus, in a real way, the motives embedded in the text of a decision are the only truly relevant motives in the life of the law.

Scholarly critics of the per curiam decision took the Court's reasons as they were given and showed that they failed to account for what the Court was doing and why it was doing it. Their major starting point was agency, where they expended a great deal of energy showing that the Court was not following the law in reaching its decision. Indeed, there was hardly a legal claim made by the Court that they did not dispute and other claims they accused the Court of failing even to consider. On the latter, they complained that the Court never considered whether Bush had standing to sue or whether entry into the election dispute required it to ignore its tradition of staying out of political questions.

While even Tribe conceded that the Court was justified in taking the case (where others would not), almost all Court critics rejected the equal protection argument, the safe harbor claim, the remedy, and the attempt to limit the reach of the decision. On the equal protection claim, they noted that the voter-intent standard was not made up by the state court but was taken from statutes and precedents, that it is a widely used standard never before challenged by the courts, that it is at least as clear as, say, a "reasonable doubt" standard used to convict people in capital cases, and that for the state court to change this standard might have violated Article II in any case. The Warren-era precedents cited by the per curiam, they noted, bore little resemblance to the Florida recount case, since no identifiable parties were harmed by the standard, and certainly no traditionally recognized parties. Furthermore, they noted that subsequent cases added an intent requirement which the majority conveniently ignored (until after the case was over). And even if the Court recognized an equal protection problem with the recount, it ignored a larger equal protection problem with the original count, whereby the use of different voting technologies ensured that identifiable classes of voters (notably Democrats, minorities, and the poor) had a much greater chance of having their votes rejected to start with; therefore, the critics argued, the majority's decision actually prevented the redressing of a much more significant equal protection problem than they purported to address.

Even defenders of the Court were not willing to defend the majority's safe harbor deadline ruling, and critics noted that the idea that Florida (or the Florida Supreme Court or the Florida legislature) would want to meet that optional deadline at any cost—including awarding the state's electors to the wrong candidate—was preposterous. And it was strange, indeed, that the per curiam failed to defer to the state court on any other issue besides this one, and this where there was no firm textual support in the Florida laws for this reading.

The remedy of stopping the recounting and refusing to remand the case back to the state court to fix the constitutional problems reflected the height of hypocrisy for a court that claimed to be defending the fundamental right to vote. Indeed, despite Posner's claim that this human recount opened the door to partisanship, critics believed that enough checks and balances were in place to ensure a fair recount, with both parties participating, an opportunity for objections offered, and a judge who had previously ruled in Bush's favor presiding over the whole process. Furthermore, the recount was necessary to correct the problems with the original recount, which unfairly rejected an inordinate number of votes from Democrats, minorities, and the poor.

Not even Lund would defend the attempt to cabin the *Bush* precedent, which was based on a relatively simple proposition about recounting standards (despite the majority's protestations that it was full of complexities). Thus, critics concluded, the majority was simply making law for Bush and Bush alone (despite Scalia's stated insistence that this was not what the Court's job was), refusing to be strapped down in the future by the principles it was using to hand the election to Bush.

These agency concerns are tightly connected to purpose concerns in the critics' constructions. Why would the Court trot out such indefensible means to stop the recount and hand the election to Bush? Obviously, because they were Republicans ideologically aligned with Bush. They were acting as partisans and as supporters of a right-wing ideology. Their decision would yield a president likely to continue their conservative judicial legacies (as he had promised of Scalia and Thomas particularly), perhaps elevate one of them to the chief justice position when the aging Rehnquist retired, or at least replace them with like-minded justices. They had family and economic reasons as well, with relatives working closely with Bush and his future administration. It could not be that they intervened in the interest of justice, since throwing out the votes of those whose recount standards are being corrected is no justice. They could not even be working in the interest of order, since having the Supreme Court name the president is a greater threat to democratic order than a messy election, particularly in snatching from Congress a role given to it by the Constitution and the Electoral Act of 1887. The questionable purpose-bad agency connection was strong if it is assumed that agency was subordinated to purpose at all costs.

A construction of agents supports this particular purpose, as critics emphasized the ideological, 5-4 split in the decision and the personal and political motives of these particular justices. The disjunction between the means the majority used and the agents who used them also pointed to a questionable purpose: why would states' rights defenders, who railed against judicial activism (some adhering to originalism) and only used equal protection to strike down reverse discrimination, suddenly reverse their positions in this case, unless personal and political motives overwhelmed their judicial sensibilities? This construction was weak to the extent that, despite the conservatives' complaints about judicial activism, they in fact had been quite activist. (Critics at least could chastise them for failing to practice what they preached.) Finally, why were these agents stepping on the toes of those to whom the Constitution and the Electoral Count Act of 1887 had given the job of resolving election disputes?

Critics constructed a tight grammatical connection between ideological and partisan agents using questionable means to ensure that a Republican was appointed president and federal judicial nominator, finding them displaying attitudes of arrogance, aggression, partisanship, recklessness, and lawlessness in picking the president (and the selector of their successors); thwarting democracy; harming the Court, the Congress, and the public; and staging a judicial coup d'état. Critics would fairly ignore the scene, except to deny that a crisis was pending, emphasizing that the Electoral Count Act of 1887 provided clear direction and that no riots were threatening the republic. They did not cut the Court slack simply because time was short (as the Court and its defenders had not done in assessing the actions of the similarly hard-pressed state court). Indeed, they could use that shortened scene against the Court in noting that the stay was granted on the assumption that Bush had a substantial probability of winning the case, even though the majority had only hours to think about complex and esoteric Florida and constitutional law issues, suggesting that they could not be acting for legal reasons but rather for political ones.

Scholarly critics offered a damning construction of the motives of the majority in *Bush v. Gore*. This overall construction was bolstered by the coherence of their construction of each of the grammatical terms, whereby agents with nonneutral attitudes used questionable means to meet certain purposes in an ultimate act not necessitated by the scene. The incoherencies that cut across different acts, as we witness agents who in the past have disdained particular acts and agencies now embracing them, provide external support for the construction of purpose in this case. They enjoy the great advantage of focusing on the act in question directly, addressing what the Court said it was doing and in assessing what the Court did.

Scholarly defenders offered an apologia for the stated motives of the majority in *Bush v. Gore*, making an indirect argument about what it was doing by looking outside the decision itself—indeed, to a great extent ignoring that decision—in order to develop a plausible explanation and perhaps a justification for what the Court was doing. They must sacrifice some of the ethos of the Court in the process, at least to the extent of admitting some disingenuousness on the Court's part in acting for reasons other than those it provided. And they never really addressed why the Court refused to lay its cards on the table. Why not, indeed, admit that the Florida recounters were acting as partisans, that the partisan state court was giving them leave to do so, and that the election recount was headed for a constitutional crisis?

These may have been rocks that Court defenders were loath to look under. At best, one could argue that to make such charges against state officials would be improper for the U.S. Supreme Court. For one thing, that would require reaching factual conclusions not established in the record, and appellate courts are not concerned with reaching factual conclusions but rather about deciding legal issues. Secondly, highlighting such assumptions would undermine good federal-state relations by jumping to conclusions about state officials when they ought to be (and traditionally have been) given the benefit of the doubt.[108]

Beyond this, rhetorically, it would have proven troublesome to draw attention to concerns that state officials, including judges, were acting on their partisan biases in this case. Such a charge, obviously, could be turned back on the five conservative Republicans who sealed Bush's victory.

Finally, appealing to a constitutional crisis required a great number of assumptions—about what the recounters would do, about what the state court would do, about what Congress would do, and so forth—which would highlight the speculative nature of the concern. More troubling still, sketching out a path to constitutional crisis as Posner had done would remind readers of the per curiam that a process for such a resolution was already in place, forcing the High Court to explain why it was short-circuiting that process.

In short, Court defenders could make claims about the High Court's motives that would have proven awkward for the Court itself to present. Indeed, as Dworkin noted, these were motives it would not publicly embrace in any case. Given the arm's length at which these motives must be held from the Court, it appears that the Court defenders had the weaker and more troubling construction. At best, they could try to make the Florida Supreme Court look worse, which was the more explicit focus of Chief Rehnquist's concurring opinion.

12

Scholars Reconstruct
Rehnquist's Concurring Opinion

Several scholars defending the Court's decision to stop the recounts thought that the concurring opinion by Chief Justice Rehnquist offered a better justification for the decision than the per curiam.[1]

Rehnquist's concurring opinion, joined by Justices Thomas and Scalia, argued for intervention by the High Court by distinguishing an "ordinary election" from the election of the president of the United States, urging that the federal issues it raised justified an otherwise extraordinary intervention over issues of state law. Rehnquist examined the language of Article II and highlighted the legislature's role in the electoral process, quoting with emphasis: "'[e]ach State shall appoint, in such Manner as the *Legislature* thereof may direct' electors for President and Vice President."[2] He argued that this special empowerment of the legislature meant that "the text of the election law itself, and not just its interpretation by the courts of the States, takes on independent significance" (532). Finally, relying on the 1892 case of *McPherson v. Blacker*,[3] he claimed that "[a] significant departure from the legislative scheme for appointing Presidential electors presents a federal constitutional question" (534). Rehnquist spent most of his opinion arguing that, indeed, the Florida Supreme Court had made a significant departure from the legislative scheme, misconstruing Florida election law.

In supporting this departure from the law, Rehnquist first argued that the state court failed to give presumption to the certified winner of the election, "empty[ing] certification of all legal consequence during the contest, and in doing so depart[ing] from the provisions enacted by the Florida Legislature" (537). Next, he claimed that the state court failed to defer to the county canvassing boards, which were given the authority to decide whether to conduct a manual recount, and the secretary of state, whom the state court forced to accept late returns and whose interpretation of "legal vote" was rejected by the state court, though she was the chief election officer in the state (537). Rehnquist saved his most extensive argument to challenge the Florida court's interpretation of "legal vote," which he claimed "plainly departed from the legislative scheme":

> No reasonable person would call it "an error in the vote tabulation," Fla. Stat. § 102.166(5), or a "rejection of legal votes," Fla. Stat. § 102.168(3)(c), when electronic or electromechanical equipment performs precisely in the manner designed, and fails to count those ballots that are not marked in the manner that these voting instructions explicitly and prominently specify. (537)

Finally, Rehnquist insisted that the recount order violated the statutory scheme, because Florida law required that election results be completed by the safe harbor deadline, and "[i]n light of the inevitable legal challenges and the ensuing appeals to the Supreme Court of Florida and petitions for certiorari to this Court, the entire recounting process could not possibly be completed by that [December 12] date" (538). Based on these problems with the state court's construction of Florida law, Rehnquist concluded that they had violated Article II. These arguments constituted "additional grounds" to reverse the state court's decision, assuring readers that he and his concurring colleagues also supported the per curiam decision.

Because the concurring opinion relied on the claim that the Florida Supreme Court had badly misconstrued Florida election law, a focus on how the concurring opinion reached its conclusions centered on the state court's actions. This approach should be distinguished from that of the defenders of the per curiam who focused on the missteps of the state court, because they did so, for the most part, by going outside the per curiam's argument (with the exception of the criticism of the state court's "voter intent" standard), leading the argument away from the High Court's actions to focus on the state court's actions. This strategy of deflection typically urged that because the state court was in the wrong, the wrongs of the High Court could be overlooked—a weak argument. But in the case of the concurrence, a focus on what the High Court did in attacking the state court's actions effectively and appropriately kept the focus on the state court, even as it analyzed what the High Court did. Thus, both defenders and critics of the concurrence found themselves arguing over similar points and focusing largely on the primary term of judicial concern: agency. The debate over how the concurring opinion reached its conclusions revolved around three issues: (1) Article II's requirements for presidential elections, (2) the Florida Supreme Court's interpretation of state election law, and (3) the remedy offered by the concurring opinion.

Article II and the Law of Presidential Elections

The concurring opinion claimed that Article II of the U.S. Constitution gave state legislatures plenary power to determine the manner of selecting presidential electors, so that judicial interpretations of such election laws must stick closely to what the legislature intended. Indeed, Michael McConnell defended this reading by calling the language of Article II a notable and meaningful "departure" from other constitutional provisions on governance:

> Article II, Section 1, Clause 2 of the U.S. Constitution provides: "Each State shall appoint, in such Manner as the Legislature Thereof May Direct, a Number of Electors." By specifying "the Legislature" as the source of state law, this Clause departs from the usual principle of federal constitutional law, which allows the people of each state to determine for themselves how to allocate power among their state governing institutions. This puts the federal court in the awkward and unusual position of having to determine for itself whether a state court's "interpretation" of state law is an authentic reading of the legislative will.[4]

McConnell focused on the language of the constitutional provision to suggest that this particular enactment was distinct from other enactments (in giving power to the legislature rather than the people) and that this difference was meaningful in its unique grant of power—a grant that creates awkwardness for the federal courts, since they must defend the state legislature's authentic will.

McConnell suggested that "[t]here is no relevant legislative history explaining why the framers of the Constitution made this departure"—no scene to explain the purpose of this act.[5] Posner agreed, noting that "there is no evidence that the choice of this word [legislature] (rather than simply of *state*) was deliberate, or that the framers of the Constitution foresaw the use of this provision of Article II to limit the scope of state judicial intervention in the selection of a state's electors."[6]

This lack of history and clear purpose led many to question whether, indeed, there was a departure here to account for, as McConnell claimed. Michael Klarman, for example, looked at where the concurrence rested its argument for departure, noting that "the concurring Justices rely entirely on the text of Article II, specifically its reference to state 'legislatures' directing the manner of choosing presidential electors." Klarman believed that "[t]his spare textual reference simply does not bear the weight the concurrence ascribes to it."[7] To challenge the textual claim, he drew an analogy:

> Article I of the Constitution declares that "all legislative Powers herein granted shall be vested in a Congress of the United States." Yet nobody has ever suggested that this language precludes judicial interpretation of congressional statutes. Indeed, since 1935 the Court never has held that this constitutional mandate that Congress exercise "all legislative power" precludes Congress from enacting vague (meaningless) statutes that essentially delegate the lawmaking power to administrative agencies and to courts.[8]

Klarman's analogy worked by taking a well-known constitutional provision that stresses the source of legislative powers, comparing it to the Article II grant of state legislative authority to determine the manner of selecting presidential electors, and suggesting that in the former case, the emphasis on legislative power had not precluded judicial interpretation, and, thus, the same might be said for the latter provision. Klarman's act-act comparison was strong in drawing on similar language but weak to the extent that the narrower grant of state legislative authority concerning the manner of selecting electors might be distinguishable. Additionally, the neat division of powers in the constitutional articles might be thought to preclude a narrow reading of Article I's grant of authority, since other branches are given authority in other sections as well, notably the courts.

Richard Epstein relied on this "spare textual reference" to provide additional unpacking of the terms of Article II. He insists that it means that

[t]he Florida legislature directs the manner in which the presidential electors are appointed, and all other actors within the Florida system have to stay within the confines of that directive. The word "direct" is a strong term whose sense is captured in the phrase "directed verdict," which refuses to let a jury stray beyond the area of permissible inferences.[9]

By qualifying the character of the term *direct* (as strong) and analogizing it to the act of directing a verdict, Epstein painted the language of Article II as emphatic in its grant of authority. The act-act analogy here gained strength only from the similarity of the words. It was weak insofar as it attempted to smuggle in a concrete, historically developed sense of directing that perhaps cannot be separated from the specific noun the term *directed* qualifies.

In the absence of locating specific legislative history on the Constitution's grant of authority to state legislators to choose the manner of selecting presidential electors, several scholars considered more general attitudes and actions of the framers. Nelson Lund, for example, who rejected the Article II argument, claimed that "[t]he framers were well aware that statutes often do require judicial interpretation in order to be applied, and federal courts ordinarily assume that state statutes mean what state courts say they mean. It would not be outlandish to interpret Article II as incorporating the same background assumption."[10] The framers' general awareness of the need for courts to interpret statutes, Lund asserted, provides a reason for believing that in this particular provision, they probably assumed the same thing (through an attitude-act construction).

Hayward Smith, recently graduated from New York University Law School, wrote a comment for *Florida State University Law Review* that challenged McConnell's claims that there was no relevant legislative history on the issue and that the language itself supported his views of the independence of the legislature in choosing electors:

> An inferential analysis of the reasoning and compromises underlying the crafting of the Elector Appointment Clause, whose language echoes that contained in a key provision of the Articles of Confederation, counsels against the assumption that the Founders understood it to create independent legislatures. Moreover, the manner in which the state legislatures exercised their federal constitutional powers in the first federal elections of 1788 indicates that the founding generation did not believe that Article II announced the independence of state legislatures.[11]

Smith admitted that the convention and ratification debates did not reveal a specific original understanding of the Article II clause's grant of power to state legislatures in choosing the manner for selecting presidential electors.[12] Therefore, Smith attempted to draw inferences to answer the following question: "[W]hen the framers debated electoral college schemes at the Federal Convention, did they express commitment to any underlying purpose or principle which might be served by independent legislatures?"[13] Smith attempted to work backward in this grammatical construction, moving from purpose to act to understand better what the act meant.

Smith reported that once the Constitutional Convention embraced the idea that an Electoral College should choose the president, the debate turned to the question of how the electors should be chosen. Smith noted that many possible means for selecting presidential electors were considered, including having them "'chosen by the people,' 'chosen by the State Executives,' 'appointed by the Legislatures of the States,' or 'chosen by the Legislatures of the States,'" before settling on a recommendation, from David Brearley's committee assigned to the question, that a state's presidential electors be chosen "in such manner as its Legislature may direct."[14] The power this language was intended to grant to the state legislatures must be seen as somewhat limited, argued Smith, because the Constitutional Convention explicitly rejected proposals to give the state legislatures more power in the process. For example, following a proposal by Elbridge Gerry of Massachusetts to allow the state legislatures themselves to choose the president directly, Smith noted, "the 'noes were so predominant' that the votes were not even counted."[15] Indeed, the final language was a compromise, for

> [e]ven with respect to an electoral college system, many delegates do not appear to have desired giving legislatures any power. Rather, delegates repeatedly proposed electoral college schemes involving popular electors. Wilson did so in June; King, Patterson, and Madison did so on July 19; and Morris did so on August 24. Gerry himself would have preferred assigning the power to choose electors to the state executives. The idea of exclusive legislative appointment of electors—perhaps embodied in the convention's brief acceptance of Ellsworth's July 19 compromise for electors appointed by state legislatures—became acceptable, it seems, only as a compromise that would placate those who, like Gerry, were opposed to direct election of anything. The near success of Morris's August 24 motion for popular electors [defeated 6-5][16] indicates that, even at that late date, many delegates would still have preferred to bypass state legislatures altogether with popular electors.[17]

Smith's argument looked at means and ends that were rejected by the Convention prior to endorsing the language we now have—the rejected means of giving all the power to the legislatures and the rejected purpose of excluding popular participation altogether. He admitted that direct popular election of the president and direct popular election of presidential electors were both rejected but framed his characterization of a compromise in noting that provisions for the legislature either to vote directly for the president or even to vote directly for electors were defeated. Of course, in choosing the manner of selecting electors, the legislatures presumably could give themselves the authority to choose the electors directly—scratching back the power Smith said the framers chose not to give them. However, there was a qualitative difference Smith emphasized here: in Article I, Section 3, the framers gave states the direct power to "chuse" members of the House of Representatives, while in Article II , Section 1, the legislatures were given "only the power to 'direct' the 'manner' of their appointment"[18]—the difference in language, presumably, reflecting a difference in power.

There was another reason the framers chose this particular language, according to Smith: they lifted it from the Articles of Confederation. Smith noted that "Article V of the Articles of Confederation . . . had provided that delegates to Congress 'shall be annually appointed in such manner as the legislature of each State shall direct.'"[19] While he warned that stronger state sovereignty under the Articles made the analogy to the present Constitution one that must be used cautiously, he insisted that it "provides a baseline understanding" from which to work.[20] He noted that despite the almost identical language of Article V and Article II, the actions of the states suggested that they did not understand this language to mean for the Articles of Confederation what the *Bush* concurrence claimed it meant in the U.S. Constitution—that legislatures had some independent, unfettered standing among state players (including the state constitutions as players) in determining the manner of selecting delegates. He noted that

> three out of four state constitutions adopted after the Articles were proposed in November 1777, but before the Federal Constitution was adopted, contained explicit provisions purporting to regulate the selection of congressional delegates. This practice was consistent with the pre-Confederation state constitutions of 1776 and 1777, of which eight out of ten had similar provisions. The Framers were certainly aware of this understanding when they settled on the language of the Elector Appointment Clause for the new Federal Constitution. Thus, the clause, like Article V of the Articles of

Confederation before it, was intended to serve federalism only in the sense that, "by virtue of their status as independent sovereigns within a federal system," states—not independent state legislatures—decided the mode by which they would appoint their electors.[21]

Smith's construction of motives was complex but compelling, involving the development of two acts. First, he constructed the act of passing Article V by emphasizing that before and after this language was crafted giving the state legislatures authority to determine the manner of choosing congressional delegates, states were putting provisions in their constitutions to regulate how their legislatures selected those delegates. Presumably, when the Articles of Confederation (and, thereby, Article V) were approved, the delegates knew that these state constitutions were regulating elections. Now, if this particular clause was meant to forbid such processes, one must wonder why three state governments defied the pending Articles of Confederation in passing such regulations. If eleven of thirteen state constitutions eventually had such provisions, one would assume that it was generally understood that the language of Article V did not forbid such regulation through state constitutions. This construction rested on an act-scene and a scene-act relationship, whereby the acts of the states in passing constitutional provisions regarding the manner of choosing congressional delegates created a scene within which such exercises of state constitutional power were implicitly accepted as appropriate. Conversely, the scene within which these exercises of constitutional power had been taken provided a backdrop against which the Articles of Confederation (and Article V particularly) were approved, affording insight into the purposes for Article V.

This construction worked well within the confines of the Articles of Confederation, suggesting a legislative purpose of not granting exclusive authority to state legislatures in this process. However, its application to the Constitution's Article II provisions required an extension of the scene created by these provisions and the states' actions preceding their approval, as well as a consideration of the importance of the linguistic agency in this case. Smith presumed—reasonably—that by adopting the same language as Article V of the first U.S. charter, Article II of the Constitution intended the same purpose as that of the Article V provision. That is, the language granting authority to the state legislatures was an agency tied to a particular purpose; and the Constitutional framers, who presumably were aware of the tradition of interpreting this language as not giving state legislatures exclusive and unfettered authority over the selection of delegates (since they were knowledgeable agents operating within this scene), would not have used this language had they intended a distinctly different purpose (such as that proposed by Chief Justice Rehnquist's concurrence). To do so would be like using a screwdriver to do some hammering (adopting an inappropriate agency). When combined with his consideration of the process by which this language was eventually adopted as a compromise, his construction of motives became compelling.

Ronald Dworkin explored the question of the framers' purposes not by looking at historical evidence but by considering generally what those purposes could *not* have been. Arguing against the idea that Article II prevented state constitutions from limiting what state legislatures could do in setting out the manner for selecting presidential electors, he asked:

> What possible point could be served by the national Constitution denying the people of Florida authority to protect their own democratic power in that way? What possible point could the framers have thought they were serving by enacting a provision with that consequence? So understood, the clause both undermines democracy and cripples state sovereignty, and has no redeeming features at all.[22]

In asking generally about purposes for this Article, Dworkin raised an act-purpose question: If their action were taken as denying the people of Florida authority to protect their own democratic power through their state constitution, then what ultimate purpose would that serve? If it would actually undermine democracy and state sovereignty, his logic went, then one should reject that purpose and a reading of the act that assumed that this was what it did.

Both Dworkin's and Smith's arguments, nonetheless, seemed to fly in the face of *Bush v. Palm Beach County Canvassing Board* (sometimes referred to as *Bush I*). In that case, a unanimous Supreme Court asked the Florida Supreme Court to explain the extent to which it was relying on the state constitution's "people power" provision to support extending the deadline for counties to turn in their vote totals beyond what Secretary of State Harris had set. The implication of the High Court's question was, as Dworkin put it, "[t]hat Article II exempts the state legislatures from the constraints of their own state constitutions in their decisions about how elections are to be run."[23] Although *Bush v. Gore* did not raise this issue directly (the state court was careful to avoid that pitfall a second time), it did carry indirect implications for the case: if the state constitution were the sole source of the Florida Supreme Court's power to review state legislation, such as election law, then Article II theoretically could trump that authority, leaving the legislature free to enact legislation without judicial oversight.[24]

Dworkin thought this was "a very bad" reading of the Article.[25] However, he conceded that

> a surprising number of lawyers and scholars (including, apparently, all nine of the Supreme Court justices) apparently think that the language quoted from Article II has a much more important consequence than that [the legislature must make election laws]. They think that it means not only that the legislature rather than some other person or group is to make the election law, but that it is to make the election law in some particularly free and unencumbered way—free, that is, from the normal background provisions and assumptions to which all its other acts of legislation are subject.[26]

Dworkin added that if this view was correct, "then the power of state court judges to review and interpret state election statutes is sharply limited."[27]

Court defenders capitalized on *Bush v. Palm Beach County Canvassing Board.* Posner, for example, argued that the Article II agency for limiting the reach of state constitutions was supported by the number of agents who endorsed it, urging that this position "actually commanded the support of all nine justices in the first opinion in the election litigation, that of December 4 [i.e., *Bush v. Palm Beach County Canvassing Board*]." He admitted that "[a] unanimous decision by the Supreme Court may well be wrong" but urged that "it is unlikely to be so far wrong as to impair the Court's authority."[28] Klarman, on the other hand, reminded his readers that the concurring opinion that endorsed this position in *Bush v. Gore* attracted a mere "plurality."[29]

Samuel Issacharoff got around *Bush v. Palm Beach County Canvassing Board* by reading it as less restrictive on judicial action than Posner seemed to allow:

> As matters stood after *Bush v. Palm Beach County Canvassing Board,* there still appeared room for the normal operation of judicial interpretation of statutes. *Bush v. Palm Beach County Canvassing Board* did not entertain the notion that the state legislative scheme would either be fully responsive to any emergency that might arise, or that it would be entirely self-revealing and consistent. In this sense, the Court rejected the more extreme argument advanced by the Bush campaign that any state judicial review or interpretation would violate the federal constitutional scheme. *Bush v. Palm Beach County Canvassing Board* does, however, appear to contemplate that state judicial review of presidential election disputes takes as its cue state legislative enactments rather than state constitutional or common law authority. What remains uncertain

is the source of remedial authority of state courts in the event of a problem in the administration of the state statutory election system.[30]

Issacharoff constructed the *Bush v. Palm Beach County Canvassing Board* court as refusing to go as far as the Bush team wanted it to go, though he admitted that there may be an independence in state election statutes that frees them from the state constitution and common law. Even here, however, he used the phrase *takes as its cue* to describe the deference to those statutes, which perhaps does not mean other sources of law are to be ignored. Finally, his emphasis on remedial authority and (like Dworkin) on the non-self-revealing nature of statutes, as well as the potential for conflicts in election laws, opened the door to judicial interpretation.

Issacharoff also provided a pragmatic argument against Article II's application in presidential election cases, which he called a "managerial" problem:

> Resting federal constitutional oversight on fidelity to preexisting election procedures necessarily involves an assessment of what prior procedures were and what alterations were actually made. Since the conduct of the elections is basically entrusted to the states, and since states in turn devolve responsibility to county level election officials, federal constitutional review of changed state election procedures would in turn require that every local and state election procedure be subject to federal judicial scrutiny. Such an approach would run counter to long-standing abstention doctrines that would have federal courts step clearly aside when matters of interpreting state law and procedures are inherent to federal questions.[31]

Issacharoff supported his last claim with a couple of Supreme Court cases elaborating the abstention doctrine.[32] His strategy here focused on necessary agencies (which would be far-reaching) described against a very large scene (which included every local and state election procedure implemented before and during or after an election in all the states). This construction relied on theoretical cases (in stressing all such procedures), instead of the smaller number in a given year that might be appealed to the federal courts. However, his description did accurately describe the depth of the waters into which the High Court was stepping for these potential cases (dramatizing that depth by taking his readers through steps down from federal to state to county levels of scrutiny). And, more important perhaps, his approach provided a purpose—of avoiding taking on what might prove unmanageable—for adhering to long-standing abstention doctrines that justified sidestepping such problems and a precedential agency for doing so.

Dworkin attacked Court defenders' reliance on *Bush v. Palm Beach County Canvassing Board* differently from Issacharoff and Smith. He did not attack its troubling managerial implications, nor did he go back to some past historical scene to figure out the framers' purposes. Instead, he turned to a general description of the act of legislating, suggesting that judicial help was required to understand what legislatures have done in a given case. Dworkin began with a description of how legislation comes to be:

> Legislation is not an act of magic. A statute does not spring, full-formed and pellucid, from the collective mind of a group of officials endowed by nature with special legislative powers. Legislation results when a group of people lucky enough to have won the last election—and not all of whom have any great understanding of what they are doing—perform some conventional act, like saying "aye," when particular words are placed before them. But what legislation they have actually enacted—what difference they have made to the law that governs the rest of us by saying "aye"—depends not just on what words were placed before them, but on a good deal else as well. It depends on background rules and practices many but not all of which are encoded in written and unwritten constitutions.[33]

Dworkin's unflattering portrait of legislators painted them not as ideal agents for rendering laws that are pellucid but as politicians engaging in some conventional act, perhaps required for lawmaking but not necessarily engaging (or collectivizing) the minds of those who partake in it.

This portrait of legislators was contrasted with a portrait of judges who must respond to challenges to such laws by individuals who believe their rights have been violated. In such cases, "it falls to state and federal judges to decide whether [a] challenge is justified."[34] Note that Dworkin's judges were passive in this instance, the challenge falling to them. They were agents with a duty to act in such cases.

Dworkin next inextricably connected the legislative act to the judicial act in insisting that "what legislation a legislature has enacted—what it has actually done—depends not only on what words the legislators had on their desks when they voted, but on what those words, in that context, mean: how, that is, they are properly interpreted." He admitted that legislatures may try to fix meaning with committee reports on intentions and the like, but he insisted that

> they cannot, in the nature of the case, anticipate or govern every issue of interpretation that may arise. Once again, in the United States, it falls to

judges to interpret vague, ambiguous, abstract, or otherwise troublesome phrases and statutes, and their interpretive decisions are crucial in fixing what law we are actually governed by.[35]

Because the legislative act in general is a limited one, not anticipating all issues of interpretation, judicial interpretation is required. Dworkin rejected the idea that judicial interpretation of this sort involves

> undo[ing] the law that the legislature has enacted. That suggestion misses the crucial point. What legislation a legislature actually *has* enacted depends on what the right answers are to the questions that, in our legal practice, judges must decide. A statute is an interpretive construction, not just a series of punctuated words.[36]

This final point blurred the line between legislative action and judicial action. What a legislature has enacted is made to depend on an act of judicial interpretation.

There was a potential terministic slip in this construction insofar as what was done by a legislature depended on what is done by a court. Two different agents (legislatures and courts) work in two different scenes (the early legislative and the later judicial) to yield a single act (or enactment) by the originating agent. Dworkin's description of a statute as "an interpretive construction" located it somewhere between those who would put meaning into it (the legislature) and those who would take meaning out of it (those applying the law). It constructed a statute as a communication to others, as partaking in a complex process that finds speakers attempting to get a message to audiences. In this construction, courts are somewhere between speakers and audiences, interpreting what legislatures say for the legal community and the public. The temporal (scenic) slippage can be sidestepped with a distinction between ontology and epistemology. Ontologically, the legislature has done what it has done; however, epistemologically, we may not yet know what it has done until an occasion arises demanding that we determine that. Thus, what legislatures do constitutes the law (literally, enacts it); what courts do interprets what has been constituted (gives us knowledge of it).

Jack Balkin also argued about the necessary role of the judiciary in the process of statutory interpretation.:

> The problem with Chief Justice Rehnquist's interpretation of Article II is that it assumes that one can divorce the Florida legislature from every other element of the Florida lawmaking process, including the Florida courts and the Florida Constitution, and that one can clearly separate what Florida law

means from what the Florida courts say it means. This is a difficult claim to sustain. The legislature only is the legislature because the Florida Constitution creates it as such. All legislative power in Florida is subject to judicial review under the Florida Constitution and statutes are subject to ordinary judicial interpretation as well as to judicial review under the requirements of the Florida Constitution. To argue otherwise would mean that in picking electors some handful of the Florida legislators could assemble as a rump session and do almost anything they wanted, because under Article II they could not be bound by what the Florida courts or the Florida Constitution said.[37]

Balkin agreed with Dworkin that separating out some statutory meaning independent of interpretation is futile—enactments must be given voice by qualified agents, in this case the state courts. He also noted that the legislature, as an agent of lawmaking, exists because of a prior constitutional enactment, so that that it cannot rise above that enactment. Indeed, the implications of ignoring the constitutional provisions that direct the legislature were teased out in the hypothetical example of a rump session that would violate constitutional directives.

Court defenders might argue that Rehnquist was carving out only one type of act for special distinction from such constraints—those involving presidential election law. It might be that this particular exception would not upset other provisions, such as those that determine whether a legislature has a proper quorum. On the other hand, as Dworkin noted, "nothing in the [U.S.] Constitution requires that states even *have* legislatures."[38] Thus, there is some background dependence on state constitutional provisions to establish the agents whom Rehnquist would free from constitutional constraints in making election laws.

While Dworkin and others stressed the inevitable role that courts must play in interpreting legislative acts, Posner argued that Article II nonetheless assumes separation between the roles: "Article II establishes a clear line of demarcation between state judicial and legislative prerogatives in the selection of a state's presidential electors, and in doing so prevents the state courts from hijacking an election by changing the rules after the outcome of the election is known."[39] Two features of this characterization are noteworthy. First, unlike Dworkin and Balkin, Posner did not speak generally about how meaning is drawn out of statutes; instead, he spoke of what Article II calls for. Thus, whether or not, in a general or practical sense, one can separate laws made from their interpretation, he insisted that Article II assumes that we can and requires that we do so. Second, he draws a distinction based on rights or powers, insisting that "state judicial and legislative *prerogatives* in the selection of presidential electors" must be distinguished. The word *prerogatives* suggests possible differences in purposes that might be realized by virtue of each branch's rights or powers to act in this area, and Posner insisted that legislative purposes must reign supreme. This difference of treatment was driven home when he used a metaphor to highlight one potential outcome of judicial prerogatives: hijacking an election by changing the rules after the outcome of the election is known.

Posner agreed that courts may be needed to interpret statutes, but he warned against allowing them to move from simply interpreting rules to changing them:

> [Although] [t]he state courts retain their ordinary powers; the Supreme Court is authorized to intervene if, in the guise of interpretation, the state courts in effect rewrite the state election law, usurping the legislature's authority. The difference between interpretive and usurpative judicial "work" on statutes is subtle, but is illuminated by comparison to the settled distinction in the law of labor arbitration between an arbitrator's interpreting a collective bargaining agreement, on the one hand, and, on the other, importing his own views of industrial justice in disregard of that agreement. The former is legitimate interpretation, and is insulated from judicial review; the latter is usurpative, and is forbidden.[40]

Grammatically, Posner would have courts rely more on the agency of statutes and less on an agent's values (which in this example he couched in the term *views of industrial justice*). This construction of proper judicial action made an assumption and an implication—assuming that one may divorce one's values (or views) from one's decision making and implying that the Florida Supreme Court, indeed, had brought its values and not, say, general judicial values, state or federal constitutional values, or other appropriate values into the process.

Posner's construction spoke to an idealized process, through which agency controls errant, passionate, and value-laden agents, to ensure that Article II's dictates are followed. However, in describing that ideal, Posner may have been stripping away too much to reflect what actually goes into judicial interpretation. Dworkin's insistence that judicial interpretation "depends on background rules and practices many but not all of which are encoded in written and unwritten constitutions" served as a warning that values may be attributed to scenes as well as agents (as part of a background), so that there is no simple, value-free agency of interpretation, even if one admits that highly personalized, esoteric values ought to be excluded from election law interpretations.

Louise Weinberg turned her focus to the agents, who she believed must have the power to get to the very heart of their statutory subjects:

> there was very little merit in their argument that the Florida Supreme Court could not interpret Florida election law in medias res. Not only must courts have the power—and, some would say, after Chief Justice Marshall, the duty—to exercise a granted jurisdiction over elections cases, but also they must have the substantive power and duty to interpret, reconcile, stay the effect of, or strike down the laws governing, elections and post-election contests within their jurisdiction. Nothing in the Constitution requires a state election code or its administration to be unmediated in these usual ways by courts.[41]

Again, Weinberg used the court critic's strategy of speaking generally about what courts must be able to do, as opposed to drawing a distinction in the kind of actions they can engage in here, as Posner and other Court defenders did. Weinberg went beyond mere power afforded to courts to speak of duty, invoking Marshall to put a mythic stamp of approval on her position.

Weinberg bolstered her case by noting congressional acknowledgment of the place for state judicial review in just such cases. Rehnquist's concurring opinion had drawn on the Electoral Count Act to bolster his interpretation:

> 3 U.S.C. § 5 informs our application of Art. II, § 1, cl. 2, to the Florida statutory scheme, which, as the Florida Supreme Court acknowledged, took that statute into account. Section 5 provides that the State's selection of electors "shall be conclusive, and shall govern in the counting of the electoral votes" if the electors are chosen under laws enacted prior to election day, and if the selection process is completed six days prior to the meeting of the electoral college. (534)

Weinberg noted that "the act of Congress on which the Rehnquist concurrence relied, enacted after the Hayes-Tilden election controversy of 1876, properly read, explicitly contemplates judicial review when state law does." Her evidence for this "proper" reading was the statute's provision that election controversies or contests may be resolved through "judicial or other methods."[42] This construction was powerful for two reasons. First, it established that another branch of government contemplated and endorsed judicial involvement in election controversies, reinforcing the idea of Court critics that any reading of Article II that cut out the judiciary was questionable. Second, because the Electoral Count Act had been invoked by Rehnquist's concurring opinion, it suggested that the chief justice was quoting selectively from the statute, ignoring an obvious provision that ran against his perspective.

Weinberg noted the potential for hypocrisy in a construction that cut out judicial oversight:

> [t]o have adopted it would have been to deny to the Florida Supreme Court the very power the Court itself was asserting: the power to make a novel post-election construction of forum election law. Moreover, it would have been to deny to the Florida Supreme Court a particular power the Court was also asserting, but with far less authority: the power of construing Florida's law.[43]

Through this agent-act perspective (whereby the High Court as a judicial agent was engaging in acts that it found inconsistent with the state court's role as judicial agent), Weinberg claimed hypocrisy on the part of the concurring opinion.

Rehnquist also attempted to support his reading of Article II through a nineteenth-century case, *McPherson v. Blacker,* in which, he claimed, "we explained that Art. II, § 1, cl. 2, 'conveys the broadest power of determination' and 'leaves it to the legislature exclusively to define the method' of appointment" (403).[44] While this description of the state legislature's agency appears to grant them broad and exclusive powers concerning appointment of electors, Court critics noted two problems with Rehnquist's claim that this precedent supported his position. First, this comment by the *McPherson* court was dicta, not a holding. Lund claimed the Court "had suggested (without deciding) that state constitutions are not authorized to constrain state legislatures in the special context of choosing presidential electors."[45] Lund's construction of this statement as a suggestion rather than a decision made it an act (or perhaps simply an attitude) that need not be heeded.

Dworkin similarly dubbed the *McPherson* position "an offhand suggestion" simply "because that issue was not before the 1892 court." This scenic language, describing the issue as not before the court, is the standard means of distinguishing holdings, which should be followed,[46] from mere dicta, which need not be heeded. He added that "it is a sign of the weakness of the Article II argument that this is as close as the Court could come to finding authority for that argument."[47]

While Court defenders could argue that dicta might be useful, even in the absence of a bona fide precedent, Balkin claimed that the *McPherson* case "cuts in both directions." He noted that in addition to stating that the legislature has broad and exclusive authority,

> [t]he [*McPherson*] Court also stated . . . that "what is forbidden or required to be done by a State" in general "is forbidden or required of the legislative power under state constitutions as they exist." In other words, the Court explained, "the [State's] legislative power is the supreme authority except as limited by the constitution of the State." Hence, if the Florida Supreme Court interpreted Florida's election code to make it consistent with the Florida Constitution, there would be no violation of Article II, Section 1, at least under the authority of *McPherson*.[48]

This was a devastating critique of Rehnquist's construction of *McPherson*, for whereas the language he cited of breadth and exclusivity granted to the state legislature by Article II was general, Balkin's contrary language from the same case specifically rejected the idea that state legislative authority trumped state constitutional authority. Weinberg noted the same contrary language in this "antique opinion."[49]

Of course, to the extent that this was dicta as well, it carried no more weight than Rehnquist's reliance on the case. However, reading the divergent passages in *McPherson* together suggests that Rehnquist's reading of the meaning of the language he quoted might need to be tempered. Dworkin offered this tempered reading (which he called "the natural reading"): "That Article [II] prevents a state constitution from assigning the general power to design elections to any body other than the state legislature, but does not extinguish the citizens' normal power to protect their rights through constitutional limits on what the legislature, in the exercise of that general power, can do."[50]

Dworkin's reading had the advantage of making the act of the *McPherson* court consistent, avoiding contradictions that the language of the court might otherwise embody. It drew on an agent-act relationship that assumed that an agent would act consistently to the extent that his or her beliefs, as an agent, control what he or she says or does.[51]

Even as they defended Rehnquist's opinion, neither Epstein nor Posner seemed to deny that some form of judicial interpretation might be required when the meaning of an election statute was contested. The question, rather, is where does a state court cross the line from mere interpretation into an Article II violation? The question is more than idle speculation, for it determines how much deference and leeway to give to the Florida Supreme Court's interpretation of Florida election law in the 2000 dispute.

Commentators drew from a paucity of sources to try to fix the meaning of Article II as more supportive or more restrictive of state court interpretation. Defenders stuck primarily to the language of section 1, clause 2, emphasizing the terms *legislature* and *direct* to suggest an emphasis on agent and a potency of agency in the provision. Critics thought this evidence threadbare and compared it with other language of the Constitution (such as Article I's grant of legislative authority) to show that this meaning was hardly plain. Smith provided a lengthy consideration of the historical evidence (which everyone else had thought nonexistent) to suggest that the purposes of the framers were not supportive of a strong, independent legislative hand in this matter and that the provision was drawn from a similar one from the Articles of Confederation which had been interpreted to allow state constitutional limitations on legislative activity. In light of Chief Justice Rehnquist's reliance on the *McPherson* precedent, critics suggested that its statements on legislative independence were mere dicta and that other passages from *McPherson* actually support the view that state constitutions may limit legislation on election laws.

As Dworkin compellingly demonstrated, legislation needs interpretation, and courts are given the responsibility for making such interpretations in contested cases. It is not simply that legislatures might not be up to writing clear laws; it is that they cannot possibly foresee all the situations where the laws they pass may get applied. And, indeed, even the Electoral Count Act relied on by Rehnquist anticipates judicial means for resolving election disputes.

It is clear enough that a reading of Article II that disallows any state judicial interpretation is unsustainable. However, a blatant departure from the statutory law on the part of the Florida Supreme Court might justify High Court intervention in such cases involving the outcome of a presidential election.

The Florida Supreme Court's Construction of State Election Law

In making his case that the Florida Supreme Court had departed from statutory requirements in its decision to order a statewide recount of undervotes, Rehnquist attempted to link this decision with the state court's earlier decision in *Palm Beach County Canvassing Board v. Harris*, drawing on previous "sins" of the Florida Supreme Court (sins recognized by a unanimous U.S. Supreme Court which vacated the decision). This allowed him to rehash the controversial change in the deadline for vote totals prior to the secretary of state's certification of the election, to emphasize the state court's inclusion of partial recounts in the certified vote totals, and to high-light statutory language that would provide a context for his interpretation of "legal vote" (536–37). The merging of these two cases is seen in two strategic places. First, Rehnquist charged that "by lengthening the protest period, [the state court] necessarily shortened the contest period for Presidential elections," making the state court blameworthy for running the re-count up against what he believed was a sacrosanct safe harbor deadline (536). Second, he brought together two different standards for justifying recounts: one for the protest period and one for the contest period, concluding:

> No reasonable person would call it "an error in the vote tabulation," Fla. Stat. § 102.166(5) [the protest standard], or a "rejection of legal votes," Fla. Stat. § 102.168(3)(c) [the contest standard], when electronic or electro-mechanical equipment performs precisely in the manner designed, and fails to count those ballots that are not marked in the manner that these [legally mandated] voting instructions explicitly and prominently specify. (537)

Epstein followed the chief justice's lead in giving a great deal of atten-tion to the protest standard, attempting to develop a context within which to interpret the meaning of "legal vote" and, in turn, to suggest that the law restricts recounts. He began by quoting the three statutory remedies for fixing an "error in vote tabulation [in the protest period] which could affect the outcome of the election":

(a) Correct the error and recount the remaining precincts with the vote tab-ulation system;
(b) Request the Department of State to verify the tabulation software; or
(c) Manually recount all ballots.[52]

Epstein drew a significant inference from this remedial statutory scheme:

> The obvious structure of the entire provision is that the three remedies are *in pari materia*. They are all directed toward the same end—the correction of errors in tabulation that arise from either human or machine error. That program can be implemented only if the definition of a properly cast ballot does not vary with the method the canvassing board chooses to rectify the error in tabulation. On this view, the sole function of the hand recount is to examine ballots to see whether they meet the standards for a ballot that is machine readable.[53]

What yoked these provisions together, Epstein insisted, was their purpose ("the same end") in correcting "errors in tabulation that arise from either human or machine error." He urged that they were, in this sense, *in pari materia* (to be construed together) because he wanted to insist that the manual counting of ballots was limited to those that were machine read-able. Punchcard ballots with hanging chads, dimples, or other possible signs of voter intent were to be ignored, he implied, because reading the provisions together meant limiting the purpose to finding machine-read-able ballots.

Later in the same essay, Epstein admitted that hanging chads or even dimples might be counted if "the dimples appear in a consistent fashion across the face of the ballot in which few, if any, of the chads are punched clear through" and if there is "evidence of equipment malfunction that prevented the stylus from working." Citing Judge Sauls's finding in the lower state court, he urged that there was no evidence of such a malfunc-tion to support the counting of dimples.[54] Nevertheless, Epstein's argument extended the concept of a vote tabulation system beyond the machines and software that would count punched ballots—covered in sections (a) and (b) of the protest remediation statute—to include the machines that were used to record voter preferences. Initially, Epstein strained to contain the definition of a legal vote by encompassing it within a shared purpose of these three provisions; but he was quickly led to a consideration of agen-cies of error, which moved from the act of counting to the original act of voting, where equipment could malfunction in recording voter choices, as well as in feeding ballots through counting machines. In light of these agencies of error, he admitted that it was "a close question as to whether these 'definite dimples in a coherent pattern' should count as errors in tabulation."[55]

Posner also discussed the statute describing the correction of errors in a protest:

The natural interpretation of this series [of three options for remediating vote counting]—which also fits in with the natural interpretation of "error in vote *tabulation*"—is that the canvassing board will first try to fix the tabu-lating machinery and only if that fails will it recount the ballots by hand. The hand recount is the if-all-else-fails alternative to the tabulating machine if the machine cannot be fixed, rather than a procedure for curing voter errors.[56]

Calling the (a), (b), and (c) options in § 102.166(5) a *series* implies that one follows another and, since the hand count is (c), that becomes a last resort. This reading drew attention away from the conjunction *or* that connects (b) to (c), which might imply simple alternatives rather than a sequence. A connecting phrase that said, "If this does not remedy the problem, then . . ." would be much more supportive of Posner's view.

Epstein, to the contrary, read the conjunction as indicating alternatives: "The conjunction that separates alternative (b) from alternative (c) is 'or,' and this suggests that the choice of remedies lies within the sound discretion of the canvassing board."[57] If the linguistic agency *or* denoted choice for Epstein, he quickly attempted to restrict that choice by arguing for a limit to the choice: "It defies comprehension, however, that the local canvassing board should have the power to make or break any candidate based simply on its choice among these three remedial options."[58] Thus, for Epstein, the canvassing board, an agent with sound discretion, may choose a remedy but may not exercise that remedy in a way that makes or breaks any candidate. Ironically, then, he would have a canvassing board conduct a hand recount just as long as it does not affect the outcome of an election afforded by a machine count, or perhaps just as long as a canvassing board does not strategically choose a remedy that favors one candidate over another. Epstein did not address the problem of how a canvassing board would know, before counting, whether a particular remedy would favor one candidate or the other, especially in a statewide recount.[59]

Unlike Epstein, Posner did not emphasize the canvassing boards' discretion in choosing these remedies, nor would he allow extensions from the voter side into the error equation:

> Voter error is not tabulator error; the voter is not the tabulator of the vote. An error in the vote tabulation is most naturally understood as an error made by the mechanical or human tabulator. More than half the votes cast in the 2000 election in Florida, including all the votes cast (other than by absentee ballot) in the four protest counties, were punchcard votes tabulated by computers that are programmed to reject ballots that are not punched through. So how could the failure of the machinery to count such ballots be thought an error in tabulation? If you put a steel bar into a meat grinder and hamburger meat doesn't come out, do you call this an error by the meat grinder?[60]

By drawing lines that attempt to cut the voter out of the tabulation process, Posner hoped to build a wall between those who use punchcards to choose candidates and those who take those cards and count them.

While Epstein was willing to admit that unreliable punchcard and other voting machines may bear some responsibility for the mistakes that led some ballots to be rejected by the machines, Posner did not; it is voter error that may lead to such miscounts. His hypothetical and metaphorical act of putting a steel bar into a meat grinder constructed a radical difference between correct and incorrect voter inputs (ballots) by suggesting that a correctly punched ballot is like meat, while an incorrectly punched ballot is like a steel bar. If the material differences between a fully punched-through ballot and one with hanging chads is subtle, the differences between meat and a steel bar are not. The analogy is an exaggeration that puts errant voters in the position of the stupid butcher who shoves a steel bar into a meat grinder.

Dworkin had the most extensive and persuasive analysis of the "error in vote tabulation" phrase. He identified three different interpretations of the phrase, beginning with the machine-error interpretation that Rehnquist and Posner defended:

> A tabulation error occurs, they [the concurrers] say, only when a device for counting votes does not function as it is designed to function. If a vote-tabulating machine is designed to count a vote when one and only one chad is fully detached from the ballot, and it does not count a ballot with a hanging chad as a vote for anyone, that is an instance of tabulation success, not tabulation error. Since there was no evidence of any substantial tabulation error understood in that way, in the counties that had undertaken manual recounts before the November 14 deadline, those recounts were pointless, because they could not have identified ballots that could lawfully be counted. They could only identify ballots in which voters had erred by not fully detaching a chad, and these ballots could not legally be counted as votes, no matter how clear an intention they displayed to vote for one candidate—even if, for example, one chad on the ballot was almost fully detached and no other chad was even dimpled.[61]

In this construction, voting (legally) is an act constituted by following all of the procedures in marking or punching a ballot that allow a machine to read that vote. As Laurence Tribe noted, "[t]he logic of that position rests on circularly defining a 'legal vote' as a ballot marked such that it can be read by a vote-counting machine."[62] Agency, or how one votes, is central here.

The Florida Supreme Court, on the other hand, used a result-error interpretation, according to Dworkin, holding that "a tabulation error occurs whenever a voter intended to vote for a particular candidate, and believed that he had, but was not recorded as voting that way."[63] In this reading, an agent's intention, or purpose, is primary. To defend the state court's decision, however, does not even require endorsing this position, argued Dworkin; one may embrace an intermediate position, which he called a process-error interpretation:

> A legislative draftsman might well use the words *error in the vote tabulation* with a different, more expanded sense than the machine-error reading allows. He might, with no violence to linguistic propriety, mean to include official errors in the whole process of recording and counting votes. He might regard an error in the instructions furnished to voters as constituting a "tabulation" error in that broader sense, for example. Suppose that in one Florida county that uses punch-card ballots some official had clearly but erroneously instructed voters that if they found they could not actually dislodge the chad, it would be enough—to make an effective vote—if they marked the chad they wanted to dislodge with an *X*. (We needn't suppose that the mistake was deliberate: The instructions might have been approved by representatives of both parties, as the butterfly ballot was approved in Palm Beach County.) A court might well construe "error in vote tabulation," as it occurs in the context of the Florida statute as a whole, to include rather than exclude this error. It would construe *tabulation* to refer to the entire process the county had established for obtaining and counting votes, not just to its process for counting them alone. It would not be outrageous for a court to take that view, particularly since it would be difficult to assign to the legislature any reason for distinguishing between instruction and machine errors in that way.[64]

If Dworkin's example of flawed voting instructions was atypical, he did better in noting that "[t]he punch card system, as we now know, is dangerously susceptible to mistake"; consequently, "[t]he punch card system almost guaranteed a significant number of mistakes, and using that system in a presidential election amounted to a process error."[65] Dworkin's process-error interpretation invoked a larger scene of voting action.

Dworkin's view of the legislative act invoked full-blooded action, featuring a draftsman writing this statute with a broader meaning. That meaning could encompass errors on the vote-recording side directly related to incorrect or inadequate voting instructions given, as well as to the use of machines that are dangerously susceptible to mistake. Dworkin invoked legislative purpose to support this broadened agency of tabulation errors, suggesting that errors on the vote-recording side presumably would be as large a concern to the legislature as errors on the vote-counting side.

Dworkin's attempt to make room for this broader interpretation of error in vote tabulation was a challenge to Rehnquist's claim that anything broader than the machine-error reading—notably, the state court's result-error reading—was "absurd." Dworkin insisted that his construction of the draftsman's act of laying down the "error in vote tabulation" standard "show[s] that the machine-error reading is not dictated by plain and indomitable semantics."[66] Dworkin, indeed, went much further in claiming that "[t]he narrowest, machine-error, reading that the three-justice concurring opinion said was 'plainly' correct is, on the contrary, indefensible."[67] He argued that neither semantics nor clear legislative intent supports this singular reading, and that

> [t]he balance it strikes between accuracy and finality shows too cheap a regard for an ideal that both the state's constitution and its central political traditions take to be of fundamental importance: that each eligible citizen must be offered a fair opportunity to vote, and that the selection of political officials should match, so far as possible, the will of those they govern. It would have been unreasonable, given the importance of those values, for the legislature to allow manual recounts when the source of suspected error was a defect in the counting machines but not when the source of suspected error was some other defect in the process, like inaccurate instructions to voters, when the latter errors could as easily be detected as the former.[68]

Dworkin here smuggled in legislative purposes that were read against the backdrop of "the state's constitution and its central political traditions"—whereby this scene filled with acts (enacting the constitution and carrying on political traditions) revealed purposes that were, in turn, used to interpret what the legislature was doing in drawing up the statute that dealt with an error in vote tabulation. Thus, constitutional and political acts that made up a scene created a purpose that provided insight into a statutory act. Because Dworkin relied on the state constitution to provide insight into legislative purposes, his earlier defense of the state constitution's proper constraint on legislative action in passing election statutes bore fruit.

The strongest defense against Dworkin's argument was to blame voters themselves for the errors. This ad hominem against errant voters, as Balkin noted, was central to Rehnquist's opinion:

> In effect, Rehnquist claimed, if a properly functioning punch card machine could not read a particular ballot, the ballot was not a "legal vote" under Florida law, no matter how clearly the voter's intention would seem to a human tabulator. Rehnquist insisted that Florida law gives detailed

instructions to voters to punch their ballots clearly and cleanly. Therefore, he concluded, voters whose votes could not be read by punch card machines have no one to blame but themselves if the votes are not counted. They simply did not follow instructions. For this reason, the Florida Supreme Court was not entitled to interpret Florida law to let state officials inquire into the intent of the voter in order to count these "improperly marked" ballots.[69]

In boiling down Rehnquist's position, Balkin revealed assumptions by Rehnquist that would be challenged by others. And although Rehnquist's construction sported a familiar and righteous "just deserts" argument, Balkin insisted that this position "changed and distorted Florida law."[70]

Tribe called Rehnquist's position (shared by Posner) a "tough-love" approach to voters in holding them responsible for the rejection of their ballots. He insists that this view

> conveniently ignores, first, that the much-lauded voting instructions were not uniform from county to county; second, that the instructions may have violated Florida law by being provided solely in English in areas with large Hispanic populations; and third, that Florida election code did not require county canvassing boards to provide voters with *any instructions whatsoever* on how to cast a ballot unless specifically requested—demonstrating the fallacy of the assumption that the legislature intended to make the right to vote depend on correctly reading a sign.[71]

Tribe's argument was supported by a news story on the lack of Spanish-language instructions and statutory language that left it to canvassing boards to decide what kind of instructions to offer.[72] He effectively shifted some of the blame from voters to the larger election system, highlighting problems in the process that tied in with Dworkin's process-error concerns.

Herman Schwartz believed that Rehnquist's toughness on voters was matched by his "exaltation of [voting] technology."[73] Rehnquist never acknowledged the gulf in accuracy between punchcard machines and optical-scan machines in the Florida election. Instead, Schwartz argued:

> The Rehnquist concurrence views Florida election technology as having performed as intended and assigns full responsibility for any uncounted ballots to the would-be voter. In place of technological subsidiarity, Rehnquist embraces technological reification. Technology is no longer an abstraction, or even a means to an end, but is identical with the system's goal. Rehnquist's logic transforms would-be voters who do not measure up to the demands of technology into nonvoters. In contrast, the Invisible Justice who

wrote the per curiam order acknowledges, if gingerly, the possibilities of flaws in Florida's technology of voting.[74]

In a bit of grammatical analysis, Schwartz noted that technology was not viewed by Rehnquist as an agency (a means to an end) but as a purpose (the system's goal). Agents who are not technologically savvy, then, become nonvoters.

Tribe made a similar point in urging that the concurrence unwisely merged technological purposes with statutory purposes: "Why should the degree of accuracy achieved by the machines automatically equal the degree of accuracy the Florida legislature intended to require in the election code?"[75] Tribe explicitly constructed voting technology as a mere agency, insisting that

> ballots are *translated* into votes; they are not *votes* as such. This is not just a matter of logic, but rather, a legislative mandate that counting all the ballots by machine is a necessary but not sufficient condition to recording all legal *votes*. Once a manual recount has been ordered, ballots transform into mere vehicles by which the election code achieves its stated end: namely, the counting of remaining votes.[76]

Tribe's construction makes ballots into agencies (vehicles) for the act of voting. Yet they are not to be confused with votes themselves. Within the context of a manual recount, he urged, these agencies support an ultimate purpose: the counting of remaining votes.

Posner claimed that the "tough-love" distinction he would draw "between errors in voting and in tabulation is important because the voter is complicit in the former error whereas the latter is invisible to the voter."[77] Such complicity was supported by Posner's emphasis on how the process was supposed to go, as was Rehnquist's. It was supportable just as far as Posner could discount the problems in the 2000 vote that Tribe and others documented, such as the failure to supply voting directions in Spanish in heavily Spanish-speaking counties. However, he backed off the implication that this was a "just deserts" argument:

> I do not suggest that the voters who failed to follow the voting instructions were seriously culpable, or even that voters who are utterly incapable, because of reading deficiencies, to follow simple and clear instructions should be disenfranchised; I argued in Chapter 1 against literacy tests for eligibility to vote. The question rather is the amount of inconvenience that a voter who, however innocently, has failed to follow directions should be entitled

to impose upon the election authorities, especially within the compressed timetable of a challenge to a Presidential election.[78]

While getting in jabs about simple and clear instructions, which Tribe would challenge, Posner hung his hat on a different and more defensible hook. He had the errant voter imposing upon the election authorities in a time-crunched scene. His term *inconvenience* was somewhat weak, considering that the sacred right to vote and have one's vote counted was at stake. His construction might have been more powerful had he collectivized the inconveniences into a monumental task of recounting, which would appear even more daunting within the time-crunched scene he described. However, indicating the collective size of the task would have hurt his case to the extent that it emphasized that not simply a lone errant voter was asking for consideration but a group of tens of thousands. That, in turn, would remind readers that something systematic seemed to have gone wrong (as was evidenced in the higher rejection rates of the punch-card system), moving responsibility away from voters and toward the scene or agency of the voting system.

Klarman provided some of the strongest support for finding that ballots mismarked by voters nonetheless can constitute legal votes, claiming that such a reading of Florida law "is consistent with the way Florida courts historically have defined legal votes, with explicit language in the Florida election code requiring that the 'intent of the voter' be ascertained with regard to damaged and defective ballots, and with the interpretation of numerous other state supreme courts."[79] Klarman supported these claims by citing numerous precedents. For example, to support the claim that this was the way Florida courts historically have defined legal votes, he cited four Florida cases: (1) a 1975 case where the court denied, "in the context of a challenge to absentee ballots, that there is any 'magic in the statutory requirements,' and insist[ed] that the 'important' question is whether 'the will of the people was effected'"; (2) a 1940 case "concluding that a ballot shall be counted 'if the will and intention of the voter can be determined,' even if the voter did not follow the instructions for marking the ballot"; (3) a 1932 case "holding that ballots that 'clearly indicate the choice of the voter' must be counted, even if 'irregular'"; and (4) a 1917 case where the court stated: "Where a ballot is so marked as to plainly indicate the voter's choice and intent in placing his marks thereon, it should be counted as marked unless some positive provision of law would be thereby violated."[80] To the extent that these precedents support the idea that mismarked ballots may contain legal votes, Klarman could argue that legal votes were excluded (triggering a contest recount) and that "error in vote tabulation" may justifiably include these uncounted ballots.

Klarman added to these precedents the statutory language of § 101.5614 (5), "providing that no ballot shall be disregarded 'if there is a clear indication of the intent of the voter as determined by the canvassing board,'" and that of § 102.166 (7), "specifying procedures for a manual recount, which include counting teams and, if necessary, county canvassing boards seeking 'to determine a voter's intent.'"[81] The former statute was frequently cited as supporting the voter intent standard; the latter was an additional source that Klarman added to his argument that the legislature intended to included ballots where the voter's intent could be discerned and that the state court was simply following this legislative agency in so holding.

Finally, Klarman reviewed decisions of other state courts to show that the Florida Supreme Court's interpretation was not unusual. For example, he cited a 1994 Connecticut decision "rejecting the view that legal votes are only those complying strictly with the ballot instructions and instead counting all ballots upon which 'the intent of the voter' is apparent 'in light of all of the available evidence disclosed by the ballot.'"[82] He quoted a South Dakota decision explaining that "the policy of the state is to count each person's vote in an effort to determine the true and actual intent of the voters."[83] He cited a 1987 Alaska case where punchcard ballots marked entirely in pen and pencil were ruled to be legal votes "because they provided clear evidence of the voters' intent."[84] With these cases, and two additional cases, Klarman showed that it was not unusual for states to search for the intent of the voter on mismarked ballots. American legal tradition supported this interpretation, he urged, drawing a reasonable agency out of an established legal scene he painted.

Klarman's reliance on a variety of precedents and on statutory language provided a well-founded agency for the Florida court to justify its interpretation of "legal vote" as including these mismarked ballots. Of course, just the fact that mismarked ballots might constitute legal votes did not mean that, under the contest statute, they had to be counted. On the other hand, it did support the idea that it was not unreasonable to decide that they should be counted.

If Court critics took Rehnquist to task for claiming that the state court's interpretation of the remedial statute was absurd, Court defenders turned the tables to note that the state court's claim that its interpretation of that statute represented its "plain meaning."[85] Both positions appeared to be overstated, though only Rehnquist was required to defend his position at all costs, because he was claiming that the Florida Supreme Court unreasonably twisted the legislature's words in violation of Article II. This battle was waged on another front as well, where critics and defenders considered who had the responsibility for interpreting statutes like the one under scrutiny.

Not surprisingly, critics and defenders reached opposite conclusions on who had the interpretive authority. Posner claimed:

> the statute itself authorizes her [the secretary of state] to interpret the statute, implying, under settled principles of Florida administrative law as of administrative law generally, that her interpretation, if reasonable, is conclusive. The election division's interpretation, which rejected voter error as a ground for extending the deadline, was reasonable and should therefore have been conclusive on the Florida supreme court.[86]

Klarman reached the opposite conclusion:

> Nor is it clear that the Florida Supreme Court owed any particular deference to the secretary of state's contrary interpretation, given the political nature of her position, the absence of any obvious agency "expertise" that would entitle her interpretation to deference, the fact that her interpretation was post hoc rather than a product of ex ante rulemaking, and the generally uncertain standard of judicial deference to agency legal interpretations called for by Florida administrative law.[87]

Note that both scholars hedged their claims a bit, with Posner not asserting a clear meaning but suggesting that the statute implies the conclusiveness of the secretary of state's interpretation, and Klarman not claiming clear meaning but suggesting that Posner's position was not clearly supported. Those hedges were necessary because the law on which they rested is ambiguous. To support his position, Posner cited two cases and a law review essay dated before the 1999 revision to the election statutes. The only post-1999 source he cited was a 2000 *Florida State University Law Review* essay on amendments to the Administrative Procedure Act (APA) of Florida. David Greenbaum and Lawrence Sellers, the authors, claimed:

> The APA provides for judicial review of agency action, and it requires the reviewing court to remand a case to the agency or to set aside agency action when it finds that the agency "has erroneously interpreted a provision of law." Nothing in the APA expressly requires the court to defer to the agency's interpretation, and the plain language in the APA does not limit

the reviewing court's authority to reverse or remand those cases in which the court determines that the agency's interpretation is "clearly" erroneous. Indeed, it has been said that the court is to review the agency's interpretation of law de novo. Nonetheless, some courts have held that a reviewing court must give "great deference" or "great weight" to an agency's construction of a statute or rule that the agency is charged with enforcing, while other courts have held that an agency's interpretation will not be overturned unless the interpretation is "clearly erroneous."[88]

The authors added that "a reviewing court will afford great weight to an agency's interpretation of a statute or rule only when it involves a matter of agency expertise, and the court will not defer to the agency's interpretation if the wording of a statute does not require any particular agency expertise."[89]

The upshot of this essay for deference to the secretary of state was much less clear than Posner suggested. Indeed, Klarman cited the same source for a summary of the "conflicting approaches that Florida courts have taken on the question of how much deference courts owe to agency legal interpretations."[90] Klarman also cited nine cases to establish that the rule of deference is less than clear, that deference is not typically given where there is no agency expertise, and that deference is greater for agency rule making than for post hoc adjudications (as in this case).[91] In construing the act of judging the statute, Klarman used agent constructions (whereby the secretary of state lacked obvious expertise and was a political officer), scene constructions (post hoc rather than ex ante), and agency constructions (with an unclear rule of deference) to suggest that the state court's failure to defer to the secretary of state was not unreasonable.

Balkin tried to resolve the issue in favor of the state court by looking to other acts of the state legislature involving judicial oversight:

> Revealingly, section 102.168 of the Florida Election Code authorizes contests of election results in the circuit courts except for elections to the state legislature, which are governed by section 102.171, in which no judicial review applies. This indicates that the Florida legislature knew perfectly well how to refrain from delegating authority to the courts when it wanted to.
>
> The very same Florida certification and contest provisions at issue in *Bush v. Gore* govern both federal and state elections conducted in Florida. There is no doubt that the Florida Supreme Court has the right to interpret those provisions in state elections; why should it be prohibited from interpreting the very same provisions in federal elections? The Florida legislature did not distinguish federal from state elections in the Florida Election Code.[92]

By demonstrating that the state legislature had explicitly limited judicial review in elections to the state legislature, Balkin concluded that it had not so limited judicial review in other elections, including federal elections that fall under the same certification and contest provisions as state elections.

Another issue involved one specific kind of deference required by the connection between the protest and the contest phases of the election battle. Rehnquist had complained that the state court ruling gave no presumption to the certified winner of the election, "empty[ing] certification of all legal consequence" (537). Both Klarman and Epstein admitted that the statute was unclear about the relationship between the protest and contest phrases. Klarman noted that "[t]he contest provisions of the Florida election code do not disclose what level of deference is owed to the Secretary of State's certification of election results, or to local canvassing boards' decisions not to conduct manual recounts."[93] Epstein conceded that "[t]he statute itself is silent on the standard of review that the circuit court in an election contest should apply to the administrative results of a protest phase."[94] The courts had not clarified this statute, either, which Klarman noted was unsurprising, "since the contest provisions were substantially overhauled in 1999."[95]

In spite of the silence and ambiguity of the statute on the relationship between the two phases, Epstein claimed that

> the issues raised at the [contest] phase are efforts to overturn incorrect decisions at the protest phase. It makes no sense to read the statute as though the contest phase is wholly unconnected with anything that went on at the protest stage. If so, then there is no need to bother to wait until the protest is over for the contest to begin.[96]

Klarman draws on the same dearth of information to conclude, to the contrary, that "[s]ince the very purpose of an election contest is to challenge the certification, it makes no sense to have a contest provision while deferring entirely to the certification."[97]

In defending their contrary claims, Epstein and Klarman drew on contrary evidence. Epstein relied on the "logical structure" of the statutes and general assumptions about administrative law. Thus, he indicated the sequential relationship between the protest and contest phrases, inferring that because one followed another, the later phase responded to the former. Specifically, he characterized the contest's acts as "efforts to overturn incorrect decisions at the protest phase."[98] If this construction of a contest was accepted, it made way for a particular agency: an "abuse of discretion" standard, which would put the onus on those who would second-guess the work of officials at the protest phase.

Klarman, on the other hand, could simply rely on the language of the statute and a bit of logic. On the latter, he claimed that one could not defer "entirely" to a certification, or else there would be no need for a contest. This construction allowed some deference to creep into the standard (something less than entire deference). However, his stronger argument came directly from the statute:

> The statutory standard for a contest to proceed, "rejection of a number of legal votes sufficient to change or place in doubt the results of the election," does not indicate that any deference at all is owed to the decisions of administrative officials. Perhaps de novo review is not the most sensible way of structuring an election contest scheme, but it is perfectly consistent with the statutory language, which the concurring opinion emphasizes is entitled to special weight in light of Article II concerns. Nor does it contravene any Florida Supreme Court precedent, since that court never before had interpreted the amended contest provisions.[99]

Klarman effectively turned Rehnquist's Article II argument against him, by stressing that special weight must be given to the language the legislature used. Because that language talked only about the rejection of legal votes and said not a word about deferring to the certified winner or the certifying officials, Klarman could claim to rely on the legislature's words and no more. He admitted that reviewing the issue anew (de novo) might not be the most sensible approach, but he could insist that that was what the statute specified.

Tribe supported Klarman's position by noting the great latitude the statute gave to the judge of election contests: "the statute stipulates that, as a remedial matter, 'the circuit judge to whom the contest is presented may fashion such orders as he or she deems necessary to ensure that each allegation in the complaint is investigated, examined, or checked, to prevent or correct any alleged wrong, and to provide any relief appropriate under such circumstances.'"[100] He added that "the contest provisions say nothing about reviewing particular certification-related rulings of the Secretary of State as though they were the rulings of an Administrative Procedure Act agency." Furthermore, he noted, "far from suggesting that decisions by the Secretary or by a canvassing board are presumed correct and are to be deemed conclusive unless found erroneous on review, [the contest provisions] merely specify that 'the canvassing board or election board shall be the proper party defendant.'"[101]

The interpretive struggle between Epstein and Rehnquist on the one hand and Klarman and Tribe on the other turns on how much context should be allowed to influence the interpretation of the legislature's words. Epstein and Rehnquist would apply standards of administrative law to find a deference requirement that is not specifically included in the statute (a scene-agency construction, where administrative law becomes part of an interpretive legal scene), while Klarman and Tribe would use the absence of any statement regarding such deference as an indication that none should be given (a narrow reading of legislative agency).

Klarman added that there was no problem with the state court's failure to defer to the county canvassing boards' decisions at the protest phase not to conduct manual recounts, because

> to overrule in the contest phase of the proceedings a local canvassing board's discretionary judgment during the protest phase not to conduct a manual recount does not nullify the statutory grant of discretion; rather, it restricts its force to elections that are not so close at the state level as to raise a doubt whether uncounted lawful votes might change the election outcome.[102]

Klarman used the distinction between total discretion and limited discretion to save the canvassing boards' discretion and reconcile it with the state court's judgment and the statutory language.

Klarman summarized the strength of the state court's position and the weakness of the concurring opinion's claim:

> Thus, the Florida Supreme Court's decision to engage in de novo review of Vice President Gore's request for manual recounts is consistent with the statutory contest language, not inconsistent with any binding Florida precedent, and reconcilable with a statutory grant of discretion to local canvassing boards not to conduct manual recounts at the protest phase of election proceedings. In what alternate universe does such an interpretation of Florida election law qualify as "absurd"?[103]

Klarman's final point cut to the heart of Rehnquist's allegation that the Florida Supreme Court had made not only a weak reading of the election statutes but an unreasonable and absurd reading. Such strong claims were critical to Rehnquist's argument, because the U.S. Supreme Court could not claim that the state court violated Article II if it merely made a less-than-ideal interpretation of the election statutes. As Justice Souter had urged, it appeared that Rehnquist was claiming that the Florida court's opinion was "so unreasonable as to transcend the accepted bounds of statutory interpretation, to the point of being a nonjudicial act."[104] Thus, limited criticism of the state court's construction would not do; only total dismissal would support the failure of the concurrence to defer to the state court's interpretation of its own laws.

Perhaps the weakest argument of the Rehnquist concurrence involved the safe harbor claim. Rehnquist acknowledged that the state court was allowed to provide "any relief appropriate" under the contest statutes but claimed that ordering relief that was very likely to miss the safe harbor deadline rendered it "inappropriate," because the state court had allegedly interpreted a legislative "wish" to take advantage of that deadline. This weak argument was used by the per curiam as well. However, Klarman effectively answered the issue with respect to the concurrence:

> The concurring opinion states that this reading of "appropriate relief" cannot be reconciled with the legislature's "wish" to take advantage of the federal safe harbor provision. Yet, as we have seen, the legislature expressed no such wish, and even if it had, reading Florida election law to elevate that wish over all competing considerations would be nonsensical.[105]

Overall, Rehnquist's construction of the Florida Supreme Court's interpretation of Florida election law as unreasonable and absurd was weak. It was not that the state court's interpretation discovered the plain meaning of the statutes, as that court implied, but it was not unsupportable, either. Even Epstein, who staunchly defended the concurrence, admitted that recording-side errors (such as failing to punch through a chad) might be included in "error in vote tabulation." Rehnquist and Posner could maintain a "tough-love" approach to voters reasonably only to the extent that they could discount or ignore problems in the voting process that shifted the blame from voters to others. Tribe especially showed that those problems were extensive. And even Posner admitted that he would not want to have such a "technological literacy" barrier to voting, though he was correct to raise the question of how much a voter should be able to ask of a time-crunched canvassing board. Two factors swing the decision in the voter's favor, though: the widespread nature of voting process problems (especially with the patently less reliable punchcard systems) and the great significance the Florida state constitution, its case law, its political traditions, and the value of American democracy as a whole place on the importance of the franchise and of finding the intent of the voters.

Critics of the concurring opinion did not have a strong explanation of the relationship between the protest phase and the contest phrase; indeed, the process they defended seemed to empty the protest phase of its significance, as Rehnquist had contended. However, they could claim to rely exclusively on the statute itself, which set the standard with no clear requirement of deference to the certified winner or to the secretary of state who certified him. While even Klarman admitted that a de novo review might not be the most sensible way of structuring an election contest scheme, he nonetheless could rely on the statute's explicit language and hold Rehnquist to the same special deference to the words of the state legislature that the chief justice demanded elsewhere.

The Concurring Opinion's Remedy for the Article II Breach

Court defenders found their strongest ground in the remedy afforded by the concurrence, at least when compared with that by the per curiam. As Posner noted of the per curiam:

> The vulnerability of the Supreme Court's remedy arises from the Court's having based its decision on the equal protection clause of the Fourteenth Amendment rather than the "Manner directed" clause of Article II. If the vice of the Florida supreme court's decision of December 8 was the standardless character of the recount that it ordered, the logical remedy was to direct that court to adopt standards; if under Florida law time did not permit this, the Florida court could be expected to dismiss the suit. Or could it? Not having shown itself to be a model of prudence, that court might not have dismissed the suit, and by pressing on with it might have precipitated a national crisis. The dilemma of what remedy to order in these circumstances would have been avoided by ruling that Article II barred the recount because the state supreme court had no basis for ordering it, whatever the criteria to be used in it. In other words, under Article II, as distinct from the equal protection clause, the appropriate judicial remedy was to bar the recount—period.[106]

Posner's contrast between the per curiam and concurring opinions' remedies showed the advantages of the latter, assuming a High Court purpose of stopping the questionable recounts or, better yet (for Posner), of stopping the Florida Supreme Court from further lawless action. This was a better remedy because it did not concede that there were any legal votes left to be counted (as the per curiam conceded there might be); thus, it did not end on a note of incompletion and frustration. The concurrence did not blame the "clock," as the per curiam had, for preventing justice from being done but blamed the state court as an errant agent in misinterpreting state law. On the other hand, blaming these state judicial agents was an outcome that was troubling to some (perhaps to Justices O'Connor and Kennedy and certainly to the dissenters), because it undermined good federal-state relations by second-guessing the state court and implying that it acted out of either incompetence or political motives.

Court critics, of course, would not concede that "error in vote tabulation" excluded those thousands of voters with mismarked and uncounted ballots. However, from a formal, legal perspective, it was more palatable to embrace a claim that the state court had exceeded its authority than a claim that the count could go on if only the safe harbor deadline did not prevent it. And because the concurring opinion did not disingenuously try to limit the precedential value of its finding in this newly minted interpretation of an article that had received almost no interpretation, the concurrence could provide remedies for similarly situated candidates in the future.

Overall, the concurrence was on weak ground in insisting on its interpretation of Article II and in urging that the state court's decision was, essentially, a nonjudicial act. It fared better on the remedy, certainly when contrasted with the majority opinion, and offered that to anyone in the future, as the per curiam had not.

Completing Construction of the Concurrence

Discussing the construction by scholars of the concurrence as an act by agents, with a purpose and an attitude, within a scene, requires much less space than coverage of its agency or means, for two reasons. First, as was the case with scholarly comments on the per curiam, comments on the concurrence looked primarily at how the author supported his position. Second, there was a great deal of grammatical overlap between the per curiam and the concurrence as acts. Three of the agents were the same. Ending the recount, stopping further action by the state court, and handing the election to Bush were purposes that could be accomplished through either the per curiam or the concurrence. The time-crunched, crisis-threatening scene was similar. And attitudes may be said to have overlapped to some extent.

Frequently, scholars constructed the concurrence by contrasting it with the per curiam. Posner was one of the most thorough in distinguishing the

two. He argued that had Rehnquist's opinion won the support of a majority, then

> [t]he justices could not have been accused of betraying their settled convic-
> tions, because none of them had ever written or joined an opinion dealing
> with the "manner directed" clause of Article II, which was last (and first) be-
> fore the Supreme Court in 1892 and because views of the clause do not di-
> vide along "liberal" and "conservative" lines, as views of the equal
> protection clause do. The justices would have eluded other criticisms as
> well, because there would have been no need for the opinion to say that the
> decision had no precedential effect, since the ground of the decision would
> have had no implications for election administration generally. The Article II
> ground, being esoteric, would not have provided a handle for criticisms that
> the general public could understand. That ground has a clear textual basis in
> the word *legislature* in Article II. The ground could be persuasively related to
> the avoidance of the looming crisis. Overriding the Florida Supreme Court
> on the basis of Article II would not be an affront to states' rights (which the
> conservative justices of the U.S. Supreme Court have tended to favor in re-
> cent years), since it would be vindicating the authority of state legislatures.
> And there would be no awkwardness in the remedy of stopping the re-
> count, since if the recount order should never have been issued, rather than
> should merely have been configured differently, there would be no occasion
> for a remand of the case to the Florida court, rather than an outright
> reversal.[107]

Posner's construction did not address Court motives directly but rather the
public motives that Rehnquist's decision would have presented. That is,
Posner concerned himself with how this alternative majority opinion
would have looked in light of who these conservative judicial agents were,
what the future scene threatened (the looming crisis), the past acts they
engaged in—acts that were part of a judicial scene associated with these
justices, and the means by which the recount and the Florida Supreme
Court would have been stopped. In short, Posner urged, Rehnquist's opinion represented a more defensible act.

Posner added a particular advantage for Justices Scalia and Thomas, for
whom the per curiam opinion was an "embarrassment," because they had
"gone out of their way in opinions and (in Scalia's case) in speeches and
articles to embrace a concept of adjudication that is inconsistent with the
majority opinion that they joined."[108] Posner noted how easy it was for
Alan Dershowitz to show Justice Scalia's hypocrisy in going along with the
limitation of the case "to present circumstances," when the justice had
written that the High Court sets precedents that ensure the rule of law "by

announcing rules [that] hedge ourselves in."[109] Scalia's position, Posner admitted, invited "charges of hypocrisy, or worse—the charge of rank partisanship leveled against Scalia by Dershowitz on insufficient evidence, but plausible enough to resonate with the millions of Americans who already profoundly distrust the good faith of all government officials."[110]

Klarman found an agent-act inconsistency in the concurring opinion itself, using hypothetical acts to throw this inconsistency into relief:

> It is almost impossible to imagine Rehnquist, Scalia, and Thomas concluding that these particular state court interpretations of state law were "absurd" in any context other than the one in which George W. Bush's election to the presidency hung in the balance. Indeed, in other settings, these three Justices have insisted that federal courts should defer even to state court interpretations of federal law unless "patently unreasonable." It takes little imagination to picture the impassioned—indeed, characteristically vitriolic—assault on judicial activism and federal overreaching that Justice Scalia might have penned had the candidates been reversed and it was Al Gore asking the United States Supreme Court to resolve a presidential election contest by repudiating a state court's interpretation of state law.[111]

Klarman cited past opinions by Thomas and Scalia to support the claim that they typically deferred to state court interpretations of federal law, emphasizing the past act-present act inconsistency. He also invoked the vitriolic image of Scalia lambasting the hypothetical Gore as appellant, an image he specifically supported with a reference to Scalia's dissent in *Planned Parenthood v. Casey,* where the justice compared the abortion decision with which he disagreed to *Dred Scott.*[112] Agent, act, and attitude fleshed out this hypothetical response to Gore and emphasized Scalia's inconsistency. Of course, Court defenders could claim this hypothetical was unrealistic, though no commentator has argued directly that the conservative justices would have ruled the same had the roles of Gore and Bush been reversed.

The motives of the concurrence were easy to construct using an agent-act relationship that located motives in the three most conservative justices on the Court finding a way to hand the election to a fellow Republican and, thereby, to ensure that future justices might be appointed in their own mold, that one of them (Scalia, perhaps) might be elevated to the chief justice position, or that Thomas's wife or Scalia's sons might prosper from victory in this case. However, as Posner noted, there might be a reduction in the charges of hypocrisy related to how they ended the recount, since Article II was fresh legal ground, while the equal protection ruling of the per curiam seemed to run against the three justices' past decisions and beliefs.

Richard Schragger tried to reduce charges of partisanship and hypocrisy in the concurring opinion by denying that the ruling ignored the justices' support for state power against the federal government: "In fact, Rehnquist's Article II argument (joined by Justices Scalia and Thomas) can be read as a defense of state power against all comers, including, most emphatically, local power. This reading is actually quite consistent with the federalist principle of state supremacy within its sphere."[113] He explained that "plenary state control of its own localities is the essence of federalism," insisting that "[a]ttention to states' rights does not translate into protection of local power; it translates into whatever the state wants local power to be."[114] This argument for past act-present act consistency and agent-act consistency was challenged by those who thought that telling a state court what its own state law meant involved federal encroachment of a different sort, though this particular distinction (similar to Rehnquist's own) was plausible.

Weinberg argued that adopting the concurring opinion as the majority opinion would have led to a different problem of inconsistency: "To have adopted it would have been to deny to the Florida Supreme Court the very power the Court itself was asserting: the power to make a novel post-election construction of forum election law."[115] Dworkin made a similar charge, noting that the concurring opinion's argument was that "[t]he Florida Supreme Court, by overruling Katherine Harris's interpretations of the Florida election statute, and then by ordering fresh manual recounts, changed the rules after the election was over, which is patently unfair." As Weinberg did, Dworkin turned the tables on this claim: "Of course, that is exactly what the critics of the Supreme Court's decision accuse the conservative justices of doing—they changed the Constitution, the critics say, so as to elect the candidate they favored. The three justices' argument can therefore be seen as a preemptive strike."[116]

The inconsistency charged here was an act-act problem: the Court said one thing and did another, criticizing a state court for doing what it did. Court defenders could draw a distinction here, however. Although both the Florida court's ruling and the position of the concurring opinion were novel, defenders might claim that only the former involved changing the law, whereas the latter involved an exposition of law that had yet to be examined. Only the lengthy consideration of agency in this Article II argument offered above could beat back this otherwise plausible distinction.

Posner tried to bolster the act of the concurring justices by finding support for its Article II ruling in the earlier *Bush v. Palm Beach County Canvassing Board* decision, insisting that that ruling "actually commanded the support of all nine justices."[117] Thus, if all of the justices supported that finding, then an agents-act relationship could be used to bolster the decision. Issacharoff noted the obvious, however, that "[t]his approach . . . ultimately garnered only three votes in *Bush v. Gore*." With this diminishment on the agents side of Posner's equation, he could insist that it "provides little basis for a robust approach to the problem of elections gone bad."[118]

Defenders and critics of the per curiam offered competing constructions of the concurring justices' attitude in the case to support or undermine the opinion. Tribe contrasted the concurrence's attitude with that of the per curiam: "Only the concurring opinion of Chief Justice Rehnquist was bold enough to declare Florida's court incapable of properly interpreting its own election code."[119] When tied to the claim that a state court could not properly interpret its own law, this characterization was a milder version of the charges that the per curiam five were overly confident, brash, brazen, and arrogant. However, Tribe's mildness was surprising, since the per curiam never questioned the Florida Supreme Court the way Rehnquist did, with his claims that their rulings were unreasonable and absurd.

University of Missouri law professor Robert Pushaw offered a construction of the High Court's attitude toward the state court's attitude—emphasizing the reactive nature of the former in a way that subtly shifted the blame to the original instigator of action or of attitude (where attitude is a precursor to action). He claimed that the High Court's "suspicion of [the state court's] political bias likely explains the unusual conclusion of Chief Justice Rehnquist and Justices Scalia and Thomas that Florida's high court had changed—not merely interpreted—its state's election statutes."[120] Pushaw's construction perhaps explained the concurring opinion, more than defended it.

Some who examined the concurring justices' attitudes looked not at the attitudes they displayed in concurring but rather in joining the per curiam. Posner, for example, suggested that they were disingenuous in joining the per curiam decision.[121] Michael Abramowicz and Maxwell Stearns, who conducted a social-scientific analysis of motives in the *Bush* case, concurred in this description, explaining that the three concurring justices joined the per curiam after "swallowing their pride on the equal protection argument."[122] They argued that the justices "acted strategically to avert a strategic play from the other side of the Court." That other side was the liberals, who might have persuaded Justices Kennedy and O'Connor to drop the safe harbor deadline and remand the case to the Florida court for a continued recount.[123]

Attacking and Defending Rehnquist and the Florida Court

Defenders of the concurring opinion had an advantage over those defending the per curiam in being able to focus simultaneously on what the state court was doing and on what the concurring justices were doing, since much of Rehnquist's argument was about "unreasonable" and "absurd" interpretations the state court made of Florida's election law. Rehnquist stressed that this was not an ordinary election but one involving the highest federal office. He relied on Article II's grant of authority to the state legislature to suggest that its words reflected special deference to that body. He used *McPherson v. Blacker* to suggest that even the state constitution could not constrain the legislature in making laws for the presidential election. He blasted the state court for departing from the legislative scheme by failing to give presumption to the certified winner, failing to defer to the canvassing boards and the secretary of state, misinterpreting "error in the vote tabulation" to include mismarked ballots (even though voting instructions had been clear and voters had only themselves to blame), and ordering a recount that would violate the safe harbor deadline, which the legislature intended to meet.

Defenders tried to construct the concurring opinion as well grounded in the law, while the state court's interpretations were problematic. They said that the specific grant of authority to legislatures in Article II to "direct" the means of choosing presidential electors was unusual and emphatic. As *Bush v. Palm Beach County Canvassing Board* had found unanimously, even the state constitution could not constrain the state legislature in making these election laws. The *McPherson* precedent supported giving broad authority to the legislature. Although legislation does not "speak for itself," that seems to be what Article II calls for, said Posner. Judges interpreting this law must not substitute their own values for those of the legislature.

Court critics thought the emphasis on *legislature* in the language was weak. The framers knew that statutes required interpretation. In any case, legislators (who are not always good at making laws) cannot write laws that foresee all applications; therefore, courts must interpret (though such interpretations are not changes but only revelations of what the law has always meant). And, as Dworkin stressed, interpretation requires a consideration of background values such as those found in state constitutions.

Even though the *Bush v. Palm Beach County Canvassing Board* court appeared to assume that Article II prevented state constitutions from limiting legislatures in choosing the manner of selecting presidential electors, this position makes no sense. It would undermine democratic values. This is perhaps why only three justices endorsed that position. Smith's analysis of the historical context of the debate over Article II suggested that the framers did not have in mind giving state legislatures special power; rather, it was a compromise that drew from similar language in the Articles of Confederation that had been read more narrowly by states organizing themselves when it was written than the concurrence suggested. Additionally, the Electoral Count Act (which Rehnquist relied on) specifically mentioned resolving election disputes "by judicial or other methods." And Rehnquist relied in *McPherson* on mere dicta, and he ignored other sections of the opinion supporting constitutional constraints on legislative authority in selecting the manner of choosing electors. If the legislature wanted to forbid judicial review, it would have done so (as it had in another election statute).

Court defenders spent a great deal of time attacking the Florida Supreme Court's decision, showing that it had transgressed Article II by rewriting what the state legislature had provided for presidential elections. "Error in the vote tabulation," notably, simply referred to machine-based errors—equipment and software—not voter-based errors (though Epstein allowed for some of these). The three remedies for errors indicated that this was the legislature's intention. Canvassing boards cannot be allowed simply to choose a method that favors their candidate; they must stick with the same definition of legal vote. Furthermore, if the voters cannot follow simple directions, it is their own fault if their votes are not counted; to require that counting is to ask too much of canvassing boards. In any case, defenders urged, the state court should have deferred to the interpretations of the secretary of state and the decisions of the canvassing boards. Certification must entail some deference, or else why wait to launch a contest? With that deference, following basic administrative law, the state court should have required an abuse of discretion standard to overturn the certification. The Florida court misconstrued Florida election law in violation of Article II.

Court critics countered that limiting errors in the vote tabulation ignored the principles of Florida's constitution and its political traditions that the voters' will should reign supreme. There is no reasonable distinction between errors caused in the vote-recording process and those in the vote-counting process, when both could be as easily remedied. Because Florida had many process problems in the election—instructions not provided in Spanish, incorrect instructions, and unreliable punchcard voting machines, among others—the cause of the errors in vote tabulation could not be laid solely at the voters' feet. Besides, Florida case law, its statutes, and the case law of many other states support finding legal votes even where ballots have been mismarked. Machine counting of ballots is a necessary but not a sufficient condition for counting all legal votes; a machine-countable vote is not the only kind of legal vote.

As for the question of deference to the secretary of state and the canvassing boards, Court critics noted that the statute says nothing about this. The case law is mixed as well. Besides, the secretary of state was a political figure (not a neutral official), she was making a post hoc judgment (not ex ante), and she had no particular expertise in this area. If Rehnquist insisted that the words of the legislature carried special significance, he should have recognized it here, where Court defenders had to stretch beyond the language of the statutes to infer that deference was due. Reading that statute shows that the judge has broad authority in remediating voting problems. Finally, the safe harbor deadline was not binding, so the court did not violate law by ordering a recount that might have gone past that date.

Court defenders did show that the remedy offered by the concurring opinion was superior to that of the per curiam. Article II had yet to be interpreted, whereas the conservative justices had said a great deal about equal protection—some of it seemingly contradicting the per curiam. Arguably, the decision supported states by supporting the legislature against local power. Without stopping the recount, as the concurrence would have afforded, a national crisis might have followed. And the concurring justices allowed their decision to stand for future use, while the per curiam tried to limit theirs. Admittedly, the concurring justices were suspicious of state court motives, and this judgment would help them stop the out-of-control court. Their only failure, perhaps, was in joining a per curiam which they did not really support.

Court critics thought the concurrence was hypocritical. The conservative justices were not supporting states' rights (as their philosophies called for) but were second-guessing a state court's interpretation of its own law. They would not have reached the conclusions they did if Gore had been the appellant; indeed, Justice Scalia likely would have lambasted Gore for suggesting federal encroachment into this state issue. These conservative justices sought to give the election to Bush, to help continue their judicial legacies, to gain appointment to the chief justice position, or even to help their relatives. They had personal and political reasons to do what they did. While accusing the Florida court of changing the law after the fact, that is what they did with Article II, which only three justices ultimately supported. These justices were bold (perhaps brazen) in challenging the Florida Supreme Court's interpretation of its own law. They may have worked strategically to ensure that Kennedy and O'Connor would not side with the liberals and allow the recount to continue.

Overall, the concurring opinion revealed too many strains to support its conclusion that the state court's ruling was unreasonable and absurd, violating Article II's grant of authority to the state legislature. Even staunch defenders acknowledged that some judicial interpretation is required for addressing unclear legislation. Despite the unanimous decision in *Bush v. Palm Beach County Canvassing Board* (perhaps the defenders' strongest support), it appears that the High Court went too far in implying that state constitutions could not constrain state legislatures. Smith's history of Article II, the Electoral Count Act's acknowledgment that disputes might be resolved through "judicial and other methods," and *McPherson*'s acknowledgment that a state constitution could limit the legislature appeared to undermine that reading, and, thereby, the overall argument of Rehnquist. For if judicial interpretation is appropriate, and if the values of the Florida constitution's "people power" provision can provide background values in interpreting ambiguous statutes, then "errors in the vote tabulation" ought to consider how the state might have contributed to those errors. Even Epstein opened the door to including recording errors, and Posner said he would not dismiss someone's vote because of technological illiteracy. If recounting mismarked ballots is an imposition, as Posner argued, surely it is an imposition that is worthwhile, from the state constitution's standpoint, especially given that the highest office in the land was at stake.

While defenders had a good argument on the relationship between the protest and the contest phases, making a de novo review a less-than-ideal approach, it was certainly not unreasonable to stick to the statute's plain language (which also supported the "people power" values of the state constitution) and simply allow the rejection of legal votes to stand as the standard for triggering a review. The broad power given to the judge in such reviews had plenty of room for even the statewide recount ordered by the state court.

As did the per curiam decision, the public motives of the concurring opinion made it too easy to see conservative judges straining the law to try to seat their preferred candidate for personal and political purposes. Although there were admittedly fewer agent-act and agent-agency contradictions here than in the per curiam (so that they were not so clearly ignoring their own stated values to reach a result), the fact that the three concurring justices also joined the per curiam opinion undermines this escape from inconsistency and makes it appear as mere political strategy to have their preferred result win the day.

13

Judging the Supreme Court and Its Judges

Judicial motives are constructed within a discursive field with enough rhetorical play in the structure of the grammar of motives for coherent stories to be developed by those who would attack or defend a particular court's actions. However, owing to the interrelatedness of the grammatical terms and of one set of acts with other sets of acts, there are limits to what can be convincingly constructed.

The flexibility in such constructions allowed the news media, editorialists, scholars, and justices to make prima facie cases for their versions of the High Court's motives in service of their own rhetorical purposes. Members of the news media, who seek first and foremost to make their stories newsworthy, were able to focus primarily on the two most dramatic terms: *act* and *agent*. They could argue for the newsworthiness of the act by stressing that it was historic, unexpected, and controversial. They could play up the drama by stressing that the High Court's agents were divided and politically allied. This drama hinted at controversial purposes, though to maintain the appearance of objectivity, the news media would not name those (although some experts they quoted would). They did not explain much about the legal bases (or agencies) of the decision, since their lay audiences would understand little about them.

Editorialists, on the other hand, could move the focus to different acts and agents, as well as purposes, to support their brief, strategic constructions. Thus, defenders of the High Court stressed the sins of the Florida court—suggesting its partisan nature, its partisan purposes, and its partisan acts, urging that the High Court was forced to act to stop the lawlessness of the state court. Those attacking *Bush v. Gore*, on the other hand, looked directly at the High Court's actions, finding them partisan, legally questionable, inconsistent with the conservatives' judicial philosophy, and seeking to put a Republican in the White House or pack the Court with conservatives.

Most scholarly constructions of Court motives focused on agency—the primary concern of legal thinkers—with some Court defenders questioning the state court's means for reaching its conclusions and most Court critics questioning the High Court's means for reaching its contrary conclusions. They dug deep into related acts as well, constructing the acts of state and federal legislators, constitutional framers, voters, county canvassing boards, Florida's secretary of state, the litigants, and others. Scholarly defenders also turned to scene to justify judicial intervention—a scene created by the state court and one that might be realized in the form of a constitutional or political crisis.

The High Court itself began this motivational tug-of-war by constructing motives to suggest that it was following the law and rendering justice, with dissenters picking out particular grammatical elements for reconstruction (especially agency) that suggested that the majority justices were falling short of their proper judicial duty.

A range of rhetorical strategies was used by rhetors with different and often competing views of the controversial decision in *Bush v. Gore*. Those strategies had to work within the grammar of motives, which limits what one can say about one element of an act, given relations among all pentadic terms and between different acts. Taken as a whole, the arguments and counterarguments over motives in this case provide something of a proving ground for what can be convincingly argued about what the Court was doing and why it was doing it, as characterizations competed with one another and with the elements of action as a whole. Thus, one rhetor's scene threatened by constitutional crisis competed with another's scene of orderly democratic processes, and both jockeyed for consistency with the agents, acts, purposes, and agencies constructed by others. Theoretically, one could examine all constructions of all terms for all acts connected to

Bush v. Gore and find out which embody the most coherent and convincing case for Supreme Court motives.[1] Such an "overall coherence" standard is implicit in the idea of the unity of action which undergirds the grammar of motives. That is not to say that action itself is unitary in this sense; however, in interpreting action, that unity, reinforced by the grammar of motives, is assumed. The grammar of motives is not deterministic in accounting for action; rather, it is terministic, shaping what we can *say* about that action.[2]

Unfortunately, the theoretical possibility of finding the most coherent construction of motives yields to practical challenges of assessing that coherence. The level of precision in assessing grammatical fit is not such that one can claim sufficient rigor to dispel all concerns about judgment and bias, though one certainly can make a compelling case. In my own reconstruction of the Court's motives below, my actions may be judged against my ethos as a particular kind of agent (a scholar with liberal leanings), just as I have demonstrated the motives of the High Court have been judged. I can only hope that my acts and agencies dispel concerns about my agent status. And my readers should add to their own meta-analyses of this liberal scholar constructing a conservative court their own status as agents of a particular stripe engaging in the act of interpretation, checking their own biases. Ultimately, we all rest most readily on judgments that we convince ourselves are reflective of the reality we must embrace. With that existential flourish, I turn now to what I believe is the most coherent reconstruction of motives for the *Bush* court. I rely on the foregoing analyses to support my otherwise truncated case for the best reading of motives in *Bush v. Gore*.

What Was the Court Doing, and Why?

Because we are judging judicial action, the appropriate starting point in assessing motives is agency. How judges reach their conclusions is the primary basis for assessing the reasonableness and legitimacy of their decisions, in legal tradition. The most important question is whether those rulings follow the law. In the *Bush* case, a number of legal agencies were invoked by the majority to support its conclusions. The stay applied an irreparable harm standard to justify stopping the recount and an assumption that Bush had a substantial probability of prevailing in the case. The per curiam relied on (1) an assertion that using different recount substandards was unfair, (2) a novel equal protection ruling, (3) a rejection of the punchcard problem as a competing equal protection concern, (4) finding a mandatory safe harbor deadline seriously limited the time for a recount, (5) urging that there was no time to restart the recount (because of the safe harbor deadline, as well as a long list of actions that needed to be taken), and (6) limiting the precedential value of the case. The concurring opinion, touted as a better legal basis for the decision by several Court defenders, urged that Article II grants plenary power to state legislatures and insisted that the state court had usurped the legislative authority.

The "irreparable harm" standard invoked by the stay failed to consider the balance of harms, never mentioning the fact that Gore might be denied an election victory because the stay cut the counting short. Scalia's opinion actually relied on Bush's *claim* to the presidency, rather than some ground that he had a *legal* right to that office. Furthermore, the harm to Bush was speculative, since it was by no means clear that Bush would lose his lead if the recounting continued. (Indeed, it was the position of many Court defenders that Bush would have won anyway.) Finally, the majority's intervention itself cast a cloud over Bush's presidency, so that the act of the stay itself caused the kind of harm the majority claimed to be trying to avert.

The majority did have a persuasive argument for harm *if* it knew at the time it issued the stay that the recount would be found unconstitutional. The argument by critics that the American public had a right to information about the recounting—even if the recounting itself and the outcomes it revealed were invalid—was a weak one. As a practical matter, it *would* be difficult to reverse a Gore victory in the recount if the Court later ruled that the process was constitutionally flawed, making the Court's motives even more suspicious than they were in this case.

However, the suggestion that the majority knew at the time of the stay that the recounting would be found to be unconstitutional is troubling. Given the esoteric state and federal issues involved in the case, there was no way for the majority to have known, less than twenty-three hours after the state court decision was handed down, how the appeal would turn out, unless they had made up their minds before even cursorily examining the law or counsels' arguments. Jumping to this conclusion without thinking through the complex legal issues reveals a great deal about the majority's motives in the case. It suggests that they did not really care about *how* they would reach a verdict for Bush, only *that* they would do so. At best, they had a hunch that the recount was constitutionally flawed, but that hardly justified stopping the recount without considering its impact on Gore.

Additional agency problems arise with the per curiam itself. One could argue from a simple gut sense of justice that recounting ballots using different substandards seems unreasonable and unfair. However, four considerations lessen this sense of unfairness. First is Laurence Tribe's argument that, indeed, different counties may have different needs with respect to recounting because of differences in the types of machines they used, different histories of servicing those machines (whereby, for example, some machines may have suffered from chad buildup that made punching through ballots more difficult), different ballots (such as the notorious butterfly ballot, which was hard for elderly voters to interpret), different past experiences by canvassing boards with various standards (leading them to prefer one over another), and so forth. Jeffrey Toobin's description of a county with punchcards that looked like pages of Braille suggested how those experiences might influence a canvassing board to decide to use one method or another: if my county is inundated with ballots like Toobin describes, which obviously contain votes without punched-through chads, I would be more likely to adapt a standard that gives voice to those voters, especially if I were aware that old voting machines, incorrect or untranslated voting instructions, and inadequate voter assistance at the polls contributed to this problem. I believe that Justice Souter reflected his lack of imagination and made a critical concession to the majority when he claimed: "I can conceive of no legitimate state interest served by these differing treatments of the expressions of voters' fundamental rights. The differences appear wholly arbitrary."[3] There *were* differences that could justify using different recount standards.

In addition to these different circumstances—which those on the ground involved in the recounts were certainly better positioned to judge than the U.S. Supreme Court or even the Florida Supreme Court—setting a uniform substandard was problematic. As soon as one sets such a standard, one potentially rejects counting a ballot that nonetheless might clearly reveal the intent of the voter. Thus, if one calls for only counting chads with two dislodged corners, what does one do with the ballot with a pregnant chad and a written message that says, "I vote for Gore," as Dworkin asked? Strictly following such a substandard would violate the law laid down by the state legislature, to seek the "clear intent of the voter," which Chief Justice Rehnquist's position on the primacy of text-based law should have us reject.

Third, Dworkin's insight into the act of recounting lessens the concern over different counties using different rules of thumb: neither a strict nor a loose standard is inherently advantageous to the voters whose ballots are under review, since the goal of recounting is to discover the intent of the voter, and that intent may be contradicted by failing to count a vote (say, because it is weakly punched) or by counting a vote that was not intended (because a loose standard reads intention where there is none). Dworkin brilliantly revealed a hidden assumption that everyone else seemed to be making: that using a looser standard was somehow giving a break to voters. That attitude is problematic, not only because it relies on a wrong-headed view of the search for voter intent but because it implicitly acknowledges that there are voters trying to cast ballots who have fallen short. Those assuming that a looser standard is more forgiving who, nonetheless, deny that forgiveness are saying, effectively: "We know you wanted to vote for a candidate, but we are not willing to concede your voting intent (even if we can infer it) because you failed to follow the rules." I disagree with the sentiment entirely, because it would use hypertechnical rules (not authorized under Florida law) to thwart the most important means for citizen participation in democracy.

A fourth problem with the unfairness argument is that it was based not on what the recounters whose actions were halted were doing but on what earlier, different recounters had done. As the per curiam explained:

> [T]estimony at trial . . . revealed that at least one county changed its evaluative standards during the counting process. Palm Beach County, for example, began the process with a 1990 guideline which precluded counting completely attached chads, switched to a rule that considered a vote to be legal if any light could be seen through a chad, changed back to the 1990 rule, and then abandoned any pretense of a per se rule, only to have a court order that the county consider dimpled chads legal.[4]

This description involved the recount by county canvassing boards during the protest period, not during the contest period. Instead of canvassing boards, the state supreme court had ordered Judge Terry Lewis to oversee the recount, and he put teams of judges on the job. Thus, there were (1) judges, not canvassing boards, and (2) a single magistrate, Judge Lewis, who would address any objections on particular ballots. At best, the per curiam's argument was about what providing the general standard "clear intent of the voter" might allow at the county level. But it entirely ignored the current recount's oversight by a single magistrate—a magistrate, it is worth noting, who already had ruled in Bush's favor in an earlier case. So, ultimately, the complaint was not about actual unfairness but only about potential unfairness, and that where more restrictive conditions applied.

If the unfairness argument was weak, so was the majority's claim that these potentially divergent counting standards represented an equal protection violation. It is not that extending equal protection to include equal treatment of ballots in recounting is an inherently bad idea. Some liberal scholars noted that this could be a welcome extension of equal rights cases in going beyond race-based requirements. But it is problematic in the existing law it threatened, in the precedents it relied on, and in its use by this group of justices.

Vincent Bugliosi was justifiably suspicious of court motives in finding that recount standards need to be uniform when for more than two centuries (or at least, say, since the passage of the Fourteenth Amendment), the High Court had been "quiet as a mouse" on the issue. Worse still, as Stevens had noted, some thirty-three states had relied on that silence in implementing similar standards for counting ballots. The result was that this new equal protection finding meant that all those states needed to change their laws—a major challenge to the status quo that there should be very good reasons for overturning. (Limiting the precedential value of the case potentially avoided that.)

The precedents the per curiam invoked for this extension were far afield of the *Bush* case. They involved identifiable groups suffering tangible harm intentionally inflicted: voters in urban districts versus those in rural districts, voters harmed as a group by uneven apportionment of voting districts, and poor voters harmed by a poll tax. Although these cases involved disparate treatment, they did not involve arbitrary treatment, which the majority was attempting to draw out of them. The majority did not explain the source of its "arbitrary and disparate treatment" approach (and no precedents have used this approach) but left it to its readers to figure out how to pull this square peg out of a round hole. The image was not one of an intelligent court waiting for its slow readers to figure out an obvious connection but a court unsure of how to connect the precedents to the case at hand that simply skipped over the tough part of making that connection. The per curiam threw out an inappropriate description—"arbitrary"—and hoped its readers would assume a connection to those precedents.

The per curiam failed to provide a more accurate account of the precedents, which involved intentional harm to identifiable groups of voters with shared interests (e.g., those in urban areas, the poor). That more accurate account would challenge the Court to explain what interests were shared by overvoters versus undervoters, voters under one recount substandard versus those under another, and voters in early recount counties versus voters in later recount counties. If a state legislature dominated by representatives from rural areas wanted to keep a rule that gave its districts a greater share of state power than those from urban districts, it is clear why they would seek to do that and whose ox was being gored by virtue of it. But what interests do overvoters share in common? If no one substandard was more accurate in assessing voter intent (because a loose standard might identify more false positives and a strict standard might miss more intended votes), what disadvantage do counties with one substandard have versus those with another? The question of unequal treatment in early versus late recount counties is a bit more complicated and requires extended treatment.

The per curiam's complaint noted that three counties selected by Gore for sample and, later, full recounts during the protest phase received different treatment from all of the other counties falling under the Florida Supreme Court's statewide recount in the contest phase. These fuller recounts represent a noteworthy difference of treatment, the per curiam said, because

> the recounts in these three counties were not limited to so-called undervotes but extended to all of the ballots. The distinction has real consequences. A manual recount of all ballots identifies not only those ballots which show no vote but also those which contain more than one, the so-called overvotes. Neither category will be counted by the machine.[5]

In addition to the uncounted votes in this group, the per curiam complained, there were votes that should not have been counted by the machines, which a manual recount theoretically might reject: "the citizen who marks two candidates, only one of which is discernable [sic] by the machine, will have his vote counted even though it should have been read as an invalid ballot."[6] I will address the overvote exclusion problem and simply note of this last silly point that I believe that a vote-counting machine's ability to distinguish a voter's selection where two chads have been fiddled with is less than a human's ability to draw those distinctions, so there would never be an overvote recorded as a vote by a machine but not by a human recounter. And, of course, the High Court could draw no evidence from the trial court (which established facts in the case) to show that such a discrepancy had ever occurred or was likely to occur.

There are a number of problems with labeling the overvote exclusion outside the three early recount counties as an equal protection problem. First, the different treatment of ballots in those counties was not arbitrary but based on statutory provisions allowing recounts in counties selected by the candidates. The law did not mandate that any particular counties be chosen for or excluded from recounts; selections were based on candidates' concerns about which counties might contain votes for them that were missed because of the counting processes employed in the election. Bush had the same opportunity to call for recounts but chose not to recount any (following his strategy of urging that the election was over and all counting had been completed).

It is true that the Florida Supreme Court (rather than the statutory law) mandated including totals from these early recount counties (with their overvotes included) in the vote totals. But exactly what would the High Court have the state court do with these votes—legal under Florida's voter intent definition? Should the state court have said, "Yes, we realize these are legal votes under our law, but we must exclude them because we did not count the overvote ballots for all counties in the contest phase"? This is very similar to the problem faced by the judge ruling on the case where thousands of absentee ballot applications for Republicans had been filled out by GOP party officials—in plain violation of Florida law—but nonetheless were permitted to be included in final totals because the remedy of throwing out thousands of otherwise legal votes seemed too extreme. In supporting the inclusion of these votes, in the face of protests by Gore's lawyers, the state court acted consistently.

Per curiam defenders might claim that this equal protection problem could have been addressed had the state court simply ordered the recounting of overvote ballots as well, as the High Court suggested. But there were very good reasons for excluding those ballots, the most persuasive of which was the fact that at trial, no one produced evidence to suggest that overvote ballots containing legal votes had been excluded. Indeed, the large number of overvote ballots were very stingy in yielding additional votes, as media recounts showed. Using the court's broad authority to fashion "any relief appropriate under such circumstances," the exclusion of these hard-to-mine, legally insignificant ballots in a recount with a quickly closing window of opportunity was prudent.

A final consideration, which the ill-informed High Court failed to understand, is that many counties already had made provisions to ensure that overvote ballots were counted. The wealthier counties had ballot readers at polling stations that would automatically spit back ballots containing over-votes, giving voters trying to deposit their errant ballots a chance to correct them.[7] Tribe noted that thirty-four counties already had corrected overvote ballots in the original vote count.[8] Thus, it was not the three counties alone that had counted overvotes but dozens more. The consequence was that without a court-ordered recount of any kind, some counties would have treated their voters differently by conducting these recounts. And despite the fact that dozens of counties were involved in this differential treatment of voters, the High Court did not call for a correction of this equal protection problem. The conservative justices might plead ignorance about these differences, but that just reinforced the idea that they should have kept their federal noses out of this state business in the first place.

In addition to relying on questionable precedents, the majority conveniently had forgotten that equal protection law had been modified since the 1960s cases they cited were heard, and such changes were notably endorsed by the majority justices. *Washington v. Davis*, which was joined by then-Associate Justice Rehnquist, held that:

> The central purpose of the Equal Protection Clause of the Fourteenth Amendment is the prevention of official conduct discriminating on the basis of race. It is also true that the Due Process Clause of the Fifth Amendment contains an equal protection component prohibiting the United States from invidiously discriminating between individuals or groups. *Bolling* v. *Sharpe*, 347 U.S. 497 (1954). But our cases have not embraced the proposition that a law or other official act, without regard to whether it reflects a racially discriminatory purpose, is unconstitutional *solely* because it has a racially disproportionate impact.[9]

By extension, just the fact that one recounting substandard was used in a particular county, while another was used in a different county, did not mean that a discriminatory purpose (and certainly not a racially discriminatory purpose) was at work. Indeed, it is hard to imagine any discriminatory purpose that might be attributed to the Florida Supreme Court or the Florida legislature for allowing counties to determine their own substandards for recounting. By choosing not to go beyond the "clear intent of the voter," the state court did not discriminate against anyone. Nor could the recounting teams in each county be charged with purposefully discriminating against others in choosing a recount standard. All teams had the same purpose: to get an accurate count (or, at least, this is what the High Court assumed). And Judge Lewis stood ready to provide consistency in judging disputed ballots.

In 1995, all five majority justices, as well as Justices Souter and Breyer, emphasized a particular requirement for equal protection claims. Rejecting such a claim in *U.S. v. Hays*, they complained: "Appellees point us to no authority for the proposition that an equal protection challenge may go forward in federal court absent the showing of individualized harm, and we decline appellees' invitation to approve that proposition in this litigation."[10] Obviously, there was no individualized harm about which to complain. Using either a loose standard or a strict standard did not clearly benefit or harm anyone, since both standards sought the voter's intent in their own ways.

Most damning to the majority's 1960s construction of equal protection law was that Justice Kennedy, author of the per curiam, proclaimed a year after *Bush*, in *Board of Trustees of the University of Alabama et al. v. Patricia Garrett et al.*, that "the failure of a state to revise policies now seen as incorrect [fails to] constitute the purposeful and intentional action required to make out a violation of the equal protection clause."[11] This marked the height of hypocrisy by the majority justices, who conveniently adjusted the current equal protection standard just long enough to apply it to Bush's case, then switched back as soon as the case was over.

Even if this novel equal protection holding were deemed defensible in ensuring fairness and the nonarbitrary treatment of voters, the High Court's decision to gloss over the much greater equal protection problem of different voting technologies was indefensible. The per curiam itself recognized the "unfortunate" problem that punchcard voting machines rejected a higher number of ballots than newer voting technologies. Indeed, when the rejection rate for ballots in one county was sixty-eight times higher than in a contiguous county using better voting technology, that was worthy of judicial notice, especially when the high-rejection-rate county (Gadsden) was Florida's only black-majority county, while the other was majority white. Because the old punchcard machines were used in poorer, more Democratic counties with larger minority populations, this problem, unlike the recount standard problem, harmed identifiable groups of voters (notably, those traditionally protected by equal protection law) by ensuring that they had less chance to have their voices heard in the political process. If ever there were a classic Warren-style case of an equal protection violation, this was it.

But the per curiam glossed over this problem by noting that county canvassing boards, using their "expertise," may make such choices without violating equal protection. The fact that such expertise yielded voting technology purchases correlated with the wealth of a county (where richer counties got the newer, more reliable voting machines) appeared not to concern the justices. Apparently, the state, as ultimate overseer of elections, had no responsibility to help those counties financially so they could make better choices and avoid treating minorities, Democrats, and the poor differently from other voters. This position, I believe, was indefensible. And it turned on an inconsistency: the High Court's willingness to defer to county officials changed markedly when they moved from their choice of voting technologies—even technologies that ensure that their voters had a much greater chance of having their ballots rejected—to choosing substandards for recounting ballots. The insistence that the counties be reined in on the latter, which had minor and unpredictable consequences, but not the former, which had significant and predictable consequences, was unreasonable. It suggested that the High Court was driven by something besides the desire to ensure fairness under the law.

Because of the significant differences in the accuracy of different voting technologies, the original vote count was flawed. By refusing to allow the recounts to go forward, the majority ensured that the original vote count— which undercounted votes from Democrats, minorities, and the poor— would not be corrected. Thus, the majority's decision contributed to unfairness in the election, rather than alleviating it.

To ensure that no correction would happen, the High Court offered the weakest argument of all: that the Florida legislature had mandated that Florida's vote count be completed by the safe harbor deadline. No scholar thought that deadline was mandatory—not even Nelson Lund—as indeed it was not. Because no Florida statute mandated that deadline, the per curiam asserted that the Florida Supreme Court had held that the deadline was sacrosanct under Florida law. This deference to the Florida court was at odds with the majority justices' rejection of almost everything else the Florida court said and with the concurring justices' insistence that Florida's written law trumped whatever the state court said about that law. Nowhere had the state court suggested that the optional deadline trumped every other consideration—certainly not ensuring an accurate vote count. On the contrary, they insisted that the state's highest goal in its voting laws was to find the will of the voters.

Ironically, any deference to the safe harbor deadline suggested by the state court was coerced out of it by *Bush v. Palm Beach County Canvassing Board*, which demanded state court recognition of the deadline. In retrospect, this functioned as a Catch–22, with the majority justices effectively setting up the state court to acknowledge that deadline, allowing them to insist later that the state court recognized it as part of state law. December 18, the day the Electoral College met, should have been the earliest deadline insisted on by the High Court. Even that date is not mandatory under federal law, though some concession to the advantages of ensuring a smooth transition for the highest office in the land probably should be made.

To bolster its case that there was no time to recount, the per curiam had described an exhaustive process for conducting a legal recount:

> It would require not only the adoption (after opportunity for argument) of adequate statewide standards for determining what is a legal vote, and practicable procedures to implement them, but also orderly judicial review of any disputed matters that might arise. In addition, the Secretary of State has advised that the recount of only a portion of the ballots requires that the vote tabulation equipment be used to screen out undervotes, a function for which the machines were not designed. If a recount of overvotes were also required, perhaps even a second screening would be necessary. Use of the equipment for this purpose, and any new software developed for it, would have to be evaluated for accuracy by the Secretary of State, as required by Fla. Stat. § 101.015 (2000).[12]

Given the Bush team's efforts to drag out the process and run out the clock, the per curiam's description of the need for an opportunity for argument on the statewide standard and for orderly judicial review of any disputed matter that might arise, not to mention the possible development of new software, the novel use of existing hardware, and the actual task of recounting, suggested a monumental challenge in the time-starved scene. But, I believe, the argument succeeded too well on this score. It becomes hard to imagine any recount that would meet constitutional standards, even if the contest period had been started at the earliest possible time and the partisan secretary of state had been cooperative rather than obstructive. In a practical sense, then, it is hard to imagine a recount of a disputed election ever going forward without a prior development of procedures for all of these contingencies. In short, the per curiam's position erased the possibility for remediation in a questionable election of this sort. Such justice is ideal—and not realistic. As Stevens had complained of the per curiam's refusal to allow the state court to leave the recount substandards to the individual counties, the High Court's demands did not give the state government enough "play in its joints" to operate effectively in the real world.[13]

Finally, the per curiam's attempt to limit the precedential value of the case was indefensible. The principle, as Bugliosi showed, did not present "complexities" that would prevent its ready application to cases in the future. Rather, the majority justices did not want to be held to their own ruling in the future. They realized that this ruling would overturn a huge number of state laws. Normally, the prospective implications of a Supreme Court decision act as a brake on precipitous action; in this case, the High Court essentially made federal law for one person: George W. Bush. This constituted unforgivable hypocrisy on the part of the High Court, especially Justice Scalia, who insisted that the Court's primary role was to set down precedents.

Posner suggested that the concurring justices—Rehnquist, Scalia, and Thomas—were more hypocritical than Justices Kennedy and O'Connor, because they joined an opinion with which they did not really agree. Indeed, their divergent take on the problems of the 2000 election controversy suggested that their joining the two unnamed justices in the majority was a strategic move to prop up a conservative decision that otherwise would be splintered and even more questionable than the 5-4 alignment they cobbled together. But there were serious problems in their own position as well.

The concurring opinion's argument that Article II gave plenary authority to the state legislature had the advantage of leaning on *Bush v. Palm Beach County Canvassing Board*'s unanimous decision, which implied that even a state's constitution might not limit the authority of the state legislature to enact laws directing the manner of choosing presidential electors. However, when push came to shove, that implication was endorsed by only three justices. Rehnquist's reliance on italicizing the word *legislature* in Article II to stress the significance of this grant of power was easily challenged by italicizing the word *State* in the same provision. With a bit of historical research—which only the young Hayward Smith was clever enough to conduct—a good case was made that the Founding Fathers did not think they were giving plenary authority to the state legislatures but only responsibility for devising election processes. That should convince the originalists in the concurrence, along with the undeniable need for unclear legislation to be interpreted by courts. Indeed, the authors of the Electoral Count Act, who lived half again closer to the days of the Founding Fathers than we do, assumed election disputes would be resolved "by judicial or other means."

But Rehnquist was unfairly picking and choosing the legal evidence. Thus, he cited language from *McPherson v. Blacker* suggesting that the state legislature had unfettered authority under Article II but ignored language in the same decision that suggested that state constitutions could constrain legislative actions in selecting the manner of choosing electors.

Rehnquist's case against the Florida Supreme Court was seriously overstated. He strained to suggest that the state court's interpretations of state law were absurd and unreasonable, when the best he could hope for was to show that they were different from his own preferred readings. His most damning critique involved the interpretation of "error in vote tabulation." To exclude voter-based errors from this definition, Rehnquist had to ignore several statutes and long-standing state court decisions that found that mismarked ballots could still be legal votes, to paint a picture of an efficient Florida voting system based on legal requirements rather than on grubby election realities (well documented in the news media by this point), and an implicit argument that voters too stupid to follow directions deserved to have their ballots thrown out.

Even Posner realized that this last, implicit argument was not one he wanted to be associated with, as he assured his readers that neither technological proficiency nor literacy (the older, rejected test) should be standards for judging who was deserving of having his or her vote counted. However, Posner brought that test in through the back door by agreeing with Rehnquist that voting directions were clear, incorrectly punched ballots were largely the fault of voters, and those voters could ask only so much of the poor canvassing boards that had to try to interpret their failed attempts to vote, especially in a presidential race where, he insisted, time was of the essence. This last point about not overburdening the canvassing boards does effectively make the technological proficiency of voters a basis for rejecting ballots, despite Posner's protest to the contrary.

The problem with these attempts to shift blame to voters was that they ignored very well-documented failures on the part of election officials. The Civil Rights Commission Report on the election, as well as numerous news reports, demonstrated that election officials did not provide ballots in Spanish in counties with high Hispanic populations, that poll workers were often poorly trained or unable to provide timely aid to voters having problems, that some ballots (especially the infamous butterfly ballot) were confusing, that voting instructions printed in the newspaper in one case were wrong, and that the punchcard voting machines were especially prone to error.

Rehnquist attempted to pare down the broad grant of authority Florida's legislature gave to the state court to "fashion such orders as he or she deems necessary to ensure that each allegation in the complaint is investigated, examined, or checked, to prevent or correct any alleged wrong, and to provide any relief appropriate under such circumstances."[14] On the other hand, he tried to broaden the authority of the secretary of state, beyond what the statutes and precedents clearly declare, in asserting that the state court was required to defer to her interpretations of election law.

Rehnquist did demonstrate that other interpretations of Florida election law were possible. He did not demonstrate that his own interpretations were better. And he certainly did not demonstrate that the Florida Supreme Court's interpretations were absurd and unreasonable. Thus, even if he had made a persuasive case for Article II's assignment of plenary authority to the state legislature (which he did not), he would not have demonstrated that the state court contravened the state legislature's intentions in this case.

It is not unusual for a Supreme Court decision to include a weak argument in support of a decision. The Court not infrequently stretches a reasonable interpretation of a rule, selectively represents the facts in a case, ignores an obvious precedent, or otherwise engages in questionable judgments in order to ensure that justice is done in the individual case, that an unclear law is settled for the future, that existing law is not disturbed, and so forth. What was highly unusual in the *Bush* case was that the High Court simultaneously ignored its responsibilities to the past, the present, and the future—to following the law, to doing justice, and to laying down clear precedents. There were no such tradeoffs here to explain the half-dozen weak arguments offered for the decision. Both the per curiam and concurring opinions were shot through with serious problems. The High Court's justification for its controversial ruling was thoroughly unpersuasive. Thus, it is not surprising that Stuart Taylor's one-year anniversary assessment of the per curiam decision found one conservative thinker admitting that the equal protection argument was "laughable" and that the decision would have been very different had Gore been the one asking for a halt to the recounts.[15]

Given these questionable means, what kind of purpose can be assigned to the majority's actions? Before turning to this means-ends relationship, one should briefly consider other grammatical connections that shed light on this crucial terministic relationship. First, it should be acknowledged that these judicial agents were intelligent and knowledgeable about the law. And if age or a want of sufficient intelligence were a problem, they had the aid of some of the smartest law clerks in the country. Thus, it must be assumed that they knew that the legal means they invoked to support their decision were weak.

Defenders might object that the incredibly limited scene for the formulation of these arguments and the writing of the opinions—a few days, at best—ensured that the arguments would not be stellar. Scholarly critics, on the other hand, have had months or even years to ponder the issues and reveal their weaknesses. However, that scene-agency argument itself is weak, because the intelligence of the agents and the discursive scene ensured that the weaknesses of these arguments were plain enough to the conservative majority. These justices had demonstrated their sharp intellects frequently during oral arguments. Their long experience as judges had honed their ability to sniff out weaknesses in legal arguments, and the three or four clerks assigned to each justice ensured that they had energetic counsel in forming these arguments. And if they still missed the problems in their arguments, the four dissenting opinions (which they should have read before the majority opinion was issued) highlighted most of the weaknesses that scholars would later elaborate at length.

An additional agent consideration involves the alleged gulf between what these justices said and did and their judicial philosophies. In many ways, the conservative justices acted out of character with respect to their stated beliefs about the law and about the role of the judiciary. No one would have thought that a conservative majority that was very stingy in its equal protection rulings would find an equal protection violation of this sort. The insistence by the Court that its decision to tell a state court how to interpret its own law did not conflict with the justices' well-known support for states' rights (noted in several cases, such as that which struck down the Violence against Women Act) is hard to accept. Scalia's hypocrisy concerning limiting the precedential value of this case has been noted. On the other hand, the conservative majority was not playing against character in its activism in this case. Despite what may have been assumed about this conservative Court and what its justices may have uttered about the importance of judicial restraint, they have rarely refrained from taking on controversial issues that a less activist Court might avoid. Thus, they were out of judicial character on equal protection, states' rights, and the limitation of the precedential value of the decision, if not on judicial activism.

The upshot of these considerations is that the majority justices offered arguments for their positions that they knew were weak. And they took positions that flew in the face of earlier positions they had taken and principles they had articulated. Why did they not offer stronger arguments that were better attuned to their judicial philosophies? The obvious answer is that there *were* no stronger or different arguments that yielded the result they sought. Several scholarly defenders, with plenty of time to ponder the issues, have not been able to develop a persuasive defense of the decision that rested on legal grounds. Despite the dearth of good legal arguments to support the decision, the Court plowed ahead, apparently allowing purpose to drive agency, rather than the other way around. In most fields of discourse, this is a perfectly legitimate approach: decide the goal you want to reach, and then figure out a way to get there. But this is not acceptable in judicial discourse, where the law is supposed to dictate the outcome, rather than the other way around.

A number of purposes have been proposed to explain or justify the Court's actions, from the selfless to the selfish. At the selfless end, Court defenders claimed that the majority took a hit to its credibility in order to prevent a constitutional and political crisis. At the selfish end, Court critics insisted that the conservative majority members wanted to make Bush president because they wanted a Republican president, particularly as a means to ensure the continuation of their conservative agenda on the Court by appointing more conservatives like themselves and perhaps elevating one of them to the chief justice position in the future.

Purposes cannot be scrutinized in the same way agencies can be scrutinized; they must be drawn out of agencies, scenes, agents, acts, and attitudes. Because the High Court knowingly used weak arguments to support its decision, the purpose must have been very important. For, as even defenders recognized, this kind of intervention by the Supreme Court was likely to provoke an avalanche of criticism, particularly in light of these weak arguments. Defenders painted the conservative majority as obviously recognizing that such criticism would be forthcoming but taking stalwart action nevertheless. Indeed, in keeping with the construction of these judicial agents as intelligent, I must concede that they probably were aware that serious criticism would follow. Whether this makes them noble or foolish is another question.

On the other hand, there was reason to believe that this criticism would come primarily from legal scholars, rather than from the American public. Given the images of recounting teams on television holding up ballots to the light in what appeared like some odd, interpretive ritual, the majority justices probably suspected that a sizable portion of the public had a gut sense that the process was flawed anyway. And the public certainly would not be in a position to second-guess the legal arguments offered by the Court. The news media could have been expected to gloss over the legal arguments—they typically do so—though they might play up the drama of the election-ending decision and quote complaints from legal scholars. Generally, the Court probably expected to catch some flak for its decision, but it probably did not assume that the criticism would be fatal to its ethos or long-lived.[16] So the conservative majority knowingly used weak arguments, for which it was prepared to face considerable scholarly criticism. For what purpose or purposes would the Court make such a sacrifice?

A purpose of avoiding a constitutional or political crisis assumes that the Court recognized the possibility of future scenarios such as those suggested by Posner and others. Indeed, the justices may have viewed even the recounting that was going on when they issued the stay as chaotic and threatening. Apologists for the Court made a good case for the *Bush* majority's distrust of some democratic processes, illustrated by the Rehnquist Court's rejection of "fusion" candidates in California. They also probably thought that the Florida Supreme Court was somewhat out of control—at least outside the High Court's control—when it responded to being spanked by the High Court in *Bush v. Palm Beach County Canvassing Board* by supporting requests for even more recounting. I do not believe this was a concern that was carefully pondered, weighing probabilities about how everything might end up. I think an attitude of arrogance and anger probably made the Court feel that processes under way were chaotic and problematic, if only because they would not cease without intervention.

Furthermore, I do not believe that the High Court carefully considered the legal arguments behind the state court's actions to determine that it was out of control and needed to be stopped—in the name of the law—for the good of the country. Instead, I suspect the majority had a vague sense that there was a problem, though those feelings probably were amplified by the majority's political concerns about what was unfolding, notably Bush's disappearing lead in light of an extension of the recounts by a state court dominated by Democrats.

The record shows that the conservative five had never hidden their political loyalties. Alan Dershowitz documented well the strong party connections of all of the majority justices. The prime example was Justice O'Connor, a longtime Republican party loyalist, who, Dershowitz showed, had been willing to let her name be used in ethically troubling party fundraising, who evinced anger and frustration at the possibility of a Gore presidency, and who had reasons to want to retire and be replaced by a Republican.

This last point adds personal purposes to the larger political ones. If a Republican president would ensure that the majority's preferred political party prevailed in the election, it also ensured that the jurisprudential legacies built up by the aging Rehnquist and O'Connor (more than twenty-nine and nineteen years on the High Court, respectively) would be preserved; that the radically new direction forged by them, Scalia, Kennedy, and Thomas would be continued; and that Scalia and Kennedy would have a shot at the chief justice position. It is not clear whether these justices had the foresight to recognize the Catch-22 they were creating for themselves: that given the self-serving appearance of the decision and the scathing attacks on their motives, Rehnquist and O'Connor would have to postpone any retirement plans for four more years to avoid the charge that they were feathering their own judicial nests.

A final agency consideration pushes the interpretation of the conservative majority's purposes toward the troublesome political and personal objectives suggested here. The decision that there was no time for recounting, which rested on the weakest of foundations (the safe harbor argument), suggested that not only did the majority justices want the "chaotic" recounting ended quickly, they wanted it ended permanently. The price they paid for this refusal to allow the recounting to continue was the loss of Justices Souter and Breyer from their majority. That is, had the majority been willing to let the recount be restarted under constitutionally acceptable standards, this likely would have been a true 7-2 decision, which would have muffled a great deal of the criticism of the Court by bolstering the majority's numbers and erasing at least two dissenting opinions. The significance of this trade-off the majority accepted in refusing to permit recounts to continue is hard to overstate. They sacrificed legitimacy for the decision, accepted a stain on their reputations, and ensured a rejection of their linchpin safe harbor claim by even their staunchest supporters in order to ensure that the recount would not restart.

Why the sacrifice? Is it because the Court believed a constitutional and political crisis would likely have followed? I do not believe so. Had the recounting begun again under new standards, it might well have been completed by December 18.[17] It would have been harder for the Florida legislature to intervene, given the High Court's endorsement of a recount with a remedy that checked the concerns about unfairness in the recount standards.[18] It would have been less likely that two competing slates of electors would have confronted Congress in January. Without that hot potato, the transition would have gone much more smoothly.

Posner, of course, rejected this scenario. He tried to justify permanently stopping the recounting—despite what he admitted was a fatally flawed safe harbor argument by the per curiam—because he thought that every political and judicial agent involved in the postelection struggle would have fought to the death for his or her own partisan ends, creating a crisis. Thus, even with a Supreme Court solution that I suggest would calm the political waters in Florida, he thought the Florida legislature would have plowed ahead with its own slate of electors for Bush.[19] Not only that, but he must have assumed that there would have been a slate for Gore coming out of a Court-sanctioned recount to compete with this new slate for Bush.[20] For if there were two competing Florida slates sent to Congress and both of them were for Bush, how would the crisis maintain its steam?

Obviously, it is hard to square this assumption with Posner's earlier, lengthy argument in his book that even with a recount, Bush would have won the election. This was an Achilles' heel for Posner's pragmatic, "rough justice" defense of the outcome of *Bush v. Gore*. He could not credibly argue both that Bush would have won the election anyway and that allowing new recounts with clear substandards to go forward would lead to a crisis. But he ran into critical problems if he gave up either of these mutually exclusive positions. If Bush would not have won the election in a new recount, then the High Court's actions—which Posner admitted were legally unsupportable on the grounds offered by the majority—effectively stole the election from Gore. It was hard to justify avoiding a crisis that might delay the transition of presidential power if that entailed transferring that power to a man who had not won the election. Even if we knew, say, that an enemy was going to capture one of our military planes, would anyone argue that it would be better to place the wrong man in the Oval Office simply to avoid a two-week power vacuum (or, more to the point, to avoid having an acting president for a couple of weeks)? It is not as if such a replacement would lack credibility under the Constitution.

On the other hand, Posner's justification for Supreme Court intervention—his alternative to the legal reasons they offered—rested on the pragmatic avoidance of a crisis; yet this crisis would not be realized if two competing slates from Florida both supported Bush. Congress would not have dragged out a debate on a moot point while the nation sat on pins and needles wondering when the interminable postelection struggle would end.

Indeed, with two slates of electors for Bush, the Bush transition team could do its job with the knowledge that it had secured the White House.

Although I reject Posner's elaborate, highly speculative, and contradictory worst-case scenario, his concerns did reveal another possible purpose for the conservative majority. If either a Supreme Court abstention from Bush's appeal or a decision to allow the recounts to continue would lead to troubling political fights, might not the avoidance of those very fights, rather than (or in addition to) a general aversion to democratic disorder, have been another purpose of the majority? I believe a good case can be made that the conservative majority took a bullet not for the country but for the Republican Party.

Suppose the Florida legislature had speedily approved its own slate for Bush just in case things did not go its way in the recounts. Posner admitted that more voters in Florida intended to vote for Gore than for Bush. Whether or not the recount yielded a victory for Gore, the majority of voters would be justifiably incensed if its supposedly representative body of legislators approved a separate slate of electors for Bush. The unprecedented spectacle of a state legislature trampling on the will of the majority of its voters would likely lead to a backlash against the Republicans, and perhaps against Florida Governor Jeb Bush. This would be fueled by a knowledge that punchcard voting machines, the butterfly ballot, the purging of alleged felons from voting rolls, inadequate resources at polls on Election Day, and other problems—many of which could be laid at the door of Republican officials—had snatched victory from Democrats' hands. Voters might rightly feel that Gore had a moral right to the presidency, regardless of who might have legally won the post.

No doubt more troubling to the High Court would be the political fallout of a fight in Congress should two actually competing slates (one for Gore, one for Bush) meet it on January 6. The debate would undoubtedly review all the Election Day problems in Florida, many of which the Democrats would lay at the door of Jeb Bush, George W. Bush's campaign in Florida, and the Florida Republicans. Americans would be glued to the television to hear from their representatives about how many African-Americans had been erroneously purged from voter rolls as felons, how Republican staffers had been flown into Miami to intimidate the county recounters, how the police had set up barricades on Election Day to stop and query all motorists in one of the few black precincts in Florida, how a Republican county canvassing board director had permitted corrections on thousands of absentee ballot applications for Republicans but not for Democrats, how even Pat Buchanan admitted that thousands of votes for him in Broward County had actually been intended for Gore, how half a million more Americans voted for Gore than for Bush, and how the Bush campaign apparently was planning to challenge the election if it received a majority of the popular vote but not a majority of the electoral votes (as Gore had).[21] This train of incompetence and political maneuverings would be particularly vivid in the Senate, which the Democrats still controlled. The picture would be one of the voters' will quashed through incompetence and outright political tricks.

Posner's simple story of party members readily voting their party's line did not adequately consider the political Armageddon into which Republicans would step if they simply rejected such concerns out of hand and voted their man into office. Posner had argued that just the fact that more Florida voters intended to vote for Gore than for Bush did not mean that Gore had a legal right to the presidency. But Congress does not deal merely in legalities, as the Supreme Court is supposed to do; moral arguments and political arguments carry weight. And so they should.

Certainly, the pressure from Republican leaders in Congress would be high for their party members to toe the line. Republicans who had serious concerns about replacing an electoral slate that was the product of a Court-certified election recount of ballots with one that a highly partisan Republican state legislature passed would face excruciating arm twisting. That itself would lead to bad feelings among Republicans, if not outright defiance of their leaders in some cases. If these "conscientious objectors" nonetheless endorsed their party's candidate, they could face serious repercussions from Democrats in their districts and other voters worried about the fairness of the election. If they rejected their party's position, they could face alienation from its ranks.

Democrats in Congress would not face the same dilemma. They could vote for their candidate—the one a recount of ballots showed to be victorious—with little fallout. The charges that a partisan state supreme court had eked out a victory for Gore could be dismissed by reference to a 7-2 U.S. Supreme Court decision—endorsed by the most conservative members of the Court—that legitimized the final recount. They could insist that not only was the will of the voters ensured, but a moral victory was won over unfortunate and costly mistakes (such as the butterfly ballot) and the questionable tactics of the Republicans (such as zealous felon purging and the Miami "Brooks Brothers riot"). Clearly, a recount that led to a Bush-Gore showdown in Congress could have hurt the Republicans badly.

But did these conservative Republican justices have enough foresight and political savvy to anticipate such a political train wreck? If not, before the majority decided to take this case, there were plenty of people who could have helped one or more of them understand the political implications. Dershowitz showed how politically connected the majority justices were. During the monthlong postelection battle, it would be surprising if they could escape the speculation about a possible congressional showdown going on inside the Beltway.

It is not that the majority justices necessarily sought out or were buttonholed by their party colleagues. The point is that none of the justices was isolated in a judicial ivory tower, above the political fray. It would be surprising if none of the five, in casual conversations over the postelection struggle, had discussed the political implications of the election being thrown to Congress. Certainly, Posner attributed to the majority the ability to foresee political consequences leading to chaos and crisis, which he asserted they sought to avoid. If they could foresee Posner's fanciful train of events, they certainly could foresee the consequences outlined here. And if they could foresee them, they might have sought to avoid them.

Ultimately, I believe the conservative majority justices made the enormous sacrifice of the legitimacy of a 7-2 decision and of a stain on their personal reputations in order to ensure that no more recounts were conducted. I believe they voted to stay the recounts when Bush was only 154 votes ahead of Gore and in danger of losing his lead, because they wanted him to be president of the United States in order to preserve their conservative majority and legacy. After eight years and two Supreme Court appointments by President Clinton, they wanted to ensure that the Court's conservative judicial philosophy, their legacy, and the rightward movement of the Court begun during the Reagan and Bush I years continued. I believe they wanted to avoid the political upheaval of following the procedures mandated by the Electoral Count Act—handing off any electoral disputes to Congress—because that would likely hurt the Republican Party and might put Gore in the White House.

Perhaps they tried to deceive themselves about these underlying partisan and political motives by focusing their anger and wrath on a Democrat-dominated state court whose arguments they summarily rejected. But they could not have believed that they actually knew the strength of those arguments when the stay was issued. Ironically, they appear to have attributed their own partisan motives to the Democrats on the Florida Supreme

Court, using a familiar agent-purpose logic to assure themselves that the state court, like them, was defending its party's interests.

I reject constructions by those apologists for the High Court who admitted that the conservative justices were flouting the law but were doing so to counteract a partisan state court. This "pox on both houses" argument ignored some critical differences in the actions of the two courts. The conservative majority ruled against Gore in every case that came before them—three out of three. The state court ruled for Gore in some cases and issues and against Gore in other cases and issues. Had the state court simply been looking for a way to make Gore the winner in Florida, it could have latched on to the 20,000 absentee ballot forms filled out by Republican operatives in plain violation of Florida law. Rejecting thousands of Republican votes, while controversial, would have the benefit of drawing on clear state law forbidding those practices and would have assured Gore of a relatively large victory in the state.[22]

The conservative majority ignored clear precedents (such as *Washington v. Davis*) and clear statutes (notably the Electoral Count Act, which gave responsibility for resolving such election disputes to Congress). The state court followed well-established state law on "intent of the voter," appealed to noble ideals in Florida's constitution, and reasonably interpreted several poorly written statutes.

The conservative majority's decision yielded justice for no one— certainly not the voters whose uncounted ballots were thrown out and certainly not Bush, who had no constitutional right to win an election that, as Louise Weinberg convincingly argued, was still contested and incomplete when the Supreme Court halted the recount forever. On the other hand, if some of the Florida Supreme Court's motives did serve its political interests in giving Gore a chance of winning the White House, they simultaneously served the interests of voters whose ballots had been rejected through the unequal distribution of voting technologies in the state. This could not be a more clear-cut case of protecting the equal rights of a state's citizens, where identifiable groups—including traditionally protected minorities and the poor—were unquestionably harmed by voting systems that, even the per curiam admitted, rejected an "unfortunate number of ballots." The fact that meeting these equal protection purposes also could support political goals attributable to the state court's Democratic majority is beside the point. It is hard to complain about an outcome that fits a court's political aspirations when it also yields justice and provides reasonable evidence that the court was following the law.

A final useful distinction between the federal and state court decisions is their immediate outcomes. The conservative majority at the U.S. Supreme Court knew that ending the recounts would award the election to Bush. The state court only knew that continuing the recounts would unearth more votes, which might or might not lead to Gore's election. Perhaps it was the hope of the state court that Gore would win; but it was a certainty for the High Court that the Texas Republican would ascend to the highest office in the land.

The Legacy of Bush v. Gore

What this analysis reveals about judicial motives in this case raises serious questions about the implications of *Bush v. Gore* for American democracy. Chief among these is the role that sincerity and transparency should play in judicial decisions. Dworkin and Posner took different positions on this issue. Dworkin told a story about clerking for Judge Learned Hand, when one day the esteemed judge announced with confidence to his young aide that he would reach a particular verdict in a case. However, Dworkin reported, that confidence soon diminished:

> He set himself to writing the opinion. I watched him, from my desk opposite his, scribbling furiously on a yellow pad with his amazing eyebrows earnestly furrowed. He threw the sheets away, and began again. And then all over again. Finally, he looked up at me. "It won't write," he said. "We're going the other way."[23]

The most coherent explanation of what the majority justices in *Bush v. Gore* were doing and why they were doing it has them prejudging a case of enormous consequence, stopping a recount that would likely have finalized the presidential election of 2000, and putting together the best arguments they could muster to justify the precipitous action they took. But when they found that the decision they were pledged to reach would not write, they plowed ahead anyway, driven by political purposes and attitudes of anger and arrogance.

Posner, the majority's greatest defender, insisted that their disingenuous arguments were justified by the possibility that if the route to settling such controversies laid down by Congress over a century ago were followed, then everything that might go wrong would go wrong, that every agent who could act on behalf of crass political motives would do so, and that delaying the installation of Bush as president would have been harmful to the country. But, of course, the per curiam opinion said nothing about such consequences, much less using them to justify its decision. Nonetheless, Posner defended this consequentialist approach, which he used to support the outcome of *Bush v. Gore* and to justify the concurrence of Rehnquist, Scalia, and Thomas in the per curiam, insisting: "If all that matters are consequences, then dishonesty, which might seem the correct term for subscribing to a judicial opinion that one thinks all wrong [as these three justices did], while no doubt regrettable becomes just another factor in the calculus of decision."[24]

Dworkin insisted that Posner's defense fell because it failed the test of sincerity and transparency. Judges themselves must be persuaded by the arguments they offer to justify their decisions. They must be sincere about their own persuasion by the arguments, following those arguments that they find most persuasive, and they must present those same arguments in their opinions, rather than some other arguments for public consumption that serve as cover for hidden motives.

There are several problems with Posner's endorsement of disingenuous arguments as a cover for alternative motives. First, it is a highly cynical approach that essentially laughs behind the backs of Americans who believe in the myth of the rule of law. Such hypocrisy is the cousin of the corrupt politician who tells voters what they want to hear and then makes secret deals with special interests that undermine the public interest. It sets the American public up as a group to be controlled with lies, rather than reasoned with. It reflects an "I know better than you" attitude that places public servants—and surely judges are public servants—above public scrutiny.

Of course, it is true that the average American cannot hope to fathom the nuances of constitutional law. Judges, legal scholars, and legal professionals are like nuclear engineers in this sense—experts to whom we must defer to some extent. However, that technical barrier to understanding cannot justify disingenuous pandering or the failure to make a persuasive case for one's position. Just as in nuclear engineering, there are experts ready to serve the public by scrutinizing what this most powerful public institution does, some of them supporting the congressional oversight role. With a news media less focused on drama and more concerned about the substance of decisions, the public could come to at least a rudimentary understanding of what was at stake and what was done in its name.[25]

John Yoo and other defenders of the decision have noted that the American public has largely forgiven the High Court—if polls are any indication—after a brief drop in credibility immediately following the decision.[26] This means, they contend, that the Court's place in the tripartite system of government is secure, and no lasting damage has been done. Indeed, if such national polls are used as the sole measure of confidence in the Supreme Court, then perhaps they are right.

However, there is a group that has not clearly forgiven the Court. While white Americans have long identified with the government and its institutions, African-Americans have not. The history of disenfranchising them has only recently been changed by efforts such as the Voting Rights Act of 1965. Any African-American older than sixty still carries memories of the days when literacy tests and poll taxes were used to keep black citizens from voting. African-American trust in the political system is understandably fragile. Unsurprisingly, then, African-Americans saw the Court's decision very differently from the majority. A CBS poll conducted on the eve of George W. Bush's inauguration as president found that while 51 percent of Americans believed his presidency was legitimate, only 12 percent of African-Americans believed so.[27] New York Democratic Congressman Charles Rangel explained this distrust by charging that the halt to the Florida recounts may have led to "the greatest mass disenfranchisement of African-Americans since passage of the Voting Rights Act of 1965."[28] That concern over disenfranchisement led the Congressional Black Caucus alone to challenge Florida's electoral slate on January 6, 2001, revealing, columnist James Caroll urged, "that the wound of race has been opened by this dispute, whether white people see it or not."[29] If democracy's progress is measured by how the least powerful in a society feel about the system they live under, then *Bush v. Gore* may have set American democracy back several decades.

Even if we ignore minority concerns and base our evaluation of the threat to the democratic system on how a majority of citizens feel about the High Court's motives, is such public acquiescence in a bad decision—a decision most Americans poorly understand—a sign that American democracy is in good shape, as Yoo implied? In a democracy, I believe, the answer must be an emphatic no. Democratic governments, like other governments, wield power—regulating commerce, waging wars, creating alliances, and so on. Democratic governments are unique in making citizens ultimately responsible for their own governance. Although America's republican form of democracy employs elected officials to run the government—including federal judges appointed by those officials—the system relies on a transparency that makes government accountability possible. The Founding Fathers were skeptical that government officials would always act in the public interest, so they instituted checks and balances (including a free press) to ensure that the actions of government officials are scrutinized and curbed when necessary.

Judicial opinions, which announce the reasoning of a court in a given case, offer one of the few windows into the workings of the judiciary. These provide the moment of truth for the judiciary—the place where what judges do in the name of the government is most susceptible to democratic scrutiny. If it becomes acceptable for a court to lie about what it is doing and why it is doing it, then the public and other branches of government will not be able to scrutinize this public institution. It will become a Star-chamber—a place of secret and arbitrary judgments that affect the lives of citizens without the benefit of disclosure that allows for informed scrutiny.

The opportunity for informed scrutiny is particularly important in the case of *Bush v. Gore.* Effectively, in shutting down the vote recount, the U.S. Supreme Court took upon itself the political decision of who was to serve as president of the United States. If any case calls for informed public scrutiny, it is one that overrides the votes of 50 million Americans. To lie about the reasons for reaching this decision is little different, in kind, from stuffing a ballot box to ensure that one's preferred candidate wins: the means (dishonesty) and the ends (electing a preferred candidate) are the same.

The consequences of placing George W. Bush in office rather than Al Gore have been enormous. Gore would not have backed out of the Kyoto Global Warming Treaty, the ABM Treaty, or the Geneva Convention's rules against torture. He would not have endorsed massive tax cuts, supported the elimination of the estate tax, or signed off on huge deficit spending by a Republican Congress. He would have pushed for raising the minimum wage and enforcing environmental regulations, while rejecting calls for constitutional amendments banning flag burning and gay marriage. Gore would not have taken the country to war in Iraq on questionable evidence of weapons of mass destruction, gaining the enmity of the international community, leaving the United States and Iraq with tens of thousands of casualties, and miring the nation in a seemingly interminable conflict.

On the other hand, assuming that the September 11, 2001, attacks still went forward, it is not known whether Gore would have been a strong leader willing to take all necessary actions to protect American citizens; however, Americans' civil liberties might face fewer challenges from a Gore administration. Assuming that Congress still went to the Republicans, there might have been gridlock (which might or might not have been a good thing). The Republicans certainly would have held more congressional investigations into executive actions. Gore would not have escaped legislative scrutiny had he appended hundreds of "signing statements" to laws, effectively changing congressional enactments, as Bush has done. And it is certain that Gore would not have gone longer than John Quincy Adams before vetoing a bill, and that first veto would not have been one that stymied stem cell research.

Finally, the jurisprudential legacies of the conservative majority would not have received the boost they did from Bush's two appointments to the Supreme Court. It is likely that the possibility of overruling *Roe v. Wade* and other landmarks of the Warren and Burger Courts would be much more remote than they are now.

Whether these differences would be good or bad depends on one's viewpoint. But without a doubt, the action taken by the High Court to support a Bush presidency and to undermine a Gore presidency have had significant consequences, which will be felt for decades. It was not the High Court's place to shape the country's future in this aggressive way, certainly not if the ideal of living under the rule of law is to be attained.

If the Supreme Court succeeded in hiding its true motives in deciding this case, it does not matter as far as future law is concerned. What judges *say* about what they are doing and why they are doing it is a primary source for judges, lawyers, and the public to figure out what the law *is* on an issue, particularly when those judges sit on the U.S. Supreme Court, which has jurisdiction over every other court in the land. Those motives are fixed in a text that explains the law of equal protection. Future litigants, lawyers, and judges can invoke those motives in urging what the law is in future cases. The legacy of *Bush v. Gore* will live on, in spite of the per curiam's efforts to end it with the 2000 election.

Notes

Introduction

1. See, for example, Anne Gearan, "Few Scars Remain from Bush v. Gore," Associated Press, December 11, 2001. Tony Mauro marked the change with two contrasting images in an article commemorating the first anniversary of the *Bush v. Gore* decision: "A year ago, ground zero was the U.S. Supreme Court, where the fate of the presidential election of 2000 was decided. Today, of course, ground zero is in New York City—the hole where the World Trade Center towers once stood." The anniversary of the controversial decision "passed largely unnoted, in the media or elsewhere." "High Court's Political Position Debated One Year after 'Bush v. Gore,'" *American Lawyer Media*, December 19, 2001. Mark Miller, writing for the *National Review*, claimed that after September 11, 2001, "all questions of legitimacy suddenly vanished. In an instant, the controversy over hanging chads came to seem remote and inconsequential. The warnings about the stability of the American constitutional order were rendered utterly beside the point as the country absorbed far greater blows and survived with its constitutional integrity intact." "Florida Refought," September 2, 2002.

2. The official margin of victory was 537 votes out of nearly 6 million.

3. On the creation of the ballot, see Jeffrey Toobin, *Too Close to Call: The Thirty-Six-Day Battle to Decide the 2000 Election* (New York: Random House, 2001), 13–15. In addition to the apparent mistakes in voting for Buchanan (at a rate six times the number in Duval County, Buchanan's north Florida stronghold), more than 19,000 ballots were spoiled through "overvoting," whereby voters punched through two holes for their presidential choice, either because they thought they needed to vote for both Democratic presidential candidate Al Gore and vice-presidential candidate Joseph Lieberman or because they realized they had voted for Buchanan (whose hole appeared to the upper right of the Democratic ticket) and punched a second hole to "correct" their vote. See Jeff Greenfield, *Oh, Waiter! One Order of Crow!* (New York: G. P. Putnam's Sons, 2001), 214. Conservative federal court judge Richard A. Posner admitted that the butterfly ballot was

confusing: "A voter who wanted to vote for Gore had to punch the third chad down; if he punched the second, which was almost level with the word 'Democratic' above Gore and Lieberman's names, he was voting for Buchanan. This would be an easy mistake to make, especially for an inexperienced voter or one with poor eyesight, even though the butterfly format enables larger type and in that respect helps people with poor eyesight." *Breaking the Deadlock: The 2000 Election, the Constitution, and the Court* (Princeton, N.J.: Princeton University Press, 2001), 83. Harvard law professor and Gore attorney Laurence H. Tribe insisted that "televised pictures of the butterfly ballot made clear to millions of Americans how easy it had been to lose one's franchise in Florida." "Erog .v Hsub and Its Disguises: Freeing *Bush v. Gore* from Its Hall of Mirrors," *Harvard Law Review* 115 (2001): 180. Even Pat Buchanan admitted on *The Today Show* that the high number of votes he received were probably meant for Gore. Susan Martin and David Ballinrud, "Long Run to the White House," *St. Petersburg Times,* December 14, 2000.

4. The lack of reliability in the punchcard voting systems in Florida was noted in *Bush v. Gore,* 121 S. Ct. 525, 552 (2000). Pamela A. Karlan quoted a study by political scientist Henry E. Brady that showed that the overvotes (ballots showing votes for more than one presidential candidate) were substantially higher for punchcard voting systems in Florida as well, with three to four rejections in optical-scanner counties versus twenty-five rejections for punchcard counties. "The Newest Equal Protection: Regressive Doctrine on a Changeable Court," in *The Vote: Bush, Gore, and the Supreme Court* Cass R. Sunstein and Richard A. Epstein, eds. (Chicago: University of Chicago Press, 2001), 90. Michael W. McConnell noted that "Every voting system has its flaws, but in ordinary cases the effects are randomly distributed. The problem in Florida arose because the optical scanning system is predominantly used in more Republican areas, while the punchcard system is predominantly used in more Democratic areas. Thus, the errors were not randomly distributed." "Two-and-a-Half Cheers for *Bush v. Gore,*" in Sunstein and Epstein, *The Vote,* 116. Some county-to-county discrepancies were enormous. Paul M. Schwartz noted that "voters in Florida's Gadsden County had a sixty-eight times greater chance of having their votes invalidated than voters in adjoining Leon County." "Voting Technology and Democracy," *New York University Law Review* 77 (2002): 625.

5. Adrian Walker, "Civics Lesson a Harsh One," *Boston Globe,* December 14, 2000, B1.
6. The U.S. Commission on Civil Rights report on the Florida election notes that of the 100 precincts with the highest numbers of disqualified ballots, 83 were majority-black precincts. Furthermore, African-Americans were ten times more likely to have their ballots rejected than whites. *Voting Irregularities in Florida during the 2000 Presidential Election* (Washington, D.C.: GPO, 2001), chap. 9.
7. Ibid., chap. 1.
8. Ibid., chap. 2.
9. Fla. Stat. § 101.62(1)(b) provides that requests for absentee ballots must include nine items of information (and these lacked item 4, the voter registration number) and that they must be filled out by "the elector, a member of the elector's immediate family, or the elector's legal guardian." Obviously, Republican Party officials do not fall into one of these required categories. Two cases acknowledged these legal violations, *Jacobs v. Seminole County Canvassing Board*, 773 So. 2d 519, 522 (Fla. 2000) (per curiam) and *Taylor v. Martin County Canvassing Board*, 773 So. 2d 517, 519 (Fla. 2000) (per curiam). But both insisted there was substantial compliance with the law and avoided the almost impossible task of fashioning a reasonable remedy.
10. The applications for absentee ballots prepared by the Republican Party for its members had been misprinted, leaving off the voter identification information. Michael Cooper, "Democrats See Hope in Absentee Ballot Application Trials," in Correspondents of the New York Times, *36 Days: The Complete Chronicle of the 2000 Presidential Election Crisis* (New York: Times Books, 2001), 244–46 (originally published December 6, 2000).
11. Richard Pérez-Peña, "Furor Erupts over 218 Votes in Nassau County," in Correspondents, *36 Days,* 173–74 (originally published November 26, 2000).
12. Richard Pérez-Peña, "Furor over Absentee Ballots," in Correspondents, *36 Days,* 96–98 (originally published November 18, 2000); Toobin, *Too Close to Call,* 131. Democrats, on the other hand, circulated a four-page memo directing their operatives to challenge ballots that did not meet the strict requirements of the law. A furor erupted over this memo after Republicans leaked it to the press and Republicans charged the Democrats with trying to disenfranchise members of the military. However, Clay Roberts, who worked in Harris's Division of Elections, reportedly told the Democratic lawyer who drafted the

memo that it represented "a correct statement of the law." David A. Kaplan, *The Accidental President: How 413 Lawyers, 9 Supreme Court Justices, and 5,963,110 Floridians (Give or Take a Few) Landed George W. Bush in the White House* (New York: William Morrow, 2001), 161. Several months later, a *New York Times* investigation revealed that the Bush campaign had its own fifty-two-page memo telling its operatives "how to challenge 'illegal' civilian votes that they assumed would be for Mr. Gore and also how to defend equally defective military ballots." David Barstow and Don Van Natta Jr., "Examining the Vote: How Bush Took Florida: Mining the Overseas Absentee Vote," *New York Times,* July 15, 2001, 1.

13. Posner, *Breaking the Deadlock,* 88.

14. Less than a week after the decision was handed down, Tony Mauro reported that the decision "exposed [the Court] to sharp criticism, the likes of which it had not felt even from past controversial decisions on abortion and racial justice." "Is Bush v. Gore Finished for the Supreme Court? Don't Bet on It," *Legal Intelligencer,* December 18, 2000. Ronald Dworkin reported: "I know of no other instance in which so many distinguished academic and professional critics have criticized the Court in such angry and intemperate language, or even suggested, as they did in this case, that some justices had decided for personal and self-serving reasons." "Introduction," in *A Badly Flawed Election: (Debating)* Bush v. Gore, *the Supreme Court and American Democracy,* Ronald Dworkin, ed., (New York: New Press, 2002), 1. See also Posner, *Breaking the Deadlock,* 88–89. Douglas Kellner agreed that the decision "has been fiercely criticized by the legal community." *Grand Theft 2000: Media Spectacle and a Stolen Election* (New York: Rowman & Littlefield, 2001), 98, n. 9. Conservative judge Richard Posner, who defended the decision, noted that the decision had inspired "a great deal of criticism." *Breaking the Deadlock,* 3.

15. The largest collection of them, 443 law professors, signed their names to a full-page advertisement in the January 13, 2001, edition of the *New York Times* denouncing the decision as politically partisan (A7). Their protest was moved to a Web site (www.the-rule-of-law.com), which included a lengthy resolution condemning the decision and demanding congressional censure of the Court. Through 2001, their numbers stood at 673 law professors from 137 different American law schools.

16. A search of the Lexis-Nexis Academic Universe database on July 31, 2006, yielded 1,629 law journal articles citing *Bush v. Gore.* Many of

these articles mention the case only in passing, but scores of them address the issues raised by the decision, with a large majority criticizing the Court's reasoning.

17. Three of these books were consistently critical of the Court's ruling in *Bush v. Gore:* Vincent Bugliosi, *The Betrayal of America: How the Supreme Court Undermined the Constitution and Chose Our President* (New York: Nation Books, 2001); Kellner, *Grand Theft 2000;* and Alan Dershowitz, *Supreme Injustice: How the High Court Hijacked Election 2000* (New York: Oxford University Press, 2001). Seven other books include significant criticism of that decision: Jack N. Rakove, ed., *The Unfinished Election of 2000: Leading Scholars Examine America's Strangest Election* (New York: Basis Books, 2001); Howard Gillman, ed., *The Votes That Counted: How the Court Decided the 2000 Presidential Election* (Chicago: University of Chicago Press, 2001); Bruce A. Ackerman, ed., *Bush v. Gore: The Question of Legitimacy* (New Haven, Conn.: Yale University Press, 2001); Samuel Issacharoff, Pamela S. Karlan, and Richard H. Pildes, eds., *When Elections Go Bad: The Law of Democracy and the Presidential Election of 2000* (Washington, D.C.: Foundation Press, 2001); E. J. Dionne Jr. and William Kristol, eds., *Bush v. Gore: The Court Cases and the Commentary* (Washington, D.C.: Brookings Institution Press, 2001); Sunstein and Epstein, *The Vote;* and Dworkin, *A Badly Flawed Election.*

18. Greenfield, *Oh, Waiter!* 298.

19. "How History Will View the Court," *Newsweek,* September 17, 2001, 35.

20. "The Supreme Court Commits Suicide," *New Republic,* December 25, 2000, 18.

21. Bugliosi, *The Betrayal of America,* 41, 61.

22. "How History Will View the Court." Only Posner attempted a book-length defense of the *Bush v. Gore* decision, yet he did not defend the grounds offered by the majority decision. He noted that the question of whether the Court's decision was correct "is a close one, perhaps unanswerable, and so the possibility that the Court's critics are right and the court lacked adequate grounds for halting the recount ordered by the Florida supreme court cannot be gainsaid." Posner, *Breaking the Deadlock,* 147. He defended the decision on other grounds. Nelson Lund, who clerked for Justice Sandra Day O'Connor and was associate counsel to President George Bush from 1989 to 1992, was one of the only scholars to mount a serious defense of the majority decision on its own terms.

23. Quoted in Nathaniel Hernandez, "Trial Lawyers and Profs Issue Split Opinion on Federal Election Ruling," *Chicago Lawyer* (February 2001): 8.

24. John C. Yoo, "In Defense of the Court's Legitimacy," in Sunstein and Epstein, *The Vote,* 239.

25. Miller, "Florida Refought."

26. This sentiment was ingrained in American political ideology by Thomas Paine in *Common Sense:* "But where says some is the king of America? I'll tell you Friend, he reigns above, and doth not make havoc of mankind like the Royal of Britain. Yet that we may not appear to be defective even in earthly honors, let a day be solemnly set apart for proclaiming the charter; let it be brought forth placed on the divine law, the word of God; let a crown be placed thereon, by which the world may know, that so far as we approve of monarchy, that in America the law is king. For as in absolute governments the king is law, so in free countries the law ought to be king; and there ought to be no other."

27. See William Lewis, "Of Innocence, Exclusion, and the Burning of Flags: The Romantic Realism of the Law," *Southern Communication Journal* 60 (1994): 4–21.

Chapter 1. Judicial Motives in American Jurisprudence

This chapter draws on material first published in three different journals, as well as my dissertation, "Judicial Invention in Cases Contributing to the Development of Corporate Criminal Liability: A Multi-Dimensional Dramatistic Analysis," University of Iowa, 1988 (directed by John R. Lyne). The published sources include the following: "Instantiating 'The Law' and its Dissents in Korematsu v United States: A Dramatistic Analysis of Judicial Discourse," *Quarterly Journal of Speech* 87, no. 1 (2001): 1–24; "On the Rhetorical Analysis of Judicial Discourse and More: A Response to Lewis," *Southern Communication Journal* 61, no. 2 (Winter 1995): 166–73 (reproduced here by kind permission of the Southern States Communication Association); and "Coming to Terms with Kenneth Burke's Pentad," *American Communication Journal* 1, no. 3 (May 1998).

1. Opening Statement before the Senate Judiciary Committee, *New York Times,* September 17, 1987, A28. This statement continues a tradition which, Ronald A. Cass noted, harkens back to "David Hume's *Essays* and the 1780 Constitution of Massachusetts, written by John Adams,

both declaring the aspiration to 'a government of laws and not of men.'" Cass noted that this phrase has been "invoked over and over to describe the rule of law, among philosophers, legal scholars, politicians, and ordinary citizens." *The Rule of Law in America* (Baltimore, Md.: Johns Hopkins University Press, 2001), 2.

2. "The Law Is Left Twisting Slowly in the Wind," *Los Angeles Times,* December 17, 2000.

3. David A. Strauss, *"Bush v. Gore:* What Were They Thinking," in *The Vote: Bush, Gore, and the Supreme Court,* Cass R. Sunstein and Richard A. Epstein, eds. (Chicago: University of Chicago Press, 2001), 204.

4. Michael W. McConnell, "Two-and-a-Half Cheers for Bush v. Gore," in Sunstein and Epstein, *The Vote,* 100.

5. *Journal of Philosophy, Psychology and Scientific Methods* 15, no. 24 (November 21, 1918): 652.

6. Of course, the "flexibility" of law includes more than the constitutional law that concerned Reed. Richard Posner's "pragmatist" views represent this last group, expressing legal skepticism when he claimed that "law could do with some demystification." Richard A. Posner, "Bush v. Gore as Pragmatic Adjudication," in *A Badly Flawed Election: Bush v. Gore, the Supreme Court and American Democracy,* Ronald Dworkin, ed. (New York: New Press, 2002), 202.

7. *The Federalist Papers,* no. 78, in *Great Books of the Western World,* Robert Maynard Hutchins, ed. (Chicago: Encyclopedia Britannica, 1952), 43: 230, 233.

8. Max Lerner, "Constitution and Court As Symbols," *Yale Law Journal* 46 (1937): 1290–1349; Jerome Frank, *Courts on Trial: Myth and Reality in American Justice* (New York: Atheneum, 1969) and "The Cult of the Robe," *Saturday Review of Literature,* October 13, 1945, 12–13 and 80–81; Gregory Casey, "The Supreme Court and Myth: An Empirical Investigation," *Law and Society Review* 8 (1974): 385–419; Roger Cobb and Charles Elder, "Symbolic Identification and Political Behavior," *American Politics Quarterly* 4 (1976): 305–32; Carl McMurray and Malcolm B. Parsons, "Public Attitudes toward the Representational Robes of Legislators and Judges," *Midwest Journal of Political Science* 9 (1965): 167–85; Harry P. Stumpf, "The Political Efficacy of Judicial Symbolism," *Western Political Quarterly* 19 (1966): 293–303.

9. Linda Greenhouse, "Rehnquist, in New Arena, Appears at Home," *New York Times,* January 7, 1999; Charles Krauthammer, "The Winner in Bush v. Gore? It's Chief Justice Rehnquist, Who Runs the Most Trusted Institution in the U.S.," *Time,* December 18, 2000.

10. The 1805 case was against Justice Samuel Chase, a partisan who vigorously enforced the Sedition Acts (passed by John Adams's administration) against Republican editors and politicians. More recently, movements for the impeachment of Chief Justice Earl Warren and Justice William O. Douglas failed as well. Richard Ellis, "Impeachment," in *The Oxford Companion to the Supreme Court of the United States,* Kermit L. Hall, ed. (Cambridge, U.K.: Oxford University Press, 1992), s.v.

11. Ronald Dworkin, *Taking Rights Seriously* (Cambridge, Mass.: Harvard University Press, 1977), 3.

12. The exceptional cases of President Andrew Jackson's refusal to enforce the Court's decision in *Worcester v. Georgia,* 31 U.S. (6 Pet.) 512 (1832), and President Abraham Lincoln's ignoring of the habeas corpus ruling in *Ex Parte Merryman,* F. Cas. 9387 (1861), simply prove the rule. See Kermit L. Hall, "Jackson, Andrew," *Oxford Companion to the Supreme Court,* s.v.; and Harold M. Hyman, "Lincoln, Abraham," *Oxford Companion to the Supreme Court,* s.v.

13. The term is from Thomas Lessl, "The Priestly Voice," *Quarterly Journal of Speech* 75 (1989): 183–97.

14. Of course, in the constitutive sense that what the Supreme Court says is law becomes precedent that must be followed by lower courses, what they say the law is *is* the law. The distinction here is that the Supreme Court typically asserts that its characterizations of law are not novel but simply reflective of what the law was prior to its decision.

15. This phrase is applied to "Platonic models of authority" in the human sciences by Michael Calvin McGee and John R. Lyne in "What Are Nice Folks Like You Doing in a Place Like This? Some Entailments of Treating Knowledge Claims Rhetorically," in *The Rhetoric of the Human Sciences,* John S. Nelson, Allan Megill, and Donald N. McCloskey, eds. (Madison: University of Wisconsin Press, 1987), 393.

16. In fact, this is the heart of the criticism by the critical legal studies movement.

17. See, for example, John R. Lyne, "Claiming the High Ground: Universalist Rhetoric in a Post-Modern Context," in *Argument in Controversy,* Donn W. Parson, ed. (Annandale, Va.: Speech Communication Association, 1991), 55.

18. Assuming that a widespread recognition that the rule of law does not constrain and a straightforward adoption of some social agenda rather than another, one gets "sincerity" of the sort referred to here.

University of Texas law professor Sandford Levinson tried to articulate this problem in discussing harder forms of legal realism, noting: "Full-scale realism leaves one without the ability to argue that legal arguments can be assessed by their conformity to norms that can be invoked, by judges and others, to discipline the vagaries of political choice." Sandford Levinson, "Return of Legal Realism," *The Nation*, January 8, 2001.

19. The distinction between constructing and reconstructing acts is sometimes blurry. Here the term *reconstructing* is used to stress that a given act already has an obvious or standard construction which a court's *re*construction would try to alter. Archbishop Richard Whately would say that existing constructions have "presumption," though this is a metaphorical and nonlegal sense of presumption, intended to convey the sense of rhetorical deference given to existing constructions. See Richard Whately, *Elements of Rhetoric* (1828; reprint, Carbondale, Ill.: Southern Illinois University Press, 1963).

20. 53 U.S. (12 How.) 443 (1851).

21. 23 U.S. (10 Wheat.) 428 (1825).

22. Ibid., 429.

23. Ibid., 454–55.

24. Ibid., 455.

25. Ibid., 456.

26. Ibid., 456.

27. This may seem a heretical claim to those who have devoted decades to the analysis of deductive, analogical, and inductive reasoning in legal discourse. Those forms of reasoning and argument are significant in judicial discourse; however, characterization makes the use of those forms possible. For some purposes, it may be valuable to see analysis of characterization in judicial opinions as a form of micro-analysis, which focuses on words, phrases, metaphors, and the like, whereas analysis of formal reasoning processes is more of a macro-analysis, which to some extent takes the work done at the micro level as a given.

28. Characterization can work in concert with syllogistic and analogical forms of reasoning, by bringing into alignment elements in major and minor premises or in two analogized things. For example, strategic characterizations of facts may help audiences see how they fit into general categories that are used in major premises or may help to show how two disparate situations actually are similar enough to justify an analogy.

29. *Embodying* needs to be clarified somewhat at this point. While judicial motives are typically constructed in judicial opinions, that discourse is not the only standard against which judicial motives are assessed. Judges typically come to cases with prior reputations—as Republicans and Democrats, strict constructionists and activist judges, First Amendment guardians and states' rights advocates, European-American males and Jewish-American females, and so forth. Judges must be sensitive to the ways in which their motives may be constructed by others based upon the reputations they bring to the decisions. So, for example, a criticism of the *Bush v. Gore* majority was that they violated their own prior statements about equal protection law and their own principles as defenders of states' rights. Thus, motives are not merely characterized but embodied by judges who are judged using extrajudicial or extradecisional factors.

30. *Bush v. Gore* involved the review of a Florida State Supreme Court ruling concerning Florida law. Normally, great deference is given to state courts in interpreting their own law; thus, the *Bush v. Gore* majority had to characterize the actions of the Florida high court carefully to justify its intervention and overruling.

31. See Edward H. Levi, *An Introduction to Legal Reasoning* (Chicago: University of Chicago Press, 1949).

32. Again, *The Genesee Chief* provides an example, whereby "eminent" jurists (including Justice Joseph Story) are characterized as "sadly mistaken," because the case before them did not press them to think harder about the real purpose behind the common-law tradition of limiting the admiralty jurisdiction to "the ebb and flow of the tide." The *Bush v. Gore* decision is unusual in inspiring dissents and outside criticisms that imply or state outright that the majority decision was driven by personal interests.

33. *Korematsu v. United States*, 323 U.S. 214, 243 (1944).

34. Dramatism was most fully developed in Kenneth Burke, *A Grammar of Motives* (1945; reprint, Berkeley: University of California Press, 1969). For a review of scholarly applications of pentadic criticism, see Clarke Rountree, "Coming to Terms with Kenneth Burke's Pentad," *American Communication Journal* 1, no. 3 (May 1998).

35. Burke, *A Grammar*, xv.

36. Ibid.

37. See Ibid., 443. The original terms of analysis constitute the dramatistic pentad; the addition of attitude makes this a hexad. Whether attitude is necessary to action, as the other terms are, is unclear. Insofar

as an attitude functions as "incipient action" or as a substitute for action, this term represents a logical extension of the term *act*. In any case, the term seems useful, if not necessary, for certain types of analysis.

38. Kenneth Burke, "Dramatism," in *Drama in Life: The Uses of Communication in Society,* James E. Combs and Michael W. Mansfield, eds. (New York: Hastings House, 1976), 9; Conversations with Kenneth Burke, video interviews, Department of Communication Studies, University of Iowa, 1987, time index 3:53.

39. Burke, *A Grammar,* xix.

40. The term *configuration* here is not meant to stress form over content in the establishment of motives. The pentadic terms have, as Burke notes, "certain formal interrelationships . . . by reason of their role as attributes of a common ground or substance" (Burke, *A Grammar,* xix), and those interrelationships ensure that putting one term first, or stressing it more, or describing its qualities more fully, or suggesting explicitly that it dominates other terms, will take away from the significance of other terms, in a zero-sum calculus. In theory, it might be possible to characterize motives in a given case in a way that gives equal weight to each of the pentadic terms and leaves those trying to understand action with a sense of mixed motives; in practice, achieving such terministic impartiality is difficult, not simply because our worldviews tend to lead us to certain assumptions about action that color the most scientific interpretations but also because something has to come first (either in the linear sequencing of texts describing actions and motives or in "catching our eye" as we perceive elements of action).

41. Burke himself has applied the pentadic terms to analyses of paraphrases (*A Grammar,* 16), myths (*A Grammar,* 63), colloquialisms (*A Grammar,* 24), jokes (Conversations, 0:14), and dreams (*A Grammar,* 301), among other things.

42. Jane Blankenship and her colleagues provided an exception to this focus on the verbal in considering the transformation of Ronald Reagan's image on camera into an element of the scene of the Republican presidential primary debates. Jane Blankenship, Marlene G. Fine, and Leslie K. Davis, "The 1980 Republican Primary Debates: The Transformation of Actor to Scene," *Quarterly Journal of Speech* 69 (1983): 25–36. Burke has never limited himself to the analysis of strictly verbal texts; consider, for example, his analyses of cartoons (Conversations, 4:11), action in plays (*A Grammar,* 3–7), and dreams (*A Grammar,* 301).

43. *Motive* in the sense defined here does not exist outside a text that places the elements of action into a configuration, strategic or otherwise. That begs the difficult question of what a text is. Rhetorical critics typically solve this knotty problem by positing some rhetorical artifact as the text under analysis—a transcript of a speech, a videotape recording of a campaign advertisement, or (here) the official record of a Supreme Court opinion. Volumes could be written on the shortcomings of this approach. In the case of the analysis here, the use of the *Bush v. Gore* text can be justified because the written record of the Supreme Court decision *is* the crucial text for those who interpret the motives of the Supreme Court in an attempt to understand what the law is on a given issue. Many constructing the Court's motives in *Bush v. Gore* will expand this text to consider related acts. For individuals interpreting motives, the text is framed by their own perception and consciousness. Thus, they may witness spontaneous acts such as children playing in the park, interpreting the motives of the child who leaps off the swing as it reaches its apex (and the one who refuses to do so) or more complex acts such as their legislator explaining her actions in voting for a certain bill (where the legislator's motive for so construing her motives is considered). In the case of both critics and lay observers of motives, it is impossible to say exactly where the text ends, since we interpret texts within contexts, which are informed by our earlier experiences of similar contexts, which were informed by our earlier experiences of similar contexts, and so on, ad infinitum. Such contexts educate us about what kinds of agents there are, what they are likely to do, where they are likely to go, what agencies they typically employ, what attitudes they carry, and why they act; what kinds of scenes there are, how they influence action, what attitudes they inspire, who will be found in them, and so forth, for all the pentadic terms. Rhetorical critics attempt to bring to light what they perceive as the most rhetorically significant aspects of a given context in understanding a given text's construction of motives.

44. A complete analysis would look at each term in relation to every other term for a total of fifteen combinations (scene-act, scene-agent, scene-agency, scene-purpose, scene-attitude, act-agent, act-agency, act-purpose, act-attitude, agent-agency, agent-purpose, agent-attitude, agency-purpose, agency-attitude, and purpose-attitude), or thirty if these terministic influences are considered in reverse (e.g., the scene contains the act [scene-act], but an act may create a scene

[act-scene]). The number of ratios analyzed should be determined by the text under study, since some rhetors may ignore certain terms and ratios altogether.

45. Burke, *A Grammar,* 12.

46. Ibid., xviii; emphasis in original.

47. See Clarke Rountree, "Instantiating 'The Law' and Its Dissents in *Korematsu v. United States:* A Dramatistic Analysis of Judicial Discourse," *Quarterly Journal of Speech* 87 (February 2001): 1–24.

48. Burke, "Dramatism," 450.

49. The functioning of such pentadic relationships is deceptively simple but rhetorically complex. Characterizing a scene alone may make an audience think, "We've got to do X (which is required by such scenes)!" In this sense, it is a sort of persuasion that works unconsciously, surreptitiously, or at least indirectly. Rhetors can insist that they were "dragged" by an audience to the conclusion that their characterization made appropriate. But characterizing a scene also may be used as a prelude to directly calling for action, so that a rhetor makes the ground fertile for his or her recommendation.

50. Burke, *A Grammar* 13, quoting *Korematsu v. United States,* 323 U.S. 214, 220 (1944).

51. Part of what it means to be a member of a given culture is understanding such terministic expectations. It allows such sexist expressions as "What's a nice girl like you doing in a place like this?" (an agent-scene relationship) to be understandable.

52. 410 U.S. 113, 124 (1973).

53. Ibid., 172 (1973) (Rehnquist, J., dissenting).

54. Ibid., 125 (1973).

Chapter 2. The Road to Bush v. Gore

1. "2000 Presidential Election: Popular Vote Totals," National Archives and Records Administration, www.nara.gov/fedreg/elctcoll/2000popres .html.

2. Jeff Greenfield, *Oh, Waiter! One Order of Crow!* (New York: G. P. Putnam's Sons, 2001), 58.

3. Part of the error was an added digit on the Jacksonville returns, which gave Gore a 43,023-to-1,026 lead in place of the actual 4,302-to-1,026 lead. David A. Kaplan, *The Accidental President: How 413 Lawyers, 9 Supreme Court Justices, and 5,953,110 (Give or Take a Few)*

Floridians Landed George W. Bush in the White House (New York: William Morrow, 2001), 10–11.

4. Ibid., 12–26.

5. Bush's 1,784-vote original lead dropped to 300 on November 14, after Harris certified the first vote tallies, jumped to 930 on November 18, after the overseas ballots were added in, and fell to 537 when Harris certified the final vote on November 26. The 154-vote lead was the unofficial tally when the U.S. Supreme Court stopped the recounts on December 9. See Correspondents of the New York Times, *36 Days: The Complete Chronicle of the 2000 Presidential Election Crisis* (New York: Times Books, 2001), 174; and Kevin Sack, "Federal Court Had Just Voted for Recount," in Correspondents, *36 Days,* 279 (originally published December 10, 2000).

6. Frank Bruni, "As Bush Lead Shrinks to 327 He Urges Gore to Concede," in Correspondents, *36 Days,* 28–29 (originally published November 11, 2000).

7. David Firestone and Michael Cooper, "Bush Sues in Federal Court to Stop Recount," in Correspondents, *36 Days,* 39–42 (originally published November 11, 2000); Kevin Sack, "Federal Judge Defers to State Court," in Correspondents, *36 Days,* 62 (originally published November 14, 2000); Todd S. Purdum, "Florida Court Rules for Recounts and Bush Goes Federal Again," in Correspondents, *36 Days,* 86 (originally published November 17, 2000); and Todd S. Purdum, "Bush Hammered in Several Courts," in Correspondents, *36 Days,* 94 (originally published November 18, 2000).

8. Todd S. Purdum and David Firestone, "Democrats Scramble over Tuesday Deadline," in Correspondents, *36 Days,* 60 (originally published November 14, 2000).

9. Jeffrey Toobin, *Too Close to Call: The Thirty-Six-Day Battle to Decide the 2000 Election* (New York: Random House, 2001), 69. See also Kaplan, *The Accidental President,* 64, 106–109, esp. 108 on this particular quotation.

10. Toobin, *Too Close to Call,* 75.

11. Political Staff of the Washington Post, *Deadlock: The Inside Story of America's Closest Election* (New York: Public Affairs, 2001), ix; Dana Canedy, "After a Partial Recount, Broward County Drops the Whole Idea," in Correspondents, *36 Days,* 65 (originally published November 14, 2000).

12. Todd S. Purdum, "Democrats Dispute Friday Deadline," in Correspondents, *36 Days,* 70–71 (originally published November 15, 2000); Dana

Canedy, "Broward County Panel Reconsiders Manual Countywide Recount," in Correspondents, *36 Days*, 74–75 (originally published November 15, 2000); Richard L. Berke, "Harris Stymies Gore's Recount Strategy," in Correspondents, *36 Days*, 78–79 (originally published November 16, 2000); Richard A. Posner, *Breaking the Deadlock: The 2000 Election, the Constitution, and the Court* (Princeton, N.J.: Princeton University Press, 2001), 94.

13. Harris's specific statement (included in a memorandum to county election officials) was as follows: "With regard to the status of overseas absentee ballots, they must have been executed as of last Tuesday. They must bear a foreign postmark as provided in Section 101.62(7), and they must be received by the supervisors of elections by midnight Friday. They are not required, however, to be postmarked on or prior to last Tuesday [November 7, Election Day]" "Counting the Vote: Memo Outlining Overseas Rules," *New York Times*, November 18, 2000, A11. See also Richard Pérez-Peña, "Furor over Absentee Ballots," in Correspondents, *36 Days*, 96–97 (originally published November 18, 2000); and Richard Pérez-Peña, "Military Ballots Merit a Review, Lieberman Says," in Correspondents, *36 Days*, 112 (originally published November 20, 2000). Many county election officials ignored the secretary's order. Pérez-Peña, "Furor over Absentee Ballots," 97–98.

14. Pérez-Peña, "Furor over Absentee Ballots," 98; and Michael Moss, "Seminole County Absentee Case Goes to Court," in Correspondents, *36 Days*, 118 (originally published November 21, 2000).

15. *Gore v. Harris*, 772 So. 2d 1243, 1248 (Fla. 2000); Richard Pérez-Peña, "Furor Erupts over 218 Votes in Nassau County," in Correspondents, *36 Days*, 173 (originally published November 27, 2000).

16. David Firestone, "Two Setbacks for Gore in Florida Courts," in Correspondents, *36 Days*, 215 (originally published December 2, 2000).

17. Michael Cooper, "Gore Loses Both Absentee Ballot Suits," in Correspondents, *36 Days*, 271–72 (originally published December 9, 2000).

18. Amid charges that they were trying to throw out the ballots of military personnel, Democratic vice-presidential candidate Joseph Lieberman asked that the canvassing boards reconsider their decision to throw out military votes lacking a postmark. Pérez-Peña, "Military Ballots Merit a Review," 111.

19. Purdum, "Democrats Dispute," 70–71.

20. Purdum, "Florida Court Rules for Recounts," 85–86.

21. Purdum, "Bush Hammered," 94.

22. *Gore v. Harris*.

23. *Fladell v. Palm Beach County Canvassing Board,* 772 So. 2d 1240 (Fla. 2000).

24. Paul Gigot, conservative columnist for the *Wall Street Journal,* called this a "bourgeois riot," which he asserted, approvingly, had caused the Miami-Dade canvassing board to "cave." "Burgher Rebellion," *Wall Street Journal,* November 24, 2000, quoted in Alan Dershowitz, *Supreme Injustice: How the High Court Hijacked Election 2000* (New York: Oxford University Press, 2001), 37.

25. Firestone, "Two Setbacks," 215.

26. *Bush v. Palm Beach County Canvassing Board,* 121 S. Ct. 471 (2000) (per curiam).

27. *Bush v. Gore,* 121 S. Ct. 512 (2000) (stay order).

28. *Bush v. Gore,* 121 S. Ct. 525 (2000).

29. Richard L. Berke and Katharine Q. Seelye, "Gore Bows Out and Urges Unity," in Correspondents, *36 Days,* 310 (originally published December 14, 2000).

30. Alison Mitchell, "Over Some Objections, Congress Certifies Electoral Vote," *New York Times,* January 7, 2001.

31. 772 So. 2d 1220 (Fla. 2000). The facts of this case, as reviewed below, are laid out in pages 1225–27 of the decision. Further page number references to this case will be made in the text.

32. *Bush v. Palm Beach County Canvassing Board,* 121 S Ct 510 (2000).

33. Federal law requires that overseas ballots be received within ten days of the election and this requirement supersedes Florida's seven-day requirement for all other votes.

34. Purdum, "Florida Court Rules," 85–87.

35. Fla. Stat. § 102.166(5).

36. Quoting the Division of Elections' advisory opinion at 772 So. 2d 1220, 1228.

37. Fla. Stat. § 102.166 (4)(b).

38. The choice of this specific deadline was not explained in the opinion. However, after the U.S. Supreme Court remanded the case back to the Florida Supreme Court for further explanation of the basis of the decision, the state court explained that the canvassing boards would have had until November 18 to submit their totals even without a protest, because final certification could not occur until the federal deadline for overseas ballots was met. Because the Division of Elections' misinterpretation of the election code on November 13 deprived the canvassing boards of five days for recounting, the state court's November 21 decision gave those five days back, creating a

new deadline of November 26. See *Palm Beach County Canvassing Board v. Harris,* 772 So. 2d 1273, 1290 (2000) (corrected).

39. Petition for Writ of Certiorari, *Bush v. Palm Beach County Canvassing Board,* No. 00–836 (filed November 22, 2000), 18–20, quoting U.S. Const. Art II § I, cl 2.

40. Ibid., 12–18.

41. Ibid., 20–26.

42. Linda Greenhouse, "Highest Court, Surprisingly, Agrees to Hear Bush's Appeal," in Correspondents, *36 Days,* 150 (originally published November 25, 2000).

43. *Siegel v. LePore,* 121 S. Ct. 510 (2000). The Supreme Court's rejection of the appeal was "without prejudice," ensuring that Bush could renew the appeal if necessary.

44. During oral arguments, given that the certification had taken place naming Bush the winner in Florida, Justice Stephen G. Breyer asked, "Is there any respect in which this really makes a difference?" Linda Greenhouse, "Sharp Questioning Reveals a Deeply Divided Court," in Correspondents, *36 Days,* 206 (originally published December 2, 2000). See also Elizabeth Garrett, "Leaving the Decision to Congress," in *The Vote: Bush, Gore, and the Supreme Court,* Cass R. Sunstein and Richard A. Epstein, eds. (Chicago: University of Chicago Press, 2001), 45–56.

45. *Bush v. Palm Beach County Canvassing Board,* 121 S. Ct. 471, 475 (2000).

46. *Gore v. Harris,* 772 So. 2d 1243 (Fla. 2000). Further page number references to this decision will be made in the text.

47. *Gore v. Harris,* 1248. Nassau County's automatic recounts included 218 fewer ballots than the original Election Night totals. For most counties' recounts, the number of votes went higher, presumably because the chads in incompletely punched ballots fell out during their second run through the machines. See Pérez-Peña, "Furor Erupts," 173–74.

48. There is a strong chance that this prediction will become a self-fulfilling prophecy, since the court granting the stay can take whatever actions are necessary to make it true; thus, the means for granting the stay could become the ends of the final decision in the case. Of course, that cannot be a *public* motive for judicial decision making, since finding for a petitioner to preserve the credibility of a stay order is letting the tail wag the dog. But, undoubtedly, there is a bit of judicial face at stake (an agent concern, linking stay-based agencies and appellate decision-based purposes across two acts).

49. *Bush v. Gore,* 121 S. Ct. 512 (2000) (stay order). Further references to this stay order will be made in the text.

50. David A. Strauss, *"Bush v. Gore:* What Were They Thinking?" in Sunstein and Epstein, *The Vote,* 189.
51. Quoting *National Socialist Party of America v. Skokie,* 434 U.S. 1327, 1328 (1977) (Stevens, J., in chambers), at 513.
52. For a recent recitation of these rules, see *Rubin v. United States,* 524 U.S. 1301 (1998).

Chapter 3. The U.S. Supreme Court Decides the Election

1. Douglas Kellner, *Grand Theft 2000: Media Spectacle and a Stolen Election* (New York: Rowman & Littlefield, 2001), 99–100.
2. Jeff Greenfield, *Oh, Waiter! One Order of Crow!* (New York: G. P. Putnam's Sons, 2001), 286–87.
3. *Bush v. Gore,* 121 S. Ct. 525 (2000). Further references to this case will be made in the text.
4. The landmark First Amendment decision in *Brandenburg v. Ohio,* 395 U.S. 444 (1969), was a rare major per curiam decision, though it was unanimous.
5. Justice Kennedy appears to have been the primary author of the majority opinion. See Alan Dershowitz, *Supreme Injustice: How the High Court Hijacked Election 2000* (New York: Oxford University Press, 2001), 163.
6. Only the minority concurring opinion of Chief Justice Rehnquist, joined by Justices Scalia and Thomas, urged that an Article II violation had occurred.
7. Noted in *Gore v. Harris,* 772 So. 2d 1243, 1255 (Fla. 2000) (emphasis added).
8. Actually, the majority goes a bit further in stating that the state legislature has the "power to appoint members of the Electoral College" (529). Article II, Section 1, says that "Each *State* shall appoint" the electors (emphasis added). However, since the state legislature could choose itself to make this appointment, it ultimately may exercise this power.
9. 383 U.S. 663 (1966).
10. 377 U.S. 533 (1964).
11. Clarke Rountree, "Instantiating 'The Law' and Its Dissents in *Korematsu v. United States:* A Dramatistic Analysis of Judicial Discourse," *Quarterly Journal of Speech* 87 (2001): 7.
12. *Gore v. Harris,* 772 So. 2d 1243, 1262.
13. Ibid., 1248.
14. 372 U.S. 368 (1963).

15. 394 U.S. 814 (1969).
16. This ostensible requirement to identify groups is based on the identi-fication of groups in the precedent cases the majority cites and in well-developed equal protection law since those cases were decided. However, the *Bush v. Gore* decision may have created a new rule for equal protection law. See, for example, Frank Michelman, "Suspicion, or the New Prince," in *The Vote: Bush, Gore, and the Supreme Court,* Cass R. Sunstein and Richard A. Epstein, eds. (Chicago: University of Chicago Press, 2001), 129.
17. As the majority put it: "The Florida Supreme Court's decision [to ac-cept partial recounts from Miami-Dade County] thus gives no assur-ance that the recounts included in a final certification must be complete" (531–32).
18. On drawing this evil-foolish distinction, see Clarke Rountree, "The President As God, the Recession as Evil: *Actus, Status,* and the Presi-dent's Rhetorical Bind in the 1992 Elections," *Quarterly Journal of Speech* 81 (1995): 346–47.
19. In considering media coverage of the case, Kellner noted that on No-vember 22, 2000, "almost every legal authority interviewed on televi-sion doubted whether the U.S. Supreme Court would accept the Bush request [to stop the recounts] on the grounds that there was no real federal issue, that the Florida Supreme Court was the legitimate site for adjudication of state election disputes, and that there would not be enough time for the U.S. Supreme Court to deliberate and ade-quately assess the issues involved." *Grand Theft 2000,* 56. See also Michelman, "Suspicion," 131; and David A. Strauss, "*Bush v. Gore:* What Were They Thinking?" in Sunstein and Epstein, *The Vote,* 193.
20. Quoting 460 U.S. 780, 794–95, at 534 (emphasis added).
21. 146 U.S. 1 (1892).
22. The cases were *NAACP v. Alabama ex rel. Patterson,* 357 U.S. 449 (1958), and *Bouie v. City of Columbia,* 378 U.S. 347 (1964), cited at 535.
23. See U.S. Commission on Civil Rights, *Voting Irregularities in Florida During the 2000 Presidential Election* (Washington, D.C.: Government Printing Office, 2001).

Chapter 4. The Dissent Reconstructs Majority Action

1. *Bush v. Gore,* 121 S. Ct. 525, 539 (2000). Further references to this case will be made in the text.
2. 146 U.S. 1 (1892).

3. *Bush v. Gore*, 542, citing *Rivers v. Roadway Express, Inc.*, 511 U.S. 298, 312–13 (1994).

4. Obviously, a state court can get the law wrong, as the Supreme Court recognized in the civil rights cases of *NAACP v. Alabama ex rel. Patterson*, 357 U.S. 449 (1958), and *Bouie v. City of Columbia*, 378 U.S. 347 (1964), cited by Rehnquist at 535.

5. *Marbury v. Madison*, 5 U.S. (1 Cranch) 137 (1803).

6. The case is *Victor v. Nebraska*, 511 U.S. 1 (1994), quoting page 5.

7. Stevens did not mention the majority's assertion that under the Florida court order, observers were prohibited from objecting during the recount, so the mechanism by which disputed ballots would reach Judge Terry Lewis appeared problematic. However, Lewis had announced to the parties that he would hear objections at the end of the tallying, probably to ensure that Republicans did not use objections as a delaying tactic as they had before. See David Barstow and Alison Mitchell, "Republicans See a 'Mess,' Democrats See 'Smooth' Process," in Correspondents of the New York Times, *36 Days: The Complete Chronicle of the 2000 Presidential Election Crisis* (New York: Times Books, 2001), 121–22 (originally published November 21, 2000); Theodore O. Prosise and Craig R. Smith, "The Supreme Court's Ruling in *Bush v. Gore:* A Rhetoric of Inconsistency," *Rhetoric & Public Affairs* 4 (2001): 612; and David A. Kaplan, *The Accidental President: How 413 Lawyers, 9 Supreme Court Justices, and 5,953,110 (Give or Take a Few) Floridians Landed George W. Bush in the White House* (New York: William Morrow, 2001), 234.

8. Quoting *Bain Peanut Co. of Tex. v. Pinson*, 282 U.S. 499, 501 (1931), at 541.

9. Jeffrey Toobin, *Too Close to Call: The Thirty-Six-Day Battle to Decide the 2000 Election* (New York: Random House, 2001), 161.

10. Quoting *Sumner v. Mata*, 449 U.S. 539, 549 (1981), at 546.

11. Quoting *Chevron U.S.A., Inc. v. Natural Resources Defense Council, Inc.*, 467 U.S. 837, 843 (1984) at 546.

12. Citing *William & Mary Law Review* 22 (1981): 813, at 547.

13. Quoting *General Motors Corp. v. Romein*, 503 U.S. 181 (1992), at 547.

14. Quoting *Central Union Telephone Co. v. Edwardsville*, 269 U.S. 190 (1925), at 547. See also three cases cited at 547, n. 1.

15. Quoting *Lehman Brothers v. Schein*, 416 U.S. 386, 391 (1974), at 547.

16. Quoting *Arizonans for Official English v. Arizona*, 520 U.S. 43, 79 (1997), at 547.

17. Quoting *Lehman Brothers v. Schein*, at 548.

18. *Fairfax's Devisee v. Hunter's Lessee,* 12 U.S. (7 Cranch) 603 (1813).
19. The book cited was Gerald Gunther and Kathleen Sullivan, *Constitutional Law,* 13th ed. (Westbury, N.Y.: Foundation Press, 1997).
20. *Martin v. Hunter's Lessee,* 14 U.S. (1 Wheat.) 305 (1814), cited at 548. This pathmarking decision upheld section 25 of the 1789 Judiciary Act in empowering federal courts to review the final judgments of the highest state courts where federal statutes or treaties were involved or where a state law or common-law rule upheld by the state was challenged under the federal constitution.
21. *NAACP v. Alabama ex rel. Patterson,* 357 U.S. 449 (1958).
22. *Bouie v. City of Columbia,* 378 U.S. 347 (1964).
23. *Bush v. Gore,* 121 S. Ct. 525, 534 (2000) (Rehnquist, C.J., concurring), cited by Ginsburg at 549.
24. Citing *Saenz v. Roe,* 526 U.S. 489, 504, n. 17 (1999), citing *U.S. Term Limits, Inc. v. Thornton,* 514 U.S. 779, 838 (1995) (Kennedy, J., concurring).
25. Justice Souter had discussed the issue of overvotes by way of considering the work required for a recount. He relied on Justice Breyer's disposition of the issue in his dissent at 545.
26. The Florida Supreme Court followed § 101.5614(5) in looking for a "clear indication of the intent of the voter."
27. This recount was conducted by BDO Seidman, LLP, at the request of the *Miami Herald,* Knight Ridder, and *USA Today.* Richard Posner, who defended the *Bush* decision, said this was "[t]he most responsible media recount to date" *Breaking the Deadlock: The 2000 Election, the Constitution, and the Court* (Princeton, N.J.: Princeton University Press, 2001), 66. He also noted that "[a] subsequent report, on the consortium's statewide recount of undervotes, found that Bush would have won unless *only* fully punched through chads were counted." Citing Martin Merzer, "But Gore Backers Have Some Points to Argue," *Miami Herald,* April 4, 2001, A1, at 66. The consortium's findings are reported in Martin Merzer and the Staff of the Miami Herald, *The Miami Herald Report: Democracy Held Hostage* (New York: St. Martin's Press, 2001).
28. The other dissenters attacked the idea that the federal safe harbor deadline itself had some binding effect on the states, rather than the specific claim that the Florida Supreme Court itself had found that Florida law required that the safe harbor deadline be met.
29. *Bush v. Gore,* 552 (Rehnquist, C.J., concurring). Breyer cited page 41 of *McPherson,* whereas Stevens relied on page 25.

30. He introduced it not with the customary "even if" but with "in any event" (553).

31. *Black's Law Dictionary* (St. Paul, Minn.: West Publishing, 1979), 419.

32. Rehnquist had insisted that the secretary "is authorized by law to issue binding interpretations of the election code" (537).

33. *Bush v. Gore*, 537 (Rehnquist, C.J., concurring). The precedent case was *Krivanek v. Take Back Tampa Political Committee*, 625 So. 2d 840, 844 (Fla. 1993).

34. Section 97.012(1) gives the secretary of state the responsibility to "[o]btain and maintain uniformity in the application, operation, and interpretation of the election laws." Section 106.23 gives the Division of Elections, which the secretary heads, the authority for providing advisory opinions that are "binding on any person or organization who sought the opinion or with reference to whom the opinion was sought, unless material facts were omitted or misstated in the request for the advisory opinion." Obviously, just because an advisory opinion is binding on canvassing boards and others who request the opinion does not mean that it is binding on the courts. Indeed, in the *Krivanek* case cited by the chief justice, the Florida Supreme Court explicitly held that such opinions are "not binding judicial precedent"; however, the court added, "advisory opinions of affected agency heads are persuasive authority and, if the construction of law in those opinions is reasonable, they are entitled to great weight in construing the law as applied to that affected agency of government" (844). One could argue, contrary to Rehnquist, that great weight is not the same as deference.

35. Citing *In re Election of U.S. Representative for Second Congressional District*, 231 Conn. 602, 621, 653 A.2d 79, 90–91 (1994), and *Brown v. Carr*, 130 W. Va. 455, 460, 43 S.E.2d 401, 404–405 (1947), at 554.

36. Citing the Electoral Count Act of 1887, 24 Stat. 373 and 3 U.S.C. §§ 5, 6, and 16, at 555.

37. Quoting H. Rep. No. 1638, from Representative Caldwell, Select Committee on the Election of President and Vice-President, 49th Cong., 1st Sess., 2, at 556.

38. Quoting 18 Cong. Rec. 30, 31 (1886), at 556.

39. Quoting Madison's remarks of July 25, 1787 from *Elliot's Debates on the Federal Constitution*, 2d. ed., vol. 5 (1876), 363, at 556.

40. Quoting "Loth, Chief Justice John Marshall and the Growth of the American Republic 365 (1948)," at 557. Although Jackson did refuse to enforce the Court order, Kermit L. Hall insisted "[he] did not make

that statement." "Jackson, Andrew," in *The Oxford Companion to the Supreme Court of the United States,* Kermit L. Hall, ed. (Cambridge, U.K.: Oxford University Press, 1992), s.v.

41. Quoting *United States v. Butler,* 297 U.S. 1, 79 (1936) (Stone, J., dissenting), at 557.

Chapter 5. Reporters Reconstruct the Supreme Court's Action

1. Robert E. Denton Jr. and Gary C. Woodward, *Political Communication in America* (Westport, Conn.: Praeger, 1985).

2. As Kenneth Burke has argued, "Wherever there is persuasion, there is rhetoric. And wherever there is 'meaning,' there is 'persuasion.'" *A Rhetoric of Motives* (1950; reprint, Berkeley: University of California Press, 1969), 172.

3. John Aloysius Farrell, "Scalia Hints at Court's View," *Boston Globe,* December 10, 2000, A39.

4. Kenneth Burke, *A Grammar of Motives* (1945; reprint, Berkeley: University of California Press, 1969), 443.

5. Charles Lane, "High Court Fractures, and Exposes the Seams," *Washington Post,* December 10, 2000, A1.

6. Laura Mechler, "Court's Reputation for Nonpartisanship Could Be at Stake in Bush v. Gore," Associated Press, December 10, 2000.

7. Finlay Lewis, "High Court May Have Slammed Door on Gore," *San Diego Union-Tribune,* December 13, 2000, A1. See also Joan Biskupic, "Ruling Reveals Depth of Divide on the Court," *USA Today,* December 13, 2000, A3; Robert G. Kaiser, "Opinion Is Sharply Divided on Ruling's Consequences," *Washington Post,* December 14, 2000; and Anne Gearan, "Divided Supreme Court Ruling May Leave Lasting Taint on Court," Associated Press, December 13, 2000.

8. Kaiser, "Opinion Is Sharply Divided."

9. Linda Greenhouse, "Bush Prevails by Single Vote, Justices End Recount, Blocking Gore after 5-Week Struggle," *New York Times,* December 13, 2000, A1.

10. Gearan, "Divided Supreme Court Ruling."

11. Evan Thomas and Michael Isikoff, "The Truth behind the Pillars," *Newsweek,* December 25, 2000, 46.

12. Lewis, "High Court May Have Slammed Door."

13. Henry Weinstein, "Bush Wins in Supreme Court," *Los Angeles Times,* December 13, 2000, A1.

14. Charles Lane, "Decision Sharpens the Justices' Divisions," *Washington Post*, December 13, 2000, A1.

15. William Carlsen, "Split Decision May Tarnish Court's Image for Years," *San Francisco Chronicle*, December 13, 2000, A13.

16. Warren Richey, "Fairly or Not, Court Takes on Political Hue," *Christian Science Monitor*, December 14, 2000, 1.

17. Gearan, "Divided Supreme Court Ruling."

18. Biskupic, "Ruling Reveals Depth."

19. "Can the Court Recover?" *Time*, December 25, 2000, 76.

20. Biskupic, "Ruling Reveals Depth."

21. Mary Leonard and John Aloysius Farrell, "Court Majority Sides with Bush, Calls Recount Methods Unlawful," *Boston Globe*, December 13, 2000, A1.

22. Biskupic, "Ruling Reveals Depth"; Lane, "Decision Sharpens the Justices' Divisions."

23. Lyle Denniston, "Justices Rule for Bush," *Baltimore Sun*, December 13, 2000, A1.

24. Lane, "Decision Sharpens the Justices' Divisions."

25. Gearan, "Divided Supreme Court Ruling."

26. Lane, "Decision Sharpens the Justices' Divisions." See also Weinstein, "Bush Wins."

27. Lane, "Decision Sharpens the Justices' Divisions."

28. "Can the Court Recover?"

29. Greenhouse, "Bush Prevails."

30. Lewis, "High Court May Have Slammed Door."

31. Denniston, "Justices Rule."

32. Richard L. Berke, "Bush Prevails by Single Vote; Justices End Recount, Blocking Gore after 5-Week Struggle," *New York Times*, December 13, 2000, A1.

33. "Can the Court Recover?"

34. Frank J. Murray, "Court Braces for a Barrage of Criticism," *Washington Times*, December 14, 2000.

35. Anne Gearan, "Swing Votes O'Connor and Kennedy Make a Stealth Majority," Associated Press, December 13, 2000.

36. Lane, "Decision Sharpens the Justices' Divisions."

37. Linda Greenhouse, "Bush v. Gore: A Special Report, Election Case a Test and Trauma for Justices," *New York Times*, February 20, 2001, A1.

38. Marianne Lavelle and Chitra Ragavan, "And Now, the Sound and Fury," *U.S. News & World Report*, December 25, 2000.

39. Gearan, "Swing Votes."

40. Lewis, "High Court May Have Slammed Door."
41. Denniston, "Justices Rule."
42. Ibid. (emphasis added).
43. Lewis, "High Court May Have Slammed Door."
44. "Opening a Gavel of Worms," *Economist,* December 16, 2000, 2.
45. Berke, "Bush Prevails."
46. Biskupic, "Ruling Reveals Depth."
47. David G. Savage and Henry Weinstein, "Supreme Court Ruling: Right or Wrong?" *Los Angeles Times,* December 21, 2000 (emphasis added).
48. "A Delicate Balance," *Saint Louis Post-Dispatch,* July 1, 2001.
49. Leonard and Farrell, "Court Majority."
50. Gearan, "Divided Supreme Court Ruling."
51. "Opening a Gavel," 2.
52. "Can the Court Recover?"
53. "Opening a Gavel."
54. Ibid.
55. Ibid.
56. Kaiser, "Opinion Is Sharply Divided."
57. Stuart Taylor Jr., "How History Will View the Court," *Newsweek,* September 17, 2001.
58. Carlsen, "Split Decision."
59. Greenhouse, "Bush Prevails."
60. Denniston, "Justices Rule."
61. Lane, "Decision Sharpens the Justices' Divisions."
62. "Opening a Gavel" (emphasis added).
63. Leonard and Farrell, "Court Majority."
64. Lavelle and Ragavan, "And Now."
65. See, for example, Greenhouse ("Bush Prevails"), who reported that Justice Souter agreed with the majority that "the varying standards in different Florida counties for counting the punch-card ballots presented problems of both due process and equal protection."
66. Lavelle and Ragavan, "And Now."
67. Ibid.
68. *Bush v. Gore,* 121 S. Ct. 525, 542 (2000).
69. Had the Court suggested that a recount discriminated against Bush, it would have highlighted the side it was taking in the controversy, much as it had done in the much-criticized stay of the recount.
70. "Opening a Gavel."
71. Ibid.
72. "Can the Court Recover?"

73. Ibid.
74. William Glaberson, "With Critical Decision Comes Tide of Criticism," *New York Times,* December 13, 2000, A24.
75. Indeed, Linda Greenhouse of the *New York Times* ("Bush v. Gore: A Special Report") explained this apparent inconsistency months later: "And it is also obvious now that there was a general misreading of the justices' initial decision in the first appeal to discard the Bush legal team's equal-protection challenge to the Florida recount. That claim, based on the argument that a partial recount in only four counties violated the 14th Amendment by weighting some votes more than others, was then still pending in a companion case before a federal appeals court. The justices' decision to delete the equal-protection issue from the first Bush appeal reflected a conclusion that the question was not yet ripe for review rather than that it was uninteresting or irrelevant."
76. "Opening a Gavel."
77. Ibid.
78. Ibid.
79. "Can the Court Recover?"
80. Lane, "Decision Sharpens the Justices' Divisions."
81. Denniston, "Justices Rule."
82. Savage and Weinstein, "Supreme Court Ruling."
83. "Can the Court Recover?"
84. Lavelle and Ragavan, "And Now."
85. Greenhouse, "Bush v. Gore."
86. Leonard and Farrell, "Court Majority."
87. Gearan, "Divided Supreme Court Ruling."
88. David M. Shribman, "An Ordeal That Sullied All in Its Path," *Boston Globe,* December 13, 2000, A1.
89. Burke, *A Grammar,* 41–43.
90. See, for example, Biskupic, "Ruling Reveals Depth"; Lewis, "High Court May Have Slammed Door"; Gearan, "Swing Votes"; Lane, "Decision Sharpens the Justices' Divisions."
91. Lane, "Decision Sharpens the Justices' Divisions."
92. Thomas and Isikoff, "The Truth."
93. Gearan, "Swing Votes."
94. Ibid.
95. Stuart Taylor Jr., "Bush v. Gore May Be Just the Beginning," *Newsweek,* December 25, 2000.
96. Biskupic, "Ruling Reveals Depth."

97. For example, Biskupic, "Ruling Reveals Depth"; Julian Borger, "Conservative Judges Faced Possible Conflicts of Interest," *Guardian*, December 14, 2000, 4; "Can the Court Recover?"; Carlsen, "Split Decision"; Mechler, "Court's Reputation"; Lane, "Decision Sharpens the Justices' Divisions"; Taylor, "Bush v. Gore."

98. Gearan, "Swing Votes."

99. Ibid.

100. "Can the Court Recover?"

101. Carlsen, "Split Decision."

102. Warren Richey, "Fairly or Not, Court Takes On Politrical Hue," *Christian Science Monitor*, December 14, 2000, 1.

103. Denniston, "Justices Rule."

104. Jonathan Ringel, "Bush v. Gore May Leave Lasting Rancor on Court," *Fulton County Daily Report*, December 14, 2000.

105. Gearan, "Swing Votes."

106. "Can the Court Recover?"

107. Lavelle and Ragavan, "And Now."

108. Gearan, "Swing Votes" and "Divided Supreme Court Ruling"; Thomas and Isikoff, "The Truth"; Taylor, "Bush v. Gore."

109. Charles Lane, "Lay Down Law, Justices Ruled with Confidence," *Washington Post*, July 1, 2001.

110. "Can the Court Recover?"

111. Savage and Weinstein, "Supreme Court Ruling."

112. Gearan, "Divided Supreme Court Ruling."

113. Biskupic, "Ruling Reveals Depth."

114. Kaiser, "Opinion Is Sharply Divided."

115. Ibid.

116. Shribman, "An Ordeal."

117. Murray, "Court Braces."

118. Berke, "Bush Prevails."

119. Kaiser, "Opinion Is Sharply Divided."

120. Gearan, "Swing Votes."

121. See Lavelle and Ragavan, "And Now"; Weinstein, "Bush Wins."

122. Shribman, "An Ordeal."

123. Borger, "Conservative Judges."

124. Richey, "Fairly or Not."

125. Taylor, "Bush v. Gore."

126. "Can the Court Recover?"

127. Borger, "Conservative Judges."

128. The Catch-22 is that if Scalia did not help Bush, Gore might have won and left him without a chance at promotion. But if he did help Bush, it would taint any promotion with a quid pro quo appearance, making it politically untenable. Kaiser, "Opinion Is Sharply Divided."

129. Taylor, "Bush v. Gore."

130. "Can the Court Recover?"

131. Borger, "Conservative Judges." These potential family conflicts of interest were not mentioned several months later, when the *New York Times* reported that Scalia's son Eugene was nominated by Bush to be the top lawyer for the Department of Labor, and Chief Justice Rehnquist's daughter Janet was nominated inspector general of the Department of Health and Human Services. See Linda Greenhouse, "Scalia's Son Named to Bush Administration Post," *New York Times,* May 8, 2001, A22; and "Rehnquist's Daughter Nominated," *New York Times,* June 2, 2001, A9.

132. "Can the Court Recover?"

133. Linda Greenhouse, "Election Case a Test and a Trauma for Justices," *New York Times,* February 19, 2001.

134. Thomas and Isikoff, "The Truth."

135. Kaiser, "Opinion Is Sharply Divided."

136. Murray, "Court Braces."

137. Thomas and Isikoff, "The Truth."

138. Kaiser, "Opinion Is Sharply Divided."

139. Charles Lane, "Two Justices Defend Court's Intervention in Florida," *Washington Post,* March 30, 2001.

140. Ibid.

141. Paul Leavitt and Kathy Kiely, "Justices Defend Bush-Gore Ruling," *USA Today,* March 30, 2001.

142. Lane, "Two Justices Defend."

143. Ibid.

144. "Scalia Defends Election Decision," *Arizona Republic,* May 24, 2001.

145. Ibid.

146. "Justice O'Connor Holds to Center," *AP Online,* May 10, 2001.

147. Thomas and Isikoff, "The Truth."

148. Charles Lane, "Laying Down the Law, Justices Ruled With Confidence," *Washington Post,* July 1, 2001.

149. "Justice O'Connor Holds to Center."

150. "O'Connor Wishes Bush v. Gore Had Never Come Up," Reuters, January 25, 2002.

151. Charles Lane, "Ginsburg Critical on Bush v. Gore," *Washington Post,* February 3, 2001.
152. Ibid.
153. Ibid.
154. Greenhouse, "Bush v. Gore."
155. Ibid.
156. David A. Kaplan, "The 'Accidental President': Exclusive Excerpt," *Newsweek,* September 17, 2001, 28.
157. Lane provided the most in-depth consideration of Rehnquist's concurrence ("Decision Sharpens the Justices' Divisions"). Gearan ("Swing Votes") and Borger ("Conservative Judges") mentioned it briefly.

Chapter 6. Editorialists Reconstruct Bush v. Gore

1. "Catch-22 Ruling Brings Election Near Messy End," *USA Today,* December 13, 2000, 16A.
2. Jim Wooten, "A Changed Landscape: Unwarranted Judicial Activism Has Hurt, Divided the Nation," *Atlanta Journal and Constitution,* December 13, 2000, 22A.
3. Debra J. Saunders, "Court of Law vs. Court of Public Opinion," *San Francisco Chronicle,* December 13, 2000, 23A.
4. Wooten, "A Changed Landscape."
5. Charles Fried, "'A Badly Flawed Election': An Exchange," *New York Times Review of Books,* February 22, 2001.
6. Nat Hentoff, "The Supreme Court Was Right," *Washington Times,* December 25, 2000, A17.
7. Ronald D. Rotunda, "The Partisan Myth," *Christian Science Monitor,* December 15, 2000.
8. Randolph J. May, "No Danger Ahead: Even after the Decision in Bush v. Gore, Our Judiciary Is Still the Least Dangerous Branch," *Legal Times,* January 1, 2001, 43.
9. Kenneth W. Starr, "Judges and the GOP," *Wall Street Journal,* May 3, 2001, A18.
10. Fried, "A Badly Flawed Election."
11. Ibid.
12. Fried's reliance on *Village of Willowbrook v. Olech,* 120 S. Ct. 1023 (2000), is hardly unequivocal. Two problems make the inference he draws from this case troublesome. First, the Court never said that there was no distinct class involved in the case; rather, it said that it

could recognize a "class of one" or a "class of five" instead of a larger, distinct class. Second, the Court recognized that the Village of Willowbrook had shown animosity against this tiny class (a single sewer customer), whereas no finding was made that the differential counting of ballots reflected animosity toward or bias against either candidate.

13. Rotunda, "The Partisan Myth."
14. May, "No Danger Ahead."
15. Michael Uhlmann, "The Supreme Court Gets It Right," *Pittsburgh Post-Gazette*, December 13, 2000, A31.
16. Charles Krauthammer, "The Winner in Bush v. Gore? It's Chief Justice Rehnquist, Who Runs the Most Trusted Institution in the U.S.," *Time*, December 18, 2000.
17. "Finally, Bush: We Might Not All Agree with How the Supreme Court Has Ruled, but It Must Be Supported," *Newsday*, December 13, 2000, A42.
18. "Catch-22 Ruling."
19. David A. Ling, "A Pentadic Analysis of Senator Edward Kennedy's Address to the People of Massachusetts, July 25, 1969," *Central States Speech Journal* 21 (1970): 81–86.
20. May, "No Danger Ahead."
21. Uhlmann, "The Supreme Court" (emphasis added).
22. "High Court Rules for Bush," *Denver Rocky Mountain News*, December 13, 2000, 55A. This editorial makes no reference to Breyer's point that no evidence was offered at trial that there were any overvotes to be recovered.
23. Saunders, "Court of Law."
24. Uhlmann, "The Supreme Court."
25. Saunders, "Court of Law."
26. Wooten, "A Changed Landscape."
27. Saunders, "Court of Law."
28. Fried, "A Badly Flawed Election."
29. Krauthammer, "The Winner."
30. Ibid.
31. Fried, "A Badly Flawed Election."
32. Uhlmann, "The Supreme Court."
33. Fried, "A Badly Flawed Election."
34. Krauthammer, "The Winner."
35. Uhlmann, "The Supreme Court." The *Bush* majority also opted for the "foolish" characterization over the "evil" characterization.
36. Wooten, "A Changed Landscape."

37. Krauthammer, "The Winner."

38. Saunders, "Court of Law."

39. Ibid.

40. Rotunda, "The Partisan Myth."

41. Fried, "A Badly Flawed Election."

42. Hentoff, "The Supreme Court."

43. Ibid.

44. Fried, "A Badly Flawed Election."

45. Wooten, "A Changed Landscape."

46. Uhlmann, "The Supreme Court."

47. "Catch-22 Ruling."

48. K. Starr, "Judges and the GOP."

49. Fried, "A Badly Flawed Election."

50. Hentoff, "The Supreme Court."

51. Vincent Bugliosi, "None Dare Call It Treason," *The Nation*, February 5, 2001. Bugliosi published this editorial, with extended additional comments, as a book later that year. See Vincent Bugliosi, *The Betrayal of America* (New York: Nation's Books, 2001).

52. *Bush v. Gore*, 121 S. Ct. 512 (2000) (stay order) (Justice Scalia concurring).

53. Bugliosi, "None Dare."

54. Ibid.

55. Ibid.

56. Linda Greenhouse, "Collision with Politics Risks Court's Legal Credibility," *New York Times*, December 11, 2000, A1.

57. Andrew Stephen, "The Scandal of American Judges," *New Statesman*, December 18, 2000, 11.

58. Eric Foner, "Partisanship Rules," *The Nation*, January 1, 2001, 6.

59. Paul Starr, "The Betrayal," *American Prospect*, January 1, 2001.

60. Mike Godwin, "The Supreme Court Shot Itself in the Foot while Shooting Down Al Gore," *Reason*, March 2001, 50.

61. Dan Rather, "Court's Image Hurt by How, Not What, It Decided," *Houston Chronicle*, December 17, 2000.

62. "Unsafe Harbor," *New Republic*, December 25, 2000, 9.

63. Randall Kennedy, "Contempt of Court," *American Prospect*, January 1, 2001, 15.

64. Stephen, "The Scandal."

65. "Catch-22 Ruling."

66. "Supreme Illogic," *Boston Globe*, December 13, 2000, A26.

67. "'Supreme' Court?" *Denver Post*, December 13, 2000, B10.

68. Bugliosi, "None Dare."
69. "Court's Tangled Ruling Produces Clear-cut Results," *Atlanta Journal and Constitution*, December 13, 2000, 22A.
70. Jeffrey Rosen, "The Supreme Court Commits Suicide," *New Republic*, December 25, 2000, 18.
71. P. Starr, "The Betrayal."
72. "Court's Tangled Ruling."
73. Rather, "Court's Image Hurt."
74. Bugliosi, "None Dare."
75. Godwin, "The Supreme Court Shot."
76. Neal Kumar Katyal, "Politics over Principle," *Washington Post*, December 14, 2000, A35.
77. Bugliosi, "None Dare."
78. Godwin, "The Supreme Court Shot."
79. Carlos A. Ball, "The Supreme Court Stole the Show," *Gay & Lesbian Review* 3, May/June 2001.
80. Rosen, "The Supreme Court Commits."
81. "Supreme Illogic."
82. Katyal, "Politics."
83. Bugliosi, "None Dare."
84. Ibid.
85. Katyal, "Politics."
86. Godwin, "The Supreme Court Shot."
87. Rosen, "The Supreme Court Commits."
88. Godwin, "The Supreme Court Shot."
89. "Supreme Illogic."
90. P. Starr, "The Betrayal."
91. Rosen, "The Supreme Court Commits."
92. Gail Schoettler, "A Tarnished Reputation," *Denver Post*, December 24, 2000, H3.
93. Bugliosi, "None Dare."
94. Rosen, "The Supreme Court Commits."
95. Schoettler, "A Tarnished Reputation."
96. Bugliosi, "None Dare."
97. Godwin, "The Supreme Court Shot."
98. Bugliosi, "None Dare," quoting from "Can the Court Recover?"
99. Ibid.
100. "Supreme Illogic."
101. Randall Kennedy, "Contempt of Court," *American Prospect*, January 15, 2001, 15.

102. Gore Vidal, "Democratic Values," *The Nation*, January 8, 2001, 4.

103. Harold Meyerson, "The Purloined Presidency," *American Spectator*, January 1, 2001.

104. "Unsafe Harbor."

105. Kennedy, "Contempt of Court."

106. Bugliosi, "None Dare."

107. Katyal, "Politics."

108. Bugliosi, "None Dare."

109. Adrian Walker, "Civics Lesson a Harsh One," *Boston Globe*, December 14, 2000, B1.

110. "'Supreme' Court?"

111. Rather, "Court's Image Hurt."

112. Schoettler, "A Tarnished Reputation."

113. Katyal, "Politics."

114. "'Supreme' Court?"

115. "Supreme Illogic."

116. "'Supreme' Court?"

117. "Supreme Illogic."

118. "Unsafe Harbor."

119. "The Ultimate Split Decision," *San Francisco Chronicle*, December 13, 2000, A22.

120. Foner, "Partisanship Rules"; Kennedy, "Contempt of Court"; "Unsafe Harbor"; Bugliosi, "None Dare."

121. Kennedy, "Contempt of Court."

122. Ellen Goodman, "The Supreme Court's Partisan Ways: It's a Recent Myth That the High Court Is Beyond the Reach of Politics," *Pittsburgh Post-Gazette*, December 13, 2000, A31.

123. "Unsafe Harbor."

124. Schoettler, "A Tarnished Reputation."

125. Foner, "Partisanship Rules."

126. Sanford Levinson, "Return of Legal Realism," *The Nation*, January 8, 2001, 8.

127. Meyerson, "The Purloined Presidency."

128. Kennedy, "Contempt of Court."

129. Foner, "Partisanship Rules."

130. P. Starr, "The Betrayal."

131. Levinson, "Return of Legal Realism."

132. Jess Bravin, Richard B. Schmitt, and Robert S. Greenberger, "Supreme Interests: For Some Justices, the Bush-Gore Case Has a Personal Angle," *Wall Street Journal*, December 12, 2000, A1; Evan

Thomas and Michael Isikoff, "The Truth behind the Pillars," *Newsweek*,
December 25, 2000, 46.

133. Vidal, "Democratic Values," 4.
134. Rosen, "The Supreme Court Commits."
135. "Court's Tangled Ruling."
136. Walker, "Civics Lesson."
137. Vidal, "Democratic Values."
138. Walker, "Civics Lesson."
139. Stephen, "The Scandal."
140. Godwin, "The Supreme Court Shot."
141. Ibid.
142. Ibid.
143. Ibid.
144. Rotunda, "The Partisan Myth."
145. May, "No Danger Ahead."
146. "Unsafe Harbor."
147. Burke uses this spatial metaphor to capture the idea of broader and
narrower conceptions of act, scene, agent, and so forth. See *A Grammar of Motives* (1945; reprint, Berkeley: University of California Press,
1969), 77–85.

Chapter 7. Scholars Reconstruct the Stay Decision

1. Kenneth Burke, *The Rhetoric of Religion* (1970; reprint, Berkeley: University of California Press, 1961), vi.
2. A search of the Lexis-Nexis Academic Universe database on July 31,
2006, yielded 1,629 law journal articles citing *Bush v. Gore*. Many of
these articles mention the case only in passing, but scores of them address the issues raised by the decision, with a large majority criticizing
the Court's reasoning. Scholarly books on *Bush v. Gore* include:
Richard A. Posner, *Breaking the Deadlock: The 2000 Election, the Constitution, and the Court* (Princeton, N.J.: Princeton University Press, 2001);
Jack N. Rakove, ed., *The Unfinished Election of 2000: Leading Scholars Examine America's Strangest Election* (New York: Basic Books, 2001);
Howard Gillman, ed., *The Votes That Counted: How the Court Decided the
2000 Presidential Election* (Chicago: University of Chicago Press, 2001);
Bruce A. Ackerman, ed., *Bush v. Gore: The Question of Legitimacy* (New
Haven, Conn.: Yale University Press, 2001); Samuel Issacharoff,
Pamela S. Karlan, and Richard H. Pildes, eds., *When Elections Go Bad:
The Law of Democracy and the Presidential Election of 2000* (Washington,

D.C.: Foundations, 2001); Cass R. Sunstein and Richard A. Epstein, eds., *The Vote: Bush, Gore, and the Supreme Court* (Chicago: University of Chicago Press, 2001); and Ronald Dworkin, ed., *A Badly Flawed Election: (Debating) Bush v. Gore, the Supreme Court and American Democracy* (New York: New Press, 2002). Books written by scholars and those knowledgeable about the law that are better adapted to a lay audience include: Alan Dershowitz, *Supreme Injustice: How the High Court Hijacked Election 2000* (New York: Oxford University Press, 2001); Douglas Kellner, *Grand Theft 2000: Media Spectacle and a Stolen Election* (New York: Rowman & Littlefield, 2001); and Vincent Bugliosi, *The Betrayal of America: How the Supreme Court Undermined the Constitution and Chose Our President* (New York: Nation Books, 2001). The last two books are the least scholarly in style. Kellner is a philosophy professor who writes on contemporary issues for the general public. Bugliosi is the famed prosecutor of Charles Manson, who is not a scholar, though he is knowledgeable about the law.

3. Dworkin, *A Badly Flawed Election,* 1.
4. Pamela S. Karlan, "The Newest Equal Protection: Regressive Doctrine on a Changeable Court," in Sunstein and Epstein, *The Vote,* 77.
5. Posner, *Breaking the Deadlock,* 4.
6. John C. Yoo, "In Defense of the Court's Legitimacy," in Sunstein and Epstein, *The Vote,* 223.
7. Michael C. Dorf and Samuel Issacharoff, "The Presidential Election Part I: Can Process Theory Constrain Courts," *University of Colorado Law Review* 72 (Fall 2001): 943.
8. Peter Berkowitz and Benjamin Wittes, "The Professors on Bush v. Gore," *Wilson Quarterly* 25, no. 4 (Autumn 2001): 76–89.
9. Richard A. Posner, "Bush v. Gore as Pragmatic Adjudication," in Dworkin, *A Badly Flawed Election,* 187.
10. Berkowitz and Wittes, in "The Professors," insisted that "[c]onservatives . . . form only a small fraction of the legal professoriate." Posner went further to claim that constitutional law, as a field, is "both over-politicized and underspecialized," leading professors in that field "to be driven by their politics rather than by their expertise." Posner, *Breaking the Deadlock,* 5.
11. Sandford Levinson, "The Law of Politics: Bush v. Gore and the French Revolution: A Tentative List of Some Early Lessons," *Law & Contemporary Problems* 65 (Summer 2002): 10.

12. Nelson Lund, "The Unbearable Rightness of Bush v. Gore," *Cardozo Law Review* 23 (March 2002): n. 2. Lund provides an extensive bibliography of critics and defenders of the decision in this note.

13. Karlan, "The Newest Equal Protection," 77.

14. Berkowitz and Wittes, "The Professors."

15. Cass R. Sunstein, "Order without Law," in Sunstein and Epstein, *The Vote*, 210.

16. Ibid.

17. Elizabeth Garrett, "Leaving the Decision to Congress," in Sunstein and Epstein, *The Vote*, 48.

18. Ronald Dworkin, "Early Responses," in Dworkin, *A Badly Flawed Election*, 65.

19. Garrett noted that preliminary media recounts suggested Bush would have remained the winner. "Leaving the Decision," 48.

20. Ibid.

21. *Bush v. Gore*, 121 S. Ct. 512 (2000) (stay order).

22. Obviously, the stay of an execution is based on a much stronger probability that a prisoner will be put to death, though power outages, hurricanes, or other unforeseen circumstances make those anticipations of harm merely probable, though with a high degree of likelihood.

23. Dworkin, "Early Responses," 65.

24. David A. Strauss, "*Bush v. Gore:* What Were They Thinking?" *University of Chicago Law Review* 68 (2001): 742.

25. Laurence H. Tribe, "Freeing eroG v. hsuB from Its Hall of Mirrors," in Dworkin, *A Badly Flawed Election*, 142.

26. *Bush v. Gore*, 512 (stay order).

27. Strauss, "*Bush v. Gore:* What Were They Thinking?" 743.

28. *Bush v. Gore*, 512 (stay order).

29. Jack M. Balkin, "Bush v Gore and the Boundary between Law and Politics," *Yale Law Journal* 110 (June 2001): 1411. Strauss endorsed this hypothesis as well in "*Bush v. Gore:* What Were They Thinking?"

30. Lund, "The Unbearable Rightness," n. 80.

31. It is possible for a scene to persist, as is suggested when we talk about "the Elizabethan Age," for example. But in this case, the scene is made to serve particular rhetorical purposes, which it cannot do.

32. Dworkin, "Early Responses," 64.

33. Strauss, "*Bush v. Gore:* What Were They Thinking?"

Chapter 8. Scholars Reconstruct
How the Court Reached Its Decision

1. Pamela S. Karlan, "The Newest Equal Protection: Regressive Doctrine on a Changeable Court," in *The Vote: Bush, Gore, and the Supreme Court,* Cass R Sunstein and Richard A. Epstein, eds. (Chicago: University of Chicago Press, 2001), 85.

2. Gene R. Nichol Jr., "Standing for Privilege: The Failure of Injury Analysis," *Boston University Law Review* 82 (April 2002): 327.

3. Vincent Bugliosi, *The Betrayal of America: How the Supreme Court Undermined the Constitution and Chose Our President* (New York: Nation Books, 2001), 42.

4. Laurence H. Tribe, "Erog .v Hsub and Its Disguises: Freeing Bush v. Gore from Its Hall of Mirrors," *Harvard Law Review* 115 (November 2001): 229–30.

5. Ibid., 230, citing *Powers v. Ohio,* 499 U.S. 400 (1991).

6. *Powers v. Ohio,* 428 (dissent by Scalia, joined by Rehnquist) (1991). Kennedy wrote the majority opinion, which O'Connor joined, so that two from the *Bush* majority did support this position on third-party standing.

7. Karlan, "The Newest Equal Protection," 85.

8. Frank I. Michelman, "Suspicion, or the New Prince," in Sunstein and Epstein, *The Vote,* 135–36.

9. Ibid., 136. The High Court seems to have gone out of its way to avoid raising the issue of partisanship among vote counters, perhaps because it did not wish thereby, indirectly, to draw attention to the partisan implications of its own actions. Karlan reached the same conclusion ("The Newest Equal Protection," 85).

10. Nichol, "Standing for Privilege," 327.

11. Ibid., 327–28.

12. Francis X. Beytagh, "Bush v. Gore: A Case of Questionable Jurisdiction," *Florida Coastal Law Journal* 2 (2001): 369.

13. Mark Tushnet, "Justiciability and the Political Thicket, Law and Prudence in the Law of Justiciability: The Transformation and Disappearance of the Political Question Doctrine," *North Carolina Law Review* 80 (May 2002): 1229.

14. Pamela S. Karlan, "Lessons for Getting the Least Dangerous Branch Out of the Political Thicket," *Boston University Law Review* 82 (2002): 671.

15. *Baker v. Carr,* 369 U.S. 186 (1962), 217, details the following considerations for courts to decide to stay out of political issues: "[A] textually demonstrable constitutional commitment of the issue to a coordinate political department; or a lack of judicially discoverable and manageable standards for resolving it; or the impossibility of deciding without an initial policy determination of a kind clearly for nonjudicial discretion; or the impossibility of a court's undertaking independent resolution without expressing lack of the respect due coordinate branches of government; or an unusual need for unquestioning adherence to a political decision already made; or the potentiality of embarrassment from multifarious pronouncements by various departments on one question."

16. Tribe, "Freeing eroG v. hsuB from Its Hall of Mirrors," in *A Badly Flawed Election: (Debating) Bush v. Gore, the Supreme Court and American Democracy, Ronald Dworkin, ed.* (New York: New Press, 2002), 141.

17. Samuel Issacharoff, "Political Judgments," in Sunstein and Epstein, *The Vote,* 57.

18. Richard H. Pildes, "Democracy and Disorder," in Sunstein and Epstein, *The Vote,* 141.

19. Karlan, "Lessons," 671–72.

20. Issacharoff, "Political Judgments," 76.

21. Ibid., 76.

22. Nelson Lund, "The Unbearable Rightness of Bush v. Gore," *Cardozo Law Review* 23 (2001): 1255.

23. Ibid., 1256–57.

24. Louise Weinberg, "Federal Courts and Electoral Politics: When Courts Decide Elections: The Constitutionality of Bush v. Gore," *Boston University Law Review* 82 (2002): 622.

25. Richard A. Epstein, "'In Such Manner As the Legislature Thereof May Direct': The Outcome in Bush v. Gore Defended," in Sunstein and Epstein, *The Vote,* 14.

26. John C. Yoo, "In Defense of the Court's Legitimacy," in Sunstein and Epstein, *The Vote,* 239.

27. Martin D. Carcieri, "Bush v. Gore and Equal Protection," *South Carolina Law Review* 53 (Fall 2001): 65.

28. Michael W. McConnell, "Two-and-a-Half Cheers for Bush v. Gore," in Sunstein and Epstein, *The Vote,* 102.

29. Lund, "The Unbearable Rightness," 1244.

30. Kenneth Burke, *A Grammar of Motives* (1945; reprint, Berkeley: University of California Press, 1969), 21–23.

31. Richard A. Posner, *Breaking the Deadlock: The 2001 Election, the Constitution, and the Court* (Princeton, N.J.: Priceton University Press, 2001), 58–59.

32. Jeffrey Toobin, *Too Close to Call: The Thirty-Six-Day Battle to Decide the 2000 Election* (New York: Random House, 2001), 161.

33. Elsewhere, Posner himself noted that "all the undervoted ballots—and all the overvoted ones as well—had been counted (that is, tabulated) twice: once in the original machine count and the second time in the machine recount." *Breaking the Deadlock*, 99.

34. Posner himself relied on assumptions about random distributions of undervotes and overvotes when denying the likelihood that Gore would overtake Bush in a full statewide recount. See ibid., 50–53.

35. See, for example, Martin Merzer and the Staff of the Miami Herald, *The Miami Herald Report* (New York: St. Martin's Press, 2001), esp. chapter 10.

36. Tribe, "Erog v. Hsub," 202.

37. Paul M. Schwartz quoting Bob Drogin, "2 Florida Counties Show Election Day's Inequities," *Los Angeles Times*, March 12, 2001, A1, in "Voting Technology and Democracy," *New York University Law Review* 77 (June 2002): 669.

38. Ibid.

39. U.S. Commission on Civil Rights, *Voting Irregularities in Florida dDuring the 2000 Presidential Election*, Chapter 4.

40. Ibid.

41. Pildes, "Democracy and Disorder," 180.

42. Michelman, "Suspicion," 135–36.

43. Jack M. Balkin, "Bush v Gore and the Boundary between Law and Politics," *Yale Law Journal* 110 (June 2001): 1427.

44. *Bush v. Gore*, 121 S. Ct. 525, 542 (Stevens, J., dissenting).

45. Merzer, *The Miami Herald Report*, 167–68 (reporting the results of the Miami Herald/Knight Ridder/USA Today review of undervote ballots). They reported that Gore would have won by three votes if the strictest standard (only cleanly punched ballots) had been used (168).

46. Tribe, "Erog v. Hsub," 215, citing *Boardman v. Esteva*, 323 So. 2d 259, 268 (Fla. 1975).

47. Ibid., 212.

48. Ibid., 215.

49. Ronald Dworkin, "Introduction," in Dworkin, *A Badly Flawed Election*, 13.

50. Peter M. Shane, "Disappearing Democracy: How Bush v. Gore Undermined the Federal Right to Vote for Presidential Electors," *Florida State University Law Review* 29 (2001): 570.

51. Dworkin, "Introduction," 13. That ruling supported Katherine Harris's position that she had exercised her discretion in rejecting late returns.

52. Pildes, "Democracy and Disorder," 180.

53. Order on Remand from Judge Terry Lewis, December 8, 2000, 2.

54. Dworkin, "Introduction," 13.

55. Richard A. Posner, "*Bush v. Gore* as Pragmatic Adjudication," in Dworkin, *A Badly Flawed Election*, 191.

56. Lund, "The Unbearable Rightness," 1241.

57. Dworkin, "Introduction," 12.

58. Epstein, "In Such Manner," 17.

59. Schwartz, "The Supreme Court's Federalism," 660.

60. Tribe, "Erog v. Hsub," 219.

61. The topic is discussed by Aristotle in *Rhetoric*, Book II, Chapter 23, Topic 4.

62. Richard C. Schragger, "Reclaiming the Canvassing Board: Bush v. Gore and the Political Currency of Local Government," *Buffalo Law Review* 50 (Winter 2002): 400.

63. See, for example, Balkin, "Bush v Gore," 1417; Michael Klarman, "Bush v. Gore through the Lens of Constitutional History," *California Law Review* 89 (December 2001): 1742–43; Tribe, "Erog v. Hsub," 199–200.

64. Lund, "The Unbearable Rightness," n. 45.

65. Posner, *Breaking the Deadlock*, 97.

66. Tribe, "Erog v. Hsub," 200–201, citing *Beckstrom v. Volusia County Canvassing Board*, 707 So. 2d 720, 722n. 4 (Fla. 1998).

67. Posner, *Breaking the Deadlock*, 107, n. 29.

68. Schragger, "Reclaiming the Canvassing Board," n. 23, citing *Florida ex rel. Carpenter v. Barber*, 198 So. 49, 51 (Fla. 1940).

69. Michael W. McConnell, "Two-and-a-Half Cheers for *Bush v. Gore*," *University of Chicago Law Review* 68 (2001): 665.

70. Indeed, it is not clear why this section was overlooked, except perhaps that it deals explicitly with the protest phase, instead of the contest phase that concerned the state court; the scene may be taken to limit the agency.

71. *Bush v. Gore*, 121 S.Ct. 525, 541 n. 2 (2000) (Stevens, J., dissenting).

72. For example, Balkin, "Bush v Gore," 1427; Karlan, "Lessons," 185; Robert J. Pushaw Jr., "Bush v. Gore: Looking at *Baker v. Carr* in a Con-

servative Mirror," *Constitutional Commentary* 18 (Summer 2001): 170; Jamin B. Raskin, "Bandits in Black Robes: Why You Should Still Be Angry about Bush v. Gore," *Washington Monthly,* March 2001, 56; Schwartz, "The Supreme Court's Federalism," 660; Tribe, "Erog v. Hsub," 313; and Weinberg, "Federal Courts," 88.

73. Klarman, "Bush v. Gore," 1727.
74. Shane, "Disappearing Democracy," 577.
75. Ibid., 576.
76. *Bush v. Gore,* 134.
77. Tribe, "Freeing eroG v. hsuB," 124–25.
78. Ronald Dworkin, "Early Responses," in Dworkin, *A Badly Flawed Election,* 289, n. 10.
79. Tribe, "Freeing eroG v. hsuB," 125–26.
80. Cass R. Sunstein, "Introduction: Of Law and Politics," in Sunstein and Epstein, *The Vote,* 83.
81. Lund, "The Unbearable Rightness," 1246.
82. *Bush v. Gore,* 107.
83. Dworkin, "Introduction," 12.
84. Ibid., 10.
85. Lund, "The Unbearable Rightness," 1220.
86. Tushnet, "Justiciability," 30.
87. Lund, "The Unbearable Rightness," 1246–47.
88. The only mention of vote dilution in the per curiam comes in a quotation of *Reynolds v. Sims,* 377 U.S. 533, 555 (1964), at *Bush v. Gore,* 105.
89. *Bush v. Gore,* 107–8.
90. Shane, "Disappearing Democracy," 574–75.
91. Ibid., 575.
92. Tribe, "Erog v. Hsub," 236.
93. Tribe cites John Mintz and Peter Slavin, "Human Factor Was at Core of Fiasco," *Washington Post,* June 1, 2001, A1, in "Erog v. Hsub," n. 265.
94. Tribe, "Erog v. Hsub," 236.
95. Ibid, n. 265.
96. Dworkin, "Introduction," 14–15.
97. Merzer, *The Miami Herald Report,* 188.
98. Ibid., 190–96.
99. Martin Merzer, "Miami Herald-Knight Ridder-USA Today Review Finds Contest for Florida's Electoral Votes Is a Split Decision," *Miami Herald,* May 10, 2001; Merzer, *The Miami Herald Report,* 231–32. Less

than half of the undervotes in this study had no marks at all; the remainder had dimples, pinpricks, detached chads, clean punches, circles, Xs, candidates' names, and so on.

100. Balkin, "Bush v Gore," 1418.

101. Schwartz, "The Supreme Court's Federalism," 652.

102. *Bush v. Gore,* 107.

103. Ibid., 105.

104. Ibid., 104–5, 107.

105. Elizabeth Garrett, "Leaving the Decision to Congress," in Sunstein
and Epstein, *The Vote,* 46.

106. Dworkin, "Introduction," 7.

107. Bugliosi, *The Betrayal,* 45.

108. Tribe, "Freeing eroG v. hsuB," 225.

109. Epstein, "In Such Manner," 15.

110. Bugliosi, *The Betrayal,* 45–46.

111. Michael Abramowicz and Maxwell L. Stearns, "Beyond Counting
Votes: The Political Economy of Bush v. Gore," *Vanderbilt Law Review*
54 (October 2001): 1867.

112. Ibid., n. 109.

113. Tribe, "Freeing eroG v. hsuB," 225.

114. Ibid.

115. Ibid.

116. Ibid., 225–26.

117. Dworkin, "Introduction," 11.

118. Ibid.

119. Epstein, "In Such Manner," 16. The term *suspect classification* often is
used in reference to racial classifications made by the state, which the
U.S. Supreme Court deemed suspect as early as the 1938 case of *U.S.
v. Carolene Products Co.,* 304 U.S. 144. Justice Harlan Fiske Stone added
the famous footnote 4 to this case suggesting that certain legislation
"is to be subjected to more exacting judicial scrutiny under the general prohibitions of the 14th Amendment than are most other types
of legislation" (153, n. 4). The point was reinforced six years later in
the Japanese internment case, *Korematsu v. United States,* where the
majority noted: "all legal restrictions which curtail the civil rights of a
single racial group are immediately suspect [and] subject . . . to the
most rigid scrutiny" (323 U.S. 214, 216). This rigid scrutiny means
that normal deference granted to the states (or in this case, the federal
government) gives way to a shifting of the burden of proof to

government agencies that wish to employ such classifications. See also *U.S. v. Carolene Products Co.*, 304 U.S. 144 (1938).

120. Epstein, "In Such Manner," 16.

121. Ibid., 16–17.

122. As *Washington v. Davis* asserted, "The central purpose of the Equal Protection Clause of the Fourteenth Amendment is the prevention of official conduct discriminating on the basis of race." 426 U.S. 229, 239 (1976).

123. In *Harper*, the Court took care not to directly charge the state with such a racially motivated purpose. In footnote 3, it said: "While the 'Virginia poll tax was born of a desire to disenfranchise the Negro' (*Harman v. Forssenius*, 380 U.S. 528, 543), we do not stop to determine whether on this record the Virginia tax in its modern setting serves the same end."

124. Under the "strict scrutiny" standard, racial classifications are not forbidden; but a state must offer good reasons for them (i.e., respectable purposes).

125. Michelman, "Suspicion," 129.

126. Shane, "Disappearing Democracy," 552.

127. Ibid., 578.

128. Cass R. Sunstein, "Order without Law," in Sunstein and Epstein, *The Vote*, 213.

129. Issacharoff, "Political Judgments," 68.

130. Ibid.

131. Ibid.

132. *Washington v. Davis*, 429.

133. Dworkin, "Introduction," 10–11, quoting *U.S. v. Hays*, 515 U.S. 737 (1995).

134. Ibid., 10.

135. Theodore O. Prosise and Craig R. Smith, "The Supreme Court's Ruling in *Bush v. Gore:* A Rhetoric of Inconsistency," *Rhetoric & Public Affairs* 4 (2001): 610, citing *Board of Trustees of the University of Alabama v. Patricia Garrett*, 536 U.S. 356 (2001). This case involved the Americans with Disabilities Act, which the Court refused to uphold against the states without a showing of intentional discrimination.

136. Lund, "The Unbearable Rightness," 1244.

137. Ibid., n. 90.

138. Shane, "Disappearing Democracy," 535–85.

139. Ibid., 536.

140. Ibid, 552.

141. Lund, "The Unbearable Rightness," 1245.
142. Ibid.
143. *Karcher v. Daggett,* 462 U.S. 725, 727 (1983).
144. See Ibid., 744–765 (1983) (Stevens, J., concurring).
145. Lund, "The Unbearable Rightness," 1245.
146. Ibid., n. 90.
147. *U.S. v. Carolene Products Co.,* 304 U.S. 144 (1938).
148. For a recent review of the strict scrutiny standard, see Pamela S. Karlan, "Easing the Spring: Strict Scrutiny and Affirmative Action after the Redistricting Cases," 43 *William & Mary Law Review* (2002): 1577–86.
149. Gerald Gunther, *Constitutional Law,* 11th ed. (Mineola, N.Y.: Foundation Press, 1985), 594.
150. Tushnet, "Justiciability," 32.
151. Ibid.
152. Weinberg, "Federal Courts," n. 185.
153. Ibid., n. 185.
154. Ibid., n. 74.
155. McConnell, "Two-and-a-Half Cheers," in Sunstein and Epstein, *The Vote,* 115.
156. *Village of Willowbrook v. Olech,* 528 U.S. 562, 564 (2000).
157. Ibid., 565 (emphasis added). The "irrational and wholly arbitrary" and the "intentional" findings were allegations that were acknowledged by the Court for purposes of allowing the equal protection case to go forward, not final, factual findings.
158. Karlan, "The Newest Equal Protection," 77–78.
159. Ibid., 79, quoting *Shaw v. Reno,* 649.
160. Ibid., 79.
161. Tushnet endorses Karlan's approach: "The harm was that the state counted some but not all legal votes, not that some group identified by a partisan—or any other—characteristic cast the uncounted legal votes. Accordingly, the harm the Court recognized was what Professor Pamela Karlan calls "structural." That is, affecting the structure of government without adversely affecting any individual" "Justiciability," 32).
162. Heather K. Gerken, "New Wine in Old Bottles: A Comment on Richard Hasen's and Richard Briffault's Essays on Bush v. Gore," *Florida State University Law Review* 29 (2001): 413.
163. Ibid., 413, n. 32, quoting Breyer in *Nixon v. Shrink Missouri Government,* 528 U.S. 377, 401 (2000).

164. *Bush v. Gore,* 104.

165. Klarman, "Bush v. Gore," 1728–29.

166. Sunstein, "Order without Law," 214.

167. Mark Levine, "On Bush v. Gore Decision," e-mail received December 15, 2000. In a 2001 telephone conversation, Levine reported having received about 6,000 replies to his popular e-mail. FindLaw, an online legal resource, reprinted the e-mail in an article entitled "The 'Gore Exception': A Layman's Guide to the Supreme Court Decision in Bush v. Gore," December 18, 2000, http://writ.news.findlaw.com. It reported that Levine had received thousands of responses to his e-mail from forty states and several countries.

168. Issacharoff, "Political Judgments," 70.

169. Klarman, "Bush v. Gore," 1729.

170. Schwartz, "The Supreme Court's Federalism," 625.

171. Karlan, "The Newest Equal Protection," 91.

172. Lani Guinier, "And to the C Students: The Lessons of Bush v. Gore," in Dworkin, *A Badly Flawed Election,* 243.

173. Schwartz, "The Supreme Court's Federalism," 643–44.

174. McConnell, "Two-and-a-Half Cheers," in Sunstein and Epstein, *The Vote,* 117.

175. Karlan, "The Newest Equal Protection," 91.

176. Guinier, "And to the C Students," 243.

177. Sunstein, "Order without Law," 215.

178. *Bush v. Gore,* 104.

179. Ibid., 109.

180. Lund, "The Unbearable Rightness," 1250.

181. Posner, *Breaking the Deadlock,* 88.

182. Ibid., 90.

183. McConnell, "Two-and-a-Half Cheers," in Sunstein and Epstein, *The Vote,* 116.

184. Ibid., 116–17.

185. Ibid., 117.

186. Ibid., 116, n. 85.

187. *Bush v. Gore,* 110, quoting *Gore v. Harris* (slip op. at 27).

188. Dworkin, "Early Responses," 66.

189. Dworkin, "Introduction," 7.

190. Weinberg, "Federal Courts," 632–33.

191. McConnell, "Two-and-a-Half Cheers," 118.

192. Lund, "The Unbearable Rightness," 1271.

193. Levine, "On Bush v. Gore Decision"; *Bush v. Gore,* 127 (Stevens, J., dissenting). As Stevens reported, Hawaii had two slates of electors, and Congress chose the one submitted on January 4, 1961.
194. Tribe, "Freeing eroG v. hsuB," 137.
195. Klarman, "Bush v. Gore," 1732.
196. Tribe, "Freeing eroG v. hsuB," 136.
197. McConnell, "Two-and-a-Half Cheers," 118.
198. Dworkin, "Early Responses," 66.
199. Ibid., 289, n. 11.
200. Lund, "The Unbearable Rightness," 1272.
201. Ibid., 1275.
202. Ibid., 1274.
203. *Palm Beach County Canvassing Board,* 772 So. 2d, at 1289.
204. Lund, "The Unbearable Rightness," 1274, quoting *Palm Beach County Canvassing Board v. Harris,* 1286, n. 17.
205. Ibid., 1274–75, quoting *Palm Beach County Canvassing Board,* 1290, n. 22.
206. Ibid., 1275.
207. Posner, "Bush v. Gore As Pragmatic Adjudication," 192.
208. Sunstein, "Order without Law," 215.
209. Ibid.
210. Dworkin, "Early Responses," 66 (emphasis added).
211. Dworkin, "Introduction," 7.
212. David A. Strauss, *"Bush v. Gore:* What Were They Thinking?" in Sunstein and Epstein, *The Vote,* 188–89.
213. Tribe, "Freeing eroG v. hsuB," 110. The decision was handed down on the night of December 12, 2000, rather than December 11, as Tribe stated.
214. Klarman, "Bush v. Gore," 1733.
215. Ibid., 1732.
216. Ibid., 1732–33.
217. Tribe, "Lost at the Equal Protection Carnival: Nelson Lund's Carnival of Mirrors," *Constitutional Commentary* 19 (2003): 621.
218. Tribe, "Freeing eroG v. hsuB," 137, quoting *Bush v. Gore,* 532.
219. Lund, "The Unbearable Rightness," 1272.
220. For an example of the use of the "things could be worse" argument as a last-ditch effort, see my analysis of the first President Bush's reelection campaign, in Clarke Rountree, "The President As God, the Recession As Evil: *Actus, Status,* and the President's Rhetorical Bind in the 1992 Elections," *Quarterly Journal of Speech* 81 (1995): 342–44.

221. *Bush v. Gore,* 121 S.Ct. 525, 533 (2000).

222. Posner, *Breaking the Deadlock,* 209.

223. Pildes, "Democracy and Disorder," 181.

224. Weinberg, "Federal Courts," 631.

225. Ward Farnsworth, "'To Do a Great Right, Do a Little Wrong': A User's Guide to Judicial Lawlessness," *Minnesota Law Review* 86 (November 2001): 252.

226. Tribe, "Freeing eroG v. hsuB," 135.

227. Weinberg, "Federal Courts," 630.

228. Raskin, "Bandits in Black Robes," 663.

229. Bugliosi, *The Betrayal,* 44.

230. Posner, *Breaking the Deadlock,* 53.

231. Ibid., 53–54.

232. Lund, "The Unbearable Rightness," 1276.

233. Ibid., 1277.

234. Farnsworth, "To Do a Great Right," 249–50.

235. *Bush v. Gore,* 111.

236. *Bush v. Gore,* 532.

237. Sunstein, "Order without Law," 765.

238. David A. Strauss, "What Were They Thinking?" *University of Chicago Law Review,* 68 (2001): 751.

239. Posner, "Bush v. Gore As Pragmatic Adjudication," 209.

240. Issacharoff, "Political Judgments," 70.

241. Lund's extensive defense of the *Bush* decision in "The Unbearable Rightness" did not extend to the Court's attempt to limit the case to present circumstances.

242. Bugliosi, *The Betrayal,* 59.

243. Karlan, "Lessons," 695.

244. Alan Dershowitz, *Supreme Injustice: How the High Court Hijacked Election 2000* (New York: Oxford University Press, 2001), 82.

245. Strauss, *"Bush v. Gore:* What Were They Thinking?" in Sunstein and Epstein, *The Vote,* 198.

246. Tribe, "Freeing eroG v. hsuB," 131.

247. Issacharoff, "Political Judgments," 70.

248. *Smith v. Allwright,* 321 U.S. 649, 669 (1944) (Roberts, J., dissenting).

249. Karlan, "Lessons," 695.

250. Issacharoff, "Political Judgments," 70.

251. Farnsworth, "To Do a Great Right," 235.

252. Klarman, "Bush v. Gore," 1763.

253. Tribe, "Freeing eroG v. hsuB," 268. Tribe also argued: "It is no good for a court to employ reasoning that resembles a one-way, nonrefundable railroad ticket, good for this day and this destination only." Ibid., 131.

254. Dershowitz, *Supreme Injustice*, 81.

255. Ibid., quoting *United States v. Virginia*, 518 U.S. 515, 596 (1996), at 82.

256. Posner, "Bush v. Gore As Pragmatic Adjudication," 212–13.

257. Even Lund did not consider the issue of whether this deadline trumped every other consideration. He only concluded that the state court interpreted Florida law as mandating the deadline; however, this construction of state court motives is misleading.

Chapter 9. Scholars Reconstruct Why the Court Reached Its Decision

1. See Kenneth Burke, *A Grammar of Motives* (1945; reprint, Berkeley: University of California Press, 1969), 365.

2. See Richard A. Posner, "Prolegomenon to an Assessment," in *The Vote: Bush, Gore, and the Supreme Court*, Cass R. Sunstein and Richard A. Epstein, eds. (Chicago: University of Chicago Press, 2001), esp. 183.

3. Richard A. Posner, *Breaking the Deadlock: The 2000 Election, the Constitution, and the Court* (Princeton, N.J.: Princeton University Press, 2001), 133–34.

4. Ibid., 133–41.

5. Ibid., 138.

6. Richard A. Posner, "Bush v. Gore As Pragmatic Adjudication," in *A Badly Flawed Election: (Debating) Bush v. Gore, the Supreme Court and American Democracy*, Ronald Dworkin, ed. (New York: New Press, 2002), 193–95.

7. Ibid., 203.

8. Cass R. Sunstein, "Order without Law," *University of Chicago Law Review* 68 (2001): 206.

9. John C. Yoo, "In Defense of the Court's Legitimacy," in Sunstein and Epstein, *The Vote*, 239.

10. Ibid.

11. Richard A. Epstein, "'In Such Manner As the Legislature Thereof May Direct': The Outcome in Bush v. Gore Defended," in Sunstein and Epstein, *The Vote*, 21.

12. Ibid., 37.

13. Michael W. McConnell, "Two-and-a-Half Cheers," in Sunstein and Epstein, *The Vote*, 107.
14. Ronald A. Cass, *The Rule of Law in America* (Baltimore, Md.: John Hopkins University Press, 2001), 94.
15. Richard A. Posner, *Breaking the Deadlock*, 50–51. Posner believed that even with a recounting of overvotes, Gore would have lacked the necessary votes to overtake Bush (51–53).
16. McConnell, "Two-and-a-Half Cheers," 98.
17. Ward Farnsworth, "'To Do a Great Right, Do a Little Wrong': A User's Guide to Judicial Lawlessness," *Minnesota Law Review* 86 (November 2001): 239, 240–41.
18. Ibid., 245–46.
19. Ibid., 246.
20. McConnell, "Two-and-a-Half Cheers," 120.
21. Elizabeth Garrett, "Leaving the Decision to Congress," in Sunstein and Epstein, *The Vote*, 49–50.
22. Ibid., 53–54.
23. Frank Michelman, "Suspicion, or the New Prince," in Sunstein and Epstein, *The Vote*, 134.
24. Pamela S. Karlan, "The Newest Equal Protection: Regressive Doctrine on a Changeable Court," in Sunstein and Epstein, *The Vote*, 92.
25. Ronald Dworkin, "Introduction," in Dworkin, *A Badly Flawed Election*, 54.
26. Francis X. Beytagh, "Bush v. Gore: A Case of Questionable Jurisdiction," *Florida Coastal Law Journal* 2 (2001): 370.
27. Garrett, "Leaving the Decision," 54.
28. Laurence H. Tribe, "Freeing eroG v. hsuB from Its Hall of Mirrors," in Dworkin, *A Badly Flawed Election*, 150.
29. Peter M. Shane, "Disappearing Democracy: How Bush v. Gore Undermined the Federal Right to Vote for Presidential Electors," *Florida State University Law Review* 29 (2001): 584.
30. McConnell, "Two-and-a-Half Cheers," 100.
31. Peter Berkowitz and Benjamin Wittes, "The Professors on Bush v. Gore," *Wilson Quarterly* 25, no. 4 (Autumn 2001). See also John C. Yoo, "Bush v. Gore: In Defense of the Court's Legitimacy," *University of Chicago Law Review* 68 (Summer 2001): 775, n. 2.
32. Berkowitz and Wittes, "The Professors."
33. Samuel Issacharoff, "Political Judgments," in Sunstein and Epstein, *The Vote*, 69–70.
34. Sunstein, "Order without Law," 218.

35. Ibid., 222.

36. Richard A. Epstein, "Afterword: Whither Electoral Reforms in the Wake of Bush v. Gore?" in Sunstein and Epstein, *The Vote*, 253.

37. A classic case of this is *Riggs v. Palmer*, 115 N.Y. 506 (1889), where the New York State Court of Appeals refused to allow a man to inherit an estate after he was convicted of murdering his grandfather to prevent the deceased from changing the will in a way that would have cut down the grandson's inheritance. There was no precedent for such a ruling, and New York law gave preference to wills that had been signed and witnessed over "parol evidence" (oral statements) suggesting an intention to change a will. The court trumped the legislative standards with a common-law rule: that no man should profit from his own wrong.

38. Posner, "Prolegomenon to an Assessment," 183.

39. Posner admitted that neither the per curiam nor the concurring opinions are "convincing." "Bush v. Gore as Pragmatic Adjudication," 205–6.

40. Posner, *Breaking the Deadlock*, 3.

41. Issacharoff, "Political Judgments," 65, n. 36.

42. David A. Strauss, "*Bush v. Gore:* What Were They Thinking?" in Sunstein and Epstein, *The Vote*, 197.

43. Ibid., 85–186.

44. Alan Dershowitz, *Supreme Injustice: How the High Court Hijacked Election 2000* (New York: Oxford University Press, 2001), 79.

45. Vincent Bugliosi, *The Betrayal of America* (New York: Nation's Books, 2001), 44.

46. Sunstein, "Order without Law," 214.

47. Douglas A. Kellner, *Grand Theft 2000: Media Spectacle and a Stolen Election* (New York: Rowman & Littlefield, 2001), 91.

48. Michelman, "Suspicion," 128, n. 8.

49. Michelman assumed here that the Article II argument of Rehnquist is less conservative than the per curiam opinion's position, because the Article II argument requires a substitution of the Court's interpretation of Florida law for the state court's interpretation of that same law.

50. Ronald Dworkin, "Introduction," in Dworkin, *A Badly Flawed Election*, 43.

51. Ronald Dworkin, "Early Responses," in Dworkin, *A Badly Flawed Election*, 64.

52. Ibid., 64.

53. Ibid.
54. Ibid., 67.
55. Ibid., 62.
56. Tribe, "Freeing eroG v. hsuB," 146–47.
57. Ibid., 141–42.
58. Jack M. Balkin, "Bush v Gore and the Boundary between Law and Politics," *Yale Law Journal* 110 (June 2001): 1440–41.
59. Ibid., 1441, n. 98. Balkin noted here that "[t]he widely circulated story [involving O'Connor] may or may not be true, although it has been confirmed by a variety of sources close to the Court."
60. Ibid., 1407.
61. Ibid., 1408.
62. Ibid., 1408–09.
63. Theodore O. Prosise and Craig R. Smith, "The Supreme Court's Ruling in *Bush v. Gore:* A Rhetoric of Inconsistency," *Rhetoric and Public Affairs* 4 (2001): 627.
64. Michael Klarman, "Bush v. Gore through the Lens of Constitutional History," *California Law Review* 89 (2001): 1725.
65. Garrett, "Leaving the Decision," 45.
66. Ibid.
67. Louise Weinberg, "Federal Courts and Electoral Politics: When Courts Decide Elections: The Constitutionality of Bush v. Gore," *Boston University Law Review* 82 (2002): 658.
68. Ibid., 659.
69. Ibid., 660. Weinberg explains that the Janissaries were "Christian captives of the Ottoman Turks under Sultan Murad I. They were forcibly converted to Islam and subjected to rigorous training. Their elite military corps became very powerful and could name or depose sultans" (n. 192).
70. Ibid., 660.
71. Ibid., 661.

Chapter 10. Scholars Reconstruct Who Decided Bush v. Gore

1. Jack M. Balkin, "Bush v Gore and the Boundary between Law and Politics," *Yale Law Journal* 110 (June 2001): 1413.
2. Ibid., 1408, 1413, n. 22.
3. Douglas A. Kellner, *Grand Theft 2000: Media Spectacle and a Stolen Election* (New York: Rowman & Littlefield, 2001), 102.

4. Ibid., 210.

5. David A. Strauss, "*Bush v. Gore:* What Were They Thinking?" in *The Vote: Bush, Gore, and the Supreme Court,* Cass R Sunstein and Richard A. Epstein, eds. (Chicago: University of Chicago Press, 2001), 204.

6. Frank Michelman, "Suspicion, or the New Prince," in Sunstein and Epstein, *The Vote,* 125.

7. Theodore O. Prosise and Craig R. Smith, "The Supreme Court's Ruling in *Bush v. Gore:* A Rhetoric of Inconsistency," *Rhetoric and Public Affairs* 4 (2001): 628.

8. Michael W. McConnell, "Two-and-a-Half Cheers," in Sunstein and Epstein, *The Vote,* 102.

9. Ibid.

10. Samuel Issacharoff, "Political Judgments," in Sunstein and Epstein, *The Vote,* 56.

11. Michelman, "Suspicion," 123.

12. Ibid., 125.

13. Ronald A. Cass, *The Rule of Law in America* (Baltimore, Md.: Johns Hopkins University Press, 2001), 93.

14. Ibid.

15. Linda Greenhouse, "Bush Prevails by Single Vote, Justices End Recount, Blocking Gore after 5-Week Struggle," *New York Times,* December 13, 2000, A1.

16. Compare *New York Times* reporter Richard L. Berke's characterization of the decision as a "tangled and elaborate ruling." "Bush Prevails by Single Vote; Justices End Recount, Blocking Gore after 5-Week Struggle," *New York Times,* December 13, 2000, A1.

17. Cass, *The Rule of Law,* 95.

18. Ibid., 95–96.

19. Ibid., 96.

20. Ibid.

21. Consider Strauss's argument that "[t]he majority's actions in the litigation show a relentless search for some reason that could be put forward to justify a decision reversing the Florida Supreme Court." "*Bush v. Gore,*" 185–86.

22. Indeed, Gore stated that he strongly disagreed with the Supreme Court's legal verdict. Richard L. Berke and Katharine Q. Seelye, "Gore Bows Out and Urges Unity," in Correspondents of the New York Times, *36 Days: The Complete Chronicle of the 2000 Presidential Election Crisis* (New York: Times Books, 2001), 311 (originally published December 14, 2000).

23. McConnell, "Two-and-a-Half Cheers," 101–2.

24. Ibid., 104.

25. Ibid., 105.

26. Strauss, "*Bush v. Gore,*" 187.

27. Michelman, "Suspicion," 127.

28. Ibid., 130.

29. *Adarand Constructors, Inc. v. Pena,* 515 U.S. 200 (1995) and *City of Richmond v. J. A. Crosson Co.,* 488 U.S. 469 (1989).

30. Mark Levine, "On Bush v. Gore Decision," e-mail, December 15, 2000.

31. Prosise and Smith, "The Supreme Court's Ruling," 611. They cited *Printz v. U.S., United States v. Morrison, Kimel v. Florida Board of Regents,* and *Board of Trustees of the University of Alabama, et al., v. Patricia Garrett, et al.*

32. Louise Weinberg, "Federal Courts and Electoral Politics: When Courts Decide Elections: The Constitutionality of Bush v. Gore," *Boston University Law Review* 82 (2002): 616.

33. John C. Yoo, "In Defense of the Court's Legitimacy," in Sunstein and Epstein, *The Vote,* 236.

34. Ibid.

35. Ibid., 236–37.

36. Ibid., 237.

37. The cases involving the theft of trade secrets by a state university, federal attempts at gun control, and violence against women (noted by Levine) illustrate this philosophy.

38. Yoo, "In Defense," 232–33.

39. Ibid., 233.

40. As Lani Guinier complained, the Rehnquist Court decisions "(1) tolerate extreme political gerrymandering that essentially predetermines electoral outcomes when districts are drawn, thus rendering elections virtually meaningless; (2) yet apply strict scrutiny to majority-minority districts designed to provide people of color a fair opportunity to elect candidates of their choice." "And to the C Students: The Lessons of Bush v. Gore," in Ronald Dworkin, *A Badly Flawed Election: (Debating) Bush v. Gore, the Supreme Court and American Democracy* (New York: New Press, 2002), 243.

41. This is not to say that a case could not be made for the Rehnquist Court's history of intervening in state election issues. The point is that Yoo's construction did not provide adequate evidence to support that argument.

42. Quoting *Cruzan v. Director, Missouri Department of Health,* 497 U.S. 261, 300-01 (1990) (Scalia concurring), at 136.

43. Michelman, "Suspicion," 137.

44. Cass R. Sunstein, "Order without Law," in Sunstein and Epstein, *The Vote,* 213, n. 39.

45. Ibid., 213–14, n. 39.

46. Ibid., 213, n. 39.

47. Richard H. Pildes, "Democracy and Disorder," in Sunstein and Epstein, *The Vote,* citing *California Democratic Party v. Jones,* 120 S. Ct. 2402 (2000), at 148–49.

48. Ibid., 149.

49. Ibid., 150, quoting *California Democratic Party,* 2410.

50. Ibid., 154, quoting *Timmons v. Twin Cities Area New Party,* 520 U.S. 351, 367 (1997).

51. Ibid., 157–58, quoting *Education Television Commission v. Forbes,* 523 U.S. 666, 681 (1998).

52. Ibid., 156.

53. Ibid., 162.

54. Laurence Tribe, "Erog .v Hsub and Its Disguises: Freeing Bush v. Gore from Its Hall of Mirrors," *Harvard Law Review* 115 (2001): 217–18.

55. Guinier, "And to the C Students," 243–44.

56. By "least scholarly," I refer to their style rather than the substance of their arguments. All of these writers, with the exception of Levine's e-mail, used note references, for example. But they explained much more, assumed much less, and used less cautious language than that of most law review articles mentioned here.

57. Vincent Bugliosi, *The Betrayal of America: How the Supreme Court Undermined the Constitution and Chose Our President* (New York: Nation Books, 2001), 50.

58. Kellner, *Grand Theft 2000,* quoting *Newsweek*'s December 25, 2000, issue at 175.

59. Kellner, *Grand Theft 2000,* 173.

60. Alan Dershowitz, *Supreme Injustice: How the High Court Hijacked Election 2000* (New York: Oxford University Press, 2001), 156–57.

61. Ibid., 157–58.

62. Ibid., 158, quoting observers and scholars.

63. Ibid.

64. Ibid., 159.

65. Ibid.

66. Ibid., 160.

67. Ibid., 160–61.

68. Ibid., 161.

69. Bugliosi, *The Betrayal*, 50; Levine; Kellner, *Grand Theft 2000*, 107; Dershowitz, *Supreme Injustice*, 167.

70. Kellner, *Grand Theft 2000*, 107, 91.

71. Ibid., 91.

72. Dershowitz, *Supreme Injustice*, 167.

73. Ibid., quoting Posner from *Harper's Magazine*, May 2001, at 167 and 167, n. 102.

74. Ibid., quoting "an expert in these matters," at 168.

75. Ibid., quoting the *Washington Post*, at 168.

76. Ibid.

77. Ibid. 168–69.

78. Kellner, *Grand Theft 2000*, 108.

79. Ibid., 96, n. 5.

80. Kim Eisler, "Supreme Court's High Honor but Low Pay Could Send Justice Scalia Job Hunting," *Washingtonian* (March 2000): 11.

81. Levine, "On Bush v. Gore Decision"; Kellner, *Grand Theft 2000*, 91, 108; Bugliosi, *The Betrayal*, 50; Dershowitz, *Supreme Injustice*, 165.

82. Dershowitz, *Supreme Injustice*, 166.

83. Ibid., 164.

84. Ibid., 165.

85. Ibid., 164.

86. Ibid., 166.

87. Ibid.

88. Ibid.

89. Ibid., quoting Toobin.

90. Ibid., 162, quoting Novak.

91. Ibid., 163.

92. See, for example, Kellner, *Grand Theft 2000*, 108.

93. Dershowitz, *Supreme Injustice*, 169.

94. Kellner, *Grand Theft 2000*, 190.

95. Elizabeth Garrett, "Leaving the Decision to Congress," in Sunstein and Epstein, *The Vote*, 41.

96. Ibid.

97. Ibid., 41–42.

98. Ibid., 42, quoting *Duncan v. Poythress*, 657 F 2d 691, 701 (5th Cir. 1981) (quoting *Powell v. Power*, 436 F 2d 84, 86 [2d Cir. 1970]), cert. granted, 455 U.S. 937, cert. dismissed, 455 U.S. 1012 (1982).

99. Ibid., 52.

100. Ibid.
101. Michelman, "Suspicion," 133–34.
102. Issacharoff, "Political Judgments," 71.
103. Ibid., 72.
104. Quoted in ibid.
105. Pildes, "Democracy and Disorder," 144.
106. Ibid., 146, quoting U.S. Constitution, Article I, § 5.
107. Posner, *Breaking the Deadlock*, 46–47.
108. Ibid., 47.
109. Yoo, "In Defense," 240.
110. Ibid.
111. Kenneth Burke, *A Grammar of Motives* (1945; reprint, Berkeley: University of California Press, 1969), 236.
112. Issacharoff, "Political Judgments," 57.
113. Laurence H. Tribe, "Freeing Erog v. Hsub from Its Hall of Mirrors," in Dworkin, *A Badly Flawed Election*, 143.
114. Mark Tushnet, "Justiciability and the Political Thicket, Law and Prudence in the Law of Justiciability: The Transformation and Disappearance of the Political Question Doctrine," *North Carolina Law Review* (May 2002): 1230.
115. Jack M. Balkin and Sanford Levinson, "Understanding the Constitutional Revolution," *Virginia Law Review* 87 (October 2001): 1049.
116. Ward Farnsworth, "'To Do a Great Right, Do a Little Wrong': A User's Guide to Judicial Lawlessness," *Minnesota Law Review* 86 (November 2001): 257.
117. Peter M. Shane, "Disappearing Democracy: How Bush v. Gore Undermined the Federal Right to Vote for Presidential Electors," *Florida State University Law Review* 29 (2001): 579.
118. Ibid., 580.
119. Michelman, "Suspicion," 139.
120. Ibid., 132.
121. Garrett, "Leaving the Decision," 38.
122. Michelman, "Suspicion," 131.
123. Tribe, "Freeing eroG v. hsuB," 139.
124. Ibid., 110 (emphasis added).
125. Pildes, "Democracy and Disorder," 186.
126. Tribe, "Freeing eroG v. hsuB," 143.
127. Aviam Soifer, "Federal Courts and Electoral Politics: Courting Anarchy," *Boston University Law Review* 82 (June 2002): 706.
128. Posner, *Breaking the Deadlock*, 217.

129. Ibid., 219.
130. Pildes, "Democracy and Disorder," 183.
131. Strauss, *"Bush v. Gore,"* 189.
132. Ronald Dworkin, "Introduction," in Dworkin, *A Badly Flawed Election,* 19.
133. Weinberg, "Federal Courts," 641.
134. Yoo, "In Defense," 237.

Chapter 11. Scholars Reconstruct When and Where the Court Reached Its Decision and What It Was Doing

1. Richard A. Posner, *Breaking the Deadlock: The 2000 Election, the Constitution, and the Court* (Princeton, N.J.: Princeton University Press, 2001), 3.
2. Richard H. Pildes, "Democracy and Disorder," in *The Vote: Bush, Gore, and the Supreme Court,* Cass R. Sunstein and Richard A. Epstein, eds. (Chicago: University of Chicago Press, 2001), 141.
3. Ward Farnsworth, "'To Do a Great Right, Do a Little Wrong': A User's Guide to Judicial Lawlessness," *Minnesota Law Review* 86 (November 2001): 259.
4. Nelson Lund, "The Unbearable Rightness of Bush v. Gore," *Cardozo Law Review* 23 (March 2001): 1226–27.
5. Ibid., 1227.
6. Posner, *Breaking the Deadlock,* 4.
7. Ibid., ix.
8. If Posner's pragmatic philosophy, as described in *Breaking the Deadlock,* could be called a mere outgrowth or replication of his earlier writings on pragmatism, his lengthy consideration of whether the justices might rightly have considered whether to weigh which candidate (Gore or Bush) would be better for the country certainly led to an elaboration of that theory.
9. Richard A. Posner, "Bush v. Gore as Pragmatic Adjudication," in *A Badly Flawed Election: (Debating) Bush v. Gore, the Supreme Court and American Democracy,* Ronald Dworkin, ed., (New York: New Press, 2002), 201.
10. Ibid., 202.
11. Ibid., 210.
12. Ronald Dworkin, "Introduction," in Dworkin, *A Badly Flawed Election,* 39.

13. Ibid., 39.
14. Ibid.
15. Ibid., 40.
16. Ibid., 41.
17. Ibid.
18. Ibid., 42–43.
19. That is not to say that the language of accident may not be used to deflect blame from a court. In an interesting early case in which the U.S. Supreme Court overruled its own prior decision, Chief Justice Taney described the overruled decision as "an erroneous decision into which the court fell." *The Genessee Chief,* 53 U.S. 443, 456 (1851), referring to the decision in *The Thomas Jefferson,* 23 U.S. 428 (1825).
20. Posner, *Breaking the Deadlock,* ix.
21. John C. Yoo, "In Defense of the Court's Legitimacy," in Sunstein and Epstein, *The Vote,* 224.
22. Lund, "The Unbearable Rightness," 1260 (emphasis added).
23. Posner, *Breaking the Deadlock,* ix.
24. Pildes, "Democracy and Disorder," 176.
25. 530 U.S. 567 (2000).
26. Pildes, "Democracy and Disorder," 176–78.
27. Yoo, "In Defense," 224.
28. Ibid.
29. Posner, *Breaking the Deadlock,* 67–68.
30. Ibid., 68–91.
31. George L. Priest, "Reanalyzing Bush v. Gore: Democratic Accountability and Judicial Overreaching," *University of Colorado Law Review* 72 (Fall 2001): 963.
32. Ibid.
33. Kenneth Burke, *A Grammar of Motives* (1945; reprint, Berkeley: University of California Press, 1969), 52–53.
34. Priest, "Reanalyzing Bush v. Gore," 963.
35. Ibid.
36. Ibid.
37. The fallacy of composition attributes to a group—in this case, a group of decisions—characteristics only attributable to one member of the group. Priest implied that what was true of the *Bush v. Palm Beach County Canvassing Board* decision was true of the *Bush v. Gore* decision as well.
38. Priest, "Reanalyzing Bush v. Gore," 962.

39. Michael Dorf and Samuel Issacharoff, whom Priest challenged, did not rely on the Electoral Count Act's provision for congressional involvement to make their case; rather, they complained that "the majority justices erred in *Bush v. Gore* because they failed even to consider whether their intervention was necessary. They did not apply process theory or anything like it." Michael C. Dorf and Samuel Issacharoff, "Can Process Theory Constrain Courts?" *University of Colorado Law Review* 72 (Fall 2001): 941. The Electoral Count Act is an obvious consideration in this case, however, since political process theory requires that one consider whether there are alternative mechanisms for resolving such problems, and the Electoral Count Act was specifically designed to deal with disputes over votes in presidential elections.
40. Cass R. Sunstein, "Order without Law," in Sunstein and Epstein, *The Vote*, 207.
41. Pildes, "Democracy and Disorder," 161.
42. Ibid., 145.
43. The case was *Timmons v. Twin Cities Area New Party*, 520 U.S. 351 (1997).
44. Pildes, "Democracy and Disorder," 154.
45. Laurence H. Tribe, "Freeing eroG v. hsuB from Its Hall of Mirrors," in Dworkin, *A Badly Flawed Election*, 142–43.
46. Ibid.
47. Dworkin, "Introduction," 44.
48. Ibid., 44–45.
49. Ibid., 45. As Dworkin admitted, "we cannot rule out as inconceivable that the conservative justices were moved by a misplaced enthusiasm for order and stability in the democratic process rather than by more personal motives, but it hardly seems likely that they were."
50. Louise Weinberg, "Federal Courts and Electoral Politics: When Courts Decide Elections: The Constitutionality of Bush v. Gore," *Boston University Law Review* 82 (2002): n. 28.
51. Frank Michelman, "Suspicion, or the New Prince," in Sunstein and Epstein, *The Vote*, 131.
52. Sunstein, "Introduction," in Sunstein and Epstein, *The Vote*, 1.
53. Ronald Dworkin, "Early Responses," in Dworkin, *A Badly Flawed Election*, 62.
54. Jack M. Balkin and Sanford Levinson, "Understanding the Constitutional Revolution," *Virginia Law Review* 87 (October 2001): 1064.
55. Posner, "Bush v. Gore," 205–6.

56. Theodore O. Prosise and Craig R. Smith, "The Supreme Court's Ruling in *Bush v. Gore:* A Rhetoric of Inconsistency," *Rhetoric and Public Affairs* 4 (2001): 625.

57. Michael Klarman, "Bush v. Gore through the Lens of Constitutional History," *California Law Review* 89 (December 2001): 1728.

58. Ibid.

59. They are *United States v. Virginia,* 518 U.S. 515, 568 (1996) (Scalia, J., dissenting), and *Rutan v. Republican Party of Illinois,* 497 U.S. 62, 95 (1990) (Scalia, J., dissenting) (1728, n. 29).

60. Pildes, "Democracy and Disorder," 155.

61. Ibid., 161–76.

62. Ibid., 182–83.

63. Klarman, "Bush v. Gore," 1725.

64. Farnsworth, "To Do a Great Right," 260.

65. Vincent Bugliosi, *The Betrayal of America: How the Supreme Court Undermined the Constitution and Chose Our President* (New York: Nation Books, 2001), 41.

66. Klarman, "Bush v. Gore," n. 28.

67. Ibid., stating: "*Bush,* 531 U.S. at 105 (refusing to decide whether the state supreme court had authority under state statute to prescribe a more specific standard for manually counting votes); see also *Gore v. Harris,* 773 So. 2d 524, 526 (Fla. 2000) (per curiam) (noting that a more expansive definition 'would have raised an issue as to whether this Court would be substantially rewriting the Code after the election')."

68. Douglas A. Kellner, *Grand Theft 2000: Media Spectacle and a Stolen Election* (New York: Rowman & Littlefield, 2001), 103.

69. Ibid.

70. Peter M. Shane, "Disappearing Democracy: How Bush v. Gore Undermined the Federal Right to Vote for Presidential Electors," *Florida State University Law Review* 29 (2001): 550, 578.

71. Aviam Soifer, "Federal Courts and Electoral Politics: Courting Anarchy," *Boston University Law Review* 82 (June 2002): 735.

72. David A. Strauss, "*Bush v. Gore:* What Were They Thinking?" in Sunstein and Epstein, *The Vote,* 204.

73. Dworkin, "Introduction," 55.

74. Ibid.

75. Posner, "Bush v. Gore," 210.

76. Yoo, "In Defense," 225.

77. Ibid., 226–27.

78. Strauss, *"Bush v. Gore,"* 204.

79. Tribe, "Freeing eroG v. hsuB," 150.

80. Klarman, "Bush v. Gore," 1721–22.

81. Shane, "Disappearing Democracy," 581.

82. Weinberg, "Federal Courts," 627–28.

83. Ibid., 639.

84. Ibid., 640.

85. Ibid.

86. Ibid., 645–46.

87. Ibid., 657, 664.

88. Balkin and Levinson, "Understanding," 1050.

89. Ibid.

90. Weinberg, "Federal Courts," 634.

91. Francis X. Beytagh, "Bush v. Gore: A Case of Questionable Jurisdiction," *Florida Coastal Law Journal* 2 (2001): 367.

92. Priest, "Reanalyzing Bush v. Gore," 965.

93. Ibid., 965–966.

94. Ibid., 979–80.

95. Ibid., 980.

96. Shane, "Disappearing Democracy," 584.

97. Weinberg, "Federal Courts," 638.

98. Tribe, "Freeing eroG v. hsuB," 145.

99. Balkin and Levinson, "Understanding," 1102.

100. Richard A. Epstein, "'In Such Manner As the Legislature Thereof May Direct': The Outcome in Bush v. Gore Defended," in Sunstein and Epstein, *The Vote,* 14.

101. Burke, *A Grammar,* 3.

102. David A. Ling, "A Pentadic Analysis of Senator Edward Kennedy's Address to the People of Massachusetts, July 25, 1969," *Central States Speech Journal* 21 (1970): 80–86.

103. Clarke Rountree, "Coming to Terms with Kenneth Burke's Pentad," *American Communication Journal* 1.3 (1998).

104. Burke, *A Grammar* 13, quoting *Korematsu v. United States,* 323 U.S. 214, 220 (1944). My own pentadic analysis of this case stressed the importance of secondary ratios in "tying down" the Court's construction. See Clarke Rountree, "Instantiating 'The Law' and Its Dissents in *Korematsu v. United States:* A Dramatistic Analysis of Judicial Discourse," *Quarterly Journal of Speech* 87 (February 2001): 1–24.

105. *Korematsu v. United States,* 323 U.S. 214, 244 (1944) (Jackson, J., dissenting).

106. Dworkin, "Introduction," 55.
107. That is not to say that citing courts never go beyond the textually embedded motives of a precedent decision; however, when they do so,
they must enter the realm beyond a precedent court's holding, indeed
beyond its dicta, to a speculative realm that gives less and less confidence as the court's literal words are more and more discounted by
circumstances highlighted by a citing court.
108. The High Court's reluctance to assume base motives on the part of
state courts was seriously tested in *NAACP v. Alabama*, 360 U.S. 240
(1959), where the federal court overturned a contempt conviction by
Alabama against the NAACP, only to have the state court determine
that the High Court was mistaken in its assessment of the NAACP's
compliance with an order to produce membership lists (which would
have exposed its members to racially motivated retribution). Despite
this affront to the High Court, the opinion maintained a calm tone,
noting: "We take it from the record now before us that the Supreme
Court of Alabama evidently was not acquainted with the detailed
basis of the proceedings here and the consequent ground for our defined disposition" (243–44).

Chapter 12. Scholars Reconstruct
Rehnquist's Concurring Opinion

1. For example, John Yoo admitted that the per curiam was not "utterly
correct" and noted, "I vastly prefer the theory put forward by the
Chief Justice's concurrence." John C. Yoo, "In Defense of the Court's
Legitimacy," in *The Vote: Bush, Gore, and the Supreme Court*, Cass R. Sunstein and Richard A. Epstein, eds. (Chicago: University of Chicago
Press, 2001), 239. Richard Posner claimed "[t]he Article II ground for
stopping the recount was far stronger than the equal protection
ground." Richard A. Posner, "Bush v. Gore As Pragmatic Adjudication," in *A Badly Flawed Election: (Debating) Bush v. Gore, the Supreme
Court and American Democracy*, Ronald Dworkin, ed. (New York: New
Press, 2002), 210.
2. *Bush v. Gore*, 121 S. Ct. 525, 534 (2000), quoting Article II, § 1, cl. 2.
Additional references to this opinion are cited in the text.
3. 146 U.S. 1 (1892).
4. Michael W. McConnell, "Two-and-a-Half Cheers for Bush v. Gore," in
Sunstein and Epstein, *The Vote*, 103.
5. Ibid.

6. Posner, "Bush v. Gore," 210.

7. Michael Klarman, "Bush v. Gore through the Lens of Constitutional History," *California Law Review* 89 (December 2001): 1736.

8. Ibid.

9. Richard A. Epstein, "'In Such Manner As the Legislature Thereof May Direct': The Outcome in Bush v. Gore Defended," in Sunstein and Epstein, *The Vote,* 20.

10. Nelson Lund, "The Unbearable Rightness of Bush v. Gore," *Cardozo Law Review* 23 (March 2001): 1265–66.

11. Hayward H. Smith, "The Law of Presidential Elections: Issues in the Wake of Florida 2000: History of the Article II Independent State Legislature Doctrine," *Florida State University Law Review* 29 (2001): 741, n. 55.

12. Ibid., 746.

13. Ibid., 748.

14. Ibid., 752–53.

15. Ibid., 756.

16. Ibid., 751.

17. Ibid, 756–57.

18. Ibid., 754.

19. Ibid.

20. Ibid., 755.

21. Ibid., 755–56.

22. Ronald Dworkin, "Introduction," in Ronald Dworkin, *A Badly Flawed Election,* 21.

23. Ibid., 21.

24. This must be qualified, however. Perhaps this would mean that Florida courts could not invalidate election laws just because they violated the state constitution. However, it might not prevent any necessary interpretations of unclear election laws by the courts when litigants request a ruling on what the law is.

25. Dworkin, "Introduction," 19.

26. Ibid., 18.

27. Ibid., 19.

28. Posner, "Bush v. Gore," 211.

29. Klarman, "Bush v. Gore," 1736.

30. Samuel Issacharoff, "Political Judgments," in Sunstein and Epstein, *The Vote,* 62.

31. Ibid, 66.

32. These were *Railroad Commission of Texas v. Pullman Co.*, 312 U.S. 496, 501 (1941), and *Burford v. Sun Oil Co.*, 319 U.S. 315, 332–34 (1943), cited at 66, n. 39.

33. Dworkin, "Introduction," 19.

34. Ibid., 19–20.

35. Ibid., 20.

36. Ibid.

37. Jack M. Balkin, "Bush v. Gore and the Boundary between Law and Politics," *Yale Law Journal* 110 (June 2001): 1414.

38. Dworkin, "Introduction," 17–18.

39. Posner, "Bush v. Gore," 211.

40. Ibid.

41. Louise Weinberg, "Federal Courts and Electoral Politics: When Courts Decide Elections: The Constitutionality of Bush v. Gore," *Boston University Law Review* 82 (2002): 625.

42. Weinberg, "Federal Courts," 627, n. 80, quoting 3 U.S.C. § 5.

43. Ibid., 626.

44. Quoting *McPherson v. Blacker,* 146 U.S. 1, 27 (1892).

45. Lund, "The Unbearable Rightness," 1234.

46. The U.S. Supreme Court, unlike lower courts in the federal system, is not required to follow even clear-cut holdings in its own precedent cases, though it often acknowledges the pull of the principle of stare decisis (not unsettling law that is settled), even as it overturns them.

47. Dworkin, "Introduction," 286, n. 14.

48. Balkin, "Bush v. Gore," 1414–15.

49. Weinberg, "Federal Courts," n. 75.

50. Dworkin, "Introduction," 286, n. 14.

51. This is an assumption generally held about normal agents, unlike abnormal agents (such as schizophrenics), who are unable to act consistently because as agents they are inconsistent (as, say, one with multiple personalities is inconsistent).

52. Epstein, "In Such Manner," quoting Fla. Stat. Ann. § 102.166(5) at 22.

53. Ibid., 24.

54. Ibid.

55. Ibid.

56. Richard A. Posner, *Breaking the Deadlock: The 2000 Election, the Constitution, and the Court* (Princeton, N.J.: Princeton University Press, 2001), 97.

57. Epstein, "In Such Manner," 23–24.

58. Ibid., 24.

59. Assumptions that a looser recount standard would favor Gore were wrong.

60. Posner, *Breaking the Deadlock,* 96.

61. Dworkin, "Introduction," 22–23.

62. Laurence H. Tribe, "Freeing eroG v. hsuB from Its Hall of Mirrors," in Dworkin, *A Badly Flawed Election,* 117.

63. Dworkin, "Introduction," 23.

64. Ibid., 25–26.

65. Ibid., 30.

66. Ibid., 25–26.

67. Ibid., 29.

68. Ibid.

69. Balkin, "Bush v. Gore," 1417.

70. Ibid.

71. Tribe, "Freeing eroG v. hsuB," 117.

72. Laurence H. Tribe, "Erog v. Hsub and Its Disguises: Freeing Bush v. Gore from Its Hall of Mirrors," *Harvard Law Review* 115 (2001): 297, nn. 71 and 72, citing John Mintz and Peter Slevin, "Human Factor Was at Core of Fiasco," *Washington Post* June 1, 2000, A1, and Fla. Stat. ch. 101.46 (1977).

73. Herman Schwartz, "The Supreme Court's Federalism: Fig Leaf for Conservatives," *Annals of the American Academy of Political and Social Science* 574 (March 2001): 668.

74. Ibid., 658.

75. Tribe, "Freeing eroG v. hsuB," 117.

76. Ibid., 118.

77. Posner, *Breaking the Deadlock,* 98.

78. Ibid., 99–100.

79. Klarman, "Bush v. Gore," 1742–43.

80. Ibid., n. 110, quoting *Boardman v. Esteva,* 323 So. 2d 259, 267 (Fla. 1975); *State ex rel. Carpenter v. Barber,* 198 So. 49, 50–51 (Fla. 1940); *Wiggins v. State ex rel. Drane,* 144 So. 2d 62, 63 (Fla. 1932); and *Darby v. State ex rel. McCollough,* 75 So. 411, 412 (Fla. 1917) (per curiam).

81. Ibid., n. 111.

82. Ibid., n. 112, quoting *In re Election of U.S. Representative for Second Congressional Dist.,* 653 A.2d 79, 90–91 (Conn. 1994).

83. Ibid., quoting *Duffy v. Mortensen,* 497 N.W.2d 437, 439 (S.D. 1993).

84. Ibid., quoting *Fischer v. Stout,* 741 P.2d 217, 221 (Alaska 1987).

85. Dworkin argued against the absurdity claim ("Introduction," 31), while Epstein argued against the "plain meaning" claim ("In Such Manner," 25).

86. Posner, *Breaking the Deadlock,* 100.

87. Klarman, "Bush v. Gore," 1743.

88. David M. Greenbaum and Lawrence E. Sellers Jr., "1999 Amendments to the Florida Administrative Procedure Act: Phantom Menace or Much Ado about Nothing?" *Florida State University Law Review* 27 (2000): 522–23.

89. Ibid., 523.

90. Klarman, "Bush v. Gore," n. 113.

91. Ibid.

92. Balkin, "Bush v. Gore," 1415.

93. Klarman, "Bush v. Gore," 1744.

94. Epstein, "In Such Manner," 31–32.

95. Klarman, "Bush v. Gore," 1742.

96. Epstein, "In Such Manner," 31.

97. Klarman, "Bush v. Gore," 1744.

98. Epstein, "In Such Manner," 31.

99. Klarman, "Bush v. Gore," 1744.

100. Tribe, "Rrog v. Hsub," 204, quoting Fla. Stat. § 102.168(8).

101. Tribe, "Freeing eroG v. hsuB," 204–5.

102. Klarman, "Bush v. Gore," 1744.

103. Ibid.

104. *Bush v. Gore,* 543 (Souter, J., dissenting).

105. Klarman, "Bush v. Gore," 1745.

106. Posner, *Breaking the Deadlock,* 211–12.

107. Posner, "Bush v. Gore," 210–11.

108. Ibid., 211.

109. Ibid., quoting Antonin Scalia, "The Rule of Law As a Law of Rules," *University of Chicago Law Review* 56 (1980): 1179–80, at 211.

110. Ibid., 213.

111. Klarman, "Bush v. Gore," 1747.

112. Ibid., n. 131, referring to *Planned Parenthood v. Casey,* 505 U.S. 833, 995–1002 (1992) (Scalia, J., dissenting).

113. Richard C. Schragger, "Reclaiming the Canvassing Board: Bush v. Gore and the Political Currency of Local Government," *Buffalo Law Review* 50 (2002): 419.

114. Ibid., 421.

115. Weinberg, "Federal Courts," 626.

116. Dworkin, "Introduction," 16.

117. Posner, "Bush v. Gore," 211.

118. Issacharoff, "Political Judgments," 60.

119. Tribe, "Freeing eroG v. hsuB," 110.

120. Robert J. Pushaw Jr., "Bush v. Gore: Looking at Baker v. Carr in a Conservative Mirror," *Constitutional Commentary* 18 (Summer 2001): n. 222.

121. See, e.g., Posner, "Bush v. Gore," 210.

122. Michael Abramowicz and Maxwell L. Stearns, "Beyond Counting Votes: The Political Economy of Bush v. Gore," *Vanderbilt Law Review* 54 (October 2001): 1950.

123. Ibid., 1949–50.

Chapter 13. Judging the Supreme Court and Its Judges

1. Rhetors do not always offer a fully rounded statement of motives, since partial constructions often serve their purposes better.

2. Clarke Rountree, "Coming to Terms with Kenneth Burke's Pentad," *American Communication Journal* 1.3 (May 1998).

3. *Bush v. Gore*, 121 S. Ct. 525, 545 (2000).

4. Ibid., 530.

5. Ibid., 531.

6. Ibid.

7. Posner noted that "an overvote is much more likely to be caught and corrected with precinct counting than an undervote." Richard A. Posner, *Breaking the Deadlock: The 2000 Election, the Constitution, and the Court* (Princeton, N.J.: Princeton University Press, 2001), 76.

8. Laurence H. Tribe, "Erog v. Hsub and Its Disguises: Freeing *Bush v. Gore* from Its Hall of Mirrors," *Harvard Law Review* 115 (2001): 236.

9. *Washington v. Davis*, 426 U.S. 229 (1976).

10. Ronald Dworkin, "Introduction," in Ronald Dworkin, *A Badly Flawed Election: (Debating) Bush v. Gore, the Supreme Court and American Democracy* (New York: New Press, 2002), 10–11, quoting *U.S. v. Hays*, 515 U.S. 737 (1995).

11. Theodore O. Prosise and Craig R. Smith, "The Supreme Court's Ruling in *Bush v. Gore*: A Rhetoric of Inconsistency," *Rhetoric and Public Affairs* 4 (2001): 610, quoting *Board of Trustees of the University of Alabama et al. v. Patricia Garrett et al.*, 536 U.S. 356 (2001). This case involved the

Americans with Disabilities Act, which the Court refused to uphold against the states without a showing of intentional discrimination.

12. *Bush v. Gore*, 532–33.

13. Quoting *Bain Peanut Co. of Texas v. Pinson*, 282 U.S. 499, 501 (1931), in *Bush v. Gore*, 541 (Stevens, J., dissenting).

14. Fla. Stat. § 102.168 (8).

15. Stuart Taylor Jr. "How History Will View the Court," *Newsweek*, September 17, 2001.

16. The fact that the Warren Court survived the school desegregation decision, which inspired a tremendous backlash from Southern states and calls for Chief Justice Warren's impeachment, probably would not be lost on this Court. Rehnquist clerked on the Court during the early years of the *Brown* decisions.

17. It is assumed that Florida officials would act quickly, as they had done before. It is also assumed that the High Court, abandoning the need to justify ending the recounts for good, would allow some flexibility on the state court's part in rejecting delaying tactics, including spurious lawsuits by Republicans, in order to ensure a timely recount.

18. Without the charge that the recount was unfair or politically biased—that, in effect, the Florida Supreme Court was allowing partisan recounters to find enough votes to make Gore president of the United States—it is hard to see how the Florida legislature could justify an intervention that would replace its will with that of the voters.

19. Posner, *Breaking the Deadlock*, 137.

20. Ibid., n. 82.

21. On this last point, see Michael Kramer, "Bush Set to Fight an Electoral College Loss," *New York Daily News*, November 1, 2000, 6.

22. I am not suggesting that figuring out which Republican absentee votes to reject would be easy. Presumably, records from voters mailing those absentee ballots could be accessed to identify many of those that relied on illegally completed ballot request forms.

23. Dworkin, "Introduction," 54.

24. Richard A. Posner, "Bush v. Gore as Pragmatic Adjudication," in Ronald Dworkin, *A Badly Flawed Election*, 210.

25. *U.S. News & World Report* did a good job of explaining the equal protection claim, where other news sources scarcely mentioned it, much less explained it. Marianne Lavelle and Chitra Ragavan, "And Now, the Sound and Fury," *U.S. News & World Report*, December 25, 2000.

26. See, for example, John C. Yoo, "In Defense of the Court's Legitimacy," *The Vote: Bush, Gore, and the Supreme Court*, Cass R Sunstein and

Richard A. Epstein, eds. (Chicago: University of Chicago Press, 2001), 225–26.

27. Cited in R. W. Apple, "Tradition and Legitimacy," *New York Times,* January 21, 2001, 1. Lani Guinier referred to this poll and source in "And to the C Students: The Lessons of *Bush v. Gore,*" in Dworkin, *A Badly Flawed Election,* 249.

28. Charles Rangel, "Supreme Injustice," *New York Amsterdam News,* December 14, 2000, 1.

29. James Caroll, "Black Caucus Sends a Message about Justice," *Boston Globe,* January 9, 2001, A19.

Bibliography

Cases Cited

Adarand Constructors, Inc. v. Pena, 515 U.S. 200 (1995).

Anderson v. Celebrezze, 460 U.S. 780 (1983).

Arizonans for Official English v. Arizona, 520 U.S. 43 (1997).

Bain Peanut Co. of Texas v. Pinson, 282 U.S. 499 (1931).

Baker v. Carr, 369 U.S. 186 (1962).

Beckstrom v. Volusia County Canvassing Board, 707 So. 2d 720 (Fla. 1998).

Board of Trustees of the University of Alabama v. Patricia Garrett, 536 U.S. 356 (2001).

Boardman v. Esteva, 323 So. 2d 259 (Fla. 1975).

Bolling v. Sharpe, 347 U.S. 497 (1954).

Bouie v. City of Columbia, 378 U.S. 347 (1964).

Brandenburg v. Ohio, 395 U.S. 444 (1969).

Brown v. Board of Education, 347 U.S. 483 (1954).

Brown v. Carr, 130 W. Va. 455 (1947).

Burford v. Sun Oil Co., 319 U.S. 315 (1943).

Bush v. Gore, 121 S. Ct. 512 (2000) (stay order).

Bush v. Gore, 121 S. Ct. 525 (2000).

Bush v. Palm Beach County Canvassing Board, 121 S. Ct. 510 (2000).

California Democratic Party v. Jones, 120 S. Ct. 2402 (2000).

Carpenter v. Barber, 198 So. 49 (Fla. 1940).

Central Union Telephone Co. v. Edwardsville, 269 U.S. 190 (1925).

Chevron U.S.A., Inc. v. Natural Resources Defense Council, Inc., 467 U.S. 837 (1984).

City of Richmond v. J.A. Crosson Co., 488 U.S. 469 (1989).

Darby v. State ex rel. McCollough, 75 So. 411 (Fla. 1917).

Duffy v. Mortensen, 497 N.W. 2d 437 (S.D. 1993).

Duncan v. Poythress, 657 F. 2d 691 (5th Cir. 1981).

Education Television Commission v. Forbes, 523 U.S. 666 (1998).

In re Election of U.S. Representative for Second Congressional Dist., 653 A. 2d 79 (Conn. 1994).

Fairfax's Devisee v. Hunter's Lessee, 11 U.S. (7 Cranch) 603 (1813).

Fischer v. Stout, 741 P. 2d 217 (Alaska 1987).

Fladell v. Palm Beach County Canvassing Board, 772 So. 2d 1240 (Fla. 2000).

Florida ex rel. Carpenter v. Barber, 198 So. 49 (Fla. 1940).

General Motors Corp. v. Romein, 503 U.S. 181 (1992).

The Genesee Chief v. Fitzhugh, 53 U.S. (11 How.) 443 (1851).

Gideon v. Wainwright, 372 U.S. 335 (1963).

Gore v. Harris, 772 So. 2d 1243 (Fla. 2000).

Gray v. Sanders, 372 U.S. 368 (1963).

Harman v. Forssenius, 380 U.S. 528 (1965).

Harper v. Virginia Board of Election, 383 U.S. 663 (1966).

Jacobs v. Seminole County Canvassing Board, 773 So. 2d 519 (Fla. 2000).

Karcher v. Daggett, 462 U.S. 725 (1983).

Kimel v. Florida Board of Regents, 528 U.S. 62 (2000).

Korematsu v. United States, 323 U.S. 214 (1944).

Krivanek v. Take Back Tampa Political Committee, 625 So. 2d 840 (Fla. 1993).

Lehman Brothers v. Schein, 416 U.S. 386 (1974).

McCleskey v. Kemp, 481 U.S. 279 (1987).

McCulloch v. Maryland, 17 U.S. (4 Wheat.) 316 (1819).

McPherson v. Blacker, 146 U.S. 1 (1892).

Marbury v. Madison, 1 Cranch (5 U.S.) 137 (1803).

Martin v. Hunter's Lessee, 14 U.S. (1 Wheat.) 305 (1814).

Ex Parte Merryman, F. Cas. 9387 (1861).

Miranda v. Arizona, 384 U.S. 456 (1966).

Moore v. Ogilvie, 394 U.S. 814 (1969).

N.A.A.C.P. v. Alabama, 360 U.S. 240 (1959).

N.A.A.C.P. v. Alabama ex rel. Patterson, 357 U.S. 449 (1958).

National Socialist Party of America v. Skokie, 434 U.S. 1327 (1977).

Nixon v. Shrink Mo. Gov't, 528 U.S. 377 (2000).

Palm Beach County Canvassing Board v. Harris, 772 So. 2d 1220 (Fla. 2000).

Palm Beach County Canvassing Board v. Harris, 772 So. 2d 1273 (2000) (corrected).

Planned Parenthood v. Casey, 505 U.S. 833 (1992).

Plessy v. Ferguson, 163 U.S. 537 (1896).

Powell v. Power, 436 F. 2d 84 (2d Cir 1970).

Powers v. Ohio, 111 S. Ct. 1364 (1991).

Printz v. U.S., 538 U.S. 1036 (2003).

Railroad Commission of Texas v. Pullman Co., 312 U.S. 496 (1941).

Regents of the University of California v. Bakke, 437 U.S. 265 (1978).

Reynolds v. Sims, 377 U.S. 533 (1964).

Riggs v. Palmer, 115 N.Y. 506 (1889).

Rivers v. Roadway Express, Inc., 511 U.S. 298 (1994).

Roe v. Wade, 410 U.S. 113, 124 (1973).

Rubin v. United States, 524 U.S. 1301 (1998).

Rutan v. Republican Party of Illinois, 497 U.S. 62 (1990).

Saenz v. Roe, 526 U.S. 489 (1999).

Scott v. Sandford, 60 U.S. (19 How.) 393 (1857).

Shaw v. Reno, 509 U.S. 630 (1993).

Siegel v. LePore, 121 S. Ct. 510 (2000).

Smith v. Allwright, 321 U.S. 649 (1944).

Sumner v. Mata, 449 U.S. 539 (1981).

Taylor v. Martin County Canvassing Board, 773 So. 2d 517 (Fla. 2000).

The Thomas Jefferson, 23 U.S (10 Wheat.) 428 (1825).

Timmons v. Twin Cities Area New Party, 520 U.S. 351 (1997).

United States v. Butler, 297 U.S. 1 (1936).

United States v. Carolene Products Co., 304 U.S. 144 (1938).

United States v. Hays, 515 U.S. 737 (1995).

United States v. Morrison, 529 U.S. 598 (2000).

United States v. Nixon, 418 U.S. 683 (1974).

United States v. Virginia, 518 U.S. 515 (1996).

U.S. Term Limits, Inc. v. Thornton, 514 U.S. 779 (1995).

Victor v. Nebraska, 511 U.S. 1 (1994).

Village of Willowbrook v. Olech, 528 U.S. 562 (2000).

Washington v. Davis, 426 U.S. 229 (1976).

Wiggins v. State ex rel. Drane, 144 So. 2d 62 (Fla. 1932).

Worcester v. Georgia, 31 U.S. (6 Pet.) 512 (1832).

Published Works

Abel, David. "Bush v. Gore Case Compels Scholars to Alter Courses at US Law Schools." *Boston Globe,* February 3, 2001, A1

Abramowicz, Michael, and Maxwell L. Stearns. "Beyond Counting Votes: The Political Economy of Bush v. Gore." *Vanderbilt Law Review* 54 (2001): 1849–1952.

Abramson, Leslie W. "Appearance of Impropriety: Deciding When a Judge's Impartiality 'Might Reasonably Be Questioned.'" *Georgetown Journal of Legal Ethics* 14 (2000): 55–102.

――――. "Canon 2 of the Code of Judicial Conduct." *Marquette Law Review* 79 (1996): 949–91.

Ackerman, Bruce. "Anatomy of a Constitutional Coup." *London Review of Books,* February 8, 2001, 2.

Ackerman, Bruce A., ed. *Bush v. Gore: The Question of Legitimacy.* New Haven, Conn.: Yale University Press, 2002.

Adler, Renata. "Irreparable Harm: The Unexpected Origins of the Supreme Court's Worst Decision." *New Republic,* July 30, 29.

Amar, Akhil Reed. "Should We Trust Judges?" *Los Angeles Times,* December 17, 2001, M1.

Amsterdam, Anthony. "The Law Is Left Twisting Slowly in the Wind." *Los Angeles Times,* December 17, 2000.

"An Analyst's Florida Balloting Favors Bush." Associated Press, April 4, 2001.

Apple, R. W. "Tradition and Legitimacy." *New York Times,* January 21, 2001, 1.

Balkin, Jack M. "Bush v Gore, and the Boundary between Law and Politics." *Yale Law Journal* 110 (2001): 1407–58.

Balkin, Jack M., and Sanford Levinson. "Understanding the Constitutional Revolution." *Virginia Law Review* 87 (2001): 1045–1109.

Ball, Carlos A. "The Supreme Court Stole the Show." *Gay & Lesbian Review* 8, no. 3 (May/June 2001): 20–22.

Barstow, David, and Don Van Natta Jr. "Examining the Vote: How Bush Took Florida: Mining the Overseas Absentee Vote." *New York Times,* July 15, 2001, 1.

Berke, Richard L. "Bush Prevails by Single Vote; Justices End Recount, Blocking Gore after 5-Week Struggle." *New York Times,* December 13, 2000, A1.

Berkowitz, Peter, and Benjamin Wittes. "The Professors on Bush v. Gore." *Wilson Quarterly* 4 (Autumn 2001): 76–89.

Beytagh, Francis X. "Bush v. Gore: A Case of Questionable Jurisdiction." *Florida Coastal Law Journal* 2 (2001): 367–72.

Biskupic, Joan. "Ruling Reveals Depth of Divide on the Court." *USA Today,* December 13, 2000.

Blankenship, Jane, Marlene G. Fine, and Leslie K. Davis. "The 1980 Republican Primary Debates: The Transformation of Actor to Scene." *Quarterly Journal of Speech* 69 (1983): 25–36.

Borger, Julian. "Conservative Judges Faced Possible Conflicts of Interest." *The Guardian,* December 14, 2000, 4.

Bork, Robert H. "Sanctimony Serving Politics: The Florida Fiasco." *New Criterion* (March 2001): 4.

Bravin, Jess, Richard B. Schmitt, and Robert S. Greenberger. "Supreme Interests: For Some Justices, the Bush-Gore Case Has a Personal Angle." *Wall Street Journal,* December 12, 2001, A1.

Breyer, Stephen G. "Program I: Judicial Independence in the United States." *Saint Louis University Law Journal* 40 (1996): 989–96.

Bugliosi, Vincent. *The Betrayal of America: How the Supreme Court Undermined the Constitution and Chose Our President.* New York: Nation Books, 2001.

———. "None Dare Call It Treason." *The Nation,* February 1, 2001.

Burke, Kenneth. *Conversations with Kenneth Burke.* Videotape. Department of Communication Studies, University of Iowa, 1987.

———. "Dramatism." In *Drama in Life: The Uses of Communication in Society,* James E. Combs and Michael W. Mansfield, eds. New York: Hastings House, 1976, 7–17.

———. *A Grammar of Motives.* 1945, reprint Berkeley: University of California Press, 1969.

———. *A Rhetoric of Motives.* 1950, reprint Berkeley: University of California Press, 1969.

———. *The Rhetoric of Religion.* 1961, reprint Berkeley: University of California Press, 1970.

Campos, Paul. "Law Professors' Site a Real Hoot." *Rocky Mountain News (Denver),* February 27, 2001.

"Can the Court Recover?" *Time,* December 25, 2000, 76.

Carcieri, Martin D. "Bush v. Gore and Equal Protection." *South Carolina Law Review* 53 (2001): 63–82.

Carlsen, William. "Split Decision May Tarnish Court's Image for Years." *San Francisco Chronicle,* December 13, 2000, A13.

Caroll, James. "Black Caucus Sends a Message about Justice." *Boston Globe,* January 9, 2001, A19.

Casey, Gregory. "The Supreme Court and Myth: An Empirical Investigation." *Law and Society Review* 8 (1974): 385–419.

Cass, Ronald A. *The Rule of Law in America.* Baltimore, Md.: Johns Hopkins University Press, 2001.

"Catch-22 Ruling Brings Election Near Messy End." *USA Today,* December 13, 2000, 16A.

Ceasar, James W., and Andrew E. Busch. *The Perfect Tie: The True Story of the 2000 Presidential Election.* New York: Rowman and Littlefield, 2001.

Chemerinsky, Erwin. "Bush v. Gore Was Not Justifiable." *University of Notre Dame Law Review* 76 (2001): 1093–1112.

Cobb, Roger, and Charles Elder. "Symbolic Identification and Political Behavior." *American Politics Quarterly* 4 (1976): 305–32.

Cooper, Michael. "Counting the Vote: The Count." *New York Times,* December 12, 2000.

Correspondents of the New York Times. *36 Days: The Complete Chronicle of the 2000 Presidential Election Crisis.* New York: Times Books, 2001.

"The Court's Presidential Debate." *Legal Times* (December 18/25, 2000): 17.

"Court's Tangled Ruling Produces Clear-Cut Results." *Atlanta Journal and Constitution,* December 13, 2000, 22A.

Coyle, Marcia. "Gauging 'Bush v. Gore' Fallout." *National Law Journal*, December 25, 2000, A4.

Crusto, Mitchell F. "The Supreme Court's 'New' Federalism: An Anti-Rights Agenda?" *Georgia State University Law Review* 16 (2000): 517–72.

"A Delicate Balance." *Saint Louis Post-Dispatch*, July 1, 2001.

Denniston, Lyle. "Justices Rule for Bush." *Baltimore Sun*, December 13, 2000, A1.

Denton, Robert E. Jr., and Gary C. Woodward. *Political Communication in America*. Westport, Conn.: Praeger, 1985.

Dershowitz, Alan. *Supreme Injustice: How the High Court Hijacked Election 2000*. New York: Oxford University Press, 2001.

Dionne, E. J. Jr. "The Overreaching Court." *Washington Post*, February 23, 2001.

Dionne, E. J. Jr., and William Kristol. *Bush v. Gore: The Court Cases and the Commentary*. Washington, D.C.: Brookings Institution Press, 2001.

Dorf, Michael C., and Samuel Issacharoff. "Can Process Theory Constrain Courts?" *University of Colorado Law Review* 72 (2001): 923–51.

Drogin, Bob. "2 Florida Counties Show Election Day's Inequities." *Los Angeles Times*, March 12, 2001, A1.

Dworkin, Ronald. "A Badly Flawed Election." *New York Review of Books*, January 11, 2001.

_____. *A Badly Flawed Election: (Debating) Bush v. Gore, the Supreme Court and American Democracy*. New York: New Press, 2002.

_____. "Early Responses." In Dworkin, *A Badly Flawed Election*, 57–73.

_____. "Introduction." In Dworkin, *A Badly Flawed Election*, 1–55.

_____. *Taking Rights Seriously*. Cambridge, Mass.: Harvard University Press, 1977.

Dwyer, Jim. "Justice Scalia's Legal Vision Is Blinded by His Ambition." *Daily News* (New York), December 11, 2000, 4.

Eisgruber, Christopher L. "John Marshall's Judicial Rhetoric." *Supreme Court Review* (1996): 439–81.

Eisler, Kim. "Supreme Court's High Honor but Low Pay Could Send Justice Scalia Job Hunting." *Washingtonian*, March 2000, 11.

Epstein, Richard A. "Afterword: Whither Electoral Reforms in the Wake of Bush v. Gore?" In *The Vote: Bush, Gore, and the Supreme Court*, Cass R. Sunstein and Richard A. Epstein, eds. Chicago: University of Chicago Press, 2001, 241–53.

_____. "'In Such Manner As the Legislature Thereof May Direct': The Outcome in Bush v. Gore Defended." *University of Chicago Law Review* 68 (2001): 613–35.

_____. "'In Such Manner As the Legislature Thereof May Direct': The Outcome in Bush v. Gore Defended." In *The Vote: Bush, Gore, and the Supreme Court*, Cass R. Sunstein and Richard A. Epstein, eds. Chicago: University of Chicago Press, 2001, 13–37.

Farnsworth, Ward. "'To Do a Great Right, Do a Little Wrong': A User's Guide to Judicial Lawlessness." *Minnesota Law Review* 86 (2001): 227–66.

Farrell, John A. "Scalia Hints at Court's View." *Boston Globe*, December 10, 2000, A39.

"Finally, Bush: We Might Not All Agree with How the Supreme Court Has Ruled, but It Must Be Supported." *Newsday*, December 13, 2000.

Fisher, Joseph M. "A Political Case Makes Bad Law." *National Law Journal*, January 8, 2001.

Flaherty, Martin S. "The Most Dangerous Branch." *Yale Law Journal* 105 (1996): 1725–82.

"Florida Ruling Eclipsed All Others." *USA Today*, June 29, 2001.

Foner, Eric. "Partisanship Rules." *The Nation*, January 1, 2001, 6.

"443 Law Professors Say: By Stopping the Vote Count in Florida, the U.S. Supreme Court Used Its Power to Act As Political Partisans, Not Judges of a Court of Law." Advertisement. *New York Times*, January 13, 2001.

Frank, Jerome. *Courts on Trial: Myth and Reality in American Justice*. New York: Atheneum, 1969.

_____. "The Cult of the Robe." *Saturday Review of Literature*, October 13, 1945, 12–13, 80–81.

Frankel, Marvin E. "Posner v. Dershowitz." *New Leader*, September/October 2001, 7–15.

Fried, Charles. "A Badly Flawed Election: An Exchange." *New York Review of Books*, February 22, 2001, 8.

Gabel, Peter. "The Political Meaning of Bush v. Gore." *Tikkun* 16, no. 4 (July/August 2001): 33–42.

Garrett, Elizabeth. "Leaving the Decision to Congress." In *The Vote: Bush, Gore, and the Supreme Court*, Cass R. Sunstein and Richard A. Epstein, eds. Chicago: University of Chicago Press, 2001, 38–54.

Garrow, David J. "A Reliably Assertive Supreme Court." *Christian Science Monitor*, July 2, 2001.

Gearan, Anne. "Divided Supreme Court Ruling May Leave Lasting Taint on Court." Associated Press, December 13, 2000.

_____. "Few Scars Remain from Bush v. Gore." Associated Press, December 11, 2001.

_____. "Lawyer Olson Talks Bush v. Gore." Associate Press Online, May 9, 2002.

_____. "Senator Clinton Discusses Election 2000." Associated Press, July 24, 2002.

_____. "Swing Votes O'Connor and Kennedy Make a Stealth Majority." Associated Press, December 13, 2000.

Gerken, Heather K. "New Wine in Old Bottles: A Comment on Richard Hasen's and Richard Briffault's Essays on Bush v. Gore." *Florida State University Law Review* 29 (2001): 407–23.

Gillman, Howard. *The Votes That Counted: How the Court Decided the 2000 Presidential Election.* Chicago: University of Chicago Press, 2003.

Ginsburg, Ruth B. Interview by Bob Edwards. *Morning Edition,* National Public Radio, May 2, 2002.

Glaberson, William. "With Critical Decision Comes Tide of Criticism." *New York Times,* December 13, 2000, A24.

Godwin, Mike. "The Supreme Court Shot Itself in the Foot while Shooting Down Al Gore." *Reason,* March 2001, 50.

Goodman, Ellen. "The Supreme Court's Partisan Way: It's a Recent Myth That the High Court Is Beyond the Reach of Politics." *Pittsburgh Post-Gazette,* December 13, 2000, A31.

Gottlieb, Stephen E. "Court's Moral Wreck." *National Law Journal,* January 29, 2001.

Greenbaum, David M., and Lawrence E. Sellers Jr. "1999 Amendments to the Florida Administrative Procedure Act: Phantom Menace or Much Ado about Nothing?" *Florida State University Law Review* 27 (2000): 499–527.

Greene, Abner. *Understanding the 2000 Election: A Guide to the Legal Battles That Decided the Presidency.* New York: New York University Press, 2001.

Greenfield, Jeff. *"Oh, Waiter! One Order of Crow!"* New York: G. P. Putnam's Sons, 2001.

Greenhaw, Leigh Hunt. "'To Say What the Law Is': Learning the Practice of Legal Rhetoric." *Valparaiso University Law Review* 29 (1995): 861–95.

Greenhouse, Linda. 2000. "Bush Prevails by Single Vote; Justices End Recount, Blocking Gore after 5-Week Struggle." *New York Times,* December 13, 2000, A1.

_____. "Collision with Politics Risks Court's Legal Credibility." *New York Times,* December 11, 2000, A1.

_____. "Election Case a Test and Trauma for Justices." *New York Times,* February 20, 2001, A1.

_____. "Rehnquist, in New Arena, Appears at Home." *New York Times,* January 7, 1999.

———. "Scalia's Son Named to Bush Administration Post." *New York Times,* May 8, 2001, A22.

Griffin, Stephen M. "A Reply to Davis and Farnsworth." *Boston University Law Review* 82 (2002): 227–78.

Groner, Jonathan. "Will Election Case Do Damage to the Judiciary?" *Legal Times,* December 18, 2000.

Guinier, Lani. "And to the C Students: The Lessons of *Bush v. Gore.*" In *A Badly Flawed Election: (Debating) Bush v. Gore, the Supreme Court and American Democracy,* Ronald Dworkin, ed. New York: New Press, 2002, 231–62.

Gumbal, Andrew. "Supreme Court Is Condemned for 'Theft of Presidency.'" *Independent Reporter,* July 7, 2001.

Gunther, Gerald. *Constitutional Law,* 11th ed. Mineola, N.Y.: Foundation Press, 1985.

Gunther, Gerald, and Kathleen Sullivan. *Constitutional Law,* 13th ed. Westbury, N.Y.: Foundation Press, 1997.

Hall, Kermit L., ed. *Oxford Companion to the Supreme Court of the United States.* New York: Oxford University Press, 1992.

Hench, Virginia E. "The Death of Voting Rights: The Legal Disenfranchisement of Minority Voters." *Case Western Reserve* 48 (1998): 727–98.

Hentoff, Nat. "The Supreme Court Was Right; All Americans Had a Stake in Florida Election." *Washington Times,* December 25, 2000, A17.

Hernandez, Nathaniel. "Trial Lawyers and Profs Issue Split Opinion on Federal Election Ruling." *Chicago Lawyer,* February 2001, 8.

"High Court Rules for Bush." *Rocky Mountain News,* December 13, 2000.

Idleman, Scott C. "A Prudential Theory of Judicial Candor." *Texas Law Review* 73 (1995): 1307–1415.

Issacharoff, Samuel. "Political Judgments." *University of Chicago Law Review* 68 (2001): 637–56.

———. "Political Judgments." In *The Vote: Bush, Gore, and the Supreme Court,* Cass R. Sunstein and Richard A. Epstein, eds. Chicago: University of Chicago Press, 2001, 55–76.

Issacharoff, Samuel, Pamela S. Karlan, and Richard H. Pildes. *When Elections Go Bad: The Law of Democracy and the Presidential Election of 2000.* Washington, D.C.: Foundations, 2001.

Jackson, Robert. "Calls for Recusal of Thomas, Scalia Are Undue, Experts Say." *Los Angeles Times,* December 13, 2000, A25.

Jamieson, Kathleen Hall, and Paul Waldman. *Electing the President 2000: The Insider's View.* Philadelphia: University of Pennsylvania Press, 2001.

Jarvis, Robert M., Phyllis Coleman, and Johnny C. Burris. *Bush vs. Gore: The Fight for Florida Vote.* Cambridge, Mass.: Kluwer Law International, 2001.

"Justice Calls Election 'December Storm.'" *Dallas Morning News,* February 3, 2001.

"Justice O'Connor Holds to Center." Associated Press Online, May 10, 2001.

"Justice Ran Out the Clock." *Business Week,* December 25, 2000, 42.

Kaiser, Robert G. "Opinion Is Sharply Divided on Ruling's Consequences." *Washington Post,* December 14, 2000.

Kaplan, David A. *The Accidental President: How 413 Lawyers, 9 Supreme Court Justices, and 5,953,110 (Give Oor Take a Few) Floridians Landed George W. Bush in the White House.* New York: William Morrow, 2001.

Karlan, Pamela S. "Easing the Spring: Strict Scrutiny and Affirmative Action after the Redistricting Cases." *William & Mary Law Review* 43 (2002): 1577–86.

———. "Lessons for Getting the Least Dangerous Branch Out of the Political Thicket." *Boston University Law Review* 82 (2002): 667–96.

———. "The Newest Equal Protection: Regressive Doctrine on a Changeable Court." In *The Vote: Bush, Gore, and the Supreme Court,* Cass R. Sunstein and Richard A. Epstein, eds. Chicago: University of Chicago Press, 2001, 77–97.

Karlan, Pamela, and Richard Posner. "The Triumph of Expedience." *Harper's Magazine* May 2001, 31.

Katyal, Neal K. "Politics over Principle." *Washington Post,* December 14, 2000, A35.

Kellner, Douglas. *Grand Theft 2000: Media Spectacle and a Stolen Election.* New York: Rowman and Littlefield, 2001.

Kennedy, Randall. "Contempt of Court." *American Prospect,* January 1–15, 2001, 15.

Klain, Ronald A. "How Democrats Can Use Bush v. Gore." *Washington Post,* March 22, 2001.

Klarman, Michael J. "Bush v. Gore through the Lens of Constitutional History." *California Law Review* 89 (2001): 1721–62.

Kramer, Michael. "Bush Set to Fight an Electoral College Loss." *New York Daily News,* November 1, 2000, 6.

Krauthammer, Charles. "The Winner in Bush v. Gore? It's Chief Justice Rehnquist, Who Runs the Most Trusted Institution in the U.S." *Time,* December 18, 2000.

Lane, Charles. "Decision Sharpens the Justices' Divisions; Dissenters See Harm to Voting Rights and the Court's Own Legitimacy." *Washington Post,* December 13, 2000, A1.

———. "Ginsburg Critical on Bush v. Gore." *Washington Post,* February 3, 2001.

———. "High Court Fractures, and Exposes the Seams." *Washington Post,* December 10, 2000, A1.

———. "Justice Kennedy's Future Role Pondered." *Washington Post,* June 17, 2002.

———. "Lay Down Law, Justices Ruled with Confidence." *Washington Post,* July 1, 2001.

———. "O'Connor Denies Plan to Leave Supreme Court." *Washington Post,* May 2, 2001.

———. "Rehnquist: Court Can Prevent a Crisis: Chief Justice Cites 1876 Election Role." *Washington Post,* January 19, 2001, A24.

———. "Two Justices Defend Court Intervention in Florida." *Washington Post,* March 30, 2001.

Lavelle, Marianne, and Chitra Ragavan. "And Now, the Sound and Fury." *U.S. News & World Report,* December 25, 2000.

"Law Professors for the Rule of Law." www.the-rule-of-law.com.

Leavitt, Paul, and Kathy Kiely. "Justices Defend Bush-Gore Ruling." *USA Today,* March 30, 2001.

Leonard, Mary, and John A. Farrell. "Court Majority Sides with Bush, Calls Recount Methods Unlawful; the End for Gore Appears at Hand As Case Is Sent Back with No Time Left for Action." *Boston Globe,* December 13, 2000, A1.

Lerner, Max. "Constitution and Court As Symbols." *Yale Law Journal* 46 (1937): 1290–1319.

Lessl, Thomas. "The Priestly Voice." *Quarterly Journal of Speech* 75 (1989): 183–97.

Levi, Edward H. *An Introduction to Legal Reasoning.* Chicago: University of Chicago Press, 1949.

Levin, Nick. "The Kabuki Mask of Bush v. Gore." *Yale Law Journal* 111 (2001): 223–30.

Levine, Mark. "On the Bush v. Gore Decision." E-mail, December 15, 2000.

Levinson, Sanford. *Constitutional Faith.* Princeton, N.J.: Princeton University Press, 1988.

———. "The Law of Politics: Bush v. Gore and the French Revolution: A Tentative List of Some Early Lessons." *Law and Contemporary Problems* 65 (Summer 2002): 7–39.

_____. "Return of Legal Realism." *The Nation*, January 8, 2001.

Lewis, Finlay. "High Court May Have Slammed Door on Gore." *San Diego Union-Tribune*, December 13, 2000, A1.

Lewis, William. "Of Innocence, Exclusion, and the Burning of Flags: The Romantic Realism of the Law." *Southern Communication Journal* 60 (1994): 4–21.

Ling, David A. "A Pentadic Analysis of Senator Edward Kennedy's Address to the People of Massachusetts, July 25, 1969." *Central States Speech Journal* 21 (1970): 81–86.

Little, Laura E. "Loyalty, Gratitude, and the Federal Judiciary." *American University Law Review* 44 (1995): 699–755.

Liu, Kathleen. "Visiting Judge Counters Criticism of Last Year's Supreme Court Decision." *Daily Princetonian*, December 4, 2001.

Lizza, Ryan. "How Team Gore Gave Up." *New Republic*, December 25, 2000.

"Long Road to the White House." *Tampa Tribune*. December 14, 2000, 11.

Lund, Nelson. "An Act of Courage." *Weekly Standard*, December 25, 2000, 19.

_____. "The Unbearable Rightness of Bush v. Gore." *Cardozo Law Review* 23 (2001): 1219–79.

Lyne, John R. "Claiming the High Ground: Universalist Rhetoric in a Post-Modern Context." In *Argument in Controversy*, Donn W. Parson, ed. Annandale, Va.: Speech Communication Association, 1991, 53–57.

McConnell, Michael W. "A Muddled Ruling." *Wall Street Journal*, December 14, 2000, A26.

_____. "Two-and-a-Half Cheers for Bush v. Gore." *University of Chicago Law Review* 68 (2001): 665–78.

_____. "Two-and-a-Half Cheers for Bush v. Gore." In *The Vote: Bush, Gore, and the Supreme Court*, Cass R. Sunstein and Richard A. Epstein, eds. Chicago: University of Chicago Press, 2001, 98–122.

McGee, Michael Calvin, and John R. Lyne. "What Are Nice Folks Like You Doing in a Place Like This? Some Entailments of Treating Knowledge Claims Rhetorically." In *The Rhetoric of the Human Sciences*, John S. Nelson, Allan Megill, and Donald N. McCloskey, eds. Madison: University of Wisconsin Press, 1987, 381–406.

McMurray, Carl, and Malcolm B. Parsons. "Public Attitudes toward the Representational Robes of Legislators and Judges." *Midwest Journal of Political Science* 9 (1965): 167–85.

Marquis, Christopher. "Challenging a Justice." *New York Times*, December 12, 2000.

Marshall, William P. "Conservatives and the Seven Sins of Judicial Activism." *University of Colorado Law Journal* 73 (2002): 1217–55.

Martin, Susan, and David Ballinrud. "Long Run to the White House." *St. Petersburg Times,* December 14, 2000.

Mauro, Tony. "High Court Justices Take Bush v. Gore for a Spin." *The Recorder,* February 12, 2001, 3.

_____. "High Court's Political Position Debated One Year after 'Bush v. Gore.'" *American Lawyer Media,* December 19, 2001.

_____. "In Search of a Swing: A Look behind the Arguments That Led to the High Court's Most Important Political Ruling in Years." *American Lawyer,* January 2001.

_____. "Is Bush v. Gore Finished for the Supreme Court? Don't Bet on It." *Legal Intelligencer,* December 18, 2000.

_____. "Reports Persist of Heightened Tension." *New Jersey Law Journal,* February 12, 2001.

May, Randolph J. "No Danger Ahead: Even after the Decision in Bush v. Gore, Our Judiciary Is Still the Least Dangerous Branch." *Legal Times,* January 1, 2001, 43.

Meckler, Laura. "Court's Reputation for Nonpartisanship Could Be at Stake in Bush v. Gore." Associated Press, December 10, 2000.

Merzer, Martin. "But Gore Backers Have Some Points to Argue." *Miami Herald,* April 4, 2001, A1.

_____. "Miami Herald-Knight Ridder-USA Today Review Finds Contest for Florida's Electoral Votes Is a Split Decision," *Miami Herald,* May 10, 2001.

Merzer, Martin, and the Staff of the Miami Herald. *The Miami Herald Report: Democracy Held Hostage.* New York: St. Martin's Press, 2001.

Meyerson, Harold. "The Purloined Presidency." *American Spectator* January 1–15, 2001.

Michelman, Frank. 2001. "Suspicion, or the New Prince." *University of Chicago Law Review* 68 (2001): 679–94.

_____. "Suspicion, or the New Prince." In *The Vote: Bush, Gore, and the Supreme Court,* Cass R. Sunstein and Richard A. Epstein, eds. Chicago: University of Chicago Press, 2001, 123–39.

Miller, Mark. "Florida Refought." *National Review,* September 2, 2002.

Mintz, John, and Peter Slavin. "Human Factor Was at Core of Fiasco." *Washington Post,* June 1, 2001, A1.

Mitchell, Alison. "Over Some Objections, Congress Certifies Electoral Vote." *New York Times,* January 7, 2001.

Mullin, Patrick A. "The U.S. Supreme Court's Decision in Bush v. Gore Gave the Impression That the Justices Were Acting for Political Reasons." *New Jersey Law Journal,* January 8, 2001.

Murphy, William P. "Bush v. Gore: So Maybe It's Not a Christmas Carol." *Pennsylvania Law Weekly,* January 1, 2001.

Murray, Frank J. "Court Braces for a Barrage of Criticism." *Washington Times,* December 14, 2000.

Nichol, Gene R. Jr. "Standing for Privilege: The Failure of Injury Analysis." *Boston University Law Review* 82 (2002): 301–36.

"An Ordeal That Sullied All in Its Path." *Boston Globe,* December 13, 2000, A1.

"O'Connor Wishes Bush v. Gore Had Never Come Up." Reuters News Service, January 25, 2002.

"Opening a Gavel of Worms." *Economist,* December 16, 2000, 2.

Palast, Greg. "The Great Florida Ex-Con Game." *Harper's Magazine,* March 1, 2002.

Pildes, Richard H. "Democracy and Disorder." In *The Vote: Bush, Gore, and the Supreme Court,* Cass R. Sunstein and Richard A. Epstein, eds. Chicago: University of Chicago Press, 2001, 140–64.

Pimental, Richard. "A Desired Outcome in Search of a Legal Principle." *Denver Post,* December 13, 2000, B11.

Pitney, John J. Jr. "Chad All Over." *Reason* 33, no. 4 (August/September 2001): 67–71.

Political Staff of the Washington Post. *Deadlock: The Inside Story of America's Closest Election.* New York: Public Affairs, 2001.

Posner, Richard A. *Breaking the Deadlock: The 2000 Election, the Constitution, and the Court.* Princeton, N.J.: Princeton University Press, 2001.

———. "Bush v. Gore As Pragmatic Adjudication." In *A Badly Flawed Election: (Debating) Bush v. Gore, the Supreme Court and American Democracy,* Ronald Dworkin, ed. New York: New Press, 2002, 187–213.

———. "Bush v. Gore: Reply to Friedman." *Florida State University Law Review* 29 (2001): 736–871.

———. "Prolegomenon to an Assessment." *University of Chicago Law Review* 68 (2001): 719–36.

———. "Prolegomenon to an Assessment." In *The Vote: Bush, Gore, and the Supreme Court,* Cass R. Sunstein and Richard A. Epstein, eds. Chicago: University of Chicago Press, 2001, 165–83.

Powell, Thomas Reed. "The Logic and Rhetoric of Constitutional Law." *Journal of Philosophy, Psychology and Scientific Methods* 15, no. 24 (November 1918): 645–58.

Priest, George L. "Reanalyzing Bush v. Gore: Democratic Accountability and Judicial Overreaching." *University of Colorado Law Review* 72 (2001): 953–81.

Prosise, Theodore O., and Craig R. Smith. "The Supreme Court's Ruling in *Bush v. Gore:* A Rhetoric of Inconsistency." *Rhetoric and Public Affairs* 4 (2001): 605–32.

Pushaw, Robert J. Jr. "Bush v. Gore: Looking at Baker v. Carr in a Conservative Mirror." *Constitutional Commentary* 18 (2001): 359–402.

Rakove, Jack N., ed. *The Unfinished Election of 2000: Leading Scholars Examine America's Strangest Election.* New York: Basic Books, 2001.

Rangel. Charles. "Supreme Injustice." *New York Amsterdam News,* December 14, 2000, 1.

Raskin, Jamin B. "Bandits in Black Robes: Why You Should Still Be Angry about Bush v. Gore." *Washington Monthly,* March 2001, 25–28.

Rather, Dan. "Court's Image Hurt by How, Not What, It Decided." *Houston Chronicle,* December 17, 2000.

"Rehnquist's Daughter Nominated." *New York Times,* June 2, 2001.

Richey, Warren. "Court Rebounds from Bush v. Gore." *Christian Science Monitor,* July 2, 2001, 1.

———. "Fairly or Not, Court Takes on Political Hue." *Christian Science Monitor,* December 14, 2000, 1.

Ringel, Jonathan. "Bush v. Gore May Leave Lasting Rancor on Court." *Fulton County Daily Report,* December 14, 2000.

Romano, Carlin. "What We'll Remember in 2050: 9 Views on Bush v. Gore." *Chronicle of Higher Education,* January 5, 2001.

Rosen, Jeffrey. "Stephen Breyer Restrains Himself." *New Republic,* January 14, 2002.

———. "The Supreme Court Commits Suicide." *New Republic,* December 25, 2000, 18.

Rosenkranz, Joshua E.. "High Court's Misuse of the Past." *National Law Journal,* January 15, 2001.

Rotunda, Ronald D. "The Partisan Myth." *Christian Science Monitor,* December 15, 2000.

Rountree, Clarke. "Coming to Terms with Kenneth Burke's Pentad." *American Communication Journal* 1, no. 3 (May 1998).

———. "Instantiating 'the Law' and Its Dissents in *Korematsu v. United States:* A Dramatistic Analysis of Judicial Discourse." *Quarterly Journal of Speech* 87 (February 2001): 1–24.

_____. "Judicial Invention in Cases Contributing to the Development of Corporate Criminal Liability: A Multi-Dimensional Dramatistic Analysis." Ph.D. dissertation. University of Iowa, 1988.

_____. "On the Rhetorical Analysis of Judicial Discourse and More: A Response to Lewis." *Southern Communication Journal* 61 (1995): 166–73.

_____. "The President As God, the Recession As Evil: *Actus, Status,* and the President's Rhetorical Bind in the 1992 Elections." *Quarterly Journal of Speech* 81 (1995): 325–52.

Saunders, Debra J. "Court of Law vs. Court of Public Opinion." *San Francisco Chronicle,* December 13, 2000, A23.

Savage, David G. "About Bush's Last 5 Votes." *National Journal,* September 8, 2001.

_____. "The Vote Case Fallout." *American Bar Association Journal* 87 (February 2001): 32.

Savage, David G., and Henry Weinstein. "High Court in Awkward Spot over Equal Protection Ruling." *Los Angeles Times,* December 16, 2000, A1.

_____. "Supreme Court Ruling: Right or Wrong?" *Los Angeles Times,* December 21, 2000.

Scalia, Antonin. *A Matter of Interpretation: Federal Courts and the Law.* Princeton, N.J.: Princeton University Press, 1997.

"Scalia Defends Election Decision." *Arizona Republic,* May 24, 2001.

Schoettler, Gail. "A Tarnished Reputation." *Denver Post,* December 24, 2000, H3.

Schragger, Richard C. "Reclaiming the Canvassing Board: Bush v. Gore and the Political Currency of Local Government." *Buffalo Law Review* 50 (Winter 2002): 393–444.

Schwartz, Herman. "The Supreme Court's Federalism: Fig Leaf for Conservatives." *Annals of the American Academy of Political and Social Science* 574 (2001): 119–30.

Schwartz, Paul M. "Voting Technology and Democracy." *New York University Law Review* 77 (2002): 625–98.

"Senate Confirms Olson As Solicitor General." United Press International, May 24, 2001.

Shane, Peter M. "Disappearing Democracy: How Bush v. Gore Undermined the Federal Right to Vote for Presidential Electors." *Florida State University Law Review* 29 (2001): 535–85.

Shribman, David M. "An Ordeal That Sullied All in Its Path," *Boston Globe,* December 13, 2000, A1.

Simon, Roger. *Divided We Stand: How Al Gore Beat George Bush and Lost the Presidency.* New York: Crown Publishers, 2001.

Smith, Hayward H. "History of the Article II Independent State Legislature Doctrine." *Florida State University Law Review* 29 (2001): 731–85.

Soifer, Aviam. "Federal Courts and Electoral Politics: Courting Anarchy." *Boston University Law Review* 2 (2002): 699–735.

Souter, David. "Statement on Bush v. Gore." *Washington Post,* October 6, 2002.

Starr, Kenneth W. "Judges and the GOP." *Wall Street Journal,* May 3, 2001, A18.

Starr, Paul. "The Betrayal." *American Prospect,* January 1–15, 2001.

Stephen, Andrew. "The Scandal of American Judges." *New Statesman,* December 18, 2000, 11.

Stephenson, Donald Grier Jr. *Campaigns and the Court: The U.S. Supreme Court in Presidential Elections.* New York: Columbia University Press, 1999.

Stier, Lance. "Academics Debate Bush v. Gore Election Decision." *Daily Pennsylvanian,* April 23, 2001.

Strauss, David A. "What Were They Thinking?" *University of Chicago Law Review* 68 (2001): 737–56.

———. "What Were They Thinking?" In *The Vote: Bush, Gore, and the Supreme Court,* Cass R. Sunstein and Richard A. Epstein, eds. Chicago: University of Chicago Press, 2001, 184–204.

Stumpf, Harry P. "The Political Efficacy of Judicial Symbolism." *Western Political Quarterly* 19 (1966): 293–303.

Sunstein, Cass R. "Introduction: Of Law and Politics." In *The Vote: Bush, Gore, and the Supreme Court,* Cass R. Sunstein and Richard A. Epstein, eds. Chicago: University of Chicago Press, 2001, 1–12.

———. "Order without Law." *University of Chicago Law Review* 68 (2001): 757–73.

———. "Order without Law." In *The Vote: Bush, Gore, and the Supreme Court,* Cass R. Sunstein and Richard A. Epstein, eds. Chicago: University of Chicago Press, 2001, 205–22.

Sunstein, Cass R., and Richard A. Epstein, eds. *The Vote: Bush, Gore, and the Supreme Court.* Chicago: University of Chicago Press, 2001.

"'Supreme' Court?" *Denver Post,* December 13, 2000, 2D.

"Supreme Illogic." 2000. *Boston Globe,* December 13, 2000, A26.

"The Supremes, Out of Tune." *Christian Science Monitor,* December 11, 2000.

"Symposium: The Prime Time Election, from Courtroom to Newsroom: The Media and the Legal Resolution of the 2000 Presidential Election." *Cardozo Studies in Law and Literature* 13 (2001): 1–104.

Tapper, Jake. *Down and Dirty: The Plot to Steal the Presidency.* Boston: Little, Brown and Company, 2001.

Taylor, Stuart Jr. 2000. "Bush v. Gore May Be Just the Beginning." *Newsweek,* December 25, 2000.

———. "Bush v. Gore: Why the Court Was More Right Than Wrong." *National Journal,* January 6, 2001, 8.

———. "How History Will View the Court." *Newsweek,* September 17, 2001.

———. "A Supreme Moment." *Newsweek,* December 11, 2000, 32.

Thomas, Evan, and Michael Isikoff. "The Truth behind the Pillars." *Newsweek,* December 25, 2000, 46.

Toobin, Jeffrey. *Too Close to Call: The Thirty-Six-Day Battle to Decide the 2000 Election.* New York: Random House, 2001.

Tribe, Laurence H. "Erog .v Hsub and Its Disguises: Freeing Bush v. Gore from Its Hall of Mirrors." *Harvard Law Review* 115 (2001): 172–304.

———. "Freeing Erog .v Hsub from Its Hall of Mirrors." In *A Badly Flawed Election (Debating) Bush v. Gore, the Supreme Court and American Democracy,* Ronald Dworkin, ed. New York: New Press, 2002, 105–54.

———. "Lost at the Equal Protection Carnival: Nelson Lund's Carnival of Mirrors." *Constitutional Commentary* 19 (2003): 619–23.

Tushnet, Mark. "Justiciability and the Political Thicket. Law and Prudence in the Law of Justiciability: The Transformation and Disappearance of the Political Question Doctrine." *North Carolina Law Review* 80 (2002): 1203–34.

Uhlmann, Michael. "The Supreme Court Gets It Right." *Pittsburgh Post-Gazette,* December 13, 2000, A31.

"The Ultimate Split Decision." *San Francisco Chronicle,* December 13, 2000, A22.

"Unsafe Harbor." *New Republic,* December 25, 2000, 9.

U.S. Civil Rights Commission. *Voting Irregularities in Florida during the 2000 Presidential Election.* Washington, D.C.: GPO, 2001.

Vairo, George M. "Bush v. Gore." *National Law Journal,* February 12, 2001, A16.

Vidal, Gore. "Democratic Values." *The Nation,* January 8, 2001, 4.

Von Drehle, David, and James V. Grimaldi. "Careful Decision to End It." *Washington Post,* December 14, 2000.

Walker, Adrian. 2000. "Civics Lesson a Harsh One." *Boston Globe,* 14 December, B1. (downloaded from Lexis-Nexis)

Weinberg, Louise. "Federal Courts and Electoral Politics: When Courts Decide Elections: The Constitutionality of Bush v. Gore." *Boston University Law Review* 82 (2002): 609–66.

Weinstein, Henry. "Bush Wins in Supreme Court." *Los Angeles Times,* December 13, 2000, A1.

Whately, Richard. *Elements of Rhetoric.* 1828, reprint Carbondale, Ill.: Southern Illinois University Press, 1963.

Wooten, Jim. "A Changed Landscape: Unwarranted Judicial Activism Has Hurt, Divided the Nation." *Atlanta Journal and Constitution,* December 13, 2000, 22A.

Yarbrough, Tinsley E. *The Rehnquist Court and the Constitution.* New York: Oxford University Press, 2000.

Yoo, John C. "In Defense of the Court's Legitimacy." *University of Chicago Law Review* 68 (2001): 775–91.

_____. "In Defense of the Court's Legitimacy." In *The Vote: Bush, Gore, and the Supreme Court,* Cass R. Sunstein and Richard A. Epstein, eds. Chicago: University of Chicago Press, 2001, 223–40.

Zarefsky, David. "Failures of Judicial Argument: Equal Protection, Separation of Powers, and Pragmatism in the Defense of *Bush v. Gore.*" Paper presented at National Communication Association convention, Miami Beach, Fla., November 22, 2003.

Index